CONSERVATISM

CONSERVATISM

AN ANTHOLOGY OF
SOCIAL AND POLITICAL
THOUGHT FROM
DAVID HUME TO
THE PRESENT

Edited by Jerry Z. Muller

At a time when the label "conservative" is indiscriminately applied to fundamentalists, populists, libertarians, fascists, and the advocates of one or another orthodoxy, this volume offers a nuanced and historically informed presentation of what is distinctive about conservative social and political thought. It is an anthology with an argument, locating the origins of modern conservatism within the Enlightenment and distinguishing between conservatism and orthodoxy. Bringing together important specimens of European and American conservative social and political analysis from the mid-eighteenth century through our own day, *Conservatism* demonstrates that while the particular institutions that conservatives have sought to conserve have varied, there are characteristic features of conservative argument that recur over time and across national borders.

The book proceeds chronologically through the following sections: Enlightenment Conservatism (David Hume,

(continued on back flap)

CONSERVATISM

◆

AN ANTHOLOGY OF SOCIAL AND POLITICAL THOUGHT FROM DAVID HUME TO THE PRESENT

◆

EDITED BY

Jerry Z. Muller

PRINCETON UNIVERSITY PRESS

PRINCETON, NEW JERSEY

Copyright © 1997 by Princeton University Press
Published by Princeton University Press, 41 William Street,
Princeton, New Jersey 08540
In the United Kingdom: Princeton University Press,
Chichester, West Sussex

Library of Congress Cataloging-in-Publication Data
Conservatism : an anthology of social and political thought
from David Hume to the present / edited by Jerry Z. Muller.
p.   cm.
Includes bibliographical references and index.
ISBN 0-691-03712-4 (cl : alk. paper). — ISBN 0-691-03711-6 (pb : alk. paper)
1. Conservatism—History.   I. Muller, Jerry Z., 1954– .
JC573.C65   1997
320.52—dc21   96-45563

This book has been composed in Galliard

Princeton University Press books are printed
on acid-free paper and meet the guidelines for
permanence and durability of the Committee on
Production Guidelines for Book Longevity
of the Council on Library Resources

Printed in the United States of America

2 4 6 8 10 9 7 5 3

2 4 6 8 10 9 7 5 3
(Pbk.)

For my liberal teachers

◆

Robert K. Merton
George L. Mosse
Fritz Stern

CONTENTS

◆

PREFACE

◆

This book is published at a time when the word "conservative" is on many lips—whether as a label of honor or as an epithet. Yet there is a remarkable discrepancy between the contemporary impact of conservatism and the attention devoted to its history. While this applies to studies of conservative political movements, it holds especially for the study of conservative thought. To be sure, there are many fine studies of one or another conservative thinker, but scholarly works which cover more than one era or more than one national history of conservative thought are few and far between. Readers who wish to acquaint themselves with conservative thought and to acquire a critical or comparative perspective on what passes for conservatism in their own time and place, will, it is hoped, find this book of use. At a time when the label "conservative" is promiscuously applied to fundamentalists, populists, libertarians, fascists, and the advocates of one or another orthodoxy, this book may help readers to acquire a clearer and more nuanced sense of what is distinctive about conservative social and political thought. Together with liberalism, socialism, and a few other "isms," conservatism is a central strand of modern thought. Of these it is arguably the ideological tradition most in need of historical and cross-cultural illumination.

This book is an anthology with an argument, which brings together important specimens of European and American conservative social and political analysis from the mid-eighteenth century through our own day. The book argues in its introduction—and demonstrates in its contents—that there are characteristic features of conservative analysis which recur across a wide swath of time and across national borders. The institutions which conservatives have sought to conserve have varied, the major targets of conservative criticism have changed over time, and conservatism differs from one national context to another. Yet, as this anthology shows, there is an identifiable constellation of shared assumptions, predispositions, arguments, metaphors, and substantive commitments, which taken together form a distinctive conservative pattern of social and political analysis.

This volume is primarily intended as an anthology of conservative analysis on issues of what might broadly be called "public policy." It is not a collection of conservative political programs. Nor is it a history of conservative political parties or political practice. Rather, it is a compendium of conservative social and political analysis that showcases the

social scientific cast of conservative thought at the expense of more literary and romantic strands of conservatism that traffic in the nostalgic evocation of the past. The selections are composed, for the most part, of
conservative diagnoses of specific social and political issues. For it is in
response to proposed or enacted plans for radical reform that conservative thought has been most effectively articulated.

Although this volume does not provide a history of conservatism, it
does take a historical approach to the understanding of conservative
texts. That approach is based in part on the conviction that significant
works of social and political thought are in general best understood in
context. This applies especially to conservative texts. For conservative
thought has arisen primarily as a response to challenges to existing institutions, and consists in good part of attempts to refute those challenges
by historically specific analysis. Because of their characteristic emphasis
on the hidden functions and interdependence of social institutions, and
on the link of institutions to particular historical experience, conservatives have often presented their arguments through an examination of
specific social and political institutions. As a result, the more general
principles and propensities animating conservative thought are frequently lost to view. Political or social theorists who identify theory with
the analytic and deductivist style of Hobbes's *Leviathan*, Locke's *Two
Treatises of Government*, or Rawls's *Theory of Justice* are apt to complain
that works such as Edmund Burke's *Reflections on the Revolution in
France* lack theoretical content. They dismiss the theory embedded in
Burke's discussions of the Revolution of 1688 and of Marie Antoinette's
bedchamber as too hard to come by. Yet it is precisely in such details
that the substance of conservative political and social thought is often to
be found. General and abstract conservative arguments must be mined
from the particular and historical ore.

This book was conceived as a teaching tool, and not merely in the
sense that it could be used in the classroom. My hope was to recapture
some of the experience of studying each reading with a teacher who in
addition to selecting the texts would introduce each thinker, explicate
the text, and call the reader's attention to some of its most significant images, conceptual themes, and rhetorical strategies. Thus each of
the readings is prefaced by an introduction which sketches the relevant
biographical and historical contexts, and by editor's footnotes which
gloss the text, explaining potentially obscure references and calling the
reader's attention to the more general conservative arguments being advanced amid the discussion of specific historical instances.

Readings from European and American thinkers have been chosen,
not only because the volume is intended for both European and American readers, but because the juxtaposition of conservative texts from

different national traditions is itself instructive. A comparison of American conservatism to its British and continental counterparts helps to call attention to some of the peculiarities of American conservatism. But readers will also notice that the gap between American conservatism and that of England, France, or Germany has narrowed from the eighteenth century to the present as the structure of institutions which conservatives in each nation seek to conserve has become more similar.

The readings have been selected, glossed, translated, and edited with an eye to making them "user-friendly." Allusions in need of explanation are treated either in footnotes or in square brackets within the text. Translations other than those by the editor have been checked against the French or German language originals and occasionally altered in the interests of clarity or precision. In translating several of the selections anew, I have tried to recapture the meaning of the original and to render it in idiomatic English, rather than aiming at close replication of the sentence structure and vocabulary of the original document. In so doing, I have been struck again by the extent to which every translation is inevitably an interpretation. Readers should also keep in mind that the selection of particular portions of a document for inclusion is itself an act of interpretation, as is the very process of selecting some texts and authors rather than others for inclusion in the volume.

The selections in this anthology do not represent an exhaustive list of significant works of conservative social and political thought. Nor can all the authors included be definitively categorized as conservative. Some of them did not define themselves as "conservative" and in some cases their work as a whole cannot be classified as unequivocally conservative. Indeed, in almost every case an argument could be made, and has been made, that some label other than "conservative" best fits the author. Included here are portions of their work which are conservative, in the sense of continuous with the constellation of assumptions and predispositions, arguments, substantive themes, and images and metaphors defined as conservative in the introduction to this volume. If one is clever, idiosyncratic, or nominalist enough one can explain why none of these authors should be regarded as conservatives—but that is not a promising approach for an anthology of conservative thought.

The definition of what counts as conservative, then, governs the criteria of selection, and the selections bear out the definition posited in the introduction. The circularity of this procedure is defensible on pragmatic grounds: it allows for demonstration of the continuity of conservative forms of argument amid a multiplicity of styles, national cultures, and historical periods. The problem of circularity is inherent in all historical models or ideal types: the characterization of conservatism is derived from the contents of the volume, but the contents are chosen, in part, to reflect the investigator's evolving conception of conservative social and political thought. The definition adopted, which is explained in the introduction, gives short shrift to some strands of conservatism, especially the more romantic varieties. Nevertheless, the proof of the pudding is in the eating: the usefulness of the definition, it is hoped, is demonstrated by the selections that follow.

The first, analytic half of the introduction is likely to be most useful to those who already have some acquaintance with conservative social and political thought: it may help to clarify and challenge their intuitive assumptions (whether favorable or unfavorable) about conservatism. On the other hand, readers with little sense of what conservatism has been about may find this section of the introduction overly abstract. They may find it more profitable to begin halfway through the introduction, with the historical overview, or read the selections first and then consult the introduction.

The selections are organized for the most part in chronological order, with some exceptions to keep thematically related essays together. The headings under which the selections are grouped are intended to signal the themes that emerge with particular salience in each period. But since all of the themes recur in one form or another from Hume's time to our own, these headings ought to be regarded as no more than suggestive signposts. The last two selections, by Arnold Gehlen and Philip Rieff, are grouped under the heading "Between Social Science and Cultural Criticism." They appear somewhat out of chronological order because both combine a high level of abstract, social scientific analysis of the fundamental categories of conservative thought with cultural criticism of the contemporary era. Their very divergent tone and categories makes the partial convergence of their analyses all the more notable. In what is in a sense a continuation of the introductory essay, an afterword by the editor explores some of the recurrent tensions and dilemmas of conservative thought. That discussion appears at the end because it is likely to mean more to readers after they have confronted the selected texts themselves. The book ends with a "Guide to Further Reading" meant to assist those who would like to further explore the themes and authors presented in this volume.

Within the edited texts, the omission of less than a sentence is indicated by an ellipsis of three dots (. . .); the omission of anywhere from a sentence to a page is indicated by an ellipsis of four dots (. . . .); and the omission of more than a page is indicated by a line space. Words within square brackets have been added by the editor. Except where noted explicitly, footnotes without brackets are added by the editor, while the original author's footnotes are enclosed in brackets.

ACKNOWLEDGMENTS

◆

Much of the initial work on this book was undertaken when I was visiting scholar in residence at the Jerusalem Center for Public Affairs; I am grateful to the Center's President, Daniel Elazar, and to its Director-General, Zvi Marom, for their hospitality and for the stimulus of their conversation. A Faculty Research Grant from the Catholic University of America helped to defray the costs of scanning texts.

I thank Peter Berkowitz, Arthur Herman, Robert K. Merton, Virgil Nemoianu, and Fritz Stern for their comments on drafts of the introductory and concluding essays. John Danford, Jeffrey Herf, Jon Wakelyn, and Rosemarie Zagarri were good enough to put their expertise at my disposal by commenting upon introductions to particular readings. Larry Poos helped to puzzle out Latin quotes and recondite historical allusions in some of the texts. I would also like to acknowledge my debt to Albert O. Hirschman, whose book on conservative thought stimulated me to undertake my own. Whether this unintended outcome is to be accounted positive or negative I leave it for him to judge. It is once again my pleasure to thank Peter J. Dougherty, my editor at Princeton University Press, for his thoughtfulness and support on this project.

My wife, Sharon, read and provided judicious commentary upon portions of this manuscript at key points in its development. In addition to her manifest qualities which merit acknowledgment, she plays more latent functions in my life than it would be prudent to specify. Among the unexpected pleasures of working on this book was the assistance of my children in the final stage of preparing it for publication, when I discovered that the pudding of parenting is in the proofing. I thank Eli, Sara, and Seffy for helping me with my homework, and for the discernment and enthusiasm they brought to the task.

The editor is grateful to the following institutions, corporations, and individuals who have kindly granted permission to make use of copyright material:

American Enterprise Institute for Public Policy Research for material from Peter L. Berger and Richard John Neuhaus, *To Empower People*;

The University of Chicago Press for material from Friedrich A. Hayek, *New Studies in Philosophy, Politics, Economics and the History of Ideas*; from Friedrich A. Hayek, *Law, Legislation, and*

Liberty, vol. 2; and from Philip Rieff, *The Triumph of the Therapeutic*;

Duncker & Humblot GmbH for material from Carl Schmitt, *Hüter der Verfassung*;

Emory Law Journal for material from *The Journal of Public Law*;

HarperCollins Publishers for material from Joseph A. Schumpeter, *Capitalism, Socialism and Democracy*;

Vittorio Klostermann GmbH for material from Arnold Gehlen, *Anthropologische Forschung*;

Irving Kristol for "Pornography, Obscenity, and the Case for Censorship";

Hermann Lübbe for material from "Politische Gleichheitspostulate und ihre sozialen Folgen";

Routledge for material from Michael Oakeshott, *Rationalism in Politics and Other Essays*;

Transaction Publishers for material from Louis de Bonald, *On Divorce*, translated by Nicholas Davidson;

Waveland Press, Inc. for material from Edward Banfield, *The Unheavenly City Revisited*.

CONSERVATISM

INTRODUCTION

◆

WHAT IS CONSERVATIVE SOCIAL AND POLITICAL THOUGHT?

An intuitive procedure for defining conservatism is to begin by listing the institutions which conservatives have sought to conserve. That will not get us very far. For conservatives have, at one time and place or another, defended royal power, constitutional monarchy, aristocratic prerogative, representative democracy, and presidential dictatorship; high tariffs and free trade; nationalism and internationalism; centralism and federalism; a society of inherited estates, a capitalist, market society, and one or another version of the welfare state. They have defended religion in general, established churches, and the need for government to defend itself against the claims of religious enthusiasts. There are, no doubt, self-described conservatives today who cannot imagine that conservatives could defend institutions and practices other than those they hold dear. Yet they might find, to their surprise, that conservatives in their own national past have defended institutions which contemporary conservatives abhor. And were they to look beyond their own national borders, they might find that some of the institutions and practices they seek to conserve are regarded as implausible or risible by their conservative counterparts in other nations.

In one of the most perceptive scholarly analyses of the subject, Samuel Huntington argued that conservatism is best understood not as an *inherent* theory in defense of particular institutions, but as a *positional* ideology. "When the foundations of society are threatened, the conservative ideology reminds men of the necessity of some institutions and the desirability of the existing ones," Huntington suggested.[1] Rather than representing the self-satisfied and complacent acceptance of the institutional status quo, ideological conservatism arises from the anxiety that valuable institutions are endangered by contemporary developments or by proposed reforms. The awareness that the legitimacy of

[1] Samuel Huntington, "Conservatism as an Ideology," *American Political Science Review*, vol. 51, 1957, pp. 454–73.

existing institutions is under attack leads conservative theorists to attempt to provide an articulate defense of the usefulness of those institutions.[2] Huntington claimed that because "the articulation of conservatism is a response to a specific social situation. . . . The manifestation of conservatism at any one time and place has little connection with its manifestation at any other time and place." As we will see, this exaggerates the lack of continuity of conservative social and political thought.

For if the specific institutions which conservative thinkers have sought to conserve have varied over time and space, a set of conservative assumptions, themes, and images *has* endured. It is the purpose of this book to present and explicate the characteristic features of conservative analysis which were first articulated in the eighteenth century and which have consistently recurred, in a variety of national contexts, until the present day.[3]

Conservatism and Orthodoxy

It is sometimes said that conservatism is defined by the assumption "that there exists a transcendent moral order, to which we ought to try to conform the ways of society."[4] Yet the notion that human institutions should reflect some transcendent order predates conservatism, is shared by a variety of nonconservative religious ideologies, and is contested by some of the most significant and influential conservative thinkers. It will be instructive, therefore, to begin by distinguishing this conception from conservatism.

Crucial to understanding conservatism as a distinctive mode of social and political thought is the distinction between *orthodoxy* and *conservatism*. While the orthodox defense of institutions depends on belief in their correspondence to some ultimate truth, the conservative tends more skeptically to avoid justifying institutions on the basis of their ultimate foundations. The orthodox theoretician defends existing institutions and practices because they are metaphysically *true*: the truth pro-

---

[2] Or, in the formulation of Peter Berger, "[T]he facticity of the social world or of any part of it suffices for self-legitimation as long as there is no challenge. When a challenge appears, in whatever form, the facticity can no longer be taken for granted. The validity of the social order must then be explicated, both for the sake of the challengers and of those meeting the challenge. . . . The seriousness of the challenge will determine the degree of elaborateness of the answering legitimations." Peter L. Berger, *The Sacred Canopy: Elements of a Sociological Theory of Religion* (New York, 1967), p. 31.

[3] Most of the primary works referred to in this introduction are reprinted below, in whole or in part.

[4] Russell Kirk, ed., *The Portable Conservative Reader* (New York, 1982), p. xv. A similar conception in a variety of formulations appears in many works of conservative self-representation.

claimed may be based on particular revelation or on natural laws purportedly accessible to all rational men, it may be religious or secular in origin. The conservative defends existing institutions because their very existence creates a presumption that they have served some useful function, because eliminating them may lead to harmful, unintended consequences, or because the veneration which attaches to institutions that have existed over time makes them potentially usable for new purposes.[5] Although orthodox and conservative thinkers may sometimes reach common conclusions, they reach those conclusions by different intellectual routes. The distinction between conservatism and orthodoxy is often elided in conservative self-representations, at times because conservative thinkers may regard it as useful for most people to believe that existing institutions correspond closely to some ultimate truth.

As misleading as the confusion between conservatism and orthodoxy is the false dichotomy of conservatism and Enlightenment. Contrary to the frequent characterization of conservatism as the enemy of the Enlightenment, it is more historically accurate to say that there were many currents within the Enlightenment, and some of them were conservative. Indeed, conservatism as a distinct mode of thought is a product of the Enlightenment. What makes social and political arguments *conservative* as opposed to *orthodox* is that the critique of liberal or progressive arguments takes place on the enlightened grounds of the search for human happiness, based on the use of reason.

Even conservatives who purport to rest their conservatism on orthodox religious principles do not base their arguments on the traditional religious grounds of the quest for ultimate salvation. Thomas Aquinas, an orthodox Christian religious thinker, began his political thought from the premise that "since the beatitude of heaven is the end of that virtuous life which we live at present, it pertains to the king's office to promote the good life of the multitude in such a way as to make it suitable for the attainment of heavenly happiness, that is to say, he should command those things which lead to the happiness of Heaven and, as far as possible, forbid the contrary."[6] Edmund Burke, by contrast, though also a Christian, was a conservative rather than an orthodox thinker, who repeatedly cited worldly utility as the dominant criterion for politi-

---

[5] Peter Berger has distinguished "conservatives by faith" from skeptical "conservatives by lack of faith" which corresponds to the distinction between orthodoxy and conservatism suggested here. Peter L. Berger and Richard J. Neuhaus, *Movement and Revolution* (New York, 1970), p. 21.

[6] Aquinas, *De Regno*, iv (i.15) [115], translated as *St. Thomas Aquinas on Kingship* (Toronto, 1949) and quoted in Robert George, *Making Men Moral: Civil Liberties and Public Morality* (Oxford, 1993), pp. 29–30.

cal decision-making.[7] "The practical consequences of any political tenet go a great way in deciding upon its value," he noted, "Political problems do not primarily concern truth or falsehood. They relate to good or evil. What in the result is likely to produce evil, is politically false: that which is productive of good, politically is true."[8] Burke was famously averse to founding the legitimacy of institutions upon their correspondence with some metaphysical truth. In his last major work, "An Appeal from the New to the Old Whigs," for example, he wrote that "nothing universal can be rationally affirmed on any moral, or any political subject. . . . Metaphysics cannot live without definition; but prudence is cautious how she defines."[9] "Theocratic" conservative theorists such as Louis de Bonald and Joseph de Maistre were more inclined than Burke to argue that the specific institutions which they favored were rooted in divine will. But forced to address an audience for whom this argument was no longer considered persuasive, they too made their case on the basis of utility. That is why de Maistre begins his chapter on "The best species of government" in *Of the Sovereignty of the People* with a statement that could have been penned by Jeremy Bentham, the founder of the Utilitarian school of philosophy. "The best government for each nation," he writes, "is that which, in the territory occupied by this nation, is capable of producing the greatest possible sum of happiness and strength, for the greatest possible number of men, during the longest possible time."[10]

While some conservative theorists have been religious believers, and most affirm the social function of religious belief in maintaining individual morality and social cohesion, none base their social and political arguments primarily on conformity with ultimate religious truth. The search for earthly happiness, broadly construed, is one assumption

---

[7] "In reality there are two, and only two, foundations of Law; and they are both of them conditions without which nothing can give it any force; I mean equity and utility. . . . [U]tility must be understood, not of partial or limited, but of general and public utility, connected in the same manner with, and derived directly from, our rational nature." Edmund Burke, "Tracts relating to the Popery Laws" (1765), in R. B. McDowell, ed., *The Writings and Speeches of Edmund Burke: Vol. IX* (Oxford, 1991), p. 456.

[8] Edmund Burke, "An Appeal from the New to the Old Whigs" (1791), in Daniel Ritchie, ed., *Edmund Burke: Further Reflections on the Revolution in France* (Indianapolis, 1992), p. 163.

[9] Burke, "Appeal," p. 91. Without using our terminology of orthodoxy and conservatism, Leo Strauss makes a similar point about Burke, in Leo Strauss, *Natural Rights and History* (Chicago, 1953), pp. 318–20.

[10] Quoted in Garrard Graeme, "Rousseau, Maistre, and the Counter-Enlightenment," *History of Political Thought*, vol. XV, no.1, Spring 1994, pp. 97–120, esp. p. 117. As Garrard notes, "While the positions that the author of *Du Pape* defends are very conservative and supportive of the Catholic Church, the social and political functions of religion are central to his outlook, whereas strictly theological arguments are quite peripheral."

which distinguishes conservative social and political analysis from religious orthodoxy. Conservative arguments are thus utilitarian, when the term is understood loosely as the criterion of contributing to worldly well-being. Of course "Utilitarianism" also exists as a formal philosophical and political doctrine which seeks to provide measurable criteria—usually the sum total of the expressed wants of individuals—by which to make policy decisions. Conservatism parts company with this sense of "Utilitarianism" because of the conservative emphasis upon social complexity, the functional inter-relationship between social institutions, and the importance of latent functions. For these reasons and for others to be explored below, conservatives tend to be skeptical of doctrines like Utilitarianism which try to cut through complexity on the assumption that there is a single and readily ascertainable measure of human happiness.

Conservatism is also distinguished from orthodoxy by the conservative emphasis upon history. Combining the emphases on history and utility, the common denominator of conservative social and political analysis might be termed "historical utilitarianism."[11] Though the term may be unfamiliar, it usefully captures a number of characteristic features of conservative thought.

For the conservative, the historical survival of an institution or practice—be it marriage, monarchy, or the market—creates a *prima facie* case that it has served some human need. That need may be the institution's explicit purpose, but just as often it will be a need other than that to which the institution is explicitly devoted. Conservatism, as Irving Kristol notes, assumes "that institutions which have existed over a long period of time have a reason and a purpose inherent in them, a collective wisdom incarnate in them, and the fact that we don't perfectly understand or cannot perfectly explain why they 'work' is no defect in them but merely a limitation in us."[12] Or, in the words of the contemporary German philosopher, Hans Blumenberg, "What the term 'institution' conveys is, above all, a distribution of the burdens of proof. Where an institution exists, the question of its rational foundation is not, of itself, urgent, and the burden of proof always lies on the person who objects to the arrangement the institution carries with it."[13] This propensity is

---

[11] This term, with a somewhat different meaning, has been used by Jack Lively, "Introduction," to Lively, ed., *The Works of Joseph de Maistre* (New York, 1971), p. 27 and Wyger R. E. Velema, *Enlightenment and Conservatism in the Dutch Republic: The Political Thought of Elie Luzac (1721–1796)* (Assen, The Netherlands, 1993), p. 185.

[12] Irving Kristol, "Utopianism, Ancient and Modern," in his *Two Cheers for Capitalism* (New York, 1978), p. 161.

[13] Hans Blumenberg, *Work on Myth*, trans. by Robert W. Wallace (Cambridge, MA, 1985), p. 166, translation altered slightly.

captured in the dictum of the eighteenth-century German conservative, Justus Möser: "When I come across some old custom or old habit which simply will not fit into modern ways of reasoning, I keep turning around in my head the idea that 'after all, our forefathers were no fools either,' until I find some sensible reason for it . . ."[14]

The conservative emphasis on "experience" is linked to the assumption that the historical survival of an institution or practice is evidence of its fitness in serving human needs. Burke's conservatism owed a great deal to the common law tradition, which had long assumed that the common law was a body of rules which had developed historically to meet changing human needs.[15] In America, conservative Whigs like Rufus Choate (1799–1859) similarly appealed to the common law as the embodiment of historical experience.[16] Later conservatives, such as William Graham Sumner or Friedrich Hayek would defend the capitalist market on the grounds that it had proved itself the fittest institution to provide for the material basis of collective survival—another variation on the theme of historical utilitarianism.[17]

Conservative social and political thought is further distinguished from orthodoxy by what we might call its "historical consequentialism": institutions are to be judged, conservatives repeatedly assert, not by the motives and intentions of their founders, and not by their explicit purposes, but by their results in furthering human well-being.[18]

"Historical utilitarianism" is the basis of conservatism in another sense as well. Since custom and habit are important features of human conduct, some of the usefulness of a practice comes from the fact that those engaged in it are already "used" to it, and are apt to be discomfited by change. Familiarity, on this logic, breeds comfort. Thus

[14] Quoted in Karl Mannheim, "Conservative Thought," in Kurt H. Wolff, ed., *From Karl Mannheim* (New York, 1971), pp. 132–222, esp. p. 198, from Justus Möser, *Sämtliche Werke*, ed. B. R. Abeken (Berlin, 1842–43), vol. 5, p. 260.

[15] See J.G.A. Pocock, "Burke and the Ancient Constitution: A Problem in the History of Ideas," in his *Politics, Language and Time* (New York, 1973), pp. 202–32; and Harold J. Berman, "The Origins of Historical Jurisprudence: Coke, Selden, Hale," *Yale Law Review*, vol. 103, no.7 (May 1994), pp. 1651–1738.

[16] See Rufus Choate, "The Position and Functions of the American Bar, as an Element of Conservatism in the State" (1845) in *The Works of Rufus Choate*, ed. Samual Gilman Brown, vol. 1. (Boston, 1862), excerpted below. On Choate's appeal to the common law, see Daniel Walker Howe, *The Political Culture of the American Whigs* (Chicago, 1979), p. 226.

[17] See, for example, William Graham Sumner, "Sociological Fallacies" (1884), in *Earth-Hunger and Other Essays*, ed. Albert Galloway Keller (New Haven, 1914), pp. 357–64, reprinted below; and Friedrich Hayek, "The Errors of Constructivism" (1976), in his *New Studies in Philosophy, Politics, Economics and the History of Ideas* (University of Chicago, 1978), reprinted below.

[18] See the quote from Burke above. Among other examples, William Graham Sumner, "Purposes and Consequences," in *Earth Hunger*, ed. Albert Galloway Keller (New Haven, 1914), pp. 67–75.

"usage"—the fact that a practice is already in place—is often interpreted by conservatives as a presumption in favor of retaining it.[19]

In a related argument, conservatives maintain that the existence of a long historical past (or, at least, belief in the existence of a long historical past) contributes to the sense of veneration in which institutions are held. Historical continuity thus increases the emotional hold of the institution upon its members, adding emotional weight to institutionally prescribed duties. A sense of historical continuity thus adds to the stability and effective functioning of an institution and hence to its utility. In de Maistre's pithy formulation: "Custom is the mother of legitimacy."[20] David Hume articulated this connection between historical time and the effective functioning of institutions,[21] and Burke dilated upon the "benefit from considering our liberties in the light of an inheritance" as a means of procuring "reverence to our civil institutions."[22] That is one reason why conservatives recommend that reform (even radical reform) be presented in a manner which makes it appear continuous with past institutional practice.[23]

There are several recurrent arguments put forth by conservatives which combine history and utility. Conservatives contend that existing institutions ought to be maintained because their ongoing existence indicates their *superiority* in meeting human needs. Another variation asserts that while existing institutions are not *intrinsically* superior to possible alternatives, they are superior under the circumstances by virtue of their familiarity and the veneration that attends institutional continuity.

RECURRENT CONSERVATIVE ASSUMPTIONS AND PREDISPOSITIONS

What follows is an outline of the recurrent constellation of assumptions, predispositions, arguments, themes, and metaphors that characterize conservative social and political thought. None of these are exclusive to

[19] Michael Oakeshott's essay, "On being conservative," in his *Rationalism in politics and other essays* (London, 1962; Expanded edition, Indianapolis, 1991), is an extended reflection on this theme.

[20] Joseph de Maistre, *Du Pape*, livre II, chap. X, quoted in Peter Richard Rohden, *Joseph de Maistre als politischer Theoretiker* (Munich, 1929; reprinted New York, 1979), pp. 175–76, which has a good discussion of the role of time and continuity in Maistre's thought.

[21] Sheldon Wolin, "Hume and Conservatism," *American Political Science Review* 48, no. 4, 1954, pp. 999–1016, esp. p. 1008.

[22] Burke, "Reflections on the Revolution in France," in L. G. Mitchell, ed., *The Writings and Speeches of Edmund Burke: Volume VIII: The French Revolution, 1790–1794* (Oxford, 1989), p. 85; excerpted below.

[23] That is the thrust of Burke's analysis, in *Reflections on the Revolution in France*, of the departure from the line of succession during the Glorious Revolution of 1688.

conservatism, nor does every conservative analyst share them all. But it is in conservative thought that these features occur with greatest frequency and in combination with one another.

Human Imperfection

Conservative thought has typically emphasized the imperfection of the individual, an imperfection at once biological, emotional, and cognitive. More than any other animal, man is dependent upon other members of his species, and hence upon social institutions for guidance and direction.[24] Though this assumption may be grounded in a religious doctrine of original sin, it has often been argued upon entirely secular grounds, including the biological facts of limited human instinctual preparedness for survival, an argument advanced by de Bonald and developed most extensively by Arnold Gehlen.[25]

Conservatives typically contend that human moral imperfection leads men to act badly when they act upon their uncontrolled impulses, and that they require the restraints and constraints imposed by institutions as a limit upon subjective impulse. Conservatives thus are skeptical of attempts at "liberation": they maintain that liberals over-value freedom and autonomy, and that liberals fail to consider the social conditions that make autonomous individuals possible and freedom desirable.[26]

Epistemological Modesty

Conservatives have also stressed the cognitive element of human imperfection, insisting upon the limits of human knowledge, especially of the social and political world. They warn that society is too complex to lend itself to theoretical simplification, and that this fact must temper all plans for institutional innovation.[27] Such epistemological modesty may be based upon philosophical skepticism as in the case of Hume, or a

---

[24] In keeping with standard English usage, here and elsewhere the term "man" is used to refer to members of the human species, males and females included. The term "male" is reserved for circumstances in which only the masculine sex is intended.

[25] See Louis de Bonald, *On Divorce*, edited and translated by Nicholas Davidson (New Brunswick, NJ, 1992), p. 43, excerpted below; Arnold Gehlen, "Mensch und Institutionen" (1960), in Arnold Gehlen, *Anthropologische Forschung* (Hamburg, 1961), pp. 69–77; partially translated below.

[26] Anthony Quinton, *The Politics of Imperfection: The religious and secular traditions of conservative thought in England from Hooker to Oakeshott* (London, 1978), p. 13; Roger Scruton, "Introduction" to Scruton, *Conservative Texts* (London, 1991), p. 9. For a recent example of such an analysis, see Peter Berger and Richard John Neuhaus, *To Empower People: The Role of Mediating Structures in Public Policy* (Washington, D.C., 1977), excerpted below.

[27] There is a good discussion of this element of conservative thought, as well as much else, in Quinton, *The Politics of Imperfection*, p. 17.

religiously derived belief in the limits of human knowledge, as in the case of Burke or de Maistre, or on some general sense of the fallibility of human knowledge, as in the case of Friedrich Hayek or Edward Banfield.[28]

Institutions

These assumptions explain the emphasis of conservative social and political thought upon *institutions*, that is, patterned social formations with their own rules, norms, rewards, and sanctions. While liberals typically view with suspicion the restraints and penalties imposed upon the individual by institutions, conservatives are disposed to protect the authority and legitimacy of existing institutions because they believe human society cannot flourish without them. The restraints imposed by institutions, they argue, are necessary to constrain and guide human passions. Hence Burke's dictum, in his *Reflections on the Revolution in France*, that "the restraints on men, as well as their liberties, are to be reckoned among their rights." The positive value ascribed to institutions by conservatism contributes to its natural affinity for the *status quo*, in contrast to liberalism's innate hostility toward authority and establishments.

Custom, Habit, and Prejudice

Burke used the term "prejudice" to refer to rules of action which are the product of historical experience and are inculcated by habit. Like Hume and Möser before him, he argued in favor of relying upon customary moral rules even when they had not been subject to rational justification. Subsequent conservatives too assume that most men and women lack the time, energy, ability, and inclination to reevaluate or reinvent social rules. Therefore, "duty," the subjective acceptance of existing social rules conveyed through socialization and habit, is regarded as the best guide for most people, most of the time.

Historicism and Particularism

Many valuable institutions, according to conservatives, arise not from natural rights, or from universal human propensities, or from explicit contract, but rather are a product of historical development. To the extent that human groups differ, conservatives argue, the institutions

[28] Edward Banfield, "Policy Science as Metaphysical Madness" (1980), in Banfield, *Here the People Rule: Selected Essays* (2nd ed., Washington, D.C, 1991).

which they develop will differ as well. Hence the institutions which conservatives seek to conserve vary over time, and from group to group.[29] Since, for the conservative, the desirability of specific institutions is dependent upon time and place, conservatism tends to be procedural and methodological, rather than substantive.[30] Stated differently, conservatism is defined in part by its affirmation of institutions as such, rather than by its commitment to specific institutions. In facing foreign institutions and practices which differ from those of his native culture, the conservative, unlike the adherent to orthodoxy or the liberal, does not begin with the assumption that because foreign institutions differ from his own at least one set of institutions must necessarily be flawed. Rather he is inclined to suspect that the foreign institution reflects a different historical experience, and may be as useful in the foreign context as his native institutions are in their context. For the conservative, then, the fact that an institution or practice has withstood the test of time leads to a presumption of its suitability to its context.

Anti-contractualism

Unlike liberals who favor voluntary, contractual social relations, conservatives emphasize the importance of nonvoluntary duties, obligations, and allegiances. Hume, for example, argued that social contract theories of political obligation which derived the duty to obey government from the explicit will of the governed were historically untenable and had the undesirable effect of delegitimating all established governments.[31] "What would become of the World if the Practice of all moral Duties, and the Foundations of Society, rested upon having their Reasons made clear and demonstrative to every Individual?" Burke asked rhetorically in his *Vindication of Natural Society*. Here as for many other elements of conservative thought, Burke's *Reflections on the Revolution in France* provides an exemplary formulation in his redefinition of the social contract as "a partnership not only between those who are living,

[29] See, for example, Justus Möser, "Der jetzige Hang zu allgemeinen Gesetzen und Verordnungen ist der gemeinen Freiheit gefährlich" (1772), in *Justus Mösers Sämtliche Werke: Historisch-kritische Ausgabe in 14 Bänden* (Oldenburg and Berlin, 1943), vol. 5, pp. 22–27.
   Burke's analysis of American peculiarities in his speech on "Conciliation with America," provides a model of this element of conservative analysis. Edmund Burke, "Conciliation with America" (1775), in Ian Harris, ed., *Edmund Burke: Pre-Revolutionary Writings* (Cambridge, 1993), pp. 206–69, esp. pp. 220ff.
[30] See the discussion in Anthony Quinton, "Conservatism," in Robert E. Goodin and Philip Pettit, eds., *A Companion to Contemporary Political Philosophy* (Oxford, 1993).
[31] See David Hume's essays, "Of the Origin of Government," "Of the Original Contract," and "Of Passive Obedience," in *Essays Moral, Political and Literary*, ed. Eugene F. Miller (revised edition, Indianapolis, 1987), reprinted below.

but between those who are living, those who are dead, and those who are to be born."[32] Because the dissolution of the social order would mean the end of social institutions by which men's passions are guided, restrained, and perfected, Burke argued, the individual has no right to opt out of the "social contract" with the state. "Men without their choice derive benefits from that association; without their choice they are subjected to duties in consequence of these benefits; and without their choice they enter into a virtual obligation as binding as any that is actual."[33] This noncontractual basis of society, Burke wrote, was evident in other social relations as well. Marriage was a matter of choice, but the duties attendant upon marriage were not: parents and children were bound by duties which were involuntary.[34] This emphasis on the non-voluntary bases of obedience and allegiance has remained a distinctively conservative theme.

The Utility of Religion

There is no necessary link between conservatism and religious belief. Devout Christians or Jews have embraced a variety of political viewpoints, including liberalism, socialism, and nationalism, while many of the most distinguished conservative theorists have been agnostics or atheists. Conservatism arose in good part out of the need to defend existing institutions from the threat posed by "enthusiasm," that is, religious inspiration which seeks to overturn the social order. The critique of religious enthusiasm, which was central to Hume's conservatism, was later extended, first by Hume himself, and more emphatically by Burke, into a critique of political radicalism.[35]

Yet despite disagreements as to the *veracity* of religion, conservatives have tended to affirm its *social utility*. Conservatives make several arguments for the utility of religion: that it legitimates the state; that the hope of future reward offers men solace for the trials of their earthly existence and thus helps to diffuse current discontent which might disrupt the social order; and that belief in ultimate reward and punishment leads men to act morally by giving them an incentive to do so. Recognition of the social utility of religion is no reflection upon the truth or

---

[32] Burke, "Reflections," p. 147; reprinted below.
[33] Burke, "Appeal," p. 160.
[34] Ibid., pp. 160–61.
[35] On Hume, see Donald W. Livingston, *Hume's Philosophy of Common Life* (Chicago, 1984), pp. 318–23. On the theme of enthusiasm in Burke, see J.G.A. Pocock, "Edmund Burke and the Redefinition of Enthusiasm: The Context as Counter-Revolution," in François Furet and Mona Ozouf, *The French Revolution and the Creation of Modern Political Culture: Vol. 3: The Transformation of Political Culture 1789–1848* (Oxford, 1989), pp. 19–36.

falsity of religious doctrine. It is quite possible to believe that religion is false but useful. But it is also possible to believe that religion is both useful and true. Or one may believe that religion is "true" in a more rational and universalistic sense than in its particular, historical embodiments, but that those particular embodiments are necessary to make religion accessible to the mass of citizens in a way which is less rationalist and abstract than more intellectual versions of the faith.[36]

RECURRENT CONSERVATIVE ARGUMENTS

The Critique of "Theory"

Conservative theorists repeatedly decry the application to society and politics of a mode of thought which they characterize as overly abstract, rationalistic, and removed from experience. Whether termed "the abuse of reason" (by Burke), "rationalism in politics" (by Oakeshott), or "constructivism" (by Hayek), the conservative accusation against liberal and radical thought is fundamentally the same: liberals and radicals are said to depend upon a systematic, deductivist, universalistic form of reasoning which fails to account for the complexity and peculiarity of the actual institutions they seek to transform.[37]

Conservative theorists are not opposed to the use of knowledge and intellect in the analysis of social and political affairs.[38] They oppose what they regard as epistemologically pretentious forms of knowledge and analysis.[39] Radical reformers and revolutionaries are said by conservatives to be insufficiently cognizant of the complexity of life and of the need to balance conflicting considerations. They fail, conservatives contend, to understand the working of existing institutions, and take for granted the benefits of existing institutions without appreciating their prerequisites.

[36] As Hume wrote in his essay, "The Sceptic," "An abstract, invisible object, like that which *natural* religion alone presents to us, cannot long actuate the mind, or be of any moment in life. To render the passion of continuance, we must find some method of affecting the senses and imagination, and must embrace some *historical*, as well as *philosophical* account of the divinity. Popular superstitions and observances are even found to be of use in this particular." (Hume, *Essays*, p. 167.) Although Hume does not always write in his own voice in the set of four essays from which the quotation is taken, he may well be conveying his own view in this instance.

[37] See also, in this regard, Karl Mannheim's schematic comparison of late eighteenth- and early nineteenth-century natural-law thinking and counterrevolutionary thought, in Karl Mannheim, *Conservatism: A Contribution to the Sociology of Knowledge*, ed. David Kettler, Volker Meja, and Nico Stehr (London, 1986), pp. 107–9.

[38] With the exception of some romantic conservatives, who are not represented in this collection.

[39] See Quinton, *Politics of Imperfection*, pp. 12–13.

Especially suspect to conservatives are projects undertaken to reform institutions in order to make them reflect universalistic theories of natural rights, theories which are supposed to be applicable to all men at all times. Of natural rights, Burke wrote that "their abstract perfection is their practical defect. . . . [T]he restraints on men, as well as their liberties, are to be reckoned among their rights. But as the liberties and the restrictions vary with times and circumstances and admit to infinite modifications, they cannot be settled upon any abstract rule; and nothing is so foolish as to discuss them upon that principle."[40] There is no consensus among conservative theorists as to whether and in what sense natural rights may be said to exist. But most conservatives stress the hazards of rejecting existing institutions merely on the grounds that they fail to guarantee some posited natural right.

Unanticipated Consequences, Latent Functions, and the Functional Interdependence of Social Elements

The following quote from Burke's *Reflections* links the conservative critique of theory to three of the most common arrows in the quiver of conservative argument: the unanticipated negative consequences of reformist action, the importance of latent functions, and the interdependence of social elements:

> The science of constructing a commonwealth, or renovating it, or reforming it, is, like every experimental science, not to be taught *a priori*. Nor is it a short experience that can instruct us in that practical science; because the real effects of moral causes are not always immediate; but that which in the first instance is prejudicial may be excellent in its remoter operation; and its excellence may arise even from the ill effects it produces in the beginning. The reverse also happens; and very plausible schemes, with very pleasing commencements, have often shameful and lamentable conclusions. In states there are often some obscure and almost latent causes, things which appear at first view of little moment, on which a very great part of its prosperity or adversity may most essentially depend.

The subject of the unanticipated consequences of purposive social action is one of the most important themes in modern social science—and by no means a particularly conservative one.[41] Liberals tend to focus

---

[40] Burke, *Reflections*, reprinted below.

[41] See the classic article by Robert K. Merton, "The Unanticipated Consequences of Purposive Social Action" (1936), reprinted in Merton, *Sociological Ambivalence* (New York, 1976). On the use of the concept by Adam Smith, see Jerry Z. Muller, *Adam Smith in His Time and Ours* (New York, 1993), pp. 84–92.

upon the unintended *positive* consequences of actions. The most striking example of this is the competitive market, in which (if a host of conditions apply) the quest of individual actors to increase their material well-being results in an increase of the economic well-being of most of society. It is typical of conservatives, by contrast, to emphasize the unanticipated *negative* consequences of deliberate social action.[42]

Such negative consequences, conservatives typically argue, occur because reformers are unaware of the latent functions of existing practices and institutions.[43] Reformers are insufficiently cognizant, it is said, of the contribution of the practice to the preservation or adaptation of the larger social system in which it is implicated. For the larger function of a practice may be different from its explicit or avowed purpose. That contribution may be unintended by those engaged in the practice. And most important, its function may be unrecognized, or recognized only retrospectively, once the reform of the practice has brought about negative unintended consequences.

The conservative stress on the positive latent functions of practices typically arises in response to reformist diagnoses of manifest dysfunctions, that is, the costs inflicted upon individuals by the practices in question. The characteristic conservative retort to the reformer's complaint of the burdens imposed by some social practice is, "It looks bad, indeed it is bad. But it can get much worse, for reasons that you have overlooked, indeed haven't even imagined." In the 1770s, for example, Justus Möser would argue against governmental measures to do away with the social sanctions against illegitimate children, on the grounds that such measures decreased the incentives to marry, thus weakening the institution of marriage, on which so much of social well-being depended.

Among the misleading characterizations of conservative thought is the claim that it is necessarily "organic." Not all conservatives have adopted the image of society as an organism. When such imagery is used, it serves to convey in metaphorical terms what can be stated as a sociological proposition, namely, that social institutions are functionally interdependent and are often mutually sustaining, so that attempts to

---

[42] A theme explored in Albert O. Hirschman, *The Rhetoric of Reaction: Perversity, Futility, Jeopardy* (Cambridge, MA, 1991). Hirschman distinguishes three forms of negative unanticipated consequences. The *perversity* thesis maintains that "any purposive action to improve some feature of the political, social, or economic order only serves to exacerbate the condition one wishes to remedy" or, stated another way, "the attempt to push society in a certain direction will result in its moving all right, but in the opposite direction." The *futility* thesis holds that purposive attempts at social transformation will be unavailing. The *jeopardy* thesis argues that "the cost of the proposed change or reform is too high as it endangers some previous, precious accomplishment."

[43] On the concept of latent functions, see Robert K. Merton, "Manifest and Latent Functions," in *Social Theory and Social Structure*, third, enlarged edition (New York, 1968), to which my discussion is very much indebted.

reform or eliminate one institution may have unanticipated negative effects on other, valued institutions.

Together, the concepts of unanticipated negative consequences, latent functions, and functional interdependence serve as recurrent arguments against radical or wholesale reform, though not against reform as such. In fact, self-conscious conservatism has frequently sought to distinguish itself, through a commitment to orderly and timely reform, from simple reaction or wholesale preservation of the status quo.[44]

Anti-humanitarianism

Flowing from these conservative arguments regarding abstract theory, latent functions, and unanticipated consequences is a recurrent polemic of anti-humanitarianism. Whether it is David Hume noting the conflict between our subjective sense of humanity and those general rules of justice which make sustained cooperation possible, James Fitzjames Stephen decrying the religion of humanity, William Graham Sumner excoriating the confusion of purposes and consequences, or Philip Rieff lamenting the predominance of remissive over interdictory elements in the therapeutic mentality of contemporary liberalism, the complaint retains a recognizable continuity.[45] Time and again conservative analysts argue that humanitarian motivation, combined with abstraction from reality, lead reformers to policies that promote behavior which is destructive of the institutions upon which human flourishing depends. If it is institutions rather than individuals which have always been the prime object of conservative concern, it is because conservatives assume that it is the functioning of institutions upon which the well-being of individuals ultimately depends.[46]

Moral earnestness devoid of the knowledge of the institutions that make beneficent social life possible is a recipe for disaster, conservatives argue. This is the gravamen of recurrent conservative warnings about the inadequacy of "compassion" or "good intentions" in the formation of social policy. When conservatives acknowledge the tension between the demands of institutions and the needs of individuals, their thought

---

[44] Rudolf Vierhaus "Konservativ, Konservatismus," in *Geschichtliche Grundbegriffe. Historisches Lexikon zur politisch-sozialen Sprache in Deutschland*, ed. Otto Brunner, Werner Conze, Reinhart Koselleck; vol. 3 (Stuttgart, 1982), pp. 531–65, esp. p. 563.

[45] David Hume, *A Treatise of Human Nature* [1740] (Oxford, 1978), ed. L. A. Selby-Bigge, revised by P. H. Nidditch; Book III (Of Morals), Section I, p. 579. See also the useful secondary discussion in Frederick G. Whelan, *Order and Artifice in Hume's Political Philosophy* (Princeton, 1985), p. 230. James Fitzjames Stephen, *Liberty, Democracy, Fraternity* (London, 1874). William Graham Sumner, "Purposes and Consequences," in *Earth Hunger*, ed. Albert Galloway Keller (New Haven, 1914), pp. 67–75. Philip Rieff, *The Triumph of the Therapeutic* (1966); excerpted below.

[46] Scruton, "Introduction," p. 9.

may take on a tragic dimension and an insistence upon the limits of human happiness.

When conservative analysts accept the premises of their opponents regarding the desirability of human happiness but argue that happiness cannot be attained through the means proposed by progressives, the characteristic mode of conservative social and political analysis will be ironic. As in dramatic irony, the conservative analyst assumes superior insight into the actions of the progressive actor, for the conservative is aware of the gap between the progressive's intentions and the likely results of his actions.

RECURRENT SUBSTANTIVE THEMES

Although conservatism is characterized above all by its historical utilitarianism and by its recurrent assumptions and arguments, the range of institutions defended by conservatives is not unlimited, and a few have been the special object of conservative solicitude. The recurrent *substantive* themes of conservative social and political thought include:

1. a skepticism regarding the efficacy of written constitutions, as opposed to the informal, sub-political, and inherited norms and mores of society. For conservatives, the real "constitution" of society lies in its historical institutions and practices, which are inculcated primarily through custom and habit;
2. the central role of cultural manners and mores in shaping character and restraining the passions, and hence the *political* importance of the social institutions in which such manners and mores are conveyed;
3. the need of the individual for socially imposed restraint and identity, and hence skepticism regarding projects intended to liberate the individual from existing sources of social and cultural authority;
4. an emphasis on the family as the most important institution of socialization, and despite considerable divergence among conservatives over the proper roles of men and women within the family, the assertion that some degree of sexual division of labor is both inevitable and desirable;
5. the legitimacy of inequality, and the need for elites, cultural, political, and economic;
6. security of possession of property as a prime function of the political order;
7. the importance of the state as the ultimate guarantor of property and the rule of law, and hence the need to maintain political authority;

8. the ineluctability of the possibility of the use of force in international relations.

9. Conservatives have a propensity to assert that the successful functioning of a capitalist society depends on premarket and nonmarket institutions and cultural practices. Anxiety over whether the cultural effects of the market will erode these institutions and practices is the most consistent tension within conservative social and political thought.[47]

RECURRENT IMAGES AND METAPHORS

Nature and Second Nature

In the *Nicomachean Ethics*, Aristotle declared that "virtue of character results from habit [*ethos*]," and asserted that "the virtues arise in us neither by nature nor against nature, but we are by nature able to acquire them, and reach our complete perfection through habit."[48] This emphasis on custom and habit would become a hallmark of conservative social theory. It is prominent in Hume's thought,[49] but it was Burke who characteristically combined the concept with its most enduring metaphor. "Men are made of two parts, the physical and the moral," he wrote. "The former he has in common with brute creation. . . . [But] Man in his moral nature, becomes, in his progress through life, a creature of prejudice—a creature of opinions—a creature of habits, and of sentiments growing out of them. They form our second nature, as inhabitants of the country and members of the society in which Providence has placed us."[50] Conservatives have ever since made recurrent use of the trope of "second nature," employing it at various times is a rough synonym for habit, custom, and culture.[51]

---

[47] Albert Hirschman has dubbed this "the self-destruction thesis" in the eponymous essay of *Rival Views of Market Society and Other Essays* (New York, 1986), pp. 109ff. On conservative anxieties regarding the effects of capitalism, see Jerry Z. Muller, "Justus Möser and the Conservative Critique of Early Modern Capitalism," *Central European History*, vol. 23 #2/3 (June/Sept. 1990), pp. 153–78.

[48] Aristotle, *Nicomachean Ethics*, trans. Terence Irwin (Indianapolis, 1985), Book 2, chap. 1, 1, 1103a15, 1103a24-25.

[49] See the discussion in Whelan, *Order and Artifice in Hume's Political Philosophy*, p. 293.

[50] The quote is from Burke's speech of 1794 at the trial of Warren Hastings, quoted in James K. Chandler, *Wordsworth's Second Nature: A Study of the Poetry and Politics* (Chicago, 1984), p. 71.

[51] Plutarch, who in his *Rules for the Preservation of Health* declared that "Custom is almost a second nature" may have been the first to coin the metaphor. On the Roman association of custom, second nature, and law, see Donald R. Kelley, *The Human Measure: Social Thought in the Western Legal Tradition* (Cambridge, MA, 1990), p. 44.

The metaphor of "second nature" has had several functions. Conservatives assert the importance of inherited custom and culture against arguments which assume the natural or pre-social goodness of man. Only by virtue of the inculcation of culture through social institutions, conservative theorists insist, is man made decent; it is institutions which humanize him. From Hume and Burke through the twentieth-century German conservative, Arnold Gehlen, the image of second nature has served as a foil against what conservatives regard as overly optimistic and excessively rationalist accounts of moral behavior.[52] It may also be used to counter excessively pessimistic accounts of human behavior as marked by a relentless and inexorable search for power or domination. The image of "second nature" is used to convey the notion that many of the advantages of internalized cultural rules comes from the fact that they are taken for granted, and are acted upon without continuous reflection.

The dual connotations of the metaphor of "second nature" lead to an ongoing tension in the role of the conservative theorist. For insofar as the conservative theorist's role is scientific and analytic, emphasis is placed on the distinction between nature and acquired, historical, particular culture. Yet to call attention to the particularity of what is taken for granted is to raise awareness of the "artificial" feature of cultural norms, of the fact that they might be otherwise. This detracts from their taken-for-grantedness, from their perceived necessity. Yet a culture in which key norms are subject to continuous reflection and reconsideration may become incapable of inculcating the unselfconscious acceptance of norms which, conservative theorists argue, is a fundamental part of character formation.[53] Hence a recurrent temptation of conservative theorists is to conflate culture with nature, to treat "second nature" as "nature" in order to make the contingent appear inevitable.[54] This helps account for the frequent use by conservatives of the metaphor of society as an organism, a naturalistic metaphor which reinforces the belief that existing institutions are inevitable.

Transparency versus Veiling

The most important metaphor in Burke's *Reflections on the Revolution in France* is that of veiling, which became a recurrent metaphor of

---

[52] See Arnold Gehlen, "Über Kultur, Natur, und Natürlichkeit,"[1958], in Gehlen, *Anthropologische Forschung* (Reinbek, 1961); translated below.

[53] See, for example, the acute formulation by Leo Strauss (attributed by him to Burke), "by opening up a larger vista, by thus revealing the limitations of any practical pursuit, theory is liable to endanger full devotion to practice." Leo Strauss, *Natural Right and History*, p. 309.

[54] There are some suggestive remarks on this theme in Chandler, *Wordsworth's Second Nature*, pp. 67ff.

subsequent conservative thought. Burke made brilliant use of imagery not as a substitute for argument, but as a metaphorical restatement of arguments laid out elsewhere in declarative form. Burke ridicules the "great acquisitions of light" of the Enlightenment, the "new conquering empire of light and reason" and of "naked reason."[55] The imagery of veiling and drapery functions as an implicit attack on the metaphors of light and transparency which were so dominant in the discourse of his age.[56]

Burke used the metaphor of culture as a "veil," a fabric of understandings which hides the direct object of the natural passions. Culture, for Burke as for later conservatives, is a means of sublimation, restraining the expression of the passions of domination and self-gratification and diverting the passions to more elevated goals. Burke believed that the effect of the *philosophes'* relentless critique of inherited beliefs and institutions was not only to delegitimate all existing political authority, it was to tear away the veil of culture which leads men to restrain themselves, and so to leave them open to act on their more primitive and antisocial urges. The result, he feared, would be a return of man to his "natural" state, a state not elevated and benign, but brutish and barbaric.

The image of culture as a veil therefore serves much the same function as the metaphor of "second nature." Here too a tension or ambiguity is built into the metaphor. For the very image of the veil implies that there is something unpleasant or dangerous beneath the veil; the veil reminds the reader that things could be otherwise, that the redirection of desire is a contingent product of existing institutions.

The metaphor of the veil is also employed in a different sense by conservatives. As we have seen, conservatives contend that institutions and practices acquire their utility in part because their continuity over time increases their venerability. What are conservatives to do when institutional continuity has been disrupted and historical precedent has been broken? The metaphor of veiling is used to convey the proper conservative strategy for interpreting such occasions so as to preserve the illusion of continuity. Describing the Glorious Revolution of 1688, in which Parliament replaced King James with William of Orange, who was married to James's daughter Mary, Burke emphasizes that Parliament maintained all the ceremonies of regular succession, thus casting "a well-wrought veil" over the irregularities which the circumstances of the time

---

[55] There is a good analysis of this imagery in F. P. Lock, *Burke's Reflections on the Revolution in France* (London, 1985), pp. 127–28.

[56] On the Enlightenment metaphor of the "naked truth," see Hans Blumenberg, "Paradigmen zu einer Metaphorologie," *Archiv für Begriffsgeschichte*, vol. 6, 1960, pp. 7–142, esp. pp. 49–54.

had made necessary. Later, the American conservative Whig, Rufus Choate, used the same image when reflecting on the dangers of continued focus on the founding doctrine of the right of men to remake their political institutions. He cautioned that "true wisdom would advise to place the power of revolution, overturning all to begin anew, rather in the background, to throw over it a politic, well-wrought veil, to reserve it for crises, exigencies, the rare and distant days of great historical epochs. . . ."[57] This second use of the veil metaphor also has an implicit tension, for it suggests that the foundations beneath the veil may not bear the closest historical scrutiny.

It was de Maistre, with his propensity for extreme and scandalizing propositions, who typically offered the most radical proposal for veiling. Beginning with the premise "the more divine the basis of an institution, the more durable it is," he came to the conclusion, "If therefore you wish to *conserve* all, *consecrate* all."[58] The scandal and fascination of de Maistre's dictum is that it is self-subverting, for an awareness of the fact that a practice has been designated sacred by an act of will and for the sake of durability detracts from its sacredness and hence from its durability. The logic behind de Maistre's recommendation seems to be that since the reverence in which institutions are held may be weakened by the discovery of their contingent and even ignoble historical origins, it is safer to ground that reverence beyond time and beyond historical investigation.

The recurrent temptation of conservative thinkers—especially when they write to reinforce existing belief rather than to analyze the functioning of institutions—is therefore to blur the distinction between conservatism and orthodoxy: to insist that existing political institutions, social structures, and cultural practices must be conserved because they correspond to some ultimate and ineluctable metaphysical reality, rather than because of their demonstrated usefulness.

THE DIFFICULTIES OF DEFINING CONSERVATISM

One distinguished student of conservatism has suggested that it may be impossible to write a history of conservative doctrine because "too many minds have been trying to 'conserve' too many things for too many rea-

[57] Rufus Choate, "The Position And Functions Of The American Bar, As An Element Of Conservatism In The State," [1845] in Samuel Gilman Brown, ed., *The Works of Rufus Choate* (two volumes, Boston, 1862), vol. 1, pp. 414–38, excerpted below.

[58] Joseph de Maistre, *Essai sur le principe générateur des constitutions politiques et des autres institutions humaines* [1814] (Lyon and Paris, 1828), excerpted and translated below.

sons."[59] It is difficult to arrive at meaningful generalizations about the specific policies favored by conservatives. Clearly it is misguided to expect unity among conservatives on questions of first philosophical or theological principles, since a propensity to slight such questions or to regard them as futile or dangerous is a defining element of modern conservatism. Moreover, conservatism tends to be more nationally particular than liberalism or socialism, which aspire to be universal in their reach. And because conservative thought often arises as a response to attacks on existing institutions and practices, the conservative reply is determined in good part by the specific nature of those attacks, which vary across time and space. Moreover, since conservatism emphasizes the need for institutional and symbolic continuity with the particular past, its symbols and institutional ideals tend to be more tied to specific, usually national, contexts.[60] That is why some scholars regard the notion of a transnational conservatism as a self-contradiction.[61]

The conception of conservatism adopted here—as a constellation of recurrent assumptions, themes, and images—tries to do justice to the historical and national diversity of conservatism while calling attention to its continuities over time and across national contexts. It differs from two common approaches to definitions which appear either too narrow or too broad to be useful. Overly narrow are attempts to define conservatism as the defense of a historically particular set of institutions, such as a landed aristocracy and an established Church, thus restricting the label to a limited swath of recognizably conservative thought. To define conservatism as primarily a traditionalistic psychological propensity which exists in all times and places,[62] by contrast, seems too broad, since these psychological propensities may be shared by those who do not advance conservative modes of analysis.

[59] J.G.A. Pocock, "Introduction," to the Hackett edition of Edmund Burke, *Reflections on the Revolution in France*, ed. Pocock (Indianapolis, 1987), pp. vii, xlix. Klaus Epstein made a similar point about the obstacles to writing a transnational history of conservatism, but thought they could be resolved by immersion in specific national histories in order to understand what conservatives wanted to conserve in each case. Klaus Epstein, *The Genesis of German Conservatism* (Princeton, 1966), pp. 6–7.

[60] F.J.C. Hearnshaw, *Conservatism in England: An Analytical, Historical, and Political Survey* (London,1933; reprinted New York, 1967), p. 35.

[61] See, for example, Martin Greiffenhagen, *Das Dilemma des Konservatismus in Deutschland* (Munich, 1971), pp. 17–18, and the German authors cited in his footnotes who arrive at similar conclusions.

A related claim is that conservatism is invariably linked to a landed aristocracy and an established Church, and because neither institution has existed in the United States an established American conservatism is a contradiction in terms. See, for example, Bernard Crick, "The Strange Quest for An American Conservatism," *The Review of Politics* XVII, 1955, pp. 359–76. This argument is taken up in the introductions to the selections from James Madison and Rufus Choate below.

[62] On the distinction between traditionalism and conservatism, see Mannheim, *Conservatism*, especially pp. 72–73.

HISTORICAL OVERVIEW

Given the historical utilitarianism of conservative thought and the wide range of institutions it has been used to defend, an accurate understanding of conservatism requires consideration of the changing historical contexts in which it has evolved. Only when the survival of current institutions and practices is no longer taken for granted does conservatism arise to explicate the often hidden usefulness of those institutions in order to justify their continued existence. A brief indication of the changing contexts and polemical targets of conservative thought is therefore necessary. Indeed, whether or not an argument may be classified as conservative will depend in part on the context in which it is made, since the defense of institutions that are historically superannuated is the hallmark not of conservatives but of reactionaries, and in extreme cases, of cranks.

The contention that conservatism arose in opposition to the Enlightenment and to the French Revolution reflects Edmund Burke's polemical characterization of the Enlightenment in his critique of the French Revolution. Though frequently reiterated, the contention is historically untenable. So too is the conception that conservatives such as Möser and Burke were part of a distinct "counter-Enlightenment."[63] Conservatism arose not *against* the Enlightenment but *within* it.

The thought of David Hume marks a watershed in the development of conservative social and political thought into a coherent, secular doctrine. The precursors of conservatism may be found in the Anglican critique of the Puritan contention that the elect or the inspired congregation, guided by their individual interpretations of the Bible, were entitled to exercise political authority.[64] Hume began by borrowing and expanding upon this critique of the politics of religious "enthusiasm." And he went on to criticize what he saw as its secular counterparts in the philosophically implausible and politically subversive doctrines of natural rights and of voluntary contract as the sole legitimate basis of political obligation.[65] In 1757, Burke used similar terms to attack what he called the "abuse of reason" among some enlightened thinkers. On the Continent, conservative social and political thought arose as a critique of the policies of enlightened absolutism. Among the foremost practitioners of this criticism was Justus Möser, himself a part of the German

---

[63] The term was coined by Isaiah Berlin, "The Counter-Enlightenment," in his *Against the Current: Essays in the History of Ideas* (New York, 1980).

[64] Quinton, *Politics of Perfection*, p. 21. Pocock, "Edmund Burke and the Redefinition of Enthusiasm."

[65] On Hume's conservatism, see, in addition to Quinton, *Politics of Perfection*; Sheldon Wolin, "Hume and Conservatism"; Whelan, *Order and Artifice in Hume's Political Philosophy*; Livingston, *Hume's Philosophy of Common Life*.

Enlightenment, and a reformer of a conservative and corporatist tinge. (Much the same could be said of Montesquieu.) In Holland, another Enlightenment figure, Jean de Luzac, articulated politically conservative arguments opposing the claims of "patriots" for a more democratic constitution.[66] Much of post-1789 intellectual conservatism is continuous with the analytic strategies, if not with the tone, of prerevolutionary conservative analysis.

It was the democratic radicalism of the French Revolution that evoked Burke's *Reflections on the Revolution in France*, which remains the most influential work in the history of conservative thought. The attempt of the revolutionary government to annex Voltaire and Rousseau to the revolutionary cause, and Burke's identification of the Revolution with the *philosophes*, led many subsequent historians to conflate the Enlightenment and the Revolution, and both with what subsequently came to be called liberalism. Yet these conflations are mistaken and misleading on several counts. First, much of the Enlightenment was not politically radical, and few of the major figures in the Enlightenment would have favored a popular revolution. Nor were those who opposed the Revolution necessarily antipathetic to the Enlightenment. The antirevolutionary French press drew heavily on conservative strands in Enlightenment thought,[67] while Louis XVI and his minister of finance, Jacques Necker, immersed themselves in Hume's *History of England*, drawing upon Hume's defense of the Stuarts to buttress their own cause.[68] Later liberals who identified with one or another element of the Enlightenment's legacy, such as Benjamin Constant, were as likely to regret the course taken by the French Revolution as to consider themselves its heirs.

Burke's defense of monarchy, aristocracy, and the established church stamped conservative thought at the end of the eighteenth century and in the early decades of the nineteenth. Yet a similar critique of democratic radicalism appears, with a more republican but nevertheless recognizably conservative thrust, in the United States, first in the writings of the American Federalists, and later in the work of the conservative Whig critic of Jacksonianism, Rufus Choate. Hume's combination of political conservatism with the championing of commerce was to remain characteristic of subsequent British and American conservatism. By contrast, the French, Catholic strains of conservatism of de Bonald and de Maistre, as well as the romantic German strains of conservatism shared Burke's substantive commitments to monarchy, aristocracy, and

[66] See Wyger R. E. Velema, *Enlightenment and Conservatism in the Dutch Republic.*
[67] See Jeremy Popkin, *The Right-Wing Press in France, 1792–1800* (Chapel Hill, 1980).
[68] David Bongie, *David Hume: Prophet of the Counter-Revolution* (Oxford, 1965), esp. pp. 126ff.

one or another form of church establishment, while remaining less accepting of capitalist economic development than the British and American strains.

As with so many other historical developments, the phenomenon of conservatism long preceded the use of the term in political life. Terms related to "conservative" first found their way into political discourse in the title of a French weekly journal, *Le Conservateur*, founded in 1818 by François-René de Chateaubriand with the aid of Louis de Bonald. "The *Conservateur* upholds religion, the King, liberty, the Charter and respectable people (*les honnêtes gens*)," it proclaimed in its first issue.[69] In England, the label "Conservative Party" was first applied to the Tories by the publicist John Wilson Crocker in 1830.[70] In Germany the term "conservative" came into use later in the same decade: it was wielded primarily by the opponents of those designated as conservative, who were charged with seeking to preserve existing institutions at any price.[71]

The development of conservative social and political thought after the mid-nineteenth century shows a movement from substance to function: from the defense of particular institutions to the defense of institutions in general; from the defense of the landed aristocracy to a defense of elites in general; from an emphasis on the role of the established Church to the function of culture in linking the individual to communal purposes; from monarchical authority to the authority of the state in general.

In the last decades of the nineteenth century, conservatism underwent an important shift, reflecting a change in opponents and in institutional substance. The increasing dominance of industrial capitalism, the expansion of the suffrage, the rise of socialist movements and of a new brand of liberalism which was more economically redistributionist and more culturally permissive, all led to a substantial transformation of conservatism. Many of the economic institutions and policies once associated with European liberalism now became that which conservatives sought to conserve.[72] This new brand of conservatism is reflected in the works of James Fitzjames Stephen, W. H. Mallock, William Graham Sumner, and in the first selection by Joseph Schumpeter.

The rhetoric by means of which institutions were defended also changed. It placed less emphasis on the veneration of tradition as such,

---

[69] *Le Conservateur*, 5.10.1818, p. 7, quoted in Vierhaus, "Konservativ," p. 538.

[70] "International Policy" in *Quarterly Review* 42, 1830, p. 276, quoted in Vierhaus, "Konservativ," p. 539.

[71] Vierhaus, "Konservativ," p. 540.

[72] Rudolf Vierhaus, "Conservatism," *Dictionary of the History of Ideas*, vol. 1, pp. 477–85, esp. p. 484; Noël O'Sullivan, *Conservatism* (London, 1976), pp. 111–18.

while seeking to increase reverence for existing institutions by showing that they were in accord with the needs of historical development. The language of common law and of inherited tradition was increasingly abandoned in favor of the language of science. The justification of the social utility of landed elites was replaced in the work of Mallock, Stephen, and Schumpeter by a more general defense of the need for elites in the realms of economics and politics, while in the work of Matthew Arnold the defense of the established Church was transformed into a defense of cultural elites. In Germany, too, the substance of conservatism was transformed, from a defense of aristocracy, a social order based on fixed estates, and paternalist monarchism, toward an emphasis on the functions of the state as such, a transformation exemplified in the selection from Carl Schmitt.[73]

In the course of the twentieth century, conservatism was defined not only by its opposition to the radical left but by antipathy to the spread of the welfare state and attempts to bring about economic redistribution, and by skepticism regarding the solution of social problems through massive governmental action. In the late 1960s and 1970s, as established liberal institutions came under attack from the New Left, conservatives engaged in an attempt to defend such institutions, while trying to limit the purported damage of liberal policies to institutions valued by conservatives. As the selections from Kristol, Berger and Neuhaus, and Lübbe indicate, conservatives increasingly called attention to the pre-liberal and non-liberal prerequisites of a viable liberal society.

RADICAL CONSERVATISM

Conservatism can be distinguished—definitionally if not always in practice—from reaction. The conservative seeks to conserve existing institutions, usually recognizing that the process of conservation may include the need for evolutionary reform. The reactionary, by contrast, is at odds with existing institutions, and seeks to return to some institutional *status quo ante*, often in a form transfigured by memory and ideology.[74] One recurrent strand of thought which is related to conservatism yet politically and analytically distinct from both conservatism and reaction is radical conservatism. The radical conservative shares some of the concerns of more conventional conservatism, such as the need for institutional authority and continuity with the past. But he believes that the processes characteristic of modernity have destroyed the valuable legacy

---

[73] Vierhaus, "Konservativ," p. 564.

[74] On the distinction between conservatives and reactionaries, see Epstein, *Genesis of German Conservatism*, pp. 10–11.

of the past for the present, so that a restoration of the purported virtues of the past demands radical or revolutionary action. Hence the self-description of one radical conservative, Paul de Lagarde, as "too conservative not to be radical," and the credo of another, Moeller van den Bruck, who professed that "conservative means creating things that are worth conserving."[75] When the foundations of society and of existing institutions are perceived as decayed beyond restoration, the radical conservative ideology reminds men of the desirability of strong institutions, and the necessity of new ones.

Like the conservative, the radical conservative has an acute appreciation for the positive role of authoritative institutions in the life of the individual and of society. But while the conservative seeks to shore up the authority of existing institutions, these institutions lack legitimacy in the eyes of the radical conservative. For him existing institutions are unworthy of assent or incapable of garnering it. Radical conservatism is a revolt against existing institutions in the name of the need for authority.[76]

Radical conservatism unites several predilections which, in combination, make it a recognizably distinct and recurrent phenomenon. It shares with conservatism an emphasis on the role of institutions in providing restraint and direction to the individual, but seeks to create new institutions which will exert a far stronger hold on the individual than do existing ones, which because of their relative tolerance are perceived by radical conservatives as "decayed." Radical conservatives typically look to *state power* to reach their goals (except in the United States, where populism and anti-statism are more deeply ingrained on the right). These aims typically include the *reassertion of collective particularity* (of the nation, the *Volk*, the race, or the community of the faithful) against a twofold threat. The internal threat arises from ideas and institutions identified by radical conservatives as corrosive of collective particularity and incapable of providing worthy goals for the collectivity and the individuals who comprise it. These threats usually include the market, parliamentary democracy, and the pluralism of value systems which capital-

---

[75] Paul de Lagarde, *Deutsche Schriften* (Göttingen, 1878), p. 5, quoted in Rudolph Hermann, *Kulturkritik und konservative Revolution* (Tübingen, 1971), p. 241; Arthur Moeller van den Bruck, *Das dritte Reich*, 3rd ed. (Hamburg, 1931), quoted in Greiffenhagen, *Dilemma*, p. 243.

[76] The term "conservative revolution" and the notion of a revolt for authority were first articulated in Hugo von Hofmannsthal's lecture of 1927, *Das Schrifttum als geistiger Raum der Nation*; see also Fritz Stern, *The Politics of Cultural Despair: A Study in the Rise of the Germanic Ideology* (Berkeley, 1974), p. 225 and passim; and Jerry Z. Muller, *The Other God that Failed: Hans Freyer and the Deradicalization of German Conservatism* (Princeton, 1987). On comparable developments in France, see Zeev Sternhell, *La Droite Révolutionnaire 1885–1914: Les Origines françaises du Fascisme* (Paris, 1978), and Zeev Sternhell, *Neither Right nor Left: Fascist Ideology in France* (Berkeley, 1986).

ism and liberal democracy are thought to promote. But the ideas and institutions perceived as threatening may also include those of internationalist socialism, which is similarly perceived as corrosive of collective particularity. The external threat arises from powerful foreign states which are perceived as using their power to spread ideas and institutions identified by radical conservatives as corrosive.

"Radical conservatism" as we have defined it conveys the common sensibilities which European intellectuals who advocated a "conservative revolution" shared with National Socialism and with other fascist movements of the interwar period. It also calls attention to the common denominator among a range of intellectual and political movements which extend beyond Europe and beyond the interwar era.

Radical Conservatism and Conservatism Compared

Conservative social and political thought represents an attempt to halt the deteriorating legitimacy or functioning of valued institutions. Conservative theorists frequently assert that the institutions they admire are being corroded by cultural, social, or political developments. Anxiety about the legitimacy of existing institutions is shared by both conservatives and radical conservatives. But to radical conservatives, existing institutions are too decrepit to make them worth conserving. In their eyes, existing institutions lack legitimacy and fail to provide the transcendent goals which make possible the subordination of the individual to a collective purpose. Radical conservatives typically loathe the mundane, and criticize existing society for the triumph of the prosaic concerns of economic or familial life over more heroic or transcendent goals.[77] As a result, many recurrent conservative assumptions, arguments, and themes are jettisoned by radical conservatives, or transformed into radically different directions.

Take, for example, the historical utilitarianism so characteristic of conservative thought. For the radical conservative, the historical survival of an existing institution creates no presumption in its favor, and the importance of custom and habit is similarly discounted. The conservative propensity to epistemological modesty and the related arguments regarding the importance of latent functions and unanticipated negative consequences, all of which lead to caution in reform, are not only absent from the discourse of radical conservatives but scorned by them. Instead radical conservatives typically emphasize the role of "will" on

---

[77] On the theme of modern liberal society as the economization of existence in the writings of two radical conservative thinkers, see Jerry Z. Muller "Carl Schmitt, Hans Freyer, and the Radical Conservative Critique of Liberal Democracy in the Weimar Republic," *History of Political Thought*, vol. XII, no. 4, Winter 1991, pp. 695–715.

the grounds that only radical action can lead from the unworthy present to a more glorious future.[78]

Radicals of the right tend to agree with conservatives that a sense of historical continuity increases the emotional hold of an institution upon its members. But since they do not regard existing institutions as worthy, radical conservatives often turn to some mythic past as a source or object of veneration.[79] The conservative critique of theory and the conservative theme of the need to "veil" the less usable past of current institutions is transformed by radical conservatives into an embrace of myth, which is valued precisely for its irrational attraction.[80] The conservative theme of the importance of "second nature," in the sense of inherited culture, is replaced by an emphasis on nature in the most physical and mythical sense, of consanguinity and geography—blood and soil.

The distinction between conservatism and radical conservatism is in part a matter of belief and temperament, in part a matter of experience. In interwar Europe, many erstwhile radical conservatives supported fascist regimes, whether out of conviction or circumstance, before frequently becoming disillusioned with the radical regimes they had supported. After the defeat of the Axis powers some of the most acute conservative analysis and critique stemmed from those who had been radical conservatives but now saw no plausible alternative to the liberal democratic welfare state.[81]

The distinction between conservatism and radical conservatism may sometimes be one of circumstance. For a recurrent problem for conservatives is what to do when the existing institutions which conservatives value are so threatened that only radical action will preserve their essence. That threat may come from antidemocratic movements which seek to overthrow the existing order by violence. But in some historical contexts it has also come from the workings of democratic institutions, from the effects of the market, or from cultural movements. The issue is not one that can be settled abstractly: it has proven a continuing dilemma not only for conservative politics but for conservative analysis as well.

---

[78] On the voluntaristic element in radical conservative thought, see among other works, Christian Graf von Krockow, *Die Entscheidung. Eine Untersuchung über Ernst Jünger, Carl Schmitt, Martin Heidegger* (Stuttgart, 1958), and Muller, *The Other God that Failed*, p. 197.

[79] Among the most recent, and least plausible, of such myths is the embrace of the pre-Christian pagan past by the French New Right. For an overview, see Mark Wegierski, "The New Right in Europe," *Telos*, no. 98–99, 1994, pp. 55–70.

[80] Here the seminal figure was Georges Sorel. On his ubiquitous influence, see most recently Zeev Sternhell, *The Birth of Fascist Ideology* (Princeton, 1994).

[81] See Muller, *The Other God that Failed*, chapters 9, 10, and appendix.

The Inevitable Varieties of Conservatism

The content of conservatism varies not only over time and across national contexts, but often among self-proclaimed conservatives at the same time and place. The declaration that one is conservative, while it signifies a certain respect for tradition and for the value of historically evolved institutions, tells us little of operational significance. The most self-conscious conservatives have always been aware of the constructed character of tradition; they have recognized that conservatives face what Burke called a "choice of inheritance."[82] The conservation of the institutional legacy of the past inevitably involves a selection from among existing traditions and legacies. Conservative theory, like all theory, cannot be applied without judgment.[83] Decisions must be made about which historical institutions and traditions are viable under changed circumstances, decisions as to how inherited institutions and practices ought to be revised or revamped, decisions as to what should be interpreted as the core of institutions to be salvaged as opposed to the chaff which may be discarded. Even among those who regard themselves as conservative these questions will inevitably elicit a variety of responses.

The selections in this book, then, cannot provide a guide to "authentic" contemporary conservative social and political analysis. The book may, however, help to lift the study of conservative thought out of the national and ideological provincialism in which it has all too often been mired.

[82] I owe my appreciation of this point to Professor Louis Hunt.

[83] A point made by Kant in regard to theory in general, in his essay, "On the Common Saying: 'This may be true in theory, but it does not apply in practice," [1793], in Hans Reiss, ed., *Kant: Political Writings* (Cambridge, 1991), pp. 61–92.

► 1 ◄

ENLIGHTENMENT
CONSERVATISM

INTRODUCTION TO
David Hume,
"Of Justice," from *An Enquiry Concerning*
the Principles of Morals

◆

According to the medieval Christian tradition, social and political institutions had their foundation in God's creation of nature, including human nature. The idea of "natural law" had its origins in Greek and Roman philosophy, and in the thought of the greatest of the Christian scholastics, Thomas Aquinas, natural law theory was reconciled with the revealed truth of the Bible. Natural law had long been justified in part on the basis of its utility, that is, the claim that it provided the requisite rules for human flourishing, but it was to be obeyed, ultimately, because of its supposed origin in God's will.[1] Aquinas claimed that the natural law could be ascertained be the unassisted human mind not illuminated by divine revelation; but he regarded such law as grounded in divine providence, and he gave it a far more unequivocal and immutable character than had his classical predecessors.[2]

Arguments which justified contemporary political institutions as based upon the will of God continued to dominate early modern Catholic and Anglican political thought. This logic of legitimating institutions reached its apogee in the doctrine of the divine right of kings. But the rise of conflict between Catholics, Anglicans, Lutherans, Calvinists, and smaller sectarians led to disputes about how divine will was to be interpreted. Early modern thinkers were therefore forced to find grounds

---

[1] See the article by N. E. Simmonds, "Natural Law," in John Eatwell, Murray Milgate, and Peter Newman, eds., *The New Palgrave* (New York, 1987).
[2] See Leo Strauss, *Natural Right and History* (Chicago, 1953), pp. 144, 163.

other than the disputed basis of divine revelation upon which to justify government and law.

David Hume rejected all doctrines which sought to show that moral rules and political institutions reflected divine will. For Hume, such theories invoked proofs and forces about which men can know nothing.[3] Yet Hume also attacked the highly rationalist and voluntarist theory of political allegiance associated with John Locke, who treated governmental legitimacy as based upon a social contract instituted to preserve universal, natural rights. Hume's political writings present a logic of conservatism clearly distinguished from orthodoxy and based upon the utility of historically developed institutions. He offers grounds for the acceptance of political authority once its origins have been demythologized. There are good reasons for obeying governmental authority, Hume argues, though its origins are neither in divine will nor in voluntary agreement by rational human actors.

Hume was born in Edinburgh, Scotland in 1711 and died there in 1776. His friend, Adam Smith, who was with him during his last days, described Hume "as approaching as nearly to the idea of a perfectly wise and virtuous man, as perhaps the nature of human frailty will permit." (Smith's encomium outraged his religiously orthodox contemporaries, for given Hume's reputation as an atheist, Smith's tribute implied that an atheist could be virtuous.) While he lived for years in France and in England, it was in Edinburgh that Hume spent most of his life, and it was in good part under his influence that the economically backward and politically dependent nation of Scotland became a center of the Enlightenment. Hume wrote at a time when his native land had relinquished its sovereignty and independence in order to become part of the polity and economy of Britain, and had begun to prosper as a result. His works were addressed less to his Scottish countrymen than to a British and indeed European audience.

In his first book, *A Treatise of Human Nature*, published in two volumes in 1739 and 1740, Hume explored the limits of what abstract philosophy could provide, while suggesting a more historical and empirical direction for the human sciences. In his later works, *An Enquiry Concerning Human Understanding* and *An Enquiry Concerning the Principles of Morals* he tried to reach out to a larger audience by conveying many of the ideas of the *Treatise* in more accessible terms. Believing that experience, not abstract reason, was the prime source of useful knowledge about political, social, and moral life, he turned to the writing of

---

[3] Knut Haakonssen, "Hume's Political Theory," in David Fate Norton, ed., *The Cambridge Companion to Hume* (Cambridge, 1993), pp. 184, 192.

history, and to essays on social, cultural, economic, and political matters which had a large historical dimension.

Hume was a political conservative, but the regime he sought to preserve was a relatively liberal and commercial one. He valued the relative liberty and prosperity of British political and commercial institutions, yet thought that the political practice of the British was better than their dominant political theories. The Whigs who dominated British politics attributed their liberty to a purported "ancient constitution." They also celebrated the Glorious Revolution of 1688, during which the monarch, James II, a Roman Catholic, was replaced by the king's Protestant daughter and her husband, William of Orange. In accepting the crown offered by Parliament, William and Mary agreed to abide by the provisions of the Bill of Rights, which reined in the power of the monarch. Whig theorists, following the lead of John Locke, argued that the monarch ruled by the consent of his subjects. The opponents of the Whigs, the Tories, emphasized the power and hereditary nature of the monarchy, not least because they viewed a strong and hereditary monarchy as the most stable basis of government.

Hume thought that the Whigs were wrong in both their history and theory. Contrary to Whig mythology, "liberty" in its modern and valuable sense was a relatively recent development, and it owed its rise, Hume thought, not so much to the limitations upon royal power as to the growth of a stable central government. The "liberty" which Hume valued was the rule of law, in which law is known, regular, predictable, and applied equally to all. But for Hume, there could be no liberty in this sense without governmental authority.[4] Hume's cosmopolitan perspective led him to observe that the political institutions of other contemporary nations, such as those of absolutist France, also provided a substantial degree of liberty and prosperity. The prerequisite for any prosperous and liberal society, he insisted, was the security provided by stable government.

Hume combined his relatively conservative view of politics with philosophical skepticism. He believed that the notion of philosophy as the search for knowledge of ultimate reality, freed from custom and tradition, led ultimately to total skepticism.[5] His epistemological skepticism did not lead him to conclude that knowledge of the human world was futile, only that it must be based on the evidence provided by expe-

---

[4] Donald W. Livingston, "Hume's Historical Conception of Liberty," in Livingston and Nicholas Capaldi, eds., *Liberty in Hume's History of England* (Dordrecht, 1990), p. 115.

[5] Donald W. Livingston, *Hume's Philosophy of Common Life* (Chicago, 1984), chapter 1; and Livingston, "Hume's Historical Conception of Liberty," pp. 136ff. Similarly, John W. Danford, *David Hume and the Problem of Reason: Recovering the Human Sciences* (New Haven, 1990), esp. pp. 77–85.

rience and acquired through empirical analysis, rather than through deduction from abstract premises. He rejected the conception of philosophy as able to command belief and judgment independent of the received beliefs, customs, and prejudices of common life. A philosophy so divorced from experience, Hume thought, could not provide worthwhile knowledge. The role of philosophy, as Hume understood it, is not to begin by freeing itself from the beliefs and institutions of common life, but to explore the structure of common life through a combination of empirical analysis and assumptions about human nature.[6]

Hume sought to defend society against overly abstract ways of thinking that claim to criticize morality and social institutions on the basis of reason alone. And he was suspicious of political movements, religious or secular, which sought to reorder society on the basis of claims to knowledge of ultimate reality.

The rules of morality, Hume maintained, were not preordained: they developed through human experience and are in that sense "artifices." Many social institutions and conventions, Hume thought, have come about in an unplanned fashion, out of attempts to meet human needs. They come to be accepted because of their social utility, because there is some sense in which they work better. The proper role of the intellectual, as Hume saw it, is to bring to light the implicit rules and principles that exist in historically developed conventions and institutions. In morals as in other areas, Hume's most important categories for describing mental experience were "habit" or "custom," through which people assimilate the patterns of conduct and of judgment that make social life possible. It is through habit and custom, Hume maintained, that obedience to these artificial, historically evolved rules comes to seem "natural."

A central element of Hume's political thought is his theory of justice, which he first developed in his *Treatise of Human Nature*, and presented in rather more accessible form in his *Enquiry Concerning the Principles of Morals*, first published in 1751 and revised in subsequent editions, from which these selections are taken.

By "justice" Hume means a system of laws which impartially protects the life and property of all. He considered such laws the necessary condition of a civilized society, and believed that their enforcement was the most important function of government. Such laws are made necessary, Hume argues, by man's natural condition, above all by the fact of the relative scarcity of goods, and the fact that we have an inborn propensity to be partial to ourselves. The laws of justice arise to limit conflict in the

---

[6] See Livingston, *Hume's Philosophy of Common Life*, passim; and Frederick G. Whelan, *Order and Artifice in Hume's Political Philosophy* (Princeton, 1985), p. 293.

competition of self-interested individuals in search of relatively scarce goods.

Against those who believe that the most important rules of society are based directly on man's natural instincts, Hume argues that such rules arise from historical experience, are adopted because of their usefulness to society, and are in that sense "artificial" rather than "natural." They are one example of what Hume calls "conventions," by which he means rules and practices which arise not from conscious design, but evolve out of historical experience and are maintained because experience has demonstrated their efficacy. Hume then argues against what might appear to be more rational or idealistic conceptions of justice. Against those who assert that justice means equality of attainment, Hume maintains that the differences in human talents and abilities makes such a system impossible. Against those who believe that society should reward each individual according to his virtue, Hume responds that there are no grounds for judging virtue upon which all can agree. Only religious fanatics, he asserts, believe they have the knowledge to make such judgments, and their desire to redistribute property based on their conceptions of virtue or of equality renders them a threat to political stability.

David Hume,
"Of Justice," from *An Enquiry Concerning the Principles of Morals* (1751)[1]

SECTION III—*OF JUSTICE*

PART I

That Justice is useful to society, and consequently that *part* of its merit, at least, must arise from that consideration, it would be a superfluous undertaking to prove. That public utility is the *sole* origin of justice, and that reflections on the beneficial consequences of this virtue are the *sole* foundation of its merit; this proposition, being more curious and important, will better deserve our examination and enquiry.

Let us suppose, that nature has bestowed on the human race such profuse *abundance* of all *external* conveniencies, that, without any uncertainty in the event, without any care or industry on our part, every

[1] The text used for these excerpts is drawn from David Hume, *An Enquiry Conerning the Principles of Morals*, ed. J. B. Schneewind (Indianapolis, 1983).

individual finds himself fully provided with whatever his most voracious appetites can want, or luxurious imagination wish or desire. His natural beauty, we shall suppose, surpasses all acquired ornaments: The perpetual clemency of the seasons renders useless all clothes or covering: The raw herbage affords him the most delicious fare; the clear fountain, the richest beverage. No laborious occupation required: No tillage: No navigation. Music, poetry, and contemplation, form his sole business: Conversation, mirth, and friendship his sole amusement.

It seems evident, that, in such a happy state, every other social virtue would flourish, and receive tenfold encrease; but the cautious, jealous virtue of justice would never once have been dreamed of. For what purpose make a partition of goods, where every one has already more than enough? Why give rise to property, where there cannot possibly be any injury? Why call this object *mine*, when, upon the seizing of it by another, I need but stretch out my hand to possess myself of what is equally valuable? Justice, in that case, being totally USELESS, would be an idle ceremonial, and could never possibly have place in the catalogue of virtues.

We see, even in the present necessitous condition of mankind, that, wherever any benefit is bestowed by nature in an unlimited abundance, we leave it always in common among the whole human race, and make no subdivisions of right and property. Water and air, though the most necessary of all objects, are not challenged as the property of individuals; nor can any man commit injustice by the most lavish use and enjoyment of these blessings. In fertile extensive countries, with few inhabitants, land is regarded on the same footing. And no topic is so much insisted on by those, who defend the liberty of the seas, as the unexhausted use of them in navigation. Were the advantages, procured by navigation, as inexhaustible, these reasoners had never had any adversaries to refute; nor had any claims ever been advanced of a separate, exclusive dominion over the ocean.

It may happen, in some countries, at some periods, that there be established a property in water, none in land;[2] if the latter be in greater abundance than can be used by the inhabitants, and the former be found, with difficulty, and in very small quantities.

Again; suppose, that, though the necessities of human race continue the same as at present, yet the mind is so enlarged, and so replete with friendship and generosity, that every man has the utmost tenderness for every man, and feels no more concern for his own interest than for that of his fellows: It seems evident, that the USE of justice would, in this

---

[2] [Genesis, chaps. xiii and xxi.]

case, be suspended by such an extensive benevolence, nor would the divisions and barriers of property and obligation have ever been thought of. Why should I bind another, by a deed or promise, to do me any good office, when I know that he is already prompted, by the strongest inclination, to seek my happiness, and would, of himself, perform the desired service; except the hurt, he thereby receives, be greater than the benefit accruing to me? in which case, he knows, that, from my innate humanity and friendship, I should be the first to oppose myself to his imprudent generosity. Why raise land-marks between my neighbour's field and mine, when my heart has made no division between our interests; but shares all his joys and sorrows with the same force and vivacity as if originally my own? Every man, upon this supposition, being a second self to another, would trust all his interests to the discretion of every man; without jealousy, without partition, without distinction. And the whole human race would form only one family; where all would lie in common, and be used freely, without regard to property; but cautiously too, with as entire regard to the necessities of each individual, as if our own interests were most intimately concerned.

In the present disposition of the human heart, it would, perhaps, be difficult to find compleat instances of such enlarged affections; but still we may observe, that the case of families approaches towards it; and the stronger the mutual benevolence is among the individuals, the nearer it approaches; till all distinction of property be, in a great measure, lost and confounded among them. Between married persons, the cement of friendship is by the laws supposed so strong as to abolish all division of possessions: and has often, in reality, the force ascribed to it. And it is observable, that, during the ardour of new enthusiasms, when every principle is inflamed into extravagance, the community of goods has frequently been attempted: and nothing but experience of its inconveniencies, from the returning or disguised selfishness of men, could make the imprudent fanatics adopt anew the ideas of justice and of separate property. So true is it, that this virtue derives its existence entirely from its necessary *use* to the intercourse and social state of mankind. . . .

Thus, the rules of equity or justice depend entirely on the particular state and condition, in which men are placed, and owe their origin and existence to that UTILITY, which results to the public from their strict and regular observance. . . .

We are naturally partial to ourselves, and to our friends; but are capable of learning the advantage resulting from a more equitable conduct. Few enjoyments are given us from the open and liberal hand of nature; but by art, labour, and industry, we can extract them in great abundance. Hence the ideas of property become necessary in all civil society: Hence justice derives its usefulness to the public: And hence alone arises its merit and moral obligation. . . .

Part II

If we examine the *particular* laws, by which justice is directed, and property determined; we shall still be presented with the same conclusion. The good of mankind is the only object of all these laws and regulations. Not only it is requisite, for the peace and interest of society, that men's possessions should be separated; but the rules, which we follow, in making the separation, are such as can best be contrived to serve farther the interests of society.

We shall suppose, that a creature, possessed of reason, but unacquainted with human nature, deliberates with himself what RULES of justice or property would best promote public interest, and establish peace and security among mankind: His most obvious thought would be, to assign the largest possessions to the most extensive virtue, and give every one the power of doing good, proportioned to his inclination. In a perfect theocracy, where a being, infinitely intelligent, governs by particular volitions, this rule would certainly have place, and might serve to the wisest purposes: But were mankind to execute such a law; so great is the uncertainty of merit, both from its natural obscurity, and from the self-conceit of each individual, that no determinate rule of conduct would ever result from it; and the total dissolution of society must be the immediate consequence. Fanatics may suppose, *that dominion is founded on grace*, and *that saints alone inherit the earth*; but the civil magistrate very justly puts these sublime theorists on the same footing with common robbers, and teaches them by the severest discipline, that a rule, which, in speculation, may seem the most advantageous to society, may yet be found, in practice, totally pernicious and destructive.

That there were *religious* fanatics of this kind in ENGLAND, during the civil wars, we learn from history; though it is probable, that the obvious *tendency* of these principles excited such horror in mankind, as soon obliged the dangerous enthusiasts to renounce, or at least conceal their tenets. Perhaps, the *levellers*, who claimed an equal distribution of property, were a kind of *political* fanatics, which arose from the religious species, and more openly avowed their pretensions; as carrying a more plausible appearance, of being practicable in themselves, as well as useful to human society.

It must, indeed, be confessed, that nature is so liberal to mankind that, were all her presents equally divided among the species, and improved by art and industry, every individual would enjoy all the necessaries, and even most of the comforts of life; nor would ever be liable to any ills, but such as might accidentally arise from the sickly frame and constitution of his body. It must also be confessed, that, wherever we depart from this equality, we rob the poor of more satisfaction than we add to the rich, and that the slight gratification of a frivolous vanity, in one individual, frequently costs more than bread to many families, and even provinces. It may appear withal, that the rule of equality, as it would be highly *useful*, is not altogether *impracticable*; but has taken place, at least in an imperfect degree, in some republics; particularly that of SPARTA; where it was attended, it is said, with the most beneficial consequences. Not to mention, that the AGRARIAN laws, so frequently claimed in ROME, and carried into execution in many GREEK cities, proceeded, all of them, from a general idea of the utility of this principle.

But historians, and even common sense, may inform us, that, however specious [superficially attractive] these ideas of *perfect* equality may seem, they are really, at bottom, *impracticable*; and were they not so, would be extremely *pernicious* to human society.[3] Render possessions ever so equal, men's different degrees of art, care, and industry will immediately break that equality. Or if you check these virtues, you reduce society to the most extreme indigence; and instead of preventing want and beggary in a few, render it unavoidable to the whole community. The most rigorous inquisition too is requisite to watch every inequality on its first appearance; and the most severe jurisdiction, to punish and redress it. But besides, that so much authority must soon degenerate into tyranny, and be exerted with great partialities; who can possibly be possessed of it, in such a situation as is here supposed? Perfect equality of possessions, destroying all subordination, weakens extremely the authority of magistracy, and must reduce all power nearly to a level, as well as property.

We may conclude, therefore, that, in order to establish laws for the regulation of property, we must be acquainted with the nature and situation of man; must reject appearances, which may be false, though specious; and must search for those rules, which are, on the whole, most *useful* and *beneficial*. Vulgar sense and slight experience are sufficient for this purpose; where men give not way to too selfish avidity, or too extensive enthusiasm.

Who sees not, for instance, that whatever is produced or improved by a man's art or industry ought, for ever, to be secured to him, in order to give encouragement to such *useful* habits and accomplishments? That the property ought also to descend to children and relations, for the

---

[3] Hume argues that inequality is inevitable and beneficial to society.

same *useful* purpose? That it may be alienated by consent, in order to beget that commerce and intercourse, which is so *beneficial* to human society? And that all contracts and promises ought carefully to be fulfilled, in order to secure mutual trust and confidence, by which the general *interest* of mankind is so much promoted?

Examine the writers on the laws of nature;[4] and you will always find, that, whatever principles they set out with, they are sure to terminate here at last, and to assign, as the ultimate reason for every rule which they establish, the convenience and necessities of mankind. A concession thus extorted, in opposition to systems, has more authority, than if it had been made in prosecution of them. . . .

In general, we may observe, that all questions of property are subordinate to authority of civil laws, which extend, restrain, modify, and alter the rules of natural justice, according to the particular *convenience* of each community. The laws have, or ought to have, a constant reference to the constitution of government, the manners, the climate, the religion, the commerce, the situation of each society. A late author of genius, as well as learning, has prosecuted this subject at large, and has established, from these principles, a system of political knowledge, which abounds in ingenious and brilliant thoughts, and is not wanting in solidity. . . .[5]

These reflections are far from weakening the obligations of justice, or diminishing any thing from the most sacred attention to property. On the contrary, such sentiments must acquire new force from the present reasoning. For what stronger foundation can be desired or conceived for any duty, than to observe, that human society, or even human nature could not subsist, without the establishment of it; and will still arrive at greater degrees of happiness and perfection, the more inviolable the regard is, which is paid to that duty?[6]

The dilemma seems obvious: As justice evidently tends to promote public utility and to support civil society, the sentiment of justice is either derived from our reflecting on that tendency, or like hunger, thirst, and other appetites, resentment, love of life, attachment to offspring, and other passions, arises from a simple original instinct in the human breast, which nature has implanted for like salutary purposes. If

---

[4] Hume believes that it is futile to attempt to found justice on "laws of nature" which arise from some source other than their utility.

[5] Hume refers to Montesquieu, *The Spirit of the Laws*, first published in 1748. His point is that the laws of justice will vary to some degree with historical, geographical, and cultural circumstances.

[6] A rational recognition of the utility of the social practices of common life increases their legitimacy. For Hume, the utility of these practices is an important function of philosophical investigation.

the latter be the case, it follows, that property, which is the object of justice, is also distinguished by a simple, original instinct, and is not ascertained by any argument or reflection. But who is there that ever heard of such an instinct? Or is this a subject, in which new discoveries can be made? We may as well attempt to discover, in the body, new senses, which had before escaped the observation of all mankind.[7]

But farther, though it seems a very simple proposition to say, that nature, by an instinctive sentiment, distinguishes property, yet in reality we shall find, that there are required for that purpose ten thousand different instincts, and these employed about objects of the greatest intricacy and nicest discernment. For when a definition of *property is* required, that relation is found to resolve itself into any possession acquired by occupation, by industry, by prescription, by inheritance, by contract, etc. Can we think, that nature, by an original instinct, instructs us in all these methods of acquisition?

These words too, inheritance and contract, stand for ideas infinitely complicated; and to define them exactly, a hundred volumes of laws, and a thousand volumes of commentators, have not been found sufficient. Does nature, whose instincts in men are simple, embrace such complicated and artificial objects, and create a rational creature, without trusting any thing to the operation of his reason?

But even though all this were admitted, it would not be satisfactory. Positive laws can certainly transfer property. Is it by another original instinct, that we recognize the authority of kings and senates, and mark all the boundaries of their jurisdiction? Judges too, even though their sentence be erroneous and illegal, must be allowed, for the sake of peace and order, to have decisive authority, and ultimately to determine property. Have we original, innate ideas of prætors [magistrates] and chancellors and juries? Who sees not, that all these institutions arise merely from the necessities of human society?[8]

All birds of the same species, in every age and country, build their nests alike: In this we see the force of instinct. Men, in different times and places, frame their houses differently: Here we perceive the influence of reason and custom. A like inference may be drawn from comparing the instinct of generation and the institution of property. . . .[9]

---

[7] Hume's point is that unlike the innate sentiment of benevolence which we feel toward those we love, the sense of justice is learned by habit and from the experience of its utility for social life.

[8] Familial relations and relations of friendship are based on the innate sentiments of love and esteem. Authority, by contast, is not based on innate sentiments but is learned from culture; it comes to us not from nature, but from "second nature."

[9] The procreative drive is a universal part of human nature, but the laws of property vary with historical circumstance.

Appendix III—*Some Farther Considerations with Regard to Justice*

The intention of this Appendix is to give some more particular explication of the origin and nature of justice, and to mark some differences between it and the other virtues.

The social virtues of humanity and benevolence exert their influence immediately, by a direct tendency or instinct, which chiefly keeps in view the simple object, moving the affections, and comprehends not any scheme or system, nor the consequences resulting from the concurrence, imitation, or example of others. A parent flies to the relief of his child; transported by that natural sympathy, which actuates him, and which affords no leisure to reflect on the sentiments or conduct of the rest of mankind in like circumstances. A generous man chearfully embraces an opportunity of serving his friend; because he then feels himself under the dominion of the beneficent affections, nor is he concerned whether any other person in the universe were ever before actuated by such noble motives, or will ever afterwards prove their influence. In all these cases, the social passions have in view a single individual object, and pursue the safety or happiness alone of the person loved and esteemed. With this they are satisfied: In this, they acquiesce. And as the good, resulting from their benign influence, is in itself compleat and entire, it also excites the moral sentiment of approbation, without any reflection on farther consequences, and without any more enlarged views of the concurrence or imitation of the other members of society. On the contrary, were the generous friend or disinterested partriot to stand alone in the practice of beneficence; this would rather enhance his value in our eyes, and join the praise of rarity and novelty to his other more exalted merits.

The case is not the same with the social virtues of justice and fidelity. They are highly useful, or indeed absolutely necessary to the well-being of mankind: But the benefit, resulting from them, is not the consequence of every individual single act; but arises from the whole scheme or system, concurred in by the whole, or the greater part of the society. General peace and order are the attendants of justice or a general abstinence from the possessions of others: But a particular regard to the particular right of one individual citizen may frequently, considered in itself, be productive of pernicious consequences. The result of the individual acts is here, in many instances, directly opposite to that of the whole system of actions; and the former may be extremely hurtful, while the latter is, to the highest degree, advantageous. Riches, inherited from a parent, are, in a bad man's hand, the instrument of mischief. The right of succession may, in one instance, be hurtful. Its benefit arises only from the observance of the general rule; and it is sufficient, if compensation be thereby made for all the ills and inconveniencies, which flow from particular characters and situations. . . .

All the laws of nature, which regulate property, as well as all civil laws, are general, and regard alone some essential circumstances of the case, without taking into consideration the characters, situations, and connexions of the person concerned, or any particular consequences which may result from the determination of these laws, in any particular case which offers. They deprive, without scruple, a beneficent man of all his possessions, if acquired by mistake, without a good title; in order to bestow them on a selfish miser, who has already heaped up immense stores of superfluous riches. Public utility requires, that property should be regulated by general inflexible rules; and though such rules are adopted as best serve the same end of public utility, it is impossible for them to prevent all particular hardships, or make beneficial consequences result from every individual case. It is sufficient, if the whole plan or scheme be necessary to the support of civil society, and if the balance of good, in the main, do thereby preponderate much above that of evil. Even the general laws of the universe, though planned by infinite wisdom, cannot exclude all evil or inconvenience, in every particular operation.[10]

It has been asserted by some, that justice arises from HUMAN CONVENTIONS, and proceeds from the voluntary choice, consent, or combination of mankind. If by *convention* be here meant a *promise* (which is the most usual sense of the word) nothing can be more absurd than this position. The observance of promises is itself one of the most considerable parts of justice; and we are not surely bound to keep our word, because we have given our word to keep it. But if by convention be meant a sense of common interest; which sense each man feels in his own breast, which he remarks in his fellows, and which carries him in concurrence with others, into a general plan or system of actions which tends to public utility; it must be owned, that, in this sense Justice arises from human conventions.[11] For if it be allowed (what is indeed, evident) that the particular consequences of a particular act of Justice may be hurtful to the public as well as to individuals; it follows, that every man, in embracing that virtue, must have an eye to the whole plan or system,

---

[10] While the application of the general rules of justice will offend our sense of fairness in particular cases, the rules must be applied nevertheless, since their impartial enforcement is beneficial on the whole.

[11] Important social rules are based neither on our instincts, nor on rationally derived voluntary agreement, but on a sense of duty which develops from observing the actions and expectations of others.

and must expect the concurrence of his fellows in the same conduct and behaviour. Did all his views terminate in the consequences of each act of his own, his benevolence and humanity as well as his self-love, might often prescribe to him measures of conduct very different from those, which are agreeable to the strict rules of right and justice. . . .

INTRODUCTION TO
David Hume,
"Of the Origin of Government," "Of the Original Contract," and "Of Passive Obedience," from *Essays Moral, Political and Literary*

◆

Many of Hume's political essays, not to speak of his *History of England*, deal with what he took to be the proper lessons to be learned from recent English history. In the mid-seventeenth century, England had been wracked by civil war, in which a series of Protestant religious sects sought to overturn the political order and the established Church of England. In response to the challenge of what they called "enthusiasm," Anglican theorists such as Richard Hooker developed a principled defense of historical institutions which was to influence the later conservatism of Hume as well as of Burke. For Hooker, the claim of the Puritans to derive prescriptions for political action directly from the Bible made them guilty of the sin of intellectual pride.[1] In his *History of England*, Hume portrayed the Puritan revolt against the royal, Anglican regime of Charles I as an example of enthusiasm in politics. The danger of the intrusion of "enthusiasm" into politics was a frequent theme of Hume's thought, by which he meant the threat posed by religious movements which take their bearings from divine revelation rather than from experience, and which seek to reorder society based upon claims of divine inspiration.

Hume argued that governments ought to be obeyed not because they were founded on divine laws or protected natural rights, but rather on the utilitarian ground that it is generally advantageous for men to do so. But what most often induces men to obey government, Hume believed, is not the rational recognition of the public benefit that government brings, but rather custom and habit. In his epistemological writings, Hume argued that inductive reasoning, based on the assumption that the same cause would always have the same effect, cannot be demonstrated with philosophical rigor, but is accepted by the mind out of habit, and comes to be regarded as "natural." Social rules, such as those of justice, were similarly learned through habituation and become part of our second nature.[2]

---

[1] Anthony Quinton, *The Politics of Imperfection: The Religious and Secular Traditions of Conservative Thought in England from Hooker to Oakeshott* (London, 1978), pp. 25–28.

[2] See Frederick G. Whelan, *Order and Artifice in Hume's Political Philosophy* (Princeton, 1985), p. 293.

Hume understood the rationalistic theory of political legitimacy formulated by Locke and endorsed by many Whigs to be critical without being constructive. He feared that such a theory was likely to weaken allegiance based on custom and habit, without offering an alternative basis for loyalty to the very governments which made liberty possible. In his *History of England* as well as in his essays, Hume challenged the Whig interpretation of the British experience of liberty, not in order to denigrate the value of liberty, but because he thought that the Whigs misinterpreted the historical and institutional basis of British liberty.[3] Hume criticized the Whigs for so emphasizing the legitimate and necessary criticism of government that they lost sight of the fact that established government is itself a necessary prerequisite of liberty.

For Hume, then, social contract theory was an example of the sort of politics he abhorred, one based upon abstract, speculative principles, which could be used to undermine a political order but were incapable of providing a regime which could command allegiance.[4] Late in his life, Hume applied these criteria to the "Wilkes and Liberty" riots of 1768–71, which he saw as a radical and democratic challenge to the existing political order. For Hume, this was an example of a new variety of enthusiasm or metaphysical politics, motivated less by real grievances than by the attempt to remake politics according to some abstract worldview.[5] Hume thus began to transfer his critique of the politics of enthusiasm from religious movements to movements animated by secular, abstract ideologies, a process which Burke was to continue.

The following selections are from Hume's essays. The first essay, "Of the Origin of Government," was written by Hume late in life and published posthumously in the 1777 edition of his *Essays and Treatises on Several Subjects*. The other two essays were first published in 1748 in a volume entitled, *Three Essays, Moral and Political*. In the first essay, Hume offers a very general explanation of how government and obedience to government arose. The theory is entirely naturalistic: it does not depend upon divine providence or intervention. Hume's explanation is also intended as alternative to theories of voluntary social contract. Government, he argues in these essays, first comes about without conscious human intention, and then comes to be accepted for the benefits that it brings.

[3] Donald W. Livingston, "Hume's Historical Conception of Liberty," in Livingston and Nicholas Capaldi, eds., *Liberty in Hume's History of England* (Dordrecht, 1990), pp. 112–13.

[4] "Introduction," to Stuart D. Warner and Donald W. Livingston, eds., *David Hume: Political Writings* (Indianapolis, 1994), p. xiv.

[5] Donald W. Livingston, *Hume's Philosophy of Common Life* (Chicago, 1984), p. 323.

David Hume,
"Of the Origin of Government" (1777),
"Of the Original Contract" (1748),
"Of Passive Obedience" (1748)[1]

"Of the Origin of Government"

Man, born in a family, is compelled to maintain society, from necessity, from natural inclination, and from habit. The same creature, in his farther progress, is engaged to establish political society, in order to administer justice; without which there can be no peace among them, nor safety, nor mutual intercourse. We are, therefore, to look upon all the vast apparatus of our government, as having ultimately no other object or purpose but the distribution of justice, or, in other words, the support of the twelve judges.[2] Kings and parliaments, fleets and armies, officers of the court and revenue, ambassadors, ministers, and privy-counsellors, are all subordinate in their end to this part of administration. Even the clergy, as their duty leads them to inculcate morality, may justly be thought, so far as regards this world, to have no other useful object of their institution.

All men are sensible of the necessity of justice to maintain peace and order; and all men are sensible of the necessity of peace and order for the maintenance of society. Yet, notwithstanding this strong and obvious necessity, such is the frailty or perverseness of our nature! it is impossible to keep men, faithfully and unerringly, in the paths of justice. Some extraordinary circumstances may happen, in which a man finds his interests to be more promoted by fraud or rapine [theft], than hurt by the breach which his injustice makes in the social union. But much more frequently, he is seduced from his great and important, but distant interests, by the allurement of present, though often very frivolous temptations. This great weakness is incurable in human nature.[3]

Men must, therefore, endeavour to palliate [alleviate] what they cannot cure. They must institute some persons, under the appellation [title] of magistrates, whose peculiar office [designated task] it is, to point out the decrees of equity, to punish transgressors, to correct fraud and violence, and to oblige men, however reluctant, to consult their own real and permanent interests. In a word, OBEDIENCE is a new duty which

[1] The selections follow the text as established in David Hume, *Essays Moral, Political and Literary*, ed. Eugene F. Miller (revised edition, Indianapolis, 1987).

[2] A possible reference to the total number of judges on the two highest British courts; six on the Court of Common Pleas and six on the Court of King's Bench.

[3] One of Hume's recurrent references to inherent human imperfection.

must be invented to support that of JUSTICE; and the tyes [obligations] of equity must be corroborated by those of allegiance.

But still, viewing matters in an abstract light, it may be thought, that nothing is gained by this alliance, and that the factitious [made by human art rather than by nature] duty of obedience, from its very nature, lays as feeble a hold of the human mind, as the primitive and natural duty of justice. Peculiar interests and present temptations may overcome the one as well as the other. They are equally exposed to the same inconvenience. And the man, who is inclined to be a bad neighbour, must be led by the same motives, well or ill understood, to be a bad citizen and subject. Not to mention, that the magistrate himself may often be negligent, or partial, or unjust in his administration.

Experience, however, proves, that there is a great difference between the cases. Order in society, we find, is much better maintained by means of government; and our duty to the magistrate is more strictly guarded by the principles of human nature, than our duty to our fellow-citizens. The love of dominion is so strong in the breast of man, that many, not only submit to, but court all the dangers, and fatigues, and cares of government; and men, once raised to that station, though often led astray by private passions, find, in ordinary cases, a visible interest in the impartial administration of justice. The persons, who first attain this distinction by the consent, tacit or express, of the people, must be endowed with superior personal qualities of valour, force, integrity, or prudence, which command respect and confidence: and after government is established, a regard to birth, rank, and station has a mighty influence over men, and enforces the decrees of the magistrate. The prince or leader exclaims against every disorder, which disturbs his society. He summons all his partizans and all men of probity [honesty] to aid him in correcting and redressing it: and he is readily followed by all indifferent persons in the execution of his office. He soon acquires the power of rewarding these services; and in the progress of society, he establishes subordinate ministers and often a military force, who find an immediate and a visible interest, in supporting his authority. Habit soon consolidates what other principles of human nature had imperfectly founded; and men, once accustomed to obedience, never think of departing from that path, in which they and their ancestors have constantly trod, and to which they are confined by so many urgent and visible motives.[4]

But though this progress of human affairs may appear certain and inevitable, and though the support which allegiance brings to justice, be founded on obvious principles of human nature, it cannot be expected that men should beforehand be able to discover them, or foresee their

---

[4] Hume suggests the necessity of political elites, and argues that a sense of obedience arises from the experience of the utility of order and develops into habit.

operation.[5] Government commences more casually and more imperfectly. It is probable, that the first ascendant [elevation] of one man over multitudes begun during a state of war; where the superiority of courage and of genius discovers itself most visibly, where unanimity and concert are most requisite, and where the pernicious effects of disorder are most sensibly felt. The long continuance of that state, an incident common among savage tribes, enured the people to submission; and if the chieftain possessed as much equity as prudence and valour, he became, even during peace, the arbiter of all differences, and could gradually, by a mixture of force and consent, establish his authority. The benefit sensibly felt from his influence, made it be cherished by the people, at least by the peaceable and well disposed among them; and if his son enjoyed the same good qualities, government advanced the sooner to maturity and perfection; but was still in a feeble state, till the farther progress of improvement procured the magistrate a revenue, and enabled him to bestow rewards on the several instruments of his administration, and to inflict punishments on the refractory [rebellious] and disobedient. Before that period, each exertion of his influence must have been particular, and founded on the peculiar circumstances of the case. After it, submission was no longer a matter of choice in the bulk of the community, but was rigorously exacted by the authority of the supreme magistrate.

In all governments, there is a perpetual intestine [internal] struggle, open or secret, between AUTHORITY and LIBERTY; and neither of them can ever absolutely prevail in the contest. A great sacrifice of liberty must necessarily be made in every government; yet even the authority, which confines liberty, can never, and perhaps ought never, in any constitution, to become quite entire and uncontrollable. The sultan is master of the life and fortune of any individual; but will not be permitted to impose new taxes on his subjects: a French monarch can impose taxes at pleasure; but would find it dangerous to attempt the lives and fortunes of individuals. Religion also, in most countries, is commonly found to be a very intractable principle; and other principles or prejudices frequently resist all the authority of the civil magistrate; whose power, being founded on opinion, can never subvert other opinions, equally rooted with that of his title to dominion. The government, which, in common appellation, receives the appellation of free, is that which admits of a partition of power among several members, whose united authority is no less, or is commonly greater than that of any monarch; but who, in the usual course of administration, must act by general

---

[5] This is a favorite Humean theme, namely that valuable existing institutions have come about as an unintended consequence of past human action, and are retained because of their functional efficacy.

and equal laws, that are previously known to all the members and to all their subjects. In this sense, it must be owned [acknowledged] that liberty is the perfection of civil society; but still authority must be acknowledged essential to its very existence: and in those contests, which so often take place between the one and the other, the latter may, on that account, challenge the preference. Unless perhaps one may say (and it may be said with some reason) that a circumstance, which is essential to the existence of civil society, must always support itself, and needs be guarded with less jealousy, than one that contributes only to its perfection, which the indolence of men is so apt to neglect, or their ignorance to overlook.[6]

"Of the Original Contract"

As no party, in the present age, can well support itself, without a philosophical or speculative system of principles, annexed to its political or practical one; we accordingly find, that each of the factions, into which this nation is divided, has reared up a fabric of the former kind, in order to protect and cover that scheme of actions, which it pursues. The people being commonly very rude builders, especially in this speculative way, and more especially still, when actuated by party-zeal; it is natural to imagine, that their workmanship must be a little unshapely, and discover evident marks of that violence and hurry, in which it was raised. The one party,[7] by tracing up government to the DEITY, endeavour to render it so sacred and inviolate, that it must be little less than sacrilege, however tyrannical it may become, to touch or invade it, in the smallest article. The other party,[8] by founding government altogether on the consent of the PEOPLE, suppose that there is a kind of *original contract*, by which the subjects have tacitly reserved the power of resisting their sovereign, whenever they find themselves aggrieved by that authority, with which they have, for certain purposes, voluntarily entrusted him. These are the speculative principles of the two parties; and these too are the practical consequences deduced from them.

I shall venture to affirm, *That both these* systems *of speculative principles are just; though not in the sense, intended by the parties:* And, *That both the* schemes *of practical consequences are prudent; though not in the*

---

[6] Hume argues that those who value liberty tend to overlook the fact that liberty is provided by government, which in turn depends upon the authority it commands.
[7] The Tories.
[8] The Whigs.

extremes, to which each party, in opposition to the other, has commonly endeavored to carry them.

That the DEITY is the ultimate author of all government, will never be denied by any, who admit a general providence, and allow, that all events in the universe are conducted by an uniform plan, and directed to wise purposes. As it is impossible for the human race to subsist, at least in any comfortable or secure state, without the protection of government; this institution must certainly have been intended by that beneficent Being, who means the good of all his creatures: And as it has universally, in fact, taken place, in all countries, and all ages; we may conclude, with still greater certainty, that it was intended by that omniscient Being, who can never be deceived by any event or operation.[9] But since he gave rise to it, not by any particular or miraculous interposition, but by his concealed and universal efficacy; a sovereign cannot, properly speaking, be called his vice-gerent [deputy], in any other sense than every power or force, being derived from him, may be said to act by his commission. Whatever actually happens is comprehended in the general plan or intention of providence; nor has the greatest and most lawful prince any more reason, upon that account, to plead a peculiar sacredness or inviolable authority, than an inferior magistrate, or even an usurper, or even a robber and a pirate. The same divine superintendent, who, for wise purposes, invested a TITUS or a TRAJAN with authority, did also, for purposes, no doubt, equally wise, though unknown, bestow power on a BORGIA or an ANGRIA.[10] The same causes, which gave rise to the sovereign power in every state, established likewise every petty jurisdiction in it, and every limited authority. A constable, therefore, no less than a king, acts by a divine commission, and possesses an indefeasible right.

When we consider how nearly equal all men are in their bodily force, and even in their mental powers and faculties, till cultivated by education; we must necessarily allow, that nothing but their own consent could, at first, associate them together, and subject them to any authority. The people, if we trace government to its first origin in the woods and deserts, are the source of all power and jurisdiction, and voluntarily, for the sake of peace and order, abandoned their native liberty, and received laws from their equal and companion. The conditions, upon

---

[9] Hume's point is that these conclusions follow from the premise of divine providence, not that the premise is true.

[10] Titus and Trajan are generally regarded as great Roman emperors, while Cesare Borgia, who conquered and ruled parts of northern Italy in the early sixteenth century, was known for his cruelty and his lack of scruple, and Angria was the leader of a family of predatory pirates who operated off of India's Malabar coast in Hume's day. His point is that if the claim that obedience to government is based on the divine source of government, then that claim can be applied to any ruler, no matter how cruel or unjust.

which they were willing to submit, were either expressed, or were so clear and obvious, that it might well be esteemed superfluous to express them. If this, then, be meant by the *original contract*, it cannot be denied, that all government is, at first, founded on a contract, and that the most ancient rude combinations of mankind were formed chiefly by that principle. In vain, are we asked in what records this charter of our liberties is registered. It was not written on parchment, nor yet on leaves or barks of trees. It preceded the use of writing and all the other civilized arts of life. But we trace it plainly in the nature of man, and in the equality, or something approaching equality, which we find in all the individuals of that species. The force, which now prevails, and which is founded on fleets and armies, is plainly political, and derived from authority, the effect of established government. A man's natural force consists only in the vigour of his limbs, and the firmness of his courage; which could never subject multitudes to the command of one. Nothing but their own consent, and their sense of the advantages resulting from peace and order, could have had that influence.

Yet even this consent was long very imperfect, and could not be the basis of a regular administration. The chieftain, who had probably acquired his influence during the continuance of war, ruled more by persuasion than command; and till he could employ force to reduce the refractory and disobedient, the society could scarcely be said to have attained a state of civil government. No compact or agreement, it is evident, was expressly formed for general submission; an idea far beyond the comprehension of savages: Each exertion of authority in the chieftain must have been particular, and called forth by the present exigencies of the case: The sensible utility, resulting from his interposition, made these exertions become daily more frequent; and their frequency gradually produced an habitual, and, if you please to call it so, a voluntary, and therefore precarious, acquiescence in the people.[11]

But philosophers, who have embraced a party (if that be not a contradiction in terms) are not contented with these concessions. They assert, not only that government in its earliest infancy arose from consent or rather the voluntary acquiescence of the people; but also, that, even at present, when it has attained full maturity, it rests on no other foundation.[12] They affirm, that all men are still born equal, and owe allegiance to no prince or government, unless bound by the obligation and sanction of a *promise*. And as no man, without some equivalent, would forego the advantages of his native liberty, and subject himself to the

---

[11] A sense of obedience arises from the experience of its utility, then continues as habit and custom.

[12] Hume has in mind Whig theorists, particularly John Locke's *Second Treatise of Government*.

will of another; this promise is always understood to be conditional, and imposes on him no obligation, unless he meet with justice and protection from his sovereign. These advantages the sovereign promises him in return; and if he fail in the execution, he has broken, on his part, the articles of engagement, and has thereby freed his subject from all obligations to allegiance. Such, according to these philosophers, is the foundation of authority in every government; and such the right of resistance, possessed by every subject.

But would these reasoners look abroad into the world, they would meet with nothing that, in the least, corresponds to their ideas, or can warrant so refined and philosophical a system. On the contrary, we find, everywhere, princes, who claim their subjects as their property, and assert their independent right of sovereignty, from conquest or succession. We find also, everywhere, subjects, who acknowledge this right in their prince, and suppose themselves born under obligations of obedience to a certain sovereign, as much as under the ties of reverence and duty to certain parents. These connexions are always conceived to be equally independent of our consent, in PERSIA and CHINA; in FRANCE and SPAIN; and even in HOLLAND and ENGLAND, wherever the doctrines above-mentioned have not been carefully inculcated. Obedience or subjection becomes so familiar, that most men never make any enquiry about its origin or cause, more than about the principle of gravity, resistance, or the most universal laws of nature. Or if curiosity ever move them; as soon as they learn, that they themselves and their ancestors have, for several ages, or from time immemorial, been subject to such a form of government or such a family; they immediately acquiesce, and acknowledge their obligation to allegiance. Were you to preach, in most parts of the world, that political connexions are founded altogether on voluntary consent or a mutual promise, the magistrate would soon imprison you, as seditious, for loosening the ties of obedience; if your friends did not before shut you up as delirious, for advancing such absurdities. It is strange, that an act of the mind, which every individual is supposed to have formed, and after he came to the use of reason too, otherwise it could have no authority; that this act, I say, should be so much unknown to all of them, that, over the face of the whole earth, there scarcely remain any traces or memory of it.[13]

But the contract, on which government is founded, is said to be the *original contract*; and consequently may be supposed too old to fall under the knowledge of the present generation. If the agreement, by which savage men first associated and conjoined their force, be here meant, this is acknowledged to be real; but being so ancient, and being

---

[13] Contract theories of obedience to government which claim that political authority is based upon conscious and voluntary consent, therefore, are at odds with experience, which shows that obedience to political authority flows largely from custom and habit.

obliterated by a thousand changes of government and princes, it cannot now be supposed to retain any authority. If we would say any thing to the purpose, we must assert, that every particular government, which is lawful, and which imposes any duty of allegiance on the subject, was, at first, founded on consent and a voluntary compact. But besides that this supposes the consent of the fathers to bind the children, even to the most remote generations (which republican writers will never allow), besides this, I say, it is not justified by history or experience, in any age or country of the world.

Almost all the governments, which exist at present, or of which there remains any record in story, have been founded originally, either on usurpation or conquest, or both, without any pretence of a fair consent, or voluntary subjection of the people. When an artful and bold man is placed at the head of an army or faction, it is often easy for him, by employing, sometimes violence, sometimes false pretences, to establish his dominion over a people a hundred times more numerous than his partizans. He allows no such open communication, that his enemies can know, with certainty, their number or force. He gives them no leisure to assemble together in a body to oppose him. Even all those, who are the instruments of his usurpation, may wish his fall; but their ignorance of each other's intention keeps them in awe, and is the sole cause of his security. By such arts as these, many governments have been established; and this is all the *original contract*, which they have to boast of.

The face of the earth is continually changing, by the encrease of small kingdoms into great empires, by the dissolution of great empires into smaller kingdoms, by the planting of colonies, by the migration of tribes. Is there any thing discoverable in all these events, but force and violence? Where is the mutual agreement or voluntary association so much talked of?

Even the smoothest way, by which a nation may receive a foreign master, by marriage or a will, is not extremely honourable for the people; but supposes them to be disposed of, like a dowry or a legacy, according to the pleasure or interest of their rulers.

But where no force interposes, and election takes place; what is this election so highly vaunted? It is either the combination of a few great men, who decide for the whole, and will allow of no opposition: Or it is the fury of a multitude, that follow a seditious ringleader, who is not known, perhaps, to a dozen among them, and who owes his advancement merely to his own impudence, or to the momentary caprice of his fellows.

Are these disorderly elections, which are rare too, of such mighty authority, as to be the only lawful foundation of all government and allegiance?

In reality, there is not a more terrible event, than a total dissolution of government, which gives liberty to the multitude, and makes the determination or choice of a new establishment depend upon a number, which nearly approaches to that of the body of the people: For it never comes entirely to the whole body of them. Every wise man, then, wishes to see, at the head of a powerful and obedient army, a general, who may speedily seize the prize, and give to the people a master, which they are so unfit to choose for themselves. So little correspondent is fact and reality to those philosophical notions.[14]

Let not the establishment at the *Revolution* deceive us, or make us so much in love with a philosophical origin to government, as to imagine all others monstrous and irregular. Even that event was far from corresponding to these refined ideas. It was only the succession, and that only in the regal part of the government, which was then changed: And it was only the majority of seven hundred, who determined that change for near ten millions.[15] I doubt not, indeed, but the bulk of those ten millions acquiesced willingly in the determination: But was the matter left, in the least, to their choice? Was it not justly supposed to be, from that moment, decided, and every man punished, who refused to submit to the new sovereign? How otherwise could the matter have ever been brought to any issue or conclusion?

The republic of ATHENS was, I believe, the most extensive democracy, that we read of in history: Yet if we make the requisite allowances for the women, the slaves, and the strangers, we shall find, that that establishment was not, at first, made, nor any law ever voted, by a tenth part of those who were bound to pay obedience to it: Not to mention the islands and foreign dominions, which the ATHENIANS claimed as theirs by right of conquest. And as it is well known, that popular assemblies in that city were always full of licence and disorder, notwithstanding the institutions and laws by which they were checked: How much more disorderly must they prove, where they form not the established constitution, but meet tumultuously on the dissolution of the ancient government, in order to give rise to a new one? How chimerical [fanciful] must it be to talk of a choice in such circumstances?

The ACHÆANS enjoyed the freest and most perfect democracy of all antiquity; yet they employed force to oblige some cities to enter into their league, as we learn from POLYBIUS.[16]

HARRY the IVth and HARRY the VIIth of ENGLAND, had really no title to the throne but a parliamentary election; yet they never would ac-

---

[14] Note Hume's antipathy to direct democracy, and suspicion of democracy in general.
[15] The transfer of the British crown to William and Mary in 1689, Hume argues, was approved only by the seven hundred members of the parliamentary conventions, called by William, in England and Scotland.
[16] [Book ii., chapter 38.]

knowledge it, lest they should thereby weaken their authority. Strange, if the only real foundation of all authority be consent and promise!

It is in vain to say, that all governments are or should be, at first, founded on popular consent, as much as the necessity of human affairs will admit. This favours entirely my pretension. I maintain, that human affairs will never admit of this consent; seldom of the appearance of it. But that conquest or usurpation, that is, in plain terms, force, by dissolving the ancient governments, is the origin of almost all the new ones, which were ever established in the world. And that in the few cases, where consent may seem to have taken place, it was commonly so irregular, so confined, or so much intermixed either with fraud or violence, that it cannot have any great authority.

My intention here is not to exclude the consent of the people from being one just foundation of government where it has place. It is surely the best and most sacred of any. I only pretend, that it has very seldom had place in any degree, and never almost in its full extent. And that therefore some other foundation of government must also be admitted.

Were all men possessed of so inflexible a regard to justice, that, of themselves, they would totally abstain from the properties of others; they had [would have] for ever remained in a state of absolute liberty, without subjection to any magistrate or political society: But this is a state of perfection, of which human nature is justly deemed incapable.[17] Again; were all men possessed of so perfect an understanding, as always to know their own interests, no form of government had ever been submitted to, but what was established on consent, and was fully canvassed by every member of the society: But this state of perfection is likewise much superior to human nature. Reason, history, and experience shew us, that all political societies have had an origin much less accurate and regular; and were one to choose a period of time, when the people's consent was the least regarded in public transactions, it would be precisely on the establishment of a new government. In a settled constitution, their inclinations are often consulted; but during the fury of revolutions, conquests, and public convulsions, military force or political craft usually decides the controversy.

When a new government is established, by whatever means, the people are commonly dissatisfied with it, and pay obedience more from fear and necessity, than from any idea of allegiance or of moral obligation. The prince is watchful and jealous, and must carefully guard against every beginning or appearance of insurrection. Time, by degrees, removes all these difficulties, and accustoms the nation to regard, as their lawful or native princes, that family, which, at first, they considered as

---

[17] The need for government arises from the need to protect property, which, because of human imperfections, will always be a source of potential disorder.

usurpers or foreign conquerors. In order to found this opinion, they
have no recourse to any notion of voluntary consent or promise, which,
they know, never was, in this case, either expected or demanded. The
original establishment was formed by violence, and submitted to from
necessity. The subsequent administration is also supported by power,
and acquiesced in by the people, not as a matter of choice, but of obligation. They imagine not, that their consent gives their prince a title: But
they willingly consent, because they think, that, from long possession,
he has acquired a title, independent of their choice or inclination. . . .

Did one generation of men go off the stage at once, and another succeed, as is the case with silk-worms and butterflies, the new race, if they
had sense enough to choose their government, which surely is never the
case with men, might voluntarily, and by general consent, establish their
own form of civil polity, without any regard to the laws or precedents,
which prevailed among their ancestors. But as human society is in perpetual flux, one man every hour going out of the world, another coming
into it, it is necessary, in order to preserve stability in government, that
the new brood should conform themselves to the established constitution, and nearly follow the path which their fathers, treading in the foot-
steps of theirs, had marked out to them. Some innovations must necessarily have place in every human institution, and it is happy where the
enlightened genius of the age give these a direction to the side of reason,
liberty, and justice: but violent innovations no individual is entitled to
make: they are even dangerous to be attempted by the legislature: more
ill than good is ever to be expected from them: and if history affords
examples to the contrary, they are not to be drawn into precedent, and
are only to be regarded as proofs, that the science of politics affords few
rules, which will not admit of some exception, and which may not sometimes be controlled by fortune and accident[18]. . . .

But would we have a more regular, at least a more philosophical, refutation of this principle of an original contract or popular consent; perhaps, the following observations may suffice.

All *moral* duties may be divided into two kinds. The *first* are those, to
which men are impelled by a natural instinct or immediate propensity,
which operates on them, independent of all ideas of obligation, and of
all views, either to public or private utility. Of this nature are, love of
children, gratitude to benefactors, pity to the unfortunate. When we reflect on the advantage, which results to society from such humane instincts, we pay them the just tribute of moral approbation and esteem:
But the person, actuated by them, feels their power and influence, ante-
cedent to any such reflection.

---

[18] Note Hume's general strictures against radical innovation.

The *second* kind of moral duties are such as are not supported by any original instinct of nature, but are performed entirely from a sense of obligation, when we consider the necessities of human society, and the impossibility of supporting it, if these duties were neglected. It is thus *justice* or a regard to the property of others, *fidelity* or the observance of promises, become obligatory, and acquire an authority over mankind. For as it is evident, that every man loves himself better than any other person, he is naturally impelled to extend his acquisitions as much as possible; and nothing can restrain him in this propensity, but reflection and experience by which he learns the pernicious effects of that licence, and the total dissolution of society which must ensue from it. His original inclination, therefore, or instinct, is here checked and restrained by a subsequent judgment or observation.

The case is precisely the same with the political or civil duty of *allegiance*, as with the natural duties of justice and fidelity. Our primary instincts lead us, either to indulge ourselves in unlimited freedom, or to seek dominion over others: And it is reflection only, which engages us to sacrifice such strong passions to the interests of peace and public order. A small degree of experience and observation suffices to teach us, that society cannot possibly be maintained without the authority of magistrates, and that this authority must soon fall into contempt, where exact obedience is not payed to it. The observation of these general and obvious interests is the source of all allegiance, and of that moral obligation, which we attribute to it.[19]

What necessity, therefore, is there to found the duty of *allegiance* or obedience to magistrates on that of *fidelity* or a regard to promises, and to suppose, that it is the consent of each individual, which subjects him to government; when it appears, that both allegiance and fidelity stand precisely on the same foundation, and are both submitted to by mankind, on account of the apparent interests and necessities of human society? We are bound to obey our sovereign, it is said; because we have given a tacit promise to that purpose. But why are we bound to observe our promise? It must here be asserted, that the commerce and intercourse of mankind, which are of such mighty advantage, can have no security where men pay no regard to their engagements. In like manner, may it be said, that men could not live at all in society, at least in a civilized society, without laws and magistrates and judges, to prevent the encroachments of the strong upon the weak, of the violent upon the just and equitable. The obligation to allegiance being of like force and authority with the obligation to fidelity, we gain nothing by resolving the

[19] Government is obeyed not on the basis of a contract between the ruler and ruled, but out of a recognition by the ruled of the usefulness of governmental authority in maintaining peace.

one into the other. The general interests or necessities of society are sufficient to establish both.

If the reason be asked of that obedience, which we are bound to pay to government, I readily answer, *because society could not otherwise subsist:* And this answer is clear and intelligible to all mankind. Your answer is, *because we should keep our word.* But besides, that nobody, till trained in a philosophical system, can either comprehend or relish this answer: Besides this, I say, you find yourself embarrassed, when it is asked, *why we are bound to keep our word?* Nor can you give any answer, but what would, immediately, without any circuit, have accounted for our obligation to allegiance.

But to *whom is allegiance due? And who is our lawful sovereign?* This question is often the most difficult of any, and liable to infinite discussions. When people are so happy, that they can answer, *Our present sovereign, who inherits, in a direct line, from ancestors, that have governed us for many ages;* this answer admits of no reply; even though historians, in tracing up to the remotest antiquity, the origin of that royal family, may find, as commonly happens, that its first authority was derived from usurpation and violence.[20] It is confessed, that private justice, or the abstinence from the properties of others, is a most cardinal virtue: Yet reason tells us, that there is no property in durable objects, such as lands or houses, when carefully examined in passing from hand to hand, but must, in some period, have been founded on fraud and injustice. The necessities of human society, neither in private nor public life, will allow of such an accurate enquiry: And there is no virtue or moral duty, but what may, with facility, be refined away, if we indulge a false philosophy, in sifting and scrutinizing it, by every captious rule of logic, in every light or position, in which it may be placed. . . .

The general obligation, which binds us to government, is the interest and necessities of society; and this obligation is very strong. The determination of it to this or that particular prince or form of government is frequently more uncertain and dubious. Present possession has considerable authority in these cases, and greater than in private property; because of the disorders which attend all revolutions and changes of government.

We shall only observe, before we conclude, that, though an appeal to general opinion may justly, in the speculative sciences of metaphysics, natural philosophy, or astronomy, be deemed unfair and inconclusive, yet in all questions with regard to morals, as well as criticism, there is really no other standard, by which any controversy can ever be decided.

---

[20] An example of Hume's historical consequentialism: allegiance derives from a recognition of the positive effects of government, not because of its origins.

And nothing is a clearer proof, that a theory of this kind is erroneous, than to find, that it leads to paradoxes, repugnant to the common sentiments of mankind, and to the practice and opinion of all nations and all ages.[21] The doctrine, which founds all lawful government on an *original contract*, or consent of the people, is plainly of this kind; nor has the most noted of its partizans, in prosecution of it, scrupled to affirm, *that absolute monarchy is inconsistent with civil society, and so can be no form of civil government at all;*[22] and *that the supreme power in a state cannot take from any man, by taxes and impositions, any part of his property, without his own consent or that of his representatives.* What authority any moral reasoning can have, which leads into opinions so wide of the general practice of mankind, in every place but this single kingdom, it is easy to determine. . . .

"Of Passive Obedience"

[. . . .] As the obligation to justice is founded entirely on the interests of society, which require mutual abstinence from property, in order to preserve peace among mankind; it is evident, that, when the execution of justice would be attended with very pernicious consequences, that virtue must be suspended, and give place to public utility, in such extraordinary and such pressing emergencies. The maxim, *fiat Justitia et ruat Coelum*, let justice be performed, though the universe be destroyed, is apparently false, and by sacrificing the end to the means, shows a preposterous idea of the subordination [proper order] of duties. What governor of a town makes any scruple of burning the suburbs, when they facilitate the approaches of the enemy? Or what general abstains from plundering a neutral country, when the necessities of war require it, and he cannot otherwise subsist his army? The case is the same with the duty of allegiance; and common sense teaches us, that, as government binds us to obedience only on account of its tendency to public utility, that duty must always, in extraordinary cases, when public ruin would evidently attend obedience, yield to the primary and original obligation. *Salus populi suprema Lex*, the safety of the people is the supreme law. This maxim is agreeable to the sentiments of mankind in all ages: Nor is any one, when he reads of the insurrections against NERO or PHILIP the

---

[21] Hume's assumption is that political thought should seek to articulate the rules and conventions which exist in common life, rather than beginning from *a priori* premises and deducing rules of conduct.

[22] Hume here paraphrases the argument of John Locke's *Second Treatise of Government*, chapter vii, §90.

Second, so infatuated with party systems, as not to wish success to the enterprise, and praise the undertakers. Even our high monarchical party, in spite of their sublime theory, are forced, in such cases, to judge, and feel, and approve, in conformity to the rest of mankind.[23]

Resistance, therefore, being admitted in extraordinary emergencies, the question can only be among good reasoners, with regard to the degree of necessity, which can justify resistance, and render it lawful or commendable. And here I must confess, that I shall always incline to their side, who draw the bond of allegiance very close, and consider an infringement of it, as the last refuge in desperate cases, when the public is in the highest danger, from violence and tyranny. For besides the mischiefs of a civil war, which commonly attends insurrection; it is certain, that, where a disposition to rebellion appears among any people, it is one chief cause of tyranny in the rulers, and forces them into many violent measures which they never would have embraced, had every one been inclined to submission and obedience. Thus the *tyrannicide* or assassination, approved of by ancient maxims, instead of keeping tyrants and usurpers in awe, made them ten times more fierce and unrelenting; and is now justly, upon that account, abolished by the laws of nations, and universally condemned as a base and treacherous method of bringing to justice these disturbers of society.

Besides we must consider, that, as obedience is our duty in the common course of things, it ought chiefly to be inculcated; nor can any thing be more preposterous than an anxious care and solicitude stating all the cases, in which resistance may be allowed. In like manner, though a philosopher reasonably acknowledges, in the course of an argument, that the rules of justice may be dispensed with in cases of urgent necessity; what should we think of a preacher or casuist, who should make it his chief study to find out such cases, and enforce them with all the vehemence of argument and eloquence? Would he not be better employed in inculcating the general doctrine, than in displaying the particular exceptions, which we are, perhaps, but too much inclined, of ourselves, to embrace and to extend?. . .

[23] Even dyed-in-the-wool monarchists recognize that there are extreme circumstances under which rulers should be overthrown.

INTRODUCTION TO
Edmund Burke,
"Preface" to *A Vindication of Natural Society*
(Second Edition)

◆

From the beginning of his public career to its end, Edmund Burke warned of the potentially disastrous social and political results of intellect which overstretched its proper reach. In his first book, from which the selection below is drawn, Burke focused on the hazards of a frame of mind that demanded a rational justification of each institution, rejected every institution which did not meet the standards set by speculative theories of justice, and demanded that human society be reconstructed to conform to speculative criteria.

Burke was born in Dublin in 1729. After studies at Trinity College, Dublin, at his father's urging he entered the Middle Temple in London to apprentice as a lawyer. But he aspired to more intellectual fame, and at the age of twenty-six abandoned his legal studies. Young Burke burst onto the intellectual and political stage in several leaps, beginning with the publication in 1756 of *A Vindication of Natural Society.*

As one perceptive student of political thought has noted, Burke is in many ways a less philosophically rigorous Hume.[1] Burke's skepticism of the claims of abstract rationalism as a guide to worldly affairs was already evident in his youthful essays, written when he was still in his early twenties and left unpublished in his lifetime. Those who have gone through a long course of study and have mastered the principles of most sciences, he noted, "find how weak and fallacious the Grounds of many are, and how uncertain the very best."[2] "Perhaps the bottom of most things is unintelligible; and our surest reasoning, when we come to a certain point, is involved not only in obscurity but contradiction," he remarked.[3] For the young Burke, as for Hume, an awareness of the limits of human reasoning led to a principled respect for custom. "The more a man's mind is elevated above the vulgar the nearer he comes to them in the simplicity of his appearance, speech, and even not a few of his Notions. He knows his reason very well and therefore he is suspicious of it. . . . A man who considers his nature rightly will be diffident of any

---

[1] Iain Hampsher-Monk, "Introduction," to *The Political Philosophy of Edmund Burke* (New York, 1987), pp. 1–43, esp. p. 34. For the similarities between Hume and Burke, see also David Miller, *Philosophy and Ideology in Hume's Political Thought* (Oxford, 1981).

[2] H.V.F. Somerset, *A Note-Book of Edmund Burke* (Cambridge, 1957), p. 83.

[3] Ibid., p. 93.

reasonings that carry him out of the ordinary roads of Life; Custom is to be regarded with great deference especially if it be an universal Custom; even popular notions are not always to be laughed at. There is some general principle operating to produce Customs, that is a more sure guide than our Theories. They are followed indeed often on odd motives, but that does not make them less reasonable or useful."[4]

Not only was the usefulness of a custom or institution not always immediately understood, the young Burke thought, but the attempt to subject all institutions to rational scrutiny could have its own negative consequences. "It is not easily conceived what use funeral ceremonies . . . are to mankind. Trifling as they may seem, they nourish humanity, they soften in some measure the rigour of Death, and they inspire humble, sober and becoming thought. They throw a decent Veil over the weak and dishonourable circumstances of our Nature. What shall we say to that philosophy, that would strip it naked? Of such sort is the wisdom of those who talk of the Love, the sentiment, and the thousand little dalliances that pass between the Sexes, in the gross way of mere procreation. They value themselves as having made a mighty discovery; and turn all pretences to delicacy into ridicule."[5]

The image of inherited culture as a veil, without which we are left with "the weak and dishonorable circumstances of our Nature" would furnish the master metaphor of Burke's reflections on the French Revolution almost four decades later. But his attack on those who would strip away the veil are found in his first book, *A Vindication of Natural Society or, A View of the Miseries and Evils Arising to Mankind from Every Species of Artificial Society. In a Letter to Lord**** by A Late Noble Writer*, which he published anonymously in 1756 at the age of twenty-seven.

The book, as its title indicates, was both satirical and ironic. Its strategy was to combat an increasingly influenctial mode of thought which Burke regarded as fundamentally misguided, and which he tried to discredit by displaying its logical consequences. The book purported to be a posthumous tract by Viscount Bolingbroke, the recently deceased British politician and political philosopher who had served as one of Voltaire's English patrons. It revealed Burke's immersion in the writings of Voltaire, the English Deists, and Rousseau, whose "Discourse on the Arts and Sciences" and "Discourse on the Origin and Foundations of Inequality" had recently been published in France and were receiving attention in England as well.[6] Like other deists, Bolingbroke had as-

  [4] Ibid., p. 90.   [5] Ibid., p. 91.
  [6] Richard B. Sewall, "Rousseau's First Discourse in England" (*Proceedings of the Modern Language Association*, Sept. 1937), and his "Rousseau's Second Discourse in England from 1755 to 1763" (*Philological Quarterly* 17, 1938, pp. 97–114), and Peter Stanlis,

serted that God governed the world through general laws, which could be ascertained purely through human reason. Revelation in a particular time and place of the sort reported in the Old and New Testaments, the Deists held, was neither plausible nor necessary.[7] Rousseau, in his second discourse, had portrayed human history as the development from a state of nature—in which men are content, independent, and fundamentally equal to others—to a civilized state in which men are alienated, dependent, and subject to oppressive hierarchy. Burke's book takes the form of a letter from a young philosopher to an older aristocrat. The philosopher echoes the Deists and Rousseau by arguing in favor of a rationalistic and universal "natural religion" and "natural society" free of any historical or nonrational accretions. He condemns all existing social, political, and cultural institutions for their departures from this rationalist standard. Since all of human history has been based upon such irrational institutions, the philosopher argues, it is a tale of unremitting woe, and he adduces copious (if specious) evidence to show that this has been the case.

Burke's voice in *A Vindication of Natural Society* is ironic: the mode of thought promoted by rationalist intellectuals, he observes, is likely to have consequences which they do not intend and would find abhorrent. Burke warned that false claims could easily be made to seem plausible, that true claims were difficult to demonstrate conclusively, and that it was easier to destroy the veneration on which institutions depend than to create such veneration anew. Public criticism might therefore destroy the hold of custom and habit that gave institutions their utility.

So adept was Burke in entering into the mindset of this new species of critical intellectual and in recapturing his characteristic mode of thought that many readers failed to recognize Burke's ironic and satirical intentions. He was obliged to begin the second edition, of 1757, with a new preface, in which he laid out his true assumptions and intentions.

"Burke and the Sensibility of Rousseau," in his *Edmund Burke: The Enlightenment and Revolution* (New Brunswick, 1991), pp. 159–91.

[7] On English deism, see Peter Harrison, *'Religion' and the Religions in the English Enlightenment* (Cambridge, 1990).

Edmund Burke,
A Vindication of Natural Society: or, A View of the Miseries and Evils Arising to Mankind from Every Species of Artificial Society. In a Letter to Lord * * * * by a Late Noble Writer,
Preface to the Second Edition, 1757

Before the Philosophical Works of Lord Bolingbroke had appeared, great Things were expected from the Leisure of a Man, who from the splendid Scene of Action, in which his Talents had enabled him to make so conspicuous a Figure, had retired to employ those Talents in the Investigation of Truth. Philosophy began to congratulate herself upon such a Proselyte from the World of Business, and hoped to have extended her Power under the Auspices of such a Leader. In the Midst of these pleasing Expectations, the Works themselves at last appeared in *full Body*, and with great Pomp.[1] Those who searched in them for new Discoveries in the Mysteries of Nature; those who expected something which might explain or direct the Operations of the Mind; those who hoped to see Morality illustrated and enforced; those who looked for new Helps to Society and Government; those who desired to see the Characters and Passions of Mankind delineated; in short, all who consider such Things as Philosophy, and require some of them at least, in every philosophical Work, all these were certainly disappointed; they found the Land-marks of Science precisely in their former Places: And they thought they received but a poor Recompence for this Disappointment, in seeing every Mode of Religion attacked in a lively Manner, and the Foundation of every Virtue, and of all Government, sapped with great Art and much Ingenuity.[2] What Advantage do we derive from such Writings? What Delight can a Man find in employing a Capacity which might be usefully exerted for the noblest Purposes, in a sort of sullen Labour, in which, if the Author could succeed, he is obliged to own [admit], that nothing could be more fatal to Mankind than his Success?

I cannot conceive how this sort of Writers propose to compass the Designs they pretend to have in view, by the Instruments which they employ.[3] Do they pretend to exalt the Mind of Man, by proving him no better than a Beast? Do they think to enforce the Practice of Virtue, by

---

[1] Bolingbroke died in 1751, and his *Works* were published in 1754.

[2] Burke's assumption is that by attacking the revealed basis of Christianity, Bolingbroke had weakened the foundation of moral virtue and political obedience.

[3] Note Burke's ironic stance: the mode of thought promoted by rationalist intellectuals is likely to have consequences which they do not intend and would find abhorrent.

denying that vice and virtue are distinguished by good or ill Fortune here, or by Happiness or Misery hereafter?[4] Do they imagine they shall increase our Piety, and our Reliance on God, by exploding his Providence, and insisting that he is neither just nor good? Such are the Doctrines which, sometimes concealed, sometimes openly and fully avowed, are found to prevail throughout the Writings of Lord Bolingbroke; and such are the Reasonings which this noble Writer and several others have been pleased to dignify with the Name of Philosophy. If these are delivered in a specious Manner, and in a Stile above the common, they cannot want a Number of Admirers of as much Docility as can be wished for in Disciples. To these the Editor of the following little Piece has addressed it: there is no Reason to conceal the Design of it any longer.[5]

The Design was, to shew that, without the Exertion of any considerable Forces, the same Engines which were employed for the Destruction of Religion, might be employed with equal Success for the Subversion of Government; and that specious Arguments might be used against those Things which they, who doubt of every thing else, will never permit to be questioned. It is an Observation which I think *Isocrates* makes in one of his Orations against the Sophists, That it is far more easy to maintain a wrong Cause, and to support paradoxical Opinions to the Satisfaction of a common Auditory, than to establish a doubtful truth by solid and conclusive Arguments. When Men find that something can be said in favour of what, on the very Proposal, they have thought utterly indefensible, they grow doubtful of their own Reason; they are thrown into a sort of pleasing Surprize; they run along with the Speaker, charmed and captivated to find such a plentiful Harvest of Reasoning, where all seemed barren and unpromising. This is the Fairy Land of Philosophy. And it very frequently happens, that those pleasing Impressions on the Imagination, subsist and produce their Effect, even after the Understanding has been satisfied of their unsubstantial Nature.[6] There is a sort of Gloss upon ingenious Falsehoods, that dazzles the Imagination, but which neither belongs to, nor becomes the sober Aspect of truth. I have met with a Quotation in Lord *Coke's* Reports that pleased me very much, though I do not know from whence he has taken it: *"Interdum*

---

[4] Here Burke is asserting the social utility of belief in divine reward and punishment.

[5] The original edition gave no overt indication of the author's ironic stance, and was read by many contemporary readers as an ingenuous statement of Burke's own views. Subsequent readers, down to our own day, have made the same error.

[6] Burke asserts the limits of reason in determining conduct. Writings which undermine behavior developed through custom and habit are pernicious, he claims, because even if we later come to understand that there are good reasons for the actions we have performed unreflectingly, we may not be able to perform them as satisfactorily or with the same degree of assurance. Cf. the dictum of the twentieth-century American psychiatrist, Henry Stack Sullivan, "If you tell them about sublimation, they can't sublimate."

fucata falsitas, (says he) *in multis est probabilior, et saepe rationibus vincit nudam veritatem."*[7] In such Cases, the Writer has a certain Fire and Alacrity inspired into him by a Consciousness, that let it fare how it will with the Subject, his Ingenuity will be sure of Applause; and this Alacrity becomes much greater if he acts upon the offensive, by the Impetuosity that always accompanies an Attack, and the unfortunate Propensity which Mankind have to the finding and exaggerating Faults. The Editor is satisfied that a Mind which has no Restraint from a Sense of its own Weakness, of its subordinate Rank in the Creation,[8] and of the extreme Danger of letting the Imagination loose upon some Subjects, may very plausibly attack every thing the most excellent and venerable; that it would not be difficult to criticise the Creation itself; and that if we were to examine the divine Fabricks by our Ideas of Reason and Fitness, and to use the same Method of Attack by which some Men have assaulted Revealed Religion, we might with as good Colour, and with the same Success, make the Wisdom and Power of God in his Creation appear to many no better than Foolishness.[9] There is an Air of Plausibility which accompanies vulgar Reasonings and Notions taken from the beaten Circle of ordinary Experience, that is admirably suited to the narrow Capacities of some, and to the Laziness of others. But this Advantage is in great measure lost, when a painful, comprehensive Survey of a very complicated Matter, and which requires a great Variety of Considerations, is to be made; when we must seek in a profound Subject, not only for Arguments, but for new Materials of Argument, their Measures and their Method of Arrangement; when we must go out of the Sphere of our ordinary Ideas, and when we can never walk sure but by being sensible of our Blindness. And this we must do, or we do nothing, whenever we examine the Result of a Reason which is not our own.[10] Even in Matters which are, as it were, just within our Reach, what would become of the World if the Practice of all moral Duties, and the Foundations of Society, rested upon having their Reasons made clear and demonstrative to every Individual?[11]

The Editor knows that the Subject of this Letter is not so fully handled as obviously it might; it was not his Design to say all that could

---

[7] "Sometimes a painted falsehood is in many ways more credible than the naked truth, and frequently by argument vanquishes it."

[8] An example of Burke's religiously based epistemological modesty.

[9] Burke's point is that the rationalistic mode of thought characteristic of deism leads beyond the deists' belief in a providentially created world, toward atheism and the denial of any intrinsic purpose in the world.

[10] Among Burke's favorite biblical quotations was Isaiah 55:8: "For my thoughts are not your thoughts, neither are your ways my ways, saieth the Lord."

[11] Another version of the argument that rational motivation is an inadequate basis for eliciting good conduct from most men most of the time.

possibly be said. It had been inexcusable to fill a large Volume with the Abuse of Reason;[12] nor would such an Abuse have been tolerable even for a few Pages, if some Under-plot, of more Consequence than the apparent Design, had not been carried on.

Some Persons have thought that the Advantages of the State of Nature ought to have been more fully displayed. This had undoubtedly been a very ample Subject for Declamation; but they do not consider the Character of the Piece. The Writers against Religion, whilst they oppose every System, are wisely careful never to set up any of their own.[13] If some Inaccuracies in Calculation, in Reasoning, or in Method be found, perhaps these will not be looked upon as Faults by the Admirers of Lord Bolingbroke; who will, the Editor is afraid, observe much more of his Lordship's Character in such Particulars of the following Letter, than they are like to find of that rapid Torrent of an impetuous and overbearing Eloquence, and the Variety of rich Imagery for which that Writer is justly admired.

[12] Burke's assertion is that the seeming rationalism of deists and of Rousseau is not really rational at all, since it attributes to reason greater powers than are plausible.

[13] The rationalist mode of thought, Burke asserts, is capable of sapping belief in existing institutions, but not of creating new ones, a claim he would repeat in his *Reflections on the Revolution in France.*

INTRODUCTION TO
Justus Möser,
"On the Diminished Disgrace of Whores and Their Children in Our Day"

◆

In the eighteenth century, progressive intellectuals appealed to the monarchs of their day to use the central government's power to break down intermediary institutions—such as guilds, privileged corporations, and serfdom—which violated the principles of individual rights and equality before the law. These intermediary institutions found their intellectual defenders against the onslaughts of what its opponents called "enlightened despotism."

The following short essay, by Justus Möser (1720–94), a high government official in the tiny Westphalian state of Osnabrück, is a case in point.[1] Möser contributed to the leading journals of the German Enlightenment, and he came to be regarded by posterity as a father of German intellectual conservatism, not least for his critique of enlightened absolutism. Like other intellectuals of the Enlightenment, Möser sought to create and nurture an educated public capable of understanding questions of public policy. To that end he founded and edited a series of gazettes and journals in which he sought to promote the gradual reform of existing institutions in the interest of their ultimate preservation. A principled defender of the existing corporate order—which he perceived as threatened by enlightened absolutism and the spread of the market economy—he often opposed the policy prescriptions of enlightened intellectuals and their supporters in the absolutist bureaucracy. Yet he defended the traditional institutions of the corporate order on the enlightened grounds of utility and felicity.

The essay was prompted by the efforts of the enlightened Habsburg emperors of the Holy Roman Empire (of which Osnabrück was a part) to rationalize existing social institutions. It was the traditional practice among eighteenth-century guilds to demand that applicants for membership be "conceived by honorable parents in a pure bed," a stipulation which made no sense from the point of view of economic efficiency or

---

[1] For a portrait of Möser's thought, see Klaus Epstein, *The Genesis of German Conservatism* (Princeton, 1966), chap. 6. Jonathan Knudsen, *Justus Möser and the German Enlightenment* (Cambridge, 1986) discusses Möser's social, economic, and political environment, as well as his thought. On those aspects of Möser's thought relating to guilds, see Mack Walker, *German Home Towns: Community, State, and General Estate, 1648–1871* (Ithaca, 1971).

individual responsibility. An imperial ordinance of 1731, "To Remedy Abuses Among the Guilds" forbade the guilds from discriminating against applicants who were illegitimately conceived. Among the motivations behind these measures was the humanitarian desire to reduce infanticide committed by mothers of illegitimate children by reducing the stigma of illegitimacy.

Möser's response is a virtual quintessence of conservative social thought. In a few pages, it explicates the latent functions and tacit rationality of seemingly irrational practices, emphasizes the importance of the family as an institution, expresses skepticism toward attempts to directly apply abstract human rights, and argues for the importance of the allocation of social honor and respect as forces of social control. And it drips from beginning to end with irony and anti-humanitarianism.

The essay which follows in a lightly edited form was first published in 1772.

Justus Möser, "On the Diminished Disgrace of Whores and Their Children in Our Day" (1772)[1]

In some states more has been done for whores and their children in recent decades than for wives in the last millenium. Every enlightened intellectual set out as soon as possible to free illegitimate children and their mothers from all possible shame, and thought he deserved the praise of the entire human race for having freed from all reproach the poor, innocent offspring of a love that was forbidden, but all too tempting. These measures were nobly motivated: nature, humanity, and humanitarianism clearly favored them. Yet they ultimately demonstrate the power of the unpolitical philosophy of our century. Once again fashionable humanitarianism triumphed over civic sense. It was at best the application to political institutions of Christian charity, which ought to be voluntary. When it comes to civic rights, one cannot move directly from the voice of nature or abstract human rights. For in the state of nature there is no institution of marriage, and as soon as one transfers concepts from the state of nature to the state of civil association, one falls prey to a dangerous confusion, whose actual results are more detrimental than are at first imagined.

---

[1] "Über die zu unsern Zeiten verminderte Schande der Huren und Hurkinder" (1772), reprinted in *Justus Mösers Sämtliche Werke* (Oldenburg, 1945), vol. V, pp. 142–45. Translated by Jerry Z. Muller.

It is true that marriage has its burdens and discomforts, and that many prefer being single. All measures that encourage bachlerhood and allow the single person all the pleasures of marriage without its burdens are therefore impolitic and against the real interests of the state, since it is an established truth that more children are born in one marriage than from three illicit sexual unions. It is impolitic to give the children of whores the same honor as the legitimately born, since by so doing one destroys one of the strongest incentives for marriage. It is impolitic to give to the unhappy mothers of these illegitimate children the same respect which they previously enjoyed, since the fear of losing that respect is a means of encouraging marriage. It is impolitic to bestow upon the unmarried the same benefits as the married, since the family household contributes more to the state and is more beneficial to it than are bachelors.

Our ancestors, who were guided by experience rather than by theories, always demanded a certificate of honorable birth before they admitted someone into their guilds and clubs; they married only daughters honorably born; they burdened the offspring of illegitimate love with their ongoing disdain; they wove garlands for pristine brides and found thousands of ways to adorn their wedding days. Why did they go to such lengths? Precisely to reserve all honor and all civic benefits for matrimony, in order to encourage it. Had someone sought to show our ancestors that illegitimate children on the whole displayed more genius than others or that they were entirely innocent of the guilt of their parents; had someone sought to demonstrate to them by reference to the principles of savages that the greatest whores must of necessity have been the most beautiful, attractive, and charming, since they were so widely sought; then our ancestors would have answered, "These arguments are correct in the state of nature, but they are inappropriate for the design of a civil society."

Don't imagine, incidentally, that our ancestors did not recognize the hardships which have motivated our progressive intellectuals to sympathy with the whores. The sack in which our ancestors drowned those who committed infanticide to free themselves from their shame shows only too clearly how they accepted the accompanying effects of disgrace when it was necessary for the general welfare of matrimony. It shows quite clearly that they too understood the human heart, but regarded it as more prudent to make the punishment extraordinary and terrifying, rather than diminish the disgrace in the least. Our new intellectuals, by contrast, diminish the disgrace without making the punishment as severe as our ancestors had done; it is doubtful they will attain their goal [of diminishing the disgrace of illegitimacy] without eliminating matrimony entirely and granting an unmarried mother the same advantages as her married counterpart.

So long as this is not the case—until the disdain which one displays to a loose wench is eradicated by some new type of education; so long as every honorable man shrinks from marrying such a person—until then the strongest temptation to commit infanticide will continue, thwarting the efforts of progressive legislators.

In addition, matrimony is always a highly important means to check vice and preserve virtue. In states where marriage loses its value, the punishment of crime must become harsher. Diminishing the disgrace of a crime which will always be tempting seems to me to be of doubtful value, since by so doing one creates the need for harsher punishments.

Just as the disgrace with which our ancestors burdened a whore in order to preserve legitimacy was rational and appropriate, so too is the blot which they placed upon illegitimate offspring. The same logic holds: the advantages which accrue to those conceived by married parents must be sacred to anyone who wishes to encourage matrimony. Divine law provides a disincentive to sin by decreeing that the transgressions of the fathers are borne by their children unto the fourth generation; why does the progressive philosophical legislator seek to improve upon the divine one?

A law which makes illegitimate children equal to legitimate ones is a policy error so momentous that I don't see how the humanitarianism of our age can forgive it.

INTRODUCTION TO
Justus Möser,
"No Promotion According to Merit"

◆

Justus Möser's vision of society was a corporatist and inegalitarian one, in which inequality rested largely on inherited status, and status included honor, property, and power. Only the existence of a hierarchy of ranks allowed one to know one's place, Möser believed. Belonging to an estate or rank was supposed to bring with it a sense of equality to those of equal rank, a sense of deference to those of higher rank, and a sense of superiority combined with responsibility toward those of lower rank.

The son of a prominent official in the bishopric of Osnabrück, Möser participated in the governance of Osnabrück from 1744 until his death in 1794. While he was still a university student, Möser was appointed as secretary of the estate of the nobles, and later was promoted to the position of syndic, which made him the most important representative of aristocratic interests in the bishopric. While serving in this capacity, he was appointed by the ruling house of Hanover as its administrative representative in Osnabrück in 1764. For the last three decades of his life he was the leading government official in the bishopric.

Within the government of Prussia and other enlightened monarchies, there was a growing movement toward the creation of a professional civil service, open, in theory at least, to men of all origins, in which promotion would be based on merit. It was with this seemingly rational principle that Möser took issue in the essay below. In the process, he tried to demonstrate the inherent advantages of existing customs governing bureaucratic advancement, in which social origins and seniority were known to weigh more heavily than professional merit. Möser's piece, whimsical in tone, conveys the potential social and psychological costs of what would come to be called the principle of "careers open to talent" and has since been termed "meritocracy."

Justus Möser,
"No Promotion According to Merit" (c. 1770)[1]

To an Officer:

While it touches me, dear friend, that your merit is so little recognized, still, your demand that the State should solely look to true merit is, if I may have your kind permission to say so, the strangest product of an hour's idle contemplation. I, for one, should—paid or not—never remain within a State in which it is a rule to award all honors solely on the basis of merit. Rewarded, I should not have the heart to appear before a friend for fear of humiliating him; and unrewarded, I should live under some sort of public calumny, because everybody would say of me, That man has no merits. Believe me, so long as we remain human, it is better that from time to time fortune and favor distribute the prizes, than that human wisdom award them to each according to his merit—birth and age are better determinants of rank in this world than is true worth. Yet, I shall dare to say that public service could not even exist if every promotion were based solely on merit. For all those who shared the hopes of the promoted—and this would quite naturally include all who had any sort of a good opinion of themselves—would consider themselves offended and calumniated. Their minds would turn against him, against the service, and even against their chief; they would erupt in hate and enmity; and within a short period, all civil and military services would witness those resignations which can now be observed only in the courts or the universities, where the fame of personal merits is more closely considered and consequently produces all the above faults. On the other hand, contemplate the case where this man is promoted because of his high birth, that man because of his seniority in service, and from time to time, other men are promoted by happy chance: Here, everybody will be free to flatter himself that merit is not the measure of the world; nobody can regard himself as calumniated; self-love acquiesces, and we think that time and fortune will bring up our turn, too. With these thoughts, we drive away our grief, get new hopes, continue to work, suffer the fortunate; and public service is not impeded. The ensign does not attempt to harm the lieutenant secretly, and the latter does not try to harm the captain, because superior has not been placed above inferior merely according to merit. The greatest measure

---

[1] "Keine Beförderung nach Verdiensten," "No Promotion According to Merit" (c. 1770), English translation by Hans W. Baade, appeared in *The Journal of Public Law*, vol. 12 (1963), pp. 185–92. The original German version is in *Justus Mösers Sämtliche Werke* (Oldenburg, 1945), vol. V, pp. 161–64.

of discord is found among generals, because the conduct of campaigns often requires great merit. But this discord would be pervasive if all officers were promoted in accordance with the principles that govern the choice of generals for operative tasks.

And how many injustices would be perpetrated by a state in the guise of furthering merit! The prince is not always a judge with deep insight; even from his vantage point, he cannot see everything. One prince would see merit in a favorite, another in a mistress; and probably the bland dilettante would replace the modest artist, the pleasant flatterer would win out over the quiet man of integrity, the feverish maker of projects would replace the experienced economist, and glamour would always win out over truth. The prince, if against all probability he is the most excellent man in insight and righteousness, would at the least find himself in the greatest embarrassment, or, under the pretext of rewarding merit, would have to act like an oriental despot who made a slave his first minister, confused all classes of men, and made himself a monster. Whoever wants to live quietly in the world, to taste the sweetness of friendship, he who desires to retain the approval of the righteous and to further great causes, would have to deny his own merit and to guard carefully against all external recognition of it.

If we humans were not constituted so that each has the best opinion of himself, it might of course be otherwise. But so long as we retain our present nature and passions, and so long as it is, so to speak, necessary that each retain a good opinion of himself, promotion based on merit seems to me the very means of bringing confusion into everything. Even today, it is a sort of law in the military that the older officer has to seek retirement when a younger one is advanced over him. What, then, would happen if advancement went according to merit—if suddenly the adjutant who now is attached to an older general as an adviser were placed ahead of the general and of everybody else? Would they not all be publicly condemned and incapacitated from further service if merit decided everything?

Granted, a great king of our times has found a means for putting minds at rest in cases such as these. He often bypasses the order of seniority, prefers a more capable person to an older one; and some time later, he promotes the person passed by in such a flattering manner that every man who is passed over for promotion is always in doubt whether the king is only saving him a better promotion or is passing him over for lack of merit. But this device will ever have to be regarded as exceptional; it only serves the prince who is qualified by insight and experience to use it wisely. For in the hands of any other man, it would be most dangerous for the tranquillity of men and a clear path to most extreme slavery.

You answer that great merit is always accompanied by modesty and moderation, and that with the aid of these virtues, the fortunate would easily placate the unfortunate and smother the feelings of hatred and envy which to the detriment of the service could develop in the hearts of all persons passed by. However, as soon as merit is publicly recognized and rewarded, modesty and moderation are taken to be mere acts of political wisdom; and they will be of no effect. I would even say that modesty often increases the offense to the unrewarded, because he not infrequently wishes to find fault with the fortunate in order to be able to hate him with more righteous equanimity; that is the way men are. Besides, the State does not weigh merit as a teacher of morals would. The former justifiably gives great talents, even if accompanied by pride and lack of modesty, preference over less talented modesty.

A State that does not have many more men of merit than can be rewarded with public office would be a very unhappy one. If this be so, it would always be unpleasant for many people to have to imagine that those receiving awards are also the best among them and that each decoration also designated the best knight. Now people can think to their comfort: fortune and not merit has elevated these; or to speak the words of the poet: a great star covers that small heart. But if everything went according to merit, this so necessary comfort would completely disappear, and the cobbler who is happy to hammer at his lasts so long as he can flatter himself that he would be doing something entirely different from mending the Lady Mayor's slippers if merit were respected in this world could not possibly be happy.

Therefore, dear friend, give up your romantic thoughts of the happiness of a State where everything goes according to merit. When men rule and where men serve, birth and age, or seniority of service, are still the safest and the least offensive rules for promotion. The creative genius, or the man of real virtue, will not be harmed by this rule; but an exception of this kind is very rare and will also only give offense to evil souls.

► 2 ◄

THE CRITIQUE OF
REVOLUTION

INTRODUCTION TO
Edmund Burke,
Reflections on the Revolution in France

◆

Though it would be a mistake to designate Edmund Burke the founder of modern conservative social and political analysis, it would be no exaggeration to characterize his *Reflections on the Revolution in France* of 1790 as the single most influential work of conservative thought published from his day to ours. The book struck every chord of conservative sentiment, rung every chime of conservative analysis, and enunciated virtually every subsequent theme of conservative ideology.[1]

After solidifying his intellectual reputation with the publication in 1757 of *A Philosophical Enquiry into the Origin of our Ideas of the Sublime and Beautiful*, Burke began his political involvement in 1759. For the next three decades he served as the brain for a body of parliamentarians associated with the Marquis of Rockingham, a great landowner and politician. As the intellectual engine of the Rockingham Whigs, Burke's function was to enunciate principles, to influence Parliament through his speeches and reports, and to influence extra-Parliamentary opinion through his own publications and through the accounts of his speeches in the press. Burke served to articulate the principles which were to transform what had begun as a collection of members of Parliament linked by connection and interest into a coherent party united by princi-

---

[1] Among the best discussions of Burke's conservatism are Iain Hampsher-Monk, "Introduction," to *The Political Philosophy of Edmund Burke*, ed. Iain Hampsher-Monk (New York, 1987), pp. 1–43; and the same author's chapter on Burke in his *A History of Modern Political Thought* (Oxford, 1992). Also essential is the important article by J.G.A. Pocock, "The political economy of Burke's analysis of the French Revolution," in his *Virtue, Commerce, and History* (Cambridge, 1985), pp. 193–212.

ple as well.[2] The Rockingham Whigs aimed at government led by the landed aristocracy but open to mercantile and commercial interests. They sought to preserve the power of parliament from royal encroachment. And they opposed attempts to expand the political influence of the unpropertied many, whether through more equal and democratic representation or through the influence of mob action.

Until the publication of *Reflections on the Revolution in France*, Burke was better known as a critic than as a defender of the existing British administration. On the eve of the French Revolution, Burke was most closely associated in the public mind with his decade-long campaign against the British East India Company, in its day the largest commercial enterprise in Britain. Burke sought to punish leading figures of the Company for what he saw as their predatory behavior toward the people of India. With the coming of the Revolution in France, and in the face of widespread support for the revolution within the British intelligentsia and within his own party, Burke devoted himself to a critique of the theory and practice of the French revolutionaries, and to a principled defense of British institutions. In offering a critical analysis of the origins and dynamics of the Revolution and a pessimistic prognosis of its likely course, Burke challenged the dominant prorevolutionary sentiment among the makers of British public opinion.

In 1765, Voltaire, the greatest propagandist of the French Enlightenment, wrote to his comrade-in-arms, d'Alembert, that "people clamor against the *philosophes*. They are right; for if opinion is the queen of the world, the *philosophes* govern that queen."[3] Burke, too, was very conscious of the fact that the spread of commercially distributed means of information had made "public opinion" into an ever more important factor in politics, and that what counted as "public opinion" was heavily influenced by intellectuals. In his analysis of the origins of the French Revolution, Burke maintained that the principal actors included "monied men" and "men of letters." "[A]s money increases and circulates, and as the circulation of news, in politicks and letters, becomes more and more diffused, the persons who diffuse this money, and this intelligence, become more and more important," he observed.[4] The circulation of newspapers, he noted, was "infinitely more efficacious and

---

[2] On Burke's role in the Rockingham Whigs in this period, see Paul Langford, "Introduction," to Paul Langford, ed., *The Writings and Speeches of Edmund Burke: Volume II: Party, Parliament and the American Crisis 1766–1774* (Oxford, 1981).

[3] Voltaire to d'Alembert, 1765; quoted in Peter Gay, *Voltaire's Politics: The Poet as Realist* (New York, 1964), p. 34.

[4] Burke, "Thoughts on French Affairs" (1791), in L. G. Mitchell, ed., *The Writings and Speeches of Edmund Burke: Volume VIII: The French Revolution, 1790–1794* (Oxford, 1989), p. 346.

extensive than ever they were. And they are a more important instrument than generally is imagined. They are a part of the reading of all, they are the whole of the reading of the far greater number. . . . Let us only suffer any person to tell us his story, morning and evening, but for one twelvemonth, and he will become our master."[5] What distinguishes Burke's treatment of the subject is his awareness—which he shared with Voltaire—that the "public opinion" often hailed as the voice of public reason and good sense was in fact the voice of men of letters. "Public opinion" in other words, was increasingly coming to mean *published opinion*, which endowed men of letters with a new and potentially ominous significance, as Burke stressed in his writings after 1789.

In November of 1790 Burke published his great work of contemporary polemic on which he had labored for almost a year. *Reflections on the Revolution in France* took the form of a letter to a young French correspondent who had written to Burke soliciting his opinion on the revolutionary events in France. The product was a masterpiece of literary composition, introducing ideas and metaphors early in the work which recur throughout its more than two hundred pages. The epistolary framework allowed Burke a certain informality that increases the book's accessibility. Burke also presented the book as a response to a sermon by Richard Price, a Unitarian minister and writer on philosophical, mathematical, and political subjects, who had delivered a sermon praising the French Revolution before the London Revolutionary Society. Price thus became the personification of all that Burke found objectionable, a foil for Burke's *Reflections*.

In his early *Vindication of Natural Society*, Burke had ridiculed the propensity of some enlightened intellectuals to judge institutions by abstract principles, and had insisted that the attempt to do so would delegitimate all existing institutions without being able to create better ones in their place. This presumption conditioned his initial response to news of the revolution in France, and served as the leitmotif of his analysis thereafter. *Reflections on the Revolution in France* is a critique of the revolutionary mentality which attempts to create entirely new structures on the basis of rational, abstract principles, a mentality which Burke contrasted unfavorably to his own conception of legitimate reform as building upon existing, historical institutions.

Burke attributed the revolution in France to the combined influence of men of letters and financiers of government debt. In conjunction, he charged, they were subverting the intellectual and institutional basis of a civilized society. By stripping away the veil of culture and by undermining the traditional institutions of the aristocracy and the Church

---

[5] "Thoughts on French Affairs," p. 348.

which had supported that veil, the intellectual and financial speculators were leading France into disaster, Burke argued. The result, he feared, would be a return of man to his "natural" state, a state not elevated and benign, but brutish and barbaric.

The question of public revenue looms large in Burke's analysis, as it did in the Revolution itself. From its earliest meetings, the National Assembly was faced with the problem of France's enormous financial debts. In September 1789, a dramatic suggestion was advanced by Dupont, the deputy for Nemours and a close associate of the reformist former minister Turgot and the school of political economists known as the Physiocrats. Dupont proposed that the government begin collecting the revenues on Church property, while at the same time taking responsibility for Church expenses.[6] On November 2, the Assembly approved a bill which declared that "all ecclesiastical properties are at the disposal of the Nation, which undertakes to provide in an appropriate manner funds to meet the expenses of the Church, stipends for its ministers, and relief for the poor." These properties were to provide the backing for a new form of government paper, the "*assignat*," which the revolutionary government used to pay the holders of government debt.

The principal opponent of the proposal to expropriate the property of the Church was the king's chaplain, the abbé Maury. "To reestablish credit, you have proposed putting the capitalists in place of the holders of benefices, and the holders of benefices in place of the capitalists," he declared. By using the Church's property to pay off the state's debts, he charged, the Assembly was transferring the Church's legacy to the holders of state debt (*créanciers*), many of whom, his listeners knew, were foreigners.[7] And in expropriating the Church's holdings, Maury claimed, the Assembly was destroying the basic right of property.

Burke, who appears to have consulted the published proceedings of the National Assembly, adopted this analysis, and it figures centrally in his characterization of the Revolution.[8] His stressed that in France, power had fallen into the hands of social outsiders who owned the public debt, and that these men were incapable of governing.

Burke's contention was based upon his own sociology of knowledge. There was a mentality inherent in the way of life of each class, Burke thought, and the mentality which led to success in finance was, in isolation, disastrous for government. "The monied interest is in its nature

[6] Florin Aftalion, *The French Revolution: An Economic Interpretation* (Cambridge, 1990), pp. 57–58.

[7] *Moniteur*, vol. II, p. 54 (Oct. 13, 1789). See also Louis Bergeron, "National Properties," in François Furet and Mona Ozouf, eds., *A Critical Dictionary of the French Revolution* (Cambridge, MA, 1989), p. 512.

[8] On Burke's sources of information during the writing of his "Reflections," see F. P. Lock, *Burke's Reflections on the Revolution in France* (London, 1985), pp. 44–45.

more ready for any adventure; and its possessors more disposed to new enterprizes of any kind. Being of a recent acquisition, it falls in more naturally with any novelties. It is therefore the kind of wealth which will be resorted to by all who wish for change."[9] Men of finance, according to Burke, share this propensity to innovation with "a new description of men . . . the political Men of Letters" with whom they had become allied. Politicized French intellectuals, Burke maintained, were motivated by the desire to destroy the Christian religion, and he predicted, quite accurately, that they would soon attempt to eliminate the established Church entirely.

In the *Reflections* as elsewhere in his writings, Burke makes use of imagery to serve not as a substitute for argument, but as a metaphorical restatement of arguments laid out elsewhere in declarative form. The most important metaphor in the *Reflections* is that of veiling and drapery, which serves to counter the metaphors of light and transparency so dominant in the age of Enlightenment.[10] Burke thus returned to his early metaphor of culture as a "veil," a fabric of understandings which hides the direct object of the natural passions. Culture, in other words, is a means of sublimation, of diverting the passions to more elevated goals, and of creating restrictions on the expression of the passions of domination and self-gratification.

For Burke, the Revolution's attack on the institutional bases of the Church and the aristocracy threatened to destroy the "manners" on which a decent commercial society depended. Having spent over a decade lamenting the impact upon the population of India of domination by young Britons whose avarice was unrestrained by either the laws or the cultural codes of their native land, he now interpreted the French Revolution through this prism. The destruction of the power of the aristocracy and of the influence of the Church, he claimed, would unleash avarice and the will to exploit others for one's own pleasure—it would lead, as he put it, to "rapine" and to "rape."

To Burke, it seemed that the French intelligentsia in 1788 and 1789 had done everything he had warned against three decades earlier. They had engaged in a wholesale critique of all the premises of their major

---

[9] Edmund Burke, "Reflections on the Revolution in France" (1790), in L. G. Mitchell, ed., *The Writings and Speeches of Edmund Burke: Volume VIII*, pp. 159–60. In the *Reflections*, Burke conjectured that in France men of finance regarded the landed nobility with rancor because the newly rich resented the disdain with which they were viewed by the nobility, and were prevented from joining it. (*Reflections*, p. 159.) But as he became more immersed in French affairs, he gave less weight to this explanation. ("Thoughts on French Affairs," pp. 346–47.)

[10] On the Enlightenment metaphor of the "naked truth," see Hans Blumenberg, "Paradigmen zu einer Metaphorologie," *Archiv für Begriffsgeschichte*, vol. 6, 1960, pp. 7–142, esp. pp. 49–54.

institutions, and they had done so publicly. Although he thought their critique radically exaggerated, Burke recognized that its effectiveness did not depend on its accuracy. For, as he had noted in his *Vindication of Natural Society*, even a mistaken critique of existing institutions could have negative consequences by eroding their legitimation in weak minds. Now, Burke asserted, the French would live with the results of the fairy land of philosophy, results which they had not anticipated but which he could. The French men of letters had delegitimated the monarchy, the aristocracy, and the taxing powers of the state in the eyes of the larger public.[11] As a result, they were left with a government drained of authority and no longer capable of collecting taxes or conducting commerce. The result, he predicted, would be ongoing instability and the threat of anarchy, which would be controlled only by the massive use of force, and eventually, military rule. It is important to remember that Burke made these predictions long before the Terror, the execution of Louis XVI, the massacre of over one hundred thousand civilians in the Vendée, or the rise of Napoléon.

Edmund Burke,
Reflections on the Revolution in France (1790)[1]

. . . I flatter myself that I love a manly, moral, regulated liberty as well as any gentleman of that society,[2] be he who he will; and perhaps I have given as good proofs of my attachment to that cause, in the whole course of my public conduct. I think I envy liberty as little as they do, to any other nation.[3] But I cannot stand forward, and give praise or blame to any thing which relates to human actions, and human concerns, on a simple view of the object, as it stands stripped of every relation, in all the nakedness and solitude of metaphysical abstraction.[4] Circumstances

---

[11] See on this process Keith Michael Baker, "Inventing the French Revolution," in his *Inventing the French Revolution: Essays on French Political Culture in the Eighteenth Century* (Cambridge, 1992).

[1] The text used for these excerpts is drawn from *The Writings and Speeches of Edmund Burke: Vol. VIII, The French Revolution, 1790–1794* (Oxford, 1989), ed. L. G. Mitchell, textual ed. William B. Todd.

[2] The Revolutionary Society of London, which adopted the resolutions congratulating the French revolutionaries on November 4, 1789.

[3] During the 1770s, Burke had defended the American colonists, and he had spent most of the 1780s defending the people of India against what he saw as the depredations of British rule there.

[4] Here Burke begins his critique of abstract theory, which remains the central theme of the book.

(which with some gentlemen pass for nothing) give in reality to every political principle its distinguishing colour, and discriminating effect. The circumstances are what render every civil and political scheme bene- ficial or noxious to mankind.[5] Abstractedly speaking, government, as well as liberty, is good; yet could I, in common sense, ten years ago, have felicitated France on her enjoyment of a government (for she then had a government) without enquiry what the nature of that govern- ment was, or how it was administered? Can I now congratulate the same nation upon its freedom? Is it because liberty in the abstract may be classed amongst the blessings of mankind, that I am seriously to felici- tate a madman, who has escaped from the protecting restraint and wholesome darkness of his cell, on his restoration to the enjoyment of light and liberty? Am I to congratulate an highwayman and murderer, who has broke prison, upon the recovery of his natural rights? This would be to act over again the scene of the criminals condemned to the gallies, and their heroic deliverer, the metaphysic Knight of the Sorrow- ful Countenance.[6]

When I see the spirit of liberty in action, I see a strong principle at work; and this, for a while, is all I can possibly know of it. The wild *gas*, the fixed air is plainly broke loose: but we ought to suspend our judg- ment until the first effervescence is a little subsided, till the liquor is cleared, and until we see something deeper than the agitation of a trou- bled and frothy surface. I must be tolerably sure, before I venture pub- licly to congratulate men upon a blessing, that they have really received one. Flattery corrupts both the receiver and the giver; and adulation is not of more service to the people than to kings. I should therefore sus- pend my congratulations on the new liberty of France, until I was in- formed how it had been combined with government; with public force; with the discipline and obedience of armies; with the collection of an effective and well-distributed revenue; with morality and religion; with the solidity of property; with peace and order; with civil and social man- ners. All these (in their way) are good things too; and, without them, liberty is not a benefit whilst it lasts, and is not likely to continue long. The effect of liberty to individuals is, that they may do what they please: We ought to see what it will please them to do, before we risk congratu- lations, which may be soon turned into complaints.[7] Prudence would dictate this in the case of separate insulated private men; but liberty, when men act in bodies, is *power*. Considerate people, before they de-

---

[5] An example of Burke's historicism and particularism. The value of particular institu- tions, practices, and rights can only be assessed in their relationship with other institutions.

[6] *Don Quixote* by Miguel Cervantes.

[7] The critique of "doing as one pleases" as a flawed conception of liberty would be echoed by many later conservatives. See the selections from Rufus Choate and Matthew Arnold later in this volume.

clare themselves, will observe the use which is made of *power*, and particularly of so trying a thing as *new* power in *new* persons, of whose principles, tempers, and dispositions, they have little or no experience, and in situations where those who appear the most stirring in the scene may possibly not be the real movers.

Sollicitous chiefly for the peace of my own country, but by no means unconcerned for yours, I wish to communicate more largely, what was at first intended only for your private satisfaction.[8] I shall still keep your affairs in my eye, and continue to address myself to you. Indulging myself in the freedom of epistolary intercourse, I beg leave to throw out my thoughts, and express my feelings, just as they arise in my mind, with very little attention to formal method. I set out with the proceedings of the Revolution Society; but I shall not confine myself to them. Is it possible I should? It looks to me as if I were in a great crisis, not of the affairs of France alone, but of all Europe, perhaps of more than Europe. All circumstances taken together, the French revolution is the most astonishing that has hitherto happened in the world.[9] The most wonderful things are brought about in many instances by means the most absurd and ridiculous; in the most ridiculous modes; and apparently, by the most contemptible instruments. Everything seems out of nature in this strange chaos of levity and ferocity, and of all sorts of crimes jumbled together with all sorts of follies. In viewing this monstrous tragi-comic scene, the most opposite passions necessarily succeed, and sometimes mix with each other in the mind; alternate contempt and indignation; alternate laughter and tears; alternate scorn and horror. . . .

[T]he political Divine proceeds dogmatically to assert,[10] that by the principles of the Revolution the people of England have acquired three fundamental rights, all which, with him, compose one system, and lie together in one short sentence; namely, that we have acquired a right

1. "To Choose our own governors."
2. "To cashier them for misconduct."
3. "To frame a government for ourselves."

---

[8] These words are addressed to the "Gentleman in Paris" who is the rhetorical recipient of Burke's letter.

[9] It is precisely because Burke recognizes the attraction of the events in France for many of his readers that he is compelled to offer a lengthy critical analysis.

[10] [P. 34 of *Discourse on the Love of our Country*, by Dr. Price.] Burke discusses the implications of the Glorious Revolution as interpreted by Rev. Richard Price in his sermon delivered to the Revolutionary Society, an organization founded in 1788 to celebrate the centenary of the Revolution of 1688. The sermon was first delivered in a Unitarian Church known as the "Old Jewry" because of its location in an area of London once inhabited by Jews. In refuting Price's interpretation, Burke advances his own conception of how reform is to be brought about, and how radical change is to be presented.

This new, and hitherto unheard-of bill of rights, though made in the name of the whole people, belongs to those gentlemen and their faction only. The body of the people of England have no share of it. They utterly disclaim it. They will resist the practical assertion of it with their lives and fortunes. They are bound to do so by the laws of their country, made at the time of that very Revolution, which is appealed to in favour of the fictitious rights claimed by the society which abuses its name.

These gentlemen of the Old Jewry, in all their reasonings on the Revolution of 1688, have a revolution which happened in England about forty years before, and the late French revolution, so much before their eyes, and in their hearts, that they are constantly confounding all the three together.[11] It is necessary that we should separate what they confound. . . .

Unquestionably there was at the Revolution, in the person of King William, a small and temporary deviation from the strict order of a regular hereditary succession; but it is against all genuine principles of jurisprudence to draw a principle from a law made in a special case, and regarding an individual. . . .

The two houses,[12] in the act of King William, did not thank God that they had found a fair opportunity to assert a right to choose their own governors, much less to make an election the *only lawful* title to the crown. Their having been in a condition to avoid the appearance of it, as much as possible, was by them considered as a providential escape. They threw a politic, well-wrought veil over every circumstance tending to weaken the rights, which in the meliorated order of succession they meant to perpetuate; or which might furnish a precedent for any future departure from what they had then settled for ever . . . [in order] that they might preserve a close conformity to the practice of their ancestors. . . .[13]

It is far from impossible to reconcile, if we do not suffer ourselves to be entangled in the mazes of metaphysic sophistry,[14] the use both of a

[11] Though nominally devoted to commemorating the Revolution of 1688, the Revolutionary Society, Burke suggests, is actually devoted to more radical theories, including the republican theories of the English Civil War and the doctrines of the French Revolution.

[12] The Lords and the Commons.

[13] Rather than trumpeting their departure from tradition, Burke asserts, they went to great lengths to stress their continuity with past practice, although they had in fact departed from it by replacing the Roman Catholic King James II with his Protestant son-in-law. Burke intends to contrast the English reformers of 1688–89 with the revolutionaries of contemporary France. The former brought about reform without delegitimating the traditional sources of authority in the eyes of the populace. The French revolutionaries, by contrast, have made their case in a manner with delegitimates all existing political authority and will lead to anarchy, Burke predicts, before order is restored by force.

[14] Seductive but false wisdom. Throughout the work, Burke will refer to French and English intellectual supporters of the Revolution whom he seeks to discredit as "sophisters."

fixed role and an occasional deviation; the sacredness of an hereditary principle of succession in our government, with a power of change in its application in cases of extreme emergency. Even in that extremity (if we take the measure of our rights by our exercise of them at the Revolution) the change is to be confined to the peccant [faulty] part only; to the part which produced the necessary deviation; and even it is to be effected without a decomposition of the whole civil and political mass, for the purpose of originating a new civil order out of the first elements of society.

A state without the means of some change is without the means of its conservation. Without such means it might even risk the loss of that part of the constitution which it wished the most religiously to preserve. The two principles of conservation and correction operated strongly at the two critical periods of the Restoration and Revolution, when England found itself without a king. At both those periods the nation had lost the bond of union in their ancient edifice; they did not, however, dissolve the whole fabric. On the contrary, in both cases they regenerated the deficient part of the old constitution through the parts which were not impaired. They kept these old parts exactly as they were, that the part recovered might be suited to them. They acted by the ancient organized states in the shape of their old organization, and not by the organic *moleculae* of a disbanded people. At no time, perhaps, did the sovereign legislature manifest a more tender regard to that fundamental principle of British constitutional policy, than at the time of the Revolution, when it deviated from the direct line of hereditary succession. The crown was carried somewhat out of the line in which it had before moved; but the new line was derived from the same stock. It was still a line of hereditary descent; still an hereditary descent in the same blood, though an hereditary descent qualified with protestantism. When the legislature altered the direction, but kept the principle, they shewed that they held it inviolable. . . .

The gentlemen of the Society for Revolutions see nothing in that of 1688 but the deviation from the constitution; and they take the deviation from the principle for the principle. They have little regard to the obvious consequences of their doctrine, though they must see, that it leaves positive authority in very few of the positive institutions of this country. When such an unwarrantable maxim is once established, that no throne is lawful but the elective, no one act of the princes who preceded their aera of fictitious election can be valid. Do these theorists mean to imitate some of their predecessors, who dragged the bodies of our ancient sovereigns out of the quiet of their tombs? Do they mean to attaint and disable backwards all the kings that have reigned before the Revolution, and consequently to stain the throne of England with the blot of a continual usurpation? Do they mean to invalidate, annul, or to call into question, together with the titles of the whole line of our kings, that great body of our statute law which passed under those whom they treat as usurpers? to annul laws of inestimable value to our liberties—of as great value at least as any which have passed at or since the period of the Revolution? If kings, who did not owe their crown to the choice of their people, had no title to make laws, what will become of the statute *de tallagio non concedendo?*—of the *petition of right?*—of the act of *habeas corpus?* . . . .[15]

The people of England will not ape the fashions they have never tried; nor go back to those which they have found mischievous on trial. They look upon the legal hereditary succession of their crown as among their rights,[16] not as among their wrongs; as a benefit, not as a grievance; as a security for their liberty, not as a badge of servitude. They look on the frame of their commonwealth, *such as it stands*, to be of inestimable value; and they conceive the undisturbed succession of the crown to be a pledge of the stability and perpetuity of all the other members of our constitution.

I shall beg leave, before I go any further, to take notice of some paltry artifices, which the abettors of election as the only lawful title to the crown, are ready to employ, in order to render the support of the just principles of our constitution a task somewhat invidious. These sophisters substitute a fictitious cause, and feigned personages, in whose favour they suppose you engaged, whenever you defend the inheritable nature of the crown. It is common with them to dispute as if they were in a conflict with some of those exploded fanatics of slavery, who formerly maintained, what I believe no creature now maintains, "that the crown is held by divine, hereditary, and indefeasible right."[17]—These old fanatics of single arbitrary power dogmatized as if hereditary royalty was the only lawful government in the world, just as our new fanatics of popular arbitrary power, maintain that a popular election is the sole law-

---

[15] *De Tallagio non Concedendo* (1297), the Petition of Right (1628), and *Habeas Corpus* (1679) were all viewed as major steps along the road of guaranteeing the rights and liberties of the individual. Burke suggests that the legitimacy of the laws depends on the legitimacy of the governments that adopted them, and if the legitimacy of those governments is to be measured by the standards proclaimed by Price and other radicals, then many of the legal institutions which the radicals value will be called into question. The application of their standards, then, would have unintended negative consequences not anticipated by the radicals.

[16] "Rights" were usually treated by liberals as guarantees which restricted governmental power. Burke, by contrast, suggests that there is a right to be restrained by governmental power, a theme to which he will return. This is one of many cases in which Burke engages in terminological reversal, that is, taking the terms of his liberal opponents and reversing their connotations.

[17] This was a traditional Tory argument.

ful source of authority. The old prerogative enthusiasts, it is true, did speculate foolishly, and perhaps impiously too, as if monarchy had more of a divine sanction than any other mode of government; and as if a right to govern by inheritance were in strictness *indefeasible* in every person, who should be found in the succession to a throne, and under every circumstance, which no civil or political right can be. But an absurd opinion concerning the king's hereditary right to the crown does not prejudice one that is rational, and bottomed upon solid principles of law and policy. If all the absurd theories of lawyers and divines were to vitiate the objects in which they are conversant, we should have no law, and no religion, left in the world. But an absurd theory on one side of a question forms no justification for alledging a false fact, or promulgating mischievous maxims on the other.[18]. . .

No government could stand a moment, if it could be blown down with any thing so loose and indefinite as an opinion of *"misconduct"* . . . .

The ceremony of cashiering kings, of which these gentlemen talk so much at their ease, can rarely, if ever, be performed without force. It then becomes a case of war, and not of constitution. Laws are commanded to hold their tongues amongst arms; and tribunals fall to the ground with the peace they are no longer able to uphold. The Revolution of 1688 was obtained by a just war, in the only case in which any war, and much more a civil war, can be just. "Justa bella quibus *necessaria.*"[19] The question of dethroning, or, if these gentlemen like the phrase better, "cashiering kings," will always be, as it has always been, an extraordinary question of state, and wholly out of the law; a question (like all other questions of state) of dispositions, and of means, and of probable consequences, rather than of positive rights. As it was not made for common abuses, so it is not to be agitated by common minds. The speculative line of demarcation, where obedience ought to end, and resistance must begin, is faint, obscure, and not easily definable. It is not a single act, or a single event, which determines it. Governments must be abused and deranged indeed, before it can be thought of; and the prospect of the future must be as bad as the experience of the past. When things are in that lamentable condition, the nature of the disease is to indicate the remedy to those whom nature has qualified to administer in extremities this critical, ambiguous, bitter portion to a distempered

[18] Though orthodox arguments on behalf of existing institutions may be flawed and implausible, there may be good arguments to be made in favor of such institutions on the grounds of historical utility. Burke accepts that the traditional Tory argument in favor of monarchy is absurd and based upon implausible faith. But he suggests rhetorically that by insisting upon a set of abstract principles without regard to historical context, the radical proponents of elective monarchy demonstrate that they too are "fanatical" and "enthusiastic."

[19] "Wars are just when they are necessary." Livy, *History of Rome.* IX, 1.

state. Times and occasions, and provocations, will teach their own lessons. The wise will determine from the gravity of the case; the irritable
from sensibility to oppression; the high-minded from disdain and indignation at abusive power in unworthy hands; the brave and bold from the
love of honourable danger in a generous cause: but, with or without
right, a revolution will be the very last resource of the thinking and the
good.

The third head of right, asserted by the pulpit of the Old Jewry,
namely, the "right to form a government for ourselves," has, at least, as
little countenance from any thing done at the Revolution, either in precedent or principle, as the two first of their claims. The Revolution was
made to preserve our *ancient* indisputable laws and liberties, and that
ancient constitution of government which is our only security for law
and liberty.[20] If you are desirous of knowing the spirit of our constitution, and the policy which predominated in that great period which has
secured it to this hour, pray look for both in our histories, in our records, in our acts of parliament, and journals of parliaments, and not in
the sermons of the Old Jewry, and the after-dinner toasts of the Revolution Society.—In the former you will find other ideas and another
language. Such a claim is as ill-suited to our temper and wishes as it is
unsupported by any appearance of authority.[21] The very idea of the fab-
rication of a new government, is enough to fill us with disgust and horror. We wished at the period of the Revolution, and do now wish, to
derive all we possess as *an inheritance from our forefathers*. Upon that
body and stock of inheritance we have taken care not to inoculate any
cyon [graft any shoot] alien to the nature of the original plant. All the
reformations we have hitherto made, have proceeded upon the principle
of reference to antiquity; and I hope, nay I am persuaded, that all those
which possibly may be made hereafter, will be carefully formed upon
analogical precedent, authority, and example.

Our oldest reformation is that of Magna Charta. You will see that Sir
Edward Coke,[22] that great oracle of our law, and indeed all the great
men who follow him, to Blackstone,[23] are industrious to prove the pedi-

---

[20] Burke is appealing here to the argument of precedent, which was central to British
Common Law. In the seventeenth century, the argument was extended to political institutions, maintaining that British constitutional practice derived from and was continuous
with practices which had existed since time immemorial.

[21] Burke here argues that the sort of abstract political claims put forward by the radicals
is both contrary to the peculiarities of British national culture, which tends to value historical precedent, and is at odds with the need to develop reverence for institutions. Presumably in other political cultures different modes of argumentation would be more
appropriate.

[22] Sir Edward Coke (1552–1634), leading constitutional lawyer, author of the *Institutes
of the Laws of England*, and an opponent of all attempts to diminish the competence of the
Common Law.

[23] [See Blackstone's Magna Charta printed at Oxford, 1759.] Sir William Blackstone

gree of our liberties. They endeavour to prove, that the ancient charter, the Magna Charta of King John,[24] was connected with another positive charter from Henry I, and that both the one and the other were nothing more than a re-affirmation of the still more ancient standing law of the kingdom. In the matter of fact, for the greater part, these authors appear to be in the right; perhaps not always: but if the lawyers mistake in some particulars, it proves my position still the more strongly; because it demonstrates the powerful prepossession towards antiquity, with which the minds of all our lawyers and legislators, and of all the people whom they wish to influence, have been always filled; and the stationary policy of this kingdom in considering their most sacred rights and franchises as an *inheritance*.

In the famous law of the 3d of Charles I called the *Petition of Right*,[25] the parliament says to the king, "Your subjects have *inherited* this freedom," claiming their franchises not on abstract principles "as the rights of men," but as the rights of Englishmen, and as a patrimony derived from their forefathers. Selden,[26] and the other profoundly learned men, who drew this petition of right, were as well acquainted, at least, with all the general theories concerning the "rights of men," as any of the discoursers in our pulpits, or on your tribune; full as well as Dr. Price, or as the Abbé Seyes.[27] But, for reasons worthy of that practical wisdom which superseded their theoretic science, they preferred this positive, recorded, *hereditary* title to all which can be dear to the man and the citizen, to that vague speculative right, which exposed their sure inheritance to be scrambled for and torn to pieces by every wild litigious spirit. . . .

You will observe, that from Magna Charta to the Declaration of Right, it has been the uniform policy of our constitution to claim and assert our liberties, as an *entailed inheritance* derived to us from our forefathers, and to be transmitted to our posterity; as an estate specially belonging to the people of this kingdom without any reference whatever to any other more general or prior right. By this means our constitution preserves an unity in so great a diversity of its parts. We have an inheritable crown; an inheritable peerage; and an house of commons and a people inheriting privileges, franchises, and liberties, from a long line of ancestors.

(1723–80) the leading authority of his day on English law . His *Commentaries on the Laws of England*, published in four volumes between 1765 and 1769, became the standard text on the subject.

[24] The Magna Carta, granted by King John in 1215, later came to be seen as embodying the very ideal of English liberties.

[25] The Petition of Right of 1628.

[26] John Selden (1584–1654), a distinguished jurist and legal historian, took part in the parliamentary opposition to James I and Charles I.

[27] Abbé Emmanuel-Joseph Sieyès (1748–1836), was author of *What is the Third Estate?*, the most significant political pamphlet of the early stage of the French Revolution.

This policy appears to me to be the result of profound reflection; or rather the happy effect of following nature, which is wisdom without reflection, and above it.[28] A spirit of innovation is generally the result of a selfish temper and confined views. People will not look forward to posterity, who never look backward to their ancestors.[29] Besides, the people of England well know, that the idea of inheritance furnishes a sure principle of conservation, and a sure principle of transmission; without at all excluding a principle of improvement. It leaves acquisition free; but it secures what it acquires. Whatever advantages are obtained by a state proceeding on these maxims, are locked fast as in a sort of family settlement; grasped as in a kind of mortmain for ever.[30] By a constitutional policy, working after the pattern of nature, we receive, we hold, we transmit our government and our privileges, in the same manner in which we enjoy and transmit our property and our lives. The institutions of policy, the goods of fortune, the gifts of Providence, are handed down, to us and from us, in the same course and order. Our political system is placed in a just correspondence and symmetry with the order of the world, and with the mode of existence decreed to a permanent body composed of transitory parts; wherein, by the disposition of a stupendous wisdom, moulding together the great mysterious incorporation of the human race, the whole, at one time, is never old, or middle-aged, or young, but in a condition of unchangeable constancy, moves on through the varied tenour of perpetual decay, fall, renovation, and progression. Thus, by preserving the method of nature in the conduct of the state, in what we improve we are never wholly new; in what we retain we are never wholly obsolete. By adhering in this manner and on those principles to our forefathers, we are guided not by the superstition of antiquarians, but by the spirit of philosophic analogy. In this choice of inheritance we have given to our frame of polity the image of a relation in blood; binding up the constitution of our country with our dearest domestic ties; adopting our fundamental laws into the bosom of our family affections; keeping inseparable, and cherishing with the warmth of all their combined and mutually reflected charities, our state, our hearths, our sepulchres, and our altars.[31]

[28] An example of the conflation of "nature" with inherited conventions.

[29] Pride in one's past leads to greater responsibility toward the future, and hence, Burke thinks, to greater caution in reform. This theme is one which Burke will go on to express in a variety of formulations in the course of the book.

[30] Mortmain was a legal device which allowed a corporation perpetual control over some property.

[31] Political institutions, Burke suggests, are "inherited" in the same way as property is inherited within the family. This description is meant both to *argue* that the British conception of political institutions as an inheritance from the collective past increases reverence for such institutions, and to *evoke* such reverence.

Through the same plan of a conformity to nature in our artificial institutions, and by calling in the aid of her unerring and powerful instincts, to fortify the fallible and feeble contrivances of our reason, we have derived several other, and those no small benefits, from considering our liberties in the light of an inheritance.[32] Always acting as if in the presence of canonized forefathers, the spirit of freedom, leading in itself to misrule and excess, is tempered with an awful gravity. This idea of a liberal descent[33] inspires us with a sense of habitual native dignity, which prevents that upstart insolence almost inevitably adhering to and disgracing those who are the first acquirers of any distinction. By this means our liberty becomes a noble freedom. It carries an imposing and majestic aspect. It has a pedigree and illustrating ancestors. It has its bearings and its ensigns armorial [emblems of nobility]. It has its gallery of portraits; its monumental inscriptions; its records, evidences, and titles. We procure reverence to our civil institutions on the principle upon which nature teaches us to revere individual men; on account of their age; and on account of those from whom they are descended. All your sophisters cannot produce any thing better adapted to preserve a rational and manly freedom than the course that we have pursued, who have chosen our nature rather than our speculations, our breasts rather than our inventions, for the great conservatories and magazines of our rights and privileges.[34]

You might, if you pleased, have profited of our example, and have given to your recovered freedom a correspondent dignity. Your privileges, though discontinued, were not lost to memory. Your constitution, it is true, whilst you were out of possession, suffered waste and dilapidation; but you possessed in some parts the walls, and in all the foundations of a noble and venerable castle. You might have repaired those walls; you might have built on those old foundations. . . .[35]

You had all these advantages in your ancient states; but you chose to act as if you had never been moulded into civil society, and had everything to begin anew.[36] You began ill, because you began by despising

[32] A very subtle sentence, which argues for the utility of regarding "artificial" institutions *as if* they were natural.

[33] That is, descent from free men, rather than from slaves or serfs.

[34] Burke insists that British institutions, even when they are renovated, have a greater emotional hold over their subjects because their continuity with the past is emphasized. By making their appeal on the basis of abstract, natural, and universal rights while discrediting all of their past and present political institutions, Burke goes on to suggest, the French are dooming their innovations.

[35] The metaphor of the need to build upon solid foundations will be a recurrent one in the rest of the book. It is meant to suggest that innovation must take place in a manner that is (or, at least, appears to be) continuous with past practice.

[36] In 1788, the King had called a meeting of the three Estates General, comprised of the clergy, the nobility, and commoners, respectively. It was the unwillingness of the repre-

everything that belonged to you. You set up your trade without a capital. If the last generations of your country appeared without much lustre in your eyes, you might have passed them by, and derived your claims from a more early race of ancestors. Under a pious predilection for those ancestors, your imaginations would have realized in them a standard of virtue and wisdom, beyond the vulgar practice of the hour: and you would have risen with the example to whose imitation you aspired. Respecting your forefathers, you would have been taught to respect yourselves. You would not have chosen to consider the French as a people of yesterday, as a nation of low-born servile wretches until the emancipating year of 1789. In order to furnish, at the expence of your honour, an excuse to your apologists here for several enormities of yours, you would not have been content to be represented as a gang of Maroon slaves,[37] suddenly broke loose from the house of bondage, and therefore to be pardoned for your abuse of the liberty to which you were not accustomed and ill fitted. Would it not, my worthy friend, have been wiser to have you thought, what I, for one, always thought you, a generous and gallant nation, long misled to your disadvantage by your high and romantic sentiments of fidelity, honour, and loyalty; that events had been unfavourable to you, but that you were not enslaved through any illiberal or servile disposition; that in your most devoted submission, you were actuated by a principle of public spirit, and that it was your country you worshipped, in the person of your king? Had you made it to be understood, that in the delusion of this amiable error you had gone further than your wise ancestors; that you were resolved to resume your ancient privileges, whilst you preserved the spirit of your ancient and your recent loyalty and honour; or, if diffident of yourselves, and not clearly discerning the almost obliterated constitution of your ancestors, you had looked to your neighbours in this land, who had kept alive the ancient principles and models of the old common law of Europe meliorated and adapted to its present state—by following wise examples you would have given new examples of wisdom to the world. You would have rendered the cause of liberty venerable in the eyes of every worthy mind in every nation. You would have shamed despotism from the earth, by shewing that freedom was not only reconcileable, but as, when well disciplined it is, auxiliary to law. . . .

Believe me, Sir, those who attempt to level, never equalize.[38] In all societies, consisting of various descriptions of citizens, some description

---

sentatives of the Third Estate to accept this arrangement which led to the formation of a single National Assembly in June 1789. Burke asserts that this was an error.

[37] A term applied to communities of fugitive slaves in the colonies.

[38] Here Burke insists upon the need for, and the inevitability of, elites.

must be uppermost. The levellers therefore only change and pervert the natural order of things; they load the edifice of society, by setting up in the air what the solidity of the structure requires to be on the ground. The associations of tailors and carpenters, of which the republic (of Paris, for instance) is composed, cannot be equal to the situation, into which, by the worst of usurpations, an usurpation on the prerogatives of nature, you attempt to force them.

The chancellor of France at the opening of the states, said, in a tone of oratorial flourish, that all occupations were honourable. If he meant only, that no honest employment was disgraceful, he would not have gone beyond the truth. But in asserting, that any thing is honourable, we imply some distinction in its favour. The occupation of an hair-dresser, or of a working tallow-chandler, cannot be a matter of honour to any person—to say nothing of a number of other more servile employments. Such descriptions of men ought not to suffer oppression from the state; but the state suffers oppression, if such as they, either individually or collectively, are permitted to rule. In this you think you are combating prejudice, but you are at war with nature.

I do not, my dear Sir, conceive you to be of that sophistical captious spirit, or of that uncandid dulness, as to require, for every general observation or sentiment, an explicit detail of the correctives and exceptions, which reason will presume to be included in all the general propositions which come from reasonable men. You do not imagine, that I wish to confine power, authority, and distinction to blood, and names, and titles. No, Sir. There is no qualification for government, but virtue and wisdom, actual or presumptive. Wherever they are actually found, they have, in whatever state, condition, profession, or trade, the passport of Heaven to human place and honour. Woe to the country which would madly and impiously reject the service of the talents and virtues, civil, military, or religious, that are given to grace and to serve it; and would condemn to obscurity everything formed to diffuse lustre and glory around a state. Woe to that country too, that passing into the opposite extreme, considers a low education, a mean contracted view of things, a sordid mercenary occupation, as a preferable title to command. Everything ought to be open; but not indifferently to every man. No rotation; no appointment by lot; no mode of election operating in the spirit of sortition or rotation, can be generally good in a government conversant in extensive objects. Because they have no tendency, direct or indirect, to select the man with a view to the duty, or to accommodate the one to the other, I do not hesitate to say, that the road to eminence and power, from obscure condition, ought not to be made too easy, nor a thing too much of course. If rare merit be the rarest of all rare things, it ought to pass through some sort of probation. The temple of honour ought to be seated on an eminence. If it be open through virtue, let it be remembered too, that virtue is never tried but by some difficulty, and some struggle.

Nothing is a due and adequate representation of a state, that does not represent its ability, as well as its property. But as ability is a vigorous and active principle, and as property is sluggish, inert, and timid, it never can be safe from the invasions of ability, unless it be, out of all proportion, predominant in the representation. It must be represented too in great masses of accumulation, or it is not rightly protected. The characteristic essence of property, formed out of the combined principles of its acquisition and conservation, is to be *unequal*. The great masses therefore which excite envy, and tempt rapacity, must be put out of the possibility of danger. Then they form a natural rampart about the lesser properties in all their gradations. The same quantity of property, which is by the natural course of things divided among many, has not the same operation. Its defensive power is weakened as it is diffused. In this diffusion each man's portion is less than what, in the eagerness of his desires, he may flatter himself to obtain by dissipating the accumulations of others. The plunder of the few would indeed give but a share inconceivably small in the distribution to the many. But the many are not capable of making this calculation; and those who lead them to rapine [theft], never intend this distribution.

The power of perpetuating our property in our families is one of the most valuable and interesting circumstances belonging to it, and that which tends the most to the perpetuation of society itself.[39] It makes our weakness subservient to our virtue; it grafts benevolence even upon avarice. The possessors of family wealth, and of the distinction which attends hereditary possession (as most concerned in it) are the natural securities for this transmission. With us, the house of peers is formed upon this principle. It is wholly composed of hereditary property and hereditary distinction; and made therefore the third of the legislature; and in the last event, the sole judge of all property in all its subdivisions. The house of commons too, though not necessarily, yet in fact, is always so composed in the far greater part. Let those large proprietors be what they will, and they have their chance of being amongst the best, they are at the very worst, the ballast in the vessel of the commonwealth. For though hereditary wealth, and the rank which goes with it, are too much idolized by creeping sycophants, and the blind abject admirers of power, they are too rashly slighted in shallow speculations of the petulant, as-

---

[39] Here Burke ties together two key themes in conservative thought, the centrality of the family as a socializing institution for the formation of moral character, and the protection of private property, which serves as a means of expressing familial commitments.

suming, short-sighted coxcombs of philosophy. Some decent regulated preeminence, some preference (not exclusive appropriation) given to birth, is neither unnatural, nor unjust, nor impolitic. . . .

The Revolution Society has discovered that the English nation is not free. They are convinced that the inequality in our representation is a "defect in our constitution so *gross and palpable*, as to make it excellent chiefly in *form and theory*."[40] . . . .

These gentlemen value themselves on being systematic; and not without reason. They must therefore look on this gross and palpable defect of representation, this fundamental grievance (so they call it) as a thing not only vicious in itself, but as rendering our whole government absolutely *illegitimate*, and not at all better than a downright *usurpation*. . . .

It is no wonder therefore, that with these ideas of everything in their constitution and government at home, either in church or state, as illegitimate and usurped, or, at best as a vain mockery, they look abroad with an eager and passionate enthusiasm.[41] Whilst they are possessed by these notions, it is vain to talk to them of the practice of their ancestors, the fundamental laws of their country, the fixed form of a constitution, whose merits are confirmed by the solid test of long experience, and an increasing public strength and national prosperity. They despise experience as the wisdom of unlettered men; and as for the rest, they have wrought underground a mine that will blow up at one grand explosion all examples of antiquity, all precedents, charters, and acts of parliament. They have "the rights of men." Against these there can be no prescription; against these no agreement is binding; these admit no temperament, and no compromise: any thing withheld from their full demand is so much of fraud and injustice. Against these their rights of men let no government look for security in the length of its continuance, or in the justice and lenity of its administration. The objections of these speculatists, if its forms do not quadrate with their theories, are as valid against such an old and beneficent government as against the most violent tyranny, or the greenest usurpation. . . .

Far am I from denying in theory; full as far is my heart from withholding in practice (if I were of power to give or to withhold) the *real* rights of men. In denying their false claims of right, I do not mean to injure those which are real, and are such as their pretended rights would totally destroy. If civil society [government] be made for the advantage of man, all the advantages for which it is made become his right. It is an institu-

---

[40] [*Discourse on the Love of our Country*, 3d ed. p. 39.]
[41] Burke's use of the term enthusiasm is meant to suggest an irrational intoxication with one's own ideas, at the expense of shared and collective experience.

tion of beneficence; and law itself is only beneficence acting by a rule. Men have a right to live by that rule; they have a right to justice; as between their fellows, whether their fellows are in politic function or in ordinary occupation. They have a right to the fruits of their industry; and to the means of making their industry fruitful. They have a right to the acquisitions of their parents; to the nourishment and improvement of their offspring; to instruction in life, and to consolation in death. Whatever each man can separately do, without trespassing upon others, he has a right to do for himself; and he has a right to a fair portion of all which society, with all its combinations of skill and force, can do in his favour. In this partnership all men have equal rights; but not to equal things.[42] He that has but five shillings in the partnership, has as good a right to it, as he that has five hundred pound has to his larger proportion. But he has not a right to an equal dividend in the product of the joint stock; and as to the share of power, authority, and direction which each individual ought to have in the management of the state, that I must deny to be amongst the direct original rights of man in civil society; for I have in my contemplation the civil social man, and no other. It is a thing to be settled by convention.

If civil society be the offspring of convention, that convention must be its law.[43] That convention must limit and modify all the descriptions of constitution which are formed under it. Every sort of legislative, judicial, or executory power are its creatures. They can have no being in any other state of things; and how can any man claim, under the conventions of civil society, rights which do not so much as suppose its existence? Rights which are absolutely repugnant to it? One of the first motives to civil society, and which becomes one of its fundamental rules, is *that no man should be judge in his own cause*. By this each person has at once divested himself of the first fundamental right of uncovenanted man, that is, to judge for himself, and to assert his own cause. He abdicates all right to be his own governor. He inclusively, in a great measure, abandons the right of self-defence, the first law of nature. Men cannot enjoy the rights of an uncivil and of a civil state together. That he may obtain justice he gives up his right of determining what it is in points the most essential to him. That he may secure some liberty, he makes a surrender in trust of the whole of it.

Government is not made in virtue of natural rights, which may and do exist in total independence of it; and exist in much greater clearness, and in a much greater degree of abstract perfection: but their abstract perfection is their practical defect. By having a right to everything, they want

---

[42] Here Burke takes the theory of the social contract and gives it his own, inegalitarian interpretation.

[43] Burke's logic here is explicitly Humean.

everything.[44] Government is a contrivance of human wisdom to provide for human *wants*. Men have a right that these wants should be provided for by this wisdom. Among these wants is to be reckoned the want, out of civil society, of a sufficient restraint upon their passions. Society requires not only that the passions of individuals should be subjected, but that even in the mass and body as well as in the individuals, the inclinations of men should frequently be thwarted, their will controlled, and their passions brought into subjection. This can only be done *by a power out of themselves*, and not, in the exercise of its function, subject to that will and to those passions which it is its office to bridle and subdue. In this sense the restraints on men, as well as their liberties, are to be reckoned among their rights.[45] But as the liberties and the restrictions vary with times and circumstances, and admit of infinite modifications, they cannot be settled upon any abstract rule; and nothing is so foolish as to discuss them upon that principle.[46]

The moment you abate any thing from the full rights of men, each to govern himself, and suffer any artificial positive limitation upon those rights, from that moment the whole organization of government becomes a consideration of convenience. This it is which makes the constitution of a state, and the due distribution of its powers, a matter of the most delicate and complicated skill. It requires a deep knowledge of human nature and human necessities, and of the things which facilitate or obstruct the various ends which are to be pursued by the mechanism of civil institutions. The state is to have recruits to its strength, and remedies to its distempers. What is the use of discussing a man's abstract right to food or to medicine? The question is upon the method of procuring and administering them. In that deliberation I shall always advise to call in the aid of the farmer and the physician, rather than the professor of metaphysics.

The science of constructing a commonwealth, or renovating it, or reforming it, is, like every other experimental science, not to be taught *a priori* [on the basis of principles prior to experience].[47] Nor is it a short experience that can instruct us in that practical science; because the real effects of moral causes are not always immediate; but that which in the

---

[44] Here and in the sentences which follow, Burke is playing on the two meanings of the word "want," which can mean both to "desire" and to "lack." Thinking in terms of a "right" to everything, he means to suggest, will unleash unfulfillable desires, and will create a lack of those institutional restraints which men require.

[45] Another example of Burke's reversal of the connotations of the key terms of his opponents. "Rights" are usually identified with restrictions on government; Burke contends that there is a right to be restricted *by* government.

[46] A pithy quintessence of historicist utilitarianism.

[47] Burke now presents the theoretical meat of his critique of abstract and universal forms of political and social theory.

first instance is prejudicial may be excellent in its remoter operation; and its excellence may arise even from the ill effects it produces in the beginning. The reverse also happens; and very plausible schemes, with very pleasing commencements, have often shameful and lamentable conclusions.[48] In states there are often some obscure and almost latent causes, things which appear at first view of little moment, on which a very great part of its prosperity or adversity may most essentially depend.[49] The science of government being therefore so practical in itself, and intended for such practical purposes, a matter which requires experience, and even more experience than any person can gain in his whole life, however sagacious and observing he may be, it is with infinite caution that any man ought to venture upon pulling down an edifice which has answered in any tolerable degree for ages the common purposes of society, or on building it up again, without having models and patterns of approved utility before his eyes.

These metaphysic rights entering into common life, like rays of light which pierce into a dense medium, are, by the laws of nature, refracted from their straight line. Indeed in the gross and complicated mass of human passions and concerns, the primitive rights of men undergo such a variety of refractions and reflections, that it becomes absurd to talk of them as if they continued in the simplicity of their original direction. The nature of man is intricate; the objects of society are of the greatest possible complexity; and therefore no simple disposition or direction of power can be suitable either to man's nature, or to the quality of his affairs. When I hear the simplicity of contrivance aimed at and boasted of in any new political constitutions, I am at no loss to decide that the artificers [craftsmen] are grossly ignorant of their trade, or totally negligent of their duty. The simple governments are fundamentally defective, to say no worse of them. If you were to contemplate society in but one point of view, all these simple modes of polity are infinitely captivating. In effect each would answer its single end much more perfectly than the more complex is able to attain all its complex purposes. But it is better that the whole should be imperfectly and anomalously answered, than that, while some parts are provided for with great exactness, others might be totally neglected, or perhaps materially injured, by the over-care of a favourite member.[50]

The pretended rights of these theorists are all extremes; and in proportion as they are metaphysically true, they are morally and politically

---

[48] Deliberate actions, Burke suggests, have negative consequences which are both unintended and unanticipated.

[49] A statement of the concept of latent functions.

[50] The recognition of social complexity, therefore, demands epistemological modesty and caution in reform.

false. The rights of men are in a sort of *middle*, incapable of definition, but not impossible to be discerned. The rights of men in governments are their advantages; and these are often in balances between differences of good; in compromises sometimes between good and evil, and sometimes, between evil and evil. Political reason is a computing principle; adding, subtracting, multiplying, and dividing, morally and not metaphysically or mathematically, true moral denominations.

By these theorists the right of the people is almost always sophistically confounded with their power. The body of the community, whenever it can come to act, can meet with no effectual resistance; but till power and right are the same, the whole body of them has no right inconsistent with virtue, and the first of all virtues, prudence. Men have no right to what is not reasonable, and to what is not for their benefit. . . .

History will record,[51] that on the morning of the 6th of October 1789, the king and queen of France, after a day of confusion, alarm, dismay, and slaughter, lay down, under the pledged security of public faith, to indulge nature in a few hours of respite, and troubled melan·choly repose. From this sleep the queen was first startled by the voice of the centinel at her door, who cried out to her, to save herself by flight— that this was the last proof of fidelity he could give—that they were upon him, and he was dead. Instantly he was cut down. A band of cruel ruffians and assassins, reeking with his blood, rushed into the chamber of the queen, and pierced with an hundred strokes of bayonets and poniards the bed, from whence this persecuted woman had but just time to fly almost naked, and through ways unknown to the murderers had escaped to seek refuge at the feet of a king and husband, not secure of his own life for a moment.

This king, to say no more of him, and this queen, and their infant children (who once would have been the pride and hope of a great and generous people) were then forced to abandon the sanctuary of the most splendid palace in the world, which they left swimming in blood,

---

[51] On October 5, 1789, at a time of rising hunger, a crowd of several thousand made up primarily of market women who blamed their plight on an aristocratic plot to starve them, set off from Paris for the royal palace at Versailles, armed with cannon, pikes, and muskets. Following behind was a brigade of rebellious National Guardsmen, determined to bring the royal family back to Paris, the better to subject it to the pressures of the Parisian populace. The next morning, after some failed negotiations, the crowd broke into the royal apartments, were fired upon by the guards, and killed two of them, including the guard stationed outside the Queen's chamber. Their heads were stuck on spears and paraded around the courtyard. After further scuffling, the incident ended with a piece of political theater staged by Lafayette, in which the King and Queen appeared on the balcony and greeted the crowd. The royal family, having narrowly escaped with its life, acceded to the crowd's demand and accompanied it back to Paris, where the royal family took up residence in the Tuileries palace.

polluted by massacre, and strewed with scattered limbs and mutilated carcases. Thence they were conducted into the capital of their kingdom. Two had been selected from the unprovoked, unresisted, promiscuous slaughter, which was made of the gentlemen of birth and family who composed the king's body guard. These two gentlemen, with all the parade of an execution of justice, were cruelly and publickly dragged to the block, and beheaded in the great court of the palace. Their heads were stuck upon spears, and led the procession; whilst the royal captives who followed in the train were slowly moved along, amidst the horrid yells, and shrilling screams, and frantic dances, and infamous contumelies [verbal abuse], and all the unutterable abominations of the furies of hell, in the abused shape of the vilest of women. After they had been made to taste, drop by drop, more than the bitterness of death, in the slow torture of a journey of twelve miles, protracted to six hours, they were, under a guard, composed of those very soldiers who had thus conducted them through this famous triumph, lodged in one of the old palaces of Paris now converted into a Bastile for kings. . . .

Although this work of our new light and knowledge, did not go to the length, that in all probability it was intended it should be carried; yet I must think, that such treatment of any human creatures must be shocking to any but those who are made for accomplishing Revolutions. But I cannot stop here. Influenced by the inborn feelings of my nature, and not being illuminated by a single ray of this new-sprung modern light, I confess to you, Sir, that the exalted rank of the persons suffering, and particularly the sex, the beauty, and the amiable qualities of the descendant of so many kings and emperors, with the tender age of royal infants, insensible only through infancy and innocence of the cruel outrages to which their parents were exposed, instead of being a subject of exultation, adds not a little to my sensibility on that most melancholy occasion. . . .

I hear, and I rejoice to hear, that the great lady, the other object of the triumph, has borne that day (one is interested that beings made for suffering should suffer well) and that she bears all the succeeding days, that she bears the imprisonment of her husband, and her own captivity, and the exile of her friends, and the insulting adulation of addresses, and the whole weight of her accumulated wrongs, with a serene patience, in a manner suited to her rank and race, and becoming the offspring of a sovereign distinguished for her piety and her courage; that like her she has lofty sentiments; that she feels with the dignity of a Roman matron; that in the last extremity she will save herself from the last disgrace, and that if she must fall, she will fall by no ignoble hand.

It is now sixteen or seventeen years since I saw the queen of France, then the dauphiness, at Versailles; and surely never lighted on this orb, which she hardly seemed to touch, a more delightful vision. I saw her just above the horizon, decorating and cheering the elevated sphere she just began to move in,—glittering like the morning-star, full of life, and splendor, and joy. Oh! what a revolution! and what an heart must I have, to contemplate without emotion that elevation and that fall! Little did I dream when she added titles of veneration to those of enthusiastic, distant, respectful love, that she should ever be obliged to carry the sharp antidote against disgrace concealed in that bosom; little did I dream that I should have lived to see such disasters fallen upon her in a nation of gallant men, in a nation of men of honour and of cavaliers. I thought ten thousand swords must have leaped from their scabbards to avenge even a look that threatened her with insult.—But the age of chivalry is gone.[52]—That of sophisters, oeconomists, and calculators,[53] has succeeded; and the glory of Europe is extinguished for ever. Never, never more, shall we behold that generous loyalty to rank and sex, that proud submission, that dignified obedience, that subordination of the heart, which kept alive, even in servitude itself, the spirit of an exalted freedom. The unbought grace of life, the cheap defence of nations, the nurse of manly sentiment and heroic enterprize is gone! It is gone, that sensibility of principle, that chastity of honour, which felt a stain like a wound, which inspired courage whilst it mitigated ferocity, which ennobled whatever it touched, and under which vice itself lost half its evil, by losing all its grossness.

This mixed system of opinion and sentiment had its origin in the antient chivalry; and the principle, though varied in its appearance by the varying state of human affairs, subsisted and influenced through a long succession of generations, even to the time we live in. If it should ever be totally extinguished, the loss I fear will be great. It is this which has given its character to modern Europe. It is this which has distinguished

[52] Leading historians of Burke's day, especially William Robertson and John Millar, had depicted "chivalry" as a revolution in manners within the feudal world, which restrained the will of barbarian warriors toward the weak, the female sex, and toward one another. It was a revolution in which men of power came to subordinate themselves, in part at least, to the moral demands of Christianity, as expressed in canon law and as interpreted by men of learning. The result was a society in which the will of the powerful was restrained by cultural codes of conduct which had their origin in and drew support from the Church. In this paragraph and the next, Burke argues that cultural mores are crucial to the maintenance of a peaceful and flourishing society, that these mores have historically been conveyed by the institutions of the Church and of the nobility, and that without them society will require greater governmental force to maintain order.

[53] Richard Price, the butt of Burke's repeated references to "sophisters" was also an expert on compound interest. Burke here expresses his fear that the values of self-interest will come to dominate over all other forms of human behavior, with, he thinks, disastrous effects for society. This is one of several instances in the book in which Burke, though a supporter of commercial society, expresses the fear that the cultural consequences of capitalism may undermine the institutions necessary to preserve a decent society.

it under all its forms of government, and distinguished it to its advantage, from the states of Asia, and possibly from those states which flourished in the most brilliant periods of the antique world. It was this which, without confounding ranks, had produced a noble equality, and handed it down through all the gradations of social life. It was this opinion which mitigated kings into companions, and raised private men to be fellows with kings. Without force, or opposition, it subdued the fierceness of pride and power; it obliged sovereigns to submit to the soft collar of social esteem, compelled stern authority to submit to elegance, and gave a domination, vanquisher of laws, to be subdued by manners.

But now all is to be changed.[54] All the pleasing illusions, which made power gentle, and obedience liberal, which harmonized the different shades of life, and which, by a bland assimilation, incorporated into politics the sentiments which beautify and soften private society, are to be dissolved by this new conquering empire of light and reason. All the decent drapery of life is to be rudely torn off. All the superadded ideas, furnished from the wardrobe of a moral imagination, which the heart owns, and the understanding ratifies, as necessary to cover the defects of our naked shivering nature, and to raise it to dignity in our own estimation, are to be exploded as a ridiculous, absurd, and antiquated fashion.

On this scheme of things, a king is but a man; a queen is but a woman; a woman is but an animal; and an animal not of the highest order. All homage paid to the sex in general as such, and without distinct views, is to be regarded as romance and folly. Regicide, and parricide, and sacrilege, are but fictions of superstition, corrupting jurisprudence by destroying its simplicity. The murder of a king, or a queen, or a bishop, or a father, are only common homicide; and if the people are by any chance, or in any way gainers by it, a sort of homicide much the most pardonable, and into which we ought not to make too severe a scrutiny.

On the scheme of this barbarous philosophy, which is the offspring of cold hearts and muddy understandings, and which is as void of solid wisdom, as it is destitute of all taste and elegance, laws are to be supported only by their own terrors, and by the concern, which each individual may find in them, from his own private speculations, or can spare to them from his own private interests. In the groves of their academy, at the end of every vista, you see nothing but the gallows. Nothing is left

---

[54] Burke here presents a theory of culture as a sublimation of more primitive human drives, especially those of sex and domination. The attempt of some enlightened thinkers to expose man's true nature as a creature of the passions, Burke suggests, will serve to dissolve the redirection of drives provided by culture. Without the restraint provided by culture, the intrinsic imperfections of human nature will be unleashed. The result will be mass desublimation, leading to rape and other forms of violence.

which engages the affections on the part of the commonwealth. On the principles of this mechanic philosophy, our institutions can never be embodied, if I may use the expression, in persons; so as to create in us love, veneration, admiration, or attachment. But that sort of reason which banishes the affections is incapable of filling their place.[55] These public affections, combined with manners, are required sometimes as supplements, sometimes as correctives, always as aids to law. The precept given by a wise man, as well as a great critic, for the construction of poems, is equally true as to states. *Non satis est pulchra esse poemata, dulcia sunto.*[56] There ought to be a system of manners in every nation which a well-formed mind would be disposed to relish. To make us love our country, our country ought to be lovely.

But power, of some kind or other, will survive the shock in which manners and opinions perish; and it will find other and worse means for its support. The usurpation which, in order to subvert antient institutions, has destroyed antient principles, will hold power by arts similar to those by which it has acquired it. When the old feudal and chivalrous spirit of *Fealty*, which, by freeing kings from fear, freed both kings and subjects from the precautions of tyranny, shall be extinct in the minds of men, plots and assassinations will be anticipated by preventive murder and preventive confiscation, and that long roll of grim and bloody maxims, which form the political code of all power, not standing on its own honour, and the honour of those who are to obey it. Kings will be tyrants from policy when subjects are rebels from principle.

When antient opinions and rules of life are taken away, the loss cannot possibly be estimated.[57] From that moment we have no compass to govern us; nor can we know distinctly to what port we steer. Europe undoubtedly, taken in a mass, was in a flourishing condition the day on which your Revolution was compleated. How much of that prosperous state was owing to the spirit of our old manners and opinions is not easy to say; but as such causes cannot be indifferent in their operation, we must presume, that, on the whole, their operation was beneficial.

We are but too apt to consider things in the state in which we find them, without sufficiently adverting [paying attention] to the causes by

[55] Burke suggests that rationalism can undermine existing institutions and practices, without being able to replace them with new institutions or practices which are capable of exerting an emotional hold.

[56] "It is not enough that poems be beautiful, they must also be charming." A quote from Horace, *De Arte Poetica*, which Burke uses to convey the notion that institutions must exert an emotional hold if they are to be effective.

[57] What follows is a long meditation on latent functions, the unanticipated consequences that arise from a failure to recognize the latent functions of institutions, and the need for a recognition of the limits of our knowledge, all of which is a prescription for caution in reform.

which they have been produced, and possibly may be upheld. Nothing is more certain, than that our manners, our civilization, and all the good things which are connected with manners, and with civilization, have, in this European world of ours, depended for ages upon two principles; and were indeed the result of both combined; I mean the spirit of a gentleman, and the spirit of religion. The nobility and the clergy, the one by profession, the other by patronage, kept learning in existence, even in the midst of arms and confusions, and whilst governments were rather in their causes than formed. Learning[58] paid back what it received to nobility and to priesthood; and paid it with usury, by enlarging their ideas and by furnishing their minds. Happy if they had all continued to know their indissoluble union, and their proper place! Happy if learning, not debauched by ambition, had been satisfied to continue the instructor, and not aspired to be the master![59] Along with its natural protectors and guardians, learning will be cast into the mire, and trodden down under the hoofs of a swinish multitude.

If, as I suspect, modern letters owe more than they are always willing to own to antient manners, so do other interests which we value full as much as they are worth. Even commerce, and trade, and manufacture, the gods of our oeconomical politicians, are themselves perhaps but creatures; are themselves but effects, which, as first causes, we choose to worship. They certainly grew under the same shade in which learning flourished.[60] They too may decay with their natural protecting principles. With you, for the present at least, they all threaten to disappear together. Where trade and manufactures are wanting to a people, and the spirit of nobility and religion remains, sentiment supplies, and not always ill supplies their place; but if commerce and the arts should be lost in an experiment to try how well a state may stand without these old fundamental principles, what sort of a thing must be a nation of gross, stupid, ferocious, and at the same time, poor and sordid barbarians, destitute of religion, honour, or manly pride, possessing nothing at present, and hoping for nothing hereafter?

You see, Sir, that in this enlightened age I am bold enough to confess, that we [Englishmen] are generally men of untaught feelings; that instead of casting away all our old prejudices, we cherish them to a very considerable degree, and, to take more shame to ourselves, we cherish

---

[58] By "learning" Burke means classical thought, and philosophy more generally, as well as men of learning.

[59] The proper role of men of learning (such as himself), Burke thinks, is as intellectual guides to gentlemen.

[60] The learning and the manners which are preserved by the nobility and the church, Burke suggests, provide the cultural and institutional prerequisites for commercial society.

them because they are prejudices; and the longer they have lasted, and the more generally they have prevailed, the more we cherish them.[61] We are afraid to put men to live and trade each on his own private stock of reason; because we suspect that this stock in each man is small, and that the individuals would be better to avail themselves of the general bank and capital of nations, and of ages. Many of our men of speculation, instead of exploding general prejudices, employ their sagacity to discover the latent wisdom which prevails in them.[62] If they find what they seek, and they seldom fail, they think it more wise to continue the prejudice, with the reason involved, than to cast away the coat of prejudice, and to leave nothing but the naked reason; because prejudice, with its reason, has a motive to give action to that reason, and an affection which will give it permanence. Prejudice is of ready application in the emergency; it previously engages the mind in a steady course of wisdom and virtue, and does not leave the man hesitating in the moment of decision, sceptical, puzzled, and unresolved. Prejudice renders a man's virtue his habit; and not a series of unconnected acts. Through just prejudice, his duty becomes a part of his nature.[63]

Your literary men, and your politicians, and so do the whole clan of the enlightened[64] among us, essentially differ in these points. They have no respect for the wisdom of others; but they pay it off by a very full measure of confidence in their own. With them it is a sufficient motive to destroy an old scheme of things, because it is an old one. As to the new, they are in no sort of fear with regard to the duration of a building run up in haste; because duration is no object to those who think little or nothing has been done before their time, and who place all their hopes in discovery. They conceive, very systematically, that all things which give perpetuity are mischievous, and therefore they are at inexpiable war with all establishments. They think that government may vary like modes of dress, and with as little ill effect. That there needs no principle of attachment, except a sense of present conveniency, to any constitution of the state. They always speak as if they were of opinion that there is a singular species of compact between them and their magistrates, which binds the magistrate, but which has nothing reciprocal in it, but that the majesty of the people has a right to dissolve it without any reason, but its will. Their attachment to their country itself, is only so far as it agrees with some of their fleeting projects; it begins and

---

[61] Here Burke presents another of his reversals of the connotations of polemical terms. For most enlightened thinkers, the term "prejudice" was one of opprobrium. Burke offers a more positive conception of the role of prejudice.

[62] A conception of the role of the intellectual similar to that of Hume and Möser.

[63] Here prejudice is connected with the theme of "second nature."

[64] Burke here uses the term "enlightened" to apply to those intellectuals, such as Price, with whom he believes himself to be fundamentally at odds.

ends with that scheme of polity which falls in with their momentary opinion. . . .

We know, and what is better we feel inwardly, that religion is the basis of civil society, and the source of all good and of all comfort.[65] In England we are so convinced of this, that there is no rust of superstition, with which the accumulated absurdity of the human mind might have crusted it over in the course of ages, that ninety-nine in an hundred of the people of England would not prefer to impiety.[66] We shall never be such fools as to call in an enemy to the substance of any system to remove its corruptions, to supply its defects, or to perfect its construction. If our religious tenets should ever want a further elucidation, we shall not call on atheism to explain them. . . .

We know, and it is our pride to know, that man is by his constitution a religious animal; that atheism is against, not only our reason but our instincts; and that it cannot prevail long. But if, in the moment of riot, and in a drunken delirium from the hot spirit drawn out of the alembick of hell, which in France is now so furiously boiling, we should uncover our nakedness by throwing off that Christian religion which has hitherto been our boast and comfort, and one great source of civilization amongst us, and among many other nations, we are apprehensive (being well aware that the mind will not endure a void) that some uncouth, pernicious, and degrading superstition, might take place of it. . . .

On these ideas, instead of quarrelling with establishments, as some do, who have made a philosophy and a religion of their hostility to such institutions, we cleave closely to them. We are resolved to keep an established church, an established monarchy, an established aristocracy, and an established democracy,[67] each in the degree it exists, and in no greater. . . .

[65] In a footnote, Burke offers a quotation from Cicero, *De Legibus*, 1.2., in the original Latin, which in translation reads:

"So let our citizens be convinced of this at the outset: that the gods are the lords and rulers of all things, that all that is done is done by their might, dominion, and authority, and that they are the benefactors of mankind; that they notice the character of each individual, what he does, of what wrong he is guilty, with what intention and with what piety he tends to his ritual observances; and that they take note of the pious and the impious. For surely minds imbued with these beliefs will not reject opinions which are useful and true."

This quotation from Cicero is used by Burke to argue for the social utility of belief in religion in general and above all in a divinity who knows our actions and rewards and punishes accordingly. It comes, significantly, from a non-Christian source, an indication that Burke is arguing here not for the truth of any particular variety of Christianity, but for the social utility of religion in general.

[66] Here Burke seems to argue that it is better to condone intellectually primitive and preposterous forms of popular Christian faith and practice than to risk undermining the utility of religion by destroying such faith.

[67] The House of Commons was seen as the democratic element in the British system of government.

[O]ne of the first and most leading principles on which the common-wealth and the laws are consecrated,[68] is lest the temporary possessors and life-renters in it, unmindful of what they have received from their ancestors, or of what is due to their posterity, should act as if they were the entire masters; that they should not think it amongst their rights to cut off the entail, or commit waste on the inheritance, by destroying at their pleasure the whole original fabric of their society; hazarding to leave to those who come after them, a ruin instead of an habitation—and teaching these successors as little to respect their contrivances, as they had themselves respected the institutions of their forefathers. By this unprincipled facility of changing the state as often, and as much, and in as many ways as there are floating fancies or fashions, the whole chain and continuity of the commonwealth would be broken. No one genera-tion could link with the other. Men would become little better than the flies of a summer.

And first of all the science of jurisprudence, the pride of the human intellect, which, with all its defects, redundancies, and errors, is the col-lected reason of ages, combining the principles of original justice with the infinite variety of human concerns, as a heap of old exploded errors, would be no longer studied.[69] Personal self-sufficiency and arrogance (the certain attendants upon all those who have never experienced a wis-dom greater than their own) would usurp the tribunal. Of course, no certain laws, establishing invariable grounds of hope and fear, would keep the actions of men in a certain course, or direct them to a certain end. Nothing stable in the modes of holding property, or exercising function, could form a solid ground on which any parent could specu-late in the education of his offspring, or in a choice for their future es-tablishment in the world. No principles would be early worked into the habits. As soon as the most able instructor had completed his laborious course of institution, instead of sending forth his pupil, accomplished in a virtuous discipline, fitted to procure him attention and respect, in his place in society, he would find everything altered; and that he had turned out a poor creature to the contempt and derision of the world, ignorant of the true grounds of estimation. Who would insure a tender and delicate sense of honour to beat almost with the first pulses of the heart, when no man could know what would be the test of honour in a nation, continually varying the standard of its coin? No part of life would retain its acquisitions. Barbarism with regard to science and liter-ature, unskilfulness with regard to arts and manufactures, would infalli-bly succeed to the want of a steady education and settled principle; and

---

[68] Through their connection with an established church.

[69] Here Burke emphasizes the necessity of law in general, and conveys a conception of British common law as the product of adaptation to human needs.

thus the commonwealth itself would, in a few generations, crumble away, be disconnected into the dust and powder of individuality, and at length dispersed to all the winds of heaven.

To avoid therefore the evils of inconstancy and versatility, ten thousand times worse than those of obstinacy and the blindest prejudice, we have consecrated the state, that no man should approach to look into its defects or corruptions but with due caution; that he should never dream of beginning its reformation by its subversion; that he should approach to the faults of the state as to the wounds of a father, with pious awe and trembling solicitude. By this wise prejudice we are taught to look with horror on those children of their country who are prompt rashly to hack that aged parent in pieces, and put him into the kettle of magicians, in hopes that by their poisonous weeds, and wild incantations, they may regenerate the paternal constitution, and renovate their father's life.

Society is indeed a contract.[70] Subordinate contracts for objects of mere occasional interest may be dissolved at pleasure—but the state ought not to be considered as nothing better than a partnership agreement in a trade of pepper and coffee, callico or tobacco, or some other such low concern, to be taken up for a little temporary interest, and to be dissolved by the fancy of the parties. It is to be looked on with other reverence; because it is not a partnership in things subservient only to the gross animal existence of a temporary and perishable nature. It is a partnership in all science; a partnership in all art; a partnership in every virtue, and in all perfection. As the ends of such a partnership cannot be obtained in many generations, it becomes a partnership not only between those who are living, but between those who are living, those who are dead, and those who are to be born. Each contract of each particular state is but a clause in the great primaeval contract of eternal society, linking the lower with the higher natures, connecting the visible and invisible world, according to a fixed compact sanctioned by the inviolable oath which holds all physical and all moral natures, each in their appointed place. . . .

Along with the monied interest, a new description of men had grown up, with whom that interest soon formed a close and marked union; I mean the political Men of Letters.[71] Men of Letters, fond of distinguish-

---

[70] Once again, Burke reverses the terminology of his opponents. He takes the doctrine of the social contract, which emphasized the voluntary consent of the governed, and turns it into a metaphor of involuntary obligation.

[71] Turning to the forces which have displaced the established church and the established nobility in France, Burke offers his analysis of the central role of intellectuals. Freed from the patronage, and hence control, of the Church, the nobility, and the monarchy, Burke claims, the French intellectuals have sought to replace the cultural authority of the Church with their own authority.

ing themselves, are rarely averse to innovation. Since the decline of the life and greatness of Lewis the XIVth, they were not so much cultivated either by him, or by the regent, or the successors to the crown; nor were they engaged to the court by favours and emoluments so systematically as during the splendid period of that ostentatious and not impolitic reign. What they lost in the old court protection, they endeavoured to make up by joining in a sort of incorporation of their own; to which the two academies of France, and afterwards the vast undertaking of the Encyclopaedia,[72] carried on by a society of these gentlemen, did not a little contribute.

The literary cabal had some years ago formed something like a regular plan for the destruction of the Christian religion. This object they pursued with a degree of zeal which hitherto had been discovered only in the propagators of some system of piety. They were possessed with a spirit of proselytism in the most fanatical degree; and from thence, by an easy progress, with the spirit of persecution according to their means. What was not to be done towards their great end by any direct or immediate act, might be wrought by a longer process through the medium of opinion. To command that opinion, the first step is to establish a dominion over those who direct it. They contrived to possess themselves, with great method and perseverance, of all the avenues to literary fame. Many of them indeed stood high in the ranks of literature and science. The world had done them justice; and in favour of general talents forgave the evil tendency of their peculiar principles. This was true liberality; which they returned by endeavouring to confine the reputation of sense, learning, and taste to themselves or their followers. I will venture to say that this narrow, exclusive spirit has not been less prejudicial to literature and to taste, than to morals and true philosophy. These Atheistical fathers have a bigotry of their own; and they have learnt to talk against monks with the spirit of a monk. But in some things they are men of the world. The resources of intrigue are called in to supply the defects of argument and wit. To this system of literary monopoly was joined an unremitting industry to blacken and discredit in every way, and by every means, all those who did not hold to their faction. To those who have observed the spirit of their conduct, it has long been clear that nothing was wanted but the power of carrying the intolerance of the tongue and of the pen into a persecution which would strike at property, liberty, and life.

[72] The *Encyclopédie* , edited by Denis Diderot and Jean d'Alembert, and published between 1751 and 1772, with contributions by many luminaries of the French Enlightenment, was an attempt to gather together useful and reliable knowledge on a wide range of topics, theoretical and applied. It was intended as work of reference as well as of social and ideological critique, and was put on the Index of the Catholic Church in 1759.

The desultory and faint persecution carried on against them, more from compliance with form and decency than with serious resentment, neither weakened their strength, nor relaxed their efforts. The issue of the whole was, that what with opposition, and what with success, a violent and malignant zeal, of a kind hitherto unknown in the world, had taken an entire possession of their minds, and rendered their whole conversation, which otherwise would have been pleasing and instructive, perfectly disgusting. A spirit of cabal, intrigue, and proselytism, pervaded all their thoughts, words, and actions. And, as controversial zeal soon turns its thoughts on force, they began to insinuate themselves into a correspondence with foreign princes; in hopes, through their authority, which at first they flattered, they might bring about the changes they had in view. To them it was indifferent whether these changes were to be accomplished by the thunderbolt of despotism, or by the earthquake of popular commotion. The correspondence between this cabal, and the late king of Prussia,[73] will throw no small light upon the spirit of all their proceedings.[74] For the same purpose for which they intrigued with princes, they cultivated, in a distinguished manner, the monied interest of France; and partly through the means furnished by those whose peculiar offices gave them the most extensive and certain means of communication, they carefully occupied all the avenues to opinion.

Writers, especially when they act in a body, and with one direction, have great influence on the public mind; the alliance therefore of these writers with the monied interest[75] had no small effect in removing the popular odium and envy which attended that species of wealth. These writers, like the propagators of all novelties, pretended to a great zeal for the poor, and the lower orders, whilst in their satires they rendered hateful, by every exaggeration, the faults of courts, of nobility, and of priesthood. They became a sort of demagogues. They served as a link to unite, in favour of one object, obnoxious wealth to restless and desperate poverty. . . .

We do not draw the moral lessons we might from history.[76] On the contrary, without care it may be used to vitiate our minds and to destroy

---

[73] The reference is to Frederick II of Prussia (1712–86), who corresponded with several of the leading French thinkers and invited them to his court at Sans-Souci, where Voltaire spent several years.

[74] [I do not choose to shock the feeling of the moral reader with any quotation of their vulgar, base and profane language.]

[75] [Their connection with Turgot and almost all the people of the finance.] Anne-Robert-Jacques Turgot (1727–81), a leading writer on economic issues and contributor to the *Encyclopédie*, served as minister of finance (controller general) from 1774 to 1776, and led efforts to reform government finance. By "the monied interest" Burke refers to those bankers and financiers who lent funds to the government.

[76] The paragraph that follows begins as a sermon on the ineradicability of human vice,

our happiness. In history a great volume is unrolled for our instruction, drawing the materials of future wisdom from the past errors and infirmities of mankind. It may, in the perversion, serve for a magazine, furnishing offensive and defensive weapons for parties in church and state, and supplying the means of keeping alive, or reviving dissensions and animosities, and adding fuel to civil fury. History consists, for the greater part, of the miseries brought upon the world by pride, ambition, avarice, revenge, lust, sedition, hypocrisy, ungoverned zeal, and all the train of disorderly appetites, which shake the public with the same

> ————troublous storms that toss
> The private state, and render life unsweet.[77]

These vices are the *causes* of those storms. Religion, morals, laws, prerogatives, privileges, liberties, rights of men, are the *pretexts*. The pretexts are always found in some specious appearance of a real good. You would not secure men from tyranny and sedition, by rooting out of the mind the principles to which these fraudulent pretexts apply? If you did, you would root out everything that is valuable in the human breast. As these are the pretexts, so the ordinary actors and instruments in great public evils are kings, priests, magistrates, senates, parliaments, national assemblies, judges, and captains. You would not cure the evil by resolving, that there should be no more monarchs, nor ministers of state, nor of the gospel; no interpreters of law; no general officers; no public councils. You might change the names. The things in some shape must remain. A certain *quantum* of power must always exist in the community, in some hands, and under some appellation. Wise men will apply their remedies to vices, not to names; to the causes of evil which are permanent, not to the occasional organs by which they act, and the transitory modes in which they appear. Otherwise you will be wise historically, a fool in practice. Seldom have two ages the same fashion in their pretexts and the same modes of mischief. Wickedness is a little more inventive. Whilst you are discussing fashion, the fashion is gone by. The very same vice assumes a new body. The spirit transmigrates; and, far from losing its principle of life by the change of its appearance, it is renovated in its new organs with the fresh vigour of a juvenile activity. It walks abroad; it continues its ravages; whilst you are gibbeting the carcass, or demolishing the tomb. You are terrifying yourself with ghosts and apparitions, whilst your house is the haunt of robbers. It is thus with all those, who, attending only to the shell and husk of history, think they are

---

then goes on to suggest that the threat posed by religious intolerance is now being superseded by an intolerance of religion.

[77] From Edmund Spenser, *The Faerie Queene*, II, canto 7. xiv.

waging war with intolerance, pride, and cruelty, whilst, under colour of abhorring the ill principles of antiquated parties, they are authorizing and feeding the same odious vices in different factions, and perhaps in worse. . . .

[Monastic orders had long been criticized for their apparent remove from productive social life, and for their control over substantial landed wealth. By a decree of February 13, 1790, the National Assembly declared that monastic vows were no longer recognized by law, and authorized anyone who wished to leave a monastery or convent to do so. Burke's observations on the dissolution of the monastic orders present an analysis of how conservative reformers ought to deal with institutions widely regarded as superannuated.]

When men are encouraged to go into a certain mode of life by the existing laws, and protected in that mode as in a lawful occupation— when they have accommodated all their ideas, and all their habits to it— when the law had long made their adherence to its rules a ground of reputation, and their departure from them a ground of disgrace and even of penalty—I am sure it is unjust in legislature, by an arbitrary act, to offer a sudden violence to their minds and their feelings; forcibly to degrade them from their state and condition, and to stigmatize with shame and infamy that character and those customs which before had been made the measure of their happiness and honour. If to this be added an expulsion from their habitations, and a confiscation of all their goods, I am not sagacious enough to discover how this despotic sport, made of the feelings, consciences, prejudices, and properties of men, can be discriminated from the rankest tyranny.

If the injustice of the course pursued in France be clear, the policy of the measure, that is, the public benefit to be expected from it, ought to be at least as evident, and at least as important. To a man who acts under the influence of no passion, who has nothing in view in his projects but the public good, a great difference will immediately strike him, between what policy would dictate on the original introduction of such institutions, and on a question of their total abolition, where they have cast their roots wide and deep, and where by long habit things more valuable than themselves are so adapted to them, and in a manner interwoven with them, that the one cannot be destroyed without notably impairing the other.[78] He might be embarrassed, if the case were really such as sophisters represent it in their paltry style of debating. But in this, as in most questions of state, there is a middle. There is something else than

[78] Although the original justification for an institution may no longer be acceptable, Burke argues, it may be prudent to preserve the institution because of its interconnection with other, more justifiable institutions.

the mere alternative of absolute destruction, or unreformed existence. *Spartam nactus es; hanc exorna.*[79] This is, in my opinion, a rule of profound sense, and ought never to depart from the mind of an honest reformer. I cannot conceive how any man can have brought himself to that pitch of presumption, to consider his country as nothing but *carte blanche,*[80] upon which he may scribble whatever he pleases. A man full of warm speculative benevolence may wish his society otherwise constituted than he finds it; but a good patriot and a true politician, always considers how he shall make the most of the existing materials of his country. A disposition to preserve, and an ability to improve, taken together, would be my standard of a statesman. Everything else is vulgar in the conception, perilous in the execution.

There are moments in the fortune of states when particular men are called to make improvements by great mental exertion. In those moments, even when they seem to enjoy the confidence of their prince and country, and to be invested with full authority, they have not always apt instruments. A politician, to do great things, looks for a *power*, what our workmen call a *purchase*[81] and if he finds that power, in politics as in mechanics he cannot be at a loss to apply it. In the monastic institutions, in my opinion, was found a great *power* for the mechanism of politic benevolence. There were revenues with a public direction; there were men wholly set apart and dedicated to public purposes, without any other than public ties and public principles; men without the possibility of converting the estate of the community into a private fortune; men denied to self-interests, whose avarice is for some community; men to whom personal poverty is honour, and implicit obedience stands in the place of freedom. In vain shall a man look to the possibility of making such things when he wants them. The winds blow as they list. These institutions are the products of enthusiasm; they are the instruments of wisdom. Wisdom cannot create materials; they are the gifts of nature or of chance; her pride is in the use. The perennial existence of bodies corporate and their fortunes, are things particularly suited to a man who has long views; who meditates designs that require time in fashioning; and which propose duration when they are accomplished. He is not deserving to rank high, or even to be mentioned in the order of great statesmen, who, having obtained the command and direction of such a power as existed in the wealth, the discipline, and the habits of such corporations, as those which you have rashly destroyed, cannot find any way of converting it to the great and lasting benefit of his country. On the view

[79] "Sparta is your lot, now adorn it." From Cicero, *Letter to Atticus*, iv.6. An admonition to make the most of given institutions.

[80] A blank sheet of paper.

[81] A hold or position of advantage for exerting pressure.

of this subject a thousand uses suggest themselves to a contriving mind. To destroy any power, growing wild from the rank productive force of the human mind, is almost tantamount, in the moral world, to the destruction of the apparently active properties of bodies in the material. It would be like the attempt to destroy (if it were in our competence to destroy) the expansive force of fixed air in nitre, or the power of steam, or of electricity, or of magnetism. These energies always existed in nature, and they were always discernible. They seemed, some of them unserviceable, some noxious, some no better than a sport to children; until contemplative ability combining with practic skill, tamed their wild nature, subdued them to use, and rendered them at once the most powerful and the most tractable agents, in subservience to the great views and designs of men. Did fifty thousand persons, whose mental and whose bodily labour you might direct, and so many hundred thousand a year of a revenue, which was neither lazy nor superstitious, appear too big for your abilities to wield? Had you no way of using the men but by converting monks into pensioners? Had you no way of turning the revenue to account, but through the improvident resource of a spendthrift sale? If you were thus destitute of mental funds, the proceeding is in its natural course. Your politicians do not understand their trade; and therefore they sell their tools.

But the institutions[82] savour of superstition in their very principle; and they nourish it by a permanent and standing influence. This I do not mean to dispute; but this ought not to hinder you from deriving from superstition itself any resources which may thence be furnished for the public advantage. You derive benefits from many dispositions and many passions of the human mind, which are of as doubtful a colour in the moral eye, as superstition itself. It was your business to correct and mitigate everything which was noxious in this passion, as in all the passions. But is superstition the greatest of all possible vices? In its possible excess I think it becomes a very great evil. It is, however, a moral subject; and of course admits of all degrees and all modifications. Superstition is the religion of feeble minds; and they must be tolerated in an intermixture of it, in some trifling or some enthusiastic shape or other, else you will deprive weak minds of a resource found necessary to the strongest. The body of all true religion consists, to be sure, in obedience to the will of the sovereign of the world; in a confidence in his declarations; and an imitation of his perfections. The rest is our own.[83] It may be prejudicial

---

[82] I.e., the monasteries.

[83] Burke maintains that monotheistic religion is "true" in a more rational and universalistic sense than its particular, historical embodiments, but that those particular embodiments, and even their more irrationalist variants, are necessary to make religion accessible to the mass of citizens in a way which is more concrete than intellectually austere versions of the faith.

to the great end; it may be auxiliary. Wise men, who as such, are not *admirers* (not admirers at least of the *Munera Terrae*)[84] are not violently attached to these things, nor do they violently hate them. Wisdom is not the most severe corrector of folly. They are the rival follies, which mutually wage so unrelenting a war; and which make so cruel a use of their advantages, as they can happen to engage the immoderate vulgar on the one side or the other in their quarrels. Prudence would be neuter; but if, in the contention between fond attachment and fierce antipathy concerning things in their nature not made to produce such heats, a prudent man were obliged to make a choice of what errors and excesses of enthusiasm he would condemn or bear, perhaps he would think the superstition which builds, to be more tolerable than that which demolishes—that which adorns a country, than that which deforms it—that which endows, than that which plunders—that which disposes to mistaken beneficence, than that which stimulates to real injustice—that which leads a man to refuse to himself lawful pleasures, than that which snatches from others the scanty subsistence of their self-denial. Such, I think, is very nearly the state of the question between the ancient founders of monkish superstition, and the superstition of the pretended philosophers of the hour[85]. . . .

[I]n these gentlemen[86] there is nothing of the tender parental solicitude which fears to cut up the infant for the sake of an experiment. In the vastness of their promises, and the confidence of their predictions, they far outdo all the boasting of empirics [charlatans]. The arrogance of their pretensions, in a manner provokes, and challenges us to an enquiry into their foundation. . . .

A leading member of the assembly,[87] M. Rabaud de St. Etienne, has expressed the principle of all their proceedings as clearly as possible. Nothing can be more simple:—*"Tous les établissemens en France couronnent le malheur du peuple: pour le rendre heureux il fault le renouveler; changer ses idées; changer ses loix; changer ses moeurs; . . . changer les hommes; changer les choses; changer les mots . . . tout détruire; oui, détruire puisque tout est à recréer."*[88] This gentleman was chosen president in an assembly not sitting at the *Quinze vingt*, or the *Petites Maisons*[89] and

---

[84] "The gifts of the earth"; Horace, *Odes*, II. xiv. 10.

[85] Burke returns to the theme that the revolutionary rationalists display all the fanaticism and distance from reality that they attribute to their monkish opponents.

[86] The French revolutionaries and their English supporters.

[87] This paragraph appears as a footnote in Burke's text.

[88] "All the establishments in France crown the unhappiness of the people. In order to make the people happy they must be renewed: change their ideas; change their laws; change their manners; . . . change the men; change things; change words . . . destroy everything; yes, destroy everything, so that all may be created anew."

[89] *Les Quinze-Vingts* was a hospital for the blind, the *Petit Masions* for the insane.

composed of persons giving themselves out to be rational beings; but neither his ideas, language, or conduct, differ in the smallest degree from the discourses, opinions, and actions of those within and without the assembly, who direct the operations of the machine now at work in France.

But is it in destroying and pulling down that skill is displayed? Your mob can do this as well at least as your assemblies. The shallowest understanding, the rudest hand, is more than equal to that task. Rage and frenzy will pull down more in half an hour, than prudence, deliberation, and foresight can build up in an hundred years. The errors and defects of old establishments are visible and palpable. It calls for little ability to point them out; and where absolute power is given, it requires but a word wholly to abolish the vice and the establishment together. The same lazy but restless disposition, which loves sloth and hates quiet, directs these politicians, when they come to work, for supplying the place of what they have destroyed. To make everything the reverse of what they have seen is quite as easy as to destroy. No difficulties occur in what has never been tried. Criticism is almost baffled in discovering the defects of what has not existed; and eager enthusiasm, and cheating hope, have all the wide field of imagination in which they may expatiate with little or no opposition.[90]

At once to preserve and to reform is quite another thing. When the useful parts of an old establishment are kept, and what is superadded is to be fitted to what is retained, a vigorous mind, steady persevering attention, various powers of comparison and combination, and the resources of an understanding fruitful in expedients are to be exercised; they are to be exercised in a continued conflict with the combined force of opposite vices; with the obstinacy that rejects all improvement, and the levity that is fatigued and disgusted with everything of which it is in possession. But you may object—"A process of this kind is slow. It is not fit for an assembly, which glories in performing in a few months the work of ages. Such a mode of reforming, possibly might take up many years." Without question it might; and it ought. It is one of the excellencies of a method in which time is amongst the assistants, that its operation is slow, and in some cases almost imperceptible. If circumspection and caution are a part of wisdom, when we work only upon inanimate matter, surely they become a part of duty too, when the subject of our demolition and construction is not brick and timber, but sentient beings, by the sudden alteration of whose state, condition, and

---

[90] Plans for the wholesale reform of institutions, Burke argues, will run into unanticipated difficulties because of the failure of the revolutionaries to consider the complexity of social institutions.

habits, multitudes may be rendered miserable. But it seems as if it were the prevalent opinion in Paris, that an unfeeling heart, and an undoubting confidence, are the sole qualifications for a perfect legislator. Far different are my ideas of that high office. The true lawgiver ought to have an heart full of sensibility. He ought to love and respect his kind, and to fear himself. It may be allowed to his temperament to catch his ultimate object with an intuitive glance; but his movements towards it ought to be deliberate. Political arrangement, as it is a work for social ends, is to be only wrought by social means. There mind must conspire with mind. Time is required to produce that union of minds which alone can produce all the good we aim at. Our patience will achieve more than our force. If I might venture to appeal to what is so much out of fashion in Paris, I mean to experience, I should tell you, that in my course I have known, and, according to my measure, have co-operated with great men; and I have never yet seen any plan which has not been mended by the observations of those who were much inferior in understanding to the person who took the lead in the business. By a slow but well sustained progress, the effect of each step is watched; the good or ill success of the first, gives light to us in the second; and so, from light to light, we are conducted with safety through the whole series. We see, that the parts of the system do not clash. The evils latent in the most promising contrivances are provided for as they arise. One advantage is as little as possible sacrificed to another. We compensate, we reconcile, we balance. We are enabled to unite into a consistent whole the various anomalies and contending principles that are found in the minds and affairs of men. From hence arises, not an excellence in simplicity, but one far superior, an excellence in composition. Where the great interests of mankind are concerned through a long succession of generations, that succession ought to be admitted into some share in the councils which are so deeply to affect them. If justice requires this, the work itself requires the aid of more minds than one age can furnish. It is from this view of things that the best legislators have been often satisfied with the establishment of some sure, solid, and ruling principle in government; a power like that which some of the philosophers have called a plastic nature; and having fixed the principle, they have left it afterwards to its own operation. . . .

Old establishments are tried by their effects. If the people are happy, united, wealthy, and powerful, we presume the rest. We conclude that to be good from whence good is derived.[91] In old establishments various correctives have been found for their aberrations from theory. Indeed they are the results of various necessities and expediencies. They

[91] A pithy formulation of historical consequentialism.

are not often constructed after any theory; theories are rather drawn from them. In them we often see the end best obtained, where the means seem not perfectly reconcilable to what we may fancy was the original scheme. The means taught by experience may be better suited to political ends than those contrived in the original project. They again re-act upon the primitive constitution, and sometimes improve the design itself from which they seem to have departed. I think all this might be curiously exemplified in the British constitution. At worst, the errors and deviations of every kind in reckoning are found and computed, and the ship proceeds in her course. This is the case of old establishments; but in a new and merely theoretic system, it is expected that every contrivance shall appear, on the face of it, to answer its end; especially where the projectors are no way embarrassed with an endeavor to accommodate the new building to an old one, either in the walls or on the foundations. . . .

The effects of the incapacity shewn by the popular leaders in all the great members of the commonwealth are to be covered with the "all-atoning name" of liberty. In some people I see great liberty indeed; in many, if not in the most, an oppressive degrading servitude. But what is liberty without wisdom, and without virtue? It is the greatest of all possible evils; for it is folly, vice, and madness, without tuition or restraint. Those who know what virtuous liberty is, cannot bear to see it disgraced by incapable heads, on account of their having high-sounding words in their mouths. Grand, swelling sentiments of liberty, I am sure I do not despise. They warm the heart; they enlarge and liberalise our minds; they animate our courage in a time of conflict. Old as I am, I read the fine raptures of Lucan and Corneille with pleasure. Neither do I wholly condemn the little arts and devices of popularity. They facilitate the carrying of many points of moment; they keep the people together; they refresh the mind in its exertions; and they diffuse occasional gaiety over the severe brow of moral freedom. Every politician ought to sacrifice to the graces; and to join compliance with reason. But in such an undertaking as that in France, all these subsidiary sentiments and artifices are of little avail. To make a government requires no great prudence. Settle the seat of power; teach obedience: and the work is done. To give freedom is still more easy. It is not necessary to guide; it only requires to let go the rein. But to form *a free government*, that is, to temper together these opposite elements of liberty and restraint in one consistent work, requires much thought, deep reflection, a sagacious, powerful, and combining mind. This I do not find in those who take the lead in the national assembly. Perhaps they are not so miserably deficient as they appear. I rather believe it. It would put them below the common level of human understanding. But when the leaders choose to make themselves bidders at an auction of popularity, their talents, in the construction of the state, will be of no service. They will become flatterers instead of legislators; the instruments, not the guides of the people. If any of them should happen to propose a scheme of liberty, soberly limited, and defined with proper qualifications, he will be immediately outbid by his competitors, who will produce something more splendidly popular. Suspicions will be raised of his fidelity to his cause. Moderation will be stigmatized as the virtue of cowards; and compromise as the prudence of traitors; until, in hopes of preserving the credit which may enable him to temper and moderate on some occasions, the popular leader is obliged to become active in propagating doctrines, and establishing powers, that will afterwards defeat any sober purpose at which he ultimately might have aimed.[92]

But am I so unreasonable as to see nothing at all that deserves commendation in the indefatigable labours of this assembly? I do not deny that among an infinite number of acts of violence and folly, some good may have been done. They who destroy everything certainly will remove some grievance. They who make everything new, have a chance that they may establish something beneficial. To give them credit for what they have done in virtue of the authority they have usurped, or which can excuse them in the crimes by which that authority has been acquired, it must appear, that the same things could not have been accomplished without producing such a revolution. Most assuredly they might; because almost every one of the regulations made by them, which is not very equivocal, was either in the cession of the king, voluntarily made at the meeting of the states, or in the concurrent instructions to the orders.[93] Some usages have been abolished on just grounds; but they were such that if they had stood as they were to all eternity, they would little detract from the happiness and prosperity of any state. The improvements of the national assembly are superficial, their errors fundamental.

Whatever they are, I wish my countrymen rather to recommend to our neighbours the example of the British constitution, than to take models from them for the improvement of our own. In the former they

---

[92] Burke's prediction of the radicalization of the Revolution under the pressure of the Parisian crowd proved remarkably prescient, and enhanced the book's credibility as an analysis of the forces at work in the Revolution.

[93] The most useful reforms, Burke argues, were already made in May and June 1789, before the fall of the Bastille. At the royal session of the Estates-General on June 23, the King announced a program of extensive reforms, which included the assent of representative bodies to all taxation, and a move toward equality of taxation. But the program left intact royal power and unequal representation through three separate orders (Clergy, Nobility, and Third Estate), and was rejected by the assembled delegates.

have got an invaluable treasure. They are not, I think, without some causes of apprehension and complaint; but these they do not owe to their constitution, but to their own conduct. I think our happy situation owing to our constitution; but owing to the whole of it, and not to any part singly; owing in a great measure to what we have left standing in our several reviews and reformations, as well as to what we have altered or superadded. Our people will find employment enough for a truly patriotic, free, and independent spirit, in guarding what they possess, from violation. I would not exclude alteration neither; but even when I changed, it should be to preserve. I should be led to my remedy by a great grievance. In what I did, I should follow the example of our ancestors. I would make the reparation as nearly as possible in the style of the building. A politic caution, a guarded circumspection, a moral rather than a complexional timidity were among the ruling principles of our forefathers in their most decided conduct. Not being illuminated with the light of which the gentlemen of France tell us they have got so abundant a share, they acted under a strong impression of the ignorance and fallibility of mankind. He that had made them thus fallible, rewarded them for having in their conduct attended to their nature. Let us imitate their caution, if we wish to deserve their fortune, or to retain their bequests. Let us add, if we please, but let us preserve what they have left; and, standing on the firm ground of the British constitution, let us be satisfied to admire rather than attempt to follow in their desperate flights the aëronauts[94] of France. . . .

---

[94] One who sails through the air. The first balloon ascent had occurred in 1783.

INTRODUCTION TO
Louis de Bonald,
On Divorce

◆

Joseph de Maistre (1753–1821) and Louis Gabriel de Bonald (1754–1840) are the two towering figures in the tradition of French reactionary thought which begins with their reaction against the French Revolution. Like Burke, they condemned the Revolution root and branch, but unlike him they regarded Catholicism as integral to political conservatism, and placed little value on liberty.[1] Though Maistre and Bonald are often grouped together, their styles of thought and of writing could not have been more different. Bonald was traditionalist in the style and content of his conservatism. His cast of mind is orthodox even while he insists that divine law meets the test of social utility, an assumption which he drew from the Thomistic tradition of religious rationalism. His style is systematic, plodding and pedantic at times, as he seeks to demonstrate the necessary inter-relationships and parallels between obligations owed to God, to kings, and to fathers. Maistre, by contrast, delighted in extremist assertions and paradoxes, intended to shock his readers, as the first step toward making them reexamine their liberal assumptions.

Louis-Gabriel-Abroise, Vicomte de Bonald, was born in 1754 into a noble family in the French town of Millau. Raised as a devout Catholic, he was educated in theology, the classics, and mathematics. Before the Revolution he served as mayor of the town, and in the early stage of the Revolution he was elected president of the newly created political *département* in which it was located. In 1791 the revolutionary government passed the Civil Constitution of the Clergy, which effectively placed the Catholic priesthood under the control of the civil government. Rather than implement a law he found despicable, Bonald fled abroad and joined the forces of the counter-Revolution. It was in exile in Heidelberg in 1796 that he published his major work, the *Theory of Power, Political and Religious*, which struck the themes of his subsequent works. Having returned to France in the late 1790s, he published *On Divorce* in 1801, during the reign of Napoleon, who had been impressed with Bonald's *Theory of Power*.

---

[1] For a comparison of Burke's position to that of Maistre and Bonald, see Massimo Boffa, "La Contre-Révolution, Joseph de Maistre," in François Furet and Mona Ozouf, eds., *The French Revolution and the Creation of Modern Political Culture; Volume 3: The Transformation of Political Culture 1789–1848* (Oxford, 1989), pp. 291–308.

The task with which Maistre and Bonald saw themselves confronted was rather different than the one that had motivated Burke's *Reflections*, and the nature of their conservatism varied accordingly. Burke's primary task was to conserve a British order which was substantially intact, though subject to intellectual attack. He could thus stress the historical utilitarian arguments that the existence of an institution creates a *prima facie* case that it has served some human need, and that historical continuity is intrinsically valuable because it increases the emotional hold of an institution upon its members. Similarly, Burke could underscore the importance of habit and custom. By the time Bonald and Maistre came to write their major works, the forces of the French Revolution had already overturned or transformed many of the key institutions of the old regime. The Counter-Revolutionary conservatives, therefore, were forced to *create*, at least in theory, a regime worth conserving. They were forced by circumstances to offer a rationale other than that of historical continuity, for the institutions of the old regime had been disrupted by the Revolution. Maistre responded to the revolution by carrying to new lengths previous conservative arguments of epistemological modesty, historical particularism, and the unanticipated consequences of deliberate action.

Bonald, by contrast, sought to present a systematic institutional blueprint, modeled on the French old regime, yet avoiding the flaws that had lead to its demise. The pillars of that old/new regime were to be the Catholic Church and the restored monarchy. Yet the function of the monarchy, as Bonald conceived it, was to support the functioning of "natural" social groups, such as the family, the guild, and local government. This strain of thought was to influence both the development of sociology in France and of the French radical Right in the late nineteenth and early twentieth centuries, which sought an authoritarian political regime which would support "natural" social groups.[2] Bonald thus sought to create a new orthodoxy to plan and legitimate a restored institutional order. His books drew upon the Thomistic strain in Catholic thought which had emphasized the socializing functions of social and political institutions, and had justified them in large part on the basis of their social utility in aiding man to restrain his sinful urges and hence in bringing about the realization of man's God-given potential. Unlike

[2] For the influence of Bonald on French sociological thought, see Robert Nisbet, "De Bonald and the Concept of the Social Group," *Journal of the History of Ideas* V (1944), pp. 315–31; and his "Conservatism" in Thomas Bottomore and Robert Nisbet, eds., *A History of Sociological Analysis* (New York, 1978). For similar arguments on the later French radical right, linking a strong monarchy to the protection of local and familial sources of authority, see Charles Maurras, "Dictator and King" (1899), in J. S. McClelland, ed., *The French Right from Maistre to Maurras* (London, 1970), pp. 215–38.

Maistre, there is little room in Bonald's thought for the particularist argument that different cultures require different institutions: for Bonald, one size fits all. While Maistre emphasized the appropriateness of British institutions for Britain, Bonald condemned the British for their Protestantism, and for what he thought of as their licentious, commercial order.

Bonald's career advanced throughout the Napoleonic era and again during the Bourbon restoration. It was Bonald who in 1818, together with François René de Chateaubriand, founded the journal *Le Conservateur*, thus contributing to the use of the term "conservative" in its political sense. In 1822 he was named Minister of State and member of the Privy Council. Until his death in 1840 he was a frequent contributor to journals of politics and learned opinion.

Among Bonald's most effective works were his books, *On Divorce* and *Summation on the Question of Divorce*, both published in 1801.[3] The Constitution of 1791 stated that "the law considers marriage to be only a civil contract." Intended to assert that marriage was to be governed by civil rather than by religious law, the provision was regarded by some Frenchmen as meaning that marriage could be dissolved like any contract, and some began to divorce even before the practice was formally legalized in the new divorce law in September 1792. That law recognized divorce by mutual consent or when initiated by either party on the grounds of incompatibility or matrimonial fault. The law was further liberalized in 1794, permitting divorce for any reason whatsoever. The new divorce laws were part of the larger ideological project of the Revolution: ease in dissolving marriage was seen as an essential element of freedom, and the premises of the new law were individualistic and egalitarian. (While opposed to the indissolubility of marriage, the Revolution extolled matrimony and family. A Festival of Marriage was instituted to exalt the virtues of family life, marital fidelity, and filial piety, which were contrasted with the purported corruption of family life under the Old Regime.)[4]

Bonald demanded the repeal of legislation permitting divorce which had been adopted during the Revolution. His books had little immediate effect, but after the restoration of the Bourbon monarchy, Bonald drew on them in arguing in the Chamber of Deputies against divorce,

---

[3] On the dating of the book's composition and publication, see the "Translator's Note," in Louis de Bonald, *On Divorce*, translated and edited by Nicholas Davidson (New Brunswick, NJ, 1992), which also includes a useful introduction by the translator. Bonald's work and career is succinctly explored in Jacques Godechot, *The Counter Revolution: Doctrine and Action, 1789–1804* (Princeton, 1981).

[4] Roderick Phillips, *Putting Asunder: A History of Divorce in Western Society* (Cambridge, 1988), pp. 175–89.

and was subsequently appointed to write the report of a government commission on the subject. Due in good part to his efforts, divorce was abolished in France in 1816.

Louis de Bonald,
On Divorce, Considered in the Nineteenth Century, in Relation to the Domestic State and to the Public State of Society (1801)[1]

[FROM CHAPTER 2, "OF DOMESTIC SOCIETY"]

Man and woman both *are*; but they *are* not both the same or in an equal manner, and they differ in sex. . . .

The union of the sexes is the reason for their difference; the production of a being is the purpose of their union.

The being produced is of the same sex as one or the other of those that gave it being; but they are formed and it is to be formed; it is young and they are old. Another inequality, another similarity.

Man, woman, *little one*, considered each in itself, and without any relation between them, each form an *individual*, that is to say, a whole which cannot be divided without destroying it. . . . Father, mother, child, which express both the union of the sexes and the production of the being, can only be considered dependently on one another, and relatively to one another. A woman could exist without the existence of a man; but there is no mother if there is no father, nor a child without both of them. Each one of these ways of being presumes and recalls the other two; that is to say, they are *relative*. Considered thus, they are called *relationships*, in Latin, *ratio*; father, mother, child are *persons*, and their union forms the family. The union of the sexes, which is the foundation of all these relationships, is called *marriage*. . . .

The production of man is the purpose of the relationship between the sexes; his conservation is the purpose of the relationship between the ages, which is to say that man and woman produce the child, and the father and mother conserve it. The production and conservation of man are thus the purpose of the family, and the reason for all the relationships of sex and age which constitute it.[2]

---

[1] This translation is from Louis de Bonald, *On Divorce*, translated and edited by Nicholas Davidson (Transaction, New Brunswick, NJ, 1992). The translation has been slightly altered in a few places in the interests of clarity, after consulting the French text in *Oevres de M. de Bonald*, vol. 4 (Brussels, 1845).

[2] Bonald assumes, here and throughout, that laws and social norms are to be based on

The beast is born with an impulsion, according to some, with a knowledge, according to others; an impulsion or a knowledge which is called *instinct*, which guides each species invariably and all species infallibly in their reproduction and conservation, for which purposes each has received everything it needs. The beast is no more free not to reproduce itself than not to conserve itself. Time, manner, everything is determined for it; and whatever our lessons add to its instinct is always for our needs rather than its own, and demonstrates its industriousness much less than ours.

Man, on the contrary, is born ignorant and helpless; and if the faculty of choosing and willing which distinguishes him were not enlightened by instruction, he would have no choice; he would have an impulsion but no will, movements but no action. He would accede to certain involuntary needs, but he would be unable either to foresee danger or to protect himself from it. Unable to conserve and perhaps to reproduce himself, he would be lower than the beast, or rather he would be nothing, because he would not be what he must be, and because, unlike the beast, he has not received an instinct to take the place of his will. . . .[3]

Religion . . . merely informs us of a fact when it teaches us that we are all born with an original or native penchant for domination, called *pride*; a penchant which betrays our natural *grandeur*, and for which society is the restraint, because society includes the institutions which maintain legitimate power, conservative of beings, against men's passions, and is nothing but the protection of weakness against the abuse of strength; and modern philosophy denies both truth and reason when it says, by the voice of Jean-Jacques Rousseau, that "man is born good, and society depraves him."[4]

The physical strength of the father could not contain this penchant for independence in the other family members; for several children are stronger than a father, and a man's very life is at every moment at his wife's disposition.

What bond, then, will hold the domestic persons in the place assigned them by their duties? The *natural affections*, say the sophists, who do not fail to cite as evidence the affections of the beasts; *sympathy*, say

---

the teleological purposes of men and women, built into their natures. The unarticulated assumption in this essay is that their purpose is the reproduction of society, in both a biological and cultural sense. Neither the intentions nor the personal happiness of the husband and wife are considered primary.

[3] The argument of these last two paragraphs is taken from Thomas Aquinas, *De Regimine Principum*, Book 1, chapter 1. The theme enunciated here by Bonald, of the inadequacy of man's instinctual endowment and hence his need for culture or "second nature," would later be developed by Arnold Gehlen. See the selection included later in this volume.

[4] Note the theme of human imperfection and the need for external restraints upon the passions.

novelists; *sentiment*, say sensible souls. But if these affections are natural to us, like the need to digest and to sleep, why are there unjust fathers, ungrateful children, unfaithful wives, unkind brothers? Why have laws, when there are necessities? Is this pretended natural affection for others not too often ready to give way to affection for oneself? And far from being natural, does it never require efforts against themselves for spouses to stay united, and for children to remain obedient? These natural affections are therefore merely reasonable ones, which habit, gratitude, and above all self-love make dear, easy, and sometimes blind; and if they are reasonable affections, then they are reasoned or learned. For man is born capable of reason; but he learns to reason, and does not reason unless he has learned to do so. . . .

[FROM CHAPTER 4, "OF MARRIAGE"]

Marriage is the commitment made by two people of different sexes to unite in order to form a society called the family. . . .

If human marriage is a union with a commitment to form a society, it differs essentially from concubinage, which is a union without a commitment to form a society, and still more from vague libertinism, which is a union with an intention not to form a society.

The end of marriage is therefore not the happiness of the spouses, if by happiness one understands an idyllic pleasure of the heart and senses, which the man who loves independence finds far more readily in unions without a commitment.

Religion and the State consider in marriage only the duties it imposes; and they regard it only as the founding act of a society, since this society-to-be is, in the sacrament, the object of the blessings of religion, and, in the civil contract, the object of the clauses ratified and guaranteed by the State. . . .

The motives for indissolubility are taken from both domestic and public society, because marriage is both domestic in its principle and public in its effects.

1. Marriage is a *potential* society, the family an *actual* society. Nature has not set a term on this potential; and even when marriage does not attain its social goal, and children do not arrive, there is not a sufficient reason to break the first commitment in order to form another, because the fertility of the second marriage is just as speculative as that of the first. Once the child has arrived, the goal is fulfilled, and the society, from being potential, becomes actual.[5]

---

[5] The language of this paragraph reflects the influence of Aquinas, and the conception of man as created with an intrinsic teleological purpose.

Thus, as long as the husband and wife have no children, they could still arrive; and since marriage is formed only for the children who are to come, there is no reason to break the marriage. Once the children have arrived, the marriage has attained its goal, and there is a reason not to break the marriage. It is to be noted that even in the case of infecundity, it is not proved that the problem lies with the wife.

In a word, the reason for marriage is the production of children. Now, by breaking a first marriage in order to contract a second one, this production becomes impossible in the first without becoming more certain in the second. Therefore, there is no reason to break the marriage; and after all, whatever disposition our modern philosophers may have to assimilate man to the beasts, and whatever importance may be attached to population by these great depopulators of the universe, they would doubtless not dare to maintain that in human marriages one should, as on stud farms, proceed by *trials*.

2. The reasons against divorce drawn from public society are even stronger than those taken from domestic society.

Political power cannot guarantee the stability of the domestic persons without recognizing them; hence the necessity of the civil act, which recognizes the commitment of the man and woman, and of the birth certificate, which recognizes the father, mother, and child.

But, and I beg the reader to pay attention to this reasoning, political power only intervenes in the spouses' contract of union because it represents the unborn child, which is the sole social object of marriage, and because it accepts the commitment made by the spouses in its presence and under its guarantee to bring that child into being. It stipulates the interests of the child in the contract, since most matrimonial clauses concern the arrival of children, and since on occasion it even accepts certain special advantages, stipulated in advance, in favor of a child born in a certain order of birth or sex;[6] and as witness of the bond which is to give the child existence, it guarantees the bond's stability in order to ensure the child's conservation. The marital commitment is thus really formed between three persons who are either present or represented; for public power, which precedes the family and survives it, always represents the absent person in the family, whether the child before its birth, or the father after his death.

The commitment formed between three therefore cannot be broken by two to the prejudice of the third, since this third person is, if not the first, at least the most important; since everything relates to him alone; and since he is the *reason* for the social union of the other two,

[6] Bonald is referring here to laws of primogeniture, the right of inheritance of the oldest male to the family farm or estate.

who are no more a father or mother without the child than he is a son without them. "In ordinary societies," say the authors of the proposed Civil Code, "one stipulates for oneself; in marriage, one stipulates for another." A father and mother who divorce are thus really two strong people who conspire to rob a weak one, and the State which consents to this is an accomplice in their brigandage. This third person can never, even when present, consent to the dissolution of the society which gave him being, since he is always a *minor* in the family, even when he has reached his majority in the State, and consequently is always incapable of consenting to anything to his prejudice. . . .

Marriage is therefore indissoluble in terms of society's domestic and public relationships. It is therefore naturally indissoluble: for the natural or man's nature is made up both of the domestic and public states; and there are certainly grounds for astonishment to hear the authors of the proposed Civil Code say that *marriage is neither a civil nor a religious act, but a natural one*; for if by a natural act they mean a physical act, then marriage is nothing but a meeting of animals; and if they mean something else, then it is impossible to guess what they wish to say.

Divorce is therefore contrary to the principle of society; we shall show, in the subsequent parts of this treatise, that it is destructive in its effects on society.

[FROM CHAPTER 11, "GENERAL CONSIDERATIONS ON DIVORCE"]

Divorce is both a harsh and a false law, because it not only allows the husband the faculty of repudiating his wife, but also grants it to the wife against her husband.

Today more than ever, divorce is a weak or oppressive law for both sexes, because it delivers them to the depravity of their penchants, at the very time that the passions, exalted by the progress of the arts, most need to be contained by the severity of the laws.[7]

Divorce is only tolerated among commercial peoples because they picture domestic society, and even political society, as a commercial association, a social contract. This is only a play on words, an illusion which vanishes under the slightest scrutiny.[8]

---

[7] Here and elsewhere Bonald suggests that social and economic development, and particularly the development of commerce, creates a need for greater restraint of the passions through law.

[8] Another example of conservative anti-contractualism, with its emphasis on the non-contractual basis of society and the inadequacy of the metaphor of contract for understanding the nature of most social institutions.

Domestic society is not a commercial association, which the partners enter with equal stakes and can leave with equal results. It is a society to which the man brings the protection of strength, the woman, the needs of weakness; one power, the other duty; a society which the man enters with authority, the woman with dignity; which the man leaves with all his authority, but the woman cannot leave with all her dignity: for out of everything she brought into the society, she can only, in the event of dissolution, recover her money. And is it not supremely unjust that the woman, having entered the family with youth and fertility, may leave it with sterility and old age, and that, belonging only to the domestic state, she should be put out of the family to which she gave existence, at the time in life when nature denies her the ability to begin another one?

Marriage is therefore not an ordinary contract, since in terminating it, the two parties cannot return themselves to the same state they were in before entering into it. And if the contract is voluntary at the time it is entered into, it can no longer be voluntary, and almost never is, at the time of its termination, since the party which manifests the desire to dissolve it takes all liberty from the other party to refuse, and has only too many means to force its consent. . . .

In comparison with all these natural reasons in favor of the indissolubility of the conjugal tie, what are all the human motives which can be alleged to justify the faculty of dissolving it? What does it matter, after all, if a few individuals suffer in the course of this transient life, as long as reason, nature, and society do not suffer?[9] And if man sometimes bears with regret a chain he cannot break, does he not suffer at all moments of his life, from his passions which he cannot subdue, from his inconstancy which he cannot settle; and is the entire life of man anything but a continual struggle against his penchants? It is up to man to harmonize tempers and characters in marriage, and to forestall disorders in the family by the equanimity of his temper and the wisdom of his conduct. But when he has made his choice against all the laws of reason, and solely on the basis of whim or interest, when he has founded his life's happiness on what only makes for the pleasure of a few moments, when he himself has poisoned the sweetness of a reasonable union by weak or unjust conduct; unhappy through his own fault, has he the right to ask society to take responsibility for his errors and offenses? Must one dissolve the family in order to contrive new pleasures for his passions, or new opportunities for his inconstancy, and corrupt an entire people because of the corruption of a few?

[9] A particularly striking example of Bonald's anti-humanitarianism.

[FROM "SUMMATION ON THE DIVORCE QUESTION," 1801]

All these limitations on the availability of divorce, all the obstacles raised against it, may make divorce difficult to obtain,—but only indissolubility makes marriage honorable. And what does it matter if divorces are rare, if spouses can never be indissolubly united? It is not difficulties which must be opposed to man's desires, for difficulties only inflame them, but the impossibility of satisfying them altogether. In the course of his passions, man stops only at the barrier which halts the Almighty himself: before the impossible.

Everything which is irritating in an indissoluble marriage becomes unbearable in a marriage subject to dissolution. Spouses then are like miserable captives who have partly opened the door of their prison and are constantly engaged in widening the gap to make a way out. . . .

Finally, and this is the most specious objection: *The indissolubility of the conjugal tie is a religious law, and the civil law of France recognizes no religion.* The law of indissoluble marriage is a domestic law, as the law of abstinence is a religious law. If one views it as religious because it is consecrated by religion, why not also view as religious, why recognize as civil, the prohibition of robbery and murder, which religion also consecrates, and indeed, consecrates even more expressly and clearly than the prohibition of divorce? The reason is that the Christian religion has made dogmas of all that nature had made principles, and that marriage, as all parties agree, is naturally indissoluble[10]. . . .

Moreover, let us dare to return to principle: governments are instituted to make men better and the family stronger. . . .

[T]he opinion that the religious must be carefully separated from the civil has not yet attained prescriptive status in society, though disseminated under a thousand forms for the last century.

Government should doubtless not command everything which religion prescribes to man as personal; but it should allow nothing which religion forbids as fundamental in society, still less should it forbid anything which religion commands. Indeed, sometimes government may precede religion, and forbid what religion tolerated only for a time. Religion directs will; the civil laws repress actions. To separate the direction of wills and the repression of actions in society is to separate the soul from the body in man; it is to materialize society, to annihilate it, by destroying the principle of its strength and progress. The indestructible

---

[10] Here Bonald shows that the grounds of his argument are not religious orthodoxy, but rather social utility.

strength, the incontestable preeminence of France, consisted in this harmony of the religious and the civil, more perfect in France, perhaps, than in any other nation, and which, by giving her constitution that theocratic element which distinguished it, made the *Very Christian* State the very powerful State.

INTRODUCTION TO
Joseph de Maistre,
Essay on the Generative Principle of Political Constitutions and of Other Human Institutions

◆

As recent interpreters have recognized, Joseph de Maistre's thought is more bold and more original than Bonald's, and far less orthodox.[1] An orthodox theorist might assert that divine origin accounts for the continuity of an institution: Maistre reverses the formulation, suggesting that the continued existence of an institution is itself evidence of its divine origin. And Maistre is more radical than Burke. Burke had noted the significance of involuntary obligations; Maistre carries Burke's claim to an extreme by asserting that no permanent obligations can be dependent on the voluntary consent of those obliged. Burke asserts that the legitimacy of the political regime is strengthened by its connection with an established church: Maistre insists that the only effective way of legitimating institutions is to make them sacrosanct. Burke suggests the limits of written constitutions: Maistre insists not only that written laws are futile, but that the most important laws are not written, indeed cannot be written.

In other ways as well Maistre takes up themes from eighteenth-century enlightened conservatism and carries them to greater extremes. Hume had criticized contractual theories of political obligation for being overly rationalistic, and insisted upon the role in human affairs of less calculating modes of behavior, such as custom and habit. Maistre digs deeper into the irrational sources of political obedience, including the desire for submission and sacrifice.[2] Montesquieu and Burke had emphasized the role of shared social and cultural habits in influencing political forms. Maistre, in the essay reprinted here, argues most unequivocally that the true "constitution" of a nation is its habits, manners, and mores which embody its unarticulated assumptions. According to Maistre, the political constitution can only reflect these, not shape them.[3]

---

[1] See, for example, Isaiah Berlin, "Joseph de Maistre and the Origins of Fascism," in *The Crooked Timber of Humanity* (New York, 1990); and Owen P. Bradley, *Logics of Violence: The Social and Political Thought of Joseph de Maistre* (unpub. Ph.D. thesis, Cornell University Department of History, 1992).

[2] See especially his "Enlightenment on Sacrifices," in Jack Lively, ed., *The Works of Joseph de Maistre* (New York, 1971).

[3] On the centrality of this theme in Maistre's thought, see Francis Bayle, *Les Idées politiques de Joseph de Maistre* (Paris, 1945; reprinted New York, 1979), pp. 57–77. On Mai-

Machiavelli, and later Rousseau, had explored the political uses of religion, but thought Christianity poorly suited to the role of civil religion. Maistre is obsessed by the relationship between religion and political stability: but unlike these predecessors, he maintains that Christianity, at least in its Catholic form, is perfectly appropriate for the role. Maistre's professions of Christianity were certainly sincere. But in his writings it is the social utility of religion as an element of political cohesion which is of concern.[4]

Maistre was born in a French-speaking region of Savoy in northern Italy. His father was a recently ennobled judge. Joseph studied law, and like his father became a magistrate. Steeped in enlightenment thought and influenced by the speculative and highly unorthodox theology of the Illuminati, he nevertheless remained a committed Catholic. When the French Revolutionary armies marched into Savoy, Maistre went into Swiss exile where he continued to serve his monarch. His first major work, *Considerations on France*, was published anonymously in Switzerland in 1797. There and in subsequent works, Maistre offered an interpretation of the Revolution which synthesized his conservatism and his millenarianism by arguing that the Revolution was a product of man's sinful pride, but that its very destructiveness paved the way for a new, more Christian Europe. At the turn of the century, Maistre was dispatched by his king to the Russian court at St. Petersburg, and it was there that he wrote his most provocative work, the *Soirées of Saint Petersburg* (the dialogic form of which allowed him to offer startling assertions without necessarily subscribing to them), as well as his *Essay on the Generative Principle of Political Constitutions and of Other Human Institutions*.

The *Essay*, which restates many of the themes of the earlier *Considerations on France* in more general and concise terms, was first written in Saint Petersburg in 1809, occasioned by Maistre's opposition to the constitutional plans of the Russian reformers.[5] But the larger backdrop against which the work must be understood was the repeated failure of attempts to create a successful constitutional order in France. At the beginning of the French Revolution, the National Assembly took its famous Tennis Court Oath, in which it swore to remain assembled "until the constitution of the realm is established and consolidated on a firm foundation." The constitution adopted by the National Assembly in 1791 was suspended under pressures of war in August 1792. In June

---

stre's debt to Montesquieu's *Spirit of the Laws*, see Peter Richard Rohden, *Joseph de Maistre als politischer Theoretiker* (Munich, 1929; reprinted New York, 1979), pp. 172ff.

[4] As recognized by Bradley, *Logics of Violence*, pp. 530ff.

[5] On the background of the work, see Richard Allen Lebrun, *Throne and Altar: The Political and Religious Thought of Joseph de Maistre* (Ottawa, 1965), p. 13 and p. 55n. 58.

1793, during the Jacobin ascendancy, a new and more radically egalitarian document, "The Constitution of the Year III," was cobbled together in a few days, but was never applied because of ongoing political instability. After the fall of the Jacobins, yet another constitution, "The Constitution of the Year V," was adopted by referendum in 1795. It established a government based on a bicameral legislature and headed by five elected Directors. After a period of reliance on the army to enforce its authority, the Directory was overpowered by a young general, Napoleon Bonaparte, whose dictatorship was confirmed in yet another constitution, "The Constitution of the Year VIII," passed by referendum in 1799. In 1802 yet another constitution confirmed Napoleon as First Consul for life; two years later, he was crowned emperor of France. It was with this sequence of events in mind that Maistre penned his *Essay*.

The essay demonstrates Maistre's recurrent strategy of conflating history with nature and nature with God's will.[6] Thus existing institutions are made to seem both inevitable and a product of divine providence. In his insistence on the futility of all deliberate human action, Maistre ends up deifying historical duration.

Joseph de Maistre,
Essay on the Generative Principle of Political Constitutions and of Other Human Institutions (1814)[1]

I. One of the gravest errors of an age which embraced them all was to believe that a political constitution could be written and created *a priori*, whereas reason and experience agree that a constitution is a divine work and that it is precisely the most fundamental and essentially constitutional elements in a nation's laws that cannot be written.[2]

---

[6] In his *Essay on Sovereignty* (Book I, chapter vii), Maistre writes of "nature, time, circumstances, that is to say, God." (Quoted in Rohden, *Joseph de Maistre*, p. 179.)

[1] This translation, which is based upon the French version of the text, *Essai sur le principe générateur des constitutions politiques et des autres institutions humaines* (Lyon and Paris, 1828), draws upon two earlier English translations. The first, by an unknown translator, was published by Little and Brown in Boston in 1847, and reprinted as *Essay on the Generative Principle of Political Constitutions* by Scholars' Facsimiles and Reprints of Delmar, New York, in 1977. The second appeared in *The Works of Joseph de Maistre*, selected, translated, and introduced by Jack Lively (New York, 1971).

[2] Maistre here uses the term "constitutional" in the sense of the inherent and essential characteristics of a culture, what Montesquieu in Book 19, chapter 4 of *The Spirit of the*

II. Frenchmen have often been asked as a joke "in what book was the Salic Law[3] written?" But Jérôme Bignon replied exactly to the point, very probably without understanding how aptly, that "it was written in the hearts of Frenchmen." Indeed, if we suppose that a law of this importance exists only because it is written, then whatever authority has written it will have the right to annul it; the law would not therefore have that character of sanctity and immutability that distinguishes truly constitutional laws. The essence of a fundamental law is that no one has the right to abolish it: but how is it beyond human power if it has been made by someone? The agreement of a people is impossible, and, even if it were, an agreement is not a law and obliges no one unless there is a superior authority guaranteeing it. Locke sought the characteristic of law in the expression of combined wills, thereby upon the precise characteristic that excludes the idea of *law*. As a matter of fact, combined wills form a *regulation* and not a *law*, which necessarily and obviously presupposes a superior will enforcing obedience. "In the Hobbesian system (which has been so successful in our day under the pen of Locke), the authority of civil laws derives solely from a contract; but if there is no natural law which obliges men to carry out the laws that have been made, of what use are they? Promises, engagements, and oaths are mere words, it is as easy to break these trifling bonds as to forge them. Without the dogma of a law-giving God, all moral obligation is chimerical. Force on the one side and powerlessness on the other, that would be the only bond of human society."[4]

What a wise and profound theologian has said here of moral obligation applies with equal force to political or civil obligation. Law is properly *law* and has a genuine sanction only if it is taken as emanating from a superior will; so that its essential feature is *that it is not the will of all*. Otherwise laws would, as has just been said, be *only regulations*; and, as the author just quoted added, "Those who have been free to make contracts have not renounced the power of revoking them; and their descendants, who played no part in them, are still less bound to observe them." Consequently, primordial good sense, happily anterior to sophisms, has everywhere sought the sanction for laws in a power above men, either by recognizing that sovereignty derives from God, or by revering certain unwritten laws as coming from Him.[5]

Laws had called the "general spirit" of each nation, above all its historically developed mores and manners.

[3] The law code of the Salian Franks, the Germanic tribe from which the name "France" derives.

[4] [Bergier, *Traité historique et dogmatique de la religion*, Book III, chap. IV, paragraph 12.]

[5] Here and elsewhere Maistre is deliberately ambiguous as to whether the unwritten

III. The compilers of the Roman laws have included in the first chapter of their collection a very remarkable fragment of Greek jurisprudence. "Among the laws which govern us," says this passage, "some are written and others are not." Nothing could be simpler and nothing more profound. Is there any Turkish law expressly permitting the sovereign to send a man to his death immediately without the intermediate decision of a court? Is there any *written* law, even a religious one, which forbids this to the sovereign of Christian Europe? Yet the Turk is no more surprised to see his ruler order an immediate execution than to see him go to the mosque. Like all of Asia and even all of antiquity, he believes that the immediate power of life and death is a legitimate perquisite of the sovereign. But our kings shudder at the very idea of condemning a man to death; for, in our eyes, such a condemnation would be a vile murder, and yet I doubt if it would be possible to forbid them this power by means of a written fundamental law without it leading to evils greater than those which one wished to prevent. . . .

VII. In spite of this, we are still lectured about written constitutions and constitutional laws created *à priori*. It is impossible to conceive how a rational man can believe in such chimeras. If some scheme was carried through in England to give the cabinet a formal constitutional status, which would thus regulate and circumscribe rigorously its privileges and powers, and would include the precautions necessary to limit its influence and prevent it from abusing it, the state would be undermined.

The real *English constitution* is the public spirit, admirable, unique, infallible, and above praise, which guides all, conserves all, preserves all. What is written is nothing.

VIII. . . . [At the end of the eighteenth century,] was it not everywhere believed that a constitution is as much a work of the mind as an ode or a tragedy. Had not Thomas Paine asserted, with a profundity which enraptured the universities, that "a constitution does not exist if one cannot put it in one's pocket?" The eighteenth century, so free of self-doubt, doubted nothing: that is the rule, and I do not believe that it produced a single youth of any talent whatever who had not made three things by the time he left school—a new system of education, a constitution, and a society. If therefore a mature and talented man, deeply versed in economics and contemporary philosophy, had undertaken only the second of these projects, this in itself would have convinced me of his extreme moderation. He who put experience (at least

---

laws actually derive from God, or whether it is politically useful to regard them as of divine origin.

as he saw it) in place of foolish theories, and humbly demanded a constitution on the English model instead of drawing one up himself, I would have regarded as a veritable prodigy of wisdom and modesty. One might say, "*even this was not possible*." I know that, but he did not; and how could he have known? Name someone who could have told him.

IX. The more one examines the influence of human agency in the formation of political constitutions, the clearer it becomes that it enters only in an extremely subordinate role or as a simple instrument. I do not believe that any doubt at all remains of the incontrovertible truth of the following propositions:

1. That the fundamentals of political constitutions exist prior to all written laws.
2. That a constitutional law is and can only be the development or the sanction of a law which is preexistent and unwritten.
3. That which is most essential, most intrinsically constitutional, and really fundamental is never written and could not be written down without imperiling the state.[6]
4. That the weakness and fragility of a constitution is in direct relationship to the number of written constitutional articles.

X. We are misled on this point by a fallacy so natural that it entirely escapes our attention. Because man acts, he believes he acts on his own; and because he is conscious of his liberty, he forgets his dependence. As far as the physical order is concerned, he listens to reason; although he can, for example, plant an acorn, water it, and so on, he is capable of admitting that he does not make the oaks, since he sees that the tree grows and reaches perfection without human interference; and besides, he has not made the acorn. But in the social order in which he is a participant and actor, he begins to believe that he is really the direct author of everything that happens through him: in a sense, the trowel believes himself to be the architect. Doubtless, man is intelligent, free, and sublime, but he is nonetheless an *implement of God.* . . .

XII. Let us now consider a particular political constitution, that of England for example. Certainly it was not made *a priori*. Her statesmen never gathered together and said, "Let us create three powers, balance them in such and such a manner," and so on. No one of them ever

---

[6] Here Maistre introduces the theme that committing the previously unwritten law to writing may imperil its functioning. Presumably he means to suggest that the law loses its flexibility and adaptability to changed circumstances by becoming codified and hence specified.

thought of such a thing. The constitution is the work of circumstances, and the number of these circumstances is infinite. Roman laws, ecclesiastical laws, and feudal laws; Saxon, Norman, and Danish customs; the privileges, legal precedents, and claims of each order; wars, revolts, revolutions, conquests, and crusades; virtues and vices of every kind; all knowledge, all error, all the passions; all of these elements, acting together and forming by their intermixture and reciprocal action endlessly multiplying combinations, have finally produced after many centuries the most complex unity and the most delicate equilibrium of political forces the world has ever known.

XIII. However, since these elements . . . have fallen into such meaningful order without a single man among the multitude who have acted on this huge stage knowing what relation his actions had with the whole scheme of things or what the future was to be, it follows that these elements were guided in their fall by an unerring hand, superior to man.[7] Perhaps the greatest folly of a century of follies was to believe that fundamental laws could be written *a priori*, whereas they are obviously the work of a power above men, and the very act of writing them down, later on, is the surest sign that their real force has gone.

XIV. It is very remarkable that God, having deigned to speak to men, has himself made these truths clear in the two revelations which we owe to his goodness.[8] A very clever man, to my mind one of the most outstanding of our age because of the bitter struggle revealed in his writings between the most terrible prejudices of the age, of sect, of habit, and the purest intentions, the most righteous sentiments, the most sensitive understanding; this man has decided "that a teaching coming direct from God, or given solely on his command, must have been man's first assurance of the existence of this Being." The truth is precisely the opposite, because the prime characteristic of this teaching is not to reveal directly either the existence or the attributes of God, but to presuppose the whole of this knowledge, without our understanding why or how. Thus it does not tell us: *There is* or You *will believe in only one God eternal, omnipotent*, and so on. It says (and these are its first words) in a purely narrative form, "*In the beginning, God created* . . ." by which it supposes that this dogma is known before writing. . . .

---

[7] Maistre, like Hume, insists that valuable human institutions are not a product of deliberate human design. But while Hume attributes the durability of conventions to the experience of their social utility, Maistre treats such conventions as products of divine providence.

[8] The Old Testament and the New.

XIX. These ideas, in a broad sense, were not unknown to the philosophers of antiquity: they well understood the weakness, I would almost say the negligible role of writing in great institutions. But no one has better seen or expressed this truth than Plato, who we always find first on the track of all the great truths. According to him, first of all, "the man who owes all his education to written discourses *will only possess the appearance of wisdom*." "The spoken word," he adds, "is to writing what a man is to his portrait. The creations of the painter strike us as being lifelike, yet *if you question them, they maintain a solemn silence*. It is the same with a written work, *which does not know what to say to one man or to conceal from another*. If you attack it or insult it unreasonably, it cannot defend itself, *for its author is never there to protect it*. So that whoever imagines himself able to establish a clear and durable doctrine by the written word alone is a great fool. If he did possess the real seeds of truth, he would take great care not to believe that, *with a little black liquid and a pen*, he could make them take root among men, protect them against inclement seasons, and provide them with the necessary vitality. As for the man who undertakes to write *laws or civil constitutions*, imagining that, because he has written them down, he has been able to give them the proper clarity and stability, he disgraces himself, whatever he is, whether private citizen or legislator, and whatever men say; for he has thereby shown that he is equally ignorant of inspiration and madness, justice and injustice, good and evil. Such ignorance is disgraceful even if the entire mass of the vulgar applaud him."[9]

XXI. . . . [This shows] the profound imbecility (it is permissible to speak like Plato, who never lost his temper), the profound imbecility, as I say, of those poor people who imagine that men are the real law-givers, that laws are made of paper and that nations can be constituted by *ink*. It shows, to the contrary, that writing is invariably a sign of weakness, ignorance, or danger; that the more perfect an institution, the less it writes; so that what is truly divine has no written document as its basis, showing us that every written law is only a necessary evil, engendered by human infirmity or malice, and that it has no authority whatever if it has not received a prior and unwritten sanction. . . .

XXIII. Every right-thinking person will end by being convinced on this point, however little he reflects on an axiom equally striking for its importance and universality. This is that NOTHING GREAT HAS GREAT BEGINNINGS. No exception to this law will be found in the whole of

---

[9] [Plato, *Phaedrus*, 275–77.]

history. *Crescit occulto velut arbor oevo*;[10] this is the eternal motto of every great institution; and it follows that every false institution writes a great deal, as it is sensible of its weakness and seeks to buttress itself. From this truth results the inevitable consequence that no great and real institution can be founded on a written law, since men themselves, a succession of instruments of its founding, do not know what it is to become, and since imperceptible growth is the true sign of durability in every possible order of things. A remarkable example of this is to be found in the power of the Sovereign Pontiffs, whom I do not intend to consider here in a dogmatic light. Since the sixteenth century, a host of scholars have made prodigious efforts of erudition to establish, by going to the earliest days of Christianity, that the Bishops of Rome were not in the first centuries what they have since become; thus assuming as an agreed point that everything that is not found in primitive ages is an abuse. However, and I say this in no spirit of contention and without meaning to shock anyone, they show in this as much philosophy and true knowledge as if they sought in a babe in arms the real dimensions of a full-grown man. The sovereignty of which I am now talking was born like others and has grown like others. It is pitiful to see powerful minds straining themselves to prove that maturity is an abuse by citing infancy; whereas the very idea of any institution being adult at birth is an absurdity of the first order, a true logical contradiction. If the enlightened and generous enemies of this power (and certainly it has many of this kind) look at the question from this point of view, as I beg them with respect to do, I have no doubt that all these time-worn objections will vanish before their eyes like a mist. . . .

XXV. . . . Less than twenty-five years ago, we witnessed a solemn attempt to regenerate a great but mortally sick nation. This was the first draft of a great work, and the *preface*, so to speak, of the frightening book that we have since had to read. Every precaution had been taken. . . . Alas, all human wisdom was lacking, and everything ended in death.

XXVI. It is said, "But we know the causes of the failure of the undertaking." How so? Do you want God to send angels in human form, charged with destroying a constitution? It will always be very necessary for secondary causes to be employed; this or that, what does it matter? Every instrument is useful in the hands of the great craftsman; but so blind are men that if tomorrow some constitution-mongers came again to organize a people and to constitute it with *a little black liquid*, the crowd would again lose no time in believing in the promised miracle.

---

[10] "Growth comes from hidden sources, as the tree from the seed."

Once more, it would be said, "Nothing is lacking; all is foreseen; all is written," whereas, if everything were to be foreseen, discussed, and written, it would show the worthlessness and insubstantiality of the constitution.

XXVII. I think I have read somewhere *that there are very few sovereignties able to justify the legitimacy of their origins.* Admitting the justice of this claim, the fact that objections may be leveled against the actions of a founder in no way blemishes his successors: the shadows which to a greater or lesser degree fall across the origins of his authority are nothing but an inconvenience, a necessary consequence of a law of the moral world. If it was otherwise, it would follow that a sovereign could reign legitimately only by virtue of a deliberation of the whole people, that is to say, *by grace of the people*, which will never happen, for nothing is more true than what has been said by the author of *Considerations on France*,[11] that "the people will always accept its masters and will never choose them." It is always necessary for the origin of sovereignty to appear as being outside the sphere of human control; so that the very men who appear to be directly involved are nevertheless only circumstances. Though the beginnings of legitimacy may appear ambiguous, God clears it up through his prime minister in the affairs of this world, *time.* . . .

XXVIII. Everything therefore brings us back to the general rule: *Man cannot make a constitution, and no legitimate constitution can ever be written.* The corpus of fundamental laws that must constitute a civil or religious society have never been and never will be written. This can be done only when the society is already constituted, yet it is impossible to spell out or explain in writing certain individual articles; but almost always these declarations are the effect or the cause of very great evils, and they always cost the people more than they are worth. . . .

XL. Not only is creation not one of man's proper functions; it does not seem as if our power *unassisted* extends to the improvement of established institutions. Nothing is plainer to man than the existence of two opposed forces which ceaselessly struggle in the universe. There is no good that evil does not contaminate and corrupt; there is no evil that good does not curb and attack, in the ceaseless movement of all things toward a more perfect state. These two forces are everywhere present. They can be seen equally in the growth of plants, in the generation of animals, in the formation of languages and of empires (two things which

[11] That is, by de Maistre himself.

are inseparable), and so on. Human power extends perhaps only to re-moving or combating evil, to free the good from it, and to restore to the good the power to grow according to its nature. The celebrated Zanotti has said, "It is difficult to change things for the better." This thought hides a profound meaning under the appearance of extreme simplicity. It accords completely with another saying of Origen, which is alone worth a whole volume. "Nothing," he said, "can be changed for the better among men without divine help."[12] All men feel the truth of this, even when they are unable to articulate it. It explains the instinctive aversion toward innovation shared by all fine minds. The word *reform*, in itself and before any scrutiny, will always be suspect to the wise, and the experience of every age justifies this kind of instinct. . . .

XLI. To apply these generalizations to a particular case, it is from the sole consideration of the grave danger of innovations based on simpli-fied human theories that, without believing that I am in a position to hold a reasoned opinion on the great question of parliamentary reform which has so deeply and for such a long time stirred English minds, I nevertheless feel led to believe that this idea is disastrous and that, if the English surrender to it too readily, they will come to regret it. "But," say the partisans of reform (for this is their great argument), "the abuses are striking and incontestable: can a blatant abuse, a vice, be constitu-tional?" Yes, indisputably it can be; for every political constitution has its essential faults which spring from its nature and which cannot be sepa-rated from it; and what should make every reformer hesitate is that these faults can change with circumstances; so that by showing that they are new, one has not demonstrated that they are not necessary. What sensi-ble man will not therefore shudder to undertake such a task? Social har-mony is subject to the law of *tempering*, as is harmony when we speak of it in regard to a keyboard. Get the *fifths* carefully in tune and the *octaves* will clash, and *vice versa*. Dissonance being therefore inevitable, rather than eliminating it, which is impossible, it is necessary to *temper* it, by distributing it. Thus in both cases, *fault is an element in possible perfec-tion*. This proposition is only apparently paradoxical. "But," it will per-haps still be said, "what is the rule to distinguish an incidental fault from one which belongs to the nature of things and which is impossible to eliminate?" Men to whom nature has given tin ears pose these sort of questions, and those with an ear for music shrug their shoulders.[13]

---

[12] [Origen, *Against Celsus*, Book i, chap. xxvi.]

[13] Politically prudent men know that no definitive answer can be given—an assertion of epistemological modesty. Because reliable rules for safe reform cannot be discovered, one should be disposed against reforming away abuses, since the interdependence of social ele-ments may lead to negative unintended consequences.

XLII. It is still more necessary to take care, when it is a question of abuses, to judge political institutions only by their persisting effects and never by any of their causes, which are not important, still less by certain collateral disadvantages (if we can call them that) which so impress those of shortsighted views and prevent them from seeing things as a whole.[14] In fact, according to the hypothesis that seems to be proved, cause need not have any logical relation to effect, and the drawbacks of a good institution are themselves, as I have just said, only *the necessary dissonances.* How, therefore, can institutions be judged on the basis of their origins and their disadvantages? . . .

LVIII . . . [T]he more divine the basis of an institution, the more durable it is. It should be pointed out, for the sake of clarity, that the religious principle is in essence creative and conservative, in two ways. In the first place, as it is the most powerful influence on the human mind, it can stimulate prodigious efforts. Take, for example, a man persuaded by his religious beliefs that it is very advantageous to him that after his death his body should be preserved as far as possible as it was in life, without any prying or profane hand being able to touch it. Such a man, having brought the art of embalming to perfection, will end by constructing the pyramids of Egypt. In the second place, the religious principle, already so strong because of what it effects, is still stronger because of what it prevents, through the respect with which it surrounds everything that comes under its protection. If a simple piece of pottery is consecrated, that immediately becomes a reason for keeping it from those who might mislay or misuse it. The world is full of proofs of this truth. Etruscan vases, for example, preserved by the sanctity of the tomb, have in spite of their fragility come down to us in greater numbers than marble or bronze statues of the same period. If therefore you wish to *conserve* all, *consecrate* all.[15]

---

[14] A statement of historical consequentialism.

[15] Up till this point Maistre has argued that the unintended positive effects of human institutions should be seen as proof of their divine origins. The durability of institutions is seen as evidence of their utility, and this too is attributed to divine origins, thus sanctifying existing institutions. Now he argues that the sanctification of institutions enhances their emotional hold, and hence their durability. For Maistre then, social utility is regarded as proof of sacred origins, while the attribution of sacred origins to social institutions enhances their utility.

INTRODUCTION TO
James Madison,
"Federalist No. 49"

◆

According to some students of comparative political culture, American conservatism does not exist, indeed cannot exist. When conservatism is defined as the defense of a landed nobility, monarchy, and the established church, the absence of such institutions in the United States after 1776 (and indeed largely before that) makes the notion of American conservatism a contradiction in terms.[1] If, however, conservatism is defined by a recurrent constellation of arguments and predilections, as we have defined it, then conservatism has been an ongoing pattern in American political and social thought, going back at least to the founding of the republic.

Yet American conservatism, like conservatism in other national contexts, has been marked by its own national peculiarities. In a nation founded by an act of will as a constitutional republic, American conservatism has always been republican and constitutional in its emphasis. Indeed in an important sense, the Constitution itself is the characteristic expression of early American conservatism. For in a republic founded upon the principles of popular sovereignty and individual liberty, and upon an assertion of natural rights, American conservatism stressed the limitation of popular sovereignty, the necessity of a relatively strong federal government, and the importance of reverence for institutions nurtured by a sense of continuity with the past.

This conception of American conservatism does not contradict the famous thesis of Louis Hartz, who argued that the political culture of the United States was deeply and indelibly marked by what in Europe was called liberalism. As Hartz himself stressed, what American conservatives sought to conserve was a rather liberal society, grounded in contract, the market, and limited government.[2] The "prejudices" of Americans—the unarticulated assumptions and habitual reactions bequeathed by their collective historical experience—were liberal, as Edmund Burke had explained to his countrymen in 1775, in what remains among the most illuminating portraits of the peculiarities of American political culture.[3] Many of the governmental forms adopted in 1776 were continu-

[1] Bernard Crick, "The Strange Quest for An American Conservatism," *The Review of Politics* XVII, 1955, pp. 359–76.

[2] Louis Hartz, *The Liberal Tradition in America* (New York, 1955), p. 57.

[3] Ibid., p. 61. Cf. Edmund Burke, "Speech of Edmund Burke, Esq., On Moving his

ous with the past: they were colonial institutions without the King and the British Parliament, both of which had long seemed distant to the inhabitants of the new United States.[4] Much that seemed radical in eighteenth-century Europe was taken for granted by Americans. The notion of a written constitution, which was a radical conception in Europe, was perceived by Americans as continuous with a past in which political institutions had long been based upon agreements such as the Mayflower Compact and the Plantation Covenants of New England towns.[5]

A heritage of self-government combined with a suspicion of governmental power predisposed the Americans for representative and constitutional government. In contrast to Jefferson's perorations on universal, natural rights, some American founders were aware that the success of their revolution was grounded in particular historical experience. One prominent figure in the early republic, Gouverneur Morris, who served as American ambassador to France in 1789, wrote of the French, "They want an American constitution, without realizing they have no Americans to uphold it"—an observation which precedes Joseph de Maistre's more famous critique of the efficacy of written constitutions.[6]

There were conservative and nonconservative elements in the American founding. In many ways the Declaration of Independence and its author, Thomas Jefferson, are paradigmatic of the nonconservative elements of the founding: rationalist, universalistic, populist, suspicious of federal government power and of nonagrarian commercial development. The more conservative elements of the founding are represented by the Constitution and by the authors of the *Federalist Papers*, John Jay, Alexander Hamilton, and above all, by James Madison. It was to Jefferson that the more populist and antigovernmental currents in subsequent American political life would look, while more conservative currents, beginning with the Whigs in the first half of the nineteenth century, looked to Madison as their forebear.

Although they cooperated closely for most of their political careers, Thomas Jefferson and James Madison were men of profoundly different philosophical temperaments. Jefferson was a political visionary, suspicious of authority and of government. He drew upon Locke and upon the more rationalist trends in the French Enlightenment, in which he felt much at home. Though Madison too drew upon Locke for his fundamental beliefs about morality and rights, his political science was

---

Resolutions for Conciliation with the Colonies, March 22nd, 1775," now in Ian Harris, ed., *Burke: Pre-Revolutionary Writings* (Cambridge, 1993), esp. pp. 221–27.

[4] Hartz, *Liberal Tradition*, p. 62.

[5] Ibid., pp. 48–49.

[6] Morris, quoted in ibid., p. 38.

more deeply indebted to the Scottish Enlightenment in general and to David Hume in particular. (Jefferson, by contrast, fearing that Hume's *History of England* would "spread universal Toryism over the land," sought to suppress the work in America and had it banned from the University of Virginia.)[7] Where Jefferson valued liberation, Madison emphasized social stability; where Jefferson was given to professions of universal ideals, Madison turned his attention to institutions and their mechanisms; and Jefferson's egalitarian propensities contrasted with Madison's concern for the role of elites in government.[8] It was these Madisonian propensities which were on display in the Constitution (propensities expressed with even greater intensity by the other major author of *The Federalist*, Alexander Hamilton). In fact, Madison's own proposals were more elitist and centralist than the constitution which emerged from the Philadelphia convention called in 1787 to revise the Articles of Confederation.[9]

After having participated in a successful and in many respects conservative revolution, Madison viewed with dismay what he saw as the increasingly irresponsible behavior of the democratically elected state legislatures of the 1780s. Like future American conservatives, Madison was at pains to put the revolutionary genie back in the bottle, while the more radical Jefferson proclaimed the need for periodic collective renewal. Hence their very different reactions to "Shays's Rebellion" of 1786–87, a popular uprising in western Massachusetts made up of farmers demanding relief from the taxes imposed upon them by the eastern-dominated legislature.

The revolt was a product of the economic and political processes of the previous decade. The Revolutionary War had increased demand for many products, and as ever more Americans became involved in market-oriented production, demand for money and for credit increased. Paper currencies were introduced, leading to a general inflation. When the market declined after the war, many of those who had borrowed to in-

[7] For an examination of this episode, see Craig Walton, "Hume and Jefferson on the Uses of History," in Donald W. Livingston and James L. King, eds., *Hume: A Re-evaluation* (New York, 1976), pp. 389–403.

[8] For a good summary of the contrast between Jefferson and Madison, see Joseph J. Ellis, "Founding Brothers," *The New Republic*, Jan. 30, 1995, pp. 32–36. For a more extended discussion, see Drew R. McCoy, *The Last of the Founders: James Madison and the Republican Legacy* (Cambridge, 1989), pp. 47–65. By contrast, Lance Banning, *Jefferson and Madison: Three Conversations from the Founding* (Madison, 1995) tends to minimize the differences between the two founders. Very useful on Madison is Marvin Meyers, *The Mind of the Founder: Sources of the Political Thought of James Madison* (revised edition, Hanover, 1981), and the same author's "Founding and Revolution: A Commentary on Publius-Madison," in Stanley Elkins and Eric McKitrick, eds., *The Hofstadter Aegis* (New York, 1974), pp. 3–32.

[9] See the discussion in Forrest McDonald, *Novus Ordo Seclorum: The Intellectual Origins of the Constitution* (Lawrence, KS, 1985), pp. 205ff.

crease their production found themselves unable to repay their loans. As voters in the new republic, they turned for relief to their state legislatures, which enacted a spate of legislation on behalf of debtors. These measures alarmed the American gentry with which Madison and Hamilton identified, most of whom were creditors, and added to their sense that the pursuit of material self-interest within the state legislatures threatened the economic and political stability of the new nation.[10] Shays's Rebellion, to Madison's relief, was suppressed by the Massachusetts state militia, but it brought home to him the dangerous volatility within the democratically elected state legislatures which dominated the new republic. In addition, attempts by the Congress to raise funds from the states in order to pay back the interest on debts incurred during the Revolution met resistance from middle- and lower-class voters in the states, leading those like Madison and Hamilton, who were concerned with the fate of the central government, to attempt to strengthen its power.[11]

Prominent among the objectives of the authors of the *Federalist* was preserving popular government by limiting the role of the populace in political decision-making. In the face of their increasing dismay with the functioning of democracy in the state legislatures, the authors of the *Federalist* sought to create a federal government more insulated than the state legislatures from the winds of popular passions, and with enough authority to make participation in the federal government attractive to the elite of men of property, education, energy, and virtue.[12] The Constitution which was adopted was notable for its nondemocratic elements. Neither the President, the members of the Senate, nor the justices of the Supreme Court were to be chosen directly by the people. The President was chosen by an electoral college, senators by their state legislatures. As the guardians of the Constitution, Hamilton set the justices of the Supreme Court, a body of men appointed by the executive branch for life, who wielded great influence through the mechanism of judicial review. As Louis Hartz has noted, the Supreme Court "came as close to being a House of Lords as a purely liberal society could produce."[13]

Though James Madison was by no means the most conservative voice at the founding, it was his voice which was to remain most resonant among the conservative Whigs who came to define American conserva-

[10] Gordon S. Wood, *The Radicalism of the American Revolution* (New York, 1992), pp. 248ff.

[11] On Shays's Rebellion and its impact, see Robert A. Gross, ed., *In Debt to Shays: The Bicentennial of an Agrarian Rebellion* (Charlottesville, 1993).

[12] See on this theme Wood, *Radicalism of the American Revolution*, pp. 252–55, 261.

[13] Hartz, *Liberal Tradition in America*, p. 103.

tism in the second quarter of the nineteenth century.[14] That voice is evident in Federalist Number 49, in which Madison took it upon himself to refute one of Jefferson's more democratic proposals. In his *Notes on the State of Virginia*, Jefferson had suggested that constitutional issues be resolved by frequent recourse to the electorate. Writing under the pseudonym "Publius," Madison took Jefferson respectfully but firmly to task, with the following Humean observations.

James Madison,
"Federalist No. 49" (1788)

. . . [A]s every appeal to the people would carry an implication of some defect in the government, frequent appeals would, in great measure, deprive the government of that veneration which time bestows on everything, and without which perhaps the wisest and freest governments would not possess the requisite stability. If it be true that all governments rest on opinion, it is no less true that the strength of opinion in each individual, and its practical influence on his conduct, depends much on the number which he supposes to have entertained the same opinion. The reason of man, like man himself, is timid and cautious when left alone, and acquires firmness and confidence in proportion to the number with which its is associated. When the examples which fortify opinion are *ancient* as well as *numerous*, they are known to have a double effect. In a nation of philosophers, this consideration ought to be disregarded. A reverence for the laws would be sufficiently inculcated by the voice of enlightened reason. But a nation of philosophers is as little to be expected as the philosophical race of kings wished for by Plato. And in every other nation, the most rational government will not find it a superfluous advantage to have the prejudices of the community on its side.

The danger of disturbing the public tranquillity by interesting too strongly the public passions is a still more serious objection against a frequent reference of constitutional questions to the decision of the whole society. Notwithstanding the success which has attended the revisions of our established forms of government and which does so much honor to the virtue and intelligence of the people of America, it must be confessed that the experiments are of too ticklish a nature to be unnecessarily multiplied. We are to recollect that all the existing constitutions

[14] On the adoration of Madison among nineteenth-century American Whigs, see Daniel Walker Howe, *The Political Culture of the American Whigs* (Chicago, 1979), p. 91.

were formed in the midst of a danger which repressed the passions most unfriendly to order and concord; of an enthusiastic confidence of the people in their patriotic leaders, which stifled the ordinary diversity of opinions of great national questions; of a universal ardor for new and opposite forms, produced by a universal resentment and indignation against the ancient government; and whilst no spirit of party connected with the changes to be made, or the abuses to be reformed, could mingle its leaven in the operation. The future situations in which we must expect to be usually placed do not present any equivalent security against the danger which is apprehended.

INTRODUCTION TO
Rufus Choate,
"The Position and Functions of the American Bar, as an Element of Conservatism in the State"

◆

For Madison, as Marvin Meyers has noted, "the founding was a gentle revolution to end all revolutions, so far as the eye of reason and experience could see."[1] His warnings against taking the right to revolution too seriously echo a half century later, in the next selection by Rufus Choate.

For decades after the adoption of the Constitution, politics in most states remained the purview of elites. But as small businessmen, industrial workers, artisans, and farmers were drawn into the market economy, they took more interest in elections and in government affairs. The right to vote, which in most states had originally been restricted to property owners, was increasingly extended to all white males. By the 1820s a new, more popular brand of electioneering was developing, dominated by political professionals adept at organizing voters.

The election of Andrew Jackson to the presidency in 1828 was widely seen as a triumph for the newly enfranchised electorate, and it was marked by an egalitarianism of style and to some extent of policy. The Jacksonians challenged the ideal of a trained and professional civil service recruited from the elites of society. They insisted that governmental posts were booty belonging to the political victors. And they attacked important institutions created by the Federalists and later retained by their Democratic successors, such as the national bank and the tariff.

In response to the challenge of Jacksonianism, more conservative Americans organized themselves. In 1834, they adopted the British term "Whig" and supported the anti-Jacksonian Henry Clay as their candidate for president. But the term "Whig" came to designate more than a political party: it was a worldview, defined in good part by its contrast with Jacksonianism. While the Jacksonian Democrats championed the rights of natural man and his freedom of action, the Whigs emphasized the need for institutional direction of the passions. The Jacksonians favored equality of political participation for all white men; the Whigs respected not Anglo-Saxon blood, but what they saw as the

---

[1] Marvin Meyers, "Founding and Revolution: A Commentary on Publius-Madison," in Stanley Elkins and Eric McKitrick, eds., *The Hofstadter Aegis* (New York, 1974), pp. 3–32, 35.

civilizing effects of Anglo-Saxon institutions. They valued self-restraint and self-control, and tended to view the Democratic voters as undisciplined men who had escaped the institutional controls of European society but had not yet learned to impose internal restraint on themselves. The Whigs retained a hierarchical view of society and rued the decline of the politics of deference. They believed that those without education should defer to the more educated. And as control of politics slipped from their hands, they sought to educate the public to the necessity of a solid institutional underpinning of the social order. The political ideology of the Whigs was conveyed through a culture of speech-making, in which politicians sought to inspire in their audiences a reverence for American institutions, above all for the state, the Constitution, and the law.[2] Not surprisingly, this emphasis on the veneration of institutions spawned a vogue of Edmund Burke; during the 1830s, seven multivolume editions of his work were published in the United States.[3]

Among the most distinguished of the Whig conservatives was Rufus Choate (1799–1859) of Massachusetts. Trained as a lawyer and famed as a legal orator, Choate served as a state legislator, congressman, and from 1841 to 1845 as United States Senator.[4] Choate's career spanned the rise of the American legal profession from its chaotic condition around 1790 to a position of political and intellectual dominance by the 1830s, a rise all the more remarkable because ordinary Americans tended to hold the law in contempt.[5] Alexis de Tocqueville, who toured the United States in the 1830s, remarked that lawyers were the nearest equivalent to an aristocracy in the new nation.

Antipathy toward the law and toward political institutions in general was most intense in the frontier regions,[6] and American conservatism defined itself by contrast to the experience of the frontier. For the shifting western frontier has long been the site of antagonism toward established authority: both the lure of the frontier and its cultural impact lay in the escape from established institutions and hierarchies. In the era of the founding, revolts against the power of the federal government typically broke out in "the west," first with Shays's Rebellion in western Massachusetts, and later in the Whiskey Rebellion of 1794, which

[2] Daniel Walker Howe, *The Political Culture of the American Whigs* (Chicago, 1979), pp. 30–40. Jean V. Matthews, *Rufus Choate: The Law and Civic Virtue* (Philadelphia, 1980), pp. 71–86.

[3] Howe, *Political Culture*, p. 211.

[4] A thoughtful work on Choate as an American Whig conservative is Matthews, *Rufus Choate: The Law and Civic Virtue*.

[5] Perry Miller, *The Life of the Mind in America: From the Revolution to the Civil War* (New York, 1965), p. 109 and passim.

[6] Ibid., p. 102.

erupted in western Pennsylvania and came to encompass western Maryland and the back-country regions of Virginia and Kentucky.[7]

A further stimulus to the Whig's conservative emphasis on restricting change to the institutional channels provided by the constitution came from the "Dorr Rebellion." In an age when universal white male suffrage was increasingly becoming the norm, the state of Rhode Island retained a relatively narrow suffrage, based on property qualifications which allowed only four out of ten adult white male citizens to vote. Moreover, membership in the state's General Assembly reflected antiquated demographic patterns, so that areas which had experienced economic growth were often underrepresented. Attempts to reform the suffrage were repeatedly squashed by the state's oligarchic leadership. After two years of agitation, reformers led by the lawyer and politician John Dorr elected delegates to an unauthorized convention. It formulated a new state constitution and submitted it for ratification in an election approved only by the convention's participants. In May 1842, Dorr and the radical wing of the reformers proclaimed themselves the legitimate government and attempted to seize control of the state. They asserted that majorities had the inalienable right to change constitutions and governments at will, in the exercise of popular sovereignty. The state authorities, backed by a promise of federal support, suppressed the radicals. The next year, the elected state government formulated and ratified a relatively liberal constitution. But the Dorr revolt sparked a renewed debate about the right of revolution, and led to the rise of a more conservative institutionalism, which emphasized stability and liberty.[8]

Among the new institutions established to teach the law was the Harvard Law School. Refounded in 1829 under new leadership, it became the intellectual center of New England's emerging legal culture. In style and message, that culture continued the traditions of the Washington and Adams Federalists of the 1790s.[9] It was there, on the eve of Independence Day in 1845 that Rufus Choate delivered his address, "The Position and Functions of the American Bar, As An Element of Conservatism in the State," among the most eloquent declamations of Whig conservatism.

[7] See Thomas P. Slaughter, *The Whiskey Rebellion: Frontier Epilogue to the American Revolution* (New York, 1986).

[8] On the Dorr episode and its interpretation by contemporaries, see George M. Dennison, *The Dorr War: Republicanism on Trial, 1831–1861* (Lexington, KY, 1976). On the new emphasis on government and law, see also Daniel Rogers, *Contested Truths: Keywords in American Politics Since Independence* (New York, 1987), pp. 112–30.

[9] On the influence of the Adams Federalists, see R. Kent Newmyer, "Harvard Law School, New England Legal Culture, and the Antebellum Origins of American Jurisprudence, *Journal of American History*, vol. 74, no. 3 (Dec. 1987), pp. 814–35; and more generally Morton J. Horowitz, *The Transformation of American Law, 1780–1860* (Cambridge, MA, 1977).

Choate set out the key tenets of mid-nineteenth-century American conservatism. In his interpretation of the Revolution and of the founding he stressed the role of the constitution as an institutional limitation upon democracy, and underscored the role of government and of law as a restraint upon human passions. Like Madison's *Federalist* 49, Choate emphasized the need to develop reverence for these institutions, a reverence enhanced by their antiquity. And he stressed that while other nations might stand in need of revolution, America needed no further revolutions because it stood upon solid institutional foundations.

Rufus Choate, "The Position and Functions of the American Bar, as an Element of Conservatism in the State" (1845)[1]

There are reasons without number why we should love and honor our noble profession, and should be grateful for the necessity or felicity or accident which called us to its service.

But of these there is one, I think, which, rightly apprehended, ought to be uppermost in every lawyer's mind. . . . And that reason is, that better than any other, or as well as any other position or business in the whole subordination of life, his profession enables him to *serve the State.* . . .

[I]nstead of diffusing myself in a display of all the modes by which the profession of the law may claim to serve the State, I shall consider but a single one, and that is its agency as an element of conservation.

And is not the profession such an element of conservation? Is not this its characteristical office and its appropriate praise? Is it not so that in its nature, in its functions, in the intellectual and practical habits which it forms, in the opinions to which it conducts, in all its tendencies and influences of speculation and action, it is and ought to be professionally and peculiarly such an element and such an agent—that it contributes, or ought to be held to contribute, more than all things else, or as much as anything else, to preserve our organic forms, our civil and social order, our public and private justice, our constitutions of government, even the Union itself? In these crises through which our liberty is to pass, may not, must not, this function of conservatism become more and

---

[1] From Samuel Gilman Brown, ed., *The Works of Rufus Choate* (two volumes, Boston: Little, Brown and Company, 1862), vol. 1, pp. 414–38. Minor changes have been made in the punctuation to bring it into line with modern usage.

more developed, and more and more operative? May it not one day be written, for the praise of the American Bar, that it helped to keep the true idea of the State alive and germinant in the American mind; that it helped to keep alive the sacred sentiments of obedience and reverence and justice, of the supremacy of the calm and grand reason of the law over the fitful will of the individual and the crowd; that it helped to withstand the pernicious sophism that the successive generations, as they come to life, are but as so many successive flights of summer flies, without relations to the past or duties to the future, and taught instead that all—all the dead, the living, the unborn—were one moral person—one for action, one for suffering, one for responsibility—that the engagements of one age may bind the conscience of another; the glory or the shame of a day may brighten or stain the current of a thousand years of continuous national being? Consider the profession of the law, then, as an element of conservation in the American State. I think it is naturally such, so to speak; but I am sure it is our duty to make and to keep it such.

It may be said, I think with some truth, of the profession of the Bar, that in all political systems and in all times it has seemed to possess a twofold nature; that it has seemed to be fired by the spirit of liberty, and yet to hold fast the sentiments of order and reverence, and the duty of subordination; that it has resisted despotism and yet taught obedience; that it has recognized and vindicated the rights of man, and yet has reckoned it always among the most sacred and most precious of those rights, to be shielded and led by the divine nature and immortal reason of law; that it appreciates social progression and contributes to it, and ranks in the classes and with the agents of progression, yet evermore counsels and courts permanence and conservatism and rest. . . .

I think I may take for granted that conservatism is, in the actual circumstances of this country, the one grand and comprehensive duty of a thoughtful patriotism. I speak in the general, of course, not pausing upon little or inevitable qualifications here and there—not meaning anything so absurd as to say that this law, or that usage, or that judgment, or that custom or condition, might not be corrected or expunged—not meaning still less to invade the domains of moral and philanthropic reform, true or false. I speak of our general political system; our organic forms; our written constitutions; the great body and the general administration of our jurisprudence; the general way in which liberty is blended with order, and the principle of progression with the securities of permanence; the relation of the States and the functions of the Union—and I say of it in a mass, that conservation is the chief end, the largest duty, and the truest glory of American statesmanship.

There are nations, I make no question, whose history, condition, and dangers, call them to a different work. There are those whom everything in their history, condition, and dangers admonishes to reform fundamentally, if they would be saved. With them the whole political and social order is to be rearranged. The stern claim of labor is to be provided for. Its long antagonism with capital is to be reconciled. Property is all to be parcelled out in some nearer conformity to a parental law of nature. Conventional discriminations of precedence and right are to be swept away. Old forms from which the life is gone are to drop as leaves in autumn. Frowning towers nodding to their fall are to be taken down. Small freeholds must dot over and cut up imperial parks. A large infusion of liberty must be poured along these emptied veins and throb in that great heart. With those, the past must be resigned; the present must be convulsed, that "an immeasurable future," as Carlyle has said, "may be filled with fruitfulness and a verdant shade."

But with us the age of this mode and this degree of reform is over; its work is done. The passage of the sea, the occupation and culture of a new world, the conquest of independence—these were our eras, these our agency, of reform. In our jurisprudence of liberty, which guards our person from violence and our goods from plunder, and which forbids the whole power of the State itself to take the ewe lamb, or to trample on a blade of the grass of the humblest citizen without adequate remuneration; which makes every dwelling large enough to shelter a human life its owner's castle which winds and rain may enter but which the government cannot—in our written constitutions, whereby the people, exercising an act of sublime self-restraint, have intended to put it out of their own power forever, to be passionate, tumultuous, unwise, unjust; whereby they have intended, by means of a system of representation; by means of the distribution of government into departments, independent, coordinate for checks and balances; by a double chamber of legislation; by the establishment of a fundamental and paramount organic law; by the organization of a judiciary whose function, whose loftiest function it is to test the legislation of the day by this standard for all time—constitutions, whereby by all these means they have intended to secure a government of laws, not of men; of reason, not of will . . . these are they in which the fruits of our age and our agency of reform are embodied; and these are they by which, if we are wise,—if we understand the things that belong to our peace—they may be perpetuated. It is for this that I say the fields of reform, the aims of reform, the uses of reform here, therefore, are wholly unlike the fields, uses, and aims of reform elsewhere. Foreign examples, foreign counsel—well or ill meant—the advice of the first foreign understandings, the example of the wisest foreign nations, are worse than useless for us. Even the teachings of history are to be cautiously consulted, or the guide of human life will lead us astray. We need reform enough, Heaven knows; but it is the reformation of our individual selves, the bettering of our personal natures; it is a more intellectual industry; it is a more diffused, profound and graceful, popular, and higher culture; it is a wider development of the love and discernment of the beautiful in form, in color, in speech, and in the soul of man,—this is what we need,—personal, moral, mental reform—not civil—not political! No, no! Government, substantially as it is; jurisprudence, substantially as it is; the general arrangements of liberty, substantially as they are; the Constitution and the Union, exactly as they are,—this is to be wise, according to the wisdom of America.

To the conservation, then, of this general order of things, I think the profession of the Bar may be said to be assigned, for this reason, among others—the only one which I shall seek to develop—that its studies and employments tend to form in it and fit it to diffuse and impress on the popular mind a class of opinions—one class of opinions—which are indispensable to conservation. Its studies and offices train and arm it to counteract exactly that specific system of opinions by which our liberty must die, and to diffuse and impress those by which it may be kept alive. . . .

[W]hat are these sentiments and opinions from which the public mind of America is in danger, and which the studies and offices of our profession have fitted us and impose on us the duty to encounter and correct?

In the first place, it has been supposed that there might be detected, not yet in the general mind, but in what may grow to be the general mind, a singularly inadequate idea of the State as an unchangeable, indestructible, and, speaking after the manner of men, an immortal thing. I do not refer at this moment exclusively to the temper in which the Federal Union is regarded, though that is a startling illustration of the more general and deeper sentiment, but I refer to a larger view to what some have thought the popular or common idea of the civil State itself, its sacredness, its permanence, its ends—in the lofty phrase of Cicero, its eternity. The tendency appears to be, to regard the whole concern as an association altogether at will, and at the will of everybody. Its boundary lines, its constituent numbers, its physical, social, and constitutional identity, its polity, its law, its continuance for ages, its dissolution—all these seem to be held in the nature of so many open questions[2]. . . .

---

[2] In 1832–33 the country had been wracked by the issue of whether individual states could "nullify" federal laws, on the grounds that the union was a compact of individual states which retained sovereign rights. Since then, sectional tensions had increased with the

Having learned from Rousseau and Locke, and our own revolutionary age, its theories and its acts, that the State is nothing but a contract, rests in contract, springs from contract; that government is a contrivance of human wisdom for human wants; that the civil life, like the Sabbath, is made for man, not man for either; having only about seventy years ago laid hold of an arbitrary fragment of the British empire, and appropriated it to ourselves, which is all the country we ever had; having gone on enlarging, doubling, trebling, changing all this since, as a garment or a house; accustomed to encounter every day, at the polls, in the market, at the miscellaneous banquet of our Liberty everywhere, crowds of persons whom we never saw before, strangers in the country, yet just as good citizens as ourselves; with a whole continent before us, or half a one, to choose a home in; teased and made peevish by all manner of small, local jealousies; tormented by the stimulations of a revolutionary philanthropy;[3] enterprising, speculative, itinerant improving, "studious of change, and pleased with novelty" beyond the general habit of desultory man—it might almost seem to be growing to be our national humor to hold ourselves free at every instant, to be and do just what we please, go where we please, stay as long as we please and no longer; and that the State itself were held to be no more than an encampment of tents on the great prairie, pitched at sun-down, and struck to the sharp crack of the rifle next morning,[4] instead of a structure, stately and eternal, in which the generations may come, one after another, to the great gift of this social life.

On such sentiments as these, how can a towering and durable fabric be set up? To use the metaphor of Bacon, on such soil how can "greatness be shown"? How unlike the lessons of the masters, at whose feet you are bred! The studies of our profession have taught us that the State is framed for a duration without end—without end—till the earth and the heavens be no more. *Sic constituta civitas ut eterna!*[5] In the eye and contemplation of law, its masses may die; its own corporate being can never die. If we inspect the language of its fundamental ordinance, every word expects, assumes, foretells a perpetuity, lasting as "the great globe itself, and all which it inherit." If we go out of that record and inquire for the designs and the hopes of its founders *ab extra*, we know that they

---

rise of abolitionism in the North and the beginnings of secessionist sentiments in the southern slave states. There were also disputes over whether to annex the territories of Texas and Oregon: Whigs such as Choate tended to oppose annexation and the mentality of frontier lawlessness which they thought it promoted.

[3] A reference to abolitionism, which Choate regarded as a threat to national unity.

[4] A critical reference to the frontier mentality.

[5] "Thus may the constitution of the city be eternal."

constructed it, and bequeathed it, for the latest posterity. If we reverently rise to a conjecture of the purposes for which the Ruler of the world permitted and decreed it to be instituted, in order to discern how soon it will have performed its office and may be laid aside, we see that they reach down to the last hour of the life of the last man that shall live upon the earth; that it was designed by the Infinite Wisdom to enable the generation who framed it, and all the generations, to perfect their social, moral, and religious nature; to do and to be good; to pursue happiness; to be fitted, by the various discipline of the social life, by obedience, by worship, for the life to come. . . .

In the next place, it has been thought that there was developing itself in the general sentiment, and in the practical politics of the time, a tendency towards one of those great changes by which free States have oftenest perished,—a tendency to push to excess the distinctive and characteristic principles of our system whereby, as Aristotle has said, governments usually perish—a tendency towards transition from the republican to the democratical era, of the history and epochs of liberty.

Essentially and generally, it would be pronounced by those who discern it, a tendency to erect the actual majority of the day into the *de jure* and actual government of the day. It is a tendency to regard the actual will of that majority as the law of the State. It is a tendency to regard the shortest and simplest way of collecting that will, and the promptest and most irresistible execution of it, as the true polity of liberty. It is a tendency which, pressed to its last development, would, if considerations of mere convenience or inconvenience did not hinder, do exactly this: it would assemble the whole people in a vast mass, as once they used to assemble beneath the sun of Athens; and there, when the eloquent had spoken, and the wise and the foolish had counselled, would commit the transcendent questions of war, peace, taxation, and treaties; the disposition of the fortunes and honor of the citizen and statesman; death, banishment, or the crown of gold; the making, interpreting, and administration of the law; and all the warm, precious, and multifarious interests of the social life, to the madness or the jest of the hour.

I have not time to present what have been thought to be the proofs of the existence of this tendency; and it is needless to do so. It would be presumptuous, too, to speculate, if it has existence, on its causes and its issues. I desire to advert to certain particulars in which it may be analyzed, and through which it displays itself, for the purpose of showing that the studies, employments, and, so to say, professional politics, of the bar are essentially, perhaps availably, antagonistical to it, or moderative of it.

It is said, then, that you may remark this tendency, first, in an inclination to depreciate the uses and usurp the functions of those organic forms[6] in which the regular, definite, and legally recognized powers of the State are embodied—to depreciate the uses and usurp the function of written constitutions, limitations on the legislature, the distribution of government into departments, the independence of the judiciary, the forms of orderly proceeding, and all the elaborate and costly apparatus of checks and balances, by which, as I have said, we seek to secure a government of laws and not of men. . . .

These "organic forms" of our system—are they not in some just sense committed to your professional charge and care? In this sense, and to this extent, does not your profession approach to, and blend itself with, one, and that not the least in dignity and usefulness, of the departments of statesmanship? Are you not thus statesmen while you are lawyers, and because you are lawyers? These constitutions of government by which a free people have had the virtue and the sense to restrain themselves— these devices of profound wisdom and a deep study of man, and of the past, by which they have meant to secure the ascendency of the just, lofty, and wise, over the fraudulent, low, and insane, in the long run of our practical ties—these temperaments by which justice is promoted, and by which liberty is made possible and may be made immortal—and this *jus publicum*, this great written code of public law—are they not a part, in the strictest and narrowest sense, of the appropriate science of your profession? More than for any other class or calling in the community, is it not for you to study their sense, comprehend their great uses, and explore their historical origin and illustrations—to so hold them up as shields, that no act of legislature, no judgment of court, no executive proclamation, no order of any functionary of any description, shall transcend or misconceive them—to so hold them up before your clients and the public, as to keep them at all times living, intelligible, and appreciated in the universal mind?

Something such has, in all the past periods of our history, been one of the functions of the American Bar. To vindicate the true interpretation of the charters of the colonies, to advise what forms of polity, what systems of jurisprudence, what degree and what mode of liberty these charters permitted—to detect and expose that long succession of infringement which grew at last to the Stamp Act and Tea Tax, and compelled us to turn from broken charters to national independence—to conduct the transcendent controversy which preceded the Revolution, that grand appeal to the reason of civilization—this was the work of our first generation of lawyers. To construct the American constitutions—the higher praise of the second generation. I claim it in part for the sobriety

---

[6] The use of the term "organic forms" tends to assimilate the mechanisms prescribed by the Constitution to nature itself.

and learning of the American Bar; for the professional instinct towards the past; for the professional appreciation of order, forms, obedience, restraints; for the more than professional, the profound and wide intimacy with the history of all liberty, classical, mediaeval, and above all, of English liberty—I claim it in part for the American Bar that, springing into existence by revolution—revolution, which more than anything and all things lacerates and discomposes the popular mind—justifying that revolution only on a strong principle of natural right, with not one single element or agent of monarchy or aristocracy on our soil or in our blood—I claim it for the Bar that the constitutions of America so nobly closed the series of our victories! These constitutions owe to the Bar more than their terse and exact expression and systematic arrangements; they owe to it, in part, too, their elements of permanence; their felicitous reconciliation of universal and intense liberty with forms to enshrine and regulations to restrain it; their Anglo-Saxon sobriety and gravity conveyed in the genuine idiom, suggestive of the grandest civil achievements of that unequalled race. To interpret these constitutions, to administer and maintain them, this is the office of our age of the profession. Herein have we somewhat wherein to glory; hereby we come into the class and share in the dignity of founders of States, of restorers of States, of preservers of States. . . .

It is one of the distemperatures to which an unreasoning liberty may grow, no doubt, to regard *law* as no more nor less than just the will—the actual and present will—of the actual majority of the nation. The majority govern. What the majority pleases, it may ordain. What it ordains is law. So much for the source of law, and so much for the nature of law. But, then as law is nothing but the will of a major number, as that will differs from the will of yesterday, and will differ from that of tomorrow, and as all law is a restraint on natural right and personal independence, how can it gain a moment's hold on the reverential sentiments of the heart, and the profounder convictions of the judgment? How can it impress a filial awe; how can it conciliate a filial love; how can it sustain a sentiment of veneration; how can it command a rational and animated defense? Such sentiments are not the stuff from which the immortality of a nation is to be woven! Oppose now to this, the loftier philosophy which we have learned. In the language of our system, the law is not the transient and arbitrary creation of the major will, nor of any will. It is not the offspring of will at all. It is the absolute justice of the State, enlightened by the perfect reason of the State. That is law. Enlightened justice assisting the social nature to perfect itself by the social life. It is ordained, doubtless, that is, it is chosen, and is ascertained by the wisdom of man. But, then, it is the master-work of man. *Quoe est enim istorum oratio tam exquista, quoe sit anteponenda bene constitutoe civitati publico jure, et moribus?*[7]

By the costly and elaborate contrivances of our constitutions we have sought to attain the transcendent result of extracting and excluding haste, injustice, revenge, and folly from the place and function of giving the law, and of introducing alone the reason and justice of the wisest and the best. By the aid of time,—time which changes and tries all things; tries them, and works them pure,—we subject the law, after it is given, to the tests of old experience, to the reason and justice of successive ages and generations, to the best thoughts of the wisest and safest of reformers. And then and thus we pronounce it good. Then and thus we cannot choose but reverence, obey, and enforce it. We would grave it deep into the heart of the undying State. We would strengthen it by opinion, by manners, by private virtue, by habit . . . All that attracts us to life, all that is charming in the perfected and adorned social nature, we wisely think or we wisely dream we owe to the all-circling presence of the law. Not even extravagant do we think it to hold, that the Divine approval may sanction it as not unworthy of the reason which we derive from His own nature. Not extravagant do we hold it to say, that there is thus a voice of the people which is the voice of God.[8]

Doubtless the known historical origin of the law contributes to this opinion of it. . . . [W]hat is that law? Mainly, a body of digested rules and processes and forms, bequeathed by what is for us the old and past time, not of one age, but all the ages of the past—a vast and multifarious aggregate, some of which you trace above the pyramids, above the flood, the inspired wisdom of the primeval East; some to the scarcely yet historical era of Pythagoras, and to Solon and Socrates; more of it to the robust, practical sense and justice of Rome, the lawgiver of the nations; more still to the teeming birth time of the modern mind and life; all of it to some epoch; some of it to every epoch of the past of which history keeps the date. In the way in which it comes down to us, it seems one mighty and continuous stream of experience and reason, accumulated, ancestral, widening and deepening and washing itself clearer as it runs on, the grand agent of civilization, the builder of a thousand cities, the guardian angel of a hundred generations, our own hereditary laws.[9] To revere such a system, would be natural and professional, if it were no

---

[7] Cicero, *De re publica*, I., 2. "For what argument of your philosophers is so carefully wrought out that it should be preferred to a state firmly established under public law and custom?" (Sabine translation)

[8] Here a proverb usually read as an endorsement of popular sovereignty is interpreted to make "the voice of the people" equivalent to inherited law.

[9] Choate repeats a standard interpretation of the common law as age-old.

more. But it is reasonable, too. There is a deep presumption in favor of that which has endured so long.[10] To say of anything that it is old, and to leave the matter there—an opinion, a polity, a code, a possession, a book—is to say nothing of praise or blame. But to have lived for ages; to be alive today—in a real sense alive—alive in the hearts, in the reason of to-day; to have lived through ages, not swathed in gums and spices and enshrined in chambers of pyramids, but through ages of unceasing contact and sharp trial with the passions, interests, and affairs of the great world; to have lived through the drums and tramplings of conquests, through revolution, reform, through cycles of opinion running their round; to have lived under many diverse systems of policy, and have survived the many transmigrations from one to another; to have attended the general progress of the race, and shared in its successive ameliorations, thus to have gathered upon itself the approbation or the sentiments and reason of all civilization and all humanity,—that is, *per se*, a *prima-facie* title to intelligent regard. . . .[11]

It is certain that in the American theory, the free theory of government, it is the right of the people, at any moment of its representation in the legislature, to make all the law, and by its representatives in conventions, to make the Constitution anew. It is their right to do so peaceably and according to existing forms, and to do it by revolution against all forms. This is the theory. But I do not know that any wise man would desire to have this theory every day, or ever, acted upon up to its whole extent, or to have it eternally pressed, promulgated, panegyrized as the grand peculiarity and chief privilege of our condition.[12] Acting upon this theory, we have made our constitutions, founded our policy, written the great body of our law, set our whole government going. It worked well. It works to a charm. I do not know that any man displays wisdom or common sense, by all the while haranguing and stimulating the people to change it. I do not appreciate the sense or humanity of all the while bawling: true, your systems are all good; life, character, property, all safe,—but you have the undoubted right to rub all out and begin again. If I see a man quietly eating his dinner, I do not know why I should tell him that there is a first-rate, extreme medicine, prussic acid, aquafortis, or what not, which he has a perfectly good right to use in any quantity he pleases! If a man is living happily with his wife, I don't know why I should go and say: yes, I see; beautiful and virtuous; I congratulate you,—but let me say, you can get a perfectly legal divorce by going to Vermont, New Jersey, or Pennsylvania. True wisdom would seem to ad-

---

[10] A pithy statement of historical utilitarianism.

[11] Here the common law is portrayed as shaped by adaptation to historical experience.

[12] For a similar sentiment about the imprudence of a focus upon the right of revolution, see the conclusion of Hume's essay, "Of Passive Obedience" above.

vise the culture of dispositions of rest, contentment, conservation. True wisdom would advise to lock up the extreme medicine till the attack of the alarming malady. True wisdom would advise to place the power of revolution, overturning all to begin anew, rather in the background, to throw over it a politic, well-wrought veil,[13] to reserve it for crises, exigencies, the rare and distant days of great historical epochs. . . .

Is there not something in the study and administrative enjoyment of an elaborate, rational, and ancient jurisprudence, which tends to raise the law itself, in the professional and in the general idea, almost up to the nature of an independent, superior reason, in one sense out of the people, in one sense above them—out of and above, and independent of, and collateral to, the people of any given day? In all its vast volumes of provisions, very little of it is seen to be produced by the actual will of the existing generation. The first thing we know about it is, that we are actually being governed by it. The next thing we know is, we are rightfully and beneficially governed by it. We did not help to make it. No man now living helped to make much of it. The judge does not make it. Like the structure of the State itself, we found it around us at the earliest dawn of reason, it guarded the helplessness of our infancy, it restrained the passions of our youth, it protects the acquisitions of our manhood, it shields the sanctity of the grave, it executes the will of the departed. Invisible, omnipresent, a real yet impalpable existence, it seems more a spirit, an abstraction—the whispered yet authoritative voice of all the past and all the good—than like the transient contrivance of altogether such as ourselves. We come to think of it, not so much as a set of provisions and rules which we can unmake, amend, and annul, as of a guide whom it is wiser to follow, an authority whom it is better to obey, a wisdom which it is not unbecoming to revere, a power—a superior—whose service is perfect freedom. Thus at last the spirit of the law descends into the great heart of the people for healing and for conservation. . . .

In supposing that conservation is the grand and prominent public function of the American Bar in the State, I have not felt that I assigned to a profession, to which I count it so high a privilege to belong, a part and a duty at all beneath its loftiest claims. I shall not deny that to found a State which grows to be a nation, on the ruins of all older, or on a waste of earth where was none before, is, intrinsically and in the judgment of the world, of the largest order of human achievements. Of the chief of men are the *conditores imperiorum*.[14] But to keep the city is only

---

[13] The image comes from Burke's description of the manner in which the actors in the Glorious Revolution of 1688 disguised the departure from precedent that led to the replacement of the hereditary monarch by his daughter and son-in-law.

[14] Founders of an empire.

not less difficult and glorious than to build it. Both rise, in the estimate
of the most eloquent and most wise of Romans, to the rank of divine
achievement. I appreciate the uses and the glory of a great and timely
reform. Thrice happy and honored who leaves the Constitution better
than he found it. But to find it good and keep it so, this, too, is virtue
and praise. . . .

► 3 ◄

AUTHORITY

INTRODUCTION TO
Matthew Arnold,
Culture and Anarchy

◆

The following selections from three Victorian writers—Matthew Arnold (1822–88), James Fitzjames Stephen (1829–1898), and W. H. Mallock (1849–1923)—mark the transition to a new form of conservatism. All three recognized that the political dominance of the aristocracy and the cultural dominance of the established Church—the twin pillars of Burkean conservatism—were crumbling. Each invoked new social, political, and intellectual sources of authority, and new elites capable of wielding that authority. These three authors do not speak with one voice: in fact, they openly criticized one another. It was an attack by James Fitzjames Stephen on Arnold's conception of culture that led Arnold to deliver the lecture, "Culture and Its Enemies," that became the germ of *Culture and Anarchy*. And Mallock later satirized Arnold's religious views in his book, *The New Republic*, published in 1877. Yet despite their very real differences, all three authors stress the importance of new elites: intellectual, political, and economic.

Of these, Arnold insists most explicitly on the need for an articulate defense of authority when traditional habits of authority are crumbling. The very notion of authority was being undermined by the habits of mind associated with the politically ascendant middle classes, Arnold argued, whose minds were furnished with antigovernmental nostrums and with the mental reflexes inculcated by their faith as Dissenting Protestants. Arnold saw it as his task to keep alive the idea of truth and of the possibility of shared standards in the face of a propensity to dismiss the importance of either. Without culture, which included the rationale for defensible authority, Arnold feared that the new governing classes would lack the will to wield authority. The result, he warned, would be anarchy. *Culture and Anarchy*, then, argues that only a culture capable of articulating good reasons for authority and of punishing those who violate the law can avert a slide toward social anarchy.

Edmund Burke, to whom Arnold was intellectually indebted, had regarded the Church of England as the institution charged with transmitting the cultural past and as a cultural glue holding British society together. Arnold's father, Thomas, was a leading figure of the Broad Church current within the Church of England, which sought to retain the established Church while making it as inclusive as possible. He was also the headmaster of Rugby, a novel and remarkably influential educational institution intended to produce Christian gentlemen capable of ruling the country in a Christian spirit. Matthew Arnold continued his father's commitments, but in a more secularized fashion. Matthew looked to men of letters to supply the spiritual guidance and moral encouragement which the priesthood was no longer capable of conveying. He too sought to maintain the established Church; but having abandoned the miraculous content of traditional Christianity, he sought to reinterpret Christianity by emphasizing its moral and aesthetic rather than its theological content.

In many respects, Arnold was a political liberal as the term was understood in his day. He supported limited government, the extension of the franchise to the working classes, and the reform of the civil service to place it in the hands of educated professionals rather than aristocratic amateurs. If liberalism and the middle classes were the most frequent butts of his criticism, it was because he regarded them as the inevitable carriers of future progress. Yet he feared that the typical emphases and propensities of the liberalism of his day threatened to degrade the cultural life of the nation and perhaps undermine political order. He described himself at one point as "a liberal of the future," but he was a liberal who deeply admired Burke, and who sent his most famous work of social criticism, *Culture and Anarchy*, to the Tory leader, Benjamin Disraeli, who welcomed it warmly.[1]

Arnold recognized that the traditional politics of deference, dominated by the landed aristocracy and gentry, was passing, and that passing he did not lament. The expansion of the electorate and the elimination of many abuses of electoral districting in 1832 had enfranchised much of the middle classes, a process described by the Duke of Wellington as "a revolution by due course of law." In 1867, the Second Reform Bill extended the franchise from one million male voters to two million, bringing the vote to the upper ranks of the working classes. Although it was only a third wave of electoral reforms from 1883 to 1885 which ex-

---

[1] On Arnold's problematic political identity, see Stefan Collini, *Arnold* (New York, 1988), pp. 88–92.

tended the vote to most adult males and definitively sapped the political power of the landed elites, the writing was already on the wall when Arnold composed *Culture and Anarchy*.

The expansion of the franchise to include the upper ranges of the working classes was very much in the air as Arnold wrote. In 1865 the Reform League had been founded to extend the franchise to the working classes. In March 1866, the Liberal politician, Gladstone, introduced a bill to expand the franchise, but it met with staunch opposition from the more conservative members of his party. In July 1866, the Reform League held a mass meeting in Trafalgar Square demanding an extension of the vote. A second "monster meeting" was scheduled for the next night in Hyde Park, a park usually given over to strolls by the middle class. The government, fearful of disorder, banned the meeting in the park. Most of the crowd which had gathered at the park gates retreated to Trafalgar Square to hold their demonstration. But some rougher participants stayed behind, tore down the railings and swarmed into the park, trampling upon the flower-beds. Troops were called out to aid the police, but they took no action, and for the next several days thousands of people milled about the park. Despite the rather minor property damage, this train of events and the specter of mob violence which it evoked led to a fear of anarchy among propertied Victorians and among contemporary intellectuals. The Hyde Park incident weighed on Arnold's mind as he published a series of essays in 1867 and 1868, which he revised and collected into a book published in 1869.

To Arnold, the events in Hyde Park reflected "the deep-seated spiritual anarchy of the English people." The deference traditionally paid to the aristocracy and gentry was fading. "As feudalism, with its ideas and habits of subordination dies out," he wrote, "we are in danger of drifting toward anarchy." Arnold argued that the freedom so valued by liberals, the freedom to be left alone by government to do as one likes (what Americans mean when they respond to criticism with the dictum, "It's a free country"), had become an end in itself and a barrier to thinking about the need for shared authority. He warned that without the development of a sense of shared authority, embodied in a state which was more than the tool of a particular class, the Hyde Park riots might be a harbinger of greater social disorder. Arnold looked to an intellectual elite, a new clerisy, to articulate the basis of that shared authority.

It was as a poet that Matthew Arnold first made his name, and he wrote *Culture and Anarchy* while a visiting professor of poetry at Oxford. But it was as Inspector of Schools that he earned his bread, and the experience deepened his worries about the unfitness of the middle classes to govern. Since educational institutions run by the established Church were not under his jurisdiction, Arnold's post took him primarily to schools run by those Protestant groups which had rejected membership in the Church of England, known as "Nonconformists" or "Dissenters." They formed a leading constituency of middle-class liberalism, and it was from their ranks that major liberal leaders such as John Bright sprang. It was from his immersion in these strongholds of the lower middle class that Arnold's critique of middle-class culture and politics evolved.

The habits of mind of those who prided themselves on their dissent from the established Church, Arnold argued, left the middle class ill equipped to become the establishment itself. The emphasis on individual freedom, together with the reflexes of dissent, had resulted in a principled antipathy to authority—not only the authority of institutions, but the authority of "right reason," the belief that there are good reasons for living one way rather than another. One function of cultural criticism, for Arnold, was to offer such reasons. "Culture," as Arnold defined it, was "the pursuit of our total perfection by means of getting to know, on all matters which most concern us, the best which has been thought and said in the world; and through this knowledge, turning a stream of fresh and free thought upon our stock notions and habits." Culture, then, depends on acquaintance with the great works of the past in order to gain some critical perspective upon the present. For Arnold, the task of culture and of its bearers was not only to "criticize authority"—it was to reinforce or re-create authority by presenting good reasons for institutions and practices.

It is such a critical perspective on his contemporaries that Arnold provides in *Culture and Anarchy*, employing irony and humor as his tools. Part of his method was to choose particular individuals and events which are treated as characteristic of the larger phenomena he wishes to criticize. Though most of these individuals and events were well known to Arnold's audience, they will be foreign to most contemporary readers and are therefore identified in the notes. Once the reader overcomes this initial unfamiliarity, it becomes clear that Arnold's criticisms reach beyond his immediate targets.

The text is drawn from the J. Dover Wilson edition of *Culture and Anarchy: An Essay in Political and Social Criticism*,[2] which is based upon the first edition of 1869, but incorporates some changes of phrase from the second edition of 1875. Profitable use has been made of the notes appended by Wilson, as well as those of R. H. Super to his edition of *Culture and Anarchy* in volume five of *The Complete Prose Works of Matthew Arnold*.[3]

[2] Cambridge, 1935.
[3] Ann Arbor, 1965.

Matthew Arnold,
Culture and Anarchy (1869)[1]

[FROM CHAPTER 1: "SWEETNESS AND LIGHT"]

[Culture] is a study of perfection, and of harmonious perfection, general perfection, and perfection which consists in becoming something rather than in having something, in an inward condition of the mind and spirit, not in an outward set of circumstances,—it is clear that culture, instead of being the frivolous and useless thing which Mr. Bright,[2] and Mr. Frederic Harrison,[3] and many other Liberals are apt to call it, has a very important function to fulfil for mankind. And this function is particularly important in our modern world, of which the whole civilisation is, to a much greater degree than the civilisation of Greece and Rome, mechanical and external, and tends constantly to become more so. But above all in our own country has culture a weighty part to perform, because here that mechanical character, which civilisation tends to take everywhere, is shown in the most eminent degree. Indeed nearly all the characters of perfection, as culture teaches us to fix them, meet in this country with some powerful tendency which thwarts them and sets them at defiance. The idea of perfection as an *inward* condition of the mind and spirit is at variance with the mechanical and material civilisation in esteem with us, and nowhere, as I have said, so much in esteem as with us. The idea of perfection as a *general* expansion of the human family is at variance with our strong individualism, our hatred of all limits to the unrestrained swing of the individual's personality, our maxim of "every man for himself." Above all, the idea of perfection as a *harmonious* expansion of human nature is at variance with our want of flexibility, with our inaptitude for seeing more than one side of a thing, with our intense energetic absorption in the particular pursuit we happen to be following. So culture has a rough task to achieve in this country. Its preachers have, and are likely long to have, a hard time of it, and they will much oftener be regarded, for a great while to come, as ele-

[1] From Matthew Arnold, *Culture and Anarchy*, ed. J. Dover Wilson (Cambridge, 1935).

[2] John Bright was an influential journalist and a leading Liberal politician of the radical persuasion, who campaigned vigorously on behalf of free trade, the expansion of the franchise, electoral reform, and the disestablishment of the Church of England. During parliamentary debates on reforming the franchise, he had dismissed the pretensions of men of culture to greater political wisdom.

[3] Harrison was a Positivist (a follower of August Comte, who believed that religion and philosophy would be replaced by a science of society modeled on the natural sciences) and political radical who advocated the extension of the franchise to the working classes. He had criticized Arnold's conception of culture in an article of 1867.

gant or spurious Jeremiahs, than as friends and benefactors. That, however, will not prevent their doing in the end good service if they persevere. And meanwhile, the mode of action they have to pursue, and the sort of habits they must fight against, ought to be made quite clear for every one to see who may be willing to look at the matter attentively and dispassionately.

Faith in machinery is, I said, our besetting danger;[4] often in machinery most absurdly disproportioned to the end which this machinery, if it is to do any good at all, is to serve; but always in machinery, as if it had a value in and for itself. What is freedom but machinery? what is population but machinery? what is coal but machinery? what are railroads but machinery? what is wealth but machinery? what are, even, religious organisations but machinery? Now almost every voice in England is accustomed to speak of these things as if they were precious ends in themselves, and therefore had some of the characters of perfection indisputably joined to them. I have before now noticed Mr. Roebuck's[5] stock argument for proving the greatness and happiness of England as she is, and for quite stopping the mouths of all gainsayers. Mr. Roebuck is never weary of reiterating this argument of his, so I do not know why I should be weary of noticing it. "May not every man in England say what he likes?"—Mr. Roebuck perpetually asks; and that, he thinks, is quite sufficient, and when every man may say what he likes, our aspirations ought to be satisfied. But the aspirations of culture, which is the study of perfection, are not satisfied, unless what men say, when they may say what they like, is worth saying,—has good in it, and more good than bad. In the same way the *Times*, replying to some foreign strictures on the dress, looks, and behaviour of the English abroad, urges that the English ideal is that every one should be free to do and to look just as he likes. But culture indefatigably tries, not to make what each raw person may like, the rule by which he fashions himself; but to draw ever nearer to a sense of what is indeed beautiful, graceful, and becoming, and to get the raw person to like that. . . .

[FROM CHAPTER 2: "DOING AS ONE LIKES"]

I have been trying to show that culture is, or ought to be, the study and pursuit of perfection. . . . To complete rightly my design, it evidently remains to speak also of intelligence, or light, as a character of perfection. . . .

---

[4] As the context makes clear, by "machinery" Arnold intends techniques or means, as opposed to substantive ends or purposes.

[5] A Liberal Member of Parliament, and a disciple of the Utilitarian school of Jeremy Bentham.

When I began to speak of culture, I insisted on our bondage to machinery, on our proneness to value machinery as an end in itself, without looking beyond it to the end for which alone, in truth, it is valuable. Freedom, I said, was one of those things which we thus worshipped in itself, without enough regarding the ends for which freedom is to be desired. In our common notions and talk about freedom, we eminently show our idolatry of machinery. Our prevalent notion is, and I quoted a number of instances to prove it, that it is a most happy and important thing for a man merely to be able to do as he likes. On what he is to do when he is thus free to do as he likes, we do not lay so much stress.[6] Our familiar praise of the British Constitution under which we live, is that it is a system of checks,—a system which stops and paralyses any power in interfering with the free action of individuals. To this effect Mr. Bright, who loves to walk in the old ways of the Constitution, said forcibly in one of his great speeches, what many other people are every day saying less forcibly, that the central idea of English life and politics is *the assertion of personal liberty*. Evidently this is so; but evidently, also, as feudalism, which with its ideas and habits of subordination was for many centuries silently behind the British Constitution, dies out, and we are left with nothing but our system of checks, and our notion of its being the great right and happiness of an Englishman to do as far as possible what he likes, we are in danger of drifting towards anarchy.[7] We have not the notion, so familiar on the Continent and to antiquity, of *the State*—the nation in its collective and corporate character, entrusted with stringent powers for the general advantage, and controlling individual wills in the name of an interest wider than that of individuals.[8] We say, what is very true, that this notion is often made instrumental to tyranny; we say that a State is in reality made up of the individuals who compose it, and that every individual is the best judge of his own interests. Our leading class is all aristocracy, and no aristocracy likes the notion of a State-authority greater than itself, with a stringent administrative machinery supersed-ing the decorative inutilities of lord-lieutenancy, deputy-lieutenancy, and the *posse comitatûs*, which are all in its own hands.[9] Our middle

[6] Here Arnold echoes Burke's dictum in *Reflections on the Revolution in France*: "The effect of liberty to individuals is, that they may do what they please: We ought to see what it will please them to do, before we risk congratulations, which may be soon turned into complaints."

[7] In *Reflections on the Revolution in France*, Burke had noted the danger posed by the decline of feudal manners. Arnold now echoes the theme that the successful functioning of a liberal, capitalist society depends on nonliberal institutions and practices, but, because of changes since Burke's day, Arnold no longer believes that the traditional institutions of aristocracy and established Church are up to the task.

[8] Arnold's definition of the state is drawn from Burke. Arnold too regards it as among the most important institutions for restraining individuals.

[9] In Arnold's day, justices of the peace were drawn largely from the local, landowning

class, the great representative of trade and Dissent, with its maxims of every man for himself in business, every man for himself in religion, dreads a powerful administration which might somehow interfere with it; and besides, it has its own decorative inutilities of vestrymanship and guardianship, which are to this class what lord-lieutenancy and the county magistracy are to the aristocratic class, and a stringent administration might either take these functions out of its hands, or prevent its exercising them in its own comfortable, independent manner, as at present.

Then as to our working class. This class, pressed constantly by the hard daily compulsion of material wants, is naturally the very centre and stronghold of our national idea, that it is man's ideal right and felicity to do as he likes. I think I have somewhere related how M. Michelet[10] said to me of the people of France, that it was "a nation of barbarians civilised by the conscription." He meant that through their military service the idea of public duty and of discipline was brought to the mind of these masses, in other respects so raw and uncultivated. Our masses are quite as raw and uncultivated as the French; and so far from their having the idea of public duty and of discipline, superior to the individual's self-will, brought to their mind by a universal obligation of military service, such as that of the conscription, so far from their having this, the very idea of a conscription is so at variance with our English notion of the prime right and blessedness of doing as one likes, that I remember the manager of the Clay Cross works in Derbyshire told me during the Crimean War, when our want of soldiers was much felt and some people were talking of a conscription, that sooner than submit to a conscription the population of that district would flee to the mines, and lead a sort of Robin Hood life under ground.

For a long time, as I have said, the strong feudal habits of subordination and deference continued to tell upon the working class. The modern spirit has now almost entirely dissolved those habits, and the anarchical tendency of our worship of freedom in and for itself, of our superstitious faith, as I say, in machinery, is becoming very manifest. More and more, because of this our blind faith in machinery, because of our want of light to enable us to look beyond machinery to the end for which machinery is valuable, this and that man, and this and that body of men, all over the country, are beginning to assert and put in practice an Englishman's right to do what he likes; his right to march where he

gentry; they were appointed by the lord chancellor on the recommendation of the lord-lieutenant. Arnold is referring to the opposition of the aristocracy to the replacement of a government made up of amateurs drawn from the ranks of landed and titled elites by an effective and professional civil service.

[10] Jules Michelet, the greatest French historian of his age.

likes, meet where he likes, enter where he likes, hoot as he likes, threaten as he likes, smash as he likes.[11] All this, I say, tends to anarchy; and though a number of excellent people, and particularly my friends of the Liberal or progressive party, as they call themselves, are kind enough to reassure us by saying that these are trifles, that a few transient outbreaks of rowdyism signify nothing, that our system of liberty is one which itself cures all the evils which it works, that the educated and intelligent classes stand in overwhelming strength and majestic repose, ready, like our military force in riots, to act at a moment's notice, yet one finds that one's Liberal friends generally say this because they have such faith in themselves and their nostrums, when they shall return, as the public welfare requires, to place and power. But this faith of theirs one cannot exactly share, when one has so long had them and their nostrums at work, and sees that they have not prevented our coming to our present embarrassed condition. And one finds, also, that the outbreaks of rowdyism tend to become less and less of trifles, to become more frequent rather than less frequent; and that meanwhile our educated and intelligent classes remain in their majestic repose, and somehow or other, whatever happens, their overwhelming strength, like our military force in riots, never does act.

How, indeed, *should* their overwhelming strength act, when the man who gives an inflammatory lecture, or breaks down the park railings, or invades a Secretary of State's office, is only following an Englishman's impulse to do as he likes; and our own conscience tells us that we ourselves have always regarded this impulse as something primary and sacred? Mr. Murphy lectures at Birmingham, and showers on the Catholic population of that town "words," says the Home Secretary, Mr. Hardy, "only fit to be addressed to thieves or murderers."[12] What then? Mr. Murphy has his own reasons of several kinds. He suspects the Roman Catholic Church of designs upon Mrs. Murphy; and he says, if mayors and magistrates do not care for their wives and daughters, he does. But, above all, he is doing as he likes; or, in worthier language, asserting his personal liberty. "I will carry out my lectures if they walk over my body as a dead corpse; and I say to the Mayor of Birmingham that he is my servant while I am in Birmingham, and as my servant he must do his duty and protect me." Touching and beautiful words, which

[11] An allusion to the recent Hyde Park riots.

[12] William Murphy was a Protestant firebrand who in 1867 gave a series of anti-Catholic lectures in Birmingham. He attacked the existence of nunneries, and warned of the danger to women of the Catholic confessional, a frequent theme of Protestant anti-Catholic polemics. His inflammatory speeches often led to rioting and bloodshed. Arnold uses Murphy's speeches as an example of the type of irrational and socially destructive activity which ought to be restricted by the state but remains permitted because of an unwillingness to assert authority.

find a sympathetic chord in every British bosom! The moment it is plainly put before us that a man is asserting his personal liberty, we are half disarmed; because we are believers in freedom, and not in some dream of a right reason to which the assertion of our freedom is to be subordinated. Accordingly, the Secretary of State had to say that although the lecturer's language was "only fit to be addressed to thieves or murderers," yet, "I do not think he is to be deprived, I do not think that anything I have said could justify the inference that he is to be deprived, of the right of protection in a place built by him for the purpose of these lectures; because the language was not language which afforded grounds for a criminal prosecution." No, nor to be silenced by Mayor, or Home Secretary, or any administrative authority on earth, simply on their notion of what is discreet and reasonable! This is in perfect consonance with our public opinion, and with our national love for the assertion of personal liberty. . . .

Having, I say, at the bottom of our English hearts a very strong belief in freedom, and a very weak belief in right reason, we are soon silenced when a man pleads the prime right to do as he likes, because this is the prime right for ourselves too; and even if we attempt now and then to mumble something about reason, yet we have ourselves thought so little about this and so much about liberty, that we are in conscience forced, when our brother Philistine[13] with whom we are meddling turns boldly round upon us and asks: *Have you any light?*—to shake our heads ruefully, and to let him go his own way after all. . . .

[The Hyde Park rioter] has no visionary schemes of revolution and transformation, though of course he would like his class to rule, as the aristocratic class like their class to rule, and the middle class theirs. But meanwhile our social machine is a little out of order; there are a good many people in our paradisiacal centres of industrialism and individualism taking the bread out of one another's mouths. The rough has not yet quite found his groove and settled down to his work, and so he is just asserting his personal liberty a little, going where he likes, assembling where he likes, bawling as he likes, hustling as he likes. Just as the rest of us,—as the country squires in the aristocratic class, as the political dissenters in the middle class,—he has no idea of a State, of the nation in its collective and corporate character controlling, as government, the free swing of this or that one of its members in the name of the higher reason of all of them, his own as well as that of others. He sees the rich, the aristocratic class, in occupation of the executive government, and so

---

[13] Arnold used this term (which he adopted from the German poet and social critic Heinrich Heine) to refer to members of the middle class. It was meant to invoke their antipathy to spiritual matters.

if he is stopped from making Hyde Park a bear-garden or the streets impassable, he says he is being butchered by the aristocracy.

His apparition is somewhat embarrassing, because too many cooks spoil the broth; because, while the aristocratic and middle classes have long been doing as they like with great vigour, he has been too undeveloped and submissive hitherto to join in the game; and now, when he does come, he comes in immense numbers, and is rather raw and rough. But he does not break many laws, or not many at one time; and, as our laws were made for very different circumstances from our present (but always with an eye to Englishmen doing as they like), and as the clear letter of the law must be against our Englishman who does as he likes and not only the spirit of the law and public policy, and as Government must neither have any discretionary power nor act resolutely on its own interpretation of the law if any one disputes it, it is evident our laws give our playful giant, in doing as he likes, considerable advantage. Besides, even if he can be clearly proved to commit an illegality in doing as he likes, there is always the resource of not putting the law in force, or of abolishing it. So he has his way, and if he has his way he is soon satisfied for the time. However, he falls into the habit of taking it oftener and oftener, and at last begins to create by his operations a confusion of which mischievous people can take advantage, and which at any rate, by troubling the common course of business throughout the country, tends to cause distress, and so to increase the sort of anarchy and social disintegration which had previously commenced. And thus that profound sense of settled order and security, without which a society like ours cannot live and grow at all, sometimes seems to be beginning to threaten us with taking its departure.

Now, if culture, which simply means trying to perfect oneself, and one's mind as part of oneself, brings us light, and if light shows us that there is nothing so very blessed in merely doing as one likes, that the worship of the mere freedom to do as one likes is worship of machinery, that the really blessed thing is to like what right reason ordains, and to follow her authority, then we have got a practical benefit out of culture. We have got a much wanted principle, a principle of authority, to counteract the tendency to anarchy which seems to be threatening us.

But how to organise this authority, or to what hands to entrust the wielding of it? How to get your *State*, summing up the right reason of the community, and giving effect to it, as circumstances may require, with vigour? And here I think I see my enemies waiting for me with a hungry joy in their eyes. But I shall elude them.

The *State*, the power most representing the right reason of the nation, and most worthy, therefore, of ruling,—of exercising, when circumstances require it, authority over us all,—is for Mr. Carlyle[14] the aristocracy. For Mr. Lowe,[15] it is the middle class with its incomparable Parliament. For the Reform League, it is the working class, the class with "the brightest powers of sympathy and readiest powers of action." Now, culture, with its disinterested pursuit of perfection, culture, simply trying to see things as they are, in order to seize on the best and to make it prevail, is surely well fitted to help us to judge rightly, by all the aids of observing, reading, and thinking, the qualifications and titles to our confidence of these three candidates for authority, and can thus render us a practical service of no mean value.

So when Mr. Carlyle, a man of genius to whom we have all at one time or other been indebted for refreshment and stimulus, says we should give rule to the aristocracy, mainly because of its dignity and politeness, surely culture is useful in reminding us, that in our idea of perfection the characters of beauty and intelligence are both of them present, and sweetness and light, the two noblest of things, are united. Allowing, therefore, with Mr. Carlyle, the aristocratic class to possess sweetness, culture insists on the necessity of light also, and shows us that aristocracies, being by the very nature of things inaccessible to ideas, unapt to see how the world is going, must be somewhat wanting in light, and must therefore be, at a moment when light is our great requisite, inadequate to our needs. Aristocracies, those children of the established fact, are for epochs of concentration. In epochs of expansion, epochs such as that in which we now live, epochs when always the warning voice is again heard: *Now is the judgment of this world*—in such epochs aristocracies with their natural clinging to the established fact, their want of sense for the flux of things, for the inevitable transitoriness of all human institutions, are bewildered and helpless. Their serenity, their high spirit, their power of haughty resistance,—the great qualities of an aristocracy, and the secret of its distinguished manners and dignity, —these very qualities, in an epoch of expansion, turn against their possessors. Again and again I have said how the refinement of an aristocracy may be precious and educative to a raw nation as a kind of shadow of true refinement; how its serenity and dignified freedom from petty cares may serve as a useful foil to set off the vulgarity and hideousness of that type of life which a hard middle class tends to establish, and to help people to see this vulgarity and hideousness in their true colours. . . . But the true grace and serenity is that of which Greece and Greek art suggest the admirable ideals of perfection,—a serenity which comes from having made order among ideas and harmonised them; whereas

[14] Thomas Carlyle, perhaps the most noted man of letters of his day.

[15] Robert Lowe, a Liberal politician who was skeptical about the extension of the franchise to the working classes.

the serenity of aristocracies, at least the peculiar serenity of aristocracies of Teutonic origin, appears to come from their never having had any ideas to trouble them. And so, in a time of expansion like the present, a time for ideas, one gets, perhaps, in regarding an aristocracy, even more than the idea of serenity, the idea of futility and sterility.

One has often wondered whether upon the whole earth there is anything so unintelligent, so unapt to perceive how the world is really going, as an ordinary young Englishman of our upper class. Ideas he has not, and neither has he that seriousness of our middle class which is, as I have often said, the great strength of this class, and may become its salvation. Why, a man may hear a young Dives[16] of the aristocratic class, when the whim takes him to sing the praises of wealth and material comfort, sing them with a cynicism from which the conscience of the veriest Philistine of our industrial middle class would recoil in affright. And when, with the natural sympathy of aristocracies for firm dealing with the multitude, and his uneasiness at our feeble dealing with it at home, an unvarnished young Englishman of our aristocratic class applauds the absolute rulers on the Continent, he in general manages completely to miss the grounds of reason and intelligence which alone can give any colour of justification, any possibility of existence, to those rulers, and applauds them on grounds which it would make their own hair stand on end to listen to.

And all this time we are in an epoch of expansion; and the essence of an epoch of expansion is a movement of ideas, and the one salvation of an epoch of expansion is a harmony of ideas. The very principle of the authority which we are seeking as a defence against anarchy is right reason, ideas, light. The more, therefore, an aristocracy calls to its aid its innate forces,—its impenetrability, its high spirit, its power of haughty resistance,—to deal with an epoch of expansion, the graver is the danger, the greater the certainty of explosion, the surer the aristocracy's defeat; for it is trying to do violence to nature instead of working along with it. The best powers shown by the best men of an aristocracy at such an epoch are, it will be observed, nonaristocratical powers, powers of industry, powers of intelligence; and these powers, thus exhibited, tend really not to strengthen the aristocracy, but to take their owners out of it, to expose them to the dissolving agencies of thought and change, to make them men of the modern spirit and of the future. . . .

Surely, now, it is no inconsiderable boon which culture confers upon us, if in embarrassed times like the present it enables us to look at the ins and the outs of things in this way, without hatred and without partiality,

---

[16] A reference to the rich man in the Gospel of Luke who dined in luxury while the beggar Lazarus wanted the crumbs from his table. The term itself comes from the Latin translation of the Bible, the Vulgate.

and with a disposition to see the good in everybody all round. And I try to follow just the same course with our middle class as with our aristocracy. Mr. Lowe talks to us of this strong middle part of the nation, of the unrivalled deeds of our Liberal middle-class Parliament, of the noble, the heroic work it has performed in the last thirty years; and I begin to ask myself if we shall not, then, find in our middle class the principle of authority we want, and if we had not better take administration as well as legislation away from the weak extreme which now administers for us, and commit both to the strong middle part. I observe, too, that the heroes of middle-class Liberalism, such as we have hitherto known it, speak with a kind of prophetic anticipation of the great destiny which awaits them, and as if the future was clearly theirs. The advanced party, the progressive party, the party in alliance with the future, are the names they like to give themselves. "The principles which will obtain recognition in the future," says Mr. Miall,[17] a personage of deserved eminence among the political Dissenters, as they are called, who have been the backbone of middle-class Liberalism,—"the principles which will obtain recognition in the future are the principles for which I have long and zealously laboured. I qualified myself for joining in the work of harvest by doing to the best of my ability the duties of seed time." These duties, if one is to gather them from the works of the great Liberal party in the last thirty years, are, as I have elsewhere summed them up, the advocacy of free-trade, of parliamentary reform, of abolition of church-rates, of voluntaryism in religion and education,[18] of non-interference of the State between employers and employed, and of marriage with one's deceased wife's sister.[19]

Now I know, when I object that all this is machinery, the great Liberal middle class has by this time grown cunning enough to answer that it always meant more by these things than meets the eye; that it has had that within which passes show, and that we are soon going to see, in a Free Church and all manner of good things, what it was. But I have learned from Bishop Wilson[20] (if Mr. Frederic Harrison will forgive my again quoting that poor old hierophant of a decayed superstition): "If

---

[17] Edward Miall, politician and Congregationalist minister, was a vocal opponent of the institution of the established Church.

[18] The principle of leaving religion and education to voluntary effort rather than to the state or the established Church.

[19] The Liberal government had introduced The Deceased Wife's Sister Bill, which permitted a small class of marriages forbidden by the Church of England. Arnold seems to have regarded it as a petty measure, intended to curry favor with Dissenting voters, while needlessly calling into question the traditional religious framework which preserved the institution of marriage.

[20] Arnold is referring to the *Maxims* of Bishop Thomas Wilson (1663–1755) of the Church of England, best known for his devotional writings.

we would really know our heart let us impartially view our actions"; and I cannot help thinking that if our Liberals had had so much sweetness and light in their inner minds as they allege, more of it must have come out in their sayings and doings.

An American friend of the English Liberals says, indeed, that their Dissidence of Dissent[21] has been a mere instrument of the political Dissenters for making reason and the will of God prevail (and no doubt he would say the same of marriage with one's deceased wife's sister); and that the abolition of a State Church is merely the Dissenter's means to this end, just as culture is mine. Another American defender of theirs says just the same of their industrialism and free-trade; indeed, this gentleman, taking the bull by the horns, proposes that we should for the future call industrialism culture, and the industrialists the men of culture, and then of course there can be no longer any misapprehension about their true character; and besides the pleasure of being wealthy and comfortable, they will have authentic recognition as vessels of sweetness and light.

All this is undoubtedly specious; but I must remark that the culture of which I talked was an endeavour to come at reason and the will of God by means of reading, observing, and thinking; and that whoever calls anything else culture, may, indeed, call it so if he likes, but then he talks of something quite different from what I talked of. And, again, as culture's way of working for reason and the will of God is by directly trying to know more about them, while the Dissidence of Dissent is evidently in itself no effort of this kind, nor is its Free Church, in fact, a church with worthier conceptions of God and the ordering of the world than the State Church professes, but with mainly the same conceptions of these as the State Church has, only that every man is to comport himself as he likes in professing them,—this being so, I cannot at once accept the Nonconformity any more than the industrialism and the other great works of our Liberal middle class as proof positive that this class is in possession of light, and that here is the true seat of authority for which we are in search. . . .

Mr. Bazley[22] sums up for us, in general, the middle class, its spirit and its works, . . . and he has given us, moreover, a famous sentence, which bears directly on the resolution of our present question, whether there is light enough in our middle class to make it the proper seat of the authority we wish to establish. When there was a talk some little while

---

[21] A phrase coined by Burke in his "Speech on Conciliation with America," to describe the influence of dissenting Protestantism on American political culture.

[22] A Manchester cotton manufacturer, sometime chairman of the Manchester Chamber of Commerce, and a Liberal Member of Parliament.

ago about the state of middle class education, Mr. Bazley, as the representative of that class, spoke some memorable words: "There had been a cry that middle class education ought to receive more attention. He confessed himself very much surprised by the clamour that was raised. He did not think that class need excite the sympathy either of the legislature or the public." Now this satisfaction of Mr. Bazley with the mental state of the middle class was truly representative, and makes good his claim to stand as the beautiful and virtuous mean of that class. But it is obviously at variance with our definition of culture, or the pursuit of light and perfection, which made light and perfection consist, not in resting and being, but in growing and becoming, in a perpetual advance in beauty and wisdom. So the middle class is by its essence, as one may say, by its incomparable self-satisfaction decisively expressed through its beautiful and virtuous mean, self-excluded from wielding an authority of which light is to be the very soul.

Clear as this is, it will be made clearer still if we take some representative man as the excess of the middle class, and remember that the middle class, in general, is to be conceived as a body swaying between the qualities of its mean and of its excess, and on the whole, of course, as human nature is constituted, inclining rather towards the excess than the mean. Of its excess no better representative can possibly be imagined than the Rev. W. Cattle, a Dissenting minister from Walsall, who came before the public in connection with the proceedings at Birmingham of Mr. Murphy, already mentioned. Speaking in the midst of an irritated population of Catholics, the Rev. W. Cattle exclaimed:—"I say, then, away with the Mass! It is from the bottomless pit; and in the bottomless pit shall all liars have their part, in the lake that burneth with fire and brimstone." And again: "When all the praties were black in Ireland, why didn't the priests say the hocus-pocus over them, and make them all good again?" He shared, too, Mr. Murphy's fears of some invasion of his domestic happiness: "What I wish to say to you as Protestant husbands is, *Take care of your wives!*" And, finally, in the true vein of an Englishman doing as he likes, a vein of which I have at some length pointed out the present dangers, he recommended for imitation the example of some churchwardens at Dublin, among whom, said he, "there was a Luther and also a Melancthon," who had made very short work with some ritualist or other, hauled him down from his pulpit, and kicked him out of church. Now it is manifest, as I said in the case of Sir Thomas Bateson,[23] that if we let this excess of the sturdy English middle

[23] An aristocratic supporter of the Church of England and Conservative Member of Parliament strongly opposed to electoral reform.

class, this conscientious Protestant Dissenter, so strong, so self-reliant, so fully persuaded in his own mind, have his way, he would be capable, with his want of light—or, to use the language of the religious world, with his zeal without knowledge—of stirring up strife which neither he nor any one else could easily compose.

And then comes in, as it did also with the aristocracy, the honesty of our race, and by the voice of another middle-class man, Alderman Wilson, Alderman of the City of London and Colonel of the City of London Militia, proclaims that it has twinges of conscience, and that it will not attempt to cope with our social disorders, and to deal with a business which it feels to be too high for it. Every one remembers how this virtuous Alderman-Colonel, or Colonel-Alderman, led his militia through the London streets; how the bystanders gathered to see him pass; how the London roughs, asserting an Englishman's best and most blissful right of doing what he likes, robbed and beat the bystanders; and how the blameless warrior-magistrate refused to let his troops interfere. "The crowd," he touchingly said afterwards, "was mostly composed of fine healthy strong men, bent on mischief; if he had allowed his soldiers to interfere they might have been overpowered, their rifles taken from them and used against them by the mob; a riot, in fact, might have ensued, and been attended with bloodshed, compared with which the assaults and loss of property that actually occurred would have been as nothing." Honest and affecting testimony of the English middle class to its own inadequacy for the authoritative part one's admiration would sometimes incline one to assign to it! "Who are we," they say by the voice of their Alderman-Colonel, "that we should not be overpowered if we attempt to cope with social anarchy, our rifles taken from us and used against us by the mob, and we, perhaps, robbed and beaten ourselves? Or what light have we, beyond a free-born Englishman's impulse to do as he likes, which could justify us in preventing, at the cost of bloodshed, other free-born Englishmen from doing as they like, and robbing and beating us as much as they please?"

This distrust of themselves as an adequate centre of authority does not mark the working class, as was shown by their readiness the other day in Hyde Park to take upon themselves all the functions of government. But this comes from the working class being, as I have often said, still an embryo, of which no one can yet quite foresee the final development; and from its not having the same experience and self-knowledge as the aristocratic and middle classes. Honesty it no doubt has, just like the other classes of Englishmen, but honesty in an inchoate and untrained state; and meanwhile its powers of action, which are, as Mr. Frederic Harrison says, exceedingly ready, easily run away with it.

That it cannot at present have a sufficiency of light which comes by culture, that is, by reading, observing, and thinking, is clear from the very nature of its condition. . . .

I conclude, therefore—what, indeed, few of those who do me the honour to read this disquisition are likely to dispute,—that we can as little find in the working class as in the aristocratic or in the middle class our much-wanted source of authority, as culture suggests it to us.

Well, then, what if we tried to rise above the idea of class to the idea of the whole community, *the State*, and to find our centre of light and authority there. Every one of us has the idea of country, as a sentiment; hardly any one of us has the idea of *the State*, as a working power. And why? Because we habitually live in our ordinary selves, which do not carry us beyond the ideas and wishes of the class to which we happen to belong. And we are all afraid of giving to the State too much power, because we only conceive of the State as something equivalent to the class in occupation of the executive government, and are afraid of that class abusing power to its own purposes. . . . And with much justice; owing to the exaggerated notion which we English, as I have said, entertain of the right and blessedness of the mere doing as one likes, of the affirming oneself, and oneself just as it is. People of the aristocratic class want to affirm their ordinary selves, their likings and dislikings; people of the middle class the same, people of the working class the same. By our everyday selves, however, we are separate, personal, at war; we are only safe from one another's tyranny when no one has any power; and this safety, in its turn, cannot save us from anarchy. And when, therefore, anarchy presents itself as a danger to us, we know not where to turn.

But by our *best self*[24] we are united, impersonal, at harmony. We are in no peril from giving authority to this, because it is the truest friend we all of us can have; and when anarchy is a danger to us, to this authority we may turn with sure trust. Well, and this is the very self which culture, or the study of perfection, seeks to develop in us; at the expense of our old untransformed self, taking pleasure only in doing what it likes or is used to do, and exposing us to the risk of clashing with every one else who is doing the same! So that our poor culture—which is flouted as so unpractical, leads us to the very ideas capable of meeting the great want of our present embarrassed times! We want an authority, and we find nothing but jealous classes, checks, and a deadlock; culture suggests the idea of *the State*. We find no basis for a firm State power in our ordinary selves; culture suggests one to us in our *best self*.

---

[24] Arnold's phrase "best self" is another version of the conservative emphasis on the role of second nature, here used in the sense of culture, as a counter to baser instincts.

It cannot but acutely try a tender conscience to be accused, in a practical country like ours, of keeping aloof from the work and hope of a multitude of earnest-hearted men, and of merely toying with poetry and aesthetics. So it is with no little sense of relief that I find myself thus in the position of one who makes a contribution in aid of the practical necessities of our times. The great thing, it will be observed, is to find our *best* self, and to seek to affirm nothing but that; not,—as we English with our over-value for merely being free and busy have been so accustomed to do,—resting satisfied with a self which comes uppermost long before our best self, and affirming that with blind energy. In short, to go back yet once more to Bishop Wilson,—of these two excellent rules of Bishop Wilson's for a man's guidance: "Firstly, never go against the best light you have; secondly, take care that your light be not darkness," we English have followed with praiseworthy zeal the first rule, but we have not given so much heed to the second. We have gone manfully, the Rev. W. Cattle and the rest of us, according to the best light we have; but we have not taken enough care that this should be really the best light possible for us, that it should not be darkness. And, our honesty being very great, conscience has whispered to us that the light we were following, our ordinary self, was, indeed, perhaps, only an inferior self, only darkness; and that it would not do to impose this seriously on all the world.

But our best self inspires faith, and is capable of affording a serious principle of authority. For example. We are on our way to what the late Duke of Wellington, with his strong sagacity, foresaw and admirably described as "a revolution by due course of law."[25] This is undoubtedly,— if we are still to live and grow, and this famous nation is not to stagnate and dwindle away on the one hand, or, on the other, to perish miserably in mere anarchy and confusion,—what we are on the way to. Great changes there must be, for a revolution cannot accomplish itself without great changes; yet order there must be, for without order a revolution cannot accomplish itself by due course of law. So whatever brings risk of tumult and disorder, multitudinous processions in the streets of our crowded towns, multitudinous meetings in their public places and parks,—demonstrations perfectly unnecessary in the present course of our affairs,—our best self, or right reason, plainly enjoins us to set our faces against. It enjoins us to encourage and uphold the occupants of the executive power, whoever they may be, in firmly prohibiting them. But it does this clearly and resolutely, and is thus a real principle of

[25] Wellington made the comment in regard to the First Reform Bill, of 1832, which substantially extended the franchise.

authority, because it does it with a free conscience; because in thus provisionally strengthening the executive power, it knows that it is not doing this merely to enable Sir Thomas Bateson to affirm himself as against Mr. Bradlaugh,[26] or the Rev. W. Cattle to affirm himself as against both. It knows that it is stablishing [establishing] *the State*, or organ of our collective best self, of our national right reason; and it has the testimony of conscience that it is stablishing the State on behalf of whatever great changes are needed, just as much as on behalf of order . . .

[26] Charles Bradlaugh, radical agitator active in the demonstration which led to the Hyde Park riots.

INTRODUCTION TO
James Fitzjames Stephen,
Liberty, Equality, Fraternity

◆

Like Matthew Arnold, James Fitzjames Stephen was part of the educated Victorian middle class whose members staffed the overlapping realms of law, politics, administration, and the higher reaches of education and journalism.[1] His conservative brand of liberalism was shared with other members of this educated class in the 1860s who, like Arnold, believed that the aristocracy was no longer capable of supplying political or cultural leadership, and that the task ahead was to provide an elite of merit and education which would guide the nation into an inevitably more democratic age.[2]

Like Arnold, Stephen was born into a family of intellectual and political distinction. His grandfather had held a seat in Parliament and worked for the abolition of slavery; his father was a colonial administrator, Under-Secretary of State for India, and finally Regius Professor of Modern History at Cambridge. Born in 1829, Stephen attended Eton and Cambridge, studied for the bar, and embarked on a career which combined the practice of law with a remarkable output of topical articles in journals of elite opinion such as the *Saturday Review*, the *Pall Mall Gazette*, and the *Cornhill Magazine* (in which Arnold's essays on culture had first appeared) .

Stephen was a utilitarian, who believed that the greatest happiness of the greatest number was the test of moral action and of institutional legitimacy. But Stephen's utilitarianism, far from the mechanical, materialistic, and ahistorical doctrine of Jeremy Bentham, reflected the internal transformation of the utilitarian tradition by John Stuart Mill, who had insisted upon the inadequacy of Bentham's vision of human possibilities and his understanding of human psychology. Stephen's utilitarianism had a more Burkean cast, indeed he regarded Burke as "a utilitarian of the strongest kind."[3] Like Burke, Stephen most valued

---

[1] See Stefan Collini, *Public Moralists: Political Thought and Intellectual Life in Britain, 1850–1930* (Oxford, 1991), chapters 1 and 7.

[2] See J. F. Stephen, "Liberalism," *Cornhill Magazine* V (1862), quoted in James A. Colaiaco, *Sir James Fitzjames Stephen and the Crisis of Victorian Thought* (New York, 1983), pp. 7–8.

[3] "Burke on the English Constitution," in *Horae Sabbaticae*, Third Series (London, 1892), pp. 114–15. On Stephen's appreciation of Burke, see Colaico, *Stephen*, pp. 40ff, and K.J.M. Smith, *James Fitzjames Stephen: Portrait of a Victorian Rationalist* (Cambridge, 1988), pp. 113–16. Stephen criticized Burke for his use of the language of natural

institutions for their restraining functions. He asserted that while the Burkean suspicion of systematic reform was appropriate for conservatism when restraining institutions were experienced as fundamentally intact, the circumstances of his own day called for a more constructive conservatism. At a time when the aristocratic and middle class hold on politics was weakening, and religion seemed to be losing its plausibility, the need, as Stephen saw it, was to systematize and reinforce restraining institutions. Among these was the criminal law, to which Stephen devoted much of his energy. For as he put it in his *History of the Criminal Law*:

> In such circumstances it seems to be specially necessary for those who do care for morality to make its one unquestionable, indisputable sanction as clear, and strong, and emphatic, as words and acts can make it. A man may disbelieve in God, heaven, and hell, he may care little for mankind or society, or for the nation to which he belongs,—let him at least be plainly told what are the acts which will stamp him with infamy, hold him up to public execration, and bring him to the gallows, the gaol, or the lash.[4]

Stephen spent the years from 1869 to 1872 in India as a legal advisor to the Viceroy. There he helped to codify and consolidate the legal system imposed by the British upon India, from which he drew the lesson that power well used could be a civilizing force.

Stephen considered himself a liberal, had long admired the writings of John Stuart Mill, and had greeted Mill's *On Liberty* positively upon its publication in 1859. In that work, a manifesto of what might be called "cultural liberalism," Mill emphasized the right of the individual to differ in his conduct from the standards of the community. Stephen's more conservative temperament, reinforced by his experiences in India, led him to conclude that Mill's essay was fundamentally flawed and based on what he called a "concept of human nature [which] appears to me to be a sort of unattractive romance."[5] On the ship home from India in 1872 he composed a refutation of Mill's essay and of what he saw as the flawed and underexamined assumptions of contemporary liberalism, egalitarianism, and humanitarianism. Stephen's refutation appeared as a series of articles in the *Pall Mall*, and were published in 1873 as *Liberty*,

---

law, a theory which Stephen regarded as implausible and at odds with the utilitarian thrust of Burke's thought.

[4] James Fitzjames Stephen, *A History of the Criminal Law of England*, 3 vols. (London, 1883), iii, pp. 366–67; quoted in Colaiaco, *James Fitzjames Stephen*, p. 210.

[5] Stephen to Lady Edgerton, April 24, 1872, quoted in Smith, *James Fitzjames Stephen*, p. 161.

Equality, Fraternity, a book which took as its title the motto of the French Revolution.

It is among Stephen's virtues as a controversialist that he lays out Mill's major contentions before attempting to refute them, thereby making their presentation in this introduction superfluous. Stephen's dissatisfaction with Mill's position led him to articulate the grounds for his skepticism of all projects intended to liberate individuals from existing sources of social and cultural authority, based upon the conservative assumption that human imperfection leaves men in need of institutions to restrain, restrict, and repress their passions. The law was one such institution, but its influence, Stephen argues, is less significant than institutions such as religion and the pressure of public opinion. These themes, together with the need for elites and for authority, are presented by Stephen with great verve in a book that attained the status of a classic of conservative thought.

The excerpts reprinted below omit Stephen's footnotes, added to the second addition of 1874, in which he responded to the arguments of his critics.

James Fitzjames Stephen, *Liberty, Equality, Fraternity* (1874)[1]

The Doctrine Of Liberty In General

The object of this work is to examine the doctrines which are rather hinted at than expressed by the phrase "Liberty, Equality, Fraternity." This phrase has been the motto of more than one Republic. It is indeed something more than a motto. It is the creed of a religion, less definite than any one of the forms of Christianity, which are in part its rivals, in part its antagonists, and in part its associates, but not on that account the less powerful. It is, on the contrary, one of the most penetrating influences of the day. It shows itself now and then in definite forms, of which Positivism is the one best known to our generation, but its special manifestations give no adequate measure of its depth or width. It penetrates other creeds. It has often transformed Christianity into a system of optimism, which has in some cases retained and in others rejected Christian phraseology. It deeply influences politics and legislation. It has its solemn festivals, its sober adherents, its enthusiasts, its Anabaptists and Antinomians. The Religion of Humanity is perhaps as good a name as

---

[1] James Fitzjames Stephen, *Liberty, Equality, Fraternity* (London, 1874).

could be found for it, if the expression is used in a wider sense than the narrow and technical one associated with it by Comte. It is one of the commonest beliefs of the day that the human race collectively has before it splendid destinies of various kinds, and that the road to them is to be found in the removal of all restraints on human conduct, in the recognition of a substantial equality between all human creatures, and in fraternity or general love. These doctrines are in very many cases held as a religious faith. They are regarded not merely as truths, but as truths for which those who believe in them are ready to do battle, and for the establishment of which they are prepared to sacrifice all merely personal ends.

Such, stated of course in the most general terms, is the religion of which I take "Liberty, Equality, Fraternity" to be the creed. I do not believe it.

I am not the advocate of Slavery, Caste, and Hatred, nor do I deny that a sense may be given to the words, Liberty, Equality, and Fraternity in which they may be regarded as good. I wish to assert with respect to them two propositions.

First, that in the present day even those who use those words most rationally—that is to say, as the names of elements of social life which, like others, have their advantages and disadvantages according to time, place, and circumstance—have a great disposition to exaggerate their advantages and to deny the existence, or at any rate to underrate the importance, of their disadvantages.

Next, that whatever signification be attached to them, these words are ill-adapted to be the creed of a religion, that the things which they denote are not ends in themselves, and that when used collectively the words do not typify, however vaguely, any state of society which a reasonable man ought to regard with enthusiasm or self-devotion.

The truth of the first proposition as a mere general observation will not, in all probability, be disputed; but I attach to it a very much more specific meaning than is conveyed by a mere commonplace. I mean to assert that the most accredited current theories upon this subject, and those which have been elaborated with the greatest care, are unsound; and to give point to this, I say more specifically that the theories advanced upon the subject by Mr. John Mill in most of his later works are unsound. I have several reasons for referring specifically to him. In the first place, no writer of the present day has expressed himself upon these subjects with anything like the same amount either of system or of ability. In the second place, he is the only modern author who has handled the subject, with whom I agree sufficiently to differ from him profitably. Up to a certain point I should be proud to describe myself as his disciple, but there is a side of his teaching which is as repugnant as the rest of it is attractive to me, and this side has of late years become by far the most prominent. I do not say that the teaching of his works on Liberty, on Utilitarianism, and on the Subjection of Women is inconsistent with the teaching of his works on Logic and Political Economy; but I wish to show the grounds on which it is possible to agree with the greater part of the contents of the two works last mentioned, and even to maintain principles which they rather imply than assert, and at the same time to dissent in the strongest way from the view of human nature and human affairs which pervades the works first mentioned.

No better statement of the popular view—I might, perhaps, say of the religious dogma of liberty—is to be found than that which is contained in Mr. Mill's essay on the subject. His works on Utilitarianism and the Subjection of Women afford excellent illustrations of the forms of the doctrines of equality and fraternity to which I object. Nothing is further from my wishes than to make a captious attack upon the writings of a great man to whom I am in every way deeply indebted; but in stating the grounds of one's dissent from wide-spread and influential opinions it is absolutely necessary to take some definite statement of those opinions as a starting point, and it is natural to take the ablest, the most reasonable, and the clearest. . . .

[Mill] enunciates his own view in the following passage:

> The object of this essay [*On Liberty*] is to assert one very simple principle, as entitled to govern absolutely the dealings of society with the individual in the way of compulsion or control, whether the means used be physical force in the form of legal penalties, or the moral coercion of public opinion. That principle is that the sole end for which mankind are warranted individually or collectively in interfering with the liberty of action of any of their number is self-protection; that the only purpose for which power can be rightfully exercised over any member of a civilized community against his will is to prevent harm to others. His own good, either physical or moral, is not a sufficient warrant. He cannot rightfully be com-pelled to do or forbear because it will be better for him to do so, because it will make him happier, because in the opinions of others to do so would be wise or even right. These are good reasons for remonstrating with him, or reasoning with him, or persuading him, or entreating him, but not for compelling him, or visiting him with any evil in case he do otherwise. To justify that, the conduct from which it is desired to deter him must be calculated to produce evil to some one else. The only part of the conduct of any one for which

he is amenable to society is that which concerns others. In the part which merely concerns himself his independence is of right, absolute. Over himself, over his own body and mind, the individual is sovereign.

He points out that "this doctrine is meant to apply only to human beings in the maturity of their faculties," and that "we may leave out of account those backward states of society in which the race itself may be considered as in its nonage." He then disclaims any advantage which could be derived to his "argument from the idea of abstract right as a thing independent of utility." He adds: "I regard utility as the ultimate appeal on all ethical questions; but it must be utility in the largest sense grounded on the permanent interests of a man as a progressive being." He concludes by specifying "the appropriate region of human liberty. It comprises, first, the inward domain of consciousness; demanding liberty of conscience in the most comprehensive sense, liberty of thought and feeling; absolute freedom of opinion and sentiment on all subjects practical or speculative, scientific, moral, or theological. The liberty of expressing and publishing opinions may seem to fall under a different principle, since it belongs to that part of the conduct of an individual which concerns other people, but being almost of as much importance as the liberty of thought itself, and resting in great part on the same reasons, is practically inseparable from it. Secondly, the principle requires liberty of tastes and pursuits, of framing our plan of life to suit our own character, of doing as we like, subject to such consequences as may follow, without impediment from our fellow-creatures, so long as what we do does not harm them—even though they should think our conduct foolish, perverse, or wrong. Thirdly, from this liberty of each individual follows the liberty within the same limits of combination among individuals."

There is hardly anything in the whole essay which can properly be called proof as distinguished from enunciation or assertion of the general principles quoted. I think, however, that it will not be difficult to show that the principle stands in much need of proof. In order to make this clear it will be desirable in the first place to point out the meaning of the word liberty according to principles which I think are common to Mr. Mill and to myself. I do not think Mr. Mill would have disputed the following statement of the theory of human actions. All voluntary acts are caused by motives. All motives may be placed in one of two categories—hope and fear, pleasure and pain. Voluntary acts of which hope is the motive are said to be free. Voluntary acts of which fear is the motive are said to be done under compulsion, or omitted under restraint. A woman marries. This in every case is a voluntary action. If she regards the marriage with the ordinary feelings and acts from the ordinary motives, she is said to act freely. If she regards it as a necessity, to which she submits in order to avoid greater evil, she is said to act under compulsion and not freely.

If this is the true theory of liberty—and, though many persons would deny this, I think they would have been accepted by Mr. Mill—the propositions already stated will in a condensed form amount to this: "No one is ever justified in trying to affect any one's conduct by exciting his fears, except for the sake of self-protection;" or, making another substitution which he would also approve—"It can never promote the general happiness of mankind that the conduct of any persons should be affected by an appeal to their fears, except in the cases excepted."

Surely these are not assertions which can be regarded as self-evident, or even as otherwise than paradoxical. What is all morality, and what are all existing religions in so far as they aim at affecting human conduct, except an appeal either to hope or fear, and to fear far more commonly and far more emphatically than to hope? Criminal legislation proper may be regarded as an engine of prohibition unimportant in comparison with morals and the forms of morality sanctioned by theology.[2] For one act from which one person is restrained by the fear of the law of the land, many persons are restrained from innumerable acts by the fear of the disapprobation of their neighbours, which is the moral sanction; or by the fear of punishment in a future state of existence, which is the religious sanction; or by the fear of their own disapprobation, which may be called the conscientious sanction, and may be regarded as a compound case of the other two. Now, in the innumerable majority of cases, disapprobation, or the moral sanction, has nothing whatever to do with self-protection. The religious sanction is by its nature independent of it. Whatever special forms it may assume, the fundamental condition of it is a being intolerant of evil in the highest degree, and inexorably determined to punish it wherever it exists, except upon certain terms. I do not say that this doctrine is true, but I do say that no one is entitled to assume it without proof to be essentially immoral and mischievous. Mr. Mill does not draw this inference, but I think his theory involves it, for I know not what can be a greater infringement of his theory of liberty, a more complete and formal contradiction to it, than the doctrine that there are a court and a judge in which, and before whom, every man must give an account of every work done in the body, whether self-regarding or not. According to Mr. Mill's theory, it ought to be a good plea in the day of judgment to say "I pleased myself and hurt nobody else." Whether or not there will ever be a day of judgment is not the

---

[2] Here and elsewhere in the book, Stephen insists upon the role of religion as a spur to moral action, and above all as a prophylactic against immoral action.

question, but upon his principles the conception of a day of judgment is fundamentally immoral. A God who punished any one at all, except for the purpose of protecting others, would, upon his principles, be a tyrant trampling on liberty.

The application of the principle in question to the moral sanction would be just as subversive of all that people commonly regard as morality. The only moral system which would comply with the principle stated by Mr. Mill would be one capable of being summed up as follows: "Let every man please himself without hurting his neighbour;" and every moral system which aimed at more than this, either to obtain benefits for society at large other than protection against injury or to do good to the persons affected, would be wrong in principle. This would condemn every existing system of morals. Positive morality is nothing but a body of principles and rules more or less vaguely expressed, and more or less left to be understood, by which certain lines of conduct are forbidden under the penalty of general disapprobation, and that quite irrespectively of self-protection. Mr. Mill himself admits this to a certain extent. In the early part of his fourth chapter he says that a man grossly deficient in the qualities which conduce to his own good is "necessarily and properly a subject of distaste, or in extreme cases even of contempt," and he enumerates various inconveniences to which this would expose such a person. He adds, however: "The inconveniences which are strictly inseparable from the unfavourable judgment of others are the only ones to which a person should ever be subjected for that portion of his conduct and character which concerns his own good, but which does not affect the interests of others in their relation with him." This no doubt weakens the effect of the admission; but be this how it may, the fact still remains that morality is and must be a prohibitive system, one of the main objects of which is to impose upon every one a standard of conduct and of sentiment to which few persons would conform if it were not for the constraint thus put upon them. In nearly every instance the effects of such a system reach far beyond anything that can be described as the purposes of self-protection.

Mr. Mill's system is violated not only by every system of theology which concerns itself with morals, and by every known system of positive morality, but by the constitution of human nature itself. There is hardly a habit which men in general regard as good which is not acquired by a series of more or less painful and laborious acts. The condition of human life is such that we must of necessity be restrained and compelled by circumstances in nearly every action of our lives. Why, then, is liberty, defined as Mr. Mill defines it, to be regarded as so precious? What, after all, is done by the legislator or by the person who sets public opinion in motion to control conduct of which he disapproves—or, if the expression is preferred, which he dislikes—which is not done for us all at every instant of our lives by circumstances? The laws which punish murder or theft are substitutes for private vengeance, which, in the absence of law, would punish those crimes more severely, though in a less regular manner. If there were laws which punished incontinence, gluttony, or drunkenness, the same might be said of them. Mr. Mill admits in so many words that there are "inconveniences which are strictly inseparable from the unfavourable judgment of others." What is the distinction in principle between such inconveniences and similar ones organized, defined, and inflicted upon proof that the circumstances which call for their infliction exist? This organization, definition, and procedure make all the difference between the restraints which Mr. Mill would permit and the restraints to which he objects. I cannot see on what the distinction rests. I cannot understand why it must always be wrong to punish habitual drunkenness by fine, imprisonment, or deprivation of civil rights, and always be right to punish it by the infliction of those consequences which are "strictly inseparable from the unfavourable judgment of others." It may be said that these consequences follow, not because we think them desirable, but in the common order of nature. This answer only suggests the further question, whether nature is in this instance to be regarded as a friend or as an enemy? Every reasonable man would answer that the restraint which the fear of the disapprobation of others imposes on our conduct is the part of the constitution of nature which we could least afford to dispense with. But if this is so, why draw the line where Mr. Mill draws it? Why treat the penal consequences of disapprobation as things to be minimized and restrained within the narrowest limits? What "inconvenience," after all, is "strictly inseparable from the unfavourable judgment of others"? If society at large adopted fully Mr. Mill's theory of liberty, it would be easy to diminish very greatly the inconveniences in question. Strenuously preach and rigorously practice the doctrine that our neighbor's private character is nothing to us, and the number of unfavorable judgments formed, and therefore the number of inconveniences inflicted by them, can be reduced as much as we please, and the province of liberty can be enlarged in a corresponding ratio. Does any reasonable man wish for this? Could any one desire gross licentiousness, monstrous extravagance, ridiculous vanity, or the like, to be unnoticed, or, being known, to inflict no inconveniences which can possibly be avoided?

If, however, the restraints on immorality are the main safeguards of society against influences which might be fatal to it, why treat them as if they were bad? Why draw so strongly marked a line between social and legal penalties? Mr. Mill asserts the existence of the distinction in every form of speech. He makes his meaning perfectly clear. Yet from one end of his essay to the other I find no proof and no attempt to give the proper and appropriate proof of it. His doctrine could have been proved if it had been true. It was not proved because it was not true.

Each of these propositions may, I think, be established by referring to the commonest and most important cases of coercion for other purposes than those of self-protection. The most important of them are: (1) Coercion for the purpose of establishing and maintaining religions. (2) Coercion for the purpose of establishing and practically maintaining morality. (3) Coercion for the purpose of making alterations in existing forms of government or social institutions.

None of these can in the common use of language be described as cases of self-protection or of the prevention of harm to persons other than those coerced. Each is a case of coercion, for the sake of what the persons who exercise coercive power regard as the attainment of a good object, and each is accordingly condemned, and the first and second were no doubt intended to be condemned, by Mr. Mill's principle. . . .

As regards coercion for the purpose of establishing and maintaining religions and systems of morality it would be a waste of time to insist upon the principle that both religion and morals are good on the whole, notwithstanding the evils of various kinds which have been connected with them. Nor need I repeat what I have already said on the point that both religion and morality are and always must be essentially coercive systems. Taking these matters for granted, however, it will be desirable to consider somewhat more fully the nature of moral and religious coercion, and the manner in which they operate. If Mr. Mill's view of liberty had always been adopted and acted upon to its full extent—if it had been the view of the first Christians or of the first Mohammedans—everyone can see that there would have been no such thing as organised Christianity or Mohammedanism in the world. Even after such success as these and other religions have obtained, the morality of the vast mass of mankind is simply to do what they please up to the point at which custom puts a restraint upon them, arising from the fear of disapprobation. The custom of looking upon certain courses of conduct with aversion is the essence of morality, and the fact that this aversion may be felt by the very person whose conduct occasions it, and may be described as arising from the action of his own conscience, makes no difference which need be considered here. The important point is that such disapprobation could never have become customary unless it had been imposed upon mankind at large by persons who themselves felt it with exceptional energy, and who were in a position which enabled them to make other people adopt their principles and even their tastes and feelings.[3]

---

[3] Here Stephen presents the first of his arguments for the necessity of elites.

Religion and morals, in a word, bear, even when they are at their calmest, the traces of having been established, as we know that in fact they were, by word of command. We have seen enough of the foundation of religions to know pretty well what is their usual course. A religion is first preached by a single person or a small body of persons. A certain number of disciples adopt it enthusiastically, and proceed to force their views upon the world by preaching, by persuasion, by the force of sympathy, until the new creed has become sufficiently influential and sufficiently well organised to exercise power both over its own members and beyond its own sphere. This power, in the case of a vigorous creed, assumes many forms. It may be military power, if the early converts are fighting men; it may be power derived from threats as to a future state—and this is the commonest and most distinctive form of religious power of which we have practical experience. It may be power derived from mere superior energy of will, or from organisations which those who possess that energy are able to set on foot by means of it. But, be the special form of religious power what it will, the principle is universally true that the growth of religions is in the nature of a conquest made by a small number of ardent believers over the lukewarmness, the indifference, and the conscious ignorance of the mass of mankind. The life of the great mass of men, to a great extent the life of all men, is like a water-course guided this way or that by a system of dams, sluices, weirs, and embankments.[4] The volume and the quality of the different streams differ, and so do the plans of the works by which their flow is regulated, but it is by these works—that is to say, by their various customs and institutions—that men's lives are regulated. Now these customs are not only in their very nature restraints, but they are restraints imposed by the will of an exceedingly small numerical minority and contentedly accepted by a majority to which they have become so natural that they do not recognise them as restraints.

As for the third set of cases in which coercion is habitually employed—I mean coercion for the purpose of making alterations in existing forms of government and social institutions—it surely needs no argument to show that all the great political changes which have been the principal subject of European history for the last three centuries have been cases of coercion in the most severe form, although a large proportion of them have been described as struggles for liberty by those who were, in fact, the most vigorous wielders of power.

Mr. Mill and his disciples would be the last persons in the world to say that the political and social changes which have taken place in the world

[4] Here and elsewhere throughout his book, Stephen employs the extended metaphor of passions as water and institutions as water channels, to express the need for institutional restraint and direction of the passions.

since the sixteenth century have not on the whole been eminently beneficial to mankind; but nothing can be clearer than that they were
brought about by force, and in many instances by the force of a minority
numerically small, applied to the conduct of an ignorant or very partially
informed and for the most part indifferent majority. It would surely be
as absurd to say that the Reformation or the French Revolution was
brought about freely and not by coercion as to say that Charles I walked
freely to the block. Each of these and many other cases which might be
mentioned were struggles for political power, efforts to bring about a
change in the existing state of things, which for various reasons appeared
desirable to people who were able to carry out their designs more or less
successfully. . . .

Not only is an appeal to facts and experience opposed to Mr. Mill's
principle, but his essay contains exceptions and qualifications which are
really inconsistent with it. He says that his principle "is meant to apply
to human beings only in the maturity of their faculties," and, he adds,
"we may leave out of account those backward states of society in which
the race itself may be considered in its nonage." Despotism, he says, "is
a legitimate mode of government in dealing with barbarians, provided
the end be their improvement, and the means justified by actually effect-
ing that end. Liberty as a principle has no application to any state of
things anterior to the time when mankind have become capable of being
improved by free and equal discussion. Until then there is nothing for
them but implicit obedience to an Akbar or a Charlemagne if they are so
fortunate as to find one.[5] But as soon as mankind have attained the capacity of being guided to their own improvement by conviction or persuasion (a period long since reached in all nations with whom we need
here concern ourselves), compulsion is no longer admissible as a means
to their own good, and is justifiable only for the security of others." . . .

[Mill's argument assumes] that in all the countries which we are accustomed to call civilised the mass of adults are so well acquainted with
their own interests and so much disposed to pursue them that no compulsion or restraint put upon any of them by any others for the purpose
of promoting their interests can really promote them.

No one can doubt the importance of this assertion, but where is the
proof of it? . . . . Before he affirmed that in Western Europe and Amer-

---

[5] Akbar (1542–1605) was a Moghul ruler who extended his empire over much of the
Indian subcontinent. A Muslim, he successfully co-opted the Hindu leadership of his newly
conquered territories, developed an imperial bureaucracy, practiced religious toleration,
and set the stage for a century of relatively stable rule. Charlemagne (742–814) was a
Frankish king whose conquests and diplomacy united much of Europe into the Holy
Roman Empire. He made great efforts to improve the education of the clergy and laity in
his domains.

ica the compulsion of adults for their own good is unjustifiable, Mr. Mill ought to have proved that there are among us no considerable differences in point of wisdom, or that if there are, the wiser part of the community does not wish for the welfare of the less wise.

It seems to me quite impossible to stop short of this principle if compulsion in the case of children and "backward" races is admitted to be justifiable; for, after all, maturity and civilisation are matters of degree. One person may be more mature at fifteen than another at thirty. A nation or a particular part of a nation may make such an advance in the arts of life in half a century that other nations, or other parts of the same nation, which were equally civilised at the beginning of the period, may be relatively barbarous at the end of it.

I do not overlook the qualification contained in the passages quoted above. It fixes the limit up to which compulsion is justifiable at the "time when mankind have become capable of being improved by free and equal discussion." This expression may imply that compulsion is always or never justifiable, according to the manner in which it is construed. I am not quite sure that I know what Mr. Mill means by "equal" discussion, but was there ever a time or place at which no men could be improved on any point by free discussion? The wildest savages, the most immature youths, capable of any sort of education, are capable of being improved by free discussion upon a great variety of subjects. Compulsion, therefore, in their own interests would, at least in relation to these subjects, be unjustifiable as regards them. If boys in a school can be convinced of the importance of industry, you must never punish them for idleness. Such an interpretation of the rule would practically exclude compulsion altogether.

A narrower interpretation would be as follows. There is a period, now generally reached all over Europe and America, at which discussion takes the place of compulsion, and in which people when they know what is good for them generally do it. When this period is reached, compulsion may be laid aside. To this I should say that no such period has as yet been reached anywhere, and that there is no prospect of its being reached anywhere within any assignable time.

Where, in the very most advanced and civilised communities, will you find any class of persons whose views or whose conduct on subjects on which they are interested are regulated even in the main by the results of free discussion? What proportion of human misconduct in any department in life is due to ignorance, and what to wickedness or weakness? Of ten thousand people who get drunk, is there one who could say with truth that he did so because he had been brought to think on full deliberation and after free discussion that it was wise to get drunk? Would not every one of the ten thousand, if he told the real truth, say in some dialect or other—"I got drunk because I was weak and a fool, because I could not resist the immediate pleasure for the sake of future and indefinite advantage"? If we look at the conduct of bodies of men as expressed in their laws and institutions, we shall find that, though compulsion and persuasion go hand in hand, from the most immature and the roughest ages and societies up to the most civilised, the lion's share of the results obtained is due to compulsion, and that discussion is at most an appeal to the motives by which the strong man is likely to be actuated in using his strength. Look at our own time and country, and mention any single great change which has been effected by mere discussion. Can a single case be mentioned in which the passions of men were interested where the change was not carried by force—that is to say, ultimately by the fear of revolution? Is it in any degree true that when the brains are out a question dies? Look at small matters which involve more or less of a principle, but do not affect many men's passions, and see how much reasoning has to do with their settlement. Such questions as the admission of Jews into Parliament and the legalisation of marriage between brothers and sisters-in-law drag on and on after the argument has been exhausted, till in course of time those who take one view or the other grow into a decided majority, and settle the matter their own way. Parliamentary government is simply a mild and disguised form of compulsion. We agree to try strength by counting heads instead of breaking heads, but the principle is exactly the same. It is not the wisest side which wins, but the one which for the time being shows its superior strength (of which no doubt wisdom is one element) by enlisting the largest amount of active sympathy in its support. The minority gives way not because it is convinced that it is wrong, but because it is convinced that it is a minority.

This again suggests an observation on a different part of the passage quoted from Mr. Mill. In rough states of society he admits of Charlemagnes and Akbars, if the world is so fortunate as to have them at hand. What reason is there to suppose that Charlemagnes or Akbars owe their power to enlightenment superior to that of the persons whom they coerce? They owe it to greater force of character and to the possession of power. What they did was to suppress anarchy—to substitute the vigorous rule of one Sovereign for the jarring pretensions of a crowd of petty rulers. No doubt powerful men are generally comparatively enlightened men, as were both Charlemagne and Akbar, for knowledge is a high form of power, as light implies intense force. But power in whatever form is the essential thing. Anarchy may be mischievous in civilised as well as in uncivilised life, and the only way out of it is, by coercion. To direct that power aright is, I think, the principal object of political argument. The difference between a rough and a civilised society is not that force is used in the one case and persuasion in the other, but that force is (or ought to be) guided with greater care in the second case than in the first. President Lincoln[6] attained his objects by the use of a degree of force which would have crushed Charlemagne and his paladins and peers like so many eggshells.

The correctness of the assertion that "in all nations with whom we need here concern ourselves," the period at which "mankind have become capable of being improved by free and equal discussion has long since arrived," may be estimated by reference to two familiar points:

(1) Upon all the subjects which mainly interest men as men—religion, morals, government—mankind at large are in a state of ignorance which in favourable cases is just beginning to be conscious that it is ignorance. How far will free discussion carry such knowledge as we have on these subjects? The very most that can be hoped for—men being what they are—is to popularise, more or less, a certain set of commonplaces, which, by the condition of their existence, cannot possibly be more than half-truths. Discussion produces plenty of effects, no doubt. People hunger and thirst after theories to such a degree that whatever puts their own wishes into a compact and intelligible form will obtain from them a degree of allegiance which may be called either touching or terrible. Look at the great popular movements which discussion has provoked, and consider what approach any one of them made to the real truth. Innumerable creeds, religious and political, have swept across the world, arguing, preaching, gesticulating, and fighting. Compare the amount of recognition which the worst of them has obtained and the devotion which it has called forth with the degree of really intelligent appreciation which has been awarded to science. Millions upon millions of men, women, and children believe in Mohammed to the point of regulating their whole life by his law. How many people have understood Adam Smith?[7] Did anybody, except perhaps Mr. Buckle, ever feel any enthusiasm about him?[8]

If we wish to test the capacity of mankind at large for any sort of abstract discussion, we ought to consider the case of the minor branches of human knowledge which have been invested with some approach to a systematic character. How many people are capable of understanding

---

[6] During the American Civil War.

[7] Smith was author of *The Wealth of Nations* (1776), a work which explained how the free market functioned to most effectively meet the needs of consumers. His argument was based on "the invisible hand" of the market, a metaphor for the fact that the market mechanism had unintended positive social consequences in that it was fueled by the motive of self-interest but, by increasing productivity and reducing prices through competition, it produced what Smith called "universal opulence."

[8] Henry Thomas Buckle (1821–1862), was, in his day, an influential historian who sought to discover historical laws leading to civilizational progress.

the fundamental principles of either political economy or jurisprudence? How many people can understand the distinction between making the fundamental assumptions of political economy for the purpose of calculating the results of the unrestrained action of the desire to get rich, and regarding those assumptions as being true in fact and capable of serving as the foundations of human society? One would have thought that it was easy to distinguish between the proposition, "If your only object in trade is to make the largest possible profit, you ought always to buy in the cheapest market and sell in the dearest," and the proposition, "All men ought, under all circumstances, to buy all things in the cheapest and sell them in the dearest market." Yet how many people do in fact distinguish them? How many recognise in the faintest degree the importance of the distinction?

(2) Men are so constructed that whatever theory as to goodness and badness we choose to adopt, there are and always will be in the world an enormous mass of bad and indifferent people—people who deliberately do all sorts of things which they ought not to do, and leave undone all sorts of things which they ought to do. Estimate the proportion of men and women who are selfish, sensual, frivolous, idle, absolutely commonplace and wrapped up in the smallest of petty routines, and consider how far the freest of free discussion is likely to improve them. The only way by which it is practically possible to act upon them at all is by compulsion or restraint. Whether it is worth while to apply to them both or either I do not now inquire; I confine myself to saying that the utmost conceivable liberty which could be bestowed upon them would not in the least degree tend to improve them. It would be as wise to say to the water of a stagnant marsh, "Why in the world do not you run into the sea? you are perfectly free. There is not a single hydraulic work within a mile of you. There are no pumps to suck you up, no defined channel down which you are compelled to run, no harsh banks and mounds to confine you to any particular course, no dams and no flood-gates; and yet there you lie, putrefying and breeding fever, frogs, and gnats, just as if you were a mere slave!" The water might probably answer, if it knew how, "If you want me to turn mills and carry boats, you must dig proper channels and provide proper water-works for me."

THE DOCTRINE OF LIBERTY IN ITS APPLICATION TO MORALS

After setting forth his theory as to personal vices being left to take their own course, [Mill] proceeds as follows:

> The distinction here pointed out between the part of a person's life which concerns only himself and that which concerns others many

persons will refuse to admit. How (it may be asked) can any part of the conduct of a member of society be a matter of indifference to the other members? No person is an entirely isolated being; it is impossible for a person to do anything seriously or permanently hurtful to himself without mischief reaching at least to his near connections, and often far beyond them.

He proceeds to enforce this by highly appropriate illustrations, which I need not quote. Further on he quotes a passage from an advocate of the suppression of intemperance, of which the following is a sample: "If anything invades my social rights, certainly the traffic in strong drink does. It invades my primary right of security by constantly creating and stimulating social disorder." Upon this Mr. Mill observes:

A theory of "social rights," the like of which probably never before found its way into distinct language, being nothing short of this, that it is the absolute social right of every individual that every other individual should act in every respect precisely as he ought, that whosoever fails thereof in the smallest violates my social right and entitles me to demand from the Legislature the removal of the grievance. So monstrous a principle is far more dangerous than any single violation of liberty. . . The doctrine ascribes to all mankind a vested interest in each other's moral, intellectual, and even physical perfection, to be defined by each according to his own standard.

At the risk of appearing paradoxical, I own that the theory which appears to Mr. Mill so monstrous appears to me defective only in its language about rights and legislation, upon which I shall have more to say hereafter. It is surely a simple matter of fact that every human creature is deeply interested not only in the conduct, but in the thoughts, feelings, and opinions of millions of persons who stand in no other assignable relation to him than that of being his fellow-creatures. A great writer who makes a mistake in his speculations may mislead multitudes whom he has never seen. The strong metaphor that we are all members one of another is little more than the expression of a fact. A man would no more be a man if he was alone in the world than a hand would be a hand without the rest of the body. . . .

It is one thing however to tolerate vice so long as it is inoffensive, and quite another to give it a legal right not only to exist, but to assert itself in the face of the world as an "experiment in living" as good as another, and entitled to the same protection from law. . . .

I now pass to the manner in which civil law may and does, and as I say properly, promote virtue and prevent vice. This is a subject so wide that

I prefer indicating its nature by a few illustrations to attempting to deal with it systematically. It would, however, be easy to show that nearly every branch of civil law assumes the existence of a standard of moral good and evil which the public at large have an interest in maintaining, and in many cases enforcing—a proceeding which is diametrically opposed to Mr. Mill's fundamental principles. . . .

Perhaps the most pointed of all illustrations of the moral character of civil law is to be found in the laws relating to marriage and inheritance. They all proceed upon an essentially moral theory as to the relation of the sexes. Take the case of illegitimate children. A bastard is *filius nullius*—he inherits nothing, he has no claim on his putative father. What is all this except the expression of the strongest possible determination on the part of the Legislature to recognize, maintain, and favour marriage in every possible manner as the foundation of civilized society? It has been plausibly maintained that these laws bear hardly upon bastards, punishing them for the sins of their parents. It is not necessary to my purpose to go into this, though it appears to me that the law is right.[9] I make the remark merely for the sake of showing to what lengths the law does habitually go for the purpose of maintaining the most important of all moral principles, the principle upon which one great department of it is entirely founded. It is a case in which a good object is promoted by efficient and adequate means. . . .

Laws relating to education and to military service and the discipline of the army have a moral side of the utmost importance. Mr. Mill would be the first to admit this; indeed, in several passages of his book he insists on the fact that society has complete control over the rising generation as a reason why it should not coerce adults into morality. This surely is the very opposite of the true conclusion. How is it possible for society to accept the position of an educator unless it has moral principles on which to educate? How, having accepted that position and having educated people up to a certain point, can it draw a line at which education ends and perfect moral indifference begins? When a private man educates his family, his superiority over them is founded principally on his superior age and experience; and as this personal superiority ceases, the power which is founded upon it gradually ceases also. Between society at large and individuals the difference is of another kind. The fixed principles and institutions of society express not merely the present opinions of the ruling part of the community, but the accumulated results of centuries of experience, and these constitute a standard by which the conduct of individuals may be tried, and to which they are in a variety of

[9] An example of Stephen's anti-humanitarianism. Note that a century earlier, Justus Möser in the selection reprinted above had made the same argument in regard to bastards.

ways, direct and indirect, compelled to conform.[10] This, I think, is one of the meanings which may be attached to the assertion that education never ceases. As a child grows into a man, and as a young man grows into an old man, he is brought under the influence of successive sets of educators, each of whom sets its mark upon him. It is no uncommon thing to see aged parents taught by their grown-up children lessons learned by the children in their intercourse with their own generation. All of us are continually educating each other, and in every instance this is and must be a process at once moral and more or less coercive.

As to Mr. Mill's doctrine that the coercive influence of public opinion ought to be exercised only for self-protective purposes, it seems to me a paradox so startling that it is almost impossible to argue against it. A single consideration on the subject is sufficient to prove this. The principle is one which it is impossible to carry out. It is like telling a rose that it ought to smell sweet only for the purpose of affording pleasure to the owner of the ground in which it grows. People form and express their opinions on each other, which, collectively, form public opinion, for a thousand reasons; to amuse themselves; for the sake of something to talk about; to gratify this or that momentary feeling; but the effect of such opinions, when formed, is quite independent of the grounds of their formation. A man is tried for murder, and just escapes conviction. People read the trial from curiosity; they discuss it for the sake of the discussion; but if, by whatever means, they are brought to think that the man was in all probability guilty, they shun his society as they would shun any other hateful thing. The opinion produces its effect in precisely the same way whatever was its origin.

The result of these observations is that both law and public opinion do in many cases exercise a powerful coercive influence on morals, for objects which are good in the sense explained above, and by means well calculated to attain those objects, to a greater or less extent at a not inadequate expense. If this is so, I say law and public opinion do well, and I do not see how either the premises or the conclusion are to be disproved.

Of course there are limits to the possibility of useful interference with morals, either by law or by public opinion; and it is of the highest practical importance that these limits should be carefully observed. . . .

Legislation ought in all cases to be graduated to the existing level of morals in the time and country in which it is employed. You cannot punish anything which public opinion, as expressed in the common practice of society, does not strenuously and unequivocally condemn. To try to

[10] Here Stephen combines historical utilitarianism with an emphasis on the role of cultural manners and mores.

do so is a sure way to produce gross hypocrisy and furious reaction. To be able to punish, a moral majority must be overwhelming. Law cannot be better than the nation in which it exists, though it may and can protect an acknowledged moral standard, and may gradually be increased in strictness as the standard rises[11]. . . .

To understand the popular enthusiasm about liberty, something more is wanted than the bare analysis of the word. In poetry and popular and pathetic language of every kind liberty means both more and less than the mere absence of restraint. It means the absence of those restraints which the person using the words regards as injurious, and it generally includes more or less distinctly a positive element as well—namely, the presence of some distinct original power acting unconstrainedly in a direction which the person using the word regards as good. When used quite generally, and with reference to the present state of the political and moral world, liberty means something of this sort—The forward impulses, the energies of human nature are good; they were regarded until lately as bad, and they are now in the course of shaking off trammels of an injurious kind which had in former ages been imposed upon them. The cry for liberty, in short, is a general condemnation of the past and an act of homage to the present in so far as it differs from the past, and to the future in so far as its character can be inferred from the character of the present.

If it be asked, What is to be thought of liberty in this sense of the word, the answer would obviously involve a complete discussion of all the changes in the direction of the diminution of authority which have taken place in modern times, and which may be expected hereafter as their consequence. Such an inquiry, of course, would be idle, to say nothing of its being impossible. A few remarks may, however, be made on points of the controversy which are continually left out of sight.

The main point is that enthusiasm for liberty in this sense is hardly compatible with anything like a proper sense of the importance of the virtue of obedience, discipline in its widest sense. The attitude of mind engendered by continual glorification of the present time, and of successful resistance to an authority assumed to be usurped and foolish, is almost of necessity fatal to the recognition of the fact that to obey a real superior, to submit to a real necessity and make the best of it in good part, is one of the most important of all virtues—a virtue absolutely essential to the attainment of anything great and lasting. Every one would admit this when stated in general terms, but the gift of recognizing the

---

[11] In his emphasis on the importance of mores, Stephen expresses skepticism about the efficacy of written laws, though in a far more moderate and nuanced way than de Maistre.

necessity for acting upon the principle when the case actually arises is one of the rarest in the world. To be able to recognize your superior, to know whom you ought to honour and obey, to see at what point resistance ceases to be honourable, and submission in good faith and without mental reservation becomes the part of courage and wisdom, is supremely difficult. All that can be said about these topics on the speculative side goes a very little way. It is like the difficulty which every one who has had any experience of the administration of justice will recognize as its crowning difficulty, the difficulty of knowing when to believe and when to disbelieve a direct assertion on a matter of importance made by a person who has the opportunity of telling a lie if he is so minded.

In nearly every department of life we are brought at last by long and laborious processes, which due care will usually enable us to perform correctly, face to face with some ultimate problem where logic, analogy, experiment, all the apparatus of thought, fail to help us, but on the value of our answer to which their value depends. The questions, Shall I or shall I not obey this man? accept this principle? submit to this pressure? and the like, are of the number. No rule can help towards their decision; but when they are decided, the answer determines the whole course and value of the life of the man who gave it. Practically, the effect of the popularity of the commonplaces about liberty has been to raise in the minds of ordinary people a strong presumption against obeying anybody, and by a natural rebound to induce minds of another class to obey the first person who claims their obedience with sufficient emphasis and self-confidence. It has shattered to pieces most of the old forms in which discipline was a recognized and admitted good, and certainly it has not produced many new ones.

The practical inference from this is that people who have the gift of using pathetic language ought not to glorify the word "liberty" as they do, but ought, as far as possible, to ask themselves before going into ecstasies over any particular case of it, Who is left at liberty to do what, and what is the restraint from which he is liberated? By forcing themselves to answer this question distinctly, they will give their poetry upon the subject a much more definite and useful turn than it has at present.

Of course these remarks apply, as all such remarks must, in opposite directions. When liberty is exalted as such, we may be sure that there will always be those who are opposed to liberty as such, and who take pleasure in dwelling upon the weak side of everything which passes by the name. These persons should ask themselves the converse questions before they glorify acts of power: Who is empowered to do what, and by what means? Or, if the words chosen for eulogy are "order" and "society," it would be well for them to ask themselves, What order and what sort of society it is to which their praises refer?[12]. . .

There are a number of objects the attainment of which is desirable for men, and which collectively may be called good, happiness, or whatever else you please so long as some word is used which sufficiently marks the fact that there is a real standard towards which human conduct must be directed, if the wishes which prompt us to action, and which are the deepest part of our nature—which are, indeed, our very selves in the attitude of wishing—are to be satisfied. These objects are very numerous. They cannot be precisely defined, and they are far from being altogether consistent with each other. Health is one of them. Wealth, to the extent of such a command of material things as enables men to use their faculties vigorously, is another. Knowledge is a third. Fit opportunities for the use of the faculties is a fourth. Virtue, the state in which given sets of faculties are so related to each other as to produce good results (whatever good may mean), is the most important and the most multiform and intricate of all. Reasonable men pursue these objects or some of them openly and avowedly. They find that they can greatly help or impede each other in the pursuit by exciting each other's hopes or fears, by promising payment for this and threatening punishment for that, and by leaving other matters to individual taste. This last department of things is the department of liberty in the proper sense of the word. Binding promises and threats always imply restraint. Thus the question, How large ought the province of liberty to be? is really identical with this: In what respects must men influence each other if they want to attain the objects of life, and in what respects must they leave each other uninfluenced?

If the object is to criticize and appreciate historical events, the question between liberty and law, scepticism and protection, and the like, will have to be stated thus: What are the facts? Which of them were caused, and to what extent, by the influence of men on each other's hopes and fears? Which of them were caused by the unrestrained and unimpelled impulses of individuals towards particular objects? How far did each class of results contribute to the attainment of the objects of life? To ask these questions is to show that they cannot be answered. Discussions about liberty are in truth discussions about a negation. Attempts to solve the problems of government and society by such discussions are like attempts to discover the nature of light and heat by inquiries into darkness and cold. The phenomenon which requires and will repay study is the direction and nature of the various forces, individual and collective, which in their combination or collision with each

---

[12] In the omitted text, Stephen proceeds to criticize de Maistre as an enthusiast of order.

other and with the outer world make up human life. If we want to know what ought to be the size and position of a hole in a water pipe, we must consider the nature of water, the nature of pipes, and the objects for which the water is wanted; but we shall learn very little by studying the nature of holes. Their shape is simply the shape of whatever bounds them. Their nature is merely to let the water pass, and it seems to me that enthusiasm about them is altogether thrown away.

The result is that discussions about liberty are either misleading or idle, unless we know who wants to do what, by what restraint he is prevented from doing it, and for what reasons it is proposed to remove that restraint. . . .

▶ 4 ◀

INEQUALITY

INTRODUCTION TO
W. H. Mallock,
Aristocracy and Evolution: A Study of the Rights, the
Origin, and Social Functions of the Wealthier Classes

◆

By the 1880s the major challenge to the existing order came not only from the new and more egalitarian liberalism against which Stephen had polemicized, but from socialism and from the newly enfranchised working-class voters on which socialists drew for support. The result was a recasting of conservatism, which became increasingly focused on the themes of the protection of property and the legitimation of economic inequality arising from the capitalist market, concerns which had formerly been associated primarily with European liberalism. Within the British Conservative party, influence shifted away from the landed classes toward businessmen, and from the countryside to the suburbs. The rhetoric of conservative paternalism—according to which the traditional landed upper classes were to protect the deferential working classes—foundered on the rock of labor union involvement in politics, which in the British case was expressed first within the Liberal Party, and after 1893 in an independent Labour Party. The centrality of opposition to socialism as the core of a recast conservatism is well represented in the writings of William Hurrell Mallock.

Mallock was born in 1849 into a gentry family in Devonshire. His father, the younger son of an aristocratic family, had chosen the honorable profession of clergyman in the Church of England, a characteristic choice for men of his background. William attended Oxford, and made his mark on the literary scene in 1877 with the publication of *The New Republic*. The book satirized the religious liberalism he had found at Oxford, as exemplified by Matthew Arnold and others. Several novels and philosophical works followed in short order. Mallock's writings attracted attention, and as a clever young man he was welcomed in the country-house milieu of fashionable society.[1] Yet Mallock was eminently aware of the declining influence of the aristocracy, which he registered in his novel of 1886, *The Old Order Changes*. "Aristocracy, as a genuine power, as a visible fact in the world, may not yet be buried, perhaps; but it is dead," he wrote.[2]

Until the 1880s the majority of members of Parliament were drawn from the ranks of landowning gentlemen; their local status as notables made them the "natural" choice of the men of property who composed much of the electorate. But the Third Reform Act of 1884–85 created mass (though not yet universal) male suffrage, expanding the electorate from three to six million. Politics, once controlled by country notables, become a matter of urban numbers. It was now the cities and suburbs that sent the most members to Parliament, and in this new electorate the working class predominated.[3] The local hegemony of aristocratic landowners in the countryside was ended by the County Councils Act of 1888.

Mallock was nominated as a Conservative candidate for the Scottish borough of St. Andrews in 1883, but relinquished his candidature because he felt it more important to play the role of "providing facts and principles for politicians, rather than playing directly the part of a politician."[4] Like many conservative theorists before and after him, Mallock found that contemporary conservative politicians were intellectually inept. "Conservatism with them was no more than a vague sentiment, healthy so far as it went, but incapable of aiding them in controversy with any glib Radical opponent," he recalled in his memoirs. He discovered that when faced with the arguments of socialists and other radicals, "the Conservatives as a whole were so ignorant that they did not know, or so timorous or apathetic that they did not dare to use, the true facts, figures, or principles by the promulgation of which alone the false might be systematically discredited." Mallock decided to devote himself to the development of a more social scientifically informed and sophisticated conservatism.[5]

Mallock was closely associated with the Liberty and Property Defence League. Founded in 1882, the League attracted the support of peers, railway magnates, and other owners of large industry, as well as over two hundred business groups. Its members responded to the increasing eco-

---

[1] On Mallock's life I have relied on A. Cochrane, "William Hurrell Mallock," in the *Dictionary of National Biography, 1922–1930*, pp. 556–57; as well as on W. H. Mallock, *Memoirs of Life and Literature* (New York, 1920).

[2] Quoted in David Cannadine, *The Decline and Fall of the British Aristocracy* (New Haven, 1990), p. 30.

[3] On this process, see Cannadine, *Decline and Fall*, pp. 1–39.

[4] Mallock, *Memoirs of Life and Literature*, p. 144

[5] Ibid., pp. 210–13.

nomic interventionism of Gladstone's second government, as well as to what they saw as the threats to property from British socialists such as the Fabians (a small but influential group of intellectuals whose leaders included Sidney and Beatrice Webb, and George Bernard Shaw), the Marxist Social Democratic Federation, and the British followers of the American social reformer Henry George. The Liberty and Property Defence League attacked state intervention in the economy, and Mallock became "its most far-sighted propagandist."[6] At the same time, Mallock began to write for *The National Review*, a journal linked with the Conservative Party's Central Office. His books *Labour and the Popular Welfare* (1893) and *Classes and Masses* (1896) were used by the Conservative Central Office as textbooks for speakers combating socialism.[7]

The immediate stimulus for *Aristocracy and Evolution* was Benjamin Kidd's *Social Evolution*, published in 1894. To Mallock, the book seemed "a piece of monumental claptrap, though it was claptrap of the highest order, and was for that reason all the more pernicious." Kidd shared with Sidney Webb and the American socialist Edward Bellamy a denial that economic growth could be traced to the efforts and abilities of extraordinary individuals, from which they concluded that large disparities of income were illegitimate. These assumptions Mallock set out to refute in a series of articles published in the *Contemporary Review*, which he gathered together into book form and published as *Aristocracy and Evolution: A Study of the Rights, the Origin, and the Social Functions of the Wealthier Classes.*[8]

The selection below presents the major theme of Mallock's writings on matters economic, namely, that the material progress of the majority of men and women depended on a small elite of the talented. Material advance was therefore based on unequal contributions, and these contributions had economic inequality as their legitimate reward. Inequality was therefore both inexorable and desirable, for it provided the incentive for the talented to apply their potential talents to actual economic improvement. At the same time, Mallock returned to a Humean theme in stressing that the economy cannot and does not reward virtue.

Mallock continued his critique of socialist economics in *A Critical Examination of Socialism* (1908), in which he chastised Marx for ignoring the role of intellectual ability in his labor theory of value. Every business, he argued, depended for its success on the talents and energies by

---

[6] Harold Perkin, *The Rise of Professional Society: England Since 1880* (London, 1989), pp. 145–49.

[7] D. J. Ford, "W.H. Mallock and Socialism in England, 1880–1918," in Kenneth D. Brown, ed., *Essays in Anti-Labour History: Responses to the Rise of Labour in Britain* (London, 1974), pp. 317–42.

[8] Mallock, *Memoir*, pp. 260–68, and *Aristocracy and Evolution* (London, 1898), pp. 64ff.

which labor was directed by management, rather than by the quantity of average labor put into it. The modern development of knowledge, of industrial methods and of machinery, Mallock wrote, was the product of individuals of exceptional ability, and he stressed the role of character and management skills in accounting for the success and failure of business enterprises.

W. H. Mallock,
Aristocracy and Evolution: A Study of the Rights, the Origin, and Social Functions of the Wealthier Classes (1898)

[FROM BOOK I, CHAPTER II, "THE ATTEMPT TO MERGE THE GREAT MAN IN THE AGGREGATE"]

If all members of the community were content with existing social arrangements, it is needless to say there would be no social problems at all. Such problems are due entirely to the existence of persons who are not contented, and who desire that certain of these arrangements should be changed. It will be seen, accordingly, that the great and fundamental question which, as a practical guide, the sociologist is asked to answer, is whether or how far the changes desired by the discontented are practicable; and the first step towards ascertaining how far the arrangements in question can be turned into something which they are not, is to ascertain precisely how they have come to be what they are. . . .

In asking, therefore, how the social arrangements we have been considering have come to be what they are, we must not ask in vague and general terms why a portion of the social aggregate occupies a position which contents it, and another portion a position which exasperates it; but we must consider the individuals of which each portion, at any given time, is composed, and begin the inquiry at the point at which they begin it themselves. "Why am I—Tom or Dick or Harry—included in that portion of the aggregate which' occupies an inferior position? And why are these men—William or James or George—more fortunate than I, and included in the portion of the aggregate which occupies a superior position?" To this question there are but three possible answers. The inferior position of Tom or Dick or Harry is due to his differing from William or James or George in external circumstances, which theoretically, at all events, might all be equalised—such, for example, as his education; or it is due to his differing from them in certain congenital faculties, with respect to which men can never be made equal—as, for example, in his brain power or his physical energy; or it is due to his differing from them in external circumstances which have arisen naturally from differences in the congenital faculties of others, and which, if they could be equalised at all, could never be equalised with anything like completeness—such, for example, as the possession by William and James and George of leisured and intellectual homes secured for them by gifted fathers, and the want of such homes and fathers on the part of Tom and Dick and Harry.

The first question, accordingly, which we have to ask is as follows. Taking Tom or Dick or Harry as a type of those classes who happen to occupy an inferior position in the aggregate, and comparing him with others who happen to occupy superior positions, we have to ask how far he is condemned to the inferior position which he resents by such external circumstances as conceivably could be equalised by legislation, and how far by some congenital inferiority of his own, or circumstances naturally arising out of the congenital inferiority of others. Or we may put the question conversely, and ask how William and George and James have come to occupy the positions which Tom, Dick, and Harry envy. Do they owe their positions solely to unjust and arbitrary legislation, which a genuinely democratic parliament could and would undo? Or to exceptional abilities of their own, of which no parliament could deprive them? Or to advantages secured for them by the exceptional abilities of their fathers, which no parliament could interfere with, or, at all events, could abolish, without entering on a conflict with the instincts of human nature, and interfering with the springs of all human action?

Now that external circumstances of a kind, easily alterable by legislation, have been, and often are, responsible for many social inequalities, is a fact which we may here assume without particularly discussing it. The inquiry, therefore, narrows itself still further, and resolves itself into this: Do the congenital superiorities or inferiorities of the persons, or of parents of the persons, who at any given time are occupying in the social aggregate superior and inferior positions, play any part in the production of these social inequalities at all?

This question must plainly be the practical sociologist's starting-point; for if social inequalities are due wholly to alterable and artificial circumstances, social conditions are capable, theoretically, at all events, of being equalised; but if, on the other hand, inferior and superior positions are partly, at all events, the result of the congenital inequalities of individuals, over which no legislation can exercise the least control, then a natural limit is set to the possibilities of the leveling process; and it is the business of the sociologist, if he aspires to be a practical guide, to begin with ascertaining what these limits are. Are, then, the congenital inequalities of men a factor in the production of social inequalities, or are they not?

Now to many people it will seem that even to ask this question is superfluous. They will regard it as a matter patent to common sense that men's congenital inequalities are to a large extent the cause, in every society, of such social inequalities as exist in it; and they will possibly say that it is a mere waste of time to discuss a truth which is so self-evident. It happens, however, that the more obvious it seems to be to common sense, the more necessary it is for us to begin our present inquiry with insisting on it. . . .

[FROM BOOK II, CHAPTER 1, "THE NATURE AND THE DEGREES OF THE SUPERIORITIES OF GREAT MEN"]

[W]hen we describe great men as being a minority, or a "scattered few," we do not mean that out of every thousand men there are nine hundred and ninety-nine "ordinary" men and one genius; or that there are (let us say) seven hundred who can be described for all purposes as "ordinary," and two hundred and ninety-nine who can be for all purposes described as "stupid"; and that there is one "clever" or "great" man who towers over them like an oak tree over bramble bushes. Nor, again, do we mean that "greatness" is some single definite quality, which marks its possessor out like a white man amongst negroes. Believers in extreme democracy, who very rightly discern in the great-man theory the destruction of their favourite enthusiasms, will instinctively seek to attribute some meaning such as this to its exponents. But the great-man theory, when properly analysed and explained, will be found to comprise no such absurdities as the foregoing. When we speak of "greatness" we mean a great variety of efficiencies, which, though grouped together because they are all exceptional in degree, are nevertheless indefinitely various in kind; and, moreover, the degrees to which they are exceptional are indefinitely various also, the degree being in many cases so low that it is difficult to say whether it should be classed as exceptional at all. In short, there are as many degrees of greatness as there are of temperature; and it is as difficult to draw a line between ordinary men and men whose greatness is of a very low degree, as it is to draw a line between coldness, coolness, and low degrees of heat. But though it may be questionable whether we should call a day cool when the thermometer is at fifty-nine, and whether we should call it hot when the thermometer is at sixty-one, everybody admits that it is hot when the thermometer is at eighty-five, and cold when the thermometer registers twenty degrees of frost. In the same way, though there will be a certain number of people who may be classed as great by one judge and classed as ordinary by another, there is a certain number whose capacities, however unequal amongst themselves, set their possessors apart as indubitably greater than the majority; and we are speaking with sufficient, though we cannot speak with absolute, precision when we say that progress depends on the action of this minority.

How great the inequality is between the natural powers of men is perhaps most clearly evidenced by the case of art, and more especially the art of poetry. In certain domains of effort it may be urged that unequal results are caused by unequal circumstances, quite as much as by unequal capacities. But about poetry, at all events, this cannot be said. Some of the greatest poets the world has ever known—it is enough to instance the cases of Burns and Shakespeare—have been men of no wealth and of very imperfect education. Obviously, therefore, in poetry one man has as good a chance as another. It is no doubt often argued—and this argument has already been examined—that great poets, of whom Shakespeare is a favourite example, owe part of their greatness not to themselves, but to their age. But this does nothing to explain the differences between poets who belong to the same age, and who, all of them, in this respect, start with the same advantage. . . .

And the same inequality that exhibits itself in the domain of poetry will be found in every other domain of human effort. What can be more unequal than the gifts of different singers? In every school and university we see multitudes of young men and boys whose opportunities of learning are not only similar but identical, but of whom, in respect to assimilating what they are taught, not one in ten rises appreciably above a certain level, and not one in a hundred rises above it signally. . . . And in practical life the same phenomenon repeats itself. Let us take any department of social activity or production, on the results of which the welfare of society at any given time depends. Let us take, for instance, the work of government, or invention, or commercial enterprise. In each of these we shall find a large number of men, each doing what is in him to subserve some particular end; and we shall find a few producing results which are great both for themselves and others, and the many producing results which are uniform in their individual pettiness.

It is perfectly true that in these great departments of practical life there may not be so obvious or so widely-extended an equality of opportunity as that which prevails amongst poets, or amongst scholars in the same seminary, but in each department there will be a large number, at all events, whose opportunities are as equal as human ingenuity could make them. This is so in the French army, in the English House of Commons, and in the world of business and industry; and yet of men thus equally placed we see some doing great things, and doubling their opportunities by using them; others doing little or nothing, and throwing their opportunities away. We have accordingly in every domain of activity a sufficient number of persons with the same external advantages, to show by the extraordinary difference between the results accomplished by them how great the natural inequality between men's capacities is, and how far the efficiency of a few exceeds that of the majority. It is therefore nothing to the purpose to attribute, as many reformers do, men's inequality in efficiency to the fact that equality of opportunity is not at present as general as it theoretically might be. To extend this equality further might produce good results or bad; but in neither case would it tend to make men's capacities equal. The utmost it would do in this particular respect would be merely to widen the area of their realised inequality—to increase the number of the mountains, not to produce a plain.

It will doubtless be objected by those who would minimise natural inequalities that a man may be contemptible in one capacity, that of a poet, for instance, and yet be greater as a man than men who in one capacity are superior to him. It may, for example, be said that Frederick of Prussia, in spite of his bad poetry, was a greater man than Voltaire. This is perfectly true; but it is necessary to explain clearly that it in no way contradicts what is being here asserted. It is, on the contrary, part of it. It cannot be too emphatically said that greatness, in the only sense in which we are here considering it—that is to say as an agent of social progress—is a quality which we attribute to a man not with reference to his whole nature, but with reference solely to the objective results produced by him, so that in one domain of activity a man may be great, in another ordinary, in another decidedly stupid. What, then, we here mean by a great man is merely a man who is superior to the majority in his power of producing some given class of result, whereas the average man and the stupid are not superior to the majority in their powers of producing any.

The reader must thus entirely disabuse himself of the idea that greatness, as an agent of social progress, has any necessary resemblance to greatness as conceived of by the moralist. A man may be a great saint or a noble "moral character" who passes his life in obscurity, stretched on a bed of sickness, and incapable even of rendering the humblest help to others. He is great in virtue not of what he does, but of what he is. But greatness, as an agent of social progress, has nothing whatever to do with what a man is, except in so far as what he is enables him to do what he does. If two doctors were confronted by some terrible epidemic, and the one met it by tending the poor for nothing, and died in his unavailing efforts to save his patients, whilst the other fled from the infected district, and, solacing himself at a distance with a mistress and an excellent cook, invented a medicine by which the disease could be warded off, and proceeded to make a large fortune by selling it, though the former as a man might be incalculably better than the latter, the latter as an agent of progress would be incalculably greater than the former. . . .

This truth, which sounds brutal when plainly stated, but is really little more than a sociological truism, is constantly overlooked, and even indignantly denied, by thinkers whose emotions are more powerful than their minds. The way in which such persons reason is very easily understood. They see that a number of men by whom great social results are produced—men who make successful inventions and who found great businesses—are narrow-minded, uncultivated, and contemptible in general conversation, and that a number of other men who produce no such results are scholars, critics, thinkers, keen judges of men and things; and contrasting the brilliancy of those who have produced no great social results with the narrow ideas and dullness of those who have produced many, they proceed to argue that great social results cannot possibly require great men to produce them; or, in other words, that they might be produced by almost anybody.

But the whole of this class of objections will altogether disappear when we more closely examine what the qualities are on which the production of given social results depend. Let us take a few of these results as examples. Let us take the formulation and the popularising of some particular political demand, by which the whole course of a country's history is affected, and the increasing and cheapening the supply of some articles of popular consumption—sugar, let us say, or workmen's boots and clothing. The persons who urge the objections we are now discussing assume that all greatness, other than physical strength and dexterity, must be necessarily ethical or intellectual, and be calculated to excite our ethical or intellectual admiration. But let them consider the qualities requisite to produce such results as have just been mentioned, and they will see that no assumption could be more wide of the truth.

A man who should, without underpaying his employees, succeed in manufacturing for the poorer classes boots, jackets, or shirts better in quality and very much less in price than those which they are accustomed to buy now, would probably have to devote a large part of his life to the consideration of a particular kind of seemingly sordid detail. To a man of wide culture and brilliant imagination, the concentration of his faculties on details such as these would be impossible; and if he wished to produce any of the results in question, he would soon discover that he could not. The men who do produce them are rendered capable of doing so, not by the width of their minds, but by the exceptional narrowness. The intellectual stream flows strongly because it is confined in a narrow channel, and thus what to the superficial observer seems a sign of their inferiority, is really, so far as the results are concerned, one of the chief causes of their greatness.

> The mean man with the little thing to do
> > Sees it and does it;
> The great man with the great end to pursue
> > Dies ere he knows it.

Robert Browning very tersely puts the case thus. We have only to alter his language in one respect. Seeing that the results we have now in view are realised results or nothing, the "*mean man*," as an agent of material progress, will be the "great man," and the "great man" will be the little.

So, too, with regard to the man who affects the history of his country by formulating and popularising some particular political demand—the secret of such a man's success, in four cases out of five, will be found to lie in the greatness, not of his intellect, but of his will—in an exceptionally sanguine temperament, in exceptional courage and energy, and very likely in an exaggerated belief in his own nostrums, which, instead of being a sign of great intellectual acuteness, is incompatible with it.

No doubt social progress, as a whole, has required and does require for its production intellectual powers of the highest and rarest kind. The point here insisted on is that it is not produced by intellectual powers alone, and that intellectual powers alone would be quite unable to produce it. Thus the sorrows and disappointments of the unfortunate inventor are proverbial; and the reason is that great inventive powers are frequently accompanied by a very feeble will and a fantastic ignorance of the world, the inventor, though strong as a mind, being pitiably weak as a man. He can do everything with his inventions except make them useful to anybody. He might be practically far greater were he to lose some of his intellectual powers, could he thereby develop some of the humbler qualities in which he is wanting. As it is, he resembles a chronometer which is without a main-spring, and which is useless when compared with a ten-and-sixpenny watch. Hence the inventor has so frequently to ally himself with the man of enterprise, and only becomes great, as a social force, by doing so. Such unions are often sufficiently strange in appearance. We see some man whose intellect is the finest machine imaginable, but he is only redeemed from absolute and grotesque uselessness by his partner, who is little better than an inspired bagman. But such a bagman's gifts, however the inefficient theorist may despise them, are, though less striking than the inventor's, often quite as rare. No doubt many great inventors have the practical gifts as well as the intellectual, and their greatness, in such cases, is comprehended completely in themselves. It remains, however, an equally composite thing, no matter whether it takes two men or only one to complete it; and exceptional intellect is only one of its elements. The other qualities with which it requires to be allied, and which alone give it its practical value, such as determination, shrewdness, and a certain thickness of skin, though often remarkable individually for the exceptional degree to which they are developed, just as often unite to produce practical greatness, not because of the exceptional degree to which they are developed, but of the exceptional proportions in which they are combined. Some of the most essential of them, indeed, need not be exceptional at all, except from the fact of their association with others that are so. Much greatness, for instance, of the most powerful kind consists mainly of very ordinary sense in conjunction with extraordinary energy; and energy is often, as has already been pointed out, in proportion to the narrowness rather than to the width of the imagination.

Greatness, in short, as an agent of social progress, is in most cases not a single quality, but a peculiar combination of many; its composition varies according to the character of the results in the production of which the great men are severally more efficient than the majority; and it often depends less on the extent to which any special faculty is developed, in comparison with the same faculty as possessed by ordinary men, than it does on the degree to which each faculty is developed as compared with the others possessed by the great man himself.

When we speak of greatness, then, in the sense here attributed to the word—when we speak of great men as agents of social progress—we do not mean that the world is divided into ordinary men and heroes. The members of that minority whom we group together as great men, though some of them are, no doubt, of noble and heroic proportions, are for the most part great in relation to special results only; even in relation to these special results they are great in very various degrees, and many of them in other relations may be ordinary, or even less than ordinary. It must therefore be clearly understood that greatness, as an agent of social progress, is not an absolute thing, and that to say of any one man that he possesses more greatness than another is a statement which, taken by itself, has no definite meaning. When we say that a man is great we mean that he is exceptionally efficient in producing some particular result, which is either implied or specified—that he is great in commanding armies, or in managing hotels, or in conducting public affairs, or in cheapening and improving the manufacture of this or that commodity; and when we say that such and such a man possesses the quality of greatness to such and such a degree we mean that he produces results of a given kind, which are in such and such a degree better or more copious than results of the same kind which are produced by other people.

The inequality of men, then, in natural capacity being an obvious fact, and the nature and the degrees of their inequalities having been now generally explained, we may re-state, with a meaning more precise than was formerly possible, the fundamental proposition implied in the great-man theory, when that theory is raised from a rhetorical to a scientific formula. Progress of an appreciable kind, in any department of social activity and achievement, takes place only when, and in proportion as, some of the men who are working to produce such and such a result are more efficient in relation to that class of result than the majority; or conversely, if a community contained no man with capacities superior to those possessed by the greater number, progress in that community would be so slow as to be practically non-existent. . . .

[FROM BOOK II, CHAPTER IV, "INEQUALITY,
HAPPINESS, AND PROGRESS"]

[N]one of the arguments contained in the present work have been invoked to prove, or have any tendency to prove, that the many, as distinct from the few, in any progressive country, may not reasonably look forward to a continuous improvement in their condition—to a greater command of the comforts and luxuries of life, together with a lightening or a lessening of the labour necessary to procure them. On the contrary, the majority may look forward to an improvement in their circumstances which it is as impossible for us to imagine distinctly at the present time as it would have been for our grandfathers to imagine the telephone or the phonograph. All that has been urged in this work is as follows: That whatever may be the new advantages which the majority of mankind attain, they will attain them not by any development in their own productive powers, but solely by the talents and activity of an exceptionally gifted minority, who will enable the ordinary man to earn more whilst labouring for fewer hours, because they will, by directing his labour to more and more advantage, secure from equal labour an ever-increasing product.

The conclusion, therefore, is not that the majority in any progressive community may not look forward to indefinitely better conditions, but merely that their condition will not depend on themselves, and that, though the conditions of all may be bettered, they will never be even approximately equal. . . .

INTRODUCTION TO
Joseph A. Schumpeter,
"Aptitude and Social Mobility"

◆

Joseph Alois Schumpeter was "the most sophisticated conservative of this century"—such at least is the judgment of a prominent liberal, John Kenneth Galbraith, who knew him.[1] Galbraith's claim is plausible, for Schumpeter was among the most learned and creative social scientists of the first half of the twentieth century, whose works spanned the fields of economics, sociology, political science, and history.

Schumpeter was born in Moravia in 1883, in what was then the Austro-Hungarian empire, the scion of several generations of entrepreneurs. At the universities of Vienna and Berlin, he studied history, sociology, economics, and law. In 1905–6 he participated in a now famous seminar on Marx's economics led by Eugen von Böhm-Bawerk; other participants included Ludwig von Mises (later a leading liberal economist and political philosopher), as well as Otto Bauer and Rudolf Hilferding, who were to become leading political and intellectual figures in the Social Democratic parties of Austria and Germany. At a time when socialist parties heavily influenced by Marx were becoming major forces in German and Austrian politics, Schumpeter was unusually knowledgeable about Marx and Marxism. In 1906 Schumpeter studied with the great German economic historian, Gustav Schmoller, in Berlin. Schumpeter's intellectual origins help account for his interest in explaining the role of social and psychological factors in the development of capitalism. The work of the British eugenicists, Francis Galton and Karl Pearson, also stimulated his interest in the broader issue of the role of inherited intelligence and other traits.

In 1912 Schumpeter published a seminal work, the *Theory of Economic Development*, in which he laid out his theory of entrepreneurship. Schumpeter argued that the laws of supply and demand, which had been the focus of economics since the time of Adam Smith, as well as the more recent focus on static equilibrium associated with the Belgian economist Leon Walras, both missed the fundamental dynamic of capitalism. Capitalism needed to be understood in terms of its dynamic transformation, Schumpeter argued, and the source of that dynamism

[1] John Kenneth Galbraith, *A View from the Stands of People, Politics, Military Power and the Arts* (Boston, 1986), quoted in Richard Swedberg, *Schumpeter: A Biography* (Princeton, 1991), p. 150.

lay in the entrepreneur, a figure largely neglected in nineteenth-century economic thought.[2]

The function of the entrepreneur, in Schumpeter's theory, was to introduce economic innovation. Innovation could mean introducing new commodities or qualitatively better versions of existing ones; finding new markets, or new methods of production and distribution, or new sources of production for existing commodities, or introducing new forms of economic organization.[3] The role of the entrepreneur was to break out of the routine of habitual economic life, and this, Schumpeter argued, required a rare and extraordinary mental creativity and energy.[4]

Schumpeter understood his conception of the entrepreneur as one aspect of the larger problem of leadership and of elites in accounting for social development, an interest which he shared with James Fitzjames Stephen and W. H. Mallock, as well as with a number of early twentieth-century continental theorists such as Gaetano Mosca and Max Weber. Perhaps the best known turn-of-the-century elite theorist was Vilfredo Pareto, whose work Schumpeter much admired.[5] Pareto's essay of 1901 on "The Rise and Fall of Elites" emphasized two themes to which Schumpeter would return time and again: the inexorability of elites, and the importance of nonrational and nonlogical drives in the explanation of social action. The social scientific significance of differences of individual talent and energy became a recurrent theme of Schumpeter's work.

Some of the broader implications of Schumpeter's elitist contentions for social scientific understanding were developed in his essay on "Social Classes in an Ethnically Homogenous Environment." Although this essay was first published in 1927 when Schumpeter was a professor of economics in Bonn, its genesis lies in the decade before the First World War. It grew, Schumpeter tells us in a prefatory note, from lectures he delivered at the University of Czernowitz in 1910–11, and then in a course he offered three years later while a visiting professor at Columbia University in New York.

Here, as so often in his writings, Schumpeter praised Marx's contentions only to demonstrate the weakness of Marx's understanding of

---

[2] On the neglect of the entrepreneur in economic theory, see Fritz Redlich, "Unternehmerforschung und Weltanschauung," *Kyklos*, vol. VIII, 1955, pp. 277–300; and for more recent literature on the subject, Israel M. Kirzner, *Discovery and the Capitalist Process* (Chicago, 1985), chapter 1.

[3] Joseph Schumpeter, *The Theory of Economic Development* (New Brunswick, NJ, 1983), p. 66. This translation of the second edition of Schumpeter's book first appeared in 1934.

[4] Ibid., p. 86.

[5] See Schumpeter's essay on Pareto in Joseph Schumpeter, *Ten Great Economists from Marx to Keynes* (New York, 1951).

those contentions. Marxists were right to point to the significance of social class, he wrote, but they had an inadequate understanding of why classes came about and downplayed the reality of mobility between classes. Schumpeter insisted on the importance of "aptitude"—both inherited genetically and acquired from existing familial class position—in explaining the phenomenon of social stratification. The social mobility of families and of individuals in and out of classes, he asserted, depends primarily on the competence of their behavior. How competence is defined depends upon the requirements of the particular social system.

Joseph A. Schumpeter,
"Aptitude and Social Mobility" (1927)[1]

We shall for the moment postulate given class situations, as though every social class that ever existed were made up simply of a certain number of family units, which, for some reason or other, had chanced into their class and had persisted in it, forbidding other people access to it—in other words, as though class barriers were insurmountable. Now it is beyond dispute that within a class the relative position of families is forever shifting, that some families rise within their class, while others fall. And we are interested in the reasons why this happens. This can best be studied in individual historical situations. . . .

In the case of the capitalist bourgeoisie of Europe—say, of the post-Napoleonic period—. . . . how does it happen that one family rises, while the other falls—quite apart from accidents, to which we attribute a certain importance but not the crucial role? The rising and falling are facts. No matter which area we study, we always find that the relative position of families in the class situation we have described—other families are of no concern to us at this point—undergoes change, not in such a way that the "big" ones grow bigger and the "small" ones smaller, but typically the other way round. In the textile area of Brno, the silk region of Krefeld, the iron-working district around Birmingham, for example, certain families have maintained their position for more than half a century, in many cases considerably longer. Yet, by and large, the families

---

[1] "Die sozialen Klassen im ethnisch homogen Milieu," *Archiv für Sozialwissenschaft und Sozialpolitik*, 1927; translation, "Social Classes in an Ethnically Homogeneous Environment," now in Joseph A. Schumpeter, *The Economics and Sociology of Capitalism*, ed. Richard Swedberg (Princeton, 1991). The translation, by Heinz Norden, originally appeared in Joseph A. Schumpeter, *Imperialism and Social Classes* (1951). It has been altered by the editor in the interests of clarity and precision. The title of the selection has been supplied by the editor.

that led around the middle of the nineteenth century are not on top of the heap today. Some of those that are most successful now were then scarcely recognized as members of the class, while some of those that were most successful then are accepted only with reservations today. Manifestly, concentration and the formation of corporations complicate our analysis, and it will be well if we make a distinction between the private and one-man firm in a competitive economy on the one hand, and the modern large-scale enterprise and trust, on the other.

The characteristic feature of the private firm is the element of family property and the coincidence of family and business success. One theory which is offered to account for shifting family positions is that of the automatism of accumulation, asserted by Marx. The "capitalist" who is bigger at the outset of any period is able to exploit more profit than the smaller one. His proportionate accumulation is therefore larger, and he improves his productive apparatus more rapidly. The difference grows continuously, until the wealthier exploiter drives out the poorer exploiter through competition and expropriates him. This view is a typical example of how bias in favor of a theory blinds the theorist to the simplest facts, grotesquely distorting their proportions. Clearly, the captured surplus value *does not invest itself* but must *be invested*. This means on the one hand that it must not be consumed by the capitalist, and on the other hand that the important point is *how* it is invested. Both factors lead away from the idea of objective automatism and toward the behavior of the capitalist, and thereby to his motive, that is to say from *social* "forces" to the *individual* (either the physical individual or the individual family), from the *objective* to the *subjective*. It may be objected that the logic of the social situation forces the individual to invest his profits, that individual motivation is only a fleeting intermediate phase. This is true, as far as it goes, and must be acknowledged by any reasonable person. To be sure, the individual psyche is no more than a product, an offshoot, a reflex, and a conductor of the inner necessities of any given situation. But the crucial factor is that the social logic or objective situation does not unequivocally determine *how much* profit shall be invested, and *how* it shall be invested, *unless individual disposition is taken into account*. Yet when that is done, the logic is no longer inherent solely in the system as distinct from the individuality of the industrialist himself. Marx, in fact, in this case as in general, implies an assumption about average behavior—an assumption that includes an economic psychology, however imperfect. The automatism as such does not exist, even though we shall presently encounter its elements—saving and the improvement of the productive apparatus—as elements of the behavior of industrial families. We can speak of an automatism, with respect to an existing class position, only in the sense that ... position does have a tendency to rise on its own, to a moderate extent, and even more a tendency to maintain itself, because the well-established firm can make better deals, attract new customers and suppliers, and so on.

There is, on the other hand, the very important fact of automatic decline. This occurs invariably when a family behaves according to Marx's description—when it persists in "plowing back into the business" a set proportion of profits, without blazing new trails, without being devoted, heart and soul, to the business alone. In that case it is bound to go under in time, though often only very slowly if the business is on a solid foundation and the mode of life frugal. A steady decline and loss of ground are first observed—what is called "being crowded out of business." This decline *is* automatic, for it is not a matter of omission or commission, but flows instead from the self-actuating logic of the competitive system, by the simple fact of profits running dry. As to the question why this is so, it is answered by the theory of entrepreneurial profit. It seems to me, however, that everybody knows the type of old respectable firm, growing obsolete, despite its integrity, and slowly and inevitably sinking into limbo.

The second reason for the phenomenon with which we are concerned at the moment lies in the disposition to save, which varies from family to family. (If the term "saving" must be avoided as implying a positive value judgment, we can speak of an energetic policy of non-spending.) This serves to make the class position secure, and adherence to such a policy over several generations is the factor that in many cases turns small family enterprises into large ones. It is a policy that is very conspicuous in families that practice it. Most of us have observed members of successful business families who watch with extreme care over expenditures which members of other classes, even when their incomes are incomparably smaller, do not hesitate a moment to make. In their personal lives, such families often live with curious frugality, sometimes against a background that, for reasons of prestige, may be quite luxurious and out of keeping with their parsimony. True, of itself this does not carry much weight, though the opposite behavior is one of the most important reasons for a decline.

The third reason lies in differences in efficiency—the quality of technical, commercial, and administrative leadership of the enterprise, primarily along traditional lines. Behavior giving rise to such differences may, for our purposes, be adequately described in terms of hard-headedness, concentration on profit, authority, capacity for work, and inexorable self-discipline, especially in renouncing other aspects of life. This latter feature often escapes consideration, because the outsider is likely to observe these people in the practice of compensatory and conspicuous excesses. The significance of such efficiency lies not so much in immediate results as in increased credit ratings that open up opportunities for expansion.

For the least significant obstacle for a rising industrial family is the potential lack of capital.[2] If it is otherwise sound, the family will find that in normal times capital is virtually thrust upon it. Indeed, one may say, with Marshall, that the size of an enterprise—and here that means the position of the family—tends to adapt itself to the ability of the entrepreneur. If he exceeds his personal limitations, resultant failure will trim the size of his enterprise; if he lacks the capital to exploit such personal resources as he does possess, he is likely to find the necessary credit. But in considering this process of expansion, we come upon a fourth reason for the varying success of business dynasties. Such expansion is not simply a matter of saving and efficient routine work. What it implies is precisely departure from routine. Elaboration of an established plant, the introduction of new production methods, the opening up of new markets—indeed, the successful carrying through of new business combinations in general—all these imply risk, trial and error, the overcoming of resistance, factors lacking in the treadmill of routine. Most members of the class are handicapped in this respect. They can follow suit only when someone else has already demonstrated success in practice. Such success requires a capacity for making decisions and the vision to evaluate forcefully the elements in a given situation that are relevant to the achievement of success, while ignoring all others. The rarity of such qualifications explains why competition does not function immediately even when there are no outward barriers, such as cartels; and this circumstance, in turn, explains the size of the profits that often eventuate from such success. This is the typical pattern by which industrial fortunes were made in the nineteenth century, and by which they are made even today; and these factors typically enhance family position, both absolutely and relatively. Neither saving nor efficient management as such are the crucial factors; what is crucial is the successful accomplishment of pertinent tasks. When one studies the history of great industrial families, one almost always comes upon one or more actions of this character— actions on which the family position is founded. Mere husbanding of already existing resources, no matter how painstaking, is always characteristic of a declining position.

In the second case, that of the trustified industrial corporation, types rise that are distinct from those in family enterprises[3]. . . . In seeking to

---

[2] This paragraph summarizes themes explored at greater length in Schumpeter's earlier work, *The Theory of Economic Development*, originally published in German in 1912, and in an English translation in 1934.

[3] Here Schumpeter argues that the aptitudes required for success vary with the functions required by dominant social institutions.

understand the factors that account for the success of a corporation official, that lift him above his fellows, we find, first of all, that extraordinary physical and nervous energy have much more to do with outstanding success than is generally believed. It is a simple fact that such industrial leaders must shoulder an often unreasonable burden of current work, which takes up the greater part of the day. They come to their policy-making "conferences" and "negotiations" with different degrees of fatigue or freshness, which have an important bearing on individual success. Moreover, work that opens up new possibilities—the very basis of industrial leadership—falls into the evening and night hours, when few men manage to preserve their full force and originality. With most of them, critical receptivity to new facts has by then given way to a state of exhaustion, and only a few maintain the degree of resolution that leads to decisive action. This makes a great difference the next day. Apart from energy itself, that special kind of "vision" that marks the family entrepreneur also plays an important part—concentration on business to the exclusion of other interests, cool and hard-headed shrewdness, by no means irreconcilable with passion.

In corporate industry it is necessary to woo support, to negotiate with and handle men with consummate skill. Elections and appointments become essential elements in the individual career. These factors are not as prominent in a family enterprise, and as a result the standard type of "manager" and "president" is quite different from the proprietary factory entrepreneur of yore. The art of "advancement" counts; the skillful secretary prospers; political connections are of importance; articulateness is an asset. The man who skillfully disposes of a troublesome private matter for an important stockholder need not worry about a bungled shipment. The implications of this situation are the discrepancy between those qualities that enable a man to *reach* a leading position and those that enable him to *hold* it—a discrepancy foreign to family enterprise. There is still another discrepancy, likewise foreign to family enterprise—that between the personal success of the man at the helm and the success of the enterprise itself. If this difference does not make itself more strongly felt, this is owing largely to persistence in the class of training in the methods of individually owned business, to which even men who have no such family background are assimilated and disciplined.

We should also mention that increasing specialization and mechanization, reaching right up to the leading functions, has thrown open positions at the top to men with purely technical qualifications that would, of themselves, be inadequate to the needs of a family enterprise. A laboratory chemist, for example, may come to head a major chemical enterprise, even though he is not at all the business leader type. A giant industry may be dominated by a lawyer who would push a simple factory to the brink of bankruptcy in no time.

Here too, however, it is always "behavior" and "aptitude" that explain shifts in the relative positions which originally existed. Only in this case, these positions are primarily individual [rather than familial]. . . .

We have assumed so far that class barriers are insurmountable. This is in accord with a very widespread popular notion that not only affects our valuation and emotional reaction to matters of class, but has also gained entry into scientific circles—for the most part only as a half-conscious axiom, attaining the dimensions of an axiomatic rule only in the case of Marxist analysis. The modern radical critique of society often rests on this purported law, which we must now discuss. . . .

It is noncontroversial that the class situation in which each individual finds himself tends to limit his possibilities and tends to keep him within his class. It acts as an obstacle to any rise into a higher class, and as a pair of water wings with respect to the classes below. . . . But as soon as we consider longer periods—family histories, for example—the picture becomes different. There we encounter the fundamental fact that classes . . . never, in the long run, consist of the *same families*—even if we subtract those that become extinct or drop down to a lower class. On the contrary, there is constant turnover. Entries and exits occur continually—the latter directed both upward and downward. Class composition is forever changing, to the point where there may be a completely new set of families. The rate at which this turnover proceeds varies greatly for different historical periods and social situations. Within each situation it varies for individual classes, and within the latter for individual families. There are cases in which membership in a given class does not even endure for the lifetime of a physical individual; and others in which it lasts for many centuries. Indeed, at first glance such cases of class longevity are unduly prominent, even though they constitute quite rare abnormalities. This difference in the rate of interchange is highly instructive and of the greatest significance for the verification of our basic idea as well as for an understanding of important social questions. The process always goes on, though at times extremely slowly and almost imperceptibly, impeded by legal and other barriers which every class, for obvious reasons, seeks to erect. For the duration of its collective life, or the time during which its identity may be assumed, each class resembles a hotel or an omnibus, always full, but always of different people. . . .

The facts and considerations that have been presented or outlined may be summarized as follows:

Shifts of family position within a class are seen to take place everywhere, without exception. They cannot be explained by the operation of chance, nor by automatic mechanisms relating to outward position, but only as the consequences of the different degree to which families are qualified to solve the problems with which their social environment confronts them.

Class barriers are always, without exception, surmountable and are, in fact, surmounted, by virtue of the same qualifications and modes of behavior that bring about shifts of family position *within* the class.

The process by which the individual family crosses class barriers is the same process by which the family content of classes is formed in the first instance, and this family content is determined in no other way.

Classes themselves rise and fall according to the nature and success with which they (meaning here, their members) fulfill their characteristic function, and according to the rise and fall in the social significance of this function, or of those functions which the class members are willing and able to accept instead—the relative social significance of a function always being determined by the degree of social leadership which its fulfillment implies or creates.

These circumstances explain the evolution of individual families and the evolution of classes as such. They also explain why social classes exist at all.

We draw the following conclusions from these statements:

The ultimate foundation on which the class phenomenon rests consists of individual differences in aptitude. What is meant is not differences in an absolute sense, but differences in aptitude with respect to those functions which the environment makes "socially necessary"—in our sense—at any given time; and with respect to leadership, along lines that are in keeping with those functions. The differences, moreover, do not relate to the physical individual, but to the clan or family.

Class structure is the ranking of such individual families by their social value in accordance, ultimately, with their differing aptitudes. Actually this is more a matter of social value, once achieved, becoming firmly established. This process of entrenchment and its perpetuation constitutes a special problem that must be specifically explained—at bottom this is the immediate and specific "class problem." Yet even this entrenched position, which endures in group terms, offering the picture of a class made secure above and beyond the individual, ultimately rests on individual differences in aptitude. Entrenched positions, which constitute the class stratification of society, are attained or created by behavior, which in turn is conditioned by differential aptitudes. . . .

To establish the presence of such an "aptitude" does not confer any laurels, nor does it testify to moral worth.[4] From various points of view—religious, aesthetic, moral—it may be evaluated as negative, and

---

[4] Like Hume and Mallock before him, and like Hayek after him, Schumpeter takes pains to distinguish social reward from moral virtue.

particularly as antisocial, indeed it may be objectively antisocial, irrespective of value judgements. Success for the individual, the family, or the class does not necessarily mean success for other segments of the population or for the nation as a whole; indeed, it may mean the very opposite. The extent to which this is actually the case in any particular instance is of importance, not only for our value judgements regarding the phenomenon of class in general or regarding particular historical classes, but for our scientific knowledge of social cause and effect. Even from the examples cited in this study it is evident that in some cases success in establishing class position does represent "social achievement"—in other words, that it enhances the position of others, as well as of those responsible for the success. In other cases this is not true, while in still others the ultimate judgment must depend on a deeper analysis, based on economic theory, of the consequences of the behavior in question. . . .

"Aptitude" is "natural" or acquired. In the latter case it may be acquired individually or by family background. The relevance of these distinctions to our problem is obvious. The greater the role played by natural and family-acquired aptitude, the firmer will class position be. The firmness of class position will also be . . . greater to the degree that the acquisition of new aptitudes depends on external means, especially material means, which are themselves the result of a superior class position. . . .

Most obviously, a trait or a set of traits determines "aptitude" only for particular functions: aptitude stands in relation to particular [social] functions, as biological adaptability stands in relation to survival in a particular physical environment. There are, as is well known, specific predispositions which have virtually no relationship to other natural endowments—those having to do with music and mathematics are the examples which have been most investigated. Yet there are other talents that display themselves with regard to a multiplicity of functions—the capacity for intellectual analysis, for example. This is true above all with respect to the various manifestations of will, and there is in particular the phenomenon of a general aptitude, which is equally effective in regard to most of the practical demands of life. Spearman's studies of this quality have given rise to the theory of a "central factor,"[5] which is only a word for something which is attested to by the experience of life. . . .

In an ethnically homogeneous environment, special and general aptitudes, physical and mental, those of will and of intellect, are probably distributed according to the normal curve. This has been carefully

[5] Charles Spearman, a British researcher in the field of intelligence testing, coined the concept of general intelligence in 1904.

demonstrated with physical characteristics that are most readily susceptible to measurement, notably body height and weight. Beyond this, we have extensive experimental material only for school children. As for the capacity of adults to measure up to the tasks of daily life, we have only our general impression to go by. Further investigations would be very important in advancing class research, but our present purpose is served well enough by the fact, scarcely disputed, that individual differences in aptitude do exist and that individual aptitudes do not fall into sharply marked categories, separated by empty space, but shade by imperceptible nuances from high to low. The situation is different only when there are sharp ethnic differences, such as between Mongols and Slavs, whites or Arabs and Negroes.

If it were true that the aptitudes of individuals bore no relationship to the aptitudes of ancestors and progeny—if none were inherited and all individuals were simply sports—then the factors of social rank and of acquired aptitude would still lead to the formation of social strata which woud be relatively stable for a time. But then the course of history would have been different. If aptitudes were never heritable and always distributed according to the laws of chance, the position of classes and of families within them would clearly be far less stable than it actually is. There can scarcely be any doubt of the inheritance of physical characteristics. As for mental characteristics, we have as yet only data in the field of defects, though these are in a state of fruitful evolution. To go beyond this, on the basis of the statistical and geneological material now available, is far more difficult and dangerous. We emphasize that until this point is settled, it is quite impossible to reach a rational verdict on the cultural significance of class (or, incidentally, on most other basic questions of the social order, past or future). But the basic idea of the theory of class presented here is quite independent of whatever one thinks [about the relative significance of inherited mental aptitudes].

▶ 5 ◀

THE CRITIQUE OF
GOOD INTENTIONS

INTRODUCTION TO
William Graham Sumner,
"Sociological Fallacies," "On the Case of a
Certain Man Who Is Never Thought Of," and
"An Examination of a Noble Sentiment"

◆

In the United States as in England, conservatism was recast in response to the more egalitarian and interventionist direction of liberalism and to the rise of socialism. It was the growing opposition to capitalism and to capitalists in late nineteenth-century America which called forth a new brand of American conservatism, most convincingly articulated by William Graham Sumner.

The decades after the end of the Civil War were an era of remarkable economic growth in the United States, spurred on by railroad construction and by the development of the iron and steel industries that followed in its wake. New forms of joint stock ownership and corporate management were pioneered in the railroad corporations and spread to other sectors of the economy.[1] Before the Civil War, the United States lagged behind Britain, France, and Germany in industrial production: by 1890, the value of its manufactures was almost equal to that of the other three nations combined. The captains of these new enterprises—such as the railway and steel entrepreneur, Andrew Carnegie, John D. Rockefeller of Standard Oil, and the financier and railroad magnate J. Pierpont Morgan—amassed unprecedented fortunes. Not least because of the new technologies and organizational forms pioneered by

---

[1] Alfred D. Chandler, Jr., ed., *The Railroads: The Nation's First Big Business* (New York, 1965) and Chandler, *The Visible Hand: The Managerial Revolution in American Business* (Cambridge, MA, 1977).

those dubbed "the Robber Barons," real wages and earnings in manufacturing went up by about 50 percent from 1860 to 1890.

Drawn by economic opportunity, unskilled and semiskilled immigrants from Europe poured into the country, putting pressure on the labor market. Along with intensive industrialization came the growth of labor unions. The first labor association of consequence, the Knights of Labor, organized as a national union in 1878. The new union attacked big corporations and large fortunes, advocated abolition of national banks and the nationalization of the railroads, and called for producer and consumer cooperatives which would supplant competitive capitalism. In 1877, with the country in depression, railway workers responded to cuts in salary with what became the first major national strike. During the Great Rail Strike, railroad workers from New York to California walked off the job. Rioting led to the loss of over one hundred lives, and to the destruction of millions of dollars worth of property.

The relative poverty and squalor of the growing cities, and the great and ever more visible inequalities of wealth in what became known as "the Gilded Age" led to demands from intellectuals for social and economic reform. Lester Ward, who was to influence a generation of American social scientists, suggested in his *Dynamic Sociology* of 1883 that in the current stage of social evolution the state, under the guidance of social scientific experts, must be assigned more extensive regulatory and planning powers.[2] Laurence Gronlund's *The Cooperative Commonwealth*, published in 1884, imported Marxist ideas into American debate. "The *wage-System*, the Profit-System, the Fleecing-System, *is utterly unfit for a higher civilization*," he wrote. By contrast, all would prosper under socialism or what he called "the cooperative commonwealth." Edward Bellamy's widely read utopian novel, *Looking Backward* (1887), told Americans that their country was on the verge of catastrophe, as "riches debauched one class with idleness of mind and body, while poverty sapped the vitality of the masses by overwork, bad food, and pestilent homes." Bellamy recommended that competitive capitalism be replaced by an economic system based on "the solidarity of the race and the brotherhood of man."[3] Others looked to the Gospels for the solutions to the problems of industrial capitalism. Washington Gladden, an influential Congregationalist minister, declared that "Jesus

[2] On Ward and his influence upon the American bureaucracy, see Michael J. Lacey, "The world of the bureaus: government and the positivist project in the late nineteenth century," in Michael J. Lacey and Mary O. Furner, eds., *The State and Social Investigation in Britain the United States* (Cambridge, 1993); Dorothy Ross, *The Origins of American Social Science* (Cambridge, 1991), pp. 88–97; and Robert C. Bannister, *Sociology and Scientism* (Chapel Hill, 1987), chapter 1.

[3] Gronland and Bellamy quoted in John Garraty, *The New Commonwealth, 1877–1890* (New York, 1968), pp. 318–21.

Christ knew a great deal more about organizing society than David Ricardo ever dreamed of knowing."[4]

It was to this onslaught of egalitarianism and humanitarianism that William Graham Sumner responded in the essays reprinted below. Sumner was born in Paterson, New Jersey, in 1840, the son of recent English immigrants. After a childhood of material and emotional deprivation, he attended Yale before going on to study in Germany and at Oxford. He began his professional career as an Episcopalian pastor, and the sermonic talent for succinct and pungent formulations which he developed remained evident in the books and essays which he wrote after he abandoned the pulpit. Deeply influenced by positivistic currents which linked the social sciences to the natural sciences and insisted upon the primacy of facts, Sumner became one of the most influential intellectual figures of his age. In 1873 Sumner joined the Yale faculty, where he taught social science until his death in 1907. He produced a stream of essays which appeared in popular magazines, as well as a river of books on political economy, sociology, and public policy issues.

As opposed to those who regarded poverty as the result of the exploitation of workers by the captains of industry, Sumner asserted that the problem of poverty arose from natural scarcity. The solution to the problem, he declared, lay in the development of economic institutions that created greater productivity. It was above all those of greater intelligence and industry who were responsible for the real increase in material well-being which had already occurred and would increase in the future if the competitive market mechanism was allowed to function, he argued. In keeping with these ideals, Sumner was a vehement foe of economic protectionism and imperialism. Active in Republican politics during the 1870s, he was appalled both by the corruption of the Democratic party's urban party machines and by Republican tariff policy, which he saw as a capitulation to business interests.[5]

Sumner's essays thus argued for the legitimacy and utility of economic inequality, combined with a suspicion of government intervention in the economy as either counterproductive, corrupt, or a cover for particular economic interests. These he combined with an emphasis on the well-being of the common man as the ultimate touchstone of social policy, an emphasis shared by the tradition of political economy to which Sumner very much indebted. This combination of populist rhetoric and antipathy to government became a characteristic strand within

[4] Gladden quoted in Robert H. Wiebe, *The Search for Order, 1877–1920* (New York, 1967), p. 148.

[5] For Sumner's biography, I have drawn on the useful introduction by Robert C. Bannister to Bannister, ed., *On Liberty, Society, and Politics: The Essential Essays of William Graham Sumner* (Indianapolis, 1992).

American conservatism from the Gilded Age onward. In contrast to the earlier propensity of conservatives to favor strong government, the new conservatism tended toward suspicion of governmental authority, contempt for politicians, and glorification of the individual. The result was what one historian has called "laissez-faire conservatism," which extolled a rugged individualism more redolent of the sensibility of the frontier than the commercial humanism of Adam Smith.[6]

Sumner is often classified as a "Social Darwinist"—a term which obscures the origins and thrust of his thought. In fact, Sumner developed his major ideas without having read Darwin, and when in the 1880s he briefly employed the Darwinian vocabulary of the survival of the fittest, he was latching on to a rhetorical device used by his contemporaries of almost all political hues.[7] In fact, when Sumner spoke of "natural selection" it was usually to restate historical utilitarianism in the idiom of his age. The "selection" with which he was concerned was institutional selection. Those institutions which had survived historically—by which he meant above all the competitive market—had done so because they were more effective in promoting human survival and well-being. He argued, in addition, that such institutions "select" among men for those character qualities needed to advance them. Sumner used the term "survival of the fittest" only briefly in his long career, and when he did so, he used it to denote the prospering of those who displayed the character traits that brought success in capitalist society, namely industry, prudence, economy, and temperance.[8] By insisting upon the demonstrated utility of the existing, historically evolved institution of the market, Sumner was recasting the recurrent argument of historical utility into contemporary terms.

For Sumner, one of the distinguishing elements of social science was its concern with facts and its rejection of sentimentalism. Time and again, he criticized the confusion of moral purposes with actual consequences, while stressing the ubiquity of negative unanticipated consequences. It is these recurrent emphases that give his work its anti-humanitarian resonance. Although his works utilize almost every major conservative argument—including the necessity of elites, the importance of custom, and the significance of latent functions—it is the critique of good intentions that provides the *leitmotiv* of his work.

[6] Clinton Rossiter coined the term "laissez-faire conservatism" in his *Conservatism in America* (New York, 1955), pp. 132ff. On the gap between Adam Smith and rugged individualism, see Jerry Z. Muller, *Adam Smith in His Time and Ours: Designing the Decent Society* (Princeton, 1995).

[7] See Donald C. Bellomy " 'Social Darwinism' Revisited," in *Perspectives in American History*, New Series, vol. 1, 1984 , pp. 1–129, esp. 23–35. Among the most useful older discussions of Social Darwinism is Donald Fleming, "Social Darwinism," in Arthur M. Schlesinger, Jr., and Morton White, eds., *Paths of American Thought* (New York, 1963).

[8] Bellomy, " 'Social Darwinism' Revisited," pp. 33–34.

William Graham Sumner, "Sociological Fallacies" (1884)[1]

In the extension of modern arts and industry the mass of mankind have been taught to expect comfort and ease, if not luxury; we boast so constantly of what we have accomplished in this direction that many believe we can do away with all hardship and establish universal well-being, if we choose. In our discourses, debates, and discussions we assume that the end for which society exists is the greatest happiness of the greatest number; it is laid down as an axiom of political science that political institutions should produce that result. Our philosophers encourage this doctrine and encourage the application to themselves of this test. It is, indeed, affirmed that our civilization is a failure because poverty continues to exist, and that a society in which poverty continues to exist is fit only to have "war" made upon it with fire, sword, and dynamite by any one who is still poor. Yet here is a plain question: is there any other man in the world who is to blame for the fact that I am poor?

The triumph of civilization is in the fact that we are not all steeped in poverty and misery. The student of sociology is more and more appalled as he goes on gaining fuller knowledge of what the primitive condition of man was, and a more definite conception of what human life must once have been. A missionary who resided among the Fuegians[2] heard a shouting often at sunrise; when he asked what it meant he was told: "People very sad; cry very much." This instinctive and childlike howling with which they greeted a new day of misery is the most pathetic, and, at the same time, most rational and fit manifestation which we should expect to find among such people. Why are any of us today better off than the Fuegians? Why are we not sunk in misery and squalor, and destitute of all things fitted to serve human need and raise men out of slavery to nature? The triumph of civilization is that all of us are above that stage, and that some of us are emancipated from poverty.

It is also asserted by some that there are men or classes among us who have no share in the gains of civilization. Such an assertion rests on a great misconception of facts. There is not a person in a civilized state who does not share in the inheritance of institutions, knowledge, ideas, doctrines, etc., which come down as fruits of civilization; we take these things in by habit and routine, and suppose that they come of themselves, or are innate. It would be one immense gain from the study of

---

[1] Originally published in *The North American Review* in 1884. Reprinted from *Earth-Hunger and Other Essays*, ed. Albert Galloway Keller (New Haven, 1914).

[2] The aborigines of Tierra del Fuego, an archipelago at the southern tip of South America. Its inhabitants were known for their primitive levels of technology and social organization.

sociology if men should learn to know by what prodigious struggles all these things have been won. Every man in a civilized state inherits a status of rights which form the basis and stay of his civil existence. These rights are often called "natural"; in truth they are the product of the struggles of thousands of generations. Men, before they were capable of reflection or had developed science, had but one process for learning: that was by their mistakes and at the price of all their experiments which failed. Our inheritance of established rights is the harvested product of the few successful experiments out of thousands which failed.[3]

If we turn to look at capital, the case is not different. Every item of capital is productive of utilities which are immeasurable in amount and broad in variety; only a few of the simplest of them can be appropriated by the man who "owns" the capital. A man who tilled the ground was already comparatively far up in civilization. He began with a pointed stick or the horn of an animal; by thousands of years of experiment and invention a spade was perfected. How can we measure the utility of a spade as compared with that of the pointed stick or the horn? That question would include the greater power of production of the spade and also the lessened pain and toil of the laborer. Now, if A owns a spade today, can he make B, who has none, pay him for the use of the spade an amount in any sense proportioned to the advantage of using a spade as compared with using a pointed stick? Certainly he cannot. Neither can A, if he keeps his spade, in any manner win by the use of it a superiority over his neighbors to be measured by the superiority of the spade to the stick. All but a small margin of the gains of civilization enters into a common stock which nobody can appropriate; it goes to make up a kind of industrial atmosphere around every one born into the society. Though a man may never have handled a plow, he gets his food under the conditions of a society which possesses plows; another may never have handled a pen or a type, but he gets his reading matter under the same conditions as a man who has pens and types. The same is true of every item of capital. Knowledge of the facts of history enables us to see when we look at a coin, a knife, a lead-pencil, a match, a book, a lock, a coat, the product of thousands of generations of tireless efforts to serve human needs more completely and easily with the materials offered by the earth.

What we might call the metaphysical side of capital is its most important side in the history of civilization. Every bit of capital presents devices, methods, processes, which are of general application. If one of us has a task to perform he unconsciously begins to review the various pro-

---

[3] Sumner presents a form of historical utilitarianism, arguing that over time useful institutions and practices have survived, while those less useful have disappeared.

cesses or devices with which he is familiar, to see if he cannot employ one of them. Springs, catches, levers, cams, etc., are presented to us all the time in capital which we do not own; the devices are available for new applications. He who owns the capital cannot appropriate these; his use of capital is only the most primary and simple of all the utilities which it offers, and he cannot get out those utilities without entering into cooperation and exchange with his neighbors through which they share the primary utilities. It is interesting to watch children at play, to see the uses to which they put their toys, the combinations, plans, devices, and processes which they will work out; to notice how they use what they have seen, how they collect experience of the qualities of substances, how they bring all their knowledge to bear; and to reflect that they possess at five or six years of age a store of facts, knowledge, skill, and the like which it cost the human race thousands of years to accumulate. Most grown people use the products of civilization as unconsciously as children, and as much by habit and routine; but it is monstrous ignorance, when the point is raised for discussion, to affirm that some now do not share in the fruits of civilization.

If any one is still unconvinced of what I have here said, let him try to cut down a tree with a flint hatchet, or to produce fire with a fire drill, or to grind corn with one stone rubbed on another. Intense labor kept up over a long period was the price of everything to the primitive man; that is, he worked very hard and got very little. If a modern hod-carrier[4] had to work a fire drill until he got a light, and if he could then strike a match to get another, he would see whether he had any share in the fruits of civilization.

The sentimentalists sometimes bewail the loss of skill due to machinery and division of labor. The fact is as alleged, but it dates from a point much further back than the factory system—it dates from the dawn of civilization. The primitive man developed great skill of eye, hand, and ear, because his tools were so poor that the wear all came on his nerves. He could accomplish nothing unless his skill was high; the man, for instance, who had to fashion a flint axe by flaking off pieces under great pressure must either work very long and spoil a great many or be very skillful. When he came to bore a hole in it with a piece of horn, some sand, and water, he must work long, skillfully, and with a true eye, or he would spoil his whole work. A Swiss anthropologist has made a stone axe, with such tools as a primitive man possessed, polished but not perforated, in five hours and forty minutes of working time with intervals of rest. As tools have been perfected, men have put the work on the tools

---

[4] The term denotes a bricklayer's assistant, and is used by Sumner to mean a laborer of the lowest skill and pay.

and spared their nerves. Take, for comparison, the manufacture of a modern axe, which requires more skill than many modern processes. In saving skill we have saved men. The division of labor does not probably lessen skill, but it concentrates it in narrow lines, and produces routine and monotony. Poetry is what really suffers, but the loss is more than compensated for by poetry in literary and other purer forms; we can spare poetry from industry when we have literature, drama, or art, just as we can afford to use bolted flour when we have a meat diet.

Another notion for which there is no foundation in fact is that there was more liberty in early ages of the world or in simpler societies than there now is; that is, liberty in the sense of freedom from restraint upon choice or caprice. The primitive man had no liberty in this sense or any other. He was a slave to nature, and that meant that he was in continual terror before dangers which he did not know, could not measure, and could not guard against. All that we learn of primitive races shows us that nature is appalling to them; they have intelligence enough to believe more and fear more than brutes. If we look at their social regulations we find that these fetter the individual in relentless traditions and rules. The impulsiveness, waywardness, and self-will of the savage are delusive if they are regarded as manifestations of liberty. The development of individual liberty, and its reconciliation with social order, is one of the grandest of those developments of original antagonism into the ultimate harmony which go to make up civilization. We have not, however, by civilization emancipated individual choice and caprice; the civilized man has won the social harmony by submitting to orderly and regular industry, under which a savage would pine and die just as surely as a cotton operative would perish in Patagonia or Greenland.

Now, the achievements of the human race have been accomplished by the elite of the race;[5] there is no ground at all in history for the notion that the masses of mankind have provided the wisdom and done the work. There are, in this whole region of thought, a vast mass of dogmas and superstitions which will have to be corrected either by hard thinking or great suffering. A man is good for something only so far as he thinks, knows, tries, or works. If we put a great many men together, those of them who carry on the society will be those who use reflection and forethought, and exercise industry and self-control. Hence the dogma that all men are equal is the most flagrant falsehood and the most immoral doctrine which men have ever believed; it means that the man who has not done his duty is as good as the one who has done his duty, and it takes away all sense from the teachings of the moralists, when they instruct youth that men who pursue one line of action will go down to loss

---

[5] Here Sumner argues for the necessity and utility of elites.

and shame, and those who pursue another course will go up to honor and success. It is, on the contrary, a doctrine of the first moral and sociological importance that truth, wisdom, and righteousness come only by painstaking, study, and striving. These things are so hard that it is only the few who attain to them. These few carry on human society now as they always have done.

Hence we see that so soon as the exigencies of life are felt, men are differentiated according to their power to cope with them into "better" or "worse" with reference to personal and social value; and as soon as any conquest is achieved which contributes to civilization, the inequality between the men who won it and those who did not win it is established as a positive fact. Men are very unequal in what they get out of life, but they are still more unequal in what they put into it. The most unequal bargain has always been made by the men who have done the world's thinking for it.

In nothing have we, as yet, made so little progress as in the art of civil government, or, more generally, in our political organization. We have abandoned hereditary government because we regard it as illogical; it affords no guarantees that fit persons will hold power; it is stable, but it is not flexible or plastic. Have we, however, as yet produced political methods under democratic-republican government which afford us any guarantees that fit persons alone will obtain power? It is very certain that we have not done this. We do not fear for the stability of the civil organization. We desire flexibility and plasticity, but if we have lost the notion of fitness altogether, and are irritated by it when it is brought to our notice, we have made no step in advance.

The fact is, that the vague encouragement which has been given, for a century, to impossible dreams and senseless ambitions has produced social problems with which our sociology is in no position to cope. How far we are from it may be judged when we find it asserted that the end of society is justice. To ask what is the end of man, or society, or the earth, is to put a teleological or theological problem. Such a problem has been discussed in regard to man; if it has ever been discussed in regard to society, it is at least new. It is also idle. The scientific view of the matter is that a thing exists for reasons which lie in its antecedents and causes, not in its purposes or destiny. Human society exists because it is, and has come to be on earth because forces which were present must produce it. It is, therefore, utterly unscientific to regard man or society as a means to any further end. The state exists to provide justice, but the state is only one among a number of social organizations. It is parallel with the others, and has its own functions. To confuse the state with society is to produce a variety of errors, not the least of which is to smuggle statecraft into political economy. It is plain that, until such courses of confusion are put entirely beyond the pale of social discussions, our social science cannot make very rapid progress. The sources of confusion lie at the very beginning, and they vitiate our political economy and political science into their remotest developments. An attentive study of any of the current controversies will show that they arise from fundamentally confused or erroneous notions of society, and that they cannot be solved without a rectification, on a scientific basis, of our data and our doctrines about human life on this earth.

"On the Case of a Certain Man Who Is Never Thought Of" (1883)[6]

The type and formula of most schemes of philanthropy or humanitarianism is this: A and B put their heads together to decide what C shall be made to do for D. The radical vice of all these schemes, from a sociological point of view, is that C is not allowed a voice in the matter, and his position, character, and interests, as well as the ultimate effects on society through C's interests, are entirely overlooked. I call C the Forgotten Man. For once let us look him up and consider his case, for the characteristic of all social doctors is that they fix their minds on some man or group of men whose case appeals to the sympathies and the imagination, and they plan remedies addressed to the particular trouble; they do not understand that all the parts of society hold together and that forces which are set in action act and react throughout the whole organism until an equilibrium is produced by a readjustment of all interests and rights.[7] They therefore ignore entirely the source from which they must draw all the energy which they employ in their remedies, and they ignore all the effects on other members of society than the ones they have in view. They are always under the dominion of the superstition of government, and forgetting that a government produces nothing at all, they leave out of sight the first fact to be remembered in all social discussion—that the state cannot get a cent for any man without taking it from some other man, and this latter must be a man who has produced and saved it. This latter is the Forgotten Man.

The friends of humanity start out with certain benevolent feelings towards "the poor," "the weak," "the laborers," and others of whom they

---

[6] Originally published in William Graham Sumner, *What the Social Classes Owe to Each Other* (1883), text taken from *War and Other Essays by William Graham Sumner*, ed. Albert Galloway Keller (New Haven, 1919).

[7] A claim about the unintended consequences of social action, due to the functional interdependence of social institutions.

make pets. They generalize these classes and render them impersonal, and so constitute the classes into social pets. They turn to other classes and appeal to sympathy and generosity and to all the other noble sentiments of the human heart. Action in the line proposed consists in a transfer of capital from the better off to the worse off. Capital, however, as we have seen, is the force by which civilization is maintained and carried on. The same piece of capital cannot be used in two ways. Every bit of capital, therefore, which is given to a shiftless and inefficient member of society who makes no return for it is diverted from a reproductive use; but if it was put to reproductive use, it would have to be granted in wages to an efficient and productive laborer. Hence the real sufferer by that kind of benevolence which consists in an expenditure of capital to protect the good-for-nothing is the industrious laborer. The latter, however, is never thought of in this connection. It is assumed that he is provided for and out of the account. Such a notion only shows how little true notions of political economy have as yet become popularized. There is an almost invincible prejudice that a man who gives a dollar to a beggar is generous and kind-hearted, but that a man who refuses the beggar and puts the dollar in a savings-bank is stingy and mean. The former is putting capital where it is very sure to be wasted, and where it will be a kind of seed for a long succession of future dollars, which must be wasted to ward off a greater strain on the sympathies than would have been occasioned by a refusal in the first place. Inasmuch as the dollar might have been turned into capital and given to a laborer who, while earning it, would have reproduced it, it must be regarded as taken from the latter. When a millionaire gives a dollar to a beggar, the gain of utility to the beggar is enormous and the loss of utility to the millionaire is insignificant. Generally the discussion is allowed to rest there. But if the millionaire makes capital of the dollar, it must go upon the labor market as a demand for productive services. Hence there is another party in interest—the person who supplies productive services. There always are two parties. The second one is always the Forgotten Man, and anyone who wants to understand truly the matter in question must go and search for the Forgotten Man. He will be found to be worthy, industrious, independent, and self-supporting. He is not, technically, "poor" or "weak"; he minds his own business and makes no complaint. Consequently the philanthropists never think of him and trample on him. . . .

For our present purpose it is most important to notice that if we lift any man up we must have a fulcrum or point of reaction. In society that means that to lift one man up we push another down. The schemes for improving the condition of the working classes interfere in the competition of workmen with each other. The beneficiaries are selected by favoritism and are apt to be those who have recommended themselves to the friends of humanity by language or conduct which does not betoken independence and energy. Those who suffer a corresponding depression by the interference are the independent and self-reliant, who once more are forgotten or passed over; and the friends of humanity once more appear, in their zeal to help somebody, to be trampling on those who are trying to help themselves.

Trades-unions adopt various devices for raising wages, and those who give their time to philanthropy are interested in these devices and wish them success. They fix their minds entirely on the workmen for the time being *in* the trade and do not take note of any other *workmen* as interested in the matter. It is supposed that the fight is between the workmen and their employers, and it is believed that one can give sympathy in that contest to the workmen without feeling responsibility for anything farther. It is soon seen, however, that the employer adds the trades-union and strike risk to the other risks of his business and settles down to it philosophically because he has passed the loss along on the public. It then appears that the public wealth has been diminished and that the danger of a trade war, like the danger of a revolution, is a constant reduction of the well-being of all. So far, however, we have seen only things which could *lower* wages—nothing which could raise them. The employer is worried, but that does not raise wages. The public loses, but the loss goes to cover extra risk, and that does not raise wages.

Aside from legitimate and economic means, a trades-union raises wages by restricting the number of apprentices who may be taken into the trade. This device acts directly on the supply of laborers, and that produces effects on wages. If, however, the number of apprentices is limited, some are kept out who want to get in. Those who are in have, therefore, made a monopoly and constituted themselves a privileged class on a basis exactly analogous to that of the old privileged aristocracies. But whatever is gained by this arrangement for those who are in is won at a greater loss to those who are kept out. Hence it is not upon the masters nor upon the public that trades-unions exert the pressure by which they raise wages; it is upon other persons of the labor class who want to get into the trades, but, not being able to do so, are pushed down into the unskilled labor class. These persons, however, are passed by entirely without notice in all the discussions about trades-unions. They are the Forgotten Men. But since they want to get into the trade and win their living in it, it is fair to suppose that they are fit for it, would succeed at it, would do well for themselves and society in it; that is to say, that of all persons interested or concerned, they most deserve our sympathy and attention.

The cases already mentioned involve no legislation. Society, however, maintains police, sheriffs, and various institutions, the object of which is to protect people against themselves—that is, against their own vices. Almost all legislative effort to prevent vice is really protective of vice, because all such legislation saves the vicious man from the penalty of his vice. Nature's remedies against vice are terrible. She removes the victims without pity. A drunkard in the gutter is just where he ought to be, according to the fitness and tendency of things. Nature has set up in him the process of decline and dissolution by which she removes things which have survived their usefulness. Gambling and other less mentionable vices carry their own penalties with them.

Now we never can annihilate a penalty. We can only divert it from the head of the man who has incurred it to the heads of others who have not incurred it. A vast amount of "social reform" consists in just this operation; The consequence is that those who have gone astray, being relieved from nature's fierce discipline, go on to worse, and that there is a constantly heavier burden for the others to bear. Who are the others? When we see a drunkard in the gutter we pity him. If a policeman picks him up, we say that society has interfered to save him from perishing. "Society" is a fine word, and it saves us the trouble of thinking. The industrious and sober workman, who is mulcted of a percentage of his day's wages to pay the policeman, is the one who bears the penalty. But he is the Forgotten Man. He passes by and is never noticed, because he has behaved himself, fulfilled his contracts, and asked for nothing. . . .

"An Examination of a Noble Sentiment" (c. 1887)[8]

A noble sentiment is a very noble thing when it is genuine. A soul which would not throb in response to a noble sentiment, if it were genuine, would prove that it was base and corrupt. On the other hand, a noble sentiment, if it is not genuine, is one of the most corrupting things in the world. The habit of entertaining bogus sentiments of a plausible sound, deprives both mind and heart of sterling sense and healthful emotion. It is no psychological enigma that Robespierre, who was a hero of the eighteenth-century *sensibilité*, should have administered the Reign of Terror. People who gush are often most impervious to real

[8] Originally published in *The Independent*, c. 1887. Reprinted from *Earth-Hunger and Other Essays*, ed. Albert Galloway Keller (New Haven: Yale UP, 1914).

appeals, and to genuine emotion. It therefore seems that we must be on our guard against pretended noble sentiments, as against very dangerous pitfalls, and test them to see whether they are genuine or not.

The sentiment which I now propose to examine is this: that we ought to see to it that every one has an existence worthy of a human being, or to keep it in the form in which it is offered, a *menschenwürdiges Dasein*. It is not a matter of accident that it is stated in German. A noble sentiment often loses poetry and transcendental solemnity to such an extent, when translated into everyday English, that it might seem like begging the question of its truth and value to translate it.

The first question is: what is an existence worthy of a human being? The hod-carrier, who is earning a dollar a day, will say that it is what he could get for a dollar and a half; the mechanic at two dollars will say that it would cost three; a man whose income is a thousand dollars will say that it costs fifteen hundred. I once heard a man, whose salary was twelve thousand dollars, speak of five thousand a year as misery. A *menschenwürdiges Dasein*, therefore, at the first touch gives us the first evidence of something wrong. It sounds like a concrete and definite thing, but it is not such; a *menschenwürdiges Dasein* is the most shifting and slippery notion which the human mind can try to conceive. In general it is about fifty per cent more than each one of us is getting now, which would, for a time, mean happiness, prosperity, and welfare to us all. It is to be remembered, also, that most of the people who, not in their own opinion, but in that of their neighbors, have not a *menschenwürdiges Dasein* are those who do not like that kind of an existence or want it, but have turned their backs upon it, and are in fact rather more contented than any other class of people with their situation as they are now.

The next question is: for how many people must a *menschenwürdiges Dasein* be provided? The provision of such an existence is the first necessity which meets one of us when he comes to understand the world in which he lives, that is, he has to earn his living,—for the exceptions, those who inherit a living, are so few that they may be disregarded by the rest of us on whom this proposed duty will fall. The task of earning a living is found, generally, to be a somewhat heavy one, chiefly for the reason, as shown in the former paragraph, that a man's definition of a decent living will not stay fixed long enough for him to realize it. As soon as he thinks that he sees his way to it he wants to marry; then he becomes responsible for the *menschenwürdiges Dasein* of a number of other persons. His whole energy, his whole life long, rarely suffices to do more than meet this obligation. Such is the fate of the man who tries to guarantee a *menschenwürdiges Dasein* to himself, his wife, and his children. But the man who is to be provided with such an existence, under the new arrangement proposed, will not have any such difficulty to contend with; he is to have a living secured to him by the state, or the social reformers, or somebody else. His wife and children will obviously have as good a claim to a *menschenwürdiges Dasein* as he; their support will therefore cause him no anxiety and no burden. Therefore this class of persons will increase with great rapidity. They are, of course, all those who have neglected or refused to win a *menschenwürdiges Dasein* for themselves; and whenever it is determined that somebody else shall give it to them, it is provided that their number shall multiply indefinitely and forever.

Furthermore, in all these propositions the fact is overlooked that no humanitarian proposition is valid unless it is applied to the whole human race. If I am bound to love my fellow-man, it is for reasons which apply to Laplanders and Hottentots just as much as to my neighbor across the street; our obligation to provide a *menschenwürdiges Dasein* is just as great toward Africans or Mongolians as towards Americans. It must certainly be as wide as all *Menschen*, that is, all human beings. There are millions of people on the globe whose mode of life, whose *Dasein*, is far below that of the most miserable wretch in the United States, never has been any better than it is, never will be any better as far ahead as anybody can see, and they cannot be said to be to blame for it. It is true that they do not know that they are badly off; they do not bother their heads about a *menschenwürdiges Dasein*. They do not work much and they are quite free from care—very much more so than the average American taxpayer. But, if we are to give a *menschenwürdiges Dasein* to those who have not got it, just because they have not got it (and no other reason is alleged in connection with the proposition before us), then the persons to whom I have referred have a very much stronger claim, for they are very much further away from it.

The next question is: what will be the effect on people of securing them a *menschenwürdiges Dasein*? Plainly it must be to pauperize them, that is, to take away all hope that they can ever win such an existence for themselves. If not, and if the proposition means only that we hope and strive to make our community as prosperous as possible, and to give everybody in it as good chances as possible, then that is just what we are trying to do now, to the best of our ability, and the proposal is only an impertinence; it interrupts and disturbs us without contributing anything to the matter in hand. Now it is one of the worst social errors to pauperize people; it demoralizes them through and through; it ruins their personal character and makes them socially harmful; it lowers their aims and makes sure that they will never have good ones; it corrupts their family life and makes sure that they will entail sordid and unworthy principles of action on their children. If any argument could be brought forward for an attempt to secure to every one an existence worthy of a man, it would be that, in that way, every one among us might be worthy to be a human being; but, whenever the attempt is made, the only result will be that those who get an existence worthy of a human being in that way are sure to be morally degraded below any admissible standard of human worth.

The next question is: who is to secure the *menschenwürdiges Dasein* to the aforesaid persons? Evidently it can only be those who have already, no one knows by what struggles and self-denial, won it for themselves. This proposition, like all the others of the class to which it belongs, proposes to smite with new responsibilities, instead of rewards, the man who has done what every one ought to do. We are told what fine things would happen if every one of us would go and do something for the welfare of somebody else; but why not contemplate also the immense gain which would ensue if everybody would do something for himself? The latter is ever so much more reasonable than the former; for those who are now taking care of themselves have very little strength to spare, while those who are not now taking care of themselves might do a great deal more. The plan of securing to those who have not a *menschenwürdiges Dasein* that blessing, is a plan for leaving the latter at ease and putting more load on the former; to the society, therefore, it is doubly destructive, increasing its burdens and wasting its resources at the same time.

The next question is: what means are to be used to give a *menschenwürdiges Dasein* to everybody? To this there is no answer; we are left to conjecture. The most reasonable conjecture is that the proponents themselves do not know; they have not made up their minds; they have not really faced the question. A proposition to give everybody an existence worthy of a human being, without a specification of the measures by which it is proposed to do it, is like a proposition to make everybody handsome.

Our analysis has therefore shown that this noble sentiment is simply a bathos.[9]

---

[9] A trivial notion which gives the impression of profundity.

▶ 6 ◀

WAR

INTRODUCTION TO
T. E. Hulme,
"Essays on War"

◆

Pacifism has historically been linked with liberalism, with socialism, and with various forms of Christianity, but conservatism and pacifism are incompatible. Among the most striking refutations of pacifism are T. E. Hulme's essays on war of 1916. The significance of Hulme's essays lies not in their originality but in their sharp dissection of the premises of Hulme's pacifist opponents, and in his pithy presentation of his conservative premises.

The propensity of the liberal tradition was to regard war as unnatural and irrational, a wasteful diversion of resources from welfare to destruction, engineered by governments either through folly or for evil reasons of their own. Wars, it was repeatedly argued, arose either because of a failure of communication between nations or because their governments were dominated by a self-interested warrior class. The solution to war lay in free trade and democracy. Free trade between nations would increase communications between them, would create shared interests, and together with greater democracy, would lead to the displacement of war-oriented aristocracies by the productively oriented sections of the population. These arguments, formulated by the end of the eighteenth century and articulated by Tom Paine in *The Rights of Man* of 1791–92, were repeated in one form or another by liberals thereafter.[1] Radicals and Socialists also regarded war as irrational and indefensible, and attributed it to the interests of rival capitalist elites or to the greed of arms manufacturers eager to find outlets for their wares.

At the outbreak of the First World War in 1914, liberal, radical, and socialist opponents of the war in Britain attacked the doctrine of the

---

[1] See Michael Howard, *War and the Liberal Conscience* (Oxford, 1981), chapter 1 for an excellent and succinct account.

balance of power: the notion that Britain must go to war against Germany in order to prevent the domination of Europe by a single power. Those liberals who did support the war increasingly justified it by the argument that Germany was in the grip of a militaristic regime and a destructive philosophy which had to be destroyed to make the world "safe for democracy." The struggle was defended, in a slogan coined by H. G. Wells, as "the war to end war."[2]

Among the most talented and vociferous intellectual opponents of the war was the Cambridge philosopher, Bertrand Russell. He became a leading voice of the Union for Democratic Control, an organization of intellectuals critical of the war, and then of the pacifist No-Conscription Fellowship.[3] It was in opposition to Russell and like-minded intellectuals that T. E. Hulme took up his pen.

Born in 1883, Thomas Ernest Hulme had made a name for himself as a theorist of art and aesthetics in the years preceding the war.[4] His aesthetics, like his politics, were devoted to combating what he saw as the enervating effects of a liberal humanitarianism based on a soft-minded and romantic conception of human nature. Hulme was in contact with antiliberal and antidemocratic French thinkers, including Georges Sorel, whose tract of 1906 against the decadence of liberal parliamentarianism, *Reflections on Violence*, Hulme translated into English. Hulme presided over a salon in London, where he influenced a circle of poets—including T. S. Eliot, Ezra Pound, W. B. Yeats, and Wyndham Lewis—who combined artistic modernism with political reaction.

When war broke out in the summer of 1914, Hulme volunteered enthusiastically for the army. He arrived in France as an infantryman late in 1914, and in April 1915 he was wounded by a bullet which passed through his arm and killed the man behind him. Sobered by his war experience, he returned to England, and after spending some time in a convalescent hospital he resumed his civilian life in London. There he attended some of Russell's public speeches in opposition to the war. Hulme composed a series of short articles in response, some of which appeared in the *Cambridge Magazine* between January and March of 1916.

They reveal a mind which increasingly cherished Britain's liberal institutions, even while it feared that they were threatened by a potential German military victory. Hulme had visited Germany in 1912 and

---

[2] Ibid., p. 74.

[3] See Alan Ryan, *Bertrand Russell: A Political Life* (New York, 1988), chapter 3.

[4] Information on Hulme's life comes from the introduction by Sam Hynes to Hynes, ed., *Further Speculations by T.E. Hulme* (Minneapolis, 1955), the editor's introduction to *The Collected Writings of T.E. Hulme*, ed. Karen Csengeri (Oxford, 1994), and Alun R. Jones, *The Life and Opinions of T.E. Hulme* (Boston, 1960).

1913, and after the war broke out he was alarmed by the aggressive militarism expressed by leading German intellectuals such as Max Scheler and Werner Sombart. Hulme argued against liberal attempts to psychologize away the sources of war. And he attacked the belief of liberal pacifists that war plays no significant role in the long-run shaping of history, arguing that at times force plays a decisive role.

Hulme obtained a commission in the Royal Marine Artillery and in late 1916 he returned to the continent, now as an artilleryman. He was killed in action in Flanders in 1917, and is said to have been writing a book on gunnery at the time of his death.

T. E. Hulme,
"Essays on War" (1916)[1]

"ON LIBERTY"

[T]he pacifist never really at heart thinks that our "liberty" would be in any way endangered by the loss of this war. . . .

We assume that defeat would involve a very great curtailment of our liberty. It is evident from everything they do and say that the pacifists do not believe there is any such danger. Though they make perfunctory reference to it, they do not at heart believe in it. They take no real interest in the matter, their enthusiasm is directed to other ends. Loss of liberty in this connection is to them an empty phrase. . . .

This scepticism about the consequences of defeat springs from two sources.

(1) The fatuous belief that liberty cannot at any rate be permanently endangered, for "Germany herself will *inevitably* develop toward democracy."

(2) The inability to see that Europe will be really altered in structure by this war. The facile and false analogy with wars like the Crimean or the Franco-Prussian, which, while they increased the power of one nation, or diminished that of another, yet still left Europe a society of independent nations. *There is no analogy between this war and other wars.* A German victory means an end of Europe as a new Hellas, a society of nations. It means a Europe under German leadership. The pacifists

---

[1] T. E. Hulme, "On Liberty" (*Cambridge Magazine* V, January 22, 1916); "Inevitability Inapplicable" (*Cambridge Magazine* V, January 29, 1916); "Why We Are In Favour of This War" (*Cambridge Magazine* V, February 12, 1916); "The Framework of Europe" (*Cambridge Magazine* V, February 19, 1916); reprinted in T. E. Hulme, *Further Speculations*, ed. Sam Hynes (Minneapolis, 1955), pp. 170–92. Title supplied by the editor of this volume.

cannot see this, for, curiously enough, while they *repudiate the balance of power as a doctrine of policy, they do so because they unconsciously assume that the balance of power will take care of itself, being grounded on the nature of things.*[2] Being assumed, like democracy, to be of the nature of the law of gravitation, it would be absurd to fight for it.

I realise the source of your incredulity. "You may make out a case for the danger to liberty—but it lacks reality. Europe has had many wars—many spoke of them as a danger to liberty—but always things were much the same after."

But this time they won't be. Forget easy analogies and examine carefully the obvious facts.

You are slowly realising the nature of that irrational thing, Force. Force does settle things, does create facts, which you have henceforth to deal with. The situation round the Dardanelles has probably now crystallised. Russia will not get through to the Mediterranean, and we shall be unable always to prevent Germany's access to Asia. Another situation created by force is being prepared for us nearer home. Europe is in flux; it will settle after the war into a physical structure which will probably endure for a century.

The most accurate metaphor for the new structure that will follow the victory of Germany is that of the emergence of a mountain in a plane. You are not to think that such an emergence leaves surrounding countries unaffected. It produces the same effect on them as putting a parcel under the tablecloth would do—all of them have to live on an inclined plane.

As evidence of the existence of the intention of Germany really to alter the framework of Europe in this way, I may conveniently quote a few sentences from a recent book on the war by Max Scheler. Scheler is not a sensational journalist, or a military writer like Bernhardi, but one of the most intelligent of the younger German philosophers, and one who, moreover, belongs to the school that is beginning to have the greater influence on this generation of students.

After a long preliminary discussion on the real nature of "international" and "cosmopolitan," the main object of the war is stated to be the destruction of the balance of power: and the creation for the first time of a solidarist Continental Europe under *German military leadership*. . . . "Then we shall see the creation of a new Mediterranean culture grounded on the *military power* of Germany."

To attain this end, Russia must be finally driven out of Europe, and France completely crushed.

---

[2] Here Hulme introduces his central theme: that liberal pacifists do not recognize the conditions upon which their liberty rests.

What is the position of England then?

He attacks the Germans who are surprised and shocked at our entry into the war. "It is inevitable that England should come in. Her whole existence as an Empire was threatened by the building of the German fleet." He reproves those who, "with an imitation of English cant," have pretended that the fleet was built for defensive purposes.

"The only possible aim in the building of the German Fleet was directed against England." "Our first object always must be the destruction of the English naval supremacy, for this stands between us and the fair division of the earth. If this object is not attained now further struggles must and will follow."

"INEVITABILITY INAPPLICABLE"

I think the writer who said the war was the most important European event since the French Revolution and probably since the Reformation, was right in this point, though he has been wrong in almost everything else. You probably reject such a statement as exaggeration, because you are very much aware of the sordid motives and the petty unimaginative people who brought it about. You prefer to look at it as a small event on a very large scale. In doing so you exhibit a certain romanticism about the past, an ignorance of the way in which really great events have been brought about. But even taking the war at your estimation, the statement quoted still remains true. You admit that it is on a very large scale—it is the mere material consequences that will follow the war as a material *fact*, that create its importance. Perhaps it is better to speak of the *conditional* importance of the war. It would be comparable to the Reformation if the Germans won; if they don't it is not an important event in the same sense. Why would it then be so important? Because a German victory means an end of Europe as we know it, as a comity of nations; the whole framework would be changed. If you ask, further, why that is important, the answer is in the enormous reactions inside the beaten nations that would follow this enormous change in their external situation. When a box is turned over on to another base, the arrangement of the loose things inside alters with it. In our own case, our liberties have to a great extent depended on our securities, and our security would now have disappeared. We shall all be obliged to become conspirators.[3]

There are certain habits of thought, which make a realisation of the actual nature of Force very difficult. This applies not only to the opponents of the war, but to its supporters. Take the case of writers like

---

[3] That is, collaborators with a militarily dominant, authoritarian Germany.

Mr. Wells.[4] You remember the old story of the man who was taken ill suddenly. The strange doctor who was called in exhibited a certain hesitation. "I'm not exactly a doctor," he said, "in fact, I'm a vet. I don't know what's the matter with you, but I can give you something that will bring on blind staggers, and I can cure that all right." Now Mr. Wells had never taken the possibility of an Anglo-German war seriously—he was pacifist by profession. It was not exactly his subject then, and last August may have found him somewhat baffled as to what to say. So he gave it blind staggers, he turned it into a "war to end war," and there you are. Such writers, in dealing with a matter like war, alien to their ordinary habits of thought, are liable to pass from a fatuous optimism to a fatuous pessimism, equally distant from the real facts of the situation.

Of all these ordinary habits of thought, perhaps the one that has the most unfortunate influences is the belief in *inevitable* progress. If the world is making for "good," then "good" can never be in serious danger. This leads to a disinclination to see how big fundamental things like liberty can in any way depend on trivial material things like guns. There is no realisation of the fact that the world *may* take a wrong turning. In a pacifist lecture by Mr. Bertrand Russell, I read "the only things worth fighting for are things of the spirit, but these things are not subject to force."[5]. . . .

Consider now two specific examples of the way in which the habit of thought distorts the pacifist perception of the facts:

(1) Even admitting that the facts as put forward by you are true; even admitting that our defeat will be followed by a German hegemony, we refuse to see in this any permanent danger to liberty. To do so would be to "assume that Germany lacks the power of development . . . her *natural* line of development towards a tolerant liberalism." There is a richness of fallacy in this quotation, which makes choice somewhat embarrassing. For our purpose here, of course, the important word is *natural*. It is natural to progress; Nature herself tends of her own accord to progress, etc. This is complicated, however, by a further assumption, an example of what the Germans call the characteristic English view of mistaking *Umwelt* for *Welt*, in other words, of mistaking the conditions of our own particular environment for universally valid laws. Even if the Germans must *naturally* develop, how can we assume that they will develop towards a tolerant liberalism? Is that also part of the essential nature of the cosmos? Free trade and all. . . . Anyone who has known Germany at all intimately during recent years knows that facts go to prove the contrary.

    [4] H. G. Wells, English novelist and socialist.
    [5] Bertrand Russell, "The Philosophy of Pacifism," in *Towards Ultimate Harmony* (London, 1915), p. 9.

(2) This habit of thought hinders the perception of the facts in another way. There is a second type of pacifist, who admits that if the consequences of defeat were the hegemony of Germany and the end of Europe as a collection of independent states—that the case for war would have been proved. But he does not admit that such will be the consequences of defeat; he does not seem able to perceive this obvious fact. He cannot take the argument seriously. Why? For exactly the same reason as that given in the first case. Liberty is a "good"; so, also, is the existence of Europe as a comity of independent nations. He finds it ridiculous to fight for liberty, for there can never be any real danger to liberty. The world is inevitably developing toward liberty, and liberty is thus *natural*, and grounded on the nature of things. In exactly the same way he assumes that the comity of nations is also *natural*, and cannot be disturbed by the artificial activities of man. The matter is complicated here by (1) a habit of interpreting war by entirely *personal* categories, and (2) a misuse of facile historical metaphor. Both these things prevent men seeing the facts as they actually are. . .

(1) They tend to look on war as of the same nature and probably as caused by the same childish motives, as the struggles of a number of boys in a room. Some may get more damaged than others, but the framework of the struggle is not changed—in the end, as at the beginning, you have a number of boys in a room. Moreover, it is a mistake to punish one boy too much, as he may then turn nasty, and be a nuisance in the future. "Germany would regard defeat not as evidence of guilt . . . and would resolve to be better prepared next time."[6] Here the real nature of the situation is entirely ignored, and an interpretation—in terms of the categories appropriate only to the description of personal conduct—is substituted for it. There is no realisation of the *particular* facts of force involved, no realisation of the *actual* danger which victory avoids and—such being the nature of the forces concerned—probably avoids for good.

(2) "Beaten nations develop into the strongest. It was her defeat by Napoleon that created Prussia as a military power." Generalisation depends, I suppose, on the possibility of repetition. The amount of possible repetition in history is very small and consequently historical generalisations are necessarily very thin; but I think I hardly remember anything quite so thin as this. If I put this phrase out of my head, and look at the concrete situation at the time of the battle of Jena, and the

---

[6] "The ordinary German would regard defeat, not as evidence of his guilt, but as evidence of our artful diplomacy. He would resolve to be even better prepared next time, and would follow the advice of his militarists even more faithfully than in the past." Bertrand Russell, "The Philosophy of Pacifism," in *Towards Ultimate Harmony* (London, 1915), p. 5.

concrete situation now, I should probably fail to discover any common elements whatever. We need no such fantastic guidance from history. What is needed is merely an objective examination of the sufficiently complicated situation we have before us *today*. It will not be very difficult then to perceive that this time it is not merely that individual combatants will get more or less damaged with every possibility of recovery, but that the room in which they fight, the framework itself, will be permanently changed. Just as we *naturally* assume that all the struggling nations will recover their old positions. But this time there is nothing *natural* about it.

"Why We Are in Favour of This War"

So far all the arguments I have given in detail have been negative; I have said very little in favour of the war, but have endeavoured rather to meet the arguments of those who incline, for quite general reasons, to think all wars bad.

But before such arguments can be convincing, another step must be taken. Reasons which are sufficient to make us reject "pacifist philosophy" are *not* sufficient to make us accept this *particular* war. The fact, for example, that a high value should be attached to military heroism, has nothing to do with the justification of a particular event in which such heroism may be displayed. This is an absolutely different question.

There are, moreover, at this moment, a class of pacifists who do not accept "a pacifist philosophy," and whose reasons for objecting to the war are based on the nature and causes of *this* war itself. I was talking recently to a pacifist of this type, and what he said threw a good deal of light—for me, personally, at any rate, on the nature of a certain opposition to the war. He had no objection to killing; and conveyed the impression that he was quite prepared to fight himself in some more "ideal" type of struggle—one with some positive and definite aim—in a war, for example, which would bring about the final disappearance of capitalism. But he was not prepared to fight in *this* war, which, in as far as it was not an entirely unnecessary stupidity, was concerned with interests very far removed from any which had any real importance for the individual citizen, and more definitely the individual workman.

I admit that this attitude, if we *agree to certain tacit assumptions*, does seem justified. As the attitude is very real and fairly widespread it is perhaps worth while examining the nature of these assumptions. Though it may not be very conscious or formulated, I think it demonstrable that there is floating before the mind of the man who makes this objection a certain false conception of the character of human activities. What makes the objection possible and gives force to it is the conception of Progress. By that I do not mean merely the hope that capitalism will ultimately disappear. It is rather that progress is looked upon as *inevitable* in this sense—that the evils in the world are due to definite oppressions, and whenever any particular shackle has been removed, the evil it was responsible for has disappeared for ever, for human nature is on the whole, good, and a harmonious society is thus possible. As long as you hold this conception of the nature of history, you are bound, I think, to find nothing in *this war* which makes it worth while. But this is a false conception; the evil in the world is not merely due to the existence of oppression. It is part of the *nature* of things and just as man is not naturally good and has only achieved anything as the result of certain discipline, the "good" here does not preserve itself, but is also preserved by discipline. This may seem too simple to be worth emphasising, but I think this way of treating the objection justified, for it really does spring from this quite *abstract* matter, this false conception of the nature of evil in the world. It is only under the influence of this false conception that you demand an *ideal* war where great sacrifices are for great ends.

So it comes about that we are unable to name any great *positive* "good" for which we can be said to be fighting. But it is not necessary that we should; there is no harmony in the nature of things, so that from time to time great and useless sacrifices become necessary, merely that whatever precarious "good" the world has achieved may just be preserved. These sacrifices are as negative, barren, and as *necessary* as the work of those who repair sea-walls. In this war, then, we are fighting for no great *liberation* of mankind, for no great jump upward, but are merely accomplishing a work, which, if the nature of things was ultimately "good," would be useless, but which in this actual "vale of tears" becomes from time to time necessary, merely in order that bad may not get worse.

This method of stating the question avoids the subterfuges to which those who hold the optimistic conception of man are driven—of inventing imaginary positive "goods" which the war is to bring about "to end war" and the rest. . . .

"THE FRAMEWORK OF EUROPE"

Most of the arguments used by the pacifists in their repudiation of the balance of power as a doctrine of policy really rest on the tacit assumption that this balance will take care of itself, being grounded on the nature of things. In describing the evil consequences of the policy, they forget that the alternative is not simply the same world, minus those evils; there would be much greater evils that would follow the destruction of the balance of power.

The only alternative at the present moment to the Balance of Power is a German hegemony of Europe. The only legitimate discussion of this doctrine, then, is one which tries to estimate the relative greatness of (1) the evils which accompany the attempt to maintain the balance of power—the present war, for example; and (2) the evils which would accompany a "united Europe under German military leadership." (I quote this sentence from a book on the war by a well-known German philosopher, as describing what, in his opinion, was the object for which Germany was fighting.)

In stating the matter in this way, however, I am perhaps assuming too much. The following types of pacifists would not accept this as a true account of the things at issue.

(1) Those who deny that the Balance of Power is the only alternative to the hegemony of one Power. They have visions of something better: (a) No Powers at all, (b) a harmony of Powers.

(2) Those who deny, or fail to realise, the *possibility* of such a hegemony as a result of our defeat in this war. . . .

I want here to consider the *second* type of pacifist indicated above. How does it come about that they cannot believe in the *possibility* of a German hegemony? Why do they tend to think that the evils of such a hegemony are merely the inventions of hysterical journalists; and if not imaginary, at least, enormously exaggerated?

Many things in Europe which we have been accustomed to regard as fixed are now temporarily in a state of flux. When the war ends the new state in which it leaves these things will probably continue, fixed and permanent, for another half century. Now it is possible that the new state of Europe produced by the way may be a permanent German hegemony, with the enormous reaction which would follow this *inside* the beaten countries. The immense importance of the war lies in the fact that in a short space of time, when the world is, as it were, plastic, things are decided, which no efforts afterwards may be able to shift. All our future efforts will take place in a framework settled by the war.

One may illustrate this by a metaphor taken from the war itself. The line of trenches on the Western front has now remained practically unaltered for over a year. The position and shape of this line are the brute facts on which all calculations as to future military action have to be based. The apparently accidental details of its shape have to be taken into account, like the similarly accidental and irregular lines of some great natural obstacle, such as a range of mountains. They form the fixed data of the problem which has to be solved. But though now it seems fixed, there was a short period in which it was plastic; and all the accidental details of an outline which seems irregular as the course of a river are due to known causes operating inside that short period. The salient at one point, the concavity at another are perhaps the result of the events of an afternoon, when a general under-estimated the number of men required at one particular point, and overestimated the number required at another. This provides an accurate parallel for the relation of this war to the future of Europe. The relation between the three months of mobility and the year of stalemate is the same as that between the state of flux in which Europe now is and the fixed outlines the war will determine for the next fifty years. . . .

What are the "habits of mind" which prevent the pacifists realising this? How does it come about that they tend to disregard any description of the consequences of German hegemony? Probably for this reason—they discount all these arguments, because they are *not* really convinced that things are in a flux. They do not really believe in the possibility of any fundamental change in Europe; the change, for example, from the present state to that constituted by the hegemony of one Power. As they do not at heart believe that the effects of Force can be so irrevocable, or that such profound changes can take place, they cannot attach serious importance to any argument which postulates such a change.

At bottom, I think, their attitude is the result of the fact that they, perhaps, unconsciously, tend to think of all events of the twentieth century in Europe as taking place within the framework impressed on our minds by the history of the nineteenth. This history, in a sense, hypnotises one, and makes the possibility of radical change very difficult to conceive. With many reservations it is, on the whole, true to say that in the history of the wars of the past century and a half, the protagonists remain much the same: England, France, Prussia, Austria, and Russia. While the power of each of them has varied, none has ever established a permanent hegemony, or been able to destroy the others; Europe has always remained divided into independent states. The result of this is that we tend to think of these nations—the elements of this history—as the permanent and indestructible elements of all future history; the games may be different, but they will always be played with the same pieces. But we ought to get rid of this distorting effect of history on our minds. We, ourselves, have not had for centuries any desire to conquer any part of Europe, and we find it difficult to grasp the fact that other nations are really moved by this desire. This particular difficulty is considerably increased by the malign influence of school histories. These books so consistently represent our own acquisitions as the accidental and undesired results of the triumph of virtue over vice, that we remain ignorant not only of the amount of calculation and brute force that went to the making of the *colonial* empire, but also find it difficult to realise the fact, that at the present moment others may be thinking of creating a *European* empire by similar methods.

► 7 ◄

DEMOCRACY

INTRODUCTION TO
Carl Schmitt,
"When Parliament Cannot
be Sovereign"

◆

Conservatives have always been hostile to democracy in its original meaning of direct rule by the people. Toward representative democracy they have been suspicious. The intensity and implications of that suspicion have varied across time and national context. Where conservatives *have* accepted democratic institutions, it has usually been with scepticism toward the claims of democratic theory. Conservatives have maintained that nominally democratic institutions are most likely to work when they are restrained and counterbalanced by nondemocratic elements which allow for the formation and influence of decision-making elites. Though the degree of their statism has varied from one national context to another, conservatives have on the whole emphasized the importance of the state as a guarantor of property and of order, and as necessary to provide national defense against external military threats.

The following selection, by the twentieth century German legal and political theorist Carl Schmitt, argues that under some circumstances, parliamentary, liberal democracy is incapable of creating a government strong enough to carry out the necessary functions of the state. His analysis of the political institutions of the later stages of the Weimar Republic has implications beyond its immediate context. Schmitt's analysis drew upon criticisms of parliamentary democracy already voiced at the turn of the century by the French radical right. Similar analyses—sometimes drawing upon Schmitt, and sometimes arrived at independently— have been presented of other liberal parliamentary systems. The dilemmas which Schmitt analyzed have resurfaced more recently in the language of "public choice" theory in the attempt to explain why the

pursuit of self-interest by a plurality of social groups may result in unfavorable collective outcomes.[1]

Schmitt was born into a devoutly Catholic family in western Germany
in 1888.[2] The German Empire in which he came of age combined an
authoritarian monarchy with a constitution which enshrined liberal freedoms and a parliament which controlled taxation and revenues. Discredited by its conduct of the First World War, the monarchy was replaced
in 1918 by a republic. The new Weimar constitution created a parliamentary form of government along with an elected president who was
granted broad emergency powers. Schmitt received his law degree in
1910, began an apprenticeship in the Prussian civil service, and spent the
First World War stationed in Munich, where he served in the German
army as a legal counselor, censor, and domestic intelligence officer. It
was there that he came into contact with Max Weber, who appears to
have stimulated Schmitt to think about legal issues in more sociological
terms. Schmitt lived through the abortive attempts at revolution in postwar Munich, and in 1923 he experienced first-hand the French occupation of the Rhineland. These events made the questions of state power
and national sovereignty central to his concerns.

In the decade after the First World War, Schmitt taught law at a series
of German universities and published a succession of stimulating works
on the politics of romanticism, secularization and political theory, and
"the concept of the political." Particularly relevant to the issues explored
in the selection below are two books written in the mid-1920s, one a
critical study of the gap between the political theory of parliamentarianism and its contemporary practice, the second a work on modern constitutional theory.[3] In 1928 he assumed a professorship in Berlin and
began a more direct involvement in the politics of the Weimar Republic.
Schmitt's initial critique of parliamentarianism was linked to his opposition to the post-war Versailles treaties, which had severely limited
Germany's military might and required it to pay reparations to the victorious western powers. At first the deficiencies of parliamentary government in Weimar were of acute concern to Schmitt because he believed
that the lack of a strong central government threatened the political
independence—and, he claimed with exaggeration, the physical existence—of the German nation.

---

[1] Among the best-known presentations is that of the Nobel laureate for economics,
James Buchanan, *The Limits of Liberty* (Chicago, 1975).
[2] Biographical information on Schmitt is drawn from Paul Noack, *Carl Schmitt: Eine
Biographie* (Berlin, 1993) and Joseph W. Bendersky, *Carl Schmitt: Theorist for the Reich*
(Princeton, 1983).
[3] Carl Schmitt, *Die geistesgeschichtliche Lage des heutigen Parliamentarismus* (Berlin,
1923; second edition, 1926), translated by Ellen Kennedy as *The Crisis of Parliamentary
Democracy* (Cambridge, MA, 1985); *Verfassunglehre* (Berlin, 1927).

In his 1923 book on parliamentarianism Schmitt claimed, correctly but one-sidedly, that arguments made on behalf of representative government by nineteenth-century liberals had been based on the rationalist belief that open discussion among elected representatives would lead parliamentarians to choose the public good. Contemporary politics, by contrast, was based upon disciplined, organized parties which sought to rally voters through propagandistic appeals to the passions and through appeals to economic self-interest, Schmitt argued. Parliamentary deputies bound by party discipline did not arrive at decisions based on a rational weighing of the public good; indeed decisions were no longer made in parliament but "behind closed doors" in committees, between leaders of party factions. Schmitt adapted and expanded a critique of parliamentary institutions developed in France by Charles Maurras, of the radical right-wing *Action Française,* and by the idiosyncratic radical Georges Sorel.[4]

In a series of works beginning in 1928 and culminating in *The Protector of the Constitution* of 1931, from which the selection below is drawn, Schmitt deepened his argument and spelled out its political import, insisting that the constitution of the Weimar Republic was based on nineteenth-century social and political assumptions which no longer applied under contemporary conditions.

In the selection below, Schmitt refers to the peculiar nature of the German political parties of his day and to the relationship between politics and economics in the Weimar Republic. Most of the major parties were more than political associations: they were the political arms of distinct subcultures. Catholics, Social Democrats, Communists, and later National Socialists each had their own newspapers, labor unions, cultural associations, youth movements, and para-military organizations, and allegiance to the "bourgeois" parties of the center and right was also frequently linked to associational life. For those within each subculture, voting was regarded less as a matter of choice between plausible alternatives than as an assertion of cultural identity. In addition, there was a close link between specific political parties and economic interest groups such as blue-collar unions, white-collar unions, agrarian leagues, shopkeepers' associations, and industrialists' lobbies.

In the background of Schmitt's analysis lay the threat to political stability arising from the fact that economic conflicts in the Weimar Republic tended to be transferred to the state itself.[5] The issue of wages was

---

[4] See, for example, Maurras's "Dictator and King" of 1899, in J. S. McClelland, ed., *The French Right from de Maistre to Maurras* (London, 1970), pp. 215–38; and Georges Sorel, *Reflections on Violence* (New York, 1961; French original, 1906).

[5] The following paragraphs are based on recent scholarship summarized and advanced by Harold James, "Economic Reasons for the Collapse of the Weimar Republic," in Ian

one element of a broader conflict in which economic issues were settled by political means, as a result of which government institutions "became the subject of a political tug-of-war, as they became overloaded with expectations."[6] In 1923, the largest party, the Social Democrats—which, together with the Catholic Center party was the mainstay of almost every Weimar government—had obtained legally binding government arbitration of wage disputes. The Social Democratic leaders prided themselves on their ability to raise wages through such political means, and it was on these grounds that they justified to their members the participation of their party in the capitalist welfare state of Weimar. Social Democratic leaders feared that if they were unable to use their political power to provide increases in wages and social benefits, part of their working-class constituency might desert them for the more radical Communists—which is in fact what happened as the arrangement broke down during the Depression. Businessmen responded at first by pressuring the "bourgeois" parties to oppose the raising of wages by political means. They claimed that the rising level of wages made it impossible for them to generate the capital required for reinvestment and economic growth—a claim which economic historians tend to regard as justified. But given the relative weakness of the pro-capitalist parties, some businessmen concluded that the parliamentary system threatened the existence of their enterprises. They founded political organizations dedicated to authoritarian constitutional reforms which would limit the power of parliament and hence the ability of the parties of the left to influence the economy.

Effective parliamentary government ended in March 1930 with the dissolution of the last cabinet based upon a parliamentary majority. The issue on which the government fell, the seemingly unimportant matter of a small increase of unemployment insurance premiums and a reduction in benefits, was in fact the tip of a socioeconomic iceberg. In withholding its support from the government, the Social Democratic party acceded to the demands of its unionized constituents, who feared that this was merely the first step of a larger program by the captains of German industry to peal back existing welfare state provisions. The liberal party, with close links to business, advocated a diminution of benefits and held its ground in the belief that without cuts in public spending and in real wage rates, German industry would become uncompetitive in

---

Kershaw, ed., *Weimar: Why Did German Democracy Fail?* (New York, 1990), pp. 30–57; and Knut Borchardt, "Constraint and room for manoeuvre in the great depression of the early thirties: toward a revision of the received historical picture," and "Economic causes of the collapse of the Weimar Republic," both in Borchardt, *Perspectives on Modern German Economic History and Policy* (Cambridge, 1991), pp. 143–83.

[6] James, "Economic Reasons," p. 32.

the international market. Both the Social Democrats and the liberals feared that if they did not stand their ground, they would lose voters to more extreme parties. The result was a new cabinet headed by Heinrich Brüning, who attempted to govern through emergency powers granted by the president of the republic in keeping with the Weimar constitution. When Brüning's deflationary, belt-tightening budget was voted down by parliament in July 1930, he promulgated the budget by presidential decree, dissolved parliament, and called new elections for the latest date possible under the provisions of the constitution. That election resulted in an electoral surge for two anti-democratic parties, Hitler's National Socialists and the Communists, thus contributing to the further destabilization of the republic.

In March 1931, Schmitt published *The Protector of the Constitution*, a book in which he brought together a series of arguments which he had made in essayistic form during the previous three years. His earlier criticism of the Weimar state for its inability to rally the nation on behalf of a more activist foreign policy now gave way to an emphasis on the absolute paralysis of decision-making in the face of a splintered party system which reflected so wide a divergence of economic, religious, and political interests. The Weimar state, Schmitt argued, had become subordinated to the pluralistic social interests of society, thus robbing the state of its unity and sovereignty. As a consequence, Schmitt wrote, the state was becoming a "total state," forced by politically organized social interests to intervene in ever more areas of society. Here the term "total state" had an opprobrious connotation. It was inevitable that the state would have a large role in the economy, Schmitt agreed, yet the Weimar state was incapable of exercising the legislative authority demanded by this new reality, because parliament now served to divide the state's power among politically organized social interests. Schmitt's preferred solution in *The Protector of the Constitution* was the creation of a stronger regime independent of parliament. Its institutional locus was to be the president, ruling through the bureaucracy and with the support of the army.[7]

It was this line of reasoning which brought Schmitt to the attention of President Hindenburg's chief of staff, and then into contact with the circle around Kurt von Schleicher, a political general who played a key role behind the scenes of the presidency. Schmitt served as a legal advisor to a succession of Weimar governments which tried to rely upon presidential decree to govern the country in the face of parliamentary deadlock and the growing electoral success of the National Socialists and the Communists.

[7] Carl Schmitt, *Der Hüter der Verfassung* (Berlin, 1931), pp. 108–59.

In the end these attempts failed, and to Schmitt's dismay, Hitler became chancellor at the end of January 1933. Schmitt, who until then had regarded the Nazis as an "immature" political force, took stock of the new situation and in late April joined the Nazi party. In the years that followed he supplied legal arguments for Hitler's internal and foreign policies, and wrote works of political theory which blamed the Jews and the British for the evils of liberalism and the decline of modern state authority.[8]

This selection from Schmitt's work provides an example of a figure on the border between conservatism and radical conservatism, of a man who values institutional order but concludes that existing institutions are incapable of providing that order and must be replaced. The selection should not be regarded as the key to Schmitt's political thought, for as one recent student of Schmitt's career has rightly noted, the search for some Archimedian point around which Schmitt's wide-ranging thought pivots has inevitably failed.[9] Carl Schmitt was a highly intelligent man, but not a very consistent or coherent thinker. While political officials who knew Schmitt claimed that he understood little about day-to-day politics, and others confirm that his understanding of economics was minimal,[10] Schmitt was deeply knowledgeable about the history of European political and legal thought, and he had a knack for relating political, economic, and cultural trends to one another. As a result, interest in his work has reached well beyond the German right; the analytic constructs presented here have been utilized not only by radical conservatives, but by liberal conservatives, liberals, and socialists.[11]

[8] For the anti-Jewish and anti-English elements in Schmitt's political theory of this period, see his *Der Leviathan in der Staatslehre des Thomas Hobbes: Sinn und Fehlschlag eines politischen Symbols* (Hamburg, 1938; reprinted Cologne, 1982), esp. pp. 119–27 and *Land und Meer: Eine weltgeschichtliche Betrachtung* (Leipzig, 1942; reprinted Cologne, 1981), pp. 86–102. For the expression of related sentiments in Schmitt's personal conversations of the period, see the memoir by Nicolaus Sombart, "Spaziergänge mit Carl Schmitt," in his *Jugend in Berlin, 1933–43* (Munich, 1984), pp. 260–65. On Schmitt's career in the Third Reich, see in addition to the biographical works mentioned above Bernd Rüthers, *Carl Schmitt im Dritten Reich* (2nd edition, Munich, 1990).

[9] Dirk van Laak, "Eigentlich beliebig," *Die Zeit*, Jan. 20, 1995, p. 17.

[10] Paul Noack, *Carl Schmitt: Eine Biographie* (Berlin, 1993), pp. 106, 132.

[11] It is central, for example, to Jürgen Habermas's much-cited book, *The Structural Transformation of the Public Sphere* (Cambridge, MA, 1989; German original 1962).

Carl Schmitt,
"When Parliament Cannot be Sovereign" (1931)[1]

The present constitutional situation is characterized by the fact that many institutions and norms have been retained unchanged from the nineteenth century, despite the fact that contemporary circumstances have changed radically. . . .

The German constitutions of the nineteenth century reflect an age the basic structure of which was characterized by the great German political theorists of the time in terms of the fundamental distinction between the state and society. . . . "Society" was essentially a polemical term, a counter-conception to the then-existing monarchic "state" based on the army and the bureaucracy; "society," by contrast, was that which did not belong to this state. The state, at that time, was distinguishable from society. It was powerful enough to stand independently of the other social forces and thereby to determine their relationship to the state and to each other. Thus the many differences within the "state-free" zone of society—including confessional, cultural, and economic antagonisms—were defined in relation to the state, and could cohere into "society," if necessary only by virtue of their common contrast to the state. On the other hand, however, the state by and large assumed a position of neutrality and nonintervention with regard to religion and society, and broadly speaking respected the autonomy of these realms; the state was not so absolute and so powerful as to make everything which was not of the state insignificant. This made possible a certain balance and dualism: it was plausible to think in terms of a state which was free of religion and particular worldviews, and indeed quite agnostic; and it was plausible to think in terms of an economy free of the state and a state free of the economy. But all was defined by the state, which was visible as a concrete and distinct entity. Even today, the term "society," which has many meanings, is of interest to us here primarily to designate that which is *not* of the state, and perhaps that which is distinct from the church as well. All the significant institutions and norms of public law which were developed in Germany in the course of the nineteenth century rest upon this fundamental distinction. The fundamental dualism of state and society was reflected in conceptions of the German constitutional monarchy as constituted by the contrast between prince and people, crown and budget, government and popular representation. The

[1] The selection is excerpted from *Der Hüter der Verfassung* (Berlin, 1931), pp. 73–91, edited and translated by Jerry Z. Muller. Schmitt's footnotes have been eliminated. Title supplied by the editor.

representative institution of the people, that is, parliament, the legislative body, was conceived as a battlefield on which society and state faced one another. It was here that society would be integrated into the state, or the state into society. . . .

A "dualistic state" of this sort was a balance between two forms of state: between a governmental state [of the monarch and his bureaucracy] and a legislative state. It developed increasingly into a legislative state, as parliament, the legislative body, came to dominate the monarch's government, that is, the more that society came to dominate the existing state. . . .

Beginning in the sixteenth century, the absolute state based on the army and the bureaucracy arose out of the collapse and dissolution of the medieval, pluralistic, feudal, estate-based legal order. It was thus essentially a state of the executive and the administration. Its justification lay not in substantive norms but in its effectiveness in creating the preconditions under which valid norms could exist at all, for it was the state which put an end to the source of all disorder and civil war, namely, the struggle on behalf of ultimate norms. This state created public order and security. Only once that was in place could the legislative state develop, with its bourgeois constitution based on the rule of law[2]. . . .

According to nineteenth-century conceptions, parliament was by its very nature the true guarantor of the constitution. . . . But this position of the legislative body was only made possible by particular circumstances. It always assumed that parliament, the legislative body, the representative of the people or of society (for "the people" and "society" can only be identified with one another as long as both are contrasted to the "state") existed alongside a partner in the constitutional contract, namely, an independent, powerful, monarchic, bureaucratic state. Parliament was regarded as the true protector and guarantor of the constitution because its contractual partner, the monarchic government, was a reluctant party to the contract. The government, therefore, was regarded with mistrust; it demanded revenues and expenditures; it was seen as spendthrift, while the people's representatives were seen as frugal and tight-fisted, and on the whole this was in fact the case. For the tendency of nineteenth-century liberalism was to limit the state to a minimum, above all to prevent it whenever possible from intervening in the economy, and in general to neutralize it in regard to society and to social conflicts of interest, in order to allow society and the economy to arrive at decisions according to their immanent principles. Nineteenth-

---

[2] Schmitt uses the term "*bürgerlich-rechtsstaatlichen Verfassung*" which could also be translated as "civic constitution based on the *Rechtsstaat*." The connotation of the term *Rechtsstaat*, which was central to German liberalism, is that government officials are bound by the law and prevented from acting arbitrarily.

century liberalism stood for parties based on the free exchange of opinions and the freedom to campaign. Discussion and struggles of opinion were supposed to produce public opinion, which in turn was to determine the content of the state's will. In the social and economic realm, freedom of contract and economic liberty seemed to ensure the greatest economic prosperity because the automatic mechanisms of the free economy and the free market were supposed to be self-guided and self-regulated by economic laws (through supply and demand, exchange, price-formation, and income formation). The fundamental bourgeois liberties and rights—especially personal freedom, freedom of expression, freedom of contract and of trade, private property— . . . assumed the existence of a fundamentally noninterventionist, neutral state, which intervened at most in order to recreate the conditions of free competition when they had been damaged.

This neutral state, in the liberal sense of one which is in principal noninterventionist in regard to society and the economy, remained the presupposition of the constitution, even when exceptions were made for social and cultural policy. But the situation changed fundamentally as the tension built into the dualistic structure (of state and society, government and people) was lost with the triumph of the legislative state. As the previously assumed distinctions between state and society, government and people vanished, all the concepts and institutions which were based on these assumptions (legislation, budget, self-government) became problematic. At the same time a broader and deeper transformation began. [Through the creation of class-based and confessionally based parties] society itself was increasingly organized with a view to controlling the state. If state and society are in principle to become identical, then all social and economic problems immediately become problems of the state, and it is no longer possible to distinguish the political realm of the state from the nonpolitical realm of society. That means an end to all of the traditional contrasts which were based on the distinction between state and society and on the assumption of a neutral state. Antithetical terms which had a meaning when they corresponded to objective, distinct, concrete entities or realms—such as state and economy, state and culture, state and education, state policy and economy, state policy and education, state policy and religion, state and law, state policy and law—all lose their meaning and no longer refer to real objects. The society-become-state develops into an economic state, a cultural state, a public assistance state, a welfare state, a provisioning state; a state no longer objectively separable from society lays hold of everything that is society, that is, every aspect of social life. There is no longer a realm which the state can view with absolute neutrality in the sense of nonintervention. As the various social interest groups organize themselves into parties, the state develops into a party-state; and because there are parties determined by economic, confessional, or cultural groups, the state can no longer remain neutral in regard to economic, confessional, or cultural matters. In such a state everything becomes at least potentially an object of politics and of the state. This new state takes hold of every realm; it becomes what French jurists and soldiers have called the state of "potential armament," a state which takes hold of *everything*, not only that which is military in the narrow, technical sense, but also the industrial and economic preparations for war, and indeed the spiritual and moral education which prepares citizens for war. A leading representative of the German front-line veterans, Ernst Jünger, has introduced a pregnant phrase for this astonishing process: "total mobilization." Regardless of the specific content or the accuracy of the formulations "potential armament" and "total mobilization," one should reflect upon the significant insight which they express. For they capture a comprehensive and deep transformation: the state made up of organized social interests is in the process of changing from the neutral state of the liberal nineteenth century into a potentially total state. This powerful transformation can be conceptualized as a dialectical development in three stages: from the absolute state of the seventeenth and eighteenth centuries, through the neutral state of the liberal nineteenth century, to the total state based on the identity of state and society.

This transformation is most striking when one looks at the economic realm. It is a widely recognized and undisputed fact that the governmental share of the economy, both in comparison to its prewar dimensions, and in comparison to the private, nongovernmental economy, has become so extensive as to signify not only a quantitative increase, but a qualitative change, a "structural transformation" involving not only financial and economic matters narrowly construed but all the realms of public life. We need not become involved in disputes as to the statistics that reflect this change, such as the oft-cited figure that in 1928, 53 percent of German national income was controlled by government, because the phenomenon as a whole is indisputable and undisputed. One expert of great authority, state-secretary Professor Johannes Popitz,[3] asserts in a recent lecture on public finance that the distribution of the greater part of German national income takes place outside the self-regulating mechanism of the free economy and the free market, which has been replaced by "the decisive influence of a fundamentally extra-economic will, namely that of the state." Another distinguished expert, state-minister Saemisch, the Federal Parks Commissioner, declares that the economy

---

[3] Popitz, a friend of Carl Schmitt, was the state secretary in the federal Ministry of Finance, the highest civil service position in the ministry.

of public finance is the decisive influence on the political situation in Germany. From the economic perspective, an apt formulation of the contrast between the earlier system and the contemporary one is that we have moved from a "system of allotment" in which the state took an allotment from national income, a sort of dividend from profits, to a "system of control" in which the state—by virtue of the intimate relationship of the economy of state finance to the private economy, and because of the sharp increase of state demands and state revenues—substantially co-determines the private economy, as a shareholder and redistributor of national income, and as a producer, consumer, and employer. . . . From the perspective of political and constitutional theory, it is essential to recognize that the relation of the state to the economy is the real focus of intra-national political conflicts, and that traditional concepts based upon the separation of state and society only confuse our understanding of this situation.

In every modern state, the relationship of the state to the economy is the real subject of contemporary internal-political questions. They can no longer be answered with the old liberal principle of absolute non-intervention. With few exceptions, this is generally recognized. In the contemporary state—and the more it is a modern, industrial state, the more this applies—the economic issues are the main topic of intra-national political struggles; both internal policy and external policy are in large part economic policy, and not only when it comes to tariff and trade policy or social policy. . . . The contemporary state has a wide-reaching labor law, wage scales, and state arbitration of wage disputes which substantially influence the level of wages; it provides huge subsidies to various branches of the economy; it is a welfare and public assistance state, and as a result it is also an enormous tax and expenditure state. In Germany, in addition, it is also a reparations state, which must pay a tribute of billions to foreign states. Under these conditions, the demand for nonintervention becomes utopian and self-contradictory. For nonintervention means giving free reign to various powerful groups to struggle against one another over social and economic conflicts, struggles which are not fought by purely economic means. Nonintervention in such a case is nothing but intervention on behalf of the strongest or most reckless groups. . . .

This transformation of the state into an economic state is the most striking change compared to nineteenth-century conceptions of the state. . . .

At the very moment when parliament, the legislative body, the basis and focal point of the legislative state, seems victorious, it becomes a conflict-laden institution, and its preconditions and pre-suppositions are undermined. . . . The state now becomes what has been called the "self-organization of society," but it is doubtful that this self-organizing society can attain sufficient unity, or that unity really comes about as a result of this process of "self-organization."

The prime agents of this self-organization were to be the political parties. But it has turned out that they themselves have been transformed. In liberal constitutional thought, parties were to be based upon free campaigning; they were not to be rigid, ongoing, permanent institutions made up of thoroughly organized social groups. The very ideas of "freedom" and of "campaigning" exclude the use of social and economic pressure, they allow only for the attempt to freely convince people who are regarded as socially and economically free, culturally and intellectually independent, and capable of forming their own judgments. . . . But today, most of the large parties are either rigid, thoroughly organized structures, or are part of a complex of social organizations with an influential bureaucracy, a standing army of paid functionaries, and an entire system of supporting associations through which their clientele is bound together culturally, socially, and economically. For some citizens the turn to the "total" has already occurred, in that they are part of a network of party associations which stretch over every area of their lives, annulling the liberal idea of the separation and neutralization of realms such as religion, economic life, and education. Though not yet a total state, several of these parties strive toward totality, with social organizations that lay hold of their members beginning in early youth in order to integrate them into what Eduard Spranger has called "a total cultural program." And such total parties make up and are supported by the pluralistic state. The fact that there are a multiplicity of competing organizational complexes, which hold one another within certain bounds—the fact of a pluralistic party-state—prevents the total state from acting with the impact of the so-called "one-party states," of Soviet Russia and [Fascist] Italy. But the fact of a plurality [of parties] does not eliminate the turn toward the total; rather the process is parceled out, so to speak, in that each complex of organized social forces attempts to create a totality within itself and for its own purposes—from singing clubs and sporting clubs up to armed self-defence organizations. . . . M. J. Bonn, a clear-eyed liberal critic of these developments, has characterized this transformation as a transition toward a new feudal society of orders. . . .

In order for a parliamentary-democratic, legislative state to fulfill the requirements of its constitution . . . the parties would have to act according to the liberal conception of party, in which parties are understood as independent institutions. It is the logic of the constitutional institutions and methods of a parliamentary democracy and intrinsic to the parliamentary system of the Weimar constitution that a unified will of the state is to be created through an ongoing process of the rise and decline of egoistic interests and opinions, which lead through the wills of the parties to a coherent will of the state. The parties cannot be so rigid that they resist the process of transforming and accommodating these interests and opinions. The parties are conceived as means of state will-formation, and they are not permitted and recognized by the constitution in order for them to use their participation in government to be rewarded through compromise deals with other parties, or as a means of extortion. Parliament is supposed to be the place in which a process takes place by which the multiplicity of social, economic, cultural, and confessional conflicts, interests, and opinions is transformed into a coherent political will. There is a long-standing belief (one more liberal than democratic) that parliamentary methods are best suited to turn parties into such transformative agencies, and that it is in parliament that party egoism—thanks to the cunning of the parliamentary idea or the institution of parliament—is transformed into a means for the formation of the political will of the state, which goes beyond egoism and particular party concerns. In particular, a party which succeeds in forming the government is supposed to be forced by this very fact to attend to and govern according to broader and higher criteria, rather than according to narrow party considerations.

[But in our case], this ascent of political leaders beyond egoistic party considerations is prevented time and again by a number of factors: as a result of the type, composition, and number of parties; as a result of the already mentioned metamorphosis of the parties into rigidly organized forces with fixed administrative apparatuses and tightly controlled clienteles; and as a result of the large number of parties and factions necessary to form a majority. In contradiction to the assumptions on which the rules of the constitution are based, only such governments come to power that are a product of factional compromise; they are too weak and hemmed in to govern effectively themselves, but on the other hand have enough power to prevent others from governing. That "cunning" which the idea and institution of parliament are supposed to provide therefore no longer functions, and instead of a state with a will of its own, what actually occurs is a casting about in all directions in order to put together enough momentary and special interests [to form a parliamentary majority]. The present situation of German parliamentarianism is characterized by the fact that the formation of state will is dependent upon labile parliamentary majorities, changing from case to case, and made up of extremely heterogeneous parties. The majority is always only a majority coalition and varies according to the political issues at stake, such as foreign policy, economic policy, social policy, or cultural policy. The inadequacies and defects of this situation have been portrayed and criticized often enough: undependable majorities, governments which are incapable of governing or unreliable because of the compromises on which they are based; recurrent party and factional compromises in which each participating party expects to be rewarded for its participation at the cost of everyone else or of the state as a whole; the distribution of state, local, and other public jobs and sinecures among party associates, according to the strength of each faction or some other tactical consideration. Even parties motivated by a noble-minded political concern, which seek to put the interests of the whole over partial interests, find that—in part because of need to consider their clientele and their voters and even more because of the intrinsic pluralism of the existing system—they are forced either to take part in the ongoing traffic in compromise, or to become insignificant bystanders. . . .

The rigid social groupings which today are the agents through which the will of the state is formed, make parliament, where their exponents appear in the form of factions, into a mere reflection of the pluralistic partitioning of the state itself. Under these conditions, how are the ties of party and interest to be superseded and transformed into the necessary unity?. . . .

When parliament has become the arena for the pluralistic division of the state among a multiplicity of highly organized social groupings, and when so great an expansion of state activity has occurred that one can speak of the turn to a total state, then it is of little help to respond to the pressing questions of contemporary constitutional law with formulas which reflect the bygone circumstances of nineteenth-century constitutional monarchies, such as "the sovereignty of parliament."

INTRODUCTION TO
Joseph A. Schumpeter,
"Political Leadership and Democracy"

◆

The next selection is drawn from Joseph Schumpeter's *Capitalism, Socialism, and Democracy*, published in 1942. Schumpeter had left Europe in 1932 to join the department of economics at Harvard University. In 1935 Schumpeter began work on a book that would synthesize and add to his previous writings on politics, economics, and sociology. The result was *Capitalism, Socialism, and Democracy*, published in 1942. In the second part of the book, Schumpeter explored the gap between the theory of democracy developed in the eighteenth century and the actual functioning of modern democracy.

Schumpeter's book appeared after two decades which had seen the collapse of most of the liberal democratic regimes of interwar Europe. In the 1920s, parliamentary democracy had broken down and been replaced by either authoritarian or fascist forms of government in Italy, Spain, Portugal, Poland, Greece, Lithuania, and Yugoslavia; in the following decade the parliamentary regimes of Germany and Austria followed. Under these circumstances, Schumpeter was eminently aware that far from being "natural," democracy depended on many prerequisites; some of these, Schumpeter maintained, were at odds with the assumptions of democratic theory.

In his discussion of democracy, Schumpeter explores the gap between the claims of democratic theory and the reality of democratic practice. In the selection below, he offers an explanation as to why voters do not act according to the assumptions of democratic theorists, and explains why they cannot be expected to do so.

In his critique of traditional democratic theory, Schumpeter drew on the works of late nineteenth- and early twentieth-century elitist critics of parliamentary democracy, such as the Frenchmen Gustave Le Bon and Georges Sorel, and the Italian theorists Vilfredo Pareto and Robert Michels. But, like his older contemporary, Max Weber, Schumpeter was concerned not to eviscerate democracy but to offer a more plausible theory of how successful democracies actually worked.

Part of his answer was that democracy allowed the population not to govern, but a choice of its governors. Actual rule was conducted by those elites selected by the voters. "Democracy does not mean and cannot mean that the people actually rule in any obvious sense of the terms 'people' and 'rule.' Democracy means only that the people have the opportunity of accepting or refusing the men who are to rule them," he wrote, "One aspect of this may be expressed by saying that democracy is the rule of the politician."[1] In keeping with his emphasis on the importance of elites, Schumpeter stressed the need for politics to attract individuals of high quality. That was more likely, he thought, when there existed a relatively open upper class which was accustomed to political leadership, so that those who had succeeded in economic life, or their descendants, would channel their superior talents toward political leadership. Schumpeter attributed the success of democracy in Britain and its failure in Weimar Germany to the existence of such a class in the British case and its absence in the German one.[2] He insisted that in order for democracy to be successful, elected elites must be allowed to formulate policy with a minimum of direct involvement from the populace.

Schumpeter offered a number of further conditions for successful democracy which departed from democratic theory. Because expertise and administrative competence were indispensable under modern conditions, he stressed the need for "the services of a well-trained bureaucracy of good standing and tradition, endowed with a strong sense of duty and a no less strong *esprit de corps*."[3] He asserted that far from a method of resolving radical differences, democracy itself depended on a substantial social consensus. And he suggested that democracy requires a self-limitation of the electorate which depended on "a national character and national habits of a certain type which have not everywhere had the opportunity to evolve and which the democratic method itself cannot be relied on to produce."[4] Like previous conservative thinkers, therefore, Schumpeter was skeptical of the efficacy of written constitutions, and stressed the significance of manners and mores in explaining the success or failure of democracy.

When, in the years following the publication of *Capitalism, Socialism and Democracy*, Schumpeter toyed with the idea of writing a book on "The Meaning of Conservatism," he noted that "I am pretty sure that no conservative I have ever met would recognize himself in the picture I am going to draw." While he found himself writing for an American audience, his formative experiences had occurred in central Europe. Like many of the more cosmopolitan conservatives on the Continent, he was a great admirer of the way in which Britain's traditional elites had negotiated the transition to liberal democracy in a manner that provided a substantial degree of historical continuity. It is this unusual combination of experiences and sensibilities that accounts for the peculiarity of Schumpeter's conservatism.

[1] Joseph Schumpeter, *Capitalism, Socialism, and Democracy* (New York, 1942, second ed. 1944), pp. 284–85.
[2] Ibid., pp. 290–91.   [3] Ibid., p. 293.   [4] Ibid., pp. 294–96.

Joseph A. Schumpeter, "Political Leadership and Democracy" (1942)[1]

THE CLASSICAL DOCTRINE OF DEMOCRACY

The eighteenth-century philosophy of democracy may be couched in the following definition: the democratic method is that institutional arrangement for arriving at political decisions which realizes the common good by making the people itself decide issues through the election of individuals who are to assemble in order to carry out its will. Let us develop the implications of this. . . .

[This theory attributes] to the will of the *individual* an independence and a rational quality that are altogether unrealistic. If we are to argue that the will of the citizens *per se* is a political factor entitled to respect, it must first exist. That is to say, it must be something more than an indeterminate bundle of vague impulses loosely playing about given slogans and mistaken impressions. Everyone would have to know definitely what he wants to stand for. This definite will would have to be implemented by the ability to observe and interpret correctly the facts that are directly accessible to everyone and to sift critically the information about the facts that are not. Finally, from that definite will and from these ascertained facts a clear *and prompt* conclusion as to particular issues would have to be derived according to the rules of logical inference— with so high a degree of general efficiency moreover that one man's opinion could be held, without glaring absurdity, to be roughly as good as every other man's. And all this the modal citizen would have to perform for himself and independently of pressure groups and propaganda, for volitions and inferences that are imposed upon the electorate obviously do not qualify for ultimate data of the democratic process. The question whether these conditions are fulfilled to the extent required in order to make democracy work should not be answered by reckless assertion or equally reckless denial. It can be answered only by a laborious appraisal of a maze of conflicting evidence. . . .

It remains to answer our question about the definiteness and independence of the voter's will, his powers of observation and interpretation of facts, and his ability to draw, clearly and promptly, rational inferences from both. This subject belongs to a chapter of social psychology that might be entitled Human Nature in Politics.

[1] From the chapters entitled "The Classical Doctrine of Democracy" and "Another Theory of Democracy," in Joseph A. Schumpeter, *Capitalism, Socialism and Democracy* (New York, Harper and Row, 1950), first published in 1942. The title is supplied by the editor. All but one of the footnotes have been eliminated.

During the second half of the last century, the idea of the human personality that is a homogeneous unit and the idea of a definite will that is the prime mover of action have been steadily fading—even before the times of Théodule Ribot and of Sigmund Freud. In particular, these ideas have been increasingly discounted in the field of social sciences where the importance of the extra-rational and irrational element in our behavior has been receiving more and more attention. . . .

Economists, learning to observe their facts more closely, have begun to discover that, even in the most ordinary currents of daily life, their consumers do not quite live up to the idea that the economic textbook used to convey. On the one hand their wants are nothing like as definite and their actions upon those wants nothing like as rational and prompt. On the other hand, they are so amenable to the influence of advertising and other methods of persuasion that producers often seem to dictate to them instead of being directed by them. The technique of successful advertising is particularly instructive. There is indeed nearly always some appeal to reason. But mere assertion, often repeated, counts more than rational argument and so does the direct attack upon the subconscious which takes the form of attempts to evoke and crystallize pleasant associations of an entirely extra-rational, very frequently of a sexual nature.

The conclusion, while obvious, must be drawn with care. In the ordinary run of often repeated decisions the individual is subject to the salutary and rationalizing influence of favorable and unfavorable experience. He is also under the influence of relatively simple and unproblematical motives and interests which are but occasionally interfered with by excitement. Historically, the consumers' desire for shoes may, at least in part, have been shaped by the action of producers offering attractive footgear and campaigning for it; yet at any given time it is a genuine want, the definiteness of which extends beyond "shoes in general" and which prolonged experimenting clears of much of the irrationalities that may originally have surrounded it. Moreover, under the stimulus of those simple motives consumers learn to act upon unbiased expert advice about some things (houses, motorcars) and themselves become experts in others. It is simply not true that housewives are easily fooled in the matter of foods, *familiar* household articles, wearing apparel. And, as every salesman knows to his cost, most of them have a way of insisting on the exact article they want. . . .

And so it is with most of the decisions of daily life that lie within the little field which the individual citizen's mind encompasses with a full sense of its reality. Roughly, it consists of the things that directly concern himself, his family, his business dealings, his hobbies, his friends and enemies, his township or ward, his class, church, trade union, or any other social group of which he is an active member—the things under his personal observation, the things which are familiar to him independently of what his newspaper tells him, which he can directly influence or manage and for which he develops the kind of responsibility that is induced by a direct relation to the favorable or unfavorable effects of a course of action. . . .

[I]n spite of all the qualifications that impose themselves, there is for everyone, within a much wider horizon, a narrower field—widely differing in extent as between different groups and individuals and bounded by a broad zone rather than a sharp line—which is distinguished by a sense of reality or familiarity or responsibility. And this field harbors relatively definite individual volitions. These may often strike us as unintelligent, narrow, egotistical; and it may not be obvious to everyone why, when it comes to political decisions, we should worship at their shrine, still less why we should feel bound to count each of them for one and none of them for more than one. If, however, we do choose to worship we shall at least not find the shrine empty.

Now this comparative definiteness of volition and rationality of behavior does not suddenly vanish as we move away from those concerns of daily life in the home and in business which educate and discipline us. In the realm of public affairs there are sectors that are more within the reach of the citizen's mind than others. This is true, first, of local affairs. Even there we find a reduced power of discerning facts, a reduced preparedness to act upon them, a reduced sense of responsibility. We all know the man—and a very good specimen he frequently is—who says that the local administration is not his business and callously shrugs his shoulders at practices which he would rather die than suffer in his own office. High-minded citizens in a hortatory mood who preach the responsibility of the individual voter or taxpayer invariably discover the fact that this voter does not feel responsible for what the local politicians do. Still, especially in communities not too big for personal contacts, local patriotism may be a very important factor in "making democracy work." Also, the problems of a town are in many respects akin to the problems of a manufacturing concern. The man who understands the latter also understands, to some extent, the former. The manufacturer, grocer, or workman need not step out of his world to have a rationally defensible view (that may of course be right or wrong) on street cleaning or town halls.

Second, there are many national issues that concern individuals and groups so directly and unmistakably as to evoke volitions that are genuine and definite enough. The most important instance is afforded by issues involving immediate and personal pecuniary profit to individual voters and groups of voters, such as direct payments, protective duties, silver policies, and so on. Experience that goes back to antiquity shows that by and large voters react promptly and rationally to any such chance. But the classical doctrine of democracy evidently stands to gain little from displays of rationality of this kind. Voters thereby prove themselves bad and indeed corrupt judges of such issues, and often they even prove themselves bad judges of their own long-run interests, for it is only the short-run promise that tells politically and only short-run rationality that asserts itself effectively.

However, when we move still farther away from the private concerns of the family and the business office into those regions of national and international affairs that lack a direct and unmistakable link with those private concerns, individual volition, command of facts and method of inference soon cease to fulfill the requirements of the classical doctrine. What strikes me most of all and seems to me to be the core of the trouble is the fact that the sense of reality is so completely lost. Normally, the great political questions take their place in the psychic economy of the typical citizen with those leisure hour interests that have not attained the rank of hobbies, and with the subjects of irresponsible conversation. These things seem so far off; they are not at all like a business proposition; dangers may not materialize at all and if they should they may not prove so very serious; one feels oneself to be moving in a fictitious world.

This reduced sense of reality accounts not only for a reduced sense of responsibility but also for the absence of effective volition. One has one's phrases, of course, and one's wishes and daydreams and grumbles; especially, one has one's likes and dislikes. But ordinarily they do not amount to what we call a will—the psychic counterpart of purposeful responsible action. In fact, for the private citizen musing over national affairs there is no scope for such a will and no task at which it could develop. He is a member of an unworkable committee, the committee of the whole nation, and this is why he expends less disciplined effort on mastering a political problem than he expends on a game of bridge.[2]

The reduced sense of responsibility and the absence of effective volition in turn explain the ordinary citizen's ignorance and lack of judgment in matters of domestic and foreign policy, which are if anything more shocking in the case of educated people and of people who are successfully active in non-political walks of life than it is with uneducated

[2] [It will help to clarify the point if we ask ourselves why so much more intelligence and clear-headedness show up at a bridge table than in, say, political discussion among non-politicians. At the bridge table we have a definite task; we have rules that discipline us; success and failure are clearly defined; and we are prevented from behaving irresponsibly because every mistake we make will not only immediately tell but also be immediately allocated to us. These conditions by their failure to be fulfilled for the political behavior of the ordinary citizen, show why it is that in politics he lacks all the alertness and the judgment he may display in his profession.]

people in humble stations. Information is plentiful and readily available. But this does not seem to make any difference. Nor should we wonder at it. We need only compare a lawyer's attitude to his brief and the same lawyer's attitude to the statements of political fact presented in his newspaper in order to see what is the matter. In the one case the lawyer has qualified for appreciating the relevance of his facts by years of purposeful labor done under the definite stimulus of interest in his professional competence; and under a stimulus that is no less powerful he then bends his acquirements, his intellect, his will to the contents of the brief. In the other case, he has not taken the trouble to qualify; he does not care to absorb the information or to apply to it the canons of criticism he knows so well how to handle; and he is impatient of long or complicated argument. All of this goes to show that without the initiative that comes from immediate responsibility, ignorance will persist in the face of masses of information however complete and correct. It persists even in the face of the meritorious efforts that are being made to go beyond presenting information and to teach the use of it by means of lectures, classes, discussion groups. Results are not zero. But they are small. People cannot be carried up the ladder.

Thus the typical citizen drops down to a lower level of mental performance as soon as he enters the political field. He argues and analyzes in a way which he would readily recognize as infantile within the sphere of his real interests. He becomes a primitive again. His thinking becomes associative and affective. And this entails two further consequences of ominous significance.

First, even if there were no political groups trying to influence him, the typical citizen would in political matters tend to yield to extra-rational or irrational prejudice and impulse. The weakness of the rational processes he applies to politics and the absence of effective logical control over the results he arrives at would in themselves suffice to account for that. Moreover, simply because he is not "all there," he will relax his usual moral standards as well and occasionally give in to dark urges which the conditions of private life help him to repress. But as to the wisdom or rationality of his inferences and conclusions, it may be just as bad if he gives in to a burst of generous indignation. This will make it still more difficult for him to see things in their correct proportions or even to see more than one aspect of one thing at a time. Hence, if for once he does emerge from his usual vagueness and does display the definite will postulated by the classical doctrine of democracy, he is as likely as not to become still more unintelligent and irresponsible than he usually is. At certain junctures, this may prove fatal to his nation.

Second, however, the weaker the logical element in the processes of the public mind and the more complete the absence of rational criticism and of the rationalizing influence of personal experience and responsibility, the greater are the opportunities for groups with an ax to grind. These groups may consist of professional politicians or of exponents of an economic interest or of idealists of one kind or another or of people simply interested in staging and managing political shows. The sociology of such groups is immaterial to the argument in hand. The only point that matters here is that, Human Nature in Politics being what it is, they are able to fashion and, within very wide limits, even to create the will of the people. What we are confronted with in the analysis of political processes is largely not a genuine but a manufactured will. And often this artefact is all that in reality corresponds to the *volonté générale* [general will] of the classical doctrine. So far as this is so, the will of the people is the product and not the motive power of the political process.

The ways in which issues and the popular will on any issue are being manufactured is exactly analogous to the ways of commercial advertising. We find the same attempts to contact the subconscious. We find the same technique of creating favorable and unfavorable associations which are the more effective the less rational they are. We find the same evasions and reticences and the same trick of producing opinion by reiterated assertion that is successful precisely to the extent to which it avoids rational argument and the danger of awakening the critical faculties of the people. And so on. Only, all these arts have infinitely more scope in the sphere of public affairs than they have in the sphere of private and professional life. The picture of the prettiest girl that ever lived will in the long run prove powerless to maintain the sales of a bad cigarette. There is no equally effective safeguard in the case of political decisions. Many decisions of fateful importance are of a nature that makes it impossible for the public to experiment with them at its leisure and at moderate cost. Even if that is possible, however, judgment is as a rule not so easy to arrive at as it is in the case of the cigarette, because effects are less easy to interpret.

But such arts also vitiate, to an extent quite unknown in the field of commercial advertising, those forms of political advertising that profess to address themselves to reason. To the observer, the anti-rational or, at all events, the extra-rational appeal and the defenselessness of the victim stand out more and not less clearly when cloaked in facts and arguments. We have seen above why it is so difficult to impart to the public unbiased information about political problems and logically correct inferences from it and why it is that information and arguments in political matters will "register" only if they link up with the citizen's preconceived ideas. As a rule, however, these ideas are not definite enough to determine particular conclusions. Since they can themselves be manufactured, effective political argument almost inevitably implies the attempt to twist existing volitional premises into a particular shape and not merely the attempt to implement them or to help the citizen to make up his mind.

Thus information and arguments that are really driven home are likely to be the servants of political intent. Since the first thing man will do for his ideal or interest is to lie, we shall expect, and as a matter of fact we find, that effective information is almost always adulterated or selective and that effective reasoning in politics consists mainly in trying to exalt certain propositions into axioms and to put others out of court; it thus reduces to the psycho-technics mentioned before. The reader who thinks me unduly pessimistic need only ask himself whether he has never heard—or said himself—that this or that awkward fact must not be told publicly, or that a certain line of reasoning, though valid, is undesirable. If men who according to any current standard are perfectly honorable or even high-minded reconcile themselves to the implications of this, do they not thereby show what they think about the merits or even the existence of the will of the people?

There are of course limits to all this. And there is truth in Jefferson's dictum that in the end the people are wiser than any single individual can be, or in Lincoln's about the impossibility of "fooling all the people all the time." But both dicta stress the long-run aspect in a highly significant way. It is no doubt possible to argue that given time the collective psyche will evolve opinions that not infrequently strike us as highly reasonable and even shrewd. History however consists of a succession of short-run situations that may alter the course of events for good. If all the people can in the short run be "fooled" step by step into something they do not really want, and if this is not an exceptional case which we could afford to neglect, then no amount of retrospective common sense will alter the fact that in reality they neither raise nor decide issues but that the issues that shape their fate are normally raised and decided for them. More than anyone else the lover of democracy has every reason to accept this fact and to clear his creed from the aspersion that it rests upon make-believe.

ANOTHER THEORY OF DEMOCRACY: COMPETITION FOR POLITICAL LEADERSHIP

I think that most students of politics have by now come to accept these criticisms leveled at the classical doctrine of democracy. . . . I also think that most of them agree, or will agree before long, in accepting another theory which is much truer to life and at the same time salvages much of what sponsors of the democratic method really mean by this term. Like the classical theory, it may be put into the nutshell of a definition.

It will be remembered that our chief troubles about the classical theory centered in the proposition that "the people" hold a definite and rational opinion about every individual question and that they give effect to this opinion—in a democracy—by choosing "representatives" who will see to it that that opinion is carried out. Thus the selection of the representatives is made secondary to the primary purpose of the democratic arrangement which is to vest the power of deciding political issues in the electorate. Suppose we reverse the roles of these two elements and make the deciding of issues by the electorate secondary to the election of the men who are to do the deciding. To put it differently, we now take the view that the role of the people is to produce a government, or else an intermediate body which in turn will produce a national executive or government. And we define: the democratic method is that institutional arrangement for arriving at political decisions in which individuals acquire the power to decide by means of a competitive struggle for the people's vote.

Defense and explanation of this idea will speedily show that, as to both plausibility of assumptions and tenability of propositions, it greatly improves the theory of the democratic process. . . .

[T]he theory embodied in this definition leaves all the room we may wish to have for a proper recognition of the vital fact of leadership. The classical theory did not do this but, as we have seen, attributed to the electorate an altogether unrealistic degree of initiative which practically amounted to ignoring leadership. But collectives act almost exclusively by accepting leadership—this is the dominant mechanism of practically any collective action which is more than a reflex. Propositions about the working and the results of the democratic method that take account of this are bound to be infinitely more realistic than propositions which do not. They will not stop at the execution of a *volonté générale* but will go some way toward showing how it emerges or how it is substituted or faked. What we have termed Manufactured Will is no longer outside the theory, an aberration for the absence of which we piously pray; it enters on the ground floor as it should. . . .

[The electorate's] choice—ideologically glorified into the Call from the People—does not flow from its initiative but is shaped, and the shaping of it is an essential part of the democratic process. Voters do not decide issues. But neither do they pick their members of parliament from the eligible population with a perfectly open mind. In all normal cases the initiative lies with the candidate who makes a bid for the office of member of parliament and such local leadership as that may imply. Voters confine themselves to accepting this bid in preference to others or refusing to accept it.

► 8 ◄

THE LIMITS OF RATIONALISM

INTRODUCTION TO
Winston Churchill,
"Speech on Rebuilding the House of Commons"

◆

Winston Churchill may not be ranked among the major conservative theorists of the twentieth century, but he remains one of the most imposing politicians of the age, and his political prowess rested on a profoundly traditionalist mind which expressed itself in a rhetoric that harked back to Burke and to the eighteenth century.[1] Nowhere are these qualities more in evidence than in the selection below, a minor gem of conservative thought and rhetoric expressing the superiority of historical experience to abstract theory. It serves as a paradigm of the sort of practical wisdom which Michael Oakeshott was soon to contrast with technical knowledge in his lecture on "Rationalism in Politics."

Winston Spencer Churchill was born into a family of noble lineage steeped in political life. He was the son of Lord Randolph Churchill, who had tried and failed to become leader of the Conservative Party, and a descendent of the eighteenth-century military hero the Duke of Marlborough. Churchill spent much of his active life in politics and the military, when he was not writing biographies of his illustrious ancestors or histories of his own age.

Churchill was first elected to Parliament in 1901 as a Conservative, but dissatisfied with his party, he crossed the aisle and joined the socially reformist Liberals, before rejoining the Conservative Party after the First World War. From 1910 through 1929 he served in a range of military and cabinet posts. While supporting the social reforms of the new Liberalism, he also distinguished himself as an opponent of organized labor when it sought to challenge public order and the rule of law, first when as Home Secretary in 1911 he used troops against strikers in South

---

[1] For an incisive sketch of Churchill's mind and its reflection in his style, see Isaiah Berlin, "Winston Churchill," in Berlin, *Personal Impressions* (New York, 1981).

Wales, and then in 1926, when as Chancellor of the Exchequer he helped defeat a general strike called by the labor movement. He spent much of the decade after 1929 in eclipse; from 1935 on he opposed the leaders of his party for what he regarded as their inadequate military response to Hitler and the rise of German power, which he saw as a threat to "the permanent and abiding interests of England." His lifelong focus on matters military, his energy, and his eloquence served him and his nation when in 1940, at the age of sixty-six, he was named Prime Minister.

On the night of May 10, 1941, during the air war against Britain, the German air force bombed the House of Commons. The next morning, Churchill inspected the damage with tears in his eyes. The members of Parliament moved temporarily to the House of Lords. By the autumn of 1943 the tide of the war had turned, and Britons could look forward to eventual victory. It was under these circumstances that Prime Minister Churchill addressed the House of Commons on October 28, 1943.

Winston S. Churchill,
"Speech on Rebuilding the House of Commons,"
October 28, 1943[1]

I beg to move,

> That a Select Committee be appointed to consider and report upon plans for the rebuilding of the House of Commons, and upon such alterations as may be considered desirable while preserving all its essential features.

On the night of 10th May, 1941, with one of the last bombs of the last serious raid, our House of Commons was destroyed by the violence of the enemy, and we have now to consider whether we should build it up again, and how, and when. We shape our buildings, and afterwards our buildings shape us.[2] Having dwelt and served for more than forty years in the late Chamber, and having derived very great pleasure and advantage therefrom, I, naturally, should like to see it restored in all essentials to its old form, convenience, and dignity. I believe that will be the opinion of the great majority of its Members. It is certainly the opinion of His Majesty's Government, and we propose to support this Resolution to the best of our ability.

---

[1] From *Winston S. Churchill. His Complete Speeches, 1897–1963*, ed. Robert Rhodes James, vol. VII (New York, 1974), pp. 6869–71.
[2] A statement of latent functions, in this case of institutional architecture.

There are two main characteristics of the House of Commons which will command the approval and the support of reflective and experienced Members.[3] They will, I have no doubt, sound odd to foreign ears. The first is that its shape should be oblong and not semi-circular. Here is a very potent factor in our political life. The semi-circular assembly, which appeals to political theorists, enables every individual or every group to move round the centre, adopting various shades of pink according as the weather changes. I am a convinced supporter of the party system in preference to the group system. I have seen many earnest and ardent Parliaments destroyed by the group system. The party system is much favoured by the oblong form of Chamber. It is easy for an individual to move through those insensible gradations from Left to Right, but the act of crossing the Floor is one which requires serious consideration. I am well informed on this matter, for I have accomplished that difficult process, not only once but twice. Logic is a poor guide compared with custom. Logic, which has created in so many countries semi-circular assemblies with buildings that give to every Member, not only a seat to sit in, but often a desk to write at, with a lid to bang, has proved fatal to Parliamentary Government as we know it here in its home and in the land of its birth.

The second characteristic of a Chamber formed on the lines of the House of Commons is that it should not be big enough to contain all its Members at once without over-crowding, and that there should be no question of every Member having a separate seat reserved for him. The reason for this has long been a puzzle to uninstructed outsiders, and has frequently excited the curiosity and even the criticism of new Members. Yet it is not so difficult to understand if you look at it from a practical point of view. If the House is big enough to contain all its Members, nine-tenths of its Debates will be conducted in the depressing atmosphere of an almost empty or half-empty Chamber. The essence of good House of Commons speaking is the conversational style, the facility for quick, informal interruptions and interchanges. Harangues from a rostrum would be a bad substitute for the conversational style in which so much of our business is done. But the conversational style requires a fairly small space, and there should be on great occasions a sense of crowd and urgency. There should be a sense of the importance of much that is said, and a sense that great matters are being decided, there and then, by the House.

We attach immense importance to the survival of Parliamentary democracy. In this country this is one of our war aims. We wish to see our Parliament a strong, easy, flexible instrument of free Debate. For this

---

[3] The superiority of experience over abstract theory is the theme of the paragraphs which follow.

purpose a small Chamber and a sense of intimacy are indispensable. It is notable that the Parliaments of the British Commonwealth have to a very large extent reproduced our Parliamentary institutions in their form as well as in their spirit, even to the Chair in which the Speakers of the different Assemblies sit. We do not seek to impose our ideas on others; we make no invidious criticisms of other nations. All the same we hold none the less tenaciously to them ourselves. The vitality and the authority of the House of Commons, and its hold upon an electorate based upon universal suffrage, depend to no small extent upon its episodes and great moments, even upon its scenes and rows, which, as everyone will agree, are better conducted at close quarters. Destroy that hold which Parliament has upon the public mind and has preserved through all these changing, turbulent times, and the living organism of the House of Commons would be greatly impaired. You may have a machine, but the House of Commons is much more than a machine; it has earned and captured and held through long generations the imagination and respect of the British nation.[4] It is not free from shortcomings; they mark all human institutions. Nevertheless, I submit to what is probably not an unfriendly audience on that subject that our House has proved itself capable of adapting itself to every change which the swift pace of modern life has brought upon us. It has a collective personality which enjoys the regard of the public, and which imposes itself upon the conduct not only of individual Members but of parties. It has a code of its own which everyone knows, and it has means of its own of enforcing those manners and habits which have grown up and have been found to be an essential part of our Parliamentary life.[5]

The House of Commons has lifted our affairs above the mechanical sphere into the human sphere. It thrives on criticism, it is perfectly impervious to newspaper abuse or taunts from any quarter, and it is capable of digesting almost anything or almost any body of gentlemen, whatever be the views with which they arrive. There is no situation to which it cannot address itself with vigour and ingenuity. It is the citadel of British liberty; it is the foundation of our laws; its traditions and its privileges are as lively to-day as when it broke the arbitrary power of the Crown and substituted that Constitutional Monarchy under which we have enjoyed so many blessings. In this war the House of Commons has proved itself to be a rock upon which an Administration, without losing the confidence of the House, has been able to confront the most terrible

---

[4] Here Churchill stresses that the veneration which is the product of continuity over time enhances the emotional hold of institutions.

[5] Here Churchill emphasizes the flexibility which arises from institutionally ingrained habit and custom. Members of Parliament and parties, he claims, acquire a second nature, or what is here termed a "collective personality."

emergencies. The House has shown itself able to face the possibility of national destruction with classical composure. It can change Governments, and has changed them by heat of passion. It can sustain Governments in long, adverse, disappointing struggles through many dark, grey months and even years until the sun comes out again. I do not know how else this country can be governed than by the House of Commons playing its part in all its broad freedom in British public life. We have learned—with these so recently confirmed facts around us and before us—not to alter improvidently the physical structures which have enabled so remarkable an organism to carry on its work of banning dictatorships within this Island, and pursuing and beating into ruins all dictators who have molested us from outside.

His Majesty's Government are most anxious, and are indeed resolved, to ask the House to adhere firmly in principle to the structure and characteristics of the House of Commons we have known, and I do not doubt that that is the wish of the great majority of the Members in this the second longest Parliament of our history. If challenged, we must take issue upon that by the customary Parliamentary method of debate followed by a Division. The question of Divisions again relates very directly to the structure of the House of Commons. We must look forward to periods when Divisions will be much more frequent than they are now. Many of us have seen twenty or thirty in a single Parliamentary Sitting, and in the lobbies of the Chamber which Hitler shattered we had facilities and conveniences far exceeding those which we are able to enjoy in this lordly abode. I am, therefore, proposing in the name of His Majesty's Government that we decide to rebuild the House of Commons on its old foundations, which are intact, and in principle within its old dimensions, and that we utilise so far as possible its shattered walls.[6] That is also the most cheap and expeditious method we could pursue to provide ourselves with a habitation. . . .

[6] Note the metaphorical quality of this sentence, which harks back to Burke's insistence on the need to build on existing foundations, as an expression of institutional continuity over time.

INTRODUCTION TO
Michael Oakeshott,
"Rationalism in Politics"

◆

Among the most powerful conservative minds in postwar Britain was the philosopher Michael Oakeshott, who was born in 1901 and died in 1990. From the mid-1920s until 1949 he was a Cambridge don, teaching history and especially the history of political thought. After spending the last three years of the Second World War in the British army, he returned to Cambridge and founded *The Cambridge Journal* in 1947. Its first volume included Oakeshott's essay "Rationalism in Politics." A brief sketch of British and international political developments at the time the essay was published will help to recapture the contemporary resonance of the piece.

The postwar British election of July 1945 resulted in a major defeat for Churchill and the Conservatives, and a victory for the Labour Party under Clement Atlee. Labour promised extensive social and economic reconstruction, to be achieved through nationalization of industries, economic planning, and an extension of governmentally provided social services. The new government carried out a great deal of this program. It had long been an article of faith among socialist intellectuals that the profit motive upon which capitalism was based necessarily led to inefficiency; the solution, they believed, was for industry to be under public ownership and hence freed from the profit motive. The party's platform called for "common ownership of the means of production," and when Labour came to power it nationalized transportation industries, the electrical power industry, the ailing coal industry, the iron industry, and the hospitals.

A second element of the Labour Party program implemented by the Atlee government was the social legislation known as the "welfare state."[1] Social programs had been enacted by previous Conservative, Liberal, and Labour governments: what was new was the scope of the programs enacted. During the war years the government had commissioned a report authored by William Beveridge, a distinguished civil servant and former head of the London School of Economics and Political Science. The Beveridge Report recommended a universal social security system (one that covered all citizens) as well as a national health service, and an economic policy oriented toward eliminating unemployment.

---

[1] For a useful overview, see Arthur Marwick, *British Society Since 1945* (New York, 1982), pp. 49–63.

The report had been welcomed by some Conservatives when it was issued in 1942, but in 1945 Churchill emphasized that the economic problems of the country were too great to implement most of the suggested programs in the near future. The Labour Party enacted most of them in the years after 1945, though often in a form rather different from what Beveridge had envisioned. It created universal unemployment insurance, expanded old age insurance, and created a national health system which provided medical care for everyone at minimal cost. The government provided small payments to all mothers with two or more children. It put large sums of money into publicly built housing for the working class. And it tried to expand educational opportunities by providing free schooling for all up to the age of fifteen.

This was the immediate British context of Oakeshott's essay. On the international scene, Britain had just completed a war against German National Socialism, a war in which Oakeshott had been an active participant. When the war ended, many men of good will placed their faith in the United Nations as the preserver of world peace. By 1947 the Cold War with the Soviet Union was heating up. At the same time, the process of decolonization was beginning, with many Asian and African intellectuals looking to Communism or to European socialism for models. Oakeshott regarded all of these projects and ideologies as examples of the political "rationalism" which he set out to deflate in his essay.

Though Oakeshott is often regarded as a conservative, there are also grounds for considering him a liberal, for it was a liberal society that he set out to conserve, and he regarded "collectivism" as the greatest contemporary threat to such a society.[2] In his later works, particularly in *On Human Conduct*, published in 1975, Oakeshott developed his liberal conception of government as a civil association relatively neutral toward shared ends and purposes.[3] But, like Hume and Burke before him, he believed that contemporary liberals misapprehended the social and cultural bases of existing liberal societies.

Oakeshott's conservatism is based on a sensibility which delights in the benefits of existing institutions,[4] is deeply impressed by human imperfectability,[5] and aware that our comprehension of the institutions

---

[2] See especially his essay of 1948, "The political economy of freedom," reprinted in Michael Oakeshott, *Rationalism in Politics and other Essays* (expanded edition, Indianapolis, 1991).

[3] On the continuities and shifts of emphasis between "Rationalism in politics" and Oakeshott's later work, see Paul Franco, "Oakeshott's Critique of Rationalism Revisited," *Political Science Reviewer*, vol. XXI (Spring 1992), pp. 15–43; and more broadly Paul Franco, *The Political Philosophy of Michael Oakeshott* (New Haven, 1990).

[4] Best expressed in his lecture of 1956, "On being conservative," reprinted in *Rationalism in Politics*.

[5] See, for example, his pointed remarks in his essay of 1947, "Scientific Politics," reprinted in Michael Oakeshott, *Religion, Politics, and the Moral Life*, ed. Timothy Fuller (New Haven, 1993), pp. 97–111, esp. p. 108.

from which we benefit can never be more than partial. It is this epistemological conservatism which is at the heart of Oakeshott's essay on
"Rationalism in Politics."[6] His distinction between technical knowledge
and practical knowledge reformulates the long-standing conservative
emphasis on the limits of human knowledge and the importance of custom and habit.[7] His polemical characterization of the rationalist recalls
Burke's satirical portrait in his *Vindication of Natural Society*.

The selection below omits the portions of the essay which deal with
the philosophical and historical genesis of "rationalism in politics," as
well as some of Oakeshott's footnotes.

Michael Oakeshott,
"Rationalism in Politics" (1947)[1]

1.

The object of this essay is to consider the character and pedigree of the
most remarkable intellectual fashion of post-Renaissance Europe. The
Rationalism with which I am concerned is modern Rationalism. No
doubt its surface reflects the light of rationalisms of a more distant past,
but in its depth there is a quality exclusively its own, and it is this quality that I propose to consider, and to consider mainly in its impact
upon European politics. What I call Rationalism in politics is not, of
course, the only (and it is certainly not the most fruitful) fashion in modern European political thinking. But it is a strong and a lively manner of
thinking which, finding support in its filiation with so much else that is
strong in the intellectual composition of contemporary Europe, has
come to colour the ideas, not merely of one, but of all political persua-
sions, and to flow over every party line. By one road or another, by conviction, by its supposed inevitability, by its alleged success, or even quite
unreflectively, almost all politics today have become Rationalist or near-
Rationalist.

The general character and disposition of the Rationalist are, I think,
not difficult to identify. At bottom he stands (he always *stands*) for independence of mind on all occasions, for thought free from obligation to

[6] See the discussion in Anthony Quinton, *The Politics of Imperfection* (London, 1978),
pp. 92–96.
[7] A theme further explored in his essay of 1948, "The Tower Of Babel," reprinted in
Rationalism in Politics.

[1] From Michael Oakeshott, *Rationalism in Politics and other Essays* (expanded edition,
Indianapolis, 1991).

any authority save the authority of "reason." His circumstances in the modern world have made him contentious: he is the *enemy* of authority, of prejudice, of the merely traditional, customary or habitual. His mental attitude is at once sceptical and optimistic: sceptical, because there is no opinion, no habit, no belief, nothing so firmly rooted or so widely held that he hesitates to question it and to judge it by what he calls his "reason"; optimistic, because the Rationalist never doubts the power of his "reason" (when properly applied) to determine the worth of a thing, the truth of an opinion or the propriety of an action. Moreover, he is fortified by a belief in a "reason" common to all mankind, a common power of rational consideration, which is the ground and inspiration of argument: set up on his door is the precept of Parmenides—judge by rational argument. But besides this, which gives the Rationalist a touch of intellectual equalitarianism, he is something also of an individualist, finding it difficult to believe that anyone who can think honestly and clearly will think differently from himself.

But it is an error to attribute to him an excessive concern with *a priori* argument. He does not neglect experience, but he often appears to do so because he insists always upon it being his own experience (wanting to begin everything *de novo* [anew]), and because of the rapidity with which he reduces the tangle and variety of experience to a set of principles which he will then attack or defend only upon rational grounds. He has no sense of the cumulation of experience, only of the readiness of experience when it has been converted into a formula: the past is significant to him only as an encumbrance. He has none of that *negative capability* (which Keats attributed to Shakespeare), the power of accepting the mysteries and uncertainties of experience without any irritable search for order and distinctness, only the capability of subjugating experience; he has no aptitude for that close and detailed appreciation of what actually presents itself which Lichtenberg called *negative enthusiasm*,[2] but only the power of recognizing the large outline which a general theory imposes upon events. His cast of mind is gnostic, and the sagacity of Ruhnken's rule, *Oportet quaedam nescire*,[3] is lost upon him. There are some minds which give us the sense that they have passed through an elaborate education which was designed to initiate them into the traditions and achievements of their civilization; the immediate impression we have of them is an impression of cultivation, of the enjoyment of an inheritance. But this is not so with the mind of the Rationalist, which impresses us as, at best, a finely tempered, neutral

---

[2] Georg Christoph Lichtenberg (1742–99) was a German scientist, philosopher, and satirical critic of the German *Sturm und Drang* writers.

[3] "There are certain things it behooves one not to know." David Ruhnken (1723–98) was a scholar of classical Greek and Latin culture.

instrument, as a well-trained rather than as an educated mind. Intellectually, his ambition is not so much to share the experience of the race as to be demonstrably a self-made man. And this gives to his intellectual and practical activities an almost preternatural deliberateness and self-consciousness, depriving them of any element of passivity, removing from them all sense of rhythm and continuity and dissolving them into a succession of climacterics, each to be surmounted by a *tour de raison*.[4] His mind has no atmosphere, no changes of season and temperature; his intellectual processes, so far as possible, are insulated from all external influence and go on in the void. And having cut himself off from the traditional knowledge of his society, and denied the value of any education more extensive than a training in a technique of analysis, he is apt to attribute to mankind a necessary inexperience in all the critical moments of life, and if he were more self-critical he might begin to wonder how the race had ever succeeded in surviving. With an almost poetic fancy, he strives to live each day as if it were his first, and he believes that to form a habit is to fail. And if, with as yet no thought of analysis, we glance below the surface, we may, perhaps, see in the temperament, if not in the character, of the Rationalist, a deep distrust of time, an impatient hunger for eternity and an irritable nervousness in the face of everything topical and transitory.

Now, of all worlds, the world of politics might seem the least amenable to rationalist treatment—politics, always so deeply veined with both the traditional, the circumstantial and the transitory. And, indeed, some convinced Rationalists have admitted defeat here: Clemenceau,[5] intellectually a child of the modern Rationalist tradition (in his treatment of morals and religion, for example), was anything but a Rationalist in politics. But not all have admitted defeat. If we except religion, the greatest apparent victories of Rationalism have been in politics: it is not to be expected that whoever is prepared to carry his rationalism into the conduct of life will hesitate to carry it into the conduct of public affairs.

But what is important to observe in such a man (for it is characteristic) is not the decisions and actions he is inspired to make, but the source of his inspiration, his idea (and with him it will be a deliberate and conscious idea) of political activity.[6] He believes, of course, in the open mind, the mind free from prejudice and its relic, habit. He believes that the unhindered human "reason" (if only it can be brought to bear)

---

[4] Feat of reason.

[5] Georges Clemenceau was a French Radical politician who became premier in 1917 determined to lead his nation to victory in the First World War.

[6] The rationalist, as described by Oakeshott in this paragraph, is characterized by a lack of epistemological modesty and historical utilitarianism.

is an infallible guide in political activity. Further, he believes in argument as the technique and operation of "reason"; the truth of an opinion and the "rational" ground (not the use) of an institution is all that matters to him. Consequently, much of his political activity consists in bringing the social, political, legal and institutional inheritance of his society before the tribunal of his intellect; and the rest is rational administration, "reason" exercising an uncontrolled jurisdiction over the circumstances of the case. To the Rationalist, nothing is of value merely because it exists (and certainly not because it has existed for many generations), familiarity has no worth, and nothing is to be left standing for want of scrutiny. And his disposition makes both destruction and creation easier for him to understand and engage in, than acceptance or reform. To patch up, to repair (that is, to do anything which requires a patient knowledge of the material), he regards as waste of time; and he always prefers the invention of a new device to making use of a current and well-tried expedient. He does not recognize change unless it is a self-consciously induced change, and consequently he falls easily into the error of identifying the customary and the traditional with the changeless. This is aptly illustrated by the rationalist attitude towards a tradition of ideas. There is, of course, no question either of retaining or improving such a tradition, for both these involve an attitude of submission. It must be destroyed. And to fill its place the Rationalist puts something of his own making—an ideology, the formalized abridgment of the supposed substratum of rational truth contained in the tradition.[7]

The conduct of affairs, for the Rationalist, is a matter of solving problems, and in this no man can hope to be successful whose reason has become inflexible by surrender to habit or is clouded by the fumes of tradition. In this activity the character which the Rationalist claims for himself is the character of the engineer, whose mind (it is supposed) is controlled throughout by the appropriate technique and whose first step is to dismiss from his attention everything not directly related to his specific intentions. This assimilation of politics to engineering is, indeed, what may be called the myth of rationalist politics. And it is, of course, a recurring theme in the literature of Rationalism. The politics it inspires may be called the politics of the felt need; for the Rationalist, politics are always charged with the feeling of the moment. He waits upon circumstance to provide him with his problems, but rejects its aid in their solution. That anything should be allowed to stand between a society and the satisfaction of the felt needs of each moment in its history must

[7] The contrast between a tradition of ideas and an ideology corresponds to Oakeshott's distinction below of two types of knowledge: one complex, nuanced and practical, the other simple, clear, and technical.

appear to the Rationalist a piece of mysticism and nonsense. And his politics are, in fact, the rational solution of those practical conundrums which the recognition of the sovereignty of the felt need perpetually creates in the life of a society. Thus, political life is resolved into a succession of crises, each to be surmounted by the application of "reason." Each generation, indeed, each administration, should see unrolled before it the blank sheet of infinite possibility. And if by chance this *tabula rasa* has been defaced by the irrational scribblings of tradition-ridden ancestors, then the first task of the Rationalist must be to scrub it clean; as Voltaire remarked, the only way to have good laws is to burn all existing laws and to start afresh.[8]

Two other general characteristics of rationalist politics may be observed. They are the politics of perfection, and they are the politics of uniformity; either of these characteristics without the other denotes a different style of politics. The essence of rationalism is their combination. The evanescence of imperfection may be said to be the first item of the creed of the Rationalist. He is not devoid of humility; he can imagine a problem which would remain impervious to the onslaught of his own reason. But what he cannot imagine is politics which do not consist in solving problems, or a political problem of which there is no "rational" solution at all. Such a problem must be counterfeit. And the "rational" solution of any problem is, in its nature, the perfect solution. There is no place in his scheme for a "best in the circumstances," only a place for "the best"; because the function of reason is precisely to surmount circumstances. Of course, the Rationalist is not always a perfectionist in general, his mind governed in each occasion by a comprehensive Utopia; but invariably he is a perfectionist in detail. And from this politics of perfection springs the politics of uniformity; a scheme which does not recognize circumstance can have no place for variety. "There must in the nature of things be one best form of government which all intellects, sufficiently roused from the slumber of savage ignorance, will be irresistibly incited to approve," writes Godwin.[9] This intrepid Rationalist states in general what a more modest believer might prefer to assert only in detail; but the principle holds—there may not be one universal remedy for all political ills, but the remedy for any particular ill is as universal in its application as it is rational in its conception. If the rational solution for one of the problems of a society has been deter-

---

[8] [Cf. Plato, *Republic*, 501A. The idea that you can get rid of a law by burning it is characteristic of the Rationalist, who can think of a law only as something written down.] For a similar critique of written law, see the selection from de Maistre, above.

[9] William Godwin (1756–1836) was a radical political writer and British fellow-traveler of the French Revolution, best known for his anarchistic, hyperrationalistic work, *An Enquiry Concerning Political Justice*, first published in 1793.

mined, to permit any relevant part of the society to escape from the solution is, *ex hypothesi*, to countenance irrationality. There can be no place for preferences that is not rational preference, and all rational preferences necessarily coincide. Political activity is recognized as the imposition of a uniform condition of perfection upon human conduct.

The modern history of Europe is littered with the projects of the politics of Rationalism. The most sublime of these is, perhaps, that of Robert Owen for "a world convention to emancipate the human race from ignorance, poverty, division, sin and misery"—so sublime that even a Rationalist (but without much justification) might think it eccentric.[10] But not less characteristic are the diligent search of the present generation for an innocuous power which may safely be made so great as to be able to control all other powers in the human world,[11] and the common disposition to believe that political machinery can take the place of moral and political education. The notion of founding a society, whether of individuals or of States, upon a Declaration of the Rights of Man is a creature of the rationalist brain, so also are "national" or racial self-determination when elevated into universal principles. The project of the so-called Re-union of the Christian Churches, of open diplomacy, of a single tax, of a civil service whose members "have no qualifications other than their personal abilities," of a self-consciously planned society, the Beveridge Report,[12] the Education Act of 1944, Federalism, Nationalism, Votes for Women, the Catering Wages Act, the destruction of the Austro-Hungarian Empire, the World State (of H. G. Wells or anyone else), and the revival of Gaelic as the official language of Eire, are alike the progeny of Rationalism. The odd generation of rationalism in politics is by sovereign power out of romanticism.

2.

The placid lake of Rationalism lies before us in the character and disposition of the Rationalist, its surface familiar and not unconvincing, its waters fed by many visible tributaries. But in its depths there flows a hidden spring, which, though it was not the original fountain from which the lake grew, is perhaps the pre-eminent source of its endurance. This spring is a doctrine about human knowledge. That some such fountain lies at the heart of Rationalism will not surprise even those who

[10] Robert Owen (1771–1858) was an early socialist.

[11] A reference to the recently founded United Nations.

[12] An extremely influential report published in 1942 which proposed a system of social security for all citizens "from the cradle to the grave," and popularly regarded as the basis of the postwar British welfare state. The report was produced by a committee of senior civil servants headed by William Beveridge.

know only its surface; the superiority of the unencumbered intellect lay precisely in the fact that it could reach more, and more certain, knowledge about man and society than was otherwise possible; the superiority of the ideology over the tradition lay in its greater precision and its alleged demonstrability. Nevertheless, it is not, properly speaking, a philosophical theory of knowledge, and it can be explained with agreeable informality.

Every science, every art, every practical activity requiring skill of any sort, indeed every human activity whatsoever, involves knowledge. And, universally, this knowledge is of two sorts, both of which are always involved in any actual activity. It is not, I think, making too much of it to call them two sorts of knowledge, because (though in fact they do not exist separately) there are certain important differences between them. The first sort of knowledge I will call technical knowledge or knowledge of technique. In every art and science, and in every practical activity, a technique is involved. In many activities this technical knowledge is formulated into rules which are, or may be, deliberately learned, remembered, and, as we say, put into practice; but whether or not it is, or has been, precisely formulated, its chief characteristic is that it is susceptible of precise formulation, although special skill and insight may be required to give it that formulation. The technique (or part of it) of driving a motor car on English roads is to be found in the Highway Code, the technique of cookery is contained in the cookery book, and the technique of discovery in natural science or in history is in their rules of research, of observation and verification. The second sort of knowledge I will call practical, because it exists only in use, is not reflective and (unlike technique) cannot be formulated in rules. This does not mean, however, that it is an esoteric sort of knowledge. It means only that the method by which it may be shared and becomes common knowledge is not the method of formulated doctrine. And if we consider it from this point of view, it would not, I think, be misleading to speak of it as traditional knowledge. In every activity this sort of knowledge is also involved; the mastery of any skill, the pursuit of any concrete activity is impossible without it.

These two sorts of knowledge, then, distinguishable but inseparable, are the twin components of the knowledge involved in every concrete human activity. In a practical art, such as cookery, nobody supposes that the knowledge that belongs to the good cook is confined to what is or may be written down in the cookery book; technique and what I have called practical knowledge combine to make skill in cookery wherever it exists. And the same is true of the fine arts, of painting, of music, of poetry; a high degree of technical knowledge, even where it is both subtle and ready, is one thing; the ability to create a work of art, the ability to compose something with real music qualities, the ability to write a great sonnet, is another, and requires, in addition to technique, this other sort of knowledge. Again, these two sorts of knowledge are involved in any genuinely scientific activity. The natural scientist will certainly make use of the rules of observation and verification that belong to his technique, but these rules remain only one of the components of his knowledge; advance in scientific discovery was never achieved merely by following the rules. The same situation may be observed also in religion. It would, I think, be excessively liberal to call a man a Christian who was wholly ignorant of the technical side of Christianity, who knew nothing of creed or formulary, but it would be even more absurd to maintain that even the readiest knowledge of creed and catechism ever constituted the whole of the knowledge that belongs to a Christian. And what is true of cookery, of painting, of natural science and of religion, is no less true of politics: the knowledge involved in political activity is both technical and practical. Indeed, as in all arts which have men as their plastic material, arts such as medicine, industrial management, diplomacy, and the art of military command, the knowledge involved in political activity is pre-eminently of this dual character. Nor, in these arts, is it correct to say that whereas technique will tell a man (for example, doctor) *what* to do, it is practice which tells him *how* to do it—the "bed-side manner," the appreciation of the individual with whom he has to deal. Even in the *what*, and above all in diagnosis, there lies already this dualism of technique and practice: there is no knowledge which is not "know how." Nor, again, does the distinction between technical and practical knowledge coincide with the distinction between a knowledge of means and a knowledge of ends, though on occasion it may appear to do so. In short, nowhere, and pre-eminently not in political activity, can technical knowledge be separated from practical knowledge, and nowhere can they be considered identical with one another or able to take the place of one another.

Now, what concerns us are the differences between these two sorts of knowledge; and the important differences are those which manifest themselves in the divergent ways in which these sorts of knowledge can be expressed and in the divergent ways in which they can be learned or acquired.

Technical knowledge, we have seen, is susceptible of formulation in rules, principles, directions, maxims—comprehensively, in propositions. It is possible to write down technical knowledge in a book. Consequently, it does not surprise us that when an artist writes about his art, he writes only about the technique of his art. This is so, not because he is ignorant of what may be called the aesthetic element, or thinks it unimportant, but because what he has to say about *that* he has said already (if he is a painter) in his pictures, and he knows no other way of saying it. And the same is true when a religious man writes about his religion or a cook about cookery. And it may be observed that this character of being susceptible of precise formulation gives to technical knowledge at least the appearance of certainty: it appears to be possible to be certain about a technique. On the other hand, it is a characteristic of practical knowledge that it is not susceptible of formulation of this kind. Its normal expression is in a customary or traditional way of doing things, or, simply, in practice. And this gives it the appearance of imprecision and consequently of uncertainty, of being a matter of opinion, of probability rather than truth. It is, indeed, a knowledge that is expressed in taste or connoisseurship, lacking rigidity and ready for the impress of the mind of the learner.

Technical knowledge can be learned from a book; it can be learned in a correspondence course. Moreover, much of it can be learned by heart, repeated by rote, and applied mechanically: the logic of the syllogism is a technique of this kind. Technical knowledge, in short, can be both taught and learned in the simplest meanings of these words. On the other hand, practical knowledge can neither be taught nor learned, but only imparted and acquired. It exists only in practice, and the only way to acquire it is by apprenticeship to a master—not because the master can teach it (he cannot), but because it can be acquired only by continuous contact with one who is perpetually practicing it. In the arts and in natural science what normally happens is that the pupil, in being taught and in learning the technique from his master, discovers himself to have acquired also another sort of knowledge than merely technical knowledge, without it ever having been precisely imparted and often without being able to say precisely what it is. Thus a pianist acquires artistry as well as technique, a chess-player style and insight into the game as well as a knowledge of the moves, and a scientist acquires (among other things) the sort of judgement which tells him when his technique is leading him astray and the connoisseurship which enables him to distinguish the profitable from the unprofitable directions to explore.

Now, as I understand it, Rationalism is the assertion that what I have called practical knowledge is not knowledge at all, the assertion that, properly speaking, there is no knowledge which is not technical knowledge. The Rationalist holds that the only element of *knowledge* involved in any human activity is technical knowledge, and that what I have called practical knowledge is really only a sort of nescience [absence of knowledge] which would be negligible if it were not positively mischievous. The sovereignty of "reason," for the Rationalist, means the sovereignty of technique.

The heart of the matter is the pre-occupation of the Rationalist with certainty. Technique and certainty are, for him, inseparably joined because certain knowledge is, for him, knowledge which does not require to look beyond itself for its certainty; knowledge, that is, which not only ends with certainty but begins with certainty and is certain throughout. And this is precisely what technical knowledge appears to be. It seems to be a self-complete sort of knowledge because it seems to range between an identifiable initial point (where it breaks in upon sheer ignorance) and an identifiable terminal point, where it is complete, as in learning the rules of a new game. It has the aspect of knowledge that can be contained wholly between the two covers of a book, whose application is, as nearly as possible, purely mechanical, and which does not assume a knowledge not itself provided in the technique. For example, the superiority of an ideology over a tradition of thought lies in its appearance of being self-contained. It can be taught best to those whose minds are empty; and if it is to be taught to one who already believes something, the first step of the teacher must be to administer a purge, to make certain that all prejudices and preconceptions are removed, to lay his foundation upon the unshakable rock of absolute ignorance. In short, technical knowledge appears to be the only kind of knowledge which satisfies the standard of certainty which the Rationalist has chosen.

Now, I have suggested that the knowledge involved in every concrete activity is never solely technical knowledge. If this is true, it would appear that the error of the Rationalist is of a simple sort—the error of mistaking a part for the whole, of endowing a part with the qualities of the whole. But the error of the Rationalist does not stop there. If his great illusion is the sovereignty of technique, he is no less deceived by the apparent certainty of technical knowledge. The superiority of technical knowledge lay in its appearance of springing from pure ignorance and ending in certain and complete knowledge, its appearance of both beginning and ending with certainty. But, in fact, this in an illusion. As with every other sort of knowledge, learning a technique does not consist in getting rid of pure ignorance, but in reforming knowledge which is already there. Nothing, not even the most nearly self-contained technique (the rules of a game), can in fact be imparted to an empty mind; and what is imparted is nourished by what is already there. A man who knows the rules of one game will, on this account, rapidly learn the rules of another game; and a man altogether unfamiliar with "rules" of any kind (if such can be imagined) would be a most unpromising pupil. And just as the self-made man is never literally *self*-made, but depends upon a certain kind of society and upon a large unrecognized inheritance, so technical knowledge is never, in fact, self-complete, and can be made to appear so only if we forget the hypotheses with which it begins. And if its self-completeness is illusory, the certainty which was attributed to it on account of its self-completeness is also an illusion. . . .

3.

The deeper motivations which encouraged and developed this intellectual fashion are, not unnaturally, obscure; they are hidden in the recesses of European society. But among its other connections, it is certainly closely allied with a decline in the belief in Providence: a beneficient and infallible technique replaced a beneficient and infallible God; and where Providence was not available to correct the mistakes of men it was all the more necessary to prevent such mistakes. Certainly, also, its provenance is a society or a generation which thinks what it has discovered for itself is more important than what it has inherited, an age over-impressed with its own accomplishment and liable to those illusions of intellectual grandeur which are the characteristic lunacy of post-Renaissance Europe, an age never mentally at peace with itself because never reconciled with its past. And the vision of a technique which puts all minds on the same level provided just the short-cut which would attract men in a hurry to appear educated but incapable of appreciating the concrete detail of their total inheritance. And, partly under the influence of Rationalism itself, the number of such men has been steadily growing since the seventeenth century. Indeed it may be said that all, or almost all, the influences which in its early days served to encourage the emergence of the Rationalist character have subsequently become more influential in our civilization. . . .

[T]hough later writers were often more elaborate in their criticism, few detected more surely than Pascal that the significance of Rationalism is not its recognition of technical knowledge, but its failure to recognize any other: its philosophical error lies in the certainty it attributes to technique and in its doctrine of the sovereignty of technique; its practical error lies in its belief that nothing but benefit can come from making conduct self-conscious.

4.

It was, of course, improbable that politics should altogether escape the impress of so strong and energetic an intellectual style as that of the new Rationalism. But what, at first sight, is remarkable is that politics should have been earlier and more fully engulfed by the tidal wave than any other human activity. The hold of Rationalism upon most departments of life has varied in its firmness during the last four centuries but in politics it has steadily increased and is stronger now than at any earlier time. We have considered already the general intellectual disposition of the Rationalist when he turns to politics; what remains to be considered are the circumstances in which European politics came to surrender almost completely to the Rationalist and the results of the surrender.

That all contemporary politics are deeply infected with Rationalism will be denied only by those who choose to give the infection another name. Not only are our political vices rationalistic, but so also are our political virtues. Our projects are, in the main, rationalist in purpose and character; but, what is more significant, our whole attitude of mind in politics is similarly determined. And those traditional elements, particularly in English politics, which might have been expected to continue some resistance to the pressure of Rationalism, have now almost completely conformed to the prevailing intellectual temper, and even represent this conformity to be a sign of their vitality, their ability to move with the times. Rationalism has ceased to be merely one style in politics and has become the stylistic criterion of all respectable politics.

How deeply the rationalist disposition of mind has invaded our political thought and practice is illustrated by the extent to which traditions of behaviour have given place to ideologies, the extent to which the politics of destruction and creation have been substituted for the politics of repair, the consciously planned and deliberately executed being considered (for that reason) better than what has grown up and established itself unselfconsciously over a period of time. This conversion of habits of behaviour, adaptable and never quite fixed or finished, into comparatively rigid systems of abstract ideas, is not, of course, new; so far as England is concerned it was begun in the seventeenth century, in the dawn of rationalist politics. But, while formerly it was tacitly resisted and retarded by, for example, the informality of English politics (which enabled us to escape, for a long time, putting too high a value on political action and placing too high a hope in political achievement—to escape, in politics at least, the illusion of the evanescence of imperfection), that resistance has now itself been converted into an ideology. This is, perhaps, the main significance of Hayek's *Road to Serfdom*[13]—not the cogency of his doctrine, but the fact that it is a doctrine. A plan to resist all planning may be better than its opposite, but it belongs to the same style of politics. And only in a society already deeply infected with Rationalism will the conversion of the traditional resources of resistance to the

---

[13] Friedrich Hayek's book written in defense of the free market economy was published in 1944, and was used by Winston Churchill and other Conservative politicians in the election campaign which followed. They lost.

tyranny of Rationalism into a self-conscious ideology be considered a strengthening of those resources.[14] It seems that now, in order to participate in politics and expect a hearing, it is necessary to have, in the strict sense, a doctrine; not to have a doctrine appears frivolous, even disreputable. And the sanctity, which in some societies was the property of a politics piously attached to traditional ways, has now come to belong exclusively to rationalist politics.

Rationalist politics, I have said, are the politics of the felt need, the felt need not qualified by a genuine, concrete knowledge of the permanent interests and direction of movement of a society, but interpreted by reason and satisfied according to the technique of an ideology: they are the politics of the book. And this also is characteristic of almost all contemporary politics: not to have a book is to be without the one thing necessary, and not to observe meticulously what is written in the book is to be a disreputable politician. Indeed, so necessary is it to have a book, that those who have hitherto thought it possible to get on without one, have had, rather late in the day, to set about composing one for their own use. This is a symptom of the triumph of technique which we have seen to be the root of modern Rationalism; for what the book contains is only what it is possible to put into a book—rules of a technique. And, book in hand (because, though a technique can be learned by rote, they have not always learned their lesson well), the politicians of Europe pore over the simmering banquet they are preparing for the future; but, like jumped-up kitchen-porters deputizing for an absent cook, their knowledge does not extend beyond the written word which they read mechanically—it generates ideas in their heads but no tastes in their mouths.

Among the other evidences of Rationalism in contemporary politics, may be counted the commonly admitted claim of the "scientist" as such (the chemist, the physicist, the economist or the psychologist) to be heard in politics; because, though the knowledge involved in a science is always more than technical knowledge, what it has to offer to politics is never more than a technique. And under this influence, the intellect in politics ceases to be the critic of political habit and becomes a substitute for habit, and the life of a society loses its rhythm and continuity and is resolved into a succession of problems and crises. Folk-lore, because it is not technique, is identified with nescience, and all sense of what Burke called the partnership between present and past is lost.

There is, however, no need to labour the point that the most characteristic thing about contemporary politics is their rationalist inspiration; the prevailing belief that politics are easy is, by itself, evidence enough.

---

[14] It might of course be argued that distinctly *conservative* social and political thought owes its rise precisely to the need to combat what Oakeshott calls "Rationalism."

And if a precise example is required we need look no further for it than the proposals we have been offered for the control of the manufacture and use of atomic energy.[15] The rationalist faith in the sovereignty of technique is the presupposition both of the notion that some over-all scheme of mechanized control is possible and of the details of every scheme that has so far been projected: it is understood as what is called an "administrative" problem. But, if Rationalism now reigns almost unopposed, the question which concerns us is, What are the circumstances that promoted this state of affairs? For the significance of the triumph lies not merely in itself, but in its context.

Briefly, the answer to this question is that the politics of Rationalism are the politics of the politically inexperienced, and that the outstanding characteristic of European politics in the last four centuries is that they have suffered the incursion of at least three types of political inexperience—that of the new ruler, of the new ruling class, and of the new political society—to say nothing of the incursion of a new sex, lately provided for by Mr Shaw.[16] How appropriate rationalist politics are to the man who, not brought up or educated to their exercise, finds himself in a position to exert political initiative and authority, requires no emphasis. His need of it is so great that he will have no incentive to be sceptical about the possibility of a magic technique of politics which will remove the handicap of his lack of political education. The offer of such a technique will seem to him the offer of salvation itself; to be told that the necessary knowledge is to be found, complete and self-contained, in a book, and to be told that this knowledge is of a sort that can be learned by heart quickly and applied mechanically, will seem, like salvation, something almost too good to be true. . . .

The view I am maintaining is that the ordinary practical politics of European nations have become fixed in a vice of Rationalism, that much of their failure (which is often attributed to other and more immediate causes[17]) springs in fact from the defects of the Rationalist character when it is in control of affairs, and that (since the rationalist disposition of mind is not a fashion which sprang up only yesterday) we must not

[15] In 1946, at an early stage of the Cold War, the American delegation to the UN committee on atomic energy put forward a sweeping plan for placing the control of all nuclear material and atomic weapons in the hands of an International Atomic Development Authority. The proposal was rejected by the Soviet Union.

[16] George Bernard Shaw, the dramatist and socialist, was the author of *The Intelligent Woman's Guide to Socialism and Capitalism*, published in 1928.

[17] [War, for example. War is a disease to which a rationalist society has little resistance: it springs easily from the kind of incompetence inherent in rationalist politics. But it has certainly increased the hold of the Rationalist disposition of mind on politics, and one of the disasters of war has been the new customary application to politics of its essentially rationalist vocabulary.]

expect a speedy release from our predicament. It is always depressing for a patient to be told that his disease is almost as old as himself and that consequently there is no quick cure for it, but (except for the infections of childhood) this is usually the case. So long as the circumstances which promoted the emergence of rationalist politics remain, so long must we expect our politics to be rationalist in disposition.

I do not think that any or all of the writers whom I have mentioned are responsible for our predicament. They are the servants of circumstances which they have helped to perpetuate (on occasion they may be observed giving another turn to the screw), but which they did not create. And it is not to be supposed that they would always have approved of the use made of their books. Nor, again, am I concerned with genuinely philosophical writing about politics; in so far as that has either promoted or retarded the tendency to Rationalism in politics, it has always been through a misunderstanding of its design, which is not to recommend conduct but to explain it. To explore the relations between politics and eternity is one thing; it is something different, and less commendable, for a practical politician to find the intricacy of the world of time and contingency so unmanageable that he is bewitched by the offer of a quick escape into the bogus eternity of an ideology. Nor, finally, do I think we owe our predicament to the place which the natural sciences and the manner of thinking connected with them has come to take in our civilization. This simple diagnosis of the situation has been much put about, but I think it is mistaken. That the influence of the genuine natural scientist is not necessarily on the side of Rationalism follows from the view I have taken of the character of any kind of concrete knowledge. No doubt there are scientists deeply involved in the rationalist attitude, but they are mistaken when they think that the rationalist and the scientific points of view necessarily coincide. The trouble is that when the scientist steps outside his own field he often carries with him only his technique, and this at once allies him with the forces of Rationalism.[18] In short, I think the great prestige of the natural sciences has, in fact, been used to fasten the rationalist disposition of mind more firmly upon us, but that this is the work, not of the genuine science as such, but of the scientist who is a Rationalist in spite of his science.

5.

To this brief sketch of the character, and the social and intellectual context of the emergence of Rationalism in politics, may be added a few reflections. The generation of rationalist politics is by political inexperi-

[18] [A celebrated scientist tells us: "I am less interested than the average person in politics

ence out of political opportunity. These conditions have often existed together in European societies; they did so in the ancient world, and that world at times suffered the effects of their union. But the particular quality of Rationalism in modern politics derives from the circumstance that the modern world succeeded in inventing so plausible a method of covering up lack of political education that even those who suffered from that lack were often left ignorant that they lacked anything. Of course, this inexperience was never, in any society, universal; and it was never absolute. There have always been men of genuine political education, immune from the infection of Rationalism (and this is particularly so of England, where a political education of some sort has been much more widely spread than in some other societies); and sometimes a dim reminder of the limitations of his technique has penetrated even the mind of the Rationalist. Indeed, so impractical is a *purely* rationalist politics, that the new man, lately risen to power, will often be found throwing away his book and relying upon his general experience of the world as, for example, a business man or a trade union official. This experience is certainly a more trustworthy guide than the book—at least it is real knowledge and not a shadow—but still, it is not a knowledge of the political traditions of his society, which, in the most favourable circumstances, takes two or three generations to acquire.[19]

Nevertheless, when he is not arrogant or sanctimonious, the Rationalist can appear a not unsympathetic character. He wants so much to be right. But unfortunately he will never quite succeed. He began too late and on the wrong foot. His knowledge will never be more than half-knowledge, and consequently he will never be more than half-right. Like a foreigner or a man out of his social class, he is bewildered by a tradition and a habit of behaviour of which he knows only the surface; a butler or an observant house-maid has the advantage of him. And he conceives a contempt for what he does not understand; habit and custom appear bad in themselves, a kind of nescience of behaviour. And by some strange self-deception, he attributes to tradition (which, of course, is pre-eminently fluid) the rigidity and fixity of character which in fact belongs to ideological politics. Consequently, the Rationalist is a dangerous and expensive character to have in control of affairs, and he does most damage, not when he fails to master the situation (his politics, of course, are always in terms of mastering situations and surmounting crises), but when he appears to be successful; for the price we pay for each of his apparent successes is a firmer hold of the intellectual fashion of Rationalism upon the whole life of society.

---

because I am convinced that all political principles today are makeshifts, and will ultimately be replaced by principles of scientific knowledge."]

[19] An argument for the necessity of trans-generational elites.

Without alarming ourselves with imaginary evils, it may, I think, be said that there are two characteristics, in particular, of political Rationalism which make it exceptionally dangerous to a society. No sensible man will worry greatly because he cannot at once hit upon a cure for what he believes to be a crippling complaint; but if he sees the complaint to be of a kind which the passage of time must make more rather than less severe, he will have a more substantial cause for anxiety. And this unfortunately appears to be so with the disease of Rationalism.

First, Rationalism in politics, as I have interpreted it, involves an identifiable error, a misconception with regard to the nature of human knowledge, which amounts to a corruption of the mind. And consequently it is without the power to correct its own shortcomings; it has no homeopathic quality; you cannot escape its errors by becoming more sincerely or more profoundly rationalistic. This, it may be observed, is one of the penalties of living by the book; it leads not only to specific mistakes, but it also dries up the mind itself: living by precept in the end generates intellectual dishonesty. And further, the Rationalist has rejected in advance the only external inspiration capable of correcting his error; he does not merely neglect the kind of knowledge which would save him, he begins by destroying it. First he turns out the light and then complains that he cannot see, that he is "comme un homme qui marche seul et dans les ténèbres."[20] In short, the Rationalist is essentially ineducable; and he could be educated *out* of his Rationalism only by an inspiration which he regards as the great enemy of mankind. All the Rationalist can do when left to himself is to replace one rationalist project in which he has failed by another in which he hopes to succeed. Indeed, this is what contemporary politics are fast degenerating into: the political habit and tradition, which, not long ago, was the common possession of even extreme opponents in English politics, has been replaced by merely a common rationalist disposition of mind.

But, secondly, a society which has embraced a rationalist idiom of politics will soon find itself either being steered or drifting towards an exclusively rationalist form of education. I do not mean the crude purpose of National Socialism or Communism of allowing no education except a training in the dominant rationalist doctrine, I mean the more plausible project of offering no place to any form of education which is not generally rationalistic in character. And when an exclusively rationalist form of education is fully established, the only hope of deliverance lies in the discovery by some neglected pedant, "rummaging among old parchments and musty records," of what the world was like before the millennium overtook it.

---

[20] "Like a man who walks alone and in the darkness."

From the earliest days of his emergence, the Rationalist has taken an ominous interest in education. He has a respect for "brains," a great belief in training them, and is determined that cleverness shall be encouraged and shall receive its reward of power. But what is this education in which the Rationalist believes? It is certainly not an initiation into the moral and intellectual habits and achievements of his society, an entry into the partnership between present and past, a sharing of concrete knowledge; for the Rationalist, all this would be an education in nescience, both valueless and mischievous. It is a training in technique, a training, that is, in the half of knowledge which can be learnt from books when they are used as cribs. And the Rationalist's affected interest in education escapes the suspicion of being a mere subterfuge for imposing himself more firmly on society, only because it is clear that he is as deluded as his pupils. He sincerely believes that a training in technical knowledge is the only education worth while, because he is moved by the faith that there is no knowledge, in the proper sense, except technical knowledge. He believes that a training in "public administration" is the surest defence against the flattery of a demagogue and the lies of a dictator.

Now, in a society already largely rationalist in disposition, there will be a positive demand for training of this sort. Half-knowledge (so long as it is the technical half) will have an economic value; there will be a market for the "trained" mind which has at its disposal the latest devices. And it is only to be expected that this demand will be satisfied; books of the appropriate sort will be written and sold in large quantities, and institutions offering a training of this kind (either generally or in respect of a particular activity) will spring up.[21] And so far as our society is concerned, it is now long since the exploitation of this demand began in earnest; it was already to be observed in the early nineteenth century. But it is not very important that people should learn the piano or how to manage a farm by a correspondence course; and in any case it is unavoidable in the circumstances. What is important, however, is that the rationalist inspiration has now invaded and has begun to corrupt the genuine educational provisions and institutions of our society: some of the ways and means by which, hitherto, a genuine (as distinct from a merely technical) knowledge has been imparted have already disappeared, others are obsolescent, and others again are in process of being corrupted from the inside. The whole pressure of the circumstances of our time is in this direction. Apprenticeship, the pupil working along-

[21] [Some people regard this as the inevitable result of an industrial civilization, but I think they have hit upon the wrong culprit. What an industrial civilization needs is genuine skill; and in so far as our industrial civilization has decided to dispense with skill and to get along with merely technical knowledge it is an industrial civilization gone to the bad.]

side the master who in teaching a technique also imparts the sort of knowledge that cannot be taught, has not yet disappeared; but it is obsolescent, and its place is being taken by technical schools whose training (because it can be a training only in technique) remains insoluble until it is immersed in the acid of practice. Again, professional education is coming more and more to be regarded as the acquisition of a technique, something that can be done through the post, with the result that we may look forward to a time when the professions will be stocked with clever men, but men whose skill is limited and who have never had a proper opportunity of learning the nuances which compose the tradition and standard of behaviour which belong to a great profession.[22] One of the ways in which this sort of knowledge has hitherto been preserved (because it is a great human achievement, and if it is not positively preserved it will be lost) and transmitted is a family tradition. But the Rationalist never understands that it takes about two generations of practice to learn a profession; indeed, he does everything he can to destroy the possibility of such an education, believing it to be mischievous. Like a man whose only language is Esperanto, he has no means of knowing that the world did not begin in the twentieth century. And the priceless treasure of great professional traditions is, not negligently but purposefully, destroyed in the destruction of so-called vested interests. But perhaps the most serious rationalist attack upon education is that directed against the Universities. The demand for technicians is now so great that the existing institutions for training them have become insufficient, and the Universities are in process of being procured to satisfy the demand. The ominous phrase, "university trained men and women," is establishing itself, and not only in the vocabulary of the Ministry of Education.

To an opponent of Rationalism these are local, though not negligible, defeats, and, taken separately, the loss incurred in each may not be irreparable. At least an institution like a University has a positive power of defending itself, if it will use it. But there is a victory which the Rationalist has already won on another front from which recovery will be more difficult because, while the Rationalist knows it to be a victory, his opponent hardly recognizes it as a defeat. I mean the circumvention and appropriation by the rationalist disposition of mind of the whole field of morality and moral education. The morality of the Rationalist is the mo-

---

[22] [The army in wartime was a particularly good opportunity of observing the difference between a trained and an educated man: the intelligent civilian had little difficulty in acquiring the technique of military leadership and command, but (in spite of the cribs provided: *Advice to Young Officers*, etc.) he always remained at a disadvantage beside the regular officer, the man educated in the feelings and emotions as well as the practices of his profession.]

rality of the self-conscious pursuit of moral ideals, and the appropriate form of moral education is by precept, by the presentation and explanation of moral principles. This is presented as a higher morality (the morality of the free man: there is no end to the clap-trap) than that of habit, the unselfconscious following of a tradition of moral behaviour;[23] but, in fact, it is merely morality reduced to a technique, to be acquired by training in an ideology rather than an education in behaviour. In morality, as in everything else, the Rationalist aims to begin by getting rid of inherited nescience and then to fill the blank nothingness of an open mind with the items of certain knowledge which he abstracts from his personal experience, and which he believes to be approved by the common "reason" of mankind. He will defend these principles by argument, and they will compose a coherent (though morally parsimonious) doctrine. But, unavoidably, the conduct of life, for him, is a jerky, discontinuous affair, the solution of a stream of problems, the mastery of a succession of crises. Like the politics of the Rationalist (from which, of course, it is inseparable), the morality of the Rationalist is the morality of the self-made man and of the self-made society: it is what other peoples have recognized as "idolatry." And it is of no consequence that the moral ideology which inspires him today (and which, if he is a politician, he preaches) is, in fact, the desiccated relic of what was once the unselfconscious moral tradition of an aristocracy who, ignorant of ideals, had acquired a habit of behaviour in relation to one another and had handed it on in a true moral education. For the Rationalist, all that matters is that he has at last separated the ore of the ideal from the dross of the habit of behaviour; and, for us, the deplorable consequences of his success. Moral ideals are a sediment; they have significance only so long as they are suspended in a religious or social tradition, so long as they belong to a religious or a social life.[24] The predicament of our time is that the Rationalists have been at work so long on their project of drawing off the liquid in which our moral ideals were suspended (and pouring it away as worthless) that we are left only with the dry and gritty residue which chokes us as we try to take it down. First, we do our best to destroy parental authority (because of its alleged abuse), then we sentimentally deplore the scarcity of "good homes," and we end by creating substitutes which complete the work of destruction. And it is for this reason that, among much else that is corrupt and unhealthy, we have the spectacle of a set of sanctimonious, rationalist politicians, preaching an

---

[23] Here Oakeshott returns to the conservative theme of the importance of habit and custom.

[24] Here Oakeshott recalls the conservative theme of the interdependence of social elements, and the latent functions of institutions.

ideology of unselfishness and social service to a population in which they and their predecessors have done their best to destroy the only living root of moral behaviour; and opposed by another set of politicians dabbling with the project of converting us from Rationalism under the inspiration of a fresh rationalization of our political tradition.

INTRODUCTION TO
Friedrich Hayek,
"The Errors of Constructivism" and
The Mirage of Social Justice

◆

Friedrich August von Hayek was born in 1899 into a family of civil servants and academics in Vienna, the capital of the Austro-Hungarian empire. His interest in social science was kindled by his experience in the empire's multiethnic army during the First World War. "That's when I saw, more or less, the great empire collapse over the nationalist problem," he recalled. "I served in a battle in which eleven different languages were spoken. It's bound to draw your attention to the problems of political organization."[1] Hayek went on to study law, economics, philosophy, and psychology before focusing, provisionally as it turned out, on economics. In the 1920s and 1930s he participated in the scholarly debate about the economic plausibility of socialism.[2] That led him to explore the role of the market in conveying information in a capitalist economy, and subsequently to the broader question of the utilization of knowledge in society.[3]

Hayek (the "von" was legally abolished with the end of the Habsburg empire) was one of many talented Austrian intellectuals who emigrated abroad in search of better opportunities. Already known among professional economists for his work on price theory, in 1931 he accepted a chair at the London School of Economics and Political Science, where he was to remain for almost two decades. Hayek was a free-market oriented economist who opposed extensive government intervention in economic life. During the 1930s he became a leading opponent of the British economist John Maynard Keynes, whose more interventionist conceptions of government's role in a capitalist economy Hayek criticized on both methodological and policy grounds. Hayek was awarded the Nobel Prize for economics in 1974 for contributions that stem largely from the interwar era.

[1] F. A. Hayek, *Hayek on Hayek: An Autobiographical Dialogue*, ed. Stephen Kresge and Leif Wenar (Chicago, 1994), p. 48.

[2] Many of the major documents of the debate are collected in Friedrich A. Hayek, ed., *Collectivist Economic Planning* (London, 1935).

[3] See "Economics and Knowledge," first published in 1937 and reprinted in Hayek, *Individualism and Economic Order* (Chicago, 1980); and the essay "The Uses of Knowledge in Society," first published in 1945 in the *American Economic Review* XXXV, no. 4, and reprinted in Chiaki Nishiyama and Kurt R. Leube, eds., *The Essence of Hayek* (Stanford, 1984).

In 1944 Hayek published *The Road to Serfdom*, the polemical work that brought him a modicum of popular fame in Britain and in America, where an abridged version of Hayek's argument was published in the magazine *Readers Digest*. The book was an attack on socialism, government ownership of the means of production, and economic planning. Hayek stressed in particular that socialism, even when it was pursued with democratic intentions, tended toward governmental control over evermore spheres of life, leading toward totalitarianism. The book contended that Britain's enemy, German National Socialism, was a product of socialist roots, and that the very processes which led to the rise of Nazism in Germany were growing in strength in England and America. The book was embraced by some British Conservatives, and it found even greater resonance among conservative opponents of the New Deal in the United States. Public acclaim, however, was purchased at the price of the loss of some academic respectability, not only because leftist academics were antipathetic to Hayek's views, but because the book's level of historical accuracy and conceptual precision was well below that of Hayek's more academic works.

In 1950 Hayek moved to the University of Chicago, then as now a font of economic liberalism. In 1962 he moved to the University of Freiburg in Germany, a center of the politically conservative brand of German economic liberalism known as "Ordo-Liberalism." Though Hayek spent the bulk of his remaining years until his death in 1992 in Germany and Austria, his greatest influence was in the English-speaking world. It was in English that he published his two most significant books of political thought, *The Constitution of Liberty* of 1960, and the trilogy, *Law, Legislation, and Liberty*, published from 1973 to 1979.

The Constitution of Liberty included a critical, though not entirely hostile, examination of what had by then become known as "the welfare state." Hayek objected to what he regarded as the *abuse* of the welfare state to pursue the traditional socialist goal of equality of income. "There are common needs that can be satisfied only by collective action and which can be thus provided for without restricting individual liberty," he wrote. "It can hardly be denied that, as we grow richer, that minimum of sustenance which the community has always provided for those not able to look after themselves, and which can be provided outside the market, will gradually rise, or that government may, usefully and without doing any harm, assist or even lead in such endeavors. There is little reason why the government should not also play some role, or even take the initiative, in such areas as social insurance and education. . . . Our problem here is not so much the aims as the methods of government action."[4] He was suspicious above all of government mo-

---

[4] Friedrich A. Hayek, *The Constitution of Liberty* (Chicago, 1960), pp. 257–58.

nopolization of the provision of social, medical, or educational services. Hayek tried to show how social security (in the broad sense) could be provided in a manner that did as little damage as possible to individual freedom and to social innovation. In addition, the book attempted to articulate the principles upon which modern, liberal society was based, an inquiry continued in *Law, Legislation, and Liberty*.

The question of whether Hayek should be considered a liberal or a conservative is by no means easily answered: much depends not only on how these terms are defined, but on the stage of Hayek's thought and the elements of his thought that are highlighted.

Hayek's political thought was stamped by the brand of liberalism developed by the educated, civil service class of the Austro-Hungarian empire from which he sprang. They were secularist in outlook, and committed to economic liberalism and the rule of law. Their cosmopolitanism took the form of attachment to a monarchy which served to integrate a polyglot empire. This most economically and culturally modern sector of Habsburg society paradoxically looked to the imperial house to protect its position and its liberal project from a variety of foes: the anticapitalism of the aristocracy, the lower-middle-class Christian Socials who sought to protect the interests of artisans and shopkeepers, the Social Democrats who advocated socialism in the name of the working class, and the nationalist self-assertion of the Slavic minorities.[5] The Austrian liberals sought to administer and maintain the coherence of an empire riven by divisions of nationality, class, and religion. They stood for a liberal political order characterized by the rule of law and by the protection of property and of market exchange. And they regarded the spread of democracy as a threat to that order, since it meant the increased influence of groups which sought to destroy the liberal political order in the name of class, religious, or ethnic interests.

From this Viennese milieu Hayek took two enduring lessons: that a modern liberal society should be bound together primarily by factors other than shared cultural commitments, and that democracy could become a threat to a liberal political order. These lessons are articulated in the selections from Hayek's late work reprinted below.

Hayek asserted that a modern polity could not be based upon the bonds provided by shared religious, ethnic, or even cultural values. Such a polity could only be held together by a set of rules and institutions that

[5] See Barbara Jelavich, *Modern Austria: Empire and Republic, 1800–1986* (Cambridge, 1987), pp. 144–45; Paul Silverman, "Law and Economics in Interwar Vienna: Kelsen, Mises, and the Regeneration of Austrian Liberalism" (Ph.D. dissertation: University of Chicago, 1984), Introduction and chapter 1; and Malachi Hacohen, "The Making of the Open Society: Karl Popper, Philosophy and Politics in Interwar Vienna," two volumes (Ph.D. dissertation: Columbia University, 1993), pp. 77–90. For an evocation of this milieu, see the autobiographical reflections of Friedrich Hayek in *Hayek on Hayek*, pp. 37ff.

allowed individuals to pursue their varied projects without attempting to embody any collective goal. Those rules were above all the rules of justice, understood in the Humean sense as the protection of person, property, and contracts, without any pretension to reward individuals according to commonly shared standards of merit or virtue. For, Hayek stressed, in a modern liberal society—what he called the "Great Society"—there *are* no such shared standards. On this understanding, the great advantage of a market-based society was not only that it led to an increase in material well-being, but also that it avoided the need for cultural consensus as the basis of political life. Any attempt to design the economy to make wages conform to shared values, Hayek argued, opened the door for various groups to make endless economic claims upon the state which could only be met at the cost of destroying the capitalist economy. Moreover, it demanded shared conceptions of social justice which simply did not exist in modern society. These ideas are reflected in the second selection below, from Hayek's book of 1976, *The Mirage of Social Justice*. There Hayek distinguishes the formal and abstract legal rules required by the modern "Great Society" from the more particularistic and altruistic morality of earlier "tribal society."

Hayek's defense of the capitalist economy and his antipathy to the redistribution of income in a more egalitarian direction was in keeping with what since the late nineteenth century had come to be considered conservative positions. But his emphasis on individual liberty marked the dominant tone of his work as liberal, at least until his late works of the 1970s. Embraced after the publication of *The Road to Serfdom* by those in England and the United States who called themselves "conservative," Hayek took pains in the postscript to his next major work, *The Constitution of Liberty* of 1960, to explain "Why I Am Not a Conservative." Unlike the suspicion of change which characterized conservatives, he wrote, liberals like himself possessed "faith in the spontaneous forces of adjustment which makes the liberal accept changes without apprehension, even though he does not know how the necessary adaptations will be brought about. It is, indeed, part of the liberal attitude to assume that, especially in the economic field, the self-regulating forces of the market will somehow bring about the required adjustments to new conditions, although no one can foretell how they will do this in a particular instance."[6] He rejected conservatism on the grounds that its failure to provide "any guiding principles which can influence long-range developments" left it unable to offer an alternative to the socialistic direction in which he believed society was moving.[7] Furthermore, he noted that while the typical conservative might have strong convictions, he had "no

---

[6] Hayek, *The Constitution of Liberty*, p. 400.   [7] Ibid., pp. 398–99.

political principles which enable him to work with people whose moral values differ from his own for a political order in which both can obey their convictions. It is the recognition of such principles that permits the coexistence of different sets of values that makes it possible to build a peaceful society with a minimum of force. The acceptance of such principles means that we agree to tolerate much that we dislike."[8] And he contrasted his own skepticism and tolerance to what he believed was the conservative propensity to assert the "authority of supernatural sources of knowledge."

Yet no sooner had Hayek disavowed the conservative label than his writing began to move in a more conservative direction.[9] The change in emphasis was expressed above all in Hayek's extreme epistemological modesty. As he increasingly stressed that the major institutions he sought to conserve—the free market and the legal structure that made it possible—were the product not of rational deliberation but the unintended results of human action, Hayek seemed wary of *any* deliberate transformation that smacked of what Oakeshott had called "rationalism in politics" or what Hayek now called "constructivism." Hayek's conception of the market as a spontaneous order and his emphasis on the limits of our comprehension of it (above all because of the difficulty of identifying latent functions) appeared to preclude the reform of institutions based on rational analysis.[10] He offered an evolutionary scheme to explain the development of the institutions of the market and the rule of law, suggesting that they were adopted over time because they provided more adequately for changing human needs. He thus arrived at a historical utilitarian interpretation which had much in common with the views of Sumner.[11]

In the last decades of his life, Hayek's thought became more conservative in another sense as well. He came to regard other traditional institutions, such as religion and the bourgeois family, as possibly conveying modes of behavior that were necessary complements to the institutions of the market and the rule of law. Hayek's warming toward tradition may reflect the changed context of his later work. In late Habsburg Vienna, religion and collective traditions were sources of conflict

---

[8] Ibid., p. 402.

[9] On the conservative element of Hayek's thought, see Chadran Kukathas, *Hayek and Modern Liberalism* (Oxford, 1989), pp. 174ff.

[10] See John Gray, *Hayek on Liberty*, second edition (Oxford, 1986), pp. 70–71.

[11] Hayek's utilitarianism has been characterized as "*indirect or system utilitarian*, inasmuch as the proper role of utility is not prescriptive or practical but rather that of a standard of evaluation for the assessment of whole systems of rules or practices." John Gray, *Hayek on Liberty*, p. 59. The same might be said of most of the other conservative thinkers in this volume, whose common denominator we have characterized as "historical utilitarianism."

rather than of consensus. After two decades in Britain and another decade in the United States, Hayek may have come to believe that religion
and other cultural traditions could be compatible with the institutions
he most valued. Hayek thus moved closer to the recurrent conservative
embrace of the functional value of religion and the necessity of the family as a socializing institution. But he was never led to examine whether
the effect of the market and the liberal state might be to weaken these
institutions.

Friedrich A. Hayek,
"The Errors of Constructivism" (1970)[1]

1

It seemed to me necessary to introduce the term "constructivism" as a
specific name for a manner of thinking that in the past has often, but
misleadingly, been described as "rationalism."[2] The basic conception of
this constructivism can perhaps be expressed in the simplest manner by
the innocent sounding formula that, since man has himself created the
institutions of society and civilisation, he must also be able to alter them
at will so as to satisfy his desires or wishes. It is almost 50 years since I
first heard and was greatly impressed by this formula.

At first the current phrase that man "created" his civilisation and its
institutions may appear rather harmless and commonplace. But as soon
as it is extended, as is frequently done, to mean that man was able to do
this because he was endowed with reason, the implications become
questionable. Man did not possess reason before civilisation. The two
evolved together. We need merely to consider language, which today
nobody still believes to have been "invented" by a rational being, in
order to see that reason and civilisation develop in constant mutual interaction. But what we now no longer question with regard to language
(though even that is comparatively recent) is by no means generally accepted with regard to morals, law, the skills of handicrafts, or social institutions. We are still too easily led to assume that these phenomena,
which are clearly the results of human action, must also have been consciously designed by a human mind, in circumstances created for the

---

[1] First delivered as a lecture in January 1970 and published in German later that year,
this English version appeared in F. A. Hayek, *New Studies in Philosophy, Politics, Economics
and the History of Ideas* (Chicago, 1978). The selections are reprinted here with Hayek's
footnotes omitted.

[2] Hayek uses the term "constructivism" to mean much the same as Oakeshott's "rationalism in politics."

purposes which they serve—that is, that they are what Max Weber called *wert-rationale* products. In short, we are misled into thinking that morals, law, skills and social institutions can only be justified in so far as they correspond to some preconceived design.[3]

It is significant that this is a mistake we usually commit only with regard to the phenomena of our own civilisation. If the ethnologist or social anthropologist attempts to understand other cultures, he has no doubt that their members frequently have no idea as to the reason for observing particular rules, or what depends on it. Yet most modern social theorists are rarely willing to admit that the same thing applies also to our own civilisation. We too frequently do not know what benefits we derive from the usages of our society;[4] and such social theorists regard this merely as a regrettable deficiency which ought to be removed as soon as possible.

2

In a short lecture it is not possible to trace the history of the discussion of these problems to which I have given some attention in recent years. I will merely mention that they were already familiar to the ancient Greeks. The very dichotomy between "natural" and "artificial" formations which the ancient Greeks introduced has dominated the discussion for 2,000 years. Unfortunately, the Greeks' distinction between natural and artificial has become the greatest obstacle to further advance; because, interpreted as an exclusive alternative, this distinction is not only ambiguous but definitely false. As was at last clearly seen by the Scottish social philosophers of the eighteenth century (but the late Schoolmen had already partly seen it), a large part of social formations, although the result of human action, is not of human design. The consequence of this is that such formations, according to the interpretation of the traditional terms, could be described either as "natural," or as "artificial."

The beginning of a true appreciation of these circumstances in the sixteenth century was extinguished, however, in the seventeenth century by the rise of a powerful new philosophy—the rationalism of René Descartes and his followers, from whom all modern forms of constructivism derive. From Descartes it was taken over by that unreasonable "Age of Reason," which was entirely dominated by the Cartesian spirit. Voltaire, the greatest representative of the so-called "Age of Reason," expressed

---

[3] Reflecting upon the inability of men to rationally create such institutions, Maistre had ascribed their origin to divine providence. Hayek, like Hume, eschews divine first causes.

[4] Here Hayek introduces the theme of latent social functions, which is central to the argument that follows.

the Cartesian spirit in his famous statement: "If you want good laws, burn those you have and make yourselves new ones." Against this, the great critic of rationalism, David Hume, could only slowly elaborate the foundations of a true theory of the growth of social formations, which was further developed by his fellow Scotsmen, Adam Smith and Adam Ferguson, into a theory of phenomena that are "the result of human action but not of human design."

Descartes had taught that we should only believe what we can prove. Applied to the field of morals and values generally, his doctrine meant that we should only accept as binding what we could recognise as a rational design for a recognisable purpose. I will leave undecided how far he himself evaded difficulties by representing the unfathomable will of God as the creator of all purposive phenomena. For his successors it certainly became a human will, which they regarded as the source of all social formations whose intention must provide the justification. Society appeared to them as a deliberate construction of men for an intended purpose—shown most clearly in the writing of Descartes' faithful pupil, J.-J. Rousseau. The belief in the unlimited power of a supreme authority as necessary, especially for a representative assembly, and therefore the belief that democracy necessarily means the unlimited power of the majority, are ominous consequences of this constructivism.

3

You will probably most clearly see what I mean by "constructivism" if I quote a characteristic statement of a well-known Swedish sociologist, which I recently encountered in the pages of a German popular science journal. "The most important goal that sociology has set itself," he wrote, "is to predict the future development and to shape (*gestalten*) the future, or, if one prefers to express it in that manner, to create the future of mankind." If a science makes such claims, this evidently implies the assertion that the whole of human civilisation, and all we have so far achieved, could only have been built as a purposive rational construction.

It must suffice for the moment to show that this constructivistic interpretation of social formations is by no means merely harmless philosophical speculation, but an assertion of fact from which conclusions are derived concerning both the explanation of social processes and the opportunities for political action. The factually erroneous assertion, from which the constructivists derive such far-reaching consequences and demands, appears to me to be that the complex order of our modern society is exclusively due to the circumstance that men have been guided in their actions by foresight—an insight into the connections between cause and effect—or at least that it could have arisen through design. What I want to show is that men are in their conduct *never* guided *exclusively* by their understanding of the causal connections between particular known means and certain desired ends, but always also by rules of conduct of which they are rarely aware, which they certainly have not consciously invented, and that to discern the function and significance of this is a difficult and only partially achieved task of scientific effort.[5] Expressing this differently—it means that the success of rational striving (Max Weber's *zweckrationales Handeln*) is largely due to the observance of values, whose role in our society ought to be carefully distinguished from that of deliberately pursued goals.

I can only briefly mention the further fact, that success of the individual in the achievement of his immediate aims depends, not only on his conscious insight into causal connections, but also in a high degree on his ability to act according to rules, which he may be unable to express in words, but which we can only describe by formulating rules. All our skills, from the command of language to the mastery of handicrafts or games—actions which we "know how" to perform without being able to state how we do it—are instances of this. I mention them here only because action according to rules—which we do not explicitly know and which have not been designed by reason, but prevail because the manner of acting of those who are successful is imitated—is perhaps easier to recognise in these instances than in the field directly relevant to my present concerns.

The rules we are discussing are those that are not so much useful to the individuals who observe them, as those that (if they are *generally* observed) make all the members of the group more effective, because they give them opportunities to act within a social *order*. These rules are also mostly not the result of a deliberate choice of means for specific purposes, but of a process of selection, in the course of which groups that achieved a more efficient order displaced (or were imitated by) others, often without knowing to what their superiority was due. This social group of rules includes the rules of law, of morals, of custom and so on—in fact, all the values which govern a society. The term "value," which I shall for lack of a better one have to continue to use in this context, is in fact a little misleading, because we tend to interpret it as referring to particular aims of individual action, while in the fields to which I am referring they consist mostly of rules which do not tell us positively what to do, but in most instances merely what we ought not to do.

[5] This emphasis on the significance of tacit knowledge is one element of Hayek's epistemological modesty. It reformulates the conservative assumption in favor of habit and custom.

Those taboos of society which are not founded on any rational justification have been the favourite subject of derision by the constructivists, who wish to see them banned from any rationally designed order of society. Among the taboos they have largely succeeded in destroying are respect for private property and for the keeping of private contracts, with the result that some people doubt if respect for them can ever again be restored.

For all organisms, however, it is often more important to know what they must not do, if they are to avoid danger, than to know what they must do in order to achieve particular ends. The former kind of knowledge is usually not a knowledge of the consequences which the prohibited kind of conduct would produce, but a knowledge that in certain conditions certain types of conduct are to be avoided. Our positive knowledge of cause and effect assists us only in those fields where our acquaintance with the particular circumstances is sufficient; and it is important that we do not move beyond the region where this knowledge will guide us reliably.[6] This is achieved by rules that, without regard to the consequences in the particular instance, generally prohibit actions of a certain kind.

That in this sense man is not only a purpose-seeking but also a rule-following animal has been repeatedly stressed in the recent literature. In order to understand what is meant by this, we must be quite clear about the meaning attached in this connection to the word "rule." This is necessary because those chiefly negative (or prohibitory) rules of conduct which make possible the formation of social order are of three different kinds, which I now spell out. These kinds of rules are: (1) rules that are merely observed in fact but have never been stated in words; if we speak of the "sense of justice" or "the feeling for language" we refer to such rules which we are able to apply, but do not know explicitly; (2) rules that, though they have been stated in words, still merely express approximately what has long before been generally observed in action; and (3) rules that have been deliberately introduced and therefore necessarily exist as words set out in sentences.

Constructivists would like to reject the first and second groups of rules, and to accept as valid only the third group I have mentioned.

4

What then is the origin of those rules that most people follow but few if anyone can state in words? Long before Charles Darwin the theorists of society, and particularly those of language, had given the answer that in

---

[6] Another statement of the need for epistemological modesty.

the process of cultural transmission, in which modes of conduct are passed on from generation to generation, a process of selection takes place, in which those modes of conduct prevail which lead to the formation of a more efficient order for the whole group, because such groups will prevail over others.[7]

A point needing special emphasis, because it is so frequently misunderstood, is that by no means every regularity of conduct among individuals produces an order for the whole of society. Therefore regular individual conduct does not necessarily mean order, but only certain kinds of regularity of the conduct of individuals lead to an order for the whole. The order of society is therefore a factual state of affairs which must be distinguished from the regularity of the conduct of individuals. It must be defined as a condition in which individuals are able, on the basis of their own respective peculiar knowledge, to form expectations concerning the conduct of others, which are proved correct by making possible a successful mutual adjustment of the actions of these individuals. If every person perceiving another were either to try to kill him or to run away, this would certainly also constitute a regularity of individual conduct, but not one that led to the formation of ordered groups. Quite clearly, certain combinations of such rules of individual conduct may produce a superior kind of order, which will enable some groups to expand at the expense of others.

This effect does not presuppose that the members of the group know to which rules of conduct the group owes its superiority, but merely that it will accept only those individuals as members who observe the rules traditionally accepted by it. There will always be an amount of experience of individuals precipitated in such rules, which its living members do not know, but which nevertheless help them more effectively to pursue their ends.

This sort of "knowledge of the world" that is passed on from generation to generation will thus consist in a great measure not of knowledge of cause and effect, but of rules of conduct adapted to the environment and acting like information about the environment although they do not say anything about it. Like scientific theories, they are preserved by proving themselves useful, but, in contrast to scientific theories, by a proof which no one needs to know, because the proof manifests itself in the resilience and progressive expansion of the order of society which it makes possible. This is the true content of the much derided idea of the "wisdom of our ancestors" embodied in inherited institutions, which plays such an important role in conservative thought, but appears to the constructivist to be an empty phrase signifying nothing.

---

[7] Here Hayek offers a version of historical utilitarianism, in which the survival of an institution is taken as evidence that it has served human needs.

5

Time allows me to consider further only one of the many interesting interrelations of this kind, which at the same time also explains why an economist is particularly inclined to concern himself with these problems: the connection between rules of law and the spontaneously formed order of the market. This order is, of course, not the result of a miracle or some natural harmony of interests. It forms itself, because in the course of millennia men develop rules of conduct which lead to the formation of such an order out of the separate spontaneous activities of individuals. The interesting point about this is that men developed these rules without really understanding their functions. Philosophers of law have in general even ceased to ask what is the "purpose" of law, thinking the question is unanswerable because they interpret "purpose" to mean particular foreseeable results, to achieve which the rules were designed. In fact, this "purpose" is to bring about an abstract order—a system of abstract relations—concrete manifestations which will depend on a great variety of particular circumstances which no one can know in their entirety. Those rules of just conduct have therefore a "meaning" or "function" which no one has given them, and which social theory must try to discover.[8]

It was the great achievement of economic theory that, 200 years before cybernetics, it recognised the nature of such self-regulating systems in which certain regularities (or, perhaps better, "restraints") of conduct of the elements led to constant adaptation of the comprehensive order to particular facts, affecting in the first instance only the separate elements. Such an order, leading to the utilisation of much more information than anyone possesses, could not have been "invented." This follows from the fact that the result could not have been foreseen. None of our ancestors could have known that the protection of property and contracts would lead to an extensive division of labour, specialisation and the establishment of markets, or that the extension to outsiders of rules initially applicable only to members of the same tribe would tend towards the formation of a world economy.

All that man could do was to try to improve bit by bit on a process of mutually adjusting individual activities, by reducing conflicts through modifications to some of the inherited rules. All that he could deliberately design, he could and did create only within a system of rules, which he had not invented, and with the aim of improving an existing order. Always merely adjusting the rules, he tried to improve the combined

---

[8] For Hayek a major function of social theory is to articulate the latent functions of existing social institutions and practices.

effect of all other rules accepted in his community. In his efforts to improve the existing order, he was therefore never free arbitrarily to lay
down any new rule he liked, but had always a definite problem to solve,
raised by an imperfection of the existing order, but of an order he would
have been quite incapable of constructing as a whole. What man found
were conflicts between accepted values, the significance of which he only
partly understood, but on the character of which the results of many of
his efforts depended, and which he could only strive better to adapt to
each other, but which he could never create anew. . . .

7

The roots of socialism in constructivistic thought are obvious not only
in its original form—in which it intended through socialisation of the
means of production, distribution and exchange to make possible a
planned economy to replace the spontaneous order of the market by an
organisation directed to particular ends. But the modern form of socialism that tries to use the market in the service of what is called "social
justice," and for this purpose wants to guide the action of men, not by
rules of just conduct for the individual, but by the recognised importance of results brought about by the decisions of authority, is no less
based upon it.

The Mirage of Social Justice (1973)[9]

THE CONQUEST OF PUBLIC IMAGINATION BY "SOCIAL JUSTICE"

The appeal to "social justice" has . . . by now become the most widely
used and most effective argument in political discussion. Almost every
claim for government action on behalf of particular groups is advanced
in its name, and if it can be made to appear that a certain measure is
demanded by "social justice," opposition to it will rapidly weaken. People may dispute whether or not the particular measure is required by
"social justice." But that this is the standard which ought to guide political action, and that the expression has a definite meaning, is hardly
ever questioned. In consequence, there are today probably no political

[9] Volume 2 of Hayek's trilogy, *Law, Legislation and Liberty: A new statement of the
liberal principles of justice and political economy* (Chicago, 1976). The selections are from
chapter 9, " 'Social' or Distributive Justice."

movements or politicians who do not readily appeal to "social justice" in support of the particular measures which they advocate.

It also can scarcely be denied that the demand for "social justice" has already in a great measure transformed the social order and is continuing to transform it in a direction which those who called for it never foresaw. Though the phrase has undoubtedly helped occasionally to make the law more equal for all, whether the demand for justice in distribution has in any sense made society juster or reduced discontent must remain doubtful.

The expression of course described from the beginning the aspirations which were at the heart of socialism. Although classical socialism has usually been defined by its demand for the socialization of the means of production, this was for it chiefly a means thought to be essential in order to bring about a "just" distribution of wealth; and since socialists have later discovered that this redistribution could in a great measure, and against less resistance, be brought about by taxation (and government services financed by it), and have in practice often shelved their earlier demands, the realization of "social justice" has become their chief promise. It might indeed be said that the main difference between the order of society at which classical liberalism aimed and the sort of society into which it is now being transformed is that the former was governed by principles of just individual conduct while the new society is to satisfy the demands for "social justice"—or, in other words, that the former demanded just action by the individuals while the latter more and more places the duty of justice on authorities with power to command people what to do.

The phrase could exercise this effect because it has gradually been taken over from the socialist not only by all the other political movements but also by most teachers and preachers of morality. It seems in particular to have been embraced by a large section of the clergy of all Christian denominations, who, while increasingly losing their faith in a supernatural revelation, appear to have sought a refuge and consolation in a new "social" religion which substitutes a temporal for a celestial promise of justice, and who hope that they can thus continue their striving to do good. The Roman Catholic church especially has made the aim of "social justice" part of its official doctrine; but the ministers of most Christian denominations appear to vie with each other with such offers of more mundane aims—which also seem to provide the chief foundation for renewed ecumenical efforts.

The various modern authoritarian or dictatorial governments have of course no less proclaimed "social justice" as their chief aim. We have it on the authority of Mr. Andrei Sakharov that millions of men in Russia are the victims of a terror that "attempts to conceal itself behind the slogan of social justice."

The commitment to "social justice" has in fact become the chief outlet for moral emotion, the distinguishing attribute of the good man, and the recognized sign of the possession of a moral conscience. Though people may occasionally be perplexed to say which of the conflicting claims advanced in its name are valid, scarcely anyone doubts that the expression has a definite meaning, describes a high ideal, and points to grave defects of the existing social order which urgently call for correction. Even though until recently one would have vainly sought in the extensive literature for an intelligible definition of the term, there still seems to exist little doubt, either among ordinary people or among the learned, that the expression has a definite and well understood sense.

But the near-universal acceptance of a belief does not prove that it is valid or even meaningful any more than the general belief in witches or ghosts proved the validity of these concepts. What we have to deal with in the case of "social justice" is simply a quasi-religious superstition of the kind which we should respectfully leave in peace so long as it merely makes those happy who hold it, but which we must fight when it becomes the pretext of coercing other men. And the prevailing belief in "social justice" is at present probably the gravest threat to most other values of a free civilization.

Whether Edward Gibbon was wrong or not, there can be no doubt that moral and religious beliefs can destroy a civilization and that, where such doctrines prevail, not only the most cherished beliefs but also the most revered moral leaders, sometimes saintly figures whose unselfishness is beyond question, may become grave dangers to the values which the same people regard as unshakable. Against this threat we can protect ourselves only by subjecting even our dearest dreams of a better world to ruthless rational dissection.

It seems to be widely believed that "social justice" is just a new moral value which we must add to those that were recognized in the past, and that it can be fitted within the existing framework of moral rules. What is not sufficiently recognized is that in order to give this phrase meaning a complete change of the whole character of the social order will have to be effected, and that some of the values which used to govern it will have to be sacrificed. It is such a transformation of society into one of a fundamentally different type which is currently occurring piecemeal and without awareness of the outcome to which it must lead. It was in the belief that something like "social justice" could thereby be achieved, that people have placed in the hands of government powers which it can now not refuse to employ in order to satisfy the claims of the ever increasing number of special interests who have learnt to employ the open sesame of "social justice."[10]

I believe that "social justice" will ultimately be recognized as a will-o'-the-wisp which has lured men to abandon many of the values which in the past have inspired the development of civilization—an attempt to satisfy a craving inherited from the traditions of the small group but which is meaningless in the Great Society of free men.[11] Unfortunately, this vague desire which has become one of the strongest bonds spurring people of good will to action, not only is bound to be disappointed. This would be sad enough. But, like most attempts to pursue an unattainable goal, the striving for it will also produce highly undesirable consequences, and in particular lead to the destruction of the indispensible environment in which the traditional moral values alone can flourish, namely personal freedom.[12]

THE INAPPLICABILITY OF THE CONCEPT OF JUSTICE TO THE RESULTS OF A SPONTANEOUS PROCESS

It is now necessary clearly to distinguish between two wholly different problems which the demand for "social justice" raises in a market order.

The first is whether within an economic order based on the market the concept of "social justice" has any meaning or content whatever.

The second is whether it is possible to preserve a market order while imposing upon it (in the name of "social justice" or any other pretext) some pattern of remuneration based on the assessment of the performance or the needs of different individuals or groups by an authority possessing the power to enforce it.

The answer to each of these questions is a clear no.

Yet it is the general belief in the validity of the concept of "social justice" which drives all contemporary societies into greater and greater efforts of the second kind and which has a peculiar self-accelerating tendency: the more dependent the position of the individuals or groups is seen to become on the actions of government, the more they will insist that the governments aim at some recognizable scheme of distributive

---

[10] Hayek's fear that the ever-increasing claims on government will expand the purview and transform the nature of the state echo those of Carl Schmitt in the selection above.

[11] Hayek uses the term "Great Society" to refer to a market-based social order in which social cohesion does not occur primarily through shared values and commitments. The term "Great Society" is meant to convey his contention that such an order can incorporate a larger number and a wider variety of people than older forms of social organization (which he terms "tribal") based on shared ancestry and shared ultimate beliefs.

[12] Hayek's assumption that personal freedom is conducive to the preservation of traditional moral values is the most disputed element of his libertarian conservatism.

justice; and the more governments try to realize some preconceived pattern of desirable distribution, the more they must subject the position of the different individuals and groups to their control. So long as the belief in "social justice" governs political action, this process must progressively approach nearer and nearer to a totalitarian system.

We shall at first concentrate on the problem of the meaning, or rather lack of meaning, of the term "social justice," and only later consider the effects which the efforts to impose *any* preconceived pattern of distribution must have on the structure of the society subjected to them.

The contention that in a society of free men (as distinct from any compulsory organization) the concept of social justice is strictly empty and meaningless will probably appear as quite unbelievable to most people. Are we not all constantly disquieted by watching how unjustly life treats different people and by seeing the deserving suffer and the unworthy prosper? And do we not all have a sense of fitness, and watch it with satisfaction, when we recognize a reward to be appropriate to effort or sacrifice?

The first insight which should shake this certainty is that we experience the same feelings also with respect to differences in human fates for which clearly no human agency is responsible and which it would therefore clearly be absurd to call injustice. Yet we do cry out against the injustice when a succession of calamities befalls one family while another steadily prospers, when a meritorious effort is frustrated by some unforeseeable accident, and particularly if of many people whose endeavours seem equally great, some succeed brilliantly while others utterly fail. It is certainly tragic to see the failure of the most meritorious efforts of parents to bring up their children, of young men to build a career, or of an explorer or scientist pursuing a brilliant idea. And we will protest against such a fate although we do not know anyone who is to blame for it, or any way in which such disappointments can be prevented.

It is no different with regard to the general feeling of injustice about the distribution of material goods in a society of free men. Though we are in this case less ready to admit it, our complaints about the outcome of the market as unjust do not really assert that somebody has been unjust; and there is no answer to the question of *who* has been unjust. Society has simply become the new deity to which we complain and clamour for redress if it does not fulfil the expectations it has created. There is no individual and no cooperating group of people against which the sufferer would have a just complaint, and there are no conceivable rules of just individual conduct which would at the same time secure a functioning order and prevent such disappointments.

The only blame implicit in those complaints is that we tolerate a system in which each is allowed to choose his occupation and therefore nobody can have the power and the duty to see that the results correspond to our wishes. For in such a system in which each is allowed to use his knowledge for his own purposes the concept of "social justice" is necessarily empty and meaningless, because in it nobody's will can determine the relative incomes of the different people, or prevent that they be partly dependent on accident. "Social justice" can be given a meaning only in a directed or "command" economy (such as an army) in which the individuals are ordered what to do; and any particular conception of "social justice" could be realized only in such a centrally directed system. It presupposes that people are guided by specific directions and not by rules of just individual conduct. Indeed, no system of rules of just individual conduct, and therefore no free action of the individuals, could produce results satisfying any principle of distributive justice.

We are of course not wrong in perceiving that the effects of the processes of a free society on the fates of the different individuals are not distributed according to some recognizable principle of justice. Where we go wrong is in concluding from this that they are unjust and that somebody is to be blamed for this. In a free society in which the position of the different individuals and groups is not the result of anybody's design—or could, within such a society, be altered in accordance with a generally applicable principle—the differences in reward simply cannot meaningfully be described as just or unjust. . . .

The Rationale of the Economic Game in Which Only the Conduct of the Players But Not the Result Can Be Just

We have seen earlier that justice is an attribute of human conduct which we have learnt to exact because a certain kind of conduct is required to secure the formation and maintenance of a beneficial order of actions. . . .

The fact is simply that we consent to retain, and agree to enforce, uniform rules for a procedure which has greatly improved the chances of all to have their wants satisfied, but at the price of all individuals and groups incurring the risk of unmerited failure. With the acceptance of this procedure the recompense of different groups and individuals becomes exempt from deliberate control. It is the only procedure yet discovered in which information widely dispersed among millions of men can be effectively utilized for the benefit of all—and used by assuring to all an individual liberty desirable for itself on ethical grounds. It is a procedure which of course has never been "designed" but which we have learnt gradually to improve after we had discovered how it increased the efficiency of men in the groups who had evolved it. . . .

Here we must content ourselves with emphasizing that the results for the different individuals and groups of a procedure for utilizing more information than any one person or agency can possess, must themselves be unpredictable, and must often be different from the hopes and intentions which determined the direction and intensity of their striving; and that we can make effective use of that dispersed knowledge only if (as Adam Smith was also one of the first to see clearly) we allow the principle of negative feedback to operate, which means that some must suffer unmerited disappointment. . . .

The long and the short of it all is that men can be allowed to decide what work to do only if the remuneration they can expect to get for it corresponds to the value their services have to those of their fellows who receive them; and that *these values which their services will have to their fellows will often have no relations to their individual merits or needs.* Reward for merit earned and indication of what a person should do, both in his own and in his fellows' interest, are different things. It is not good intentions or needs but doing what in fact most benefits others, irrespective of motive, which will secure the best reward. . . .

THERE IS NO "VALUE TO SOCIETY"

[One] source of the conception that the categories of just and unjust can be meaningfully applied to the remunerations determined by the market is the idea that the different services have a determined and ascertainable "value to society," and that the actual remuneration frequently differs from the value. But though the conception of a "value to society" is sometimes carelessly used even by economists, there is strictly no such thing and the expression implies the same sort of anthropomorphism or personification of society as the term "social justice." Services can have value only to particular people (or an organization), and any particular service will have very different values for different members of the same society. To regard them differently is to treat society not as a spontaneous order of free men but as an organization whose members are all made to serve a single hierarchy of ends. This would necessarily be a totalitarian system in which personal freedom would be absent.

Although it is tempting to speak of a "value to society" instead of a man's value to his fellows, it is in fact highly misleading if we say, e.g., that a man who supplies matches to millions and thereby earns $200,000 a year is worth more "to society" than a man who supplies great wisdom or exquisite pleasure to a few thousand and thereby earns $20,000 a year. Even the performance of a Beethoven sonata, a painting by Leonardo or a play by Shakespeare have no "value to society" but a value only to those who know and appreciate them. And it has little meaning to assert that a boxer or a crooner is worth more to society than a violin virtuoso or a ballet dancer if the former renders services to millions and the latter to a much smaller group. The point is not that the true values are different, but that the values attached to the different services by different groups of people are incommensurable; all that these expressions mean is merely that one in fact receives a larger aggregate sum from a larger number of people than the other. . . .

The consideration of the different attitudes which different groups will take to the remuneration of different services incidentally also shows that the large numbers by no means grudge all the incomes higher than theirs, but generally only those earned by activities the functions of which they do not understand or which they even regard as harmful. I have never known ordinary people grudge the very high earnings of the boxer or torero, the football idol or the cinema star or the jazz king—they seem often even to revel vicariously in the display of extreme luxury and waste of such figures compared with which those of industrial magnates or financial tycoons pale. It is where most people do not comprehend the usefulness of an activity, and frequently because they erroneously regard it as harmful (the "speculator"—often combined with the belief that only dishonest activities can bring so much money), and especially where the large earnings are used to accumulate a fortune (again out of the erroneous belief that it would be desirable that it should be spent rather than invested) that the outcry about the injustice of it arises. Yet the complex structure of the modern Great Society would clearly not work if the remunerations of all the different activities were determined by the opinion which the majority holds of their value—or indeed if they were dependent on any one person's understanding or knowledge of the importance of all the different activities required for the functioning of the system. . . .

"EQUALITY OF OPPORTUNITY"

It is of course not to be denied that in the existing market order not only the results but also the initial chances of different individuals are often very different; they are affected by circumstances of their physical and social environment which are beyond their control but in many particular respects might be altered by some governmental action. The demand for equality of opportunity or equal starting conditions (*Startgerechtigkeit*) appeals to, and has been supported by, many who in general favour the free market order. So far as this refers to such facilities and opportunities as are of necessity affected by governmental decisions (such as appointments to public office and the like), the demand was indeed one of the central points of classical liberalism, usually expressed by the French phrase "*la carrière ouverte aux talents.*"[13] There is also much to be said in favour of the government providing on an equal basis the means for the schooling of minors who are not yet fully responsible citizens, even though there are grave doubts whether we ought to allow government to administer them.

But all this would still be very far from creating real equality of opportunity, even for persons possessing the same abilities. To achieve this government would have to control the whole physical and human environment of all persons, and have to endeavour to provide at least equivalent chances for each; and the more government succeeded in these endeavours, the stronger would become the legitimate demand that, on the same principle, any still remaining handicaps must be removed—or compensated for by putting extra burden on the still relatively favoured. This would have to go on until government literally controlled every circumstance which could affect any person's well-being. Attractive as the phrase of equality of opportunity at first sounds, once the idea is extended beyond the facilities which for other reasons have to be provided by government, it becomes a wholly illusory ideal, and any attempt concretely to realize it apt to produce a nightmare.

"SOCIAL JUSTICE" AND FREEDOM UNDER THE LAW

. . . Perhaps the acutest sense of grievance about injustice inflicted on one, not by particular persons but by the "system," is that about being deprived of opportunities for developing one's abilities which others enjoy. For this any difference of environment, social or physical, may be responsible, and at least some of them may be unavoidable. The most important of these is clearly inseparable from the institution of the family. This not only satisfies a strong psychological need but in general serves as an instrument for the transmission of important cultural values. There can be no doubt that those who are either wholly deprived of this benefit, or grew up in unfavourable conditions, are gravely handicapped; and few will question that it would be desirable that some public institution so far as possible should assist such unfortunate children when relatives and neighbours fail. Yet few will seriously believe (although Plato did) that we can fully make up for such a deficiency, and I trust even fewer that, because this benefit cannot be assured to all, it should, in the interest of equality, be taken from those who now enjoy it. Nor does it seem to me that even material equality could compensate for those differences in the capacity of enjoyment and of experiencing a lively interest in the cultural surroundings which a suitable upbringing confers. . . .

---

[13] "The career open to talents."

The Spatial Range of "Social Justice"

There can be little doubt that the moral feelings which express themselves in the demand for "social justice" derive from an attitude which in more primitive conditions the individual developed towards the fellow members of the small group to which he belonged. Towards the personally known member of one's own group it may well have been a recognized duty to assist him and to adjust one's actions to his needs. This is made possible by the knowledge of his person and his circumstances. The situation is wholly different in the Great or Open Society. Here the products and the services of each benefit mostly persons he does not know. The greater productivity of such a society rests on a division of labour extending far beyond the range any one person can survey. This extension of the process of exchange beyond relatively small groups, and including large numbers of persons not known to each other, has been made possible by conceding to the stranger and even the foreigner the same protection of rules of just conduct which apply to the relations to the known members of one's own small group.

This application of the same rules of just conduct to the relations to all other men is rightly regarded as one of the great achievements of a liberal society. What is usually not understood is that this extension of the same rules to the relations to all other men (beyond the most intimate group such as the family and personal friends) requires an attenuation at least of some of the rules which are enforced in the relations to other members of the smaller group. If the legal duties towards strangers or foreigners are to be the same as those towards the neighbours or inhabitants of the same village or town, the latter duties will have to be reduced to such as can also be applied to the stranger. No doubt men will always wish to belong also to smaller groups and be willing voluntarily to assume greater obligations towards self-chosen friends or companions. But such moral obligations towards some can never become enforced duties in a system of freedom under the law, because in such a system the selection of those towards whom a man wishes to assume special moral obligations must be left to him and cannot be determined by law. A system of rules intended for an Open Society and, at least in principle, meant to be applicable to all others, must have a somewhat smaller content than one to be applied in a small group. . . .

INTRODUCTION TO
Edward Banfield,
The Unheavenly City Revisited

◆

The period from the end of the Second World War through the oil shock of 1973 was an era of substantial economic growth for the capitalist economies of North America and western Europe. They were also years in which the welfare state, in its many national variants, expanded. In general, there was an attempt to provide greater social security through the extension of old age benefits and unemployment insurance, to provide more universal access to health care, and to increase vocational opportunity by expanding access to education. Another goal of the welfare state was the elimination of poverty. Among the most incisive conservative critics of this latter campaign was the American political scientist Edward Banfield.

The expansion of the American welfare state known as the "the Great Society" began during the Kennedy Administration with the Omnibus Housing Act in 1961, which aimed at the elimination of slums through "urban renewal," and the Manpower Development and Training Act, which sought to train the unemployed for skilled labor. In 1963 the socialist intellectual Michael Harrington published *The Other America*. The book focused the attention of opinion makers on the extent of ongoing poverty amid an increasingly affluent society, and led to calls for government action to eliminate poverty. Government experts assigned by President Kennedy to come up with an anti-poverty program noted the limits of what was known about effectively combatting poverty, and recommended a series of small-scale demonstration projects. But after the assassination of Kennedy, the new president, Lyndon Johnson, seeking to make his political mark, demanded that his advisors come up with something that would be "big and bold and hit the whole nation with real impact." In his State of the Union message of January 1964, Johnson proclaimed that "this administration today, here and now, declares unconditional war on poverty in America."[1]

From 1964 through 1968, federal spending on the poor rose from twelve billion dollars per annum to twenty-seven billion.[2] Programs were designed to create greater opportunities for children of the poor, especially those in black slums, on the theory that juvenile delinquency

---

[1] Allen J. Matusow, *The Unraveling of America: A History of Liberalism in the 1960s* (New York, 1984), pp. 103–24.

[2] Ibid., p. 240.

was a rational response to the lack of opportunities in impoverished urban settings. In 1965 the government launched the Job Corps, which created residential centers to train inner city youth for the job market.[3] A Community Action Program was funded with a mandate that its programs be "developed, conducted, and administered with maximum feasible participation of residents," that is, by the poor themselves. The Office of Economic Opportunity was created with widely ramified powers. After the passage of major civil rights bills in 1964 and 1965, the civil rights movement turned from desegregating the American South to demanding jobs and greater economic equality for American blacks, increasing the pressure on government to eliminate urban poverty. When asked at a Senate hearing in 1966 how long he thought it would take to win the War on Poverty, the head of President Johnson's anti-poverty program, Sargeant Shriver, replied "About ten years."

Attention to the urban poor was further heightened in August of 1966 when riots erupted in Watts, a poor black neighborhood in Los Angeles. The civil insurrection went on for five days, and was quelled with the aid of the National Guard. The next summer was more violent still, as 164 racial disturbances flared in cities across America and National Guard units occupied parts of eight major cities.[4] The problems of America's cities, it was widely claimed, were getting worse instead of better.

Edward Banfield was a distinguished political scientist at Harvard University when he published *The Unheavenly City: The Nature and Future of Our Urban Crisis* in 1970. Before coming to Harvard he had studied and taught at the University of Chicago, and he shared the skepticism of his Chicago colleague Milton Friedman regarding governmental intervention in social and economic processes. Banfield had written and edited half a dozen books on American urban politics and the problems of big cities, and had chaired a pre-inauguration Task Force on Urban Affairs for President-elect Richard M. Nixon in 1968–1969. He combined empirical social scientific analysis with a deeply conservative sensibility.

Both American liberals and conservatives in the 1960s embraced the notion of a "culture of poverty," a phrase coined by the anthropologist Oscar Lewis. To liberals, the concept suggested that the culture of the poor, which limited their upward social mobility, could be transformed by government agencies such as schools, enrichment programs for preschool children, and job training programs. In *The Unheavenly City*, Banfield too focused on the cultural determinants of class, but he was far more pessimistic about the plausibility of the suggested remedies. His

---

[3] Ibid., p. 238.   [4] Ibid., pp. 214–15.

book called attention to the significance of lower-class culture in explaining the persistence of poverty. It was not the *race* of poor blacks, but the cultural characteristics which they shared with poor whites that made the escape from poverty so difficult, he argued. But these cultural and behavioral characteristics, Banfield suggested, were more difficult to change than liberal reformers tended to assume.

Drawing upon a mountain of social scientific research on social class, Banfield contended that each class exhibits a distinct pattern of attitudes, values, and modes of behavior. Central to each pattern, he argued, was the degree of orientation toward the future. While he discussed the upper, middle, and working classes in these terms, Banfield was particularly interested in the difference between the time-orientation of these "normal" classes and that of what he called the "lower class." The members of that class, he wrote, tended to display an extreme present-orientation, which had little place for the planning and deferred gratification so essential to functioning in modern society. Much of the futility of contemporary social policy, he claimed, was based on confusing the lower class with the working class, and he sought to highlight their differences in behavior and in future orientation. "The lower-class person lives from moment to moment, he is either unable or unwilling to take account of the future or to control his impulses. Improvidence and irresponsibility are direct consequences of this failure to take the future into account . . . and these consequences have further consequences: being improvident and irresponsible, he is likely also to be unskilled, to move frequently from one dead-end job to another, to be a poor husband and father . . ." Thus the culture of lower class males, Banfield wrote, stressed "masculinity" and "action" and tended to be unstable and violent.[5] And that pattern of behavior tended to be culturally transmitted from generation to generation.

The Unheavenly City was replete with the recurrent conservative themes of human imperfection and the unanticipated negative consequences of governmental action. In focusing on the culture of the lower class as an ongoing determinant of social position, Banfield linked the recurrent conservative emphasis on the importance of manners and mores with the theme of the ineluctability of inequality. The book concluded with an ironic and anti-humanitarian message: the prime beneficiaries of government programs aimed at the elimination of urban poverty, he suggested, were the humanitarian consciences of the upper classes. As for the concrete effects of the War on Poverty programs on poverty, they were negative when they were not merely worthless.

[5] Edward C. Banfield, *The Unheavenly City Revisited* (1974, reprinted 1990), pp. 53–54, 63.

The Unheavenly City was a *succès de scandale*. The book sold one hundred thousand copies, an extraordinary number for a work of social scientific analysis. It was greeted with rage by liberal and leftist intellectuals. At a time when the American New Left was just beyond the peak of its strength and vehemence, the book and its author were vilified on campuses from coast to coast. At Harvard, the leading New Left group on campus, Students for a Democratic Society, held regular demonstrations denouncing Banfield. His scheduled lectures at a number of major universities were canceled due to threats of violence.[6] The book also generated a wave of responses by other social scientists.

In 1974, Banfield published a revised version of his book under the title *The Unheavenly City Revisited*, in which he sought to clarify his claims and complement the book's theses with additional information. The selection below is taken from the concluding chapters of that book. Banfield's footnotes have been excised.

Edward Banfield,
The Unheavenly City Revisited (1974)[1]

THE FUTURE OF THE LOWER CLASS

So long as the city contains a sizable lower class, nothing basic can be done about its most serious problems. Good jobs may be offered to all, but some will remain chronically unemployed. Slums may be demolished, but if the housing that replaces them is occupied by the lower class it will shortly be turned into new slums. Welfare payments may be doubled or tripled and a negative income tax instituted, but some persons will continue to live in squalor and misery. New schools may be built, new curricula devised, and the teacher-pupil ratio cut in half, but if the children who attend these schools come from lower-class homes, the schools will be turned into blackboard jungles, and those who graduate or drop out from them will in most cases, be functionally illiterate. The streets may be filled with armies of policemen, but violent crime and civil disorder will decrease very little. If, however, the lower class were to disappear—if, say, its members were overnight to acquire the attitudes,

---

[6] Nicholas Lemann, *The Promised Land: The Great Black Migration and How it Changed America* (New York, 1991), pp. 178–79; T. R. Marmor, "Banfield's 'Heresy,'" *Commentary*, July 1972, pp. 86–88.

[1] From Edward C. Banfield, *The Unheavenly City Revisited* (Boston, 1974; reissued Prospect Heights, IL, 1990).

motivations, and habits of the working class—the most serious and intractable problems of the city would all disappear with it.

As the last several chapters have contended, the serious problems of the city all exist in two forms—a normal-class and a lower-class form—which are fundamentally different from each other. In its normal-class form, the employment problem, for example, consists mainly of young people who are just entering the labor market and who must make a certain number of trials and errors before finding suitable jobs; in its lower-class form, it consists of people who prefer the "action" of the street to any steady job. The poverty problem in its normal-class form consists of people (especially the aged, the physically handicapped, and mothers with dependent children) whose only need in order to live decently is money; in its lower-class form it consists of people who would live in squalor and misery even if their incomes were doubled or tripled. The same is true with the other problems—slum housing, schools, crime, rioting; each is really two quite different problems. The lower-class forms of all problems are at bottom a single problem: the existence of an outlook and style of life which is radically present-oriented and which therefore attaches no value to work, sacrifice, self-improvement, or service to family, friends, or community. . . .

Whether lower-class outlook and style of life will change—or can be changed—and, if so, under what circumstances and at what rate—are questions of great interest to policymakers. As was pointed out when the concept of class culture was introduced [earlier in the book], social scientists differ as to the relative importance of "social heredity" and "social machinery" in forming class patternings of attitudes, values, and modes of behavior. As was said before, both sets of influences are undoubtedly at work and interact in complex ways; undoubtedly, too, the relative importance of these forces, as well as the nature of their interaction, differs from one group to another and from one individual to another.

Whether because (as Walter B. Miller has insisted in a brilliant essay) they have been caught up in an ideological movement or for some other reason, since the late 1950s most social scientists have discounted heavily the view that the lower-class person has been permanently damaged by having been assimilated in infancy and early childhood into a pathological culture and instead have come to view the lower-class life style as an adaptation to the realities of poverty, racial and class discrimination, bad schooling, poor or nonexistent job opportunities, and, in general, "blocked opportunities."

From the standpoint of its theorists, the War on Poverty of the 1960s represented an effort to eliminate the lower class. (That "poverty" was not to be regarded as solely, or even mainly, a matter of low income was stressed by Michael Harrington in *The Other America*, a book which did much to create the public opinion that made possible the War on Poverty. His "most important analytic point," Harrington wrote, was that *"poverty in America forms a culture, a way of life and feeling."*) Few social scientists supposed that raising incomes would of itself bring about the desired changes in the life style of "the poor." Higher incomes were a necessary but not a sufficient condition for this. It was crucial to change the "opportunity structure" in many ways: by ending racial discrimination, providing job training, improving schools, housing, and health care, and enabling and encouraging "the poor" to participate in the making of neighborhood and community decisions. A "service strategy," as it was called, would lead to higher incomes, but, what was of fundamental importance, it would change the individual's attitudes and habits, cause him to gain self-confidence and self-respect, and thus render him able and willing to move out of lower-class and into normal ("mainstream") culture.

Whatever its achievements in other directions, the War on Poverty did not change the style of life of "the poor." . . .

Even on the most optimistic assumptions as to the inducements offered them and their willingness and ability to respond to them, it is safe to say that lower-class persons will not disappear in the foreseeable future. Although a very small part of the population, they are nevertheless numerous enough to generate social problems—violent crime, for example—of great seriousness in the eyes of the society and there is at least the possibility that their numbers will increase rather than decrease in the future. It is necessary, therefore, to consider further the future of that portion of the lower class—a small one, perhaps—which will persist no matter what changes are made in "social machinery.". . .

What Can Be Done?

Often travelers, technical advisers, or "old hands" from a given country return with tales of how disorganized, dishonest, or untrustworthy the people are; but once the tales have been told, everyone settles down to a theoretical description of, or plan for, the economy of that country which does not take into account in any formal way the psychological characteristics of the people just described.—David McClelland

It will be convenient to approach the question that forms the title of this chapter by distinguishing the feasible from the acceptable. A measure is *feasible* if (and only if) government (local, state, or national)

could constitutionally implement it and if its implementation would result in the achievement of some specified goal or level of output at a cost
that is not obviously prohibitive. For example, it is not feasible for every
city dweller to have a one-acre lot (physical reality prevents), for every
child to get a high school education as distinguished from a high school
diploma (social and perhaps even biological reality prevent), to prohibit
the movement of the poor from one city to another (this would be unconstitutional), or to replace the present cities with new ones in the
space of a few years (the cost would be wildly out of relation to the
benefits). The acceptability of a measure does not depend upon its feasibility: a measure is *acceptable* if those who have authority in government
(elected or appointed officials or sometimes voters) are willing to try to
carry it into effect. Thus, a measure could be entirely feasible but quite
unacceptable or entirely acceptable and quite infeasible.

It goes without saying that it is often impossible to know in advance
whether a particular measure is either feasible or acceptable. One can
rarely be sure that the knowledge needed to make the measure "work"
is at hand or within reach; its constitutionality may be in doubt; and
there is always some possibility that unanticipated consequences will
make its cost prohibitively high. ("Cost" in this context means any undesired effect or forgone advantage, not just an outlay of money or material resources.) These practical difficulties do not affect the validity
of the distinction, however, or destroy its usefulness for purposes of
analysis.

This chapter tries to show, first, that the range of feasible measures for
dealing with the serious problems of the cities is much narrower than
one might think, and, second, that within this range hardly any of the
feasible measures are acceptable. If what is feasible is not, in general,
acceptable, the reverse is also true: what is acceptable is not, in general, feasible. Moreover, government seems to have a perverse tendency
to adopt measures which—if the analysis in the preceding chapters is not
far wrong—are the very opposite of those that one would recommend.[2]
The reasons for this perversity are to be found in the nature of American
political institutions and, especially, in the influence on public opinion
of the upper-class cultural ideal of "service" and "responsibility to the
community."[3]

Clearly, a measure is infeasible if aimed at the simultaneous attainment of mutually exclusive ends. Two persons cannot both be satisfied
if one's satisfaction is *constituted* of the other's nonsatisfaction. Insofar

[2] An example of the conservative emphasis on the unintended negative consequences of
deliberate action.

[3] Banfield annunciates the antihumanitarian theme of the critique of good intentions
that figures prominently in this chapter.

as the poverty problem, for example, has this relational character (that is, insofar as it is one of "relative deprivation"), it is insoluble. In Hollywood, Leo C. Rosten writes, "it is natural for the actress who earns $20,000 a year to envy the actress who earns $50,000 who envies the actress making $100,000. In a community where one can make $350,000 a year, $75,000 a year is not especially impressive—either to the group or the self." The same problem arises, of course, even in the least glamorous places and with people of very ordinary income. That objective differences in income can be reduced to almost nothing does not necessarily mean that the problem of relative deprivation can be solved, for the smaller objective difference in income may come to have a greater subjective importance. The same problem arises with the distribution of things other than income. It is in the nature of deference, for example, that some persons receive more than others. There is really no way to prevent those who receive relatively little from perceiving that fact and being made unhappy or suffering a loss of self-respect because of it. As Frank H. Knight has written, "The real scarcity which seriously afflicts individualistic civilization is the scarcity of such things as distinction, spectacular achievements, honor, victory, and power." Since there can never be enough of these things to go around, the problem of poverty with respect to them is logically insoluble.

There are many other major problems which, although they differ from this one in (presumably) not having a logical structure that makes them inherently insolvable, are nevertheless unsolved and, for all anyone knows, may remain so. Although an economist of the first rank, Kenneth J. Arrow, has recently said that he thinks it "most likely that the reconciliation of full employment and price stability can be significantly improved in the future," the problem appears to be one that cannot be eliminated. A problem of even greater magnitude which seems no less resistant to solution is that of ensuring that all children acquire the attitudes and skills without which they cannot live on mutually acceptable terms with society later on.[4] Albert K. Cohen, in his path-breaking book of nearly twenty years ago, *Delinquent Boys: The Culture of the Gang*, posed a series of questions which have gone unanswered:

> Of these various circumstances and features of our social system which are involved in the production of the delinquent subculture, which are subject to deliberate control? From the purely technical standpoint, exactly how is it possible to manipulate them in accordance with our wishes? How, for example, can we enable the work-

---

[4] The conservative theme of human imperfectibility is here linked to the emphasis on manners and mores.

ing-class male to compete more effectively for status in a largely middle-class world. . . ? What price are we willing to pay for this or that change?

When "solutions" are offered without specification of the means by which they are to be reached, it must be presumed that the means—if any exist—have yet to be discovered and that the "solution" is therefore infeasible. Doubtless a "change in the hearts and minds of men" would solve a great many problems. But how is it to be brought about? Except as the means are outlined and except as there is some real possibility of their being implemented, such "solutions" are mere words. They are seldom if ever labeled as such, however, even when put forward by highly professional social analysts. Consider, for example, the following, written not as a Commencement Day Oration but as a contribution to a leading journal of economics:

> We believe that resolution of the [urban] crisis is possible if political majorities are future-oriented enough to adopt constitutional reforms which not only benefit the lower classes but serve the majority's long-run self-interest. If these political majorities have the foresight to adopt fundamental, constitutional-type change, fulfillment can be harnessed to hope, and an urban society that is just, humane, and truly free can be a reality.

The authors stop there. They offer no grounds whatever for believing that political majorities *will* change their ways and they say not a word about the steps that one (who?) might take to get them to do so.

Those who use the terminology of social science may talk of changing "culture," rather than "hearts and minds." The fact is, however, that no one knows how to change the culture of any part of the population—the lower class or the upper, whites or Negroes, pupils or teachers, policemen or criminals. Moreover, even if one *did* know how, there is good reason to suppose that doing so would be infeasible on other grounds; for example, it might require unconstitutional methods, such as taking infants from their parents at birth, or entail other disadvantages that more than offset its advantages.

What can an educational psychologist, Jerome Bruner, mean by writing that the plight of the poor in our society probably cannot be changed without first changing "the society that permits such poverty to exist" and that accordingly his "first recommendation, as a common-sense psychologist and a concerned man, would be that we should transform radically the structure of our society"? Can it be that he thinks "society" is an entity having faculties enabling it to "permit" conditions to exist—that is, to exercise choice regarding them? (If so, why not criticize it for permitting *any* social problem to exist?) Assuming that society *is* able to permit, is it likely to permit "us" to transform it in such a way that it can no longer permit what it previously permitted, namely poverty? Assuming that it *will* permit this, how does one transform radically the structure of a society? (Apparently it is not always easy; Christopher Jencks remarks sadly in *Inequality* that the rate of social mobility "does not seem to respond to most of the things that social theorists expect it to respond to.") Finally, assuming that the effort would succeed, what grounds are there for supposing that the new, restructured society will not permit evils even worse than poverty?

Some "solutions" are infeasible because (1) there is no reason to expect people to do the things that would constitute a solution unless government motivates them to do them, and (2) government for one reason or another cannot so motivate them. If, as Lee Rainwater asserts, "only effective protest can change endemic patterns of police harassment and brutality, or teachers' indifference and insults, or butchers' heavy thumbs, or indifferent street cleaning and garbage disposal," then (assuming that effective protest must be carried on from *outside* the government) measures to correct these abuses lie beyond the bounds of feasibility. In other words, if there *are* solutions to these problems they are not *governmental* ones, which is to say that one cannot implement them by calling into play the state's ultimate monopoly on the use of force.

Repeal of the minimum-wage laws is certainly feasible, but elimination of the *informal* minimum wage, which would reduce unemployment among the low-skilled even more, is not. Government cannot prevent the formation of a social definition of what is a "decent" wage, and (what amounts to the same thing) it cannot prevent workers from feeling some loss of self-respect in working for "peanuts." From the standpoint of the policymaker, then, the informal minimum wage presents an insoluble problem.

In the nature of the case, it is impossible to have a very clear idea of what government can and cannot do in the way of forming public opinion. Nothing except the elimination of lower-class culture would contribute as much to a general solution of the urban problem as would certain changes in public opinion—for example, greater awareness of the importance of class-cultural and other nonracial factors in the Negro's situation and a more realistic sense of what levels of performance it is reasonable to expect from such institutions as schools and police forces and from the economy as a whole. However, it is very questionable to what extent, if at all, government can bring these changes about. It is a question also whether *if* it can bring them about it *ought* to—that is, whether the unintended and long-run effects of a strenuous exercise of its opinion-forming capacities would not be likely to change American society for the worse rather than for the better.

People often respond to government measures by making adaptations the aggregate effect of which is to render the measures ineffective or even injurious. Thus, for example, the principal obstacle in the way of permanently maintaining full employment by fiscal policy devices is that investors respond to the price outlook in such a way as to check any policy except the impossible one of a continuous and accelerating inflation. Other examples of the same phenomenon are easy to find. Subsidies to induce employers to hire "hard-core" workers achieve very little because the employers tend to make adjustments (which may be perfectly legitimate) that enable them to take the subsidies while employing workers who are not significantly different from those whom they would have employed anyway. Similarly, efforts to reduce unemployment, poverty, or slum housing in a particular city may be counterproductive in that they attract more poor workers to the city. Thus, the *Wall Street Journal* reports from Detroit:

> A massive industry effort to help avert future riots in Detroit appears to be backfiring as hundreds—possibly thousands—of unemployed persons from out of state come to the city seeking work.
>
> The result: Some out-of-staters have failed to get a job, swelling the unemployment that many believe contributed to last July's riot.
>
> Others have snapped up jobs that might have gone to the city's own so-called hard-core unemployed.

There is much to be said for the idea of giving small sums at any hour of day or night to persons, mostly youths, who might otherwise steal or kill to get the price of a few drinks or a "fix" of heroin. It would not be feasible to do this, however, because of the adaptive behavior that it would evoke. Once it became known that money was being given away (and of course the scheme would not work unless it *was* known), the demand would become too great to satisfy.

Essentially the same problem may exist with any welfare program that offers generous support to all who can be considered poor. Such a program may weaken rather than strengthen the self-esteem of its beneficiaries by reinforcing their impression that events are beyond their control. It may also encourage them to adapt to the new situation in ways that are in the long run disadvantageous to them and destructive of the welfare system itself—for example, by taking steps to make themselves eligible (the wife leaving her job, perhaps, or lying about the number of dependents) they may "swamp" the system with their numbers. As Levitan, Rein, and Marwick remark, "Adequate benefits to relieve poverty conflict with a coherent incentive system to encourage work" and "all the good will and exhortation of welfare reformers have failed to offer a viable solution . . . to the dilemma."

Some "solutions" are infeasible because the very feature(s) of social reality that constitute the problem make them impracticable. Training programs do not as a rule offer any solution to the problem of hard-core unemployment because the same qualities that make a worker hard-core also make him unable or unwilling to accept training. More generally, giving lower-class persons "really good" jobs is not a feasible way of inducing them to change their style of life, because that very style of life makes it impossible to give them "really good" jobs.

"Solutions" that deal with minor, as opposed to key or strategic, factors in a situation are also infeasible. To put the matter in another way, it does not help to create a necessary condition when there is no way of creating the sufficient conditions; similarly, in situations of multiple causation, it is of little use to set in motion a cause that contributes a trivial amount to the total effect desired when there is no way to set in motion those that would contribute a significant amount to it. It is less than likely that the McCone Commission, in its report on the background of the Watts riot, was correct in asserting that "an adequate mid-day meal is essential to a meaningful educational experience" (it may be a contributing factor, but it is certainly not *essential*). Even assuming for the sake of argument that the commission *was* correct, the conclusion does not follow that a school lunch program would have an appreciable effect on the problem of preventing riots of the sort that occurred in Watts. The school lunch program "solution," however desirable it might be on other grounds, would not touch a great many much more important causes that would make riots just as likely as ever.

The assumption that an improvement in material welfare is bound to make a major contribution to the solution of almost any social problem is a pervasive one: better nutrition, better housing, better transportation, better street cleaning and refuse removal—all such things are commonly seen as ways of reducing crime, of preventing the break-up of the family, of encouraging upward social mobility, and so on. Although one cannot often find clear evidence of it, such measures probably do have *some* such effects. Even so, the policymaker must ask with regard to them the question that was raised about midday meals: Is the contribution that this *one* cause can make to the total effect (i.e. to the "solution" of the problem) likely to be more than trivial? Following such a procedure in his discussion of the efficacy of various types of social policy in reducing the "deficits" of the average Negro, James S. Coleman finds that housing, health, and public education (for example) are fields from which the contributions are likely to be small in relation to the problem.

Even if it is feasible in all other respects, a measure lies outside the bounds of feasibility if its implementation would entail costs that more than offset its benefits. The proponents of a particular measure are usually blessed with both myopia and tunnel vision: they can see only the immediate and direct effects that would follow from the attainment of their objective; long-run or indirect effects, especially ones pertinent to what may be called background values, are quite invisible to them. Proponents of rent control, for example, see an immediate advantage to the poor in freezing rents at low levels. But they fail to see the harm that this will do to the whole community—and especially to the poor—because the harm will be indirect and more or less delayed. One immediate—but somewhat indirect and therefore hard to see—injury to the poor consists in preventing them from outbidding the nonpoor for housing that they (the poor) could afford because they would occupy it more intensively. (As Thomas Sowell points out, rent control drastically reduces any incentive real estate agents and landlords have to break down ethnic and racial barriers.) Another immediate but somewhat indirect injury to the poor is the lowering of maintenance standards and services—heat and light, for example—that occurs when the landlord is bound to get the same (fixed) rent no matter how much or little he does for his tenants. In the longer run—and therefore harder to see—are injuries to neighborhoods and to the city as a whole: the formation of slums as buildings go unrepaired year after year, the growing frustration and anger of those who cannot move because they are not permitted to compete for housing, and the decrease in the total housing supply because investors, who in the absence of rent control would build new units or rehabilitate old ones, decide to put their money elsewhere.

An important special case of infeasibility resulting from a disproportion between costs and benefits exists when the implementation of a measure would require organization of a kind unsuitable for the implementation of other, equally desirable measures. Coleman, in making this point, remarks that it is safe to say that no city will consciously unequalize schools in order to pull suburbanites back into the city or stabilize neighborhoods. It is not for lack of social organization that cities will fail to do this, he says, but because of organization that is inappropriate; whether there could be organization appropriate to solve this problem and yet not inappropriate to solve other problems he considers questionable. "Paradoxically," he concludes, "in this instance organization itself helps bring about disorganization and disintegration of the city."

There follows a list of some of the principal measures that might well be regarded as feasible by one who accepts the analysis in the previous chapters. (It will be recalled that by "feasible" is meant capable of being implemented and likely to accomplish something of more than trivial value at a cost not obviously prohibitive.) It will be seen that the list is rather short; that many of the items on it are not "constructive"—that is, they call for *not* doing something; and that far from being a comprehensive program for making the city into what one would like, it hardly begins to solve any of the problems that have been under discussion. Even if all the recommendations were carried out to the full, the urban situation would not be fundamentally improved. Feasible measures are few and unsatisfactory as compared to what it would be nice to have happen or what one would do if one were dictator. What is more to the present point, however, *hardly any of the feasible measures are acceptable.* The list is as follows:

1. Assure to all equal access to polling places, courts, and job, housing, and other markets.

2. Avoid rhetoric tending to raise expectations to unreasonable and unrealizable levels, to encourage the individual to think that "society" (e.g., "white racism"), not he, is responsible for his ills, and to exaggerate both the seriousness of social problems and the possibility of finding solutions.

3. If it is feasible to do so (the disagreement among economists has been noted earlier), use fiscal policy to keep the general unemployment level below 3 percent. In any case, remove impediments to the employment of the unskilled, the unschooled, the young, Negroes, women, and others by (a) repealing the minimum-wage and occupational licensure laws and laws that enable labor unions to exercise monopolistic powers, (b) ceasing to overpay for low-skilled public employment, (c) ceasing to harass private employers who offer low wages and unattractive (but not unsafe) working conditions to workers whose alternative is unemployment, and (d) offer wage supplements in the form of "scholarships" to enable boys and girls who have received little schooling to get jobs with employers who offer valuable on-the-job training.

4. Revise elementary and secondary school curricula so as to cover in nine grades what is now covered in twelve. Reduce the school-leaving age to fourteen (grade 9), and encourage (or perhaps even require) boys and girls who are unable or unwilling to go to college to take a full-time job or else enter military service or a civilian youth corps. Guarantee loans for higher education to all who require them. Assure the availability of serious on-the-job training for all boys and girls who choose to go to work rather than to go to college.

5. Define poverty in terms of the nearly fixed standard of "hardship," rather than in terms of the elastic one of "relative deprivation," and bring all incomes above the poverty line. Distinguish categorically between those of the poor who are competent to manage their affairs and

those of them who are not, the latter category consisting of the insane, the severely retarded, the senile, the lower class (inveterate "problem families"), and unprotected children. Make cash income transfers to the first category by means of a negative income tax, the rate structure of which gives the recipient a strong incentive to work. Whenever possible, assist the incompetent poor with goods and services rather than with cash; depending upon the degree of their incompetence, encourage (or require) them to reside in an institution or semi-institution (for example, a closely supervised public housing project).

6. Give intensive birth-control guidance to the incompetent poor.

7. Pay "problem families" to send infants and children to day nurseries and preschools, the programs of which are designed to bring the children into normal culture.

8. Regulate insurance and police practices so as to give potential victims of crime greater incentive to take reasonable precautions to prevent it.

9. Intensify police patrol in high-crime areas; permit the police to "stop and frisk" and to make misdemeanor arrests on probable cause; institute a system of "negative bail"—that is, an arrangement whereby a suspect who is held in jail and is later found innocent is paid compensation for each day of confinement.

10. Reduce drastically the time elapsing between arrest, trial, and imposition of punishment.

11. Abridge to an appropriate degree the freedom of those who in the opinion of a court are extremely likely to commit violent crimes. Confine and treat drug addicts.

12. Make it clear in advance that those who incite to riot will be severely punished.

13. Prohibit "live" television coverage of riots and of incidents likely to provoke them.

There can be little doubt that with a few exceptions these recommendations are unacceptable. A politician with a heterogeneous constituency would strenuously oppose almost all of them. In most matters, the actual course of policy is likely to be the very opposite of the one recommended, whichever party is in power. Government is more likely to promote unequal than equal access to job and housing markets either by failing to enforce laws prohibiting discrimination or by "enforcing" them in a way (for example, by "affirmative action") that is itself discriminatory. It is also more likely to raise expectations than to lower them; to emphasize "white racism" as *the* continuing cause of the Negro's handicaps rather than to de-emphasize it; to increase the minimum wage rather than to decrease or repeal it; to keep children who cannot or will not learn in school a longer rather than a shorter time; to define poverty in terms of relative deprivation rather than in terms of hardship; to deny the existence of class-cultural differences rather than to try to distinguish the competent from the incompetent poor on this basis; to reduce the potential victim's incentives to take precautions against crime rather than to increase them; to give the police less discretionary authority rather than more; to increase the time between arrest, trial, and punishment rather than to decrease it; and to enlarge the freedom of those who have shown themselves to be very likely to commit violent crimes rather than to restrict it.

One reason why these recommendations are politically out of the question is that there exist well-armed and strategically placed veto groups (as David Riesman calls them in *The Lonely Crowd*) which can prevent them from being seriously discussed, much less adopted. The recommendation of the Moynihan Report, that government try to strengthen the Negro family, is a case in point: official consideration of this idea had to stop abruptly when the civil-rights organizations and their allies objected.[5] What these organizations did with this proposal organized labor could do with one to free up the labor market, organized teachers could do with one to reduce the school-leaving age, organized social workers could do with one to define poverty in terms of hardship, and so on.

That interest groups have such power does not represent a malfunctioning of the political system. When they designed the system, the Founding Fathers took great pains to distribute power widely so that "factions" would check one another, thus preventing the rise of any sort of tyranny. The arrangement has worked remarkably well, but there is no denying that it has the defects of its virtues. One of these defects is that a small minority can often veto measures that would benefit a large majority.

Obviously, proposals are frequently adopted despite the opposition of such groups. Why does this not happen in the case of the measures recommended above? There are more prospective gainers than losers from each measure (if this were not thought to be so, the measures would not have been recommended); why, then, do not the prospective gainers organize themselves to overcome the opposition of the veto groups? At the very least, why do they not themselves function as veto groups when

---

[5] In 1965 the US Department of Labor published "The Negro Family: The Case for Action," by Daniel Patrick Moynihan, then an assistant secretary in the department. In it he called attention to the fact that the out-of-wedlock birth rate among blacks was 26 percent, which he regarded as part of "the tangle of pathology" among the black poor, along with factors such as poor school performance and high rates of male desertion, welfare dependency, and crime. The report was denounced by the left for "blaming the victim"; the vehement response to the report stilled any discussion of the state of the black family in mainstream liberal circles.

the opposites of the measures that would serve their interests are proposed? For example, if they cannot get the minimum-wage law repealed, why do they not at least prevent the rate from being raised?

Part of the answer to these questions is that in most instances the benefits from the recommended measures would be what economists call "public goods"—that is, goods such that if *anyone* benefited *everyone* would benefit. This being the case, the prospective gainers can "ride free" and therefore have little or no incentive to contribute to the support of an organization to fight for the benefits. Another part of the answer is that the voter must usually accept or reject *combinations* of measures (what the candidate or the party stands for); he cannot pick and choose, he must cast his vote one way or the other. His choice therefore turns upon his evaluation of the one or two items in the "package" that touch his primary (which in many cases means his bread-and-butter) interests most closely; if he thinks that his primary interests are well served by these one or two items, he will vote in favor of the "package" even though it contains many other items that are undesirable from the standpoint of his subsidiary interests. Thus, even if the measures recommended above would benefit every voter without exception, there would nevertheless be a unanimous vote against them if they were presented in combinations such that each voter could serve one of his primary interests only by voting against them. In their effort to bring together winning coalitions of interests, candidates and parties tend to be very much aware of such considerations.

Public opinion consists largely of opinions on subjects that do *not* touch the primary interests of the one holding the opinion, and if political choices were made only in the light of primary interests, public opinion would matter very little. In fact, of course, it matters a good deal. And there can be no doubt that it supports practically none of the recommendations on the list above. Indeed, in many matters it favors the opposite. In part, then, the perversity that government exhibits in its choice of measures reflects a corresponding perversity in public opinion.

It is pertinent to inquire, therefore, why *public opinion* is perverse. An answer sometimes given is that in matters such as these it is generally dominated by the opinion of the well-educated and well-off. These people (so the argument runs) are indifferent to or downright hostile to the interest of the less well-off and the poor. In short, the "masses" are against the recommended measures because they have been misled by an elite that is looking after its own interests.

The trouble with this theory is that with respect to most measures it runs counter to the facts. The well-off are not benefited by an increase in the minimum wage or by any other measures that price low-value labor out of the market and onto the welfare rolls. They are not benefited by laws that keep children who cannot or will not learn in schools that they (the well-off) must support. They are not benefited by the making of sweeping charges about "white racism" or by crisis-mongering of any kind.

Public opinion is indeed decisively influenced in many matters by the opinion of the well-educated and well-off. But this opinion, which reflects the "service" ideal of the upper class, tends to be altruistic. And it is precisely this altruistic bias that accounts for its perversity.[6]

The American political style was formed largely in the upper classes and, within those classes, mainly by people of dissenting-Protestant and Jewish traditions. Accordingly, it is oriented toward the future and toward moral and material progress, for the individual and for the society as a whole. The American is confident that with a sufficient effort all difficulties can be overcome and all problems solved, and he feels a strong obligation to try to improve not only himself but everything else: his community, his society, the whole world. Ever since the days of Cotton Mather, whose *Bonifacius* was a how-to-do-it book on the doing of good, service has been the American motto. To be sure, practice has seldom entirely corresponded to principles. The principles, however, have always been influential and they have sometimes been decisive. They can be summarized in two very simple rules: first, DON'T JUST SIT THERE. DO SOMETHING! and second, DO GOOD!

These two rules contribute to the perversity that characterizes the choice of measures for dealing with the urban "crisis." From the President on down everyone (almost everyone) enjoys the feeling of exhilaration when a bold step is taken, and that enjoyment is no less when, as it almost always must be, the step is taken blindfold. Believing that any problem can be solved if only we try hard enough, we do not hesitate to attempt what we do not have the least idea of how to do and what, in some instances, reason and experience both tell us cannot be done. Not recognizing any bounds to what is feasible, we are not reconciled to—indeed, we do not even perceive—the necessity, so frequently arising, of choosing the least objectionable among courses of action that are all very unsatisfactory. That some children simply cannot be taught much in school is one example of a fact that the American mind will not entertain. Our cultural ideal requires that we give every child a good education whether he wants it or not and whether he is capable of receiving it or not. If at first we don't succeed, we must try, try again. And if in the end we don't succeed, we must feel guilty for our failure. To lower the school-leaving age would be, in the terms of this secular religion, a shirking of the task for which we were chosen.

---

[6] Banfield returns to the antihumanitarian critique of good intentions.

The recommendations listed earlier are mostly unacceptable, even repellent, to public opinion because what they call for does not appear to be and (although this is beside the point) may in fact not be morally improving either to the doer or to the object of his doing. It does not appear to be improving to a youth to send him to work rather than to school, especially as this is what it is in one's interest as a taxpayer to do. It does not appear to be improving to a recidivist to keep him in jail pending trial, especially as this is what accords with one's feelings of hostility toward him. It does not appear to be improving to a slum dweller to say that if he has an adequate income but prefers to spend it for things other than housing he must not expect the public to intervene, especially as it is in one's "selfish" interest that the public not intervene. In reality, the doing of good is not so much for the benefit of those to whom the good is done as it is for that of the *doers*, whose moral faculties are activated and invigorated by the doing of it, and for that of the community, the shared values of which are ritually asserted and vindicated by the doing of it. For this reason, good done otherwise than by intention, especially good done in pursuance of ends that are selfish or even "nontuistic," [non-altruistic] is not really "good" at all. For this reason, too, actions taken from good motives count as good even when in fact they do harm. By far the most effective way of helping the poor is to keep profit-seekers competing vigorously for their trade as consumers and for their services as workers; this, however, is not a way of helping that affords members of the upper classes the chance to flex their moral muscles or the community the chance to dramatize its commitment to the values that hold it together. The way to do these things is with a War on Poverty; even if the War should turn out to have precious little effect on the incomes of the poor—indeed, even if it should *lower* their incomes—the undertaking would nevertheless represent a sort of secular religious revival that affords the altruistic classes opportunities to bear witness to the cultural ideal and, by doing so, to strengthen society's adherence to it. One recalls Macaulay's remark about the attitude of the English Puritans toward bear-baiting: that they opposed it not for the suffering that it caused the bear but for the pleasure that it gave the spectators. Perhaps it is not far-fetched to say that the present-day outlook is similar: the reformer wants to improve the situation of the poor, the black, the slum dweller, and so on, not so much to make them better off materially as to make himself and the whole society better off morally.

There is something to be said for this attitude. The Puritans were surely right in thinking it worse that people should enjoy the sufferings of animals than that animals should suffer. And the present-day reformers are surely right in thinking it more important that society display a concern for what is right and just than that the material level of the poor, which is already above the level of hardship in most cases, be raised somewhat higher. There are problems here, however. One is to keep the impulse for doing good from gushing incontinently into mass extravaganzas—domestic Marshall Plans, Freedom Budgets, and the like—into which billions are poured for no one knows what or how; surely, if it is to be morally significant, good cannot be done from motives that are contrived for the individual by people who have large organizations to maintain or foisted upon him by the mass media. Another problem is to find ways of doing good that are relatively harmless—that do not greatly injure those to whom the good is done (as, for example, children who cannot or will not learn are injured by too-long confinement in school), that are not grossly unfair to third parties (taxpayers, for example), and that do not tend to damage the consensual basis, and thus eventually the political freedom, of the society (as headline-catching official declarations about "white racism" do). Still another problem is to retain, as an element of the cultural ideal itself, what Lionel Trilling has termed moral realism—"the perception of the dangers of the moral life itself."

If the process of middle- and upper-class-ification tends to make public opinion more perverse, it also tends to make it more important. Half a century or more ago, the basis of city and state political power—and therefore, to a large extent, of national political power as well—was the machine. The bosses who ran it kept themselves in power by dispensing patronage and by trading in ethnic, sectional, and party loyalties, and therefore could pretty well disregard public opinion when it suited them to do so. Middle- and upper-class-ification rendered this system obsolete and brought into being one in which the politician, in order to compete successfully for office, has to combine offers of benefits to *classes* of voters (homeowners, taxpayers, and so on) with appeals to general ideas and conceptions of the public interest. Whereas the old system had promised personal rewards, the new one promises social reforms. Accordingly, the smoke-filled room was replaced by the talk-filled one. "The amount of talk which is now expended on all subjects of human interest is something of which a previous age has had not the smallest conception," E. L. Godkin remarked at the end of the last century, adding that "the affairs of nations and of men will be more and more regulated by talk." But even Godkin, since he did not anticipate television, had not the smallest conception of the extent to which affairs would be regulated by talk in our day.

The politician, like the TV news commentator, must always have something to say even when nothing urgently needs to be said. If he lived in a society without problems, he would have to invent some (and of course "solutions" along with them) in order to attract attention and to kindle the interest and enthusiasm needed to carry him into office and enable him, once there, to levy taxes and do the other unpopular things of which governing largely consists. Although in the society that actually exists there are many problems, there are still not enough—enough about which anyone can say or do anything very helpful—to meet his constant need for program material. Moreover, the real and important problems are not necessarily the ones that people want to hear about; a politician may be able to attract more attention and create more enthusiasm—and thus better serve his purpose, which is to generate power with which to take office and govern—by putting real problems in an unreal light or by presenting illusory ones as if they were real. The politician (again like the TV news commentator) can never publicly discuss an important matter with the seriousness that it deserves; time is short, ifs, ands, and buts make tedious listening, and there are always some in the audience who will be confused or offended by what is said and others who will try to twist it into a weapon that they can use against the speaker. Besides, the deeper a discussion goes, the less likelihood of reaching an outcome that the politician can use to generate support.

The changes brought about in the political system by the process of middle- and upper-class-ification have greatly reduced its effectiveness in finding the terms on which people will act together or even live together in peace. The upper-class ideal recommends participation as intrinsically good, but unfortunately, the more participants there are, the larger the number of issues that must be dealt with and the greater the disagreements about each. The ideal also requires that issues be settled on their merits, not by logrolling, and that their merits be conceived of in terms of general moral principles that may not, under any circumstances, be compromised. In the smoke-filled room, it was party loyalty and private interest that mainly moved men; these motives always permitted "doing business." In the talk-filled room, righteous indignation is the main motive, and therefore the longer the talk continues, the clearer it becomes to each side that the other must either be shouted down or knocked down.

If we look toward the future, it is impossible not to be apprehensive. The frightening fact is that large numbers of persons are being rapidly assimilated to the upper classes and are coming to have incomes—time as well as money—that permit them to indulge their taste for "service" and doing good in political action. Television, even more than the newspapers, tends to turn the discussion of public policy issues into a branch of the mass entertainment industry. Doing good is becoming—has already become—a growth industry, like the other forms of mass entertainment, while righteous indignation and uncompromising allegiance to principle are becoming *the* motives of political commitment. This is the way it is in the affluent, middle-class society. How will it be in the super-affluent, upper-middle-class one?

THE PROSPECT

It is impossible to avoid the conclusion that the serious problems of the cities will continue to exist in something like their present form for another twenty years at least. Even on the most favorable assumptions we shall have large concentrations of the poor and the unskilled, and—what, to repeat, is by no means the same thing—the lower class in the central cities and the larger, older suburbs. The outward movement of industry and commerce is bound to continue, leaving ever-larger parts of the inner city blighted or semi-abandoned. Even if we could afford to throw the existing cities away and build new ones from scratch, matters would not be essentially different, for the people who move into the new cities would take the same old problems with them. Eventually, the present problems of the cities will disappear or dwindle into relative unimportance; they will not, however, be "solved" by programs of the sort undertaken in the past decade. On the contrary, the tendency of such programs would be to prolong the problems and perhaps even make them worse.

For the most part, the problems in question have arisen from and are inseparably connected with developments that almost everyone welcomes: the growth and spread of affluence has enabled millions of people to move from congested cities to new and more spacious homes in the suburbs; the availability of a large stock of relatively good housing in the central cities and older suburbs has enabled the Negro to escape the semi-slavery of the rural South and, a century late, to move into industrial society; better public health measures and facilities have cut the deathrate of the lower class; the war and postwar baby boom have left the city with more adolescents and youths than ever before; and a widespread and general movement upward on the class-cultural scale has made poverty, squalor, ignorance, and brutality—conditions that have always and everywhere been regarded as inevitable in the nature of things—appear as anomalies that should be removed entirely and at once.

What stands in the way of dealing effectively with these problems (insofar as their nature admits of their being dealt with by government) is mainly the virtues of the American political system and of the American character. It is because governmental power is widely distributed that organized interests are so often able to veto measures that would benefit large numbers of people. It is the generous and public-regarding impulses of voters and taxpayers that impel them to support measures—for example, the minimum wage and compulsory high school attendance—the ultimate effect of which is to make the poor poorer and more demoralized. Our devotion to the doctrine that all men are created equal discourages any explicit recognition of class-cultural differences and leads to "democratic"—and often misleading—formulations of problems: for example, poverty as lack of income and material resources (something external to the individual) rather than as inability or unwillingness to take account of the future or to control impulses (something internal). Sympathy for the oppressed, indignation at the oppressor, and a wish to make amends for wrongs done by one's ancestors lead to a misrepresentation of the Negro as the near-helpless victim of "white racism." Faith in the perfectibility of man and confidence that good intentions together with strenuous exertions will hasten his progress onward and upward lead to bold programs that promise to do what no one knows how to do and what perhaps cannot be done, and therefore end in frustration, loss of mutual respect and trust, anger, and even coercion.

Even granting that in general the effect of government programs is to exacerbate the problems of the cities, it might perhaps be argued that they have a symbolic value that is more than redeeming. What economist Kenneth Boulding has said of national parks—that we seem to need them "as we seem to need a useless dome on the capitol, as a symbol of national identity and of that mutuality of concern and interest without which government would be naked coercion"—may possibly apply as well to Freedom Budgets, domestic Marshall Plans, and other such concoctions. That government programs do not succeed in reducing welfare dependency, preventing crime, and so on, is not a weighty objection to them if, for want of them the feeling would spread that the society is "not worth saving." There is an imminent danger, however, that the growing multitude of programs that are intended essentially as gestures of goodwill may constitute a bureaucratic juggernaut which cannot be stopped and which will symbolize not national identity and mutual concern but rather divisiveness, confusion, and inequity. If a symbol is wanted, a useless dome is in every way preferable. . . .

9

THE CRITIQUE OF
SOCIAL AND CULTURAL
EMANCIPATION

INTRODUCTION TO
Irving Kristol,
"Pornography, Obscenity, and the
Case for Censorship"

◆

"Society," wrote Burke in his *Reflections on the Revolution in France*, requires that "the inclinations of men should frequently be thwarted, their will controlled, and their passions brought into subjection. This can only be done *by a power out of themselves*; . . . In this sense the restraints on men, as well as their liberties, are to be reckoned among their rights." As we have seen, skepticism regarding attempts to liberate the individual from existing sources of social and cultural control has been among the most persistent propensities of conservative thought. It arose once again in the 1960s in regard to the censorship of pornography and obscenity: the issue of whether it is good for society and the individuals who comprise it to have the deliberate intensification of desire restricted by the law.

Two landmark cases before the Supreme Court transformed American obscenity law in the 1960s. The first concerned the publication of Henry Miller's *Tropic of Cancer* in 1964; the second, two years later, concerned the publication of an eighteenth-century erotic novel, *Memoirs of a Woman of Pleasure*, better known under the title "Fanny Hill." Justice William J. Brennan, Jr. wrote the opinion for the majority declaring that these works could not be banned as obscene. He presented three criteria for judging a work obscene: it must have "prurient appeal," be "patently offensive," and comprised of material "utterly without redeeming social value." The latter criterion made it virtually impossible to ban a work as obscene, since it was always possible to find some expert who would testify that the work in question had some redeeming social value.[1] In its loosening of the laws of obscenity, the Supreme Court was reflecting liberal opinion and the spirit of the times, in which "repression" in general was disparaged. The virtual repeal of obscenity law lifted the legal flood-gates, and within a short time the now unrestrained profit-motive led to a deluge of commercially purveyed pornographic images.[2]

Amidst a wave of what one observer called "massive desublimation" a few conservative voices defended the legitimacy of governmentally enforced constraint. Among them was Irving Kristol, then a rising star in the American intellectual firmament, who in 1971 published the essay below, "Pornography, Obscenity, and the Case for Censorship." Like previous conservative intellectuals, Kristol attempted to offer good reasons for traditional practices which had come to be challenged and seemed on the verge of elimination.

In the essay, Kristol referred to himself as a "liberal," a characterization he was soon to jettison in favor of "Neoconservative." As so often occurs in the history of political culture, the label was originally coined as a term of opprobrium but came to be embraced by its erstwhile targets. The "neo" was partly biographical and partly substantive.[3] In terms of biography, it reflected the fact that Kristol had not always identified himself as a conservative. As a college student during the last years of the Great Depression, he had briefly been a Trotskyite (though in the peculiar cultural milieu in which he came of age, this was one of the more conservative options). During the 1950s and 1960s, he wrote for and edited a series of liberal journals in England and the United States,

---

[1] On the relaxation of American pornography laws, see the extensive account by a leading protagonist, Edward de Grazia, *Girls Lean Back Everywhere: The Law of Obscenity and the Assault on Genius* (New York, 1992).

[2] On the growth of commercial pornography and its dimensions, see Bernard Arcand, *The Jaguar and the Anteater: Pornography Degree Zero*, translated by Wayne Grady (London, 1993 [French original 1991]), pp. 33–50.

[3] In the account that follows I have made use of Kristol's biographical and historical reflections in the prefaces to his books, *On the Democratic Idea in America* (New York, 1972); *Reflections of a Neoconservative* (New York, 1983), and the preface and biographical essays in his selected essays, *Neoconservatism: the Autobiography of an Idea* (New York, 1995); as well as some of the memoirs regarding various phases of Kristol's career in Christopher DeMuth and William Kristol, eds., *The Neoconservative Imagination: Essays in Honor of Irving Kristol* (Washington, D.C., 1995), which includes a bibliography of Kristol's work. An analytically acute discussion of the distinctions between neoconservatism and other varieties of American intellectual conservatism during the period under discussion is Brigitte Berger and Peter L. Berger, "Our Conservatism and Theirs," *Commentary*, vol. 82, no. 4, (October 1986), pp. 62–67. It should be kept in mind that "neoconservatism" was above all a relational term, and that as the configuration of American political and intellectual life changed, it lost much of its specificity.

at a time when anti-communism was a constitutive element of American liberalism. In 1965, Kristol, together with his friend Daniel Bell, founded the journal, *The Public Interest*, which sought to offer a critical, social scientifically informed commentary on issues of public policy at a time of growth and experimentation in the American welfare state. During the later 1960s, as elite intellectual life became increasingly anti-capitalist and moved in the direction of the "counter-culture" with its embrace of liberation from constraints, Kristol and others like him found that their defense of existing liberal institutions led them to be characterized as "neoconservatives."

"Neoconservatism," Kristol proclaimed, "aims to infuse American bourgeois orthodoxy with a new self-conscious intellectual vigor."[4] Given the prevailing intellectual norms of the late 1960s and 1970s, Kristol's laudatory use of terms such as "capitalism" and "bourgeois" was deliberately provocative. The "conservative" element of the label referred in part to Kristol's articulate defense of liberal capitalism as an economic system which worked better than known alternatives. Unlike some libertarian defenders of capitalism, Kristol did not believe that governmental measures intended to provide a degree of social security were incompatible with the market order. But, like other erstwhile liberals who contributed to *The Public Interest*, Kristol was acutely sensitive to the unanticipated negative consequences of governmental action, which he increasingly elevated from a possibility to a near certainty. Another element of Kristol's conservatism was his articulation of the proposition that a liberal and democratic society required institutions and assumptions that were neither liberal nor democratic.

Kristol had been influenced intellectually by the American cultural critic, Lionel Trilling, an Arnoldian and self-identified liberal, who never abandoned the liberal label while stressing the limitations of what he called "the liberal imagination." In the preface to his 1950 book of that title, Trilling wrote, "It has for some time seemed to me that a criticism which has at heart the interests of liberalism might find its most useful work not in confirming liberalism in its sense of general rightness but rather in putting under some degree of pressure the liberal ideas and assumptions of the present moment."[5] From the work of the conservative German émigré political philosopher Leo Strauss, Kristol took the belief that the great works of the past offered a useful tool for submitting contemporary liberal ideas and assumptions to critical scrutiny. But Kristol lacked Trilling's ongoing emotional commitment to liberalism, and did not share the sense of unease with modern bourgeois society which colored Strauss's sensibility. Moreover, he had a critical respect

---

[4] Irving Kristol, preface to *Reflections of a Neoconservative*, p. xiv.
[5] Lionel Trilling, *The Liberal Imagination* (New York, 1950), p. viii.

and taste for social scientific modes of explanation and their application to immediate issues of public policy.

These characteristics are evident in the article reprinted below, which originally appeared in *The New York Times Magazine* of March 28, 1971, and was reprinted in Irving Kristol, *Reflections of a Neoconservative* (New York, 1983).

Irving Kristol,
"Pornography, Obscenity, and the Case for Censorship" (1971)

Being frustrated is disagreeable, but the real disasters in life begin when you get what you want. For almost a century now, a great many intelligent, well-meaning, and articulate people—of a kind generally called liberal or intellectual, or both—have argued eloquently against any kind of censorship of art and/or entertainment. And within the past ten years, the courts and the legislatures of most Western nations have found these arguments persuasive—so persuasive that hardly a man is now alive who clearly remembers what the answers to these arguments were. Today, in the United States and other democracies, censorship has to all intents and purposes ceased to exist.

Is there a sense of triumphant exhilaration in the land? Hardly. There is, on the contrary, a rapidly growing unease and disquiet. Somehow, things have not worked out as they were supposed to, and many notable civil libertarians have gone on record as saying this was not what they meant at all. They wanted a world in which *Desire under the Elms*[1] could be produced, or *Ulysses*[2] published, without interference by philistine busybodies holding public office. They have got that, of course; but they have also got a world in which homosexual rape takes place on the stage, in which the public flocks during lunch hours to witness varieties of professional fornication, in which Times Square has become little more than a hideous market for the sale and distribution of printed filth that panders to all known (and some fanciful) sexual perversions.

But disagreeable as this may be, does it really matter? Might not our unease and disquiet be merely a cultural hangover—a "hang-up," as they say? What reason is there to think that anyone was ever corrupted by a book?

[1] A 1924 play by Eugene O'Neill.

[2] A novel by James Joyce, regarded as one of the greatest literary works of the twentieth century. First published in Paris in 1922, it was banned in the United States until 1933, and in the United Kingdom until 1936.

This last question, oddly enough, is asked by the very same people who seem convinced that advertisements in magazines or displays of violence on television do indeed have the power to corrupt. It is also asked, incredibly enough and in all sincerity, by people—for example, university professors and schoolteachers—whose very lives provide all the answers one could want. After all, if you believe that no one was ever corrupted by a book, you have also to believe that no one was ever improved by a book (or a play or a movie). You have to believe, in other words, that all art is morally trivial and that, consequently, all education is morally irrelevant. No one, not even a university professor, really believes that.

To be sure, it is extremely difficult, as social scientists tell us, to trace the effects of any single book (or play or movie) on an individual reader or any class of readers. But we all know, and social scientists know it too, that the ways in which we use our minds and imaginations do shape our characters and help define us as persons. That those who certainly know this are nevertheless moved to deny it merely indicates how a dogmatic resistance to the idea of censorship can—like most dogmatism—result in a mindless insistence on the absurd.

I have used these harsh terms—"dogmatism" and "mindless"—advisedly. I might also have added "hypocritical." For the plain fact is that none of us is a complete civil libertarian. We all believe that there is some point at which the public authorities ought to step in to limit the "self-expression" of an individual or a group, even where this might be seriously intended as a form of artistic expression, and even where the artistic transaction is between consenting adults. A playwright or theatrical director might, in this crazy world of ours, find someone willing to commit suicide on the stage, as called for by the script. We would not allow that—any more than we would permit scenes of real physical torture on the stage, even if the victim were a willing masochist. And I know of no one, no matter how free in spirit, who argues that we ought to permit gladiatorial contests in Yankee Stadium, similar to those once performed in the Colosseum at Rome—even if only consenting adults were involved.

The basic point that emerges is one that Walter Berns has powerfully argued: No society can be utterly indifferent to the ways its citizens publicly entertain themselves.[3] Bearbaiting and cockfighting are prohibited only in part out of compassion for the suffering animals; the main reason they were abolished was because it was felt that they debased and brutalized the citizenry who flocked to witness such spectacles. And the

---

[3] [This is as good a place as any to express my profound indebtedness to Walter Berns's superb essay "Pornography versus Democracy," in the Winter 1971 issue of *The Public Interest*.]

question we face with regard to pornography and obscenity is whether, now that they have such strong legal protection from the Supreme Court, they can or will brutalize and debase our citizenry. We are, after all, not dealing with one passing incident—one book, or one play, or one movie. We are dealing with a general tendency that is suffusing our entire culture.

I say pornography *and* obscenity because, though they have different dictionary definitions and are frequently distinguishable as "artistic" genres, they are nevertheless in the end identical in effect. Pornography is not objectionable simply because it arouses sexual desire or lust or prurience in the mind of the reader or spectator; this is a silly Victorian notion. A great many nonpornographic works—including some parts of the Bible—excite sexual desire very successfully. What is distinctive about pornography is that, in the words of D. H. Lawrence, it attempts "to do dirt on [sex] . . . [It is an] insult to a vital human relationship."

In other words, pornography differs from erotic art in that its whole purpose is to treat human beings obscenely, to deprive human beings of their specifically human dimension. That is what obscenity is all about. It is light years removed from any kind of carefree sensuality—there is no continuum between Fielding's *Tom Jones* and the Marquis de Sade's *Justine*. These works have quite opposite intentions. To quote Susan Sontag: "What pornographic literature does is precisely to drive a wedge between one's existence as a full human being and one's existence as a sexual being—while in ordinary life a healthy person is one who prevents such a gap from opening up." This definition occurs in an essay *defending* pornography—Miss Sontag is a candid as well as gifted critic—so the definition, which I accept, is neither tendentious nor censorious.

Along these same lines, one can point out—as C. S. Lewis pointed out some years back—that it is no accident that in the history of all literatures obscene words, the so-called "four-letter" words, have always been the vocabulary of farce or vituperation. The reason is clear; they reduce men and women to some of their mere bodily functions—they reduce man to his animal component, and such a reduction is an essential purpose of farce or vituperation.

Similarly, Lewis also suggested that it is not an accident that we have no offhand, colloquial, neutral terms—not in any Western European language at any rate—for our most private parts. The words we do use are either (1) nursery terms, (2) archaisms, (3) scientific terms, or (4) a term from the gutter (i.e., a demeaning term). Here I think the genius of language is telling us something important about man. It is telling us that man is an animal with a difference: He has a unique sense of privacy, and a unique capacity for shame when this privacy is violated. Our "private parts" are indeed private, and not merely because convention prescribes it. This particular convention is indigenous to the human race. In practically all primitive tribes, men and women cover their private parts; and in practically all primitive tribes, men and women do not copulate in public.

It may well be that Western society, in the latter half of the twentieth century, is experiencing a drastic change in sexual mores and sexual relationships. We have had many such "sexual revolutions" in the past—the bourgeois family and bourgeois ideas of sexual propriety were themselves established in the course of a revolution against eighteenth-century "licentiousness"—and we shall doubtless have others in the future. It is, however, highly improbable (to put it mildly) that what we are witnessing is the Final Revolution which will make sexual relations utterly unproblematic, permit us to dispense with any kind of ordered relationships between the sexes, and allow us freely to redefine the human condition. And so long as humanity has not reached that utopia, obscenity will remain a problem.

One of the reasons it will remain a problem is that obscenity is not merely about sex, any more than science fiction is about science. Science fiction, as every student of the genre knows, is a peculiar vision of power: What it is really about is politics. And obscenity is a peculiar vision of humanity: What it is really about is ethics and metaphysics.

Imagine a man—a well-known man, much in the public eye—in a hospital ward, dying an agonizing death. He is not in control of his bodily functions, so that his bladder and his bowels empty themselves of their own accord. His consciousness is overwhelmed and extinguished by pain, so that he cannot communicate with us, nor we with him. Now, it would be, technically, the easiest thing in the world to put a television camera in his hospital room and let the whole world witness this spectacle. We do not do it—at least we do not do it as yet—because we regard this as an *obscene* invasion of privacy. And what would make the spectacle obscene is that we would be witnessing the extinguishing of humanity in a human animal.

Incidentally, in the past our humanitarian crusaders against capital punishment understood this point very well. The abolitionist literature goes into great physical detail about what happens to a man when he is hanged or electrocuted or gassed. And their argument was—and is—that what happens is shockingly obscene, and that no civilized society should be responsible for perpetrating such obscenities, particularly since in the nature of the case there must be spectators to ascertain that this horror was indeed being perpetrated in fulfillment of the law.

Sex—like death—is an activity that is both animal and human. There are human sentiments and human ideals involved in this animal activity. But when sex is public, the viewer does not see—cannot see—the sentiments and the ideals. He can only see the animal coupling. And that is why, when men and women make love, as we say, they prefer to be alone—because it is only when you are alone that you can make love, as distinct from merely copulating in an animal and casual way. And that, too, is why those who are voyeurs, if they are not irredeemably sick, also feel ashamed at what they are witnessing. When sex is a public spectacle, a human relationship has been debased into a mere animal connection.

It is also worth noting that this making of sex into an obscenity is not a mutual and equal transaction but rather an act of exploitation by one of the partners—the male partner. I do not wish to get into the complicated question as to what, if any, are the essential differences—as distinct from conventional and cultural differences—between male and female. I do not claim to know the answer to that. But I do know—and I take it as a sign that has meaning—that pornography is, and always has been, a man's work; that women rarely write pornography; and that women tend to be indifferent consumers of pornography.[4] My own guess, by way of explanation, is that a woman's sexual experience is ordinarily more suffused with human emotion than is man's, that men are more easily satisfied with autoerotic activities, and that men can therefore more easily take a more "technocratic" view of sex and its pleasures. Perhaps this is not correct. But whatever the explanation, there can be no question that pornography is a form of "sexism," as the women's liberation movement calls it, and that the instinct of women's liberation has been unerring in perceiving that when pornography is perpetrated, it is perpetrated against them, as part of a conspiracy to deprive them of their full humanity.

But even if all this is granted, it might be said—and doubtless will be said—that I really ought not to be unduly concerned. Free competition in the cultural marketplace—it is argued by people who have never otherwise had a kind word to say for laissez-faire—will automatically dispose of the problem. The present fad for pornography and obscenity, it will be asserted, is just that, a fad. It will spend itself in the course of time; people will get bored with it, will be able to take it or leave it alone in a casual way, in a "mature way," and, in sum, I am being unnecessarily distressed about the whole business. The *New York Times*, in an editorial, concludes hopefully in this vein.

> In the end . . . the insensate pursuit of the urge to shock, carried from one excess to a more abysmal one, is bound to achieve its own antidote in total boredom. When there is no lower depth to descend to, ennui will erase the problem.

[4] [There are, of course, a few exceptions. *L' Histoire d' O*, for instance, was written by a woman. It is unquestionably the most *melancholy* work of pornography ever written. And its theme is precisely the dehumanization accomplished by obscenity.]

I would like to be able to go along with this line of reasoning, but I cannot. I think it is false, and for two reasons, the first psychological, the second political.

The basic psychological fact about pornography and obscenity is that it appeals to and provokes a kind of sexual regression. The sexual pleasure one gets from pornography and obscenity is autoerotic and infantile; put bluntly, it is a masturbatory exercise of the imagination, when it is not masturbation pure and simple. Now, people who masturbate do not get bored with masturbation, just as sadists do not get bored with sadism, and voyeurs do not get bored with voyeurism.

In other words, infantile sexuality is not only a permanent temptation for the adolescent or even the adult—it can quite easily become a permanent, self-reinforcing neurosis. It is because of an awareness of this possibility of regression toward the infantile condition, a regression which is always open to us, that all the codes of sexual conduct ever devised by the human race take such a dim view of autoerotic activities and try to discourage autoerotic fantasies. Masturbation is indeed a perfectly natural autoerotic activity, as so many sexologists blandly assure us today. And it is precisely because it is so perfectly natural that it can be so dangerous to the mature or maturing person, if it is not controlled or sublimated in some way. That is the true meaning of Portnoy's complaint.[5] Portnoy, you will recall, grows up to be a man who is incapable of having an adult sexual relationship with a woman; his sexuality remains fixed in an infantile mode, the prisoner of his autoerotic fantasies. Inevitably, Portnoy comes to think, in a perfectly *infantile* way, that it was all his mother's fault.

It is true that, in our time, some quite brilliant minds have come to the conclusion that a reversion to infantile sexuality is the ultimate mission and secret destiny of the human race. I am thinking in particular of Norman O. Brown,[6] for whose writings I have the deepest respect. One of the reasons I respect them so deeply is that Mr. Brown is a serious thinker who is unafraid to face up to the radical consequences of his radical theories. Thus, Mr. Brown knows and says that for his kind of salvation to be achieved, humanity must annul the civilization it has created—not merely the civilization we have today, but all civilization—so as to be able to make the long descent backward into animal innocence.

And that is the point. What is at stake is civilization and humanity, nothing less. The idea that "everything is permitted," as Nietzsche put it, rests on the premise of nihilism and has nihilistic implications. I will not pretend that the case against nihilism and for civilization is an easy

---

[5] The reference is to the novel by Philip Roth, *Portnoy's Complaint* (1969).

[6] Author of *Life against Death: The Psychoanalytical Meaning of History* (1959) and *Love's Body* (1966).

one to make. We are here confronting the most fundamental of philosophical questions, on the deepest levels. In short, the matter of pornography and obscenity is not a trivial one, and only superficial minds can take a bland and untroubled view of it.

In this connection, I must also point out, those who are primarily against censorship on liberal grounds tell us not to take pornography or obscenity seriously, while those who are for pornography and obscenity on radical grounds take it very seriously indeed. I believe the radicals—writers like Susan Sontag, Herbert Marcuse, Norman O. Brown, and even Jerry Rubin—are right, and the liberals are wrong. I also believe that those young radicals at Berkeley, some seven years ago, who provoked a major confrontation over the public use of obscene words, showed a brilliant political instinct. And once Mark Rudd could publicly ascribe to the president of Columbia a notoriously obscene relationship to his mother, without provoking any kind of reaction, the SDS [Students for a Democratic Society] had already won the day. The occupation of Columbia's buildings merely ratified their victory. Men who show themselves unwilling to defend civilization against nihilism are not going to be either resolute or effective in defending the university against anything.

I am already touching upon a political aspect of pornography when I suggest that it is inherently and purposefully subversive of civilization and its institutions. But there is another and more specifically political aspect, which has to do with the relationship of pornography and/or obscenity to democracy, and especially to the quality of public life on which democratic government ultimately rests.

Though the phrase "the quality of life" trips easily from so many lips these days, it tends to be one of those clichés with many trivial meanings and no large, serious one. Sometimes it merely refers to such externals as the enjoyment of cleaner air, cleaner water, cleaner streets. At other times it refers to the merely private enjoyment of music, painting, or literature. Rarely does it have anything to do with the way the citizen in a democracy views himself—his obligations, his intentions, his ultimate self-definition.

Instead, what I would call the "managerial" conception of democracy is the predominant opinion among political scientists, sociologists, and economists, and has, through the untiring efforts of these scholars, become the conventional journalistic opinion as well. The root idea behind this managerial conception is that democracy is a "political system" (as they say) which can be adequately defined in terms of—can be fully reduced to—its mechanical arrangements. Democracy is then seen as a set of rules and procedures, and *nothing but* a set of rules and procedures, whereby majority rule and minority rights are reconciled into a state of equilibrium. If everyone follows these rules and procedures, then a democracy is in working order. I think this is a fair description of the democratic idea that currently prevails in academia. One can also fairly say that it is now the liberal idea of democracy par excellence.

I cannot help but feel that there is something ridiculous about being this kind of a democrat, and I must further confess to having a sneaking sympathy for those of our young radicals who also find it ridiculous. The absurdity is the absurdity of idolatry—of taking the symbolic for the real, the means for the end. The purpose of democracy cannot possibly be the endless functioning of its own political machinery.[7] The purpose of any political regime is to achieve some version of the good life and the good society. It is not at all difficult to imagine a perfectly functioning democracy which answers all questions except one—namely, why should anyone of intelligence and spirit care a fig for it?

There is, however, an older idea of democracy—one which was fairly common until about the beginning of this century—for which the conception of the quality of public life is absolutely crucial. This idea starts from the proposition that democracy is a form of self-government, and that if you want it to be a meritorious polity, you have to care about what kind of people govern it. Indeed, it puts the matter more strongly and declares that if you want self-government, you are only entitled to it if that "self" is worthy of governing. There is no inherent right to self-government if it means that such government is vicious, mean, squalid, and debased. Only a dogmatist and a fanatic, an idolater of democratic machinery, could approve of self-government under such conditions.

And because the desirability of self-government depends on the character of the people who govern, the older idea of democracy was very solicitous of the condition of this character. It was solicitous of the individual self, and felt an obligation to educate it into what used to be called "republican virtue." And it was solicitous of that collective self which we call public opinion and which, in a democracy, governs us collectively. Perhaps in some respects it was nervously oversolicitous—that would not be surprising. But the main thing is that it cared, cared not merely about the machinery of democracy but about the quality of life that this machinery might generate.

And because it cared, this older idea of democracy had no problem in principle with pornography and/or obscenity. It censored them—and it did so with a perfect clarity of mind and a perfectly clear conscience. It was not about to permit people capriciously to corrupt themselves. Or,

---

[7] The distinction between the "machinery" of democracy and its cultural content recalls Matthew Arnold, *Culture and Anarchy*, elsewhere in this volume.

to put it more precisely: In this version of democracy, the people took some care not to let themselves be governed by the more infantile and irrational parts of themselves.

I have, it may be noticed, uttered that dreadful word censorship. And I am not about to back away from it. If you think pornography and/or obscenity is a serious problem, you have to be for censorship. I will go even further and say that if you want to prevent pornography and/or obscenity from becoming a problem, you have to be for censorship. And lest there be any misunderstanding as to what I am saying, I will put it as bluntly as possible: If you care for the quality of life in our American democracy, then you have to be for censorship.

But can a liberal be for censorship? Unless one assumes that being a liberal *must* mean being indifferent to the quality of American life, then the answer has to be yes, a liberal can be for censorship—but he ought to favor a liberal form of censorship.

Is that a contradiction in terms? I do not think so. We have no problem in contrasting *repressive* laws governing alcohol and drugs and tobacco with laws *regulating* (i.e., discouraging the sale of) alcohol and drugs and tobacco. Laws encouraging temperance are not the same thing as laws that have as their goal prohibition or abolition. We have not made the smoking of cigarettes a criminal offense. We have, however, and with good liberal conscience, prohibited cigarette advertising on television, and may yet, again with good liberal conscience, prohibit it in newspapers and magazines. The idea of restricting individual freedom, in a liberal way, is not at all unfamiliar to us.

I therefore see no reason why we should not be able to distinguish repressive censorship from liberal censorship of the written and spoken word. In Britain, until a few years ago, you could perform almost any play you wished, but certain plays, judged to be obscene, had to be performed in private theatrical clubs, which were deemed to have a "serious" interest in theater. In the United States, all of us who grew up using public libraries are familiar with the circumstances under which certain books could be circulated only to adults, while still other books had to be read in the library reading room, under the librarian's skeptical eye. In both cases, a small minority that was willing to make a serious effort to see an obscene play or read an obscene book could do so. But the impact of obscenity was circumscribed and the quality of public life was only marginally affected.[8]

[8] [It is fairly predictable that someone is going to object that this point of view is "elitist"—that, under a system of liberal censorship, the rich will have privileged access to pornography and obscenity. Yes, of course, they will—just as, at present, the rich have privileged access to heroin if they want it. But one would have to be an egalitarian maniac to object to this state of affairs on the grounds of equality.]

I am not saying it is easy in practice to sustain a distinction between liberal and repressive censorship, especially in the public realm of a democracy, where popular opinion is so vulnerable to demagoguery. Moreover, an acceptable system of liberal censorship is likely to be exceedingly difficult to devise in the United States today, because our educated classes, upon whose judgment a liberal censorship must rest, are so convinced that there is no such thing as a problem of obscenity, or even that there is no such thing as obscenity at all. But, to counterbalance this, there is the further, fortunate truth that the tolerable margin for error is quite large, and single mistakes or single injustices are not all that important.

This possibility of error, of course, occasions much distress among artists and academics. It is a fact, one that cannot and should not be denied, that any system of censorship is bound, upon occasion, to treat unjustly a particular work of art—to find pornography where there is only gentle eroticism, to find obscenity where none really exists, or to find both where its existence ought to be tolerated because it serves a larger moral purpose. Though most works of art are not obscene, and though most obscenity has nothing to do with art, there are some few works of art that are, at least in part, pornographic and/or obscene. There are also some few works of art that are in the special category of the comic-ironic "bawdy" (Boccaccio, Rabelais). It is such works of art that are likely to suffer at the hands of the censor. That is the price one has to be prepared to pay for censorship—even liberal censorship.

But just how high is this price? If you believe, as so many artists seem to believe today, that art is the only sacrosanct activity in our profane and vulgar world—that any man who designates himself an artist thereby acquires a sacred office—then obviously censorship is an intolerable form of sacrilege. But for those of us who do not subscribe to this religion of art, the costs of censorship do not seem so high at all.

If you look at the history of American or English literature, there is precious little damage you can point to as a consequence of the censorship that prevailed throughout most of that history. Very few works of literature—of real literary merit, I mean—ever were suppressed; and those that were, were not suppressed for long. Nor have I noticed, now that censorship of the written word has to all intents and purposes ceased in this country, that hitherto suppressed or repressed masterpieces are flooding the market. Yes, we can now read *Fanny Hill* and the Marquis de Sade. Or, to be more exact, we can now openly purchase them, since many people were able to read them even though they were publicly banned, which is as it should be under a liberal censorship. So how much have literature and the arts gained from the fact that we can all now buy them over the counter, that, indeed, we are all now encouraged to buy them over the counter? They have not gained much that I can see.

And one might also ask a question that is almost never raised: How much has literature lost from the fact that everything is now permitted? It has lost quite a bit, I should say. In a free market, Gresham's Law can work for books or theater as efficiently as it does for coinage—driving out the good, establishing the debased. The cultural market in the United States today is being preempted by dirty books, dirty movies, dirty theater. A pornographic novel has a far better chance of being published today than a nonpornographic one, and quite a few pretty good novels are not being published at all simply because they are not pornographic, and are therefore less likely to sell. Our cultural condition has not improved as a result of the new freedom. American cultural life was not much to brag about twenty years ago; today one feels ashamed for it.

Just one last point, which I dare not leave untouched. If we start censoring pornography or obscenity, shall we not inevitably end up censoring political opinion? A lot of people seem to think this would be the case—which only shows the power of doctrinaire thinking over reality. We had censorship of pornography and obscenity for 150 years, until almost yesterday, and I am not aware that freedom of opinion in this country was in any way diminished as a consequence of this fact. Fortunately for those of us who are liberal, freedom is not indivisible. If it were, the case for liberalism would be indistinguishable from the case for anarchy; and they are two very different things.

But I must repeat and emphasize: What kinds of laws we pass governing pornography and obscenity, what kind of censorship—or, since we are still a federal nation, what kinds of censorship—we institute in our various localities may indeed be difficult matters to cope with; nevertheless the real issue is one of principle. I myself subscribe to a liberal view of the enforcement problem: I think that pornography should be illegal *and* available to anyone who wants it so badly as to make a pretty strenuous effort to get it. We have lived with under-the-counter pornography for centuries now, in a fairly comfortable way. But the issue of principle, of whether it should be over or under the counter, has to be settled before we can reflect on the advantages and disadvantages of alternative modes of censorship. I think the settlement we are living under now, in which obscenity and democracy are regarded as equals is wrong; I believe it is inherently unstable; I think it will, in the long run, be incompatible with any authentic concern for the quality of life in our democracy.

INTRODUCTION TO
Peter L. Berger and Richard John Neuhaus,
To Empower People: The Role of Mediating Structures in Public Policy

◆

Among the shibboleths of radicalism in the 1960s was "liberation," national, political, cultural, and sexual. This trend called forth the perennial conservative arguments about the individual's need for institutional direction and identification. A theme appropriated from the New Left was "empowerment." In the following essay by Peter L. Berger and Richard John Neuhaus, this latter theme is linked to traditional conservative concerns about the political importance of the family, religion, and the sub-political social institutions in which manners and mores are conveyed. Montesquieu, in the eighteenth century, had coined the term "intermediary powers," but he was primarily concerned with the role of institutions such as the nobility, the Church, and the *parlements* (law courts) in limiting the absolute power of the monarch and preventing descent into unchecked despotism. It was a French liberal, Alexis de Tocqueville, who offered an account of the importance of family, religion, and civic association in maintaining the liberty and vitality of mid-nineteenth-century American democracy. Though Tocqueville was a liberal in the European context of his day, his work found great resonance among American conservatives after the Second World War. The significance of such institutions had been a mainstay of French social thinkers, including liberals such as Emile Durkheim and radical conservatives such as Charles Maurras. In German-speaking Europe, Hegel had stressed the importance of the family and of professional corporations in mediating between the individual and the state. Echoes of all of these precursors, and more, may be found in "To Empower People: The Role of Mediating Structures in Public Policy."

Peter Berger was at the time a professor of sociology at Rutgers University, who had published seminal works on the sociology of religion, the sociology of knowledge, modernization theory, and strategies of economic development.[1] Born in Vienna in 1929, Berger received his higher education in the United States.[2] His fluency in German and his

---

[1] The most important of these were *The Sacred Canopy* (1967); *The Social Construction of Reality* (1966), with Thomas Luckmann; *The Homeless Mind: Modernization and Consciousness* (1973) with Brigitte Berger and Hansfried Kellner; and *Pyramids of Sacrifice* (1974).

[2] Robert Wuthnow et al., *Cultural Analysis: The Work of Peter L. Berger, Mary Douglas,*

contact with German émigré scholars at the New School for Social Research made him a conduit for the ideas of German-speaking theorists. From Alfred Schütz (with whom he had studied at the New School) Berger adopted the phenomenological approach to social science, which emphasized recapturing the social actor's perception of social reality. From Arnold Gehlen, he adopted the concept of institutions as forming a necessary "second nature" which provides meaning, purpose, and necessary delimitation.[3] Among Berger's foremost concerns was the role of institutions such as the church and the family in the formation of individual identity under modern conditions characterized by an awareness of competing cultural systems (what Berger called "the pluralization of life-worlds").[4]

Richard John Neuhaus was a politically active theologian and the Lutheran pastor of a predominantly black church in the Bedford-Stuyvesant slum of New York City.[5] His opposition to American involvement in Vietnam led him in 1964 to participate in founding the organization, Clergy and Laymen Concerned About Vietnam. (Berger, who had been a relatively apolitical conservative,[6] was also active in the organization and opposed American involvement in the war in Vietnam, while remaining a political conservative.) From 1966 to 1968 Neuhaus worked closely with Martin Luther King, Jr., helping to convince King to come out against the war in Vietnam, and aiding in plans for what was to be the "Poor People's Campaign" to create pressure for black economic equality.[7] Neuhaus combined his opposition to the war and his commitment to black equality with a cultural conservatism, and as "the Movement" became more politically radical and culturally liberationist, he became increasingly alienated from it.

The piece that follows is drawn from *Empowering People*, an essay intended as a conceptual and programmatic introduction to a research project on "the role of mediating structures in public policy" which Berger and Neuhaus organized in 1975 at the American Enterprise Institute in Washington, then emerging as a center of neoconservatism. At

---

Michel Foucault, and Jürgen Habermas (Boston, 1984) includes a brief biographical sketch of Berger on pages 9–11, and a chapter-length discussion of his ideas, written by James Davison Hunter.

[3] See the selection from Gehlen's work which appears in translation later in this book.

[4] See particularly the essays on "Marriage and the Construction of Reality," and "In Praise of Particularity: The Concept of Mediating Structures," in Berger's collection, *Facing Up to Modernity: Excursions in Society, Politics, and Religion* (New York, 1977).

[5] For information on this period of Neuhaus's life I have drawn on his autobiographical remarks in "Remembering the Movement," in Neuhaus, *America Against Itself: Moral Vision and the Public Order* (Notre Dame, 1992).

[6] See his essay "Intellectual Conservatism: Two Paradoxes," in *Facing Up to Modernity*.

[7] Peter L. Berger and Richard John Neuhaus, *Movement and Revolution* (New York, 1970), p. 141.

about the same time, Irving Kristol wrote that neoconservatism "seeks not to dismantle the welfare state in the name of free-market economics but rather to reshape it so as to attach to it the *conservative* predispositions of the people."[8] In subsequent years, Kristol, Berger, and Neuhaus, together with other neoconservatives, called attention to the dysfunctional effects of welfare state policies. But the emphasis on "mediating institutions" as set out in the essay below was perhaps the most significant neoconservative contribution to debates on public policy. It renewed the perennial conservative skepticism regarding projects to liberate the individual from existing sources of social and cultural authority. And it restated the recurrent conservative emphasis on the family and on other sub-political institutions in which manners and mores are conveyed, a theme we have seen in Möser, Burke, and Bonald. The piece is also notable for its defense of particular, historically developed identities, and the suspicion that the destruction of those identities leads not to liberation but to existential emptiness and anomie, a proposition further developed in the selection by Hermann Lübbe which follows.

Peter L. Berger and Richard John Neuhaus, *To Empower People: The Role of Mediating Structures in Public Policy* (1977)[1]

1. MEDIATING STRUCTURES AND THE DILEMMAS OF THE WELFARE STATE

Two seemingly contradictory tendencies are evident in current thinking about public policy in America. First, there is a continuing desire for the services provided by the modern welfare state. Partisan rhetoric aside, few people seriously envisage dismantling the welfare state. The serious debate is over how and to what extent it should be expanded. The second tendency is one of strong animus against government, bureaucracy, and bigness as such. This animus is directed not only toward Washington but toward government at all levels. Although this essay is addressed to the American situation, it should be noted that a similar ambiguity about the modern welfare state exists in other democratic societies, notably in Western Europe.

---

[8] "Introduction" to Irving Kristol, *Reflections of a Neoconservative* (New York, 1982), p. xii.

[1] Peter L. Berger and Richard John Neuhaus, *To Empower People: The Role of Mediating Structures in Public Policy* (Washington, D.C., 1975).

Perhaps this is just another case of people wanting to eat their cake and have it too. It would hardly be the first time in history that the people wanted benefits without paying the requisite costs. Nor are politicians above exploiting ambiguities by promising increased services while reducing expenditures. The extravagant rhetoric of the modern state and the surrealistic vastness of its taxation system encourage magical expectations that make contradictory measures seem possible. As long as some of the people can be fooled some of the time, some politicians will continue to ride into office on such magic.

But this is not the whole story. The contradiction between wanting more government services and less government may be only apparent. More precisely, we suggest that the modern welfare state is here to stay, indeed that it ought to expand the benefits it provides—but that *alternative mechanisms are possible to provide welfare-state services.*

The current anti-government, anti-bigness mood is not irrational. Complaints about impersonality, unresponsiveness, and excessive interference, as well as the perception of rising costs and deteriorating service—these are based upon empirical and widespread experience. The crisis of New York City, which is rightly seen as more than a fiscal crisis, signals a national state of unease with the policies followed in recent decades. At the same time there is widespread public support for publicly addressing major problems of our society in relieving poverty, in education, health care, and housing, and in a host of other human needs. What first appears as contradiction, then, is the sum of equally justified aspirations. The public policy goal is to address human needs without exacerbating the reasons for animus against the welfare state.

Of course there are no panaceas. The alternatives proposed here, we believe, can solve *some* problems. Taken seriously, they could become the basis of far-reaching innovations in public policy, perhaps of a new paradigm for at least sectors of the modern welfare state.

The basic concept is that of what we are calling mediating structures. The concept in various forms has been around for a long time. What is new is the systematic effort to translate it into specific public policies. For purposes of this study, mediating structures are defined as *those institutions standing between the individual in his private life and the large institutions of public life.*

Modernization brings about an historically unprecedented dichotomy between public and private life. The most important large institution in the ordering of modern society is the modern state itself. In addition, there are the large economic conglomerates of capitalist enterprise, big labor, and the growing bureaucracies that administer wide sectors of the society, such as in education and the organized professions. All these institutions we call the *megastructures.*

Then there is that modern phenomenon called private life. It is a curious kind of preserve left over by the large institutions and in which individuals carry on a bewildering variety of activities with only fragile institutional support.

For the individual in modern society, life is an ongoing migration between these two spheres, public and private. The megastructures are typically alienating, that is, they are not helpful in providing meaning and identity for individual existence. Meaning, fulfillment, and personal identity are to be realized in the private sphere. While the two spheres interact in many ways, in private life the individual is left very much to his own devices, and thus is uncertain and anxious. Where modern society is "hard," as in the megastructures, it is personally unsatisfactory; where it is "soft," as in private life, it cannot be relied upon. Compare, for example, the social realities of employment with those of marriage.

The dichotomy poses a double crisis. It is a crisis for the individual who must carry on a balancing act between the demands of the two spheres. It is a political crisis because the megastructures (notably the state) come to be devoid of personal meaning and are therefore viewed as unreal or even malignant. Not everyone experiences this crisis in the same way. Many who handle it more successfully than most have access to institutions that *mediate* between the two spheres. Such institutions have a private face, giving private life a measure of stability, and they have a public face, transferring meaning and value to the megastructures.[2] Thus, mediating structures alleviate each facet of the double crisis of modern society. Their strategic position derives from their reducing both the anomic precariousness of individual existence in isolation from society and the threat of alienation to the public order.

Our focus is on four such mediating structures—neighborhood, family, church, and voluntary association. This is by no means an exhaustive list, but these institutions were selected for two reasons: first, they figure prominently in the lives of most Americans and, second, they are most relevant to the problems of the welfare state with which we are concerned. The proposal is that, if these institutions could be more imaginatively recognized in public policy, individuals would be more "at home" in society, and the political order would be more "meaningful." Without institutionally reliable processes of mediation, the political order becomes detached from the values and realities of individual life. Deprived of its moral foundation, the political order is "delegitimated." When that happens, the political order must be secured by coercion rather than by consent. And when that happens, democracy disappears.

---

[2] The emphasis here is on the latent functions of such institutions, that is, their contribution to personal integration and the maintenance of social order.

The attractiveness of totalitarianism—whether instituted under left-wing or right-wing banners—is that it overcomes the dichotomy of private and public existence by imposing on life one comprehensive order of meaning. Although established totalitarian systems can be bitterly disappointing to their architects as well as their subjects, they are, on the historical record, nearly impossible to dismantle. The system continues quite effectively, even if viewed with cynicism by most of the population—including those who are in charge.

Democracy is "handicapped" by being more vulnerable to the erosion of meaning in its institutions. Cynicism threatens it; wholesale cynicism can destroy it. That is why mediation is so crucial to democracy. Such mediation cannot be sporadic and occasional; it must be institutionalized in *structures*. The structures we have chosen to study have demonstrated a great capacity for adapting and innovating under changing conditions. Most important, they exist where people are, and that is where sound public policy should always begin.

This understanding of mediating structures is sympathetic to Edmund Burke's well-known claim: "To be attached to the subdivision, to love the little platoon we belong to in society, is the first principle (the germ as it were) of public affections."[3] And it is sympathetic to Alexis de Tocqueville's conclusion drawn from his observation of Americans: "In democratic countries the science of association is the mother of science; the progress of all the rest depends upon the progress it has made." Marx too was concerned about the destruction of community, and the glimpse he gives us of post-revolutionary society is strongly reminiscent of Burke's "little platoons." The emphasis is even sharper in the anarcho-syndicalist tradition of social thought.

In his classic study of suicide, Emile Durkheim describes the "tempest" of modernization sweeping away the "little aggregations" in which people formerly found community, leaving only the state on the one hand and a mass of individuals, "like so many liquid molecules," on the other. Although using different terminologies, others in the sociological tradition—Ferdinand Toennies, Max Weber, Georg Simmel, Charles Cooley, Thorstein Veblen—have analyzed aspects of the same dilemma. Today Robert Nisbet has most persuasively argued that the loss of community threatens the future of American democracy.[4]

Also, on the practical political level, it might seem that mediating structures have universal endorsement. There is, for example, little political mileage in being anti-family or anti-church. But the reality is not so

---

[3] This oft-cited quotation, from Burke's *Reflections on the Revolution in France*, refers in the original to loyalty to one's estate or rank.

[4] Robert Nisbet, *The Quest for Community* (New York, 1953; with revised preface, 1969); *The Twilight of Authority* (New York, 1975).

simple. Liberalism—which constitutes the broad center of American politics, whether or not it calls itself by that name—has tended to be blind to the political (as distinct from private) functions of mediating structures. The main feature of liberalism, as we intend the term, is a commitment to government action toward greater social justice within the existing system. (To revolutionaries, of course, this is "mere re- formism," but the revolutionary option has not been especially relevant, to date, in the American context.)

Liberalism's blindness to mediating structures can be traced to its En- lightenment roots. Enlightenment thought is abstract, universalistic, addicted to what Burke called "geometry" in social policy. The concrete particularities of mediating structures find an inhospitable soil in the lib- eral garden. There the great concern is for the individual ("the rights of man") and for a just public order, but anything "in between" is viewed as irrelevant, or even an obstacle, to the rational ordering of society. What lies in between is dismissed, to the extent it can be, as superstition, bigotry, or (more recently) cultural lag.

American liberalism has been vigorous in the defense of the pri- vate rights of individuals, and has tended to dismiss the argument that private behavior can have public consequences. Private rights are frequently defended *against* mediating structures—children's rights against the family, the rights of sexual deviants against neighborhood or small-town sentiment, and so forth. Similarly, American liberals are vir- tually faultless in their commitment to the religious liberty of individu- als. But the liberty to be defended is always that of privatized religion. Supported by a very narrow understanding of the separation of church and state, liberals are typically hostile to the claim that institutional reli- gion might have public rights and public functions. As a consequence of this "geometrical" outlook, liberalism has a hard time coming to terms with the alienating effects of the abstract structures it has multiplied since the New Deal. This may be the Achilles heel of the liberal state today.

The left, understood as some version of the socialist vision, has been less blind to the problem of mediation. Indeed, the term alienation de- rives from Marxism. The weakness of the left, however, is its exclusive or nearly exclusive focus on the capitalist economy as the source of this evil, when in fact the alienations of the socialist states, insofar as there are socialist states, are much more severe than those of the capitalist states. While some theorists of the New Left have addressed this prob- lem by using elements from the anarcho-syndicalist tradition, most so- cialists see mediating structures as something that may be relevant to a post-revolutionary future, but that in the present only distracts attention from the struggle toward building socialism. Thus the left is not very helpful in the search for practical solutions to our problem.

On the right of the political broad center, we also find little that is helpful. To be sure, classical European conservatism had high regard for mediating structures, but, from the eighteenth century on, this tradition has been marred by a romantic urge to revoke modernity—a prospect that is, we think, neither likely nor desirable. On the other hand, what is now called conservatism in America is in fact old-style liberalism. It is the laissez-faire ideology of the period before the New Deal, which is roughly the time when liberalism shifted its faith from the market to government. *Both* the old faith in the market *and* the new faith in government share the abstract thought patterns of the Enlightenment. In addition, today's conservatism typically exhibits the weakness of the left in reverse: it is highly sensitive to the alienations of big government, but blind to the analogous effects of big business. Such one-sidedness, whether left or right, is not helpful.

As is now being widely recognized, we need new approaches free of the ideological baggage of the past. The mediating structures paradigm cuts across current ideological and political divides. This proposal has met with gratifying interest from most with whom we have shared it, and while it has been condemned as right-wing by some and as left-wing by others, this is in fact encouraging. Although the paradigm may play havoc with the conventional political labels, it is hoped that, after the initial confusion of what some social scientists call "cognitive shock," each implication of the proposal will be considered on its own merits.

The argument of this essay—and the focus of the research project it is designed to introduce—can be subsumed under three propositions. The first proposition is analytical: *Mediating structures are essential for a vital democratic society.* The other two are broad programmatic recommendations: *Public policy should protect and foster mediating structures*, and *Wherever possible, public policy should utilize mediating structures for the realization of social purposes. . . .*

The analytical proposition assumes that mediating structures are the value-generating and value-maintaining agencies in society. Without them, values become another function of the megastructures, notably of the state, and this is a hallmark of totalitarianism. In the totalitarian case, the individual becomes the object rather than the subject of the value-propagating processes of society.

The two programmatic propositions are, respectively, minimalist and maximalist. Minimally, public policy should cease and desist from damaging mediating structures. Much of the damage has been unintentional in the past. We should be more cautious than we have been. As we have learned to ask about the effects of government action upon racial minorities or upon the environment, so we should learn to ask about the effects of public policies on mediating structures.[5]

The maximalist proposition ("utilize mediating structures") is much the riskier. We emphasize, "wherever possible." The mediating structures paradigm is not applicable to all areas of policy. Also, there is the real danger that such structures might be "co-opted" by the government in a too eager embrace that would destroy the very distinctiveness of their function. The prospect of government control of the family, for example, is clearly the exact opposite of our intention. The goal in utilizing mediating structures is to expand government services without producing government oppressiveness. Indeed, it might be argued that the achievement of that goal is one of the acid tests of democracy.

It should be noted that these propositions differ from superficially similar proposals aimed at decentralizing governmental functions. Decentralization is limited to what can be done *within* governmental structures; we are concerned with the structures that stand *between* government and the individual. Nor, again, are we calling for a devolution of governmental responsibilities that would be tantamount to dismantling the welfare state. We aim rather at rethinking the institutional means by which government exercises its responsibilities. The idea is not to revoke the New Deal but to pursue its vision in ways more compatible with democratic governance.

Finally, there is a growing ideology based upon the proposition that "small is beautiful." We are sympathetic to that sentiment in some respects, but we do not share its programmatic antagonism to the basic features of modern society. Our point is not to attack the megastructures but to find better ways in which they can relate to the "little platoons" in our common life.

The theme is *empowerment*.[6] One of the most debilitating results of modernization is a feeling of powerlessness in the face of institutions controlled by those whom we do not know and whose values we often do not share. Lest there be any doubt, our belief is that human beings, whoever they are, understand their own needs better than anyone else— in, say, 99 percent of all cases. The mediating structures under discussion here are the principal expressions of the real values and the real needs of people in our society. They are, for the most part, the people-

[5] The theme of the erosion of mediating institutions as unintended negative consequences of contemporary government welfare measures was developed in an influential essay by the Harvard sociologist Nathan Glazer, "The Limits of Social Policy," *Commentary*, September 1971, pp. 51–58.

[6] During the 1960s "empowerment" of the poor had been a theme of War on Poverty programs such as Mobilization for Youth and the Community Action Program. Here the authors seek to appropriate the term for their own purposes.

sized institutions. Public policy should recognize, respect, and, where possible, empower these institutions.

A word about the poor is in order. Upper-income people already have ways to resist the encroachment of megastructures. It is not their children who are at the mercy of alleged child experts, not their health which is endangered by miscellaneous vested interests, not their neighborhoods which are made the playthings of utopian planners. Upper-income people may allow themselves to be victimized on all these scores, but they do have ways to resist if they choose to resist. Poor people have this power to a much lesser degree. The paradigm of mediating structures aims at empowering poor people to do the things that the more affluent can already do, aims at spreading the power around a bit more— and to do so where it matters, in people's control over their own lives. Some may call this populism. But that term has been marred by utopianism and by the politics of resentment. We choose to describe it as the empowerment of people.

2. NEIGHBORHOOD

[. . .] The neighborhood should be seen as a key mediating structure in the reordering of our national life. As is evident in fears and confusions surrounding such phrases as ethnic purity or neighborhood integrity, the focus on neighborhood touches some of the most urgent and sensitive issues of social policy. . . .

One reason for the present confusion about individual and communal rights has been the unreflective extension of policies deriving from America's racial dilemma to other areas where they are neither practicable nor just. That is, as a nation, and after a long, tortuous, and continuing agony, we have solemnly covenanted to disallow any public regulation that discriminates on the basis of race. That national decision must in no way be compromised. At the same time, the singularity of America's racial history needs to be underscored. Public policy should be discriminating about discriminations. Discrimination is the essence of particularism and particularism is the essence of pluralism. The careless expansion of antidiscrimination rulings in order to appease every aggrieved minority or individual will have two certain consequences: first, it will further erode local communal authority and, second, it will trivialize the historic grievances and claims to justice of America's racial minorities.

In terms of communal standards and sanctions, deviance always exacts a price. Indeed, without such standards, there can be no such thing as deviance. Someone who engages in public and deviant behavior in, say, Paducah, Kentucky, can pay the social price of deviance, can persuade his fellow citizens to accept his behavior, or can move to New York City. He should not be able to call in the police to prevent the people of Paducah from enforcing their values against his behavior. (Obviously, we are not referring to the expression of unpopular political or religious views, which, like proscriptions against racial discrimination, is firmly protected by national law and consensus.) The city—variously viewed as the cesspool of wickedness or the zone of liberation—has historically been the place of refuge for the insistently deviant. It might be objected that our saying "he can move to the city" sounds like the "love it or leave it" argument of those who opposed anti-war protesters in the last decade. The whole point, however, is the dramatic difference between a nation and a neighborhood. One is a citizen of a nation and lays claim to the rights by which that nation is constituted. Within that nation there are numerous associations such as neighborhoods—more or less freely chosen—and membership in those associations is usually related to affinity. This nation is constituted as an exercise in pluralism, as the *unum* within which myriad *plures* are sustained. If it becomes national policy to make the public values of Kokomo or Salt Lake City indistinguishable from those of San Francisco or New Orleans, we have as a nation abandoned the social experiment symbolized by the phrase "E Pluribus Unum." . . . .

3. FAMILY

There are places, especially in urban areas, where life styles are largely detached from family connections. This is, one hopes, good for those who choose it. Certainly such life styles add to the diversity, the creativity, even the magic, of the city. But since a relatively small number of people inhabit these areas, it would be both foolish and undemocratic to take such life styles as guidelines for the nation. For most Americans, neighborhood and community are closely linked to the family as an institution.

The family may be in crisis in the sense that it is undergoing major changes of definition, but there is little evidence that it is in decline. High divorce rates, for example, may indicate not decline but rising expectations in what people look for in marriage and family life. The point is underscored by high remarriage rates. It is noteworthy that the counterculture, which is so critical of the so-called bourgeois family, uses the terminology of family for its new social constructions, as do radical feminists pledged to "sisterhood." For most Americans, the evidence is that involvement in the bourgeois family, however modified, will endure.

Of course, modernization has already had a major impact on the family. It has largely stripped the family of earlier functions in the areas of education and economics, for example. But in other ways, modernization has made the family more important than ever before. It is the major institution within the private sphere, and thus for many people the most valuable thing in their lives. Here they make their moral commitments, invest their emotions, plan for the future, and perhaps even hope for immortality.

There is a paradox here. On the one hand, the megastructures of government, business, mass communications, and the rest have left room for the family to be the autonomous realm of individual aspiration and fulfillment. This room is by now well secured in the legal definitions of the family. At the same time, the megastructures persistently infringe upon the family. We cannot and should not eliminate these infringements entirely. After all, families exist in a common society. We can, however, take positive measures to protect and foster the family institution, so that it is not defenseless before the forces of modernity.

This means public recognition of the family *as an institution*. It is not enough to be concerned for individuals more or less incidentally related to the family as institution. Public recognition of the family as an institution is imperative because every society has an inescapable interest in how children are raised, how values are transmitted to the next generation. Totalitarian regimes have tried—unsuccessfully to date—to supplant the family in this function. Democratic societies dare not try if they wish to remain democratic. Indeed, they must resist every step, however well intended, to displace or weaken the family institution.

Public concern for the family is not antagonistic to concern for individual rights. On the contrary, individuals need strong families if they are to grow up and remain rooted in a strong sense of identity and values. Weak families produce uprooted individuals, unsure of their direction and therefore searching for some authority. They are ideal recruits for authoritarian movements inimical to democratic society. . . .

4. CHURCH

Religious institutions form by far the largest network of voluntary associations in American society. Yet, for reasons both ideological and historical, their role is frequently belittled or totally overlooked in discussions of social policy. Whatever may be one's attitude to organized religion, this blind spot must be reckoned a serious weakness in much thinking about public policy. The churches and synagogues of America can no more be omitted from responsible social analysis than can big labor, business corporations, or the communications media. Not only are religious institutions significant "players" in the public realm, but they are singularly important to the way people order their lives and values at the most local and concrete levels of their existence. Thus they are crucial to understanding family, neighborhood, and other mediating structures of empowerment.

The view that the public sphere is synonymous with the government or the formal polity of the society has been especially effective in excluding religion from considerations of public policy. We shall return to some of the church/state controversies that have reflected and perpetuated this view; but for the moment it should be obvious that our whole proposal aims at a complex and nuanced understanding of the public realm that includes many "players" other than the state. Also, much modern social thought deriving from Enlightenment traditions has operated on one or two assumptions that tend to minimize the role of religion. The first assumption is that education and modernization make certain the decline of allegiance to institutional religion. That is, there is thought to be an inevitable connection between modernization and secularization. The second assumption is that, even if religion continues to flourish, it deals purely with the private sphere of life and is therefore irrelevant to public policy. Both assumptions need to be carefully reexamined.

The evidence, at least in America, does not support the hypothesis of the inevitable decline of religion. . . . It is perhaps relevant to understanding American society to note that on any given Sunday there are probably more people in churches than the total number of people who attend professional sports events in a whole year—or to note that there are close to 500,000 local churches and synagogues voluntarily supported by the American people.

This is not the place for a detailed discussion of various secularization theories. We are keenly aware of the need to distinguish between institutions of religion and the dynamic of religion as such in society. Let it suffice that our approach raises a strong challenge to the first assumption mentioned above, namely, that in the modern world allegiance to institutional religion must perforce decline. Public policies based upon that highly questionable, if not patently false, assumption will continue to be alienated from one of the most vital dimensions in the lives of many millions of Americans.

The second assumption—that religion deals purely with the private sphere and is therefore irrelevant to public policy—must also be challenged. Although specifically religious activities have been largely privatized, the first part of the proposition overlooks the complex ways in which essentially religious values infiltrate and influence our public thought. But even to the extent that the first part of the proposition is true, it does not follow that religion is therefore irrelevant to public policy. The family, for example, is intimately involved in the institution of religion, and since the family is one of the prime mediating structures (perhaps the prime one), this makes the church urgently relevant to public policy. Without falling into the trap of politicizing all of life, our point is that structures such as family, church, and neighborhood are all public institutions in the sense that they must be taken seriously in the ordering of the polity.

The church (here meaning all institutions of religion) is important not only to the family but also to families and individuals in neighborhoods and other associations. For example, the black community, both historically and at present, cannot be understood apart from the black church. Similarly, the much discussed ethnic community is in large part religiously defined, as are significant parts of American Jewry (sometimes, but not always, subsumed under the phenomenon of ethnicity). And of course the role of religion in small towns or rural communities needs no elaboration. In none of these instances should the religious influence be viewed as residual. Few institutions have demonstrated and continue to demonstrate perduring power comparable to that of religion. It seems that influence is residual only to the extent that the bias of secularizing culture and politics is determined to act as though it is residual. Again, these observations seem to us to be true quite apart from what we may or may not *wish* the influence of religion to be in American society. We are convinced that there is a profoundly antidemocratic prejudice in public policy discourse that ignores the role of religious institutions in the lives of most Americans.

In the public policy areas most relevant to this discussion—health, social welfare, education, and so on—the historical development of programs, ideas, and institutions is inseparable from the church. In some parts of the country, notably in the older cities of the Northeast, the great bulk of social welfare services function under religious auspices. . . . [T]he religious character of these service agencies is being fast eroded. Where government agencies are not directly taking over areas previously serviced by religious institutions, such institutions are being turned into quasi-governmental agencies through the powers of funding, certification, licensing, and the like. The loss of religious and cultural distinctiveness is abetted also by the dynamics of professionalization within the religious institutions and by the failure of the churches either to support their agencies or to insist that public policy respect their distinctiveness. The corollary to the proposition that government responsibilities must be governmentally implemented—a proposition we challenge—is that public is the opposite of sectarian. In public policy discourse sectarian is usually used as a term of opprobrium for anything religious. We contend that this usage and the biases that support it undermine the celebration of distinctiveness essential to social pluralism. . . .

The danger today is not that the churches or any one church will take over the state. The much more real danger is that the state will take over the functions of the church, except for the most narrowly construed definition of religion limited to worship and religious instruction. It is not alarmist but soberly necessary to observe that the latter has been the totalitarian pattern of modern states, whether of the left or of the right. Pluralism, including religious pluralism, is one of the few strong obstacles to that pattern's success. While those who advance this pattern may often do so inadvertently, it would be naive to ignore the fast that many of them—sundry professionals, bureaucrats, politicians—have a deep vested interest in such state expansion. The interest is not only ideological, although that is no doubt the primary interest in many cases; it is also and very practically an interest in jobs and power.

5. VOLUNTARY ASSOCIATION

The discussion of the church leads logically to the subject of the voluntary association. Of course the church is—in addition to whatever else it may be—a voluntary association. But the category of voluntary association includes many other structures that can play a crucial mediating role in society.

There is a history of debate over what is meant by a voluntary association. For our present purposes, a voluntary association is a body of people who have voluntarily organized themselves in pursuit of particular goals. (Following common usage, we exclude business corporations and other primarily economic associations.) Important to the present discussion is the subject of volunteer service. Many voluntary associations have both paid and volunteer staffing. For our purposes, the crucial point is the free association of people for some collective purpose, the fact that they may pay some individuals for doing work to this end not being decisive.

At least since de Tocqueville the importance of voluntary associations in American democracy has been widely recognized. Voluntarism has flourished in America more than in any other Western society and it is reasonable to believe this may have something to do with American political institutions. Associations create statutes, elect officers, debate, vote courses of action, and otherwise serve as schools for democracy. However trivial, wrongheaded, or bizarre we may think the purpose of some associations to be, they nonetheless perform this vital function.

Apart from this political role, voluntary associations are enormously important for what they have actually done. Before the advent of the modern welfare state, almost everything in the realm of social services was under the aegis of voluntary associations, usually religious in character. Still today there are about 1,900 private colleges and universities, 4,600 private secondary schools, 3,600 voluntary hospitals, 6,000 museums, 1,100 orchestras, 5,500 libraries and no less than 29,000 nongovernmental welfare agencies. Of course not all of these are equally important as mediating structures. Orchestras and groups promoting stamp-collecting or the preservation of antique automobiles are, however important in other connections, outside our focus here. We are interested in one type within the vast array of voluntary associations—namely, associations that render social services relevant to recognized public responsibilities. . . .

Were all these institutions taken over by the government, there might be a more uniform imposition of standards and greater financial accountability than now exists (although the monumental corruption in various government social services does not make one sanguine about the latter), but the price would be high. Massive bureaucratization, the proliferation of legal procedures that generate both public resentment and business for lawyers, the atrophying of the humane impulse, the increase of alienation—these would be some of the costs. Minimally, it should be public policy to encourage the voluntarism that, in our society, has at least slowed down these costs of modernity.

As always, the maximalist side of our approach—that is, using voluntary associations as agents of public policies—is more problematic than the minimalist. One thinks, for example, of the use of foster homes and half-way houses in the treatment and prevention of drug addiction, juvenile delinquency, and mental illness. These is reason to believe such approaches are both less costly and more effective than using bureaucratized megastructures (and their local outlets). Or one thinks of the successful resettlement of more than 100,000 Vietnam refugees in 1975, accomplished not by setting up a government agency but by working through voluntary agencies (mainly religious). This instance of using voluntary associations for public policy purposes deserves careful study. . . .

This said, it remains true that mediating structures can be co-opted by government, that they can become instruments of those interested in destroying rather than reforming American society, and that they can undermine the institutions of the formal polity. These are real risks. On the other side are the benefits described earlier. Together they constitute a major challenge to the political imagination. . . .

6. Empowerment through Pluralism

Of course, some critics will decry our proposal as "balkanization," "retribalization," "parochialization," and such. The relevance of the Balkan areas aside, we want frankly to assert that tribe and parochial are not terms of derision. That they are commonly used in a derisive manner is the result of a worldview emerging from the late eighteenth century. That worldview held, in brief, that the laws of Nature are reflected in a political will of the people that can be determined and implemented by rational persons. Those naive notions of Nature, Will, and Reason have in the last hundred years been thoroughly discredited in almost every discipline, from psychology to sociology to physics. Yet the irony is that, although few people still believe in these myths, most social thought and planning continues to act as though they were true. The result is that the enemies of particularism ("tribalism") have become an elite tribe attempting to impose order on the seeming irrationalities of the real world and operating on premises that most Americans find both implausible and hostile to their values. Social thought has been crippled and policies have miscarried because we have not developed a paradigm of pluralism to replace the discredited assumptions of the eighteenth century. We hope this proposal is one step toward developing such a paradigm[7]. . . .

This requires a new degree of modesty among those who think about social policy—not modesty in the sense of lowering our ideals in the search for meeting human needs and creating a more just society, but modesty about *our* definitions of need and justice. Every world within this society, whether it calls itself a subculture or a supraculture or simply the American culture, is in fact a subculture, is but a part of the whole. This fact needs to be systematically remembered among those who occupy the world of public policy planning and implementation.

The subculture that envisages its values as universal and its style as cosmopolitan is no less a subculture for all that. The tribal patterns evident at an Upper West Side cocktail party are no less tribal than those evident at a Polish dance in Greenpoint, Brooklyn. That the former is produced by the interaction of people trying to transcend many particularisms simply results in a new, and not necessarily more interesting, particularism. People at the cocktail party may think of themselves as liberated, and indeed they may have elected to leave behind certain particularisms into which they were born. They have, in effect, elected a new particularism. *Liberation is not escape from particularity but discov-*

---

[7] Many of the propositions in this paragraph, which go back to earlier conservative thinkers, were revived in the 1980s under the rubric of "post-modernism."

ery of the particularity that fits. Elected particularities may include life style, ideology, friendships, place of residence, and so forth. Inherited particularities may include race, economic circumstance, region, religion, and, in most cases, politics. Pluralism means the lively interaction among inherited particularities and, through election, the evolution of new particularities. The goal of public policy in a pluralistic society is to sustain as many particularities as possible, in the hope that most people will accept, discover, or devise one that fits.

INTRODUCTION TO
Hermann Lübbe,
"The Social Consequences of Attempts to
Create Equality"

◆

A major thrust of governmental policy in most western welfare states in the postwar decades was the expansion of educational opportunities. Motivated in part by the recognition that social position was increasingly dependent upon educational attainment, liberal and social-democratic parties, and often conservative parties as well, sought to expand access to higher education and to reform school systems in more egalitarian directions.[1] Yet the attempt to achieve greater educational equality created unanticipated difficulties, which are examined in the following selection by the German philosopher and social critic Hermann Lübbe.

Among the most articulate German voices calling for the expansion of educational opportunities in the 1960s was Ralf Dahrendorf, a young sociologist and liberal social theorist. Dahrendorf sought to push West Germany more rapidly along the road to modernity, with the aim of creating a more "open" society which offered its members greater equality of opportunity. In a widely read work published in 1965, Dahrendorf deplored the traditionalism of his countrymen, what he called their "complete lack of motive toward the new possibilities of life, such as upward mobility, geographic mobility, changes of political orientation or social membership."[2] In another work published shortly thereafter, Dahrendorf challenged his West German countrymen to concretize the "right to education" proclaimed in the German constitution. Like other educational reformers, he recommended the creation of a more flexible educational system which would allow students to transfer into university-oriented tracks at various stages of their education, rather than tracking them early and irrevocably into university-oriented or vocationally oriented education, a procedure which was thought to reinforce the influence of social origins. Dahrendorf also urged an expansion of the number of university students.[3] And he pointed out that upward social

---

[1] See, for example, the discussion of educational issues in the influential work of the British Labourite and later Minister of Education, C.A.R. Crosland, *The Future of Socialism* (1956; revised edition, New York, 1963).

[2] Ralf Dahrendorf, *Society and Democracy in Germany* (New York, 1967; German original, 1965), p. 414.

[3] Ralf Dahrendorf, *Bildung als Bürgerrecht: Plädoyer für eine aktive Bildungspolitik* (Hamburg, 1968).

mobility was limited not only by formal barriers but by the invisible barriers created by social expectations linked to class, gender, and traditionalist culture.[4]

No major western country went further than West Germany in efforts to extend equality of educational opportunity. In the public schools, attempts were made to eliminate early tracking into technical, vocational, and university-oriented education. In the late 1970s, the issue of whether the intermediate grades (those attended by pupils ages ten through twelve) should be tracked or comprehensive was much discussed. In some provinces, above all those governed by Social Democrats, there were efforts to eliminate tracking entirely through the replacement of the tripartite school system by comprehensive schools. School fees were abolished, university tuition was made free, and the state provided university students with a living stipend. The number of students at German universities rose from approximately 120,000 in 1950 to 280,000 in 1960, 400,000 in 1970, and then to almost 1.3 million by 1983.[5]

Yet even as access to education was being extended, the content of that education was being called into question and at times transformed. In the early 1970s, Claus Offe, a political scientist associated with the Frankfurt School of social criticism, offered a critique of contemporary society which resonated with the student New Left. He insisted that the orientation toward "achievement" or "performance" of the educational system and of the social system to which education contributed was intrinsically oppressive.[6] Meanwhile, radical educational theorists influenced by the social theorist Jürgen Habermas suggested that the school curriculum be revised to reflect the ideals of "emancipatory education." Habermas had insisted that the aim of social policy ought to be the development of "communicative competence," by which he meant the ability and willingness of individuals to expose their claims to discussion. His assumption was that only claims which could be justified through totally unprejudiced discussion should be considered as valid.[7] Habermas had formulated this as a regulative ideal of debate in a liberal society; the pedagogical theorists influenced by him concluded that in the interests of ending "domination" and increasing their "communicative competence," students were to learn to call into question the "ideologi-

---

[4] Dahrendorf, *Society and Democracy in Germany*, pp. 100–112.

[5] These figures are drawn from Jeffrey Herf, *War by Other Means: Soviet Power, West German Resistance, and the Battle of the Euromissiles* (New York, 1991), p. 68.

[6] Claus Offe, *Industry and Equality* (London, 1976; German original, 1967). The intellectual progenitor of this critique was Herbert Marcuse, who coined the term "performance principle" in his *Eros and Civilization* (Boston, 1955).

[7] This theme was developed in Jürgen Habermas, *Zur Rekonstruktion des Historischen Materialismus* (Frankfurt, 1976); parts of it have been translated in Habermas, *Communication and the Evolution of Society* (London, 1979).

cal distortion" created by the structures around them, including their own families.

These themes and developments form the backdrop of the following selection. Its author, Hermann Lübbe, began as a liberal, and his subsequent conservatism combined the attempt to defend existing liberal institutions with older conservative themes, leading him to define himself as a "liberal conservative."[8] Born in 1926, Lübbe attended university after the Second World War. Trained in philosophy, social science, and theology, Lübbe's writing combined political philosophy with contemporary social analysis. In the 1960s he was affiliated with the German Social Democrats, and from 1967 to 1970 he served as the official responsible for university affairs in the education ministry of Germany's largest state, Rhineland-Westphalia. In 1971 he became professor of philosophy and political theory at the University of Zurich, where he taught until his retirement.

Upon leaving government, Lübbe became a leading critic of the West German New Left, then at the height of its activism. In the 1970s and 1980s, he emerged as a leading polemicist and proponent of a more conservative liberalism. In contrast to those who regarded existing social institutions and cultural norms as barriers to human freedom, Lübbe insisted that there came a point at which the costs of social and cultural "emancipation" outweighed its benefits. The demand for full cultural emancipation, he argued, meant the elimination of all inherited cultural particularity that might in any way inhibit the individual's willingness and ability to consider new ideas. Taken to its logical conclusion, Lübbe argued, the demand for full emancipation meant the self-destruction of a pluralist society based on multiple sources of identity, leaving only culturally homogenous individuals "emancipated" from the past ties that gave their lives meaning. He asserted that individual and collective identity came at least in part from identification with past traditions, without which the pace of technological and social change would leave the individual disoriented, or dependent for direction upon utopian social scientific theories which promised to replace older moral traditions but could not.

The selection which follows is drawn from Lübbe's contribution to a 1984 symposium in which he brought together a number of themes from his earlier work. Returning to the conservative theme of the ineluctability of inequality, he argues that the liberal attempt to create equality of opportunity must be coupled with the acceptance of unequal outcomes based on unequal abilities. And while not hostile to the attempt to create greater equality of educational opportunity, he points out that

---

[8] See Hermann Lübbe, "Aufklärung und Gegenaufklärung," in Michael Zöller, ed., *Aufklärung heute: Bedingungen unserer Freiheit* (Zurich, 1980), p. 13.

the attempt to create equality of educational achievement and social mobility may mean the destruction of existing cultural identities. These are the trade-offs, he suggests, which must be considered in framing educational policy. Lübbe thus touches upon the themes explored in the previous selection by Berger and Neuhaus.

Hermann Lübbe,
"The Social Consequences of Attempts to Create Equality" (1984)[1]

. . . Let us explore the social consequences of a specific type of demand for equality that is particularly significant in the contemporary political context, namely the demand that educational policy ought to achieve an equality of life chances.[2] In keeping with my experience, I would like to examine the effects of this policy through some German examples.

Educational policy throughout contemporary Europe arose out of the desire to bring about not only formal, legal equality, but also socially effective equality of educational opportunity for all. Our purpose here is not to explore the considerable difficulties that this effort entails, but to call attention to the following, inevitable effect. Today we are in the process of diminishing the old, status-bound, socially determined barriers to education, which still represent obstacles for many. But if, someday, all such obstacles are eliminated, then along with the equality of educational chances brought about by political and social means, the chance would be created for the display of the actual potential of everyone, under circumstances in which those possibilities would no longer be distorted by social inequality. The educational realm is not exempt from the dialectic of every demand for equality, namely that equality of opportunity always leads to a process of differential individual achievement.[3]

Under these circumstances the competition for achievement actually increases. Precisely the egalitarian society is by necessity an achievement-

---

[1] Hermann Lübbe: "Politische Gleichheitspostulate und ihre sozialen Folgen," in Robert Kopp, ed., *Solidarität in der Welt der 80er Jahre: Leistungsgesellschaft und Sozialstaat* (Basel and Frankfurt, 1984), pp. 64–77; English version edited and translated by Jerry Z. Muller.

[2] The term "life chances," as used here, refers primarily to vocational and political opportunities.

[3] The German word *Leistung*, which Lübbe uses, has been translated here as "achievement" to comport with normal English social scientific usage; it may also be translated as "performance." What Herbert Marcuse termed "the performance principle" is close in meaning to what is normally referred to as "achievement-orientation."

oriented society. And the competition created under such conditions can in some circumstances be very harsh. Under conditions in which political and social equality of opportunity has become a reality, one will no longer be able to ascribe one's relative falling behind to social causes; instead, one will have to ascribe it to what once would have been unself-consciously called "stupidity."

One must keep this in mind in evaluating the social-psychological effects which necessarily accompany the attempt—such as the Federal Republic of Germany has now undertaken—to see to it that half of the members of each age cohort graduate from an academic high school, and that half of these go on to complete a college degree. This is part of the logic of effectively providing what Ralf Dahrendorf has called "the basic right to education." Such a process necessarily entails the intensification of competitive pressure. This effect is inevitable so long as and to the degree that social chances are dependent on educational chances; and we know of no modern industrial society, be it socialist or market-oriented, liberal or totalitarian, in which social opportunity is not dependent upon educational opportunity. This dependence is shown in plain, quantitative terms by the fact that in Germany the average income opportunities of a college graduate are twice as high as those of a high-school graduate. One needs to know little more than this fact to understand the explosion in the number of university students.

Given these linkages, educational institutions from elementary school through university become the most significant guarantors of vertical social mobility, and policy aimed at creating equality of social opportunity must address equality of educational opportunity.

If we assume, to speak in terms of ideal types, that vertical social mobility represents a system of competition and of allotting rewards on the basis of achievement, then the creation of effective equality of educational opportunity necessarily means that the school will be part of this system of achievement oriented distribution of rewards.

This applies also and indeed above all to the comprehensive schools and colleges favored by some state governments. Their explicit goal is to tear down the historical, inherited social barriers which hinder real equality of educational opportunity. Not a few of those who had promoted these new institutions were astounded by the high degree of competitiveness which arose in such schools. They could have been spared their surprise. It was predictable, through simple insight into the growing significance and salience of differences under conditions of decreasing social and institutional distance.[4] When traditional class barriers

---

[4] That is, children of different classes and different levels of ability who in the past would have been largely segregated by the educational system now interact with one another directly in the same schools.

are eliminated, the tendency to compare oneself to others increases. Put differently: legally guaranteed equality merely defines the field on which differences which cannot be eliminated through legal equality will show themselves; hence these differences will become all the more blatant. One sees then that rising competitive pressures for achievement are not an accident of modern educational policy, they are part of its very logic. . . .

In short, expectations of achievement, and the staffing of positions in the social system on the basis of achievement, are a necessary consequence of a modern society, that is, one which is differentiated and mobile, and no longer organized on the basis of inherited social estate. Why then, and under what circumstances, are such expectations of achievement declared unbearable and attacked as educationally and politically repressive? Let us acknowledge that the expectation of achievement, which is part of modern society, is experienced time and again (quite rightly) as overtaxing. As a result, the nostalgic transfiguration of the simple life in undifferentiated communities has been a recurrent theme within the culture of industrial society, from the Romantics until today, and the emotional potential of this romantic view continues to be exploited in the ideological promise of a society free of alienation. But this deeply rooted source of discontent within modern culture does not explain the protest against demands for achievement which has arisen in some liberal states. . . .

How can this be explained? My contention is this: thanks to enormous efforts of educational policy, the members of the younger generation have been given historically unprecedented egalitarian educational and vocational opportunities. But they are shielded from the insight that competition and expectations of achievement are a necessary consequence of every egalitarian system and need to be acknowledged as such. To put it another way, while the claim of equality of opportunity has become politically irresistible, our dominant ideology and educational policy refuses to recognize that equality of opportunity necessarily produces differential achievement; in fact, the dominant ideology delegitimates such differences of achievement.

A few significant examples will demonstrate this self-contradictory refusal to recognize the differential achievement necessarily produced by effective equality of opportunity.

The former Minister of Education of Lower Saxony, Peter von Oertzen,[5] recently complained that it is a terrible misunderstanding of the function of the intermediate school to treat it as a "machine for selection," rather than as an opportunity to discover and promote talents.

[5] Von Oertzen was a Social Democrat with close ties to the New Left.

This is a perplexing statement. To discover and promote talents—surely that means to discover distinctions, leading to a process of selection. But the polemical expression "machine for selection" is intended to delegitimate and hinder the social efficacy of this process of differentiation.

This self-contradictory attitude also explains the systematic attack which has been conducted for some years against the traditional system of grading. Granted that there is a certain range of imprecision in every attempt to quantify achievement. But this imprecision is by no means a legitimate reason to refuse to quantify measures of achievement. The ongoing campaign to deny the value of such quantitative measures of achievement arises above all from the refusal to acknowledge the differential achievement necessarily produced by effective equality of opportunity. The effect of this refusal is to make pupils neurotic, by disseminating the notion that the system of achievement-oriented selection is a system of repressive injustice. Under these circumstances, in which the existence of socially significant differences of achievement are denied, and the attempt to identify them is treated as illegitimate, the demand for achievement which in fact remains is perceived as an unbearable pressure; the joy of achievement withers, and so does the ability to come to terms with the limits of one's capacities. This is the real reason for the increasing inability of some young people to orient themselves within a social system differentiated by achievement, and not some objectively overly burdensome demand for achievement. It also provides the background for the audacious and cynical grading practices which have led to a shower of high grades at some institutions of higher education. Since there is an indissoluble link between equality of opportunity and differential achievement, the practice of awarding a high grade to everyone is cynical, because by eliminating measured achievement it destroys equality of opportunity.

Satisfaction through achievement on the one hand, and the ability to recognize and accept the limits of one's own abilities on the other, can only develop in a climate in which the differential outcomes of equality are publicly acknowledged in discussions of educational policy and in the broader culture. . . .

[To take another example.] The chairman of the largest German teachers' union recently referred to differences of talent discussed by educational policy-makers as "alleged" differences.

If differences of talent are really only "alleged" then here is the problem facing the teacher who must do his work informed by this ostensible truth from the head of his union. Let us say that he works in a comprehensive high school, equipped with the best educational resources, and has done his best to see a weak pupil through to graduation. Yet other pupils, those traditionally regarded as more talented, make use of the same educational opportunities and do better. Is the teacher therefore to conclude that he or someone else has acted wrongly?

Even worse is the situation faced by the comprehensive-school pupil in question. He too has given his best effort and yet experiences the fact that his fellow-pupil, with much less effort, achieves higher grades. The lower-achieving pupil cannot live with himself when everywhere he turns he hears it proclaimed as truth that differences of talent are merely "alleged". . . . One essential facet of maturity is the ability to come to terms with the limits of one's own capacities, and it is this ability which is systematically suppressed when one is taught that the real reason for one's own weaknesses always lie in someone else or in external circumstances.

So much for the analysis of the dialectic of equality as exemplified in the demand for equality of educational opportunity. What has been demonstrated by this example drawn from the realm of educational policy also holds true more generally of demands for equality: the implementation of those demands does not make people equal, it creates the legal and then the actual bases on which people can develop the natural and cultural differences of every sort which are set free.

This link is so basic that is has almost always been recognized. In the history of political theory as well as in the history of modern constitutional politics, those who demanded "equality" (above all civil equality) never assumed real equality among people; quite the contrary, they assumed that people were unequal. . . .

Now let us turn to another problem which has become prominent in discussions of educational policy, namely that formal equality of opportunity is worth little when the conditions under which the individuals are socialized do not motivate them to actually *make use* of the opportunities that are offered. The differential results of equality of opportunity are in good part the result of characteristics of the individual which one might call "contingent." Whether these contingent characteristics are natural or social in origin, they are historical; this leads some to argue that in addition to creating legal and institutional equality of opportunity, one must also try to bring about equality in regard to those characteristics which enable people to actually make use of opportunities.

This sounds abstract, so let us make it more concrete by means of a much-cited example. We know from educational statistics that according to social-statistical averages, individuals are especially limited in their ability to make use of educational opportunities when they are of rural origin, when they are female, and when they are Catholic. On this basis,

Dahrendorf has presented the oft-cited construct of the Catholic girl from the countryside: she is "emancipationally handicapped," that is, handicapped in the ability to actually make use of legal and institutional opportunities.[6]

Is there a right, or indeed an obligation, to eliminate the emancipational handicaps of certain individuals, in order to make them totally emancipationally competent? Or, on the contrary, are there limits to the demand for emancipation?

It is beyond dispute that all of us, as citizens, are subject to some extent to the demands that we become emancipationally competent and thereby culturally homogenous with others. In this sense the obligation for everyone to attend school, which arose out of the Enlightenment, can be understood as an institution of compulsory emancipation. But are there limits to this compulsion? How extensive is our right to use political and legal means to make individuals the same with regard to those characteristics required to make equal use of opportunities?

A radical answer to this question would be what we might call "the cultural-revolutionary elimination of limits on the demands for emancipation."

That solution was unsurpassably formulated by the young Karl Marx, when he declared that *political* emancipation must be superseded by *human* emancipation. *Political* emancipation was the substantive content of the Enlightenment's program of freedom, ranging from legal equality for Jews through freedom of religion and all the rest of the freedoms known to us from European constitutional history. What, by comparison, is the meaning of superseding political emancipation by what Marx called *human* emancipation? Unsatisfied with the freedom of religion provided by liberal constitutions, Marx's formula called for advancing from "religious liberty" to liberating man "from religion," and from the emancipation of the Jews to "the emancipation of mankind from Jewry."[7]

---

[6] See Ralf Dahrendorf, *Society and Democracy in Germany* (New York, 1967; German original, 1965), pp. 104–6.

[7] Marx's early essay "On the Jewish Question" was a response to the Young Hegelian, Bruno Bauer, who insisted that since the modern liberal state was a historical outgrowth of the universalistic suppositions of Christian culture, Jews had to overcome the cultural particularism inherent in Judaism before they could become citizens of the state. In his response to Bauer, Marx insisted that the problem was not with the Jews' particularistic religion, it was with a society that made what he regarded as the comforting illusions of religion necessary in the first place. The problem, as Marx understood it, was the existence of a society based on trade, that motivated the self-interest of individuals who act out of particularistic identities rather than regarding themselves as universalistic "species-beings." In calling for the emancipation of mankind from "Jewry," Marx was playing the dual meaning of "Jewry" as referring to Jews or to trade as such. His statement can

This is a prime formulation of what we have called "the cultural-revolutionary elimination of limits on the demands for emancipation." As a recent Christian philosopher has suggested, Marx is here criticizing both Christianity and Judaism "according to the criterion of communicative freedom." If this interpretation is correct, then the domination of the enlightened super-norm of so-called "communicative freedom" would be intrinsically terroristic. For it would amount to the demand to attain unlimited communicative competence through unlimited cultural emancipation from all contingent characteristics that are a result of origin, until there was nothing that we would be unwilling to put up for discussion. In terms of cultural identity this amounts to a program for the transformation of those elements of our character formed by our contingent origins as members of a particular family or religion, into a new identity in which each of us is ready and competent to engage in unlimited communication as members of a united humanity indifferent to origins. Under those circumstances, individuals would not in fact be distinguishable in terms of their ability to take advantage of their equal opportunities.

I regard this sort of cultural-revolutionary program of complete emancipation as a program for the self-destruction of a liberal culture.[8] This becomes clear when one turns once again to Dahrendorf's construct of the Catholic girl from the countryside. Measured by the ideals of an "educational society" [i.e., a society geared to educational achievement] she is indeed emancipationally handicapped. But should we then conclude that we have the right or indeed the obligation to enact the cultural-revolutionary program of the expropriation of all cultural substance for the sake of eliminating the contingent results of religious and familial origin, in order to create homogenous technical and economic competence? Should the effects of education within the family be eliminated? Should religious instruction in schools be eliminated or transformed into sessions for training in communicative freedom? Are private schools, with their particular cultural milieux, an anachronism? Are my fellow East Frisians to be declared unenlightened by virtue of the fact that they have many children, or the farmers of Westphalia declared emancipationally handicapped by virtue of their lower rates of divorce?

---

therefore be understood as a call to eliminate commerce and to eliminate particularistic identity.

For a good discussion of the issue, see Nathan Rotenstreich, "For and Against Emancipation: The Bruno Bauer Controversy," *Leo Baeck Institute Yearbook*, no. 4, 1959, pp. 3–36.

[8] Here Lübbe recurs to the conservative theme that the stability of a liberal society depends upon non-liberal institutions.

Given the inexhaustible historical and regional differentiation within our culture, one could raise an endless series of similar questions which would bring out the conceptual error of the progressivist tendency to treat cultural traditions as obstructions to emancipation which ought to be eliminated in the interests of creating effective social and cultural equality.

The conservative (and for that matter, liberal) response to the challenge of such programs of complete cultural-revolutionary emancipation can be formulated as follows: As much commonality as necessary based on the recognition of inalienable, universally valid claims; as much diversity as possible, based on the effective influence of contingent origins.

▶ 10 ◀

BETWEEN
SOCIAL SCIENCE AND
CULTURAL CRITICISM

INTRODUCTION TO
Arnold Gehlen,
"On Culture, Nature, and Naturalness" and
"Man and Institutions"

◆

Arnold Gehlen (1904–76) was among the most controversial and stimulating conservative theorists of the twentieth century. Gehlen's social
theory has been characterized as an abstract legitimation of order as
such, free of any particular content.[1] His is arguably the most sophisticated attempt in the twentieth century to explain the significance of
"second nature." Gehlen's conservatism begins not only with the assumption that there is no transcendent order: his is a thoroughly skeptical and relativistic conservatism that insists that historically developed
institutions are all that man has available to him as the source of social
order, and that there are no super-historical standards against which institutions can be measured.

Gehlen began as a radical conservative intellectual for whom National
Socialism became the god that failed.[2] Born in Leipzig, Germany, Gehlen studied philosophy and completed his *Habilitation*, the higher degree required to teach in a German university, in 1931. His early
writings adumbrate the theme that would recur in his later work,
namely, the inability of existing institutions to provide the individual

---

[1] This introduction has profited from the essays collected in Helmut Klages and Helmut
Quaritsch, eds., *Zur geisteswissenschaftlichen Bedeutung Arnold Gehlens* (Berlin, 1994).
[2] On Gehlen's career, see Jerry Z. Muller, *The Other God that Failed: Hans Freyer and
the Deradicalization of German Conservatism* (Princeton, 1987), pp. 395–99 and passim.

with a reliable and commonly shared sense of purpose. For Gehlen, the National Socialist ascension to power represented both a political and personal opportunity. He joined the Nazi party after its rise to power in 1933, and was active within its academic organizations through 1936. During the Third Reich his professional rise was meteoric, as he was named to a succession of chairs in Leipzig, Königsberg, and Vienna. During the Second World War he continued to teach while serving simultaneously in an army psychology unit.

At first Gehlen had high hopes for the new regime. Conscious of the primitiveness of National Socialist ideology, but enthused at the prospect of a new institutional order that might overcome what he regarded as the decadent subjectivism and individualism of the modern age, Gehlen set out to develop a proper philosophy of National Socialism. But his writings on the topic came under attack from Nazi ideologists, and his works after 1935 showed a greater reserve and distance from immediate questions.

In 1940 Gehlen published the first edition of his most seminal work, entitled *Man: His Nature and Place in the World*.[3] There he put forward a theory of the biological foundations of the human need for institutions, perhaps the most sophisticated attempt in the twentieth century to restate the conservative argument for the necessity of institutions on an entirely naturalistic basis. The book set forth a detailed argument regarding the *function* of institutions and the worldviews which sustained them, without offering criteria for preferring one worldview to another. In Gehlen's book it was the ability of institutions to provide their members with a firm and all-encompassing set of orientations which counted. Gehlen was concerned with the stabilizing *function* of the beliefs which legitimated institutions, not with the truth or falsity of those beliefs.

In the two decades after 1945, Gehlen continued to develop his theory of institutions, most notably in *Primitive Man and Late Culture*.[4] He also produced a stream of books and essays of cultural criticism, art criticism, and social and political analysis.

Gehlen's involvement with National Socialism influenced his professional standing after the war, and he was never appointed to a chair at a major university. No Gehlenite "school" arose in West German sociology, not least due to Gehlen's marginal position within the academy. But the influence of his thought was considerable; it extended not only

---

[3] *Der Mensch, seine Natur und seine Stellung in der Welt* (Hamburg, 1940); subsequent editions, with significant revisions were published in 1944 and 1950; a critical edition, edited by Karl-Siegbert Rehberg, was published as volume three of the *Arnold Gehlen Gesamtausgabe* (Frankfurt, 1993); the book has appeared in English translation as *Man: His Nature and Place in the World* (New York, 1988).

[4] *Urmensch und Spätkultur* (Bonn, 1956).

to conservatives, but to liberals, liberal conservatives, and independent leftists such as Jürgen Habermas.

Gehlen's theory of institutions owes a great deal to Hegel, and is in some ways an attempt to reformulate Hegel's thought on a naturalistic basis, an aspiration which led to Gehlen's self-acknowledged affinities with David Hume and with twentieth-century American Pragmatists, especially George Herbert Mead. The biological starting point of Gehlen's theory of institutions is man's unique position in the animal world.[5] Gehlen draws upon the findings of evolutionary embryology and physical anthropology, yet his approach is anti-biologistic. Indeed, he begins with Nietzsche's definition of man as "the undetermined animal." Rather than conceiving of man as determined by his biology, Gehlen stresses that in contrast to the animals, man is unprepared by his biology for survival: he owes his continued existence and his emotional well-being to institutions and the cultural norms that sustain them. Compared to most animals, man in "unfinished" at birth: much of his organic development occurs after he has left the womb. Man's unspecialized instinctual structure allows him to adapt to a remarkable range of natural environments, but it does not "program" him for a particular, stable social structure in which to develop to maturity. Man's sensory apparatus leaves him open to a wide range of stimuli, resulting in what Gehlen terms "openness to the world." This plethora of stimuli threatens to distract or overwhelm him, unless they are filtered out by institutionally conveyed mental habits. Similarly, man is "burdened" with biological drives not clearly directed by instincts, which leave him prone to anxiety unless he is "unburdened" by institutions which shape and direct these energies. Institutions then, for Gehlen, are the culturally produced forms by which human life is given coherence and continuity, thus compensating for man's lack of instinctual determination. For Gehlen, man's nature requires second nature.

Gehlen's theory develops and reformulates recurrent conservative arguments about the necessity of institutions. His contemporary cultural criticism often has a radical conservative undertone, suggesting that modern institutions are "decayed" and not up to the task of providing the sort of unquestioned certainties about the world and the individual's place in it which Gehlen associates with ancient (archaic) institutions. It is never clear from Gehlen's analysis just when he believes that this "deinstitutionalization" set in. Other theorists have adopted Gehlen's theory of institutions without accepting his negative evaluation of modern developments. But Gehlen's argument is particularly noteworthy for

---

[5] For a clear summary of Gehlen's theory of institutions, on which I have drawn in this paragraph, see Peter Berger's "Foreword" to Arnold Gehlen, *Man in the Age of Technology* (New York, 1980).

its clear presentation of the recurrent conservative lament that contemporary processes are eroding the institutions valued by conservatives.

The following selections are drawn from two articles by Gehlen, dating from 1958 and 1960. They succinctly convey themes explored more extensively in his major books: his theory of institutions, and his analysis of the institutional decay that he associated with modernity.[6]

Arnold Gehlen,
"On Culture, Nature, and Naturalness" (1958)[1]

The "Naturalness" of Cultures

One can bring together a number of anthropological perspectives into the formula that "man is by nature a cultural being". . . . At any rate, we only know of men in possession of cultural attainments, which, no matter how primitive we may find them, are still so fundamental that human existence would be unthinkable without them. The distinction between natural man and cultured man is therefore imprecise, and taken literally, quite false—only cultured humanity exists or has existed, though with an astounding range of cultural inventory.

Among the great riddles of the anthropological search for some primeval, natural culture is the incredible diversity of the forms and configurations that have been discovered. As a result of several decades of research in cultural anthropology, we know with greater certainty the enormous range of variations of cultural arrangements, values, fundamental orientations and resulting consequences. . . . The well known little book by Ruth Benedict, *Patterns of Culture*, shows this through the example of three primitive peoples, each with its particular and internally meaningful pattern. The book demonstrates such striking contrasts among peoples, which reach so to speak into the interior of the human heart, that one is almost led to believe that one is dealing with different species.

It follows from what has been said so far that we only encounter what is natural in man already suffused by cultural coloration. This proposition is often conceded, but too rarely are its implications fully taken into account. For if culture is natural to man then we never encounter human

---

[6] "*Über Kultur, Natur und Natürlichkeit*," first published in 1958, was reprinted in Arnold Gehlen, *Anthropologische Forschung. Zur Selbstbegegnung und Selbstentdeckung des Menschen* (Hamburg, 1961), pp. 78–91. "*Mensch und Institution*," first delivered as a lecture in 1960, was published in the same volume, pp. 69–77.

[1] From Arnold Gehlen, *Anthropologische Forschung* (Reinbek, 1961), edited and translated by Jerry Z. Muller.

nature as such, it is always already permeated by the effects of cultural context. The question of the essential difference between the sexes, for example, cannot be answered in general, but only within the range of a particular culture, since we are dealing in every case with a culturally determined stylization[2] of some substrate which we never encounter as such, in its primordial natural form. . . . [This applies] to virtually all axioms of cultural life: legal, religious, aesthetic, political or other norms can diverge entirely from one society to another. One is impressed by the far-reaching natural undeterminedness of man, at the very least in the sense that behavior cannot be predicted on the basis of his biology. Thus it seems to me quite impossible to define terms such as "law" or "religion" in such a way that they really encompass all the known forms of these phenomena, or what we usually classify as such. In regard to religion, for example, take the case of primitive Buddhism, a salvational religion (a salvational teaching? technique?) which knew neither gods nor a world-creator. The various cultures are as different from one another in their perspectives and structural elements as are languages; the infinite and indeed categorical dissimilarity among languages also applies to other realms of culture, such as forms of family, property, authority, and so on. That is not to say that all the constants will be overshadowed by the variations, but one can only approach the question of what is *essential* when one has come to terms with the empirical evidence. Whoever makes declarations about man, woman, property, etc. on the basis of his own naive reflections, runs the risk, even if he is a scholar, of merely generalizing the taken-for-granted assumptions of his own culture. An adequate theory of knowledge would have to take into account the problem of cultural bias along with that of personal bias.

We have recalled these problems, which are widely conceded nowadays, by way of introduction, in order now to introduce a quite simple chain of reasoning. The first link may be formulated this way: Each culture experiences the cultural norms and institutions which it has developed (for example its legal theory, its marital forms, its scale of interests, passions, and emotions) as the only natural and naturally appropriate ones. As a rule, each culture experiences the norms of another culture or society as curious, comic, peculiar, and for the most part as unnatural, perverse, anti-natural, and indeed, at the extreme end of this spectrum, as sinful and abhorrent. . . . As the psychologist Hofstätter[3] puts it in his *Introduction to Social Psychology*, "In a strongly established culture, the normative balance is taken-for-granted, and is perceived as naturally appropriate." Helmut Schelsky[4] generalizes the thesis when, in his

---

[2] That is, the molding of emotions into standard or typical patterns of behavior.

[3] Peter R. Hofstätter, a German psychologist, was a close associate of Gehlen.

[4] Helmut Schelsky was a German sociologist and close associate of Gehlen. The quote

discussion of the norms of sexual behavior, he writes, "When socially created sexual norms appear as absolute in the self-consciousness of the members of a society, then acting according to such norms is generally experienced as *natural*. But the assertion of 'naturalness' is evidence not of a biological fact, it is a sign that the norm is undoubted." And the same applies, as we have seen, more generally. Thus a society may regard as natural or taken-for-granted that there is polygamous marriage, or that women do the work in the fields because they alone "can make things grow," or that social leadership and the attached privileges must go to the elders by virtue of their long experience, or that one can "naturally" be related by blood only to one's mother and not to one's father. These are examples of assumptions the validity of which is taken for granted in other cultures but not in ours. In addition to divergent assumptions about what is "natural" there is the phenomenon of the cultural imposition of norms and valuations on truly natural facts, for example the assertion that the white race is naturally superior to every other, such that every other race can be assigned to some subordinate rank. Up through the first quarter of our century this was regarded as taken-for-granted among Germans, Englishmen, and incidentally among Americans as well. Only now do we experience how these same nations, at the same time as they lose their certainty, are inclined to accept the theory (however self-evident or implausible one holds it to be) that all races of whatever color are naturally assumed to be entitled to equality.

What has been said so far applies also to the picture that each culture has of external nature—that picture too is culturally relative. Some readily concede this in regard to the past (in regard to the ancient Greeks' view of nature, for example) without recognizing that it applies to our view of nature as well; yet the peculiar logical-mathematical and technical methods through which our view of nature is filtered are themselves a creation of West-European culture (or whatever one wants to call it.) Similarly the orientation toward abstract experiment (the invention of mechanisms that produce pure events of nature for observation) is also a product of the culture of western Europe. Originally, it was as peculiarly European as, say, war by firearms.

CONVENTIONALITY AS AN INDICATOR OF DECAYED CULTURAL STYLIZATIONS

Let us now go a step further. If the cultural forms which in a particular historical context have become second nature are shaken, some very in-

---

which follows is from Schelsky, *Soziologie der Sexualität: Über die Beziehungen zwischen Geschlecht, Moral, und Gesellschaft* (Hamburg, 1955).

teresting processes occur. This is not the place to explore the question of why and under what circumstances the self-confidence of a culture is shaken in a way that threatens its taken-for-granted assumptions. But we know that often mere contact with another culture is sufficient. Such processes have often occurred, and they are now occurring once again in Europe. What will become of the taken-for-granted norms that were experienced as natural? Hofstätter offers the correct answer, "When a tradition is in the process of becoming subject to doubt, its norms are perceived only as conformities to custom."[5]

In other words, while unbroken cultural stylizations are perceived as arising from one's own will and from one's innermost nature, shaken or superannuated cultural stylizations come to be regarded for the first time as mere conventions. To treat norms as "conventional" is to imply the arbitrariness of their claims to validity, no longer to perceive them as the only possibility, to begin to distance oneself from them. . . .

"Man and Institutions" (1960)[6]

THE UNBURDENING FUNCTION OF INSTITUTIONS

One of most significant and fundamental human characteristics is the incompleteness and uncertainty of instinctual life, the plasticity and fluidity of man's instincts. The need for institutions arises from this undeterminedness of human drives and the resulting unpredictability of human behavior. The relationship between institutions and man's instinctual endowment is captured in the following formulation: "Human instincts do not determine a particular, established pattern of behavior, as do the instincts of animals. Instead, every culture extracts particular variants out of the multiplicity of possible forms of human behavior, and elevates them to socially sanctioned behavioral norms which are binding upon all members of the group. For the individual, the existence of such culturally-created behavioral models or institutions are an unburdening, a relief from the need to make all too many decisions, a signpost through the flood of impressions and stimuli with which 'world-open' human beings are flooded."[7]

From this perspective, institutions appear as forms for the mastery of vital tasks or of circumstances which demand orderly and ongoing cooperation, such as propagation, defense, or nourishment. From another

---

[5] Peter R. Hofstätter, *Sozialpsychologie* (1956), p. 144.

[6] From Gehlen, *Anthropologische Forschung*.

[7] Gehlen is quoting an encyclopedia article by Ilse Schwidetzki, but the definition is based upon Gehlen's own, earlier work.

perspective, institutions appear as *stabilizing* forces: man is a being who is by nature unstable and at risk, overburdened by affect; institutions are the forms which make men mutually tolerable to one another and tolerable to themselves; they provide things which one can count on and rely on in oneself and in others. On one hand, it is in these institutions that the tasks of life can be pursued in common. On the other hand, it is through institutions that men orient themselves to ultimate, fixed goals of action, which brings with it an extraordinary gain in the stabilization of internal life, in that they are not forced on every occasion into emotional confrontations or decisions of principles.

The individual experiences an institution such as property or marriage as a super-personal, preexisting standard to which he adjusts; in other cases he enters into an institution such as a profession, an office, or a factory, in the consciousness that the institution in this form has long existed and will long continue to exist despite changes in the particular individuals who enter it or leave it. This theme leads into highly significant directions when one recognizes that human actions are transformed into inherent norms which come to confront individuals as an objective order, and which the individual encounters as a valid order.[8]

To summarize our theme in a few words: the forms in which men live or work with one another, in which authority is embodied, or contact with the super-sensual is encountered—they all develop into arrangements with their own emotional weight; into institutions, which ultimately gain a certain autonomy from the individuals who first gave rise to them, so that an individual's action becomes increasingly predictable when one knows his place in the social system and the social institutions of which he is a part. The demands of vocation and of family, of the state or of organizations to which one belongs, regulate not only our behavior, they reach down into our sense of self-worth and influence the decisions of our will; as a result, we are able to act without hesitation and doubt, as if automatically. Other possibilities seem inconceivable, and we act with the conviction that our response is natural. Within the interior life of the individual this creates a feeling of beneficent certitude, a vital unburdening, because on the basis of this substructure of inner habits and external customs, mental energies are free to rise upward, so to speak, they become available for particular, *personal*, unique and novel purposes. From an anthropological point of view, the concept of individual *personality* is intimately linked to that of institutions, for it is institutions which make it possible for personal qualities to develop. . . . Though institutions in a sense schematize us, by moulding and stan-

---

[8] That is, social institutions convey the message that they are legitimate and hence are perceived by the individual as "valid."

dardizing our thought and our emotions along with our actions,[9] it is this very fact that allows one the reserves of energy to be unique, within the given circumstances, that is, to act effectively, inventively, fruitfully. He who seeks to be a "personality" not *within* the given circumstances, but *regardless* of all circumstances, is bound to fail.[10]

Let us now go a step further to ask what occurs when institutions are disrupted or shattered. This happens whenever there is a historical catastrophe, be it a revolution, the collapse of a state or a social order or an entire culture, or by the violent intervention of an aggressive culture into a peaceful one. The immediate effect is a deep loss of the sense of certainty of those affected; this disorientation reaches down to their moral and spiritual centers, for there too the certainty of the taken-for-granted is disrupted. Reaching into the core of the psyche, disruption forces men to improvise, to make decisions against their will, or to dive into uncertainty with eyes shut tight, or perhaps to grasp onto one or another fundamental belief firmly and come what may in order to survive. Lack of certainty may also be affectively expressed as anxiety, obstinacy, or sensitivity.

Institutional Decay and the Exaggeration of Subjectivity

The effect of the decay of institutions on the individuals who were part of them—whether it occurs slowly or through a sudden catastrophe—is *subjectivism*. By this I do not mean self-referentiality or egocentricity, at least not in the conventional sense, but rather a self-imprisonment in which the individual experiences *his* fortuitous inner predispositions, the particular convictions and thoughts that occur to *him*, and *his* emotional reactions as if these immediate experiences were of super-personal import. Left in the lurch by institutions and thrown back on oneself, one can only react by taking the internal experiences which remain and exaggerating them into general validity, and this now occurs with such frequency that it is taken for granted. It goes hand in hand with an immediate claim on public attention. . . . The unrestrained claim for attention to one's subjectivity, which arises from this institutional impoverishment and normative confusion, goes together with a striking vulnerability and sensitivity on the part of individual subjects. Never have people been more decisively thrown back on the limited reserves of their fortuitous predispositions than today, never have these predispositions been under greater pressure, and as a result never have they been so vulner-

---

[9] This process is what Gehlen in the previous selection refers to as "stylization."

[10] That is, a certain degree of conformity to existing social institutions is a prerequisite of effective individual development.

able. In the nature of things, the condition described here is most readily grasped in the realm of culture, art and literature, but I believe that it can be generalized. In well-functioning institutions, individual sensitivities and subjective frictions are neutralized, because one makes sense of oneself on the basis of external realities. As these irritated sensibilities emerge, they cannot be relieved through so-called open discussion. And so a paradoxical situation arises: the more people make use of the fundamental freedom to speak their minds, that is to say to profess their subjectivism, the less authentic contact results. . . .

INTRODUCTION TO
Philip Rieff,
"Toward a Theory of Culture"

◆

The work of Philip Rieff, who spent most of his academic career as a professor of sociology, combines sociological theory, intellectual history, cultural criticism, and (in his later writings) religious apologetics. His writings touch upon a remarkable range of subjects, while returning time and again to a few unifying themes. He is the author of three major books: *Freud: The Mind of the Moralist* (first published in 1959), *The Triumph of the Therapeutic: Uses of Faith after Freud* (1966), and *Fellow Teachers* (1973), and of numerous essays.[1] The idiosyncrasies of his style require a rather substantial introduction to his key themes and concepts.

For the source of Rieff's central concern, one can turn to one of his earliest publications, a 1952 review of Hannah Arendt's *Origins of Totalitarianism*. In her book, Rieff found the notion that the mass murders in Nazi Germany and Stalinist Russia were "a revelation of the abyss of possibility." "Man emancipated from his particularity becomes not human but demonic," he wrote.[2] It is this presentiment that underlies much of Rieff's subsequent writing. The barrier which kept men from sliding into the "abyss of possibility" Rieff called "culture." "Everything is possible to human beings," he writes, "we are members of a culture in the sense that everything is not permitted to us, nor even conceivable by us."[3]

Against the predominant emphasis of modern liberalism and left-wing radicalism on the desirability of liberation, Rieff has stressed the typically conservative themes of the necessity for restraint and constraint, and has returned time and again to the theme of culture as a "second nature" which veils the abysmal possibilities of human nature.

---

[1] Philip Rieff, *Freud: The Mind of the Moralist* (New York, 1959); rev. ed., New York, 1961; 2nd ed., London, 1965; 3rd ed., with epilogue, "One Step Further" (Chicago, 1979). Rieff, *The Triumph of the Therapeutic: Uses of Faith after Freud* (New York, 1966); 2nd ed., with a new preface (Chicago, 1987); *Fellow Teachers* (New York, 1973), 2nd ed. published as *Fellow Teachers/Of Culture and Its Second Death*, with a new preface: "A Pretext of Proof Texts" (Chicago, 1984). Many of Rieff's essays are collected in Rieff, *The Feeling Intellect: Selected Writings*, edited and with an introduction by Jonathan B. Imber (Chicago, 1990); this volume also includes a complete bibliography of Rieff's works through 1990.

[2] "The Theology of Politics: Reflections on Totalitarianism as the Burden of Our Time," in *Feeling Intellect*, p. 89.

[3] "Toward a Theory of Culture: With Special Reference to the Psychoanalytic Case" (1972), in ibid., p. 324.

While many sociological theories have treated shared understandings of what is morally desirable and morally undesirable as key elements of social cohesion, Rieff focuses on the latter, on what each culture *forbids*, or what he calls "interdicts," which are often dismissed as "taboos."

While most contemporary theorists of culture have followed Clifford Geertz in stressing the aesthetic or symbolic nature of cultures, Rieff by contrast has insisted upon the centrality of *moral* demands in cultural systems.[4] According to Rieff, cultures are based on a shared vision of ideal moral behavior, including behavior which is forbidden. Given man's moral fallibility and frailty, transgressions are often committed, and each culture has "remissions" which allow the individual to live with having done what ought not to have been done. Remissions make it possible, in other words, to live with our frequent inability to live up to shared moral standards, while reaffirming the worth of those standards.

Rieff assumes that human beings acquire their sense of purpose and meaning from the cultures in which they live, and that cultures unable to convey such a sense of meaning leave their members feeling empty or anxious. By attaching the self to some larger set of shared goals, and by requiring that man's asocial or evil urges be repressed or redirected toward higher, ultimate purposes, cultures provide individual purpose and collective cohesion.

For Rieff, a morally desirable culture is one in which the system of moral demands is so deeply accepted by individuals that the evil instinctual possibilities of which men are always capable are generally felt to be repugnant—so repugnant that they are not even spoken of directly. Education is the process by which individuals internalize their culture's "consensus of shalt nots." The most important educational institution has traditionally been the family, where this cultural authority is first instilled.[5] Through creeds and institutions, men and women are trained in the necessary limitation of their possibilities. Depth of character, Rieff writes, occurs when cultural shalts and shalt nots become so much a part of us that we are disposed to fulfill them almost instinctively. Character in this sense leads to consistent action, and for just this reason it is the basis of social trust. The proper role of those most versed in the culture's creeds—of intellectuals—is primarily to aid in the educative process by which our culturally acquired character keeps us from sliding individually or collectively into the "abyss of possibility." According to Rieff, where intellectuals regard their mission primarily as the opening up of possibilities rather than recalling the reasons why possibilities ought to be foreclosed, they pave the way for barbarism.

[4] See the selection reprinted below, and "Toward a Theory of Culture," in *Feeling Intellect*, pp. 321–30.
[5] See *Fellow Teachers*, pp. 38, 106; "The Cultural Economy of Higher Education," in *Feeling Intellect*, pp. 247–48.

It is Rieff's contention that historical western cultures based on polit-ical or religious ideals are in the process of radical erosion.

In this process Freud plays a key if ambiguous role, which Rieff ana-lyzed in *Freud: The Mind of the Moralist.* On the one hand, the book asserted that Freud was a great mind, and a rather conservative one at that. In contrast to a widely shared impression of Freud as a legitimator of sexual revolution and instinctual expression, Rieff showed that Freud regarded the social repression of instincts as necessary and inevitable. On the other hand, Rieff portrayed Freud as the catalyst of a new cul-tural sensibility which he saw as increasingly dominant among the Amer-ican educated classes. He dubbed Freud "The first out-patient of the hospital culture in which we live," or what Rieff termed the culture of "the therapeutic." Central to the therapeutic sensibility and to Rieff's portrait of Freud was the "lowering" of authority, the premise that what men had regarded as high or ultimate was actually the expression of something lower, in this case of instincts and their sublimation. Freud's interpretation of culture and of human motivation, Rieff showed, was inevitably reductive. By interpreting all ethics of self-sacrifice and all reli-gious belief as the veiled and distorted expressions of sexuality, Freud explicitly or implicitly deflated older, nobler aspirations. Thus all social and religious goals were interpretively reconceived as veiled expressions of the instincts. For those steeped in the Freudian sensibility, to be ra-tional was to be suspicious of all altruism, of public commitments, and of religious belief. Psychoanalysis thus delegitimated inherited cultural identities, while helping to create a new cultural ideal—what Rieff called "psychological man"—committed only to "his own careful economy of the inner life."[6] For psychological man, social relationships and cultural attachments were viewed as forms of therapy. Though psychological men entered into social relationships, they did so with deep suspicion and with a constant attention to whether their investments were paying off in psychic health.

In *The Triumph of the Therapeutic* (1966), Rieff refined and rounded out the implications of the replacement of politics and religion by the therapeutic worldview. For what Rieff called "the therapeutic"—the person schooled in the analytic attitude—the highest wisdom was "to keep in touch with the options around which the conduct of his life might be organized; ideally, all options ought to be kept alive because, theoretically, all are equally advisable—or inadvisable, in given personal circumstances."[7] The therapeutic type was thus schooled against bind-ing, permanent commitments; the bottom line of every social contract, for him, was the escape clause. This applied not only to personal com-mitments, but to cultural or intellectual commitments as well. Commit-

---

[6] *Freud,* p. 356.   [7] *Triumph,* p. 50.

ment itself was viewed as a form of therapeutic self-enhancement, with each commitment to be abandoned when self-enhancement diminished.

The culture of therapy and analysis was therefore the antithesis of what Rieff regarded as high culture: by "deconverting" the individual from inherited religious and historical commands and understandings, it made the mind open and pliable, rather than stable and trustworthy. The culture of therapy was a "remissive" culture, more adept at excusing or explaining away the "shalt nots" of the past than of offering compelling reasons of its own for anti-instinctual moral behavior. It thus paved the way for the revolt against cultural constraints which Rieff saw flowering the 1960s.[8]

In Rieff's account, intellectuals were the first to adopt the culture of therapy, and have been most responsible for its diffusion into the larger culture. Abandoning their traditional role of articulating the necessity of the repression of desire for the sake of communal purposes and higher authority, intellectuals were increasingly devoted to demonstrating the arbitrariness of all restraints and authority.

The inculcation of these assumptions, Rieff claims, whether in its psychoanalytic or sociological form, makes the reappropriation of previous cultural traditions so difficult. For Rieff, then, contemporary intellectuals immersed in the critical culture of therapy can only teach one critique of meaning after another. They open the door to "liberation": and beyond the door lies the personal meaninglessness that comes from having to choose and choose again, without compelling grounds for choice.

The selections below, from *The Triumph of the Therapeutic*, convey Rieff's theory of culture, as well as his analysis of the direction of modern cultural developments.

Philip Rieff,
"Toward a Theory of Culture" (1966)[1]

To speak of a *moral* culture would be redundant. Every culture has two main functions: (1) to organize the moral demands men make upon themselves into a system of symbols that make men intelligible and

---

[8] This is the theme of *Fellow Teachers*.

[1] From Philip Rieff, *The Triumph of the Therapeutic: Uses of Faith after Freud* (New York, 1966). The excerpts are taken primarily from the original introductory chapter, "Toward a Theory of Culture," with some additions from the final chapter, "The Triumph of the Therapeutic." Most of Rieff's footnotes have been eliminated; those retained are indicated by brackets.

trustworthy to each other, thus rendering also the world intelligible and trustworthy;[2] (2) to organize the expressive remissions by which men release themselves, in some degree, from the strain of conforming to the controlling symbolic, internalized variant readings of culture that constitute individual character. The process by which a culture changes at its profoundest level may be traced in the shifting balance of controls and releases which constitute a system of moral demands.

Those who transmit the moral demand system are a cultural elite, exemplifying those demands in their character and behavior. But an elite cannot merely teach or write of the moral demand system without acting out some part of it. However the labor of exemplary enactment is divided, no culture survives long without its elite, those cadres which demonstrate the particular balance of control and remission in the culture itself. . . .

As cultures change, so do the modal types of personality that are their bearers. The kind of man I see emerging, as our culture fades into the next, resembles the kind once called "spiritual"—because such a man desires to preserve the inherited morality freed from its hard external crust of institutional discipline. Yet a culture survives principally, I think, by the power of its institutions to bind and loose men in the conduct of their affairs with reasons which sink so deep into the self that they become commonly and implicitly understood—with that understanding of which explicit belief and precise knowledge of externals would show outwardly like the tip of an iceberg.[3] Spiritualizers of religion[4] (and precisians of science) failed to take into account the degree of intimacy with which this comprehensive interior understanding was cognate with historic institutions,[5] binding even the ignorants of a culture to a great chain of meaning. These institutions are responsible for conveying the social conditions of their acceptance by men thus saved from destructive illusions of uniqueness and separateness. Having broken the outward forms, so as to liberate, allegedly, the inner meaning of the good, the beautiful, and the true, the spiritualizers, who set the pace of Western cultural life from just before the beginning to a short time after the end of the nineteenth century, have given way now to their logical and historical successors, the psychologizers, inheritors of that dualist tradition which pits human nature against social order.

[2] This system of morally laden symbols is what Rieff refers to as a "symbolic."

[3] A restatement of the concept of second nature.

[4] That is, those who attempt to preserve the moral content of religion while divesting religion of dogma and institutional forms.

[5] They failed to recognize that the inculcation of moral standards could not be divorced from the historically developed institutions through which these standards were conveyed.

Undeceived, as they think, about the sources of all morally binding address, the psychologizers, now fully established as the pacesetters of cultural change, propose to help men avoid doing further damage to themselves by preventing live deceptions from succeeding the dead ones.[6] But, in order to save themselves from falling apart with their culture, men must engender another, different and yet powerful enough in its reorganization of experience to make themselves capable again of controlling the infinite variety of panic and emptiness to which they are disposed. It is to control their dis-ease as individuals that men have always acted culturally, in good faith. Books and parading, prayers and the sciences, music and piety toward parents: these are a few of the many instruments by which a culture may produce the saving larger self, for the control of panic and the filling up of emptiness. Superior to and encompassing the different modes in which it appears, a culture must communicate ideals, setting as internalities those distinctions between right actions and wrong that unite men and permit them the fundamental pleasure of agreement. Culture is another name for a design of motives directing the self outward, toward those communal purposes in which alone the self can be realized and satisfied. . . .

The best spirits of the twentieth century have thus expressed their conviction that the original innocence, which to earlier periods was a sinful conceit, the new center, which can be held even as communities disintegrate, is the self. By this conviction a new and dynamic acceptance of disorder, in love with life and destructive of it, has been loosed upon the world. Here literature and sociology converge; for the ultimate interest of sociology, like that of psychiatry when it is not lost in a particular patient, turns on the question whether our culture can be so reconstructed that faith—some compelling symbolic of self-integrating communal purpose—need no longer superintend the organization of personality.

So long as a culture maintains its vitality, whatever must be renounced disappears and is given back bettered; Freud called this process sublimation. But, as that sage among psychiatrists Harry Stack Sullivan once said, "if you tell people how they can sublimate, they can't sublimate." The dynamics of culture are in "the unwitting part of it."[7] Now our renunciations have failed us; less and less is given back bettered. . . .

It is less the lingering of the old culture than the emergence of the new that needs diagnosis. In fact, evil and immorality are disappearing,

---

[6] By presenting all shared cultural ideals as mere "deceptions" (veils of instinctual demands), psychologizers of morality attempt to prevent deep personal commitment to any shared ideals, old or new.

[7] [Harry Stack Sullivan, "The Illusion of Personal Individuality," *Psychiatry* (1950), vol. 13, no. 1, p. 323.]

as Spencer[8] assumed they would, mainly because our culture is changing its definition of human perfection. No longer the Saint, but the instinctual Everyman, twisting his neck uncomfortably inside the starched collar of culture, is the communal ideal, to whom men offer tacit prayers for deliverance from their inherited renunciations. Freud sought only to soften the collar; others, using bits and pieces of his genius, would like to take it off. There have been forerunners of this movement—Rousseau, Boehme, Hamann, or Blake. But never before has there been such a general shifting of sides as now among intellectuals in the United States and England. Many have gone over to the enemy without realizing that they, self-considered the cultural elite, have actually become spokesmen for what Freud called the instinctual "mass." Much of modern literature constitutes a symbolic act of going over to the side of the latest, and most original, individualist. This represents the complete democratization of our culture.

It was in order to combat just such talented hostility to culture that Freud emphasized coercion and the renunciation of instinct as indispensable elements in all culture. Freud was neither an eroticist nor a democrat. His theory of culture depended upon a crossing between his idea of moral authority and an elitist inclination. "It is just as impossible," he writes, "to do without control of the mass by a minority as it is to dispense with coercion in the work of civilization." By "mass" Freud means not merely the "lazy and unintelligent," but, more importantly, those who "have no love for instinctual renunciation" and who cannot be "convinced by argument of its inevitability." That such large numbers of the cultivated and intelligent have identified themselves deliberately with those who are supposed to have no *love* for instinctual renunciation, suggests to me the most elaborate act of suicide that Western intellectuals have ever staged—those intellectuals, whether of the left or right, whose historic function it has been to assert the authority of a culture organized in terms of communal purpose, through the agency of congregations of the faithful. . . .

The debts incurred by conscience through warped and atrophied communal purposes are now being paid off at a usurious rate of interest. The lingering death of authoritarian love has left behind hatred and violence, twin widows of dead love, free to stimulate in the culturally impoverished or disenchanted energies emancipated from conviction. It is not class or race war that we have to fear so much as deadly violence between the culture classes. But the upper culture classes have already lost this most fundamental of all class struggles by their admiration for the "vitality" of the lower, that vitality being a mirror image of their own earlier dynamism. A social structure shakes with violence and shivers

---

[8] Herbert Spencer, nineteenth-century positivist and liberal.

with fears of violence not merely when that structure is callously unjust, but also when its members must stimulate themselves to feverish activity in order to demonstrate how alive they are. That there are colonies of the violent among us, devoid of any stable sense of communal purpose, best describes, I think, our present temporarily schizoid existence in two cultures—vacillating between dead purposes and deadly devices to escape boredom.

A full transition to a post-communal culture may never be achieved. It is a persuasive argument, still, that maintains there are safeguards, built into both human nature and culture, limiting the freedom of men to atomize themselves. Perhaps human nature will revolt, producing yet another version of second nature with which to fend off and curb the vitality of the present assault upon the moralizing functions of our past. Every culture must establish itself as a system of moralizing demands, images that mark the trail of each man's memory; thus to distinguish right actions from wrong the inner ordinances are set, by which men are guided in their conduct so as to assure a mutual security of contact. Culture is, indeed, the higher learning. But, this higher learning is not acquired at universities; rather, it is assimilated continuously from earliest infancy when human beings first begin to trust in those familiar responses others make to their overtures.[9] In every culture, there stands a censor, governing the opportunity of recognizing and responding to novel stimuli. That governor, inclined always to be censorious about novelty, we may call "faith." Faith is the compulsive dynamic of culture, channeling obedience to, trust in, and dependence upon authority. With more or less considered passion, men submit to the moral demand system—and, moreover, to its personifications, from which they cannot detach themselves except at the terrible cost of guilt that such figures of authority exact from those not yet so indifferent that they have ceased troubling to deny them. . . .

One main clue to the understanding of social organization is to be found in its symbolic of communal purpose; this, in turn, operates through a social system enacting that symbolic in a way at once admonitory and consoling. Each culture is its own order of therapy—a system of moralizing demands, including remissions that ease the pressures of communal purposes. Therapeutic elites before our own were predominately supportive rather than critical of culture as a moral demand system. Admonitions were the expectable predicates [conditions] of consolations; that is what is meant, nowadays, by "guilt" culture. Whenever

[9] Rieff restates the conservative theme of the importance of the family as a socializing agency.

therapeutic elites grow predominately critical then a cultural revolution may be said to be in progress. Ours is such a time. The Occident has long been such a place.

Until the present culture rose to threaten its predecessor, our demand system could be specified by the kind of creedal hedges it raised around impulses of independence or autonomy from communal purpose. In the culture preceding our own, the order of therapy was embedded in a consensus of "shalt nots." The best never lacked binding convictions, for they were the most bound, mainly by what they should not do—or even think, or dream. "Thou shalt" precipitated a sequence of operative "shalt nots." Cultic therapies of commitment never mounted a search for some new opening into experience; on the contrary, new experience was not wanted. Cultic therapy domesticated the wildness of experience. By treating some novel stimulus or ambiguity of experience in this manner, the apparently new was integrated into a restrictive and collective identity. Cultic therapies consisted, therefore, chiefly in participation mystiques severely limiting deviant initiatives. Individuals were trained, through ritual action, to express fixed wants, although they could not count thereby upon commensurate gratifications. The limitation of possibilities was the very design of salvation. . . .

In the classical Christian culture of commitment, one renunciatory mode of control referred to the sexual opportunism of individuals. Contemporary churchmen may twist and turn it while they try to make themselves heard in a culture that renders preaching superfluous: the fact remains that renunciatory controls of sexual opportunity were placed in the Christian culture very near the center of the symbolic that has not held. Current apologetic efforts by religious professionals, in pretending that renunciation as the general mode of control was never dominant in the system, reflect the strange mixture of cowardice and courage with which they are participating in the dissolution of their cultural functions. . . . Historically, the rejection of sexual individualism (which divorces pleasure and procreation) was the consensual matrix of Christian culture. It was never the last line drawn. On the contrary, beyond that first restriction there were drawn others, establishing the Christian corporate identity within which the individual was to organize the range of his experience. Individuality was hedged round by the discipline of sexuality, challenging those rapidly fluctuating imperatives established in Rome's remissive culture, from which a new order of deprivations was intended to release the faithful Christian believer. Every controlling symbolic contains such remissive functions. What is revolutionary in modern culture refers to releases from inherited doctrines of therapeutic deprivation; from a predicate of renunciatory control, enjoining releases from impulse need, our culture has shifted toward a predicate of impulse release, projecting controls unsteadily based upon an infinite variety of wants raised to the status of needs. . . .

What is moral is *not* "self-evident," as Freud declared in a letter to James Putnam.[10] What is moral becomes and remains self-evident only within a powerful and deeply compelling system of culture. . . . The death of a culture begins when its normative institutions fail to communicate ideals in ways that remain inwardly compelling, first of all to the cultural elites themselves. . . . Yet it is precisely this that the new arts and social sciences, in their very nature, cannot accomplish. They cannot create the ardent imaginations necessary to the forming of new communities. . . .

What binding address now describes our successor culture? In what does the self now try to find salvation, if not in the breaking of corporate identities and in an acute suspicion of all normative institutions? Western culture has had a literary canon, through which its character ideals were conveyed. What canons will replace the scriptural? None, I suppose. We are probably witnessing the end of a cultural history dominated by book religions and word makers. The elites of the emergent culture—if they do not destroy themselves and all culture with a dynamism they appear unable to control—are being trained in terminologies that have only the most tenuous relation to any historic culture or its incorporative self-interpretations. . . .

Our cultural revolution does not aim, like its predecessors, at victory for some rival commitment, but rather at a way of using all commitments, which amounts to loyalty toward none. . . .

Viewed traditionally, the continuing shift from a controlling to a releasing symbolic may appear as the dissolution of culture. Viewed sociologically, the dominance of releasing motifs, in which the releasers themselves evolve as new modes of control, with patterns of consumption as our popular discipline, implies a movement of Western culture away from its former configuration, toward one in which old ideological contents are preserved mainly for their therapeutic potential, as interesting deposits of past motifs of moralizing. No imperative can then develop a monopoly on sentiment, because none will be backed by a deeply ingrained sense of inner ordinances. . . .

[10] [Ernst L. Freud, ed., *Letters of Sigmund Freud* (New York, 1960), p. 308.]

AFTERWORD

◆

RECURRENT TENSIONS AND
DILEMMAS OF
CONSERVATIVE THOUGHT

We have seen that a long-term trend in the development of conservative thought has been from the defense of particular institutions to the defense of institutions in general, and the replacement of arguments for the indispensability of particular institutions (such as the Church and aristocracy), with functional arguments about the need for institutions as such. This process, most evident in the selections from Oakeshott and Gehlen, marks an ever greater self-consciousness and relativism among conservative theorists. Yet this very self-consciousness and relativism generate dilemmas of their own for conservative thinkers.

The conservative thinker, in his role as analyst, is aware that the latent functions of institutions may be more socially significant than their avowed purposes. But latent functions are by definition hidden, not apparent, unappreciated or at least not the focus of conscious attention. When previously latent functions become the articulated purpose of institutions, the institutions may cease to fulfill the very functions for which they were originally valued by conservative theorists. Conservative analysts may conclude, for example, that the most important social function of churches is as mediating institutions, providing their congregants with a sense of shared purpose and a social setting which diminishes the danger of alienation from the larger institutions of society. But a church in which most members no longer believe in God as the object of their common worship may cease to fulfill its latent social functions. The family that prays together may stay together; but members of a family that pray together in order to stay together may eventually find themselves neither praying nor staying. By emphasizing the latent functions of institutions, then, the conservative analyst may find himself unwittingly transforming and perhaps impairing the very institutions he seeks to conserve.

This results in a characteristic tension of conservative analysis. On the one hand, institutions are defended on the grounds of continuity, utility, and the unanticipated costs of radical change. Yet these institutions may be based upon beliefs which are shared by the orthodox, but not by the conservative. Conservatives who are aware that only genuine belief may be socially functional must therefore take care not to undermine such belief, indeed to strengthen it whenever possible. This leads to an implicit tension between typically conservative modes of analysis and the modes by which institutions are defended by their orthodox adherents.

It should not be imagined that these dilemmas apply only to the position of conservatives vis-à-vis religious institutions. In a polity founded in good part upon liberal or natural right axioms, the conservative analyst may be reluctant to impair the legitimacy of the regime by calling its axioms into question. An ongoing dilemma for American conservative thinkers, for example, has been their perceived need to maintain popular reverence for the Declaration of Independence despite the fact that much of its content—from self-evident truths to the dogmatic assertion that "all men are created equal"—is likely to be viewed with skepticism by many conservatives. (The favored alternative, as we have seen, has been to emphasize the Constitution and the historical legacy of the common law at the expense of the Declaration.) In such cases, conservatives may approach the claims of orthodoxy with strategies which may be termed tact, prudence, esotericism, or noble lying. Or, like Hegel or Hayek, they may attempt to rationally demonstrate that existing institutions reflect higher, historically evolving norms, thus providing grounds for belief in the legitimacy of existing institutions, with an eye to enhancing their emotional hold upon contemporaries.

Conservative social and political thought is characterized in good part by its emphasis upon the restraining role of institutions as a prerequisite of human thriving. This focus is combined with the propensity to defend existing, historically developed institutions on the grounds of their usefulness. Yet conservatism as an articulated intellectual position only arises when the legitimacy of existing institutions can no longer be taken for granted, either because those institutions are under ideological attack or because of social, political, and cultural developments that tend to undermine their authority or their functioning. The result is a propensity to historical pessimism.

Thus, while conservatism is defined in large part by its defense of existing institutions, a recurrent lament among conservative thinkers has been that newer institutions are less adequate than older or existing ones, either because they are unable to command assent, or because they provide inadequate direction to human passions. This proclivity to view contemporary history as a process of decline may already be found in Burke's lament that the age of chivalry is dead; one finds it in an extreme form in the work of Arnold Gehlen, whose book *Urmensch und Spätkultur* seemed to regard much of recorded human history as a decline from more authoritative and binding institutions. A similar theme of declining institutional effectiveness is voiced in a different key in the work of Philip Rieff. This recurrent lament expresses the propensity of conservatives to identify the decline of particular institutions with the decline of institutions per se.[1] Because the articulate defense of existing institutions usually comes about only when their stability has been challenged, and given the tendency of conservatives to identify the decline of existing institutions with the decline of institutions as such, conservatism sometimes appears as a defense of lost causes, or a fighting retreat from one institutional outpost to another.

A perennial dilemma for conservatives is when to declare the battle for a particular institution definitively lost. The defense of institutions which are irrevocably lost is characteristic of a species of conservatism which might be termed "reactionary" except that it seeks to retreat to a position preceding the *status quo ante*—"crankiness" seems a more adequate label. A comical self-caricature of this stance was provided by Evelyn Waugh. Requested by a British journal to comment on the upcoming elections of 1959, Waugh responded, "I have never voted in a parliamentary election. I shall not vote this year. . . . In the last three hundred years, particularly in the last hundred, the Crown has adopted what seems to me a very hazardous process of choosing advisers: popular election. Many great evils have resulted. . . . I do not aspire to advise my Sovereign in her choice of servants."[2] The humor of Waugh's remark comes from its self-conscious portrait of the eccentric reactionary. Less obviously comical, because less self-aware, is the sort of intellectual conservatism which insists upon reasserting values which have entirely lost their institutional moorings, as in the case of the American "Southern Agrarians" of the 1930s and their spiritual offspring who championed the idealized values of the Antebellum South long after the social structures which sustained those values had disappeared.[3]

Because of the positional nature of conservatism, later conservatives sometimes find themselves defending institutions that were decried by previous generations of conservatives. In the eighteenth century, for example, conservatives such as Möser and Burke pointed to the advantages of using criteria other than merit or initiative in determining the social

---

[1] This point is made in regard to Arnold Gehlen by Karl-Siegbert Rehberg in his article, "Existentielle Motive im Werk Arnold Gehlens," in Helmut Klages and Helmut Quaritsch, eds., *Zur geisteswissenschaftlichen Bedeutung Arnold Gehlens* (Berlin, 1994), p. 517.

[2] Evelyn Waugh, "Aspirations of a Mugwump," *Spectator*, Oct. 2, 1959, p. 435. Reprinted in Donat Gallagher, ed., *A Little Order: Evelyn Waugh, A Selection from his Journalism* (Boston, 1977), pp. 139–40.

[3] See the astute remarks in Eugene D. Genovese, *The Southern Tradition: The Achievement and Limitations of an American Conservatism* (Cambridge, MA, 1994), pp. 79–80.

and political elite. By the late nineteenth century, however, conservatives had turned to a defense of elites based upon achievement and performance. Moreover, the conservative defense of institutional order is
transferred from older institutions to newer ones, after the latter have
proved their worth by passing the test of historical experience. Reflection upon this fact might lead to the conclusion that each successive
stage of conservatism proves that the defenders of all previous stages
were wrong, since they defended institutions which subsequent generations of conservatives were to abandon. But that conclusion depends
upon the premise that there is a single institutional order best suited to
all times and all places—a premise at odds with the historical utilitarianism at the heart of conservatism. An alternative—and more conservative—understanding of the process would assert that the defense of institutions and practices which are now recognized as superannuated may
have been necessary at some other time or place. They may have been
useful to ensure cultural continuity, or to provide leadership by an established elite during an era of transition from older to new institutions.
Because of the conservative emphasis on historical particularity, therefore, it is possible to maintain that some institutions and practices were
desirable in other times and places, but are now indefensible.

Another recurrent dilemma for conservatives is how to legitimate
change which marks a break with the past. One solution, as we have
seen, is to recast or reinterpret the institutional past to make it appear
continuous with contemporary practice; or, alternatively, to formulate
innovation in a way that appears continuous with past practice, as in
legal fictions. Yet another solution to the legitimation of new or radically recast institutions is the resort to historicist explanations: the institutional rules must change, it is argued, because historical circumstances
have changed. This historicist conception has become a ubiquitous
component of modern intellectual life, and in one form or another has
been central in conservative thought as well. Yet the permeation of historicist assumptions may have the unwitting effect of undermining belief in the truth of existing institutions, or indeed in the idea of truth
as such.[4]

The need for conservatives to react to cultural, social, economic and
political change gives rise to recurrent strategies, each of which has
potential pitfalls. The strategy of pragmatic flexibility runs the risk of
trading away the fundamental substance of existing institutions in order
to avoid unpleasant conflict. The strategy of holding fast to existing institutional arrangements in their totality risks descent into political ir-

---

[4] This was the point of Allan Bloom's book, *The Closing of the American Mind* (New
York, 1987), as it was of Bloom's teacher, Leo Strauss, in *Natural Right and History* (Chicago, 1953). What answer either of them had to the dilemma remains unclear.

relevance. When the fundamental institutions valued by conservatives appear to be in imminent danger, a strategy of radical action may seem necessary, despite the conservative's sensitivity to the hazards posed by the negative unanticipated consequences of action.

> Our late experience has taught us, that many of those fundamental principles, formerly believed infallible, are either not of the importance they were imagined to be; or that we have not at all adverted [referred] to some other far more important, and far more powerful principles, which entirely over-rule those we have considered as omnipotent.[5]

So wrote Edmund Burke in a speech of 1775, in support of conciliation with those colonies soon to become known as the United States of America. It is difficult to imagine a more succinct formulation of the fundamental, intrinsic dilemma of conservatism: When does experience demand a change in the order of institutional priorities? That recurrent conservative quandary, and the variety of responses to which it gives rise, provides a persistent source of tension among conservatives, and an on-going stimulus to the reformulation of conservatism.

[5] "Speech of Edmund Burke, Esq., On Moving his Resolutions for Conciliation with the Colonies," in Ian Harris, ed., *Burke: Pre-Revolutionary Writings* (Cambridge, 1993), p. 229.

GUIDE TO FURTHER READING

◆

General Works on Conservatism

Among the most perspicacious examinations of conservative thought are Samuel Huntington, "Conservatism as an Ideology," *American Political Science Review*, vol. 51 (1957), pp. 454–73; Anthony Quinton, "Conservatism," in *A Companion to Contemporary Political Philosophy* (Oxford, 1993), ed. Robert E. Goodin and Philip Pettit; Robert Nisbet, *Conservatism: Dream and Reality* (Minneapolis, 1986); Karl Mannheim, "Conservative Thought," in Kurt H. Wolff ed., *From Karl Mannheim* (New York, 1971), pp. 132–222, and the more extensive version published as Karl Mannheim, *Conservatism: A Contribution to the Sociology of Knowledge*, ed. David Kettler, Volker Meja, and Nico Stehr (London, 1986); and Roger Scruton's introductory essay to the volume he has edited, *Conservative Texts: An Anthology* (London, 1991). On defining conservatism, see David Y. Allen, "Modern Conservatism: The Problem of Definition," *The Review of Politics*, vol. 43, no. 4 (1981), pp. 582–604. Though marred by polemically induced reductionism and some inaccuracy, Albert O. Hirschman, *The Rhetoric of Reaction* (Cambridge, 1991) is well worth consulting. (On the problems of the book, see Jerry Z. Muller, "Albert Hirschman's Rhetoric of Recrimination," *The Public Interest*, Summer 1991, pp. 81–92.)

On the history of the term "conservative" in political discourse, see Rudolf Vierhaus, "Conservatism," *Dictionary of the History of Ideas*, vol. 1, pp. 477–85; and the same author's article, "Konservativ, Konservatismus," in *Geschichtliche Grundbegriffe. Historisches Lexikon zur politisch-sozialen Sprache in Deutschland*, ed. Otto Brunner, Werner Conze, and Reinhart Koselleck (Stuttgart, 1982), vol. 3, pp. 531–65.

Conservatism in Particular National Contexts

Most significant works on conservative social and political thought remain confined to a particular national tradition. Noël O'Sullivan, *Conservatism* (London, 1976), maintains a national focus in its individual chapters on British, German, and French conservatism. Focused on the radical right, *The European Right: A Historical Profile*, ed. Hans Rogger and Eugen Weber (Berkeley, 1965), contains essays of high quality on the right in various nations.

Perhaps the best work on a particular national tradition is Anthony Quinton, *The Politics of Imperfection: The Religious and Secular Traditions of Conservative Thought in England from Hooker to Oakeshott* (London, 1978), which combines historical breadth with analytic precision. The older work by F.J.C. Hearnshaw, *Conservatism in England: An Analytical, Historical, and Political Survey* (London, 1933; reprinted, New York, 1967), is more highly partisan and includes remarkably little on the history of conservative ideas, but is of some analytic value. For an up-to-date bibliography of books and articles on English conservatism consult the footnotes of Andrew Vincent, "British Conservatism and the Problem of Ideology," *Political Studies*, vol. 42 (1994), pp. 204–27.

Histoire des droites en France, three volumes (Paris, 1992), edited by Jean-François Sirinelli, is a useful guidebook and attempt at synthesis, notable for its organization. It includes a volume of the politics of the French right, another on its political culture, and a third on its "sensibilities" toward topics such as the family, land, region, God, parliamentary institutions, and the economy. Still useful—though not particularly in the realm of ideas—is the overview by René Rémond, *The Right Wing in France from 1815 to de Gaulle* (2nd American edition, Philadelphia, 1969; first published in French in 1954). Robert Nisbet's article "Conservatism," in *A History of Sociological Analysis* (New York, 1978), ed. Tom Bottomore and Robert Nisbet, pp. 80–117, is focused on nineteenth-century French thinkers. *The French Right from Maistre to Maurras* (London, 1970), ed. J. S. McClelland, is an anthology of writings which emphasizes the work of reactionary and radical conservative theorists.

A thematic analysis of German conservatism in the nineteenth and twentieth centuries is offered by Martin Greiffenhagen, *Das Dilemma des Konservatismus in Deutschland* (Munich, 1971, second edition 1977). Kurt Lenk, *Deutscher Konservatismus* (Frankfurt, 1989), tends to project the radical conservatism of the 1920s and 1930s backward to characterize all of German conservatism. The discussion in Klaus Epstein, *The Genesis of German Conservatism* (Princeton, 1966), which covers the period from the eighteenth century through the Napoleonic era, is superior. Karl Mannheim, "Conservative Thought," in Kurt H. Wolff, ed., *From Karl Mannheim* (New York, 1971), pp. 132–22, is mainly concerned with late eighteenth- and early nineteenth-century German conservatism. On the romantic German conservative ideologist Adam Müller, see Robert M. Berdahl, *The Politics of the Prussian Nobility: The Development of a Conservative Ideology 1770–1848* (Princeton, 1988). The volume *Konservatismus*, ed. Hans Gerd Schumann (Cologne, 1974) is focused on conservatism in Germany, but includes a number of articles on trans-national patterns of conservatism. On radical conservatism in Germany, see Fritz Stern, *The Politics of Cultural Despair* (Berkeley, 1961) and Jerry Z. Muller, *The Other God that Failed: Hans Freyer and the Deradicalization of German Conservatism* (Princeton, 1987).

For the argument that American conservatism is a contradiction in terms, see Bernard Crick, "The Strange Quest for an American Conservatism," *The Review of Politics*, vol. 17, 1955, pp. 359–76. For the claim that American conservatism is fundamentally liberal, see Louis Hartz, *The Liberal Tradition in America* (New York, 1955). On the development of New England conservatism in the generation between Madison and Choate, see David Hackett Fischer, *The Revolution of American Conservatism: The Federalist Party in the Era of Jeffersonian Democracy* (New York, 1965). On conservative strands within the American Whigs, see Daniel Walker Howe, *The Political Culture of the American Whigs* (1978). The slave-owning Antebellum South developed its own peculiar brands of conservatism, focused on the paternalistic defense of slavery and the excoriation of the horrors and inherent instability of capitalist wage-labor. The contradictions of Southern conservative ideology are dissected with empathy and acuity in Eugene D. Genovese, *The Slaveholders' Dilemma: Freedom and Progress in Southern Conservative Thought, 1820–1860* (Columbia, South Carolina, 1992), the footnotes of which serve as a guide to the primary and secondary literature on the subject. The attempts by twentieth-century Southern intellectuals from the Southern Agrarians on to formulate a Southern conservatism are recapitulated and dissected by the same author in *The Southern Tradition: The Achievement and Limitations of an American Conservatism* (Cambridge, MA, 1994). On the development of American intellectual conservatism from the Second World War through the 1960s, see George H. Nash, *The Conservative Intellectual Movement in America Since 1945* (New York, 1976; second edition, Wilmington, 1996). For a hostile and incisive analysis of patterns of thought on the postwar radical right, see Richard Hofstadter, *The Paranoid Style in American Politics and Other Essays* (New York, 1965), Part I. On other strands of American conservatism, see the sections on individual American thinkers below.

Russell Kirk, *The Conservative Mind from Burke to Eliot*, seventh revised edition (Chicago, 1986; [first edition 1953]), is confined to Britain and the United States, and its emphasis is on the more romantic and reactionary strands of conservatism. Kirk's taste in conservatism, which favored literary evocation over social and political analysis, is also evident in Russell Kirk, ed., *The Portable Conservative Reader* (New York, 1982). Both volumes are well worth consulting, not least because they offer a conception of conservatism quite different from the one highlighted in this book.

David Hume

The most accessible *entré* to Hume's social and political thought is through his essays. A modern edition which includes all of Hume's essays and a very useful apparatus is David Hume, *Essays Moral, Political, and Literary*, ed. Eugene F. Miller (revised edition, Indianapolis, 1987). An edition of Hume's *An Enquiry Concerning the Principles of Morals*, ed. J. B. Schneewind (Indianapolis, 1983) includes a useful introduction. The most important portions of the *Treatise of Human Nature*, the *Enquiry*, and the essays relevant to Hume's political thought may be found in Stuart D. Warner and Donald W. Livingston, eds., *David Hume: Political Writings* (Indianapolis, 1994), which includes a helpful introduction. Hume's political thought is also conveyed in his multivolume *History of England*.

There is an excellent explication of Hume's theory of justice and its place in his thought in Knud Haakonssen, *The Science of a Legislator: The Natural Jurisprudence of David Hume and Adam Smith* (Cambridge, 1981). Haakonssen offers an overview of Hume's political thought in his essay "The Structure of Hume's political theory," in David Fate Norton, ed., *The Cambridge Companion to Hume* (Cambridge, 1993), and in his introduction to the volume of Hume's essays he has edited in the series, Cambridge Texts in the History of Political Thought. The concept of "artificial" rules in Hume's thought is treated at rather too great a length in Frederick G. Whelan, *Order and Artifice in Hume's Political Philosophy* (Princeton, 1985). A detailed and contextual study is Duncan Forbes, *Hume's Philosophical Politics* (Cambridge, 1975).

No one has done more to explicate Hume's conception of the proper role of philosophy and its relationship to "common life" than Donald W. Livingston in *Hume's Philosophy of Common Life* (Chicago, 1984). John W. Danford, *Hume and the Problem of Reason* (New Haven, 1990) explains how Hume's philosophical skepticism stamped his approach to the human sciences. Richard H. Popkin, *The High Road to Pyrrhonism* (San Diego, 1980), ed. Richard A. Watson and James E. Force, brings together a number of seminal studies on Hume and on early modern skepticism by a distinguished historian of philosophy. A valuable collection of essays, *Liberty in Hume's History of England* (Dordrecht, 1990), ed. Nicholas Capaldi and Donald W. Livingston, brings out the centrality of Hume's historical essays and of his *History of England* in understanding his political thought. Also useful is an earlier collection, *Hume: A Re-evaluation* (New York, 1976), ed. Donald W. Livingston and James T. King.

The standard biography of Hume is E. C. Mossner, *The Life of David Hume* (second edition, London, 1980). The journal *Hume Studies*, founded in 1975, is devoted to his life and thought.

Edmund Burke

All of Burke's works are relevant to an understanding of the nature of his conservatism. But the interested reader can get a jump start by reading *Burke: Pre-Revolutionary Writings*, ed. Ian Harris (Cambridge, 1993), which collects many of the most significant of Burke's writings; *Reflections on the Revolution in France*, ed. J.G.A. Pocock (Indianapolis, 1987), the best edition now available, with an excellent introduction and notes; *Further Reflections on the Revolution of France*, ed. Daniel E. Ritchie (Indianapolis, 1992), which collects Burke's most significant statements about the French Revolution aside from his *Reflections*; and *Selected Letters of Edmund Burke*, ed. Harvey C. Mansfield, Jr. (Chicago, 1984), a thematically arranged selection drawn from the ten-volume series, *The Correspondence of Edmund Burke*, ed. Thomas Copeland.

The most widely used nineteenth-century edition of Burke's works is *The Works of Edmund Burke*, published by Bohn's British Classics from 1854–89. It is now in the process of being replaced by the still incomplete *The Writings and Speeches of Edmund Burke* under the general editorship of Paul Langford. For the most part, the quality of the introductions and notes to the volumes in this edition make them indispensable for scholars; lamentably, the volume which includes *Reflections on the Revolution in France* is an exception.

The most up-to-date works on Burke's life are Stanley Ayling, *Edmund Burke: His Life and Opinions* (London, 1988), and Conor Cruise O'Brien, *The Great Melody: A Thematic Biography of Edmund Burke* (Chicago, 1992), which is particularly strong on Burke's campaign against the British East India Company, but manages to play down his conservatism.

Among the best and most up-to-date discussions of Burke's conservatism are Iain Hampsher-Monk's "Introduction," to the volume he has edited, *The Political Philosophy of Edmund Burke* (New York, 1987); and the same author's chapter on Burke in his *A History of Modern Political Thought* (Oxford, 1992). In addition to his valuable introduction to the edition of the *Reflections* noted above, J.G.A. Pocock has published a number of major studies of Burke, including "The political economy of Burke's analysis of the French Revolution," in his *Virtue, Commerce, and History* (Cambridge, 1985), pp. 193–212, and "Edmund Burke and the Redefinition of Enthusiasm: The Context as Counter-Revolution," in François Furet and Mona Ozouf, eds., *The French Revolution and the Creation of Modern Political Culture: Vol. 3: The Transformation of Political Culture 1789–1848* (Oxford, 1989), pp. 19–36. Harvey Mansfield, Jr., *Statesmanship and Party Government: A Study of Burke and Bolingbroke* (Chicago, 1965) is a particularly penetrating study. Burke had frequent recourse to the rhetoric of natural law, one of several rhetorical traditions on which he drew: scholars have differed as to how this ought to be interpreted and how much emphasis to place upon it. The most emphatic exposition of Burke as a proponent of natural law is Peter J. Stanlis, *Edmund Burke and the Natural Law* (Ann Arbor, 1958), the most subtle is Francis Canavan, *The Political Reason of Edmund Burke* (New York, 1960). More convincing than either, however, is the interpretation in the final chapter of Mansfield, *Statesmanship and Party Government*.

Justus Möser

The standard modern edition of Möser's work is *Justus Mösers Sämtliche Werke. Historisch-kritische Ausgabe in 14 Bänden* (Oldenburg/Berlin, 1943 to date).

Perhaps the best portrait of Möser's thought is in Klaus Epstein, *The Genesis of German Conservatism* (Princeton, 1966), chapter 6. Jonathan Knudsen, *Justus Möser and the German Enlightenment* (Cambridge, 1986), is an up-to-date and invaluable source on Möser's social, economic, and political environment, as well as on his thought. On those aspects of Möser's thought relating to guilds, see Mack Walker, *German Home Towns: Community, State, and General Estate, 1648–1871* (Ithaca, 1971). See also Jerry Z. Muller, "Justus Möser and the Conservative Critique of Early Modern Capitalism," *Central European History*, vol. 23, no. 2/3 (June/Sept. 1990), pp. 153–78.

Louis de Bonald

Readers interested in pursuing Bonald's argument may consult the full English translation of *On Divorce* by Nicholas Davidson (New Brunswick, NJ, 1992), which also includes a useful if uncritical introduction. The standard edition of his works is *Oeuvres complètes de M. de Bonald*, ed. Abeé Migne, 3 volumes, (Paris, 1859–64). Bonald's most substantial work, his *Theory of Power, Political and Religious*, has not been translated into English.

Bonald's work and career is succinctly explored in Jacques Godechot, *The Counter-Revolution: Doctrine and Action, 1789–1804* (Princeton, 1970 [French original, 1961]), a book that is stronger on politics than on ideas. The standard work on his life remains Henri Moulinié, *De Bonald* (Paris, 1915). For the influence of Bonald on French sociological thought, see Robert Nisbet, "De Bonald and the Concept of the Social Group," *Journal of the History of Ideas*, vol. 5 (1944), pp. 315–31. On the sociological functionalism predominant in his thought, see Robert Spaemann, *Der Ursprung der Soziologie aus dem Geist der Restauration: Studien über L.G.A. Bonald* (Munich, 1959). On Bonald's debt to Enlightenment thought, see Leigh Barclay, "Louis de Bonald, prophet of the past?" *Studies in Voltaire and the Eighteenth Century*, vol. 55 (1967), pp. 167–204.

Joseph de Maistre

The complete edition of Maistre's works is the *Oeuvres complètes de J. de Maistre* (Lyon, 1884–87). A new, critical edition is currently being published by Editions Slatkine in Geneva. A selection drawn from Maistre's major works is Jack Lively, ed., *The Works of Joseph de Maistre* (New York, 1971). *Considerations on France*, ed. and trans. by R. A. Lebrun (Cambridge, 1994), includes an introduction by Isaiah Berlin which is an abbreviated version of an essay discussed below. There is a useful recent French edition, *Considérations sur la France*, ed. Pierre Manent (Paris, 1988). Maistre's other major work, *St. Petersburg Dialogues*, has also been translated by Lebrun (Montreal, 1993).

Two classic studies of Maistre's political thought were reprinted together in 1979. They are Francis Bayle, *Les Idées politiques de Joseph de Maistre* (Paris, 1945; reprinted New York, 1979), and Peter Richard Rohden, *Joseph de Maistre als politischer Theoretiker* (Munich, 1929; reprinted New York, 1979). Isaiah Berlin, "Joseph de Maistre and the Origins of Fascism," in *The Crooked Timber of Humanity* (New York, 1990) is worth consulting, although Berlin's antipathy to his subject makes for a less empathetic and less insightful study than one has come to expect of one of the great intellectual historians of our age. A very thoughtful if diffuse study is Owen P. Bradley, *Logics of Violence: The Social and Political Thought of Joseph de Maistre* (unpub. Ph.D. thesis, Cornell University Department of History, 1992). See also Richard Allen Lebrun, *Throne and Altar: The Political and Religious Thought of Joseph de Maistre* (Ottawa, 1965), and his *Joseph de Maistre: An Intellectual Militant* (Montreal, 1988). The journal *La Revue des Études Maistriennes* was published from 1975 to 1990; some important articles from it have been translated by Richard Lebrun in *Maistre Studies* (Lanham, MD, 1988).

James Madison

The best introduction to Madison's political thought is Marvin Meyers, *The Mind of the Founder: Sources of the Political Thought of James Madison* (rev. ed., Hanover, 1981) and his "Founding and Revolution: A Commentary on Publius-Madison," in Stanley Elkins and Eric McKitrick, eds., *The Hofstadter Aegis* (New York, 1974), pp. 3–32. Hume's influence on Madison is emphasized in the sketch of the man and his intellectual development in Eric McKitrick and Stanley Elkins, *The Age of Federalism* (New York, 1993), pp. 79ff; see also Roy Branson, "James Madison and the Scottish Enlightenment," *Journal of the History of Ideas*, vol. 42 (April–June, 1979), pp. 235–50. On the incidence of Lockean and Humean conceptions in *The Federalist*, see Morton White, *Philosophy, The Federalist, and the Constitution* (Oxford, 1987), which, while analytically acute, applies a philosophically finer comb than is perhaps appropriate to the texts. David F. Epstein, *The Political Theory of The Federalist* (Chicago, 1984) is a detailed and penetrating study.

On the contrast between Jefferson and Madison, see Joseph J. Ellis, "Founding Brothers," *The New Republic*, Jan. 30, 1995, pp. 32–36. For a more extended discussion, see Drew R. McCoy, *The Last of the Founders: James Madison and the Republican Legacy* (Cambridge, 1989), pp. 47–65. By contrast, Lance Banning, *Jefferson and Madison: Three Conversations from the Founding* (Madison, 1995) tends to minimize the differences between the two.

Rufus Choate

Choate's writings and speeches are collected in Samuel Gilman Brown, ed., *The Works of Rufus Choate* (two volumes, Boston, 1862). Jean V. Matthews, *Rufus Choate: The Law and Civic Virtue* (Philadelphia, 1980) is a thoughtful book on Choate as American Whig conservative. Also useful is Daniel Walker Howe, *The Political Culture of the American Whigs* (Chicago, 1979).

Matthew Arnold

The standard editions of Arnold's works are *The Complete Prose Works of Matthew Arnold*, ed. R. H. Super, eleven volumes published by the University of Michigan Press in Ann Arbor from 1960–1977; and *The Poems of Matthew Arnold*, ed. Kenneth Allot, second edition revised by Miriam Allott (London, 1979). The edition of *Culture and Anarchy* included in volume seven of *The Complete Prose Works* comes with extensive explanatory notes. The most recent edition, edited by Samuel Lipman and published in 1994 by Yale University Press in New Haven, includes a brief introduction to Arnold's life, a helpful glossary of proper names and events, and four essays by contemporary intellectuals on the historical context and present relevance (or lack thereof) of Arnold's book. Some of Arnold's most important additional essays in cultural criticism— "Democracy" (1861), "The Function of Criticism at the Present Time" (1864), "Equality" (1878), and "Civilisation in the United States" (1888)—can be found in the volume *Matthew Arnold*, ed. Miriam Allott and Robert H. Super (Oxford, 1986), in the Oxford Authors series.

Stefan Collini, *Arnold* (New York, 1988) is the best short introduction to his life and thought and includes a guide to further reading. Lionel Trilling, *Matthew Arnold*, first published in 1939 and reprinted thereafter, remains indispensable. Of the many other secondary works on Arnold, Sidney Coulling, *Matthew Arnold and His Critics: A Study of Arnold's Controversies* (Athens, Ohio, 1974) is especially useful. Park Honan, *Matthew Arnold: A Life* (Cambridge, 1983) is the most up-to-date biography.

James Fitzjames Stephen

Liberty , Equality, and Fraternity is now available in two editions, each worthwhile. The University of Chicago edition of 1991 is largely reproduced from the edition published by Cambridge University Press in 1967 with notes by R. J. White; it also includes three short essays by Stephen that complement the themes of the book, and an introductory essay by Richard A. Posner relating the book to present American controversies. The Liberty Fund edition, edited by Stuart D. Warner (Indianapolis, 1993), includes a thematic introduction, a comparative table of subjects to Stephen's book and Mill's *On Liberty*, and a brief bibliography; the editor has wisely moved Stephen's "Preface to the Second Edition" to the end of the work. Among Stephen's most substantial works was his *History of the Criminal Law of England* (three volumes, London, 1883); a collection of his pieces for the *Saturday Review*, *Horae Sabbaticae* (three volumes, London, 1892), makes for good reading and provides his critical assessments of past political theorists, including Hobbes, Burke, and de Maistre.

Two fine secondary works on Stephen's life and intellectual development are James A. Colaiaco, *Sir James Fitzjames Stephen and the Crisis of Victorian Thought* (New York, 1983), and K.J.M. Smith, *James Fitzjames Stephen: Portrait of a Victorian Rationalist* (Cambridge, 1988). There is a nineteenth-century biography by Stephen's brother, Leslie Stephen, *The Life of Sir James Fitzjames Stephen* (London, 1895).

W. H. Mallock

The themes in the excerpts reprinted in this volume from Mallock's *Aristocracy and Evolution: A Study of the Rights, the Origin, and Functions of the Wealthier Classes* (London, 1898) were pursued at greater length in *A Critical Examination of Socialism*, first published in 1908 and reprinted by Transaction Publishers (New Brunswick, NJ, 1989). An excerpt from Mallock's satire on Victorian cultural life, *The New Republic* (London, 1877), may be found in Russell Kirk, ed., *The Portable Conservative Reader*.

On Mallock's career, see his Memoirs *of Life and Literature* (New York, 1920), and D. J. Ford, "W. H. Mallock and Socialism in England, 1880–1918," in Kenneth D. Brown, ed., *Essays in Anti-Labour History: Responses to the Rise of Labour in Britain* (London, 1974). On his skirmishes with the Fabians, see Albert V. Tucker, "W. H. Mallock and Late Victorian Conservatism," in *University of Toronto Quarterly*, vol. 31, no. 2 (1962), pp. 223–41. For a Fabian response to Mallock, see [George] Bernard Shaw, *Socialism and Superior Brains: A Reply to Mr. Mallock* (New York and London, 1910).

William Graham Sumner

On Liberty, Society, and Politics: The Essential Essays of William Graham Sumner, ed. Robert C. Bannister (Indianapolis, 1992) is a good place to begin the study of Sumner. It reprints a representative sample of Sumner's essays from the various stages of his career, and includes a sketch of his life as well as a bibliographical essay. Six volumes of Sumner's essays were edited by his student and colleague, Albert G. Keller. Sumner's most important systematic work of sociology is his *Folkways*, first published in 1906, and in print in a number of more recent editions.

Bruce Curtis, *William Graham Sumner* (Boston, 1981) provides an overview of Sumner's life and the development of his doctrines. Among the most influential treatments of Sumner is that of Richard Hofstadter, *Social Darwinism in American Thought* (Philadelphia, 1944; rev. ed. Boston, 1956). The issue of Sumner's "Social Darwinism" is examined by Robert C. Bannister in *Social Darwinism: Science and Myth* (Philadelphia, 1979) and at greater length in Donald C. Bellomy, "'Social Darwinism' Revisited," in *Perspectives in American History*, New Series, vol. 1 (1984), pp. 1–129, which argues convincingly that Hofstadter's characterization of Sumner as a Social Darwinist is misleading: Sumner used the phrase "survival of the fittest" only briefly, Bellomy shows, and did so at a time when a wide range of social theorists made use of Darwinian terminology. Among the most useful older discussions of Social Darwinism is Donald Fleming, "Social Darwinism," in Arthur M. Schlesinger, Jr., and Morton White, eds., *Paths of American Thought* (New York, 1963).

Joseph Schumpeter

Schumpeter produced seminal works in economic theory, sociological theory, history, and the intellectual history of economics, as well as a substantial stream of contemporary commentary. Many of his most significant essays are now available in Joseph A. Schumpeter, *The Economics and Sociology of Capitalism* (Princeton, 1991) ed. Richard Swedberg, including, "Social Classes in an Ethnically Homogeneous Environment," and Schumpeter's important historical studies on "The Crisis of the Tax State" and "The Sociology of Imperialism." His first and perhaps greatest contribution to economic theory came in *The Theory of Economic Development* (New Brunswick, NJ, 1983), first published in German in 1906. But his most influential and widely read book has been *Capitalism, Socialism and Democracy*, first published in 1942 and still available in print in a number of languages. The book was written for a broad audience, and incorporates many ideas from Schumpeter's previous works. Perhaps the most influential portion of the book is Part Two, "Can Capitalism Survive?" in which Schumpeter puts forth the argument that capitalism will be superseded by socialism not because of capitalism's economic inadequacies, but because it creates the social and cultural preconditions for its own delegitimization. Neil McInnes, "Wrong for Superior Reasons," *The National Interest*, no. 39 (Spring 1995), pp. 85–96, provides a thoughtful overview on the ongoing reception of *Capitalism, Socialism and Democracy*.

There are now several biographies of Schumpeter. Richard Swedberg, *Schumpeter: A Biography* (Princeton, 1991) is perhaps the best introduction to the man and his thought. For additional information, consult Robert Loring Allen, *Opening Doors: The Life and Work of Joseph Schumpeter*, two volumes (New Brunswick, NJ, 1991); Wolfgang F. Stolper, *Joseph Alois Schumpeter: The Public Life of a Private Man* (Princeton, 1994); and Erich Schneider, *Joseph A. Schumpeter, Leben und Werk eines großen Sozialökonomen* (Tübingen, 1970). Eduard März, *Joseph Schumpeter: Scholar, Teacher and Politician* (New Haven, 1991) is an illuminating collection of the author's essays on Schumpeter's thought and career. An expensive but useful collection of articles on Schumpeter's work is *J.A. Schumpeter: Critical Assessments*, ed. John Cunningham Wood, four volumes (London and New York, 1991). Massimo M. Augello,

Joseph Alois Schumpeter: A Reference Guide (Berlin, 1990) lists over 1,900 secondary works on one or another aspect of his thought. For an introduction to Schumpeter's economics, most readers will profit from the relevant chapter of Robert Heilbroner, *The Worldly Philosophers*, sixth edition (New York, 1986).

T. E. Hulme

The Collected Writings of T.E. Hulme, ed. Karen Csengeri (Oxford, 1994) supersedes earlier collections of Hulme's writings, and the editor's introduction provides a brief and accurate account of Hulme's life and of his intellectual development. In place of the "Essays on War" reprinted here, the volume reproduces a longer and more detailed version which appeared under the title "War Notes" as published in the magazine *New Age* in 1915–16, and adds explanatory notes. Alun R. Jones, *The Life and Opinions of T.E. Hulme* (Boston, 1960) contains additional biographical information, but is less than acute on Hulme's thought. Superior is the analysis of Hulme's ideas in Leslie Susser, "Right Wings Over Britain: T.E. Hulme and the Intellectual Rebellion against Democracy," in Zeev Sternhell, ed., *The Intellectual Revolt Against Liberal Democracy* (Jerusalem, 1996).

Carl Schmitt

Some of the same qualities that have made Carl Schmitt's work stimulating to intellectuals in a variety of disciplines and across the political spectrum necessarily frustrate the attempt to form a coherent picture of his thought. His books cover a range of fields, including political theory, philosophy, theology, literature, and intellectual history, in addition to immediate issues of politics and of constitutional and international law. Schmitt was a powerful rhetorician, and his works abound in key terms and definitions which are often striking but upon close inspection turn out to be ambiguous. The problem is compounded by the fact that Schmitt himself sometimes used his key terms in opposite senses over time. The great mirage of scholarship on Schmitt is that his writings in these diverse fields and across seven decades fit together into a coherent whole. For all these reasons, it is especially important to place Schmitt's writings into their political and cultural contexts in order to understand their meaning and import.

For Schmitt's skepticism about the viability of parliamentary democracy, see his early work, *Die geistesgeschichtliche Lage des heutigen Parliamentarismus* (Berlin, 1923; 2nd edition, 1926), translated by Ellen Kennedy as *The Crisis of Parliamentary Democracy* (Cambridge, MA, 1985); the English translation includes a very useful introductory essay by Ellen Kennedy which helps to orient Schmitt's thought within the debates of the Weimar era. The literal translation of the title, "The Intellectual-Historical Status of Contemporary Parliamentarianism" more accurately reflects the book's contents. Schmitt's most extended discussion of liberal theory and what he saw as its weaknesses is in his volume on constitutional theory, *Verfassunglehre* (Berlin, 1928). His subsequent efforts move toward greater concreteness, in *Der Hüter der Verfassung* (Berlin, 1931), and in the related essays collected in *Verfassungsrechtliche Aufsätze aus den*

Jahren 1924–1954 (Berlin, 1958), and *Positionen und Begriffe im Kampf mit Weimar-Genf-Versailles* (Berlin, 1940).

A number of Schmitt's other works of the 1920s have been translated into English. These include *Der Begriff des Politischen* (Berlin, 1927), translated by George Schwab as *The Concept of the Political* (New Brunswick, NJ, 1976; with a new foreword and appendix, Chicago, 1996); *Politische Theologie* (Berlin, 1979), translated by George Schwab as *Political Theology: Four Chapters on the Concept of Sovereignty* (Cambridge, MA, 1985); and *Politische Romantik* (Berlin, 1919), translated by Guy Oakes as *Political Romanticism* (Cambridge, MA, 1986).

The most up-to-date biography of Schmitt is Paul Noack, *Carl Schmitt: Eine Biographie* (Berlin, 1993), which includes a select bibliography of Schmitt's works and secondary books about him. Also useful for biographical purposes is Joseph W. Bendersky, *Carl Schmitt: Theorist for the Reich* (Princeton, 1983). On Schmitt's career in the Third Reich, see also Bernd Rüthers, *Carl Schmitt im Dritten Reich* (2nd edition, Munich, 1990). On his postwar activities and influence, see Dirk van Laak, *Gespräche in der Sicherheit des Schweigens: Carl Schmitt in der politischen Geistesgeschichte der frühen Bundesrepublik* (Berlin, 1993).

Among the more insightful interpreters of Schmitt's thought is Günther Mashke. A former radical leftist turned radical rightist, Mashke shares Schmitt's fundamental antiliberal sympathies, which has made him an unusually sensitive reader of Schmitt's work. Especially worthwhile, because relatively unpolemical, is Maschke's essay "Drei Motive im Anti-Liberalismus Carl Schmitts," in Klaus Hansen and Hans Lietzmann, eds., *Carl Schmitt und die Liberalismuskritik* (Opladen, 1988), pp. 55–79. Maschke's *Der Tod des Carl Schmitt. Apologie und Polemik* (Vienna, 1987), while both polemical and apologetic as its title implies, provides a critical overview of recent writing on Schmitt in several languages. Also polemical, though from the opposite side, but analytically trenchant is the chapter on Schmitt in Stephen Holmes, *The Anatomy of Antiliberalism* (Cambridge, MA, 1993). A discussion of the key themes of the *Verfassungslehre* and their centrality in Schmitt's thought of the Weimar era is found in William E. Scheuermann, "Carl Schmitt's Critique of Liberal Constitutionalism," *The Review of Politics*, vol. 58, no. 2 (1996), pp. 299–322. On the radical conservative elements of Schmitt's thought, see Jerry Z. Muller "Carl Schmitt, Hans Freyer, and the Radical Conservative Critique of Liberal Democracy in the Weimar Republic," *History of Political Thought*, vol. 12, no. 4 (Winter 1991), pp. 695–715. Of varying but generally high quality are the essays and discussions included in *Complexio Oppositorum. Über Carl Schmitt* (Berlin, 1988), ed. Helmut Quaritsch, which includes bibliographical information.

Michael Oakeshott

The place to begin the study of Oakeshott's political thought is with the expanded edition of *Rationalism in Politics and Other Essays*, edited by Timothy Fuller and published by Liberty Press (Indianapolis, 1991). Along with the essays originally collected in the first edition of 1962, the expanded edition includes six additional essays, a useful foreword by Timothy Fuller, and a bibliography of Oakeshott's principal works and selected secondary books and articles. The two essays most closely related to "Rationalism in Politics" are "Political Education," and "On being Conservative." At the time of his death, Oakeshott left a number of books, essays, and lecture series unpublished. They have been edited by Timothy Fuller and published posthumously by Yale University Press. The book, *The Politics of Faith and the Politics of Skepticism* (New Haven, 1996) dates from the same period as *Rationalism in Politics* and expands upon the theme of the political consequences of epistemological modesty. Oakeshott's most systematic work of political philosophy is *On Human Conduct* (Oxford, 1975).

Among the more significant studies of Oakeshott's political thought are Josiah Lee Auspitz, "Individuality, Civility, and Theory: The Philosophical Imagination of Michael Oakeshott," part of a symposium on Oakeshott's thought in *Political Theory*, vol. 4, no. 3 (August 1976); Paul Franco, "Oakeshott's Critique of Rationalism Revisited," in *The Political Science Reviewer*, vol. 21 (Spring 1992), pp. 15–44, and his *The Political Philosophy of Michael Oakeshott* (New Haven, 1990); and John Gray, "Oakeshott on law, liberty, and civil association," in Gray, *Liberalisms: Essays in Political Philosophy* (New York, 1989). Robert Grant, *Oakeshott* (London, 1990), contains a brief biographical chapter as well as a brief overview of Oakeshott's works.

Irving Kristol

Irving Kristol's favored genre has been the essay of contemporary cultural and political commentary, and his four books are each collections of previously published essays. *Neoconservatism: The Autobiography of an Idea: Selected Essays, 1949–1995* (New York, 1995), is the most recent and most comprehensive, reprinting most (but not all) of the essays included in his earlier collections. It also includes a long autobiographical introductory essay, and reprints a number of earlier autobiographical sketches. His previously published collections of essays are *On the Democratic Idea in America* (New York, 1972); *Two Cheers for Capitalism* (New York, 1978); and *Reflections of a Neoconservative* (New York, 1983). For a complete bibliography of his published works through 1994, see *The Neoconservative Imagination: Essays in Honor of Irving Kristol* (Washington, D.C., 1995), ed. Christopher DeMuth and William Kristol. The volume also includes a number of biographical memoirs by friends; those by Nathan Glazer and Peregrine Worsthorne are particularly telling. On the development of neoconservatism, see Mark Gerson, *The Neoconservative Vision: From the Cold War to the Culture Wars* (Lanham, MD, 1996). Another trenchant conservative analysis of the topic of the Kristol essay reprinted here is by Walter Berns, "Obscenity and Public Morality," in his *The First Amendment and the Future of American Democracy* (Chicago, 1985).

Peter Berger and Richard John Neuhaus

The entire original text of *Empowering People: The Role of Mediating Structures in Public Policy*, together with a recent meditation by the authors and a series of reflections on the theme by sympathetic commentators may be found in Peter L.

Berger and Richard John Neuhaus, *To Empower People: From State to Civil Society*, ed. Michael Novak (Washington, D.C., 1996).

Of Berger's many other books, those most germane to this subject are his *Facing Up to Modernity: Excursions in Society, Politics, and Religion* (New York, 1977); Peter L. Berger, Brigitte Berger, and Hansfried Kellner, *The Homeless Mind: Modernization and Consciousness* (New York, 1973); and Brigitte Berger and Peter L. Berger, *The War over the Family* (New York, 1983). Also related and highly significant in their own right are *The Sacred Canopy: Elements of a Sociological Theory of Religion* (New York, 1967) and *The Capitalist Revolution* (New York, 1986). Robert Wuthnow et al., *Cultural Analysis: The Work of Peter L. Berger, Mary Douglas, Michel Foucault, and Jürgen Habermas* (Boston, 1984) includes a brief biographical sketch of Berger and a chapter-length discussion of his ideas by James Davison Hunter.

Neuhaus's preferred genre has been the essay of contemporary religious, cultural, and political commentary. He has also been active as an editor of volumes on contemporary theological and cultural issues. His most extended foray, and most influential work, is *The Naked Public Square: Religion and Democracy in America* (Grand Rapids, MI, 1984; 2nd edition 1986). His collection *America Against Itself: Moral Vision and the Public Order* (Notre Dame, 1992), includes some biographical reflections.

Hermann Lübbe

While Lübbe has written a number of books of political theory and intellectual history, his favored genre is the essay, in which he brings philosophical and historical reflection to bear upon contemporary issues. His reflections most closely related to the essay translated in this volume may be found in his "Aufklärung und Gegenaufklärung," in Michael Zöller, ed., *Aufklärung Heute: Bedingungen unserer Freiheit* (Zurich, 1980), and his collection of essays, *Fortschritts-Reaktionen: Über konservative und destruktive Modernität* (Graz, 1987). *Endstation Terror. Rückblick auf lange Märsche* (1978) is a collection of his polemics against the German New Left. The critique of utopian moralism has been an ongoing theme in his work, pursued in *Politischer Moralismus: Der Triumph der Gesinnung über die Urteilskraft* (Berlin, 1987), and in *Der Lebenssinn der Industriegesellschaft* (Berlin, 1990). The issue of secularization and the sense in which religious claims may be maintained under modern conditions has been a frequent topic of Lübbe's work, most extensively pursued in *Religion nach der Aufklärung* (Graz, 1986). For a critique of Lübbe from one of his most frequent targets on the left, see Jürgen Habermas, "Neoconservative Cultural Criticism in the United States and West Germany," first published in German in 1982 and translated in the collection of his essays entitled *The New Conservatism: Cultural Criticism and the Historians' Debate* (Cambridge, MA, 1989), esp. pp. 35–45.

Friedrich Hayek

Hayek's most extended works of political and social thought are *The Constitution of Liberty* (Chicago, 1960), and the three-volume *Law, Legislation and*

Liberty (Chicago, 1973–79). Many of his seminal essays are collected in *The Essence of Hayek*, ed. Chiaki Nishiyama and Kurt R. Leube (Stanford, 1984), which includes a brief biographical introduction. More information on Hayek's life can be gleaned from F. A. Hayek, *Hayek on Hayek: An Autobiographical Dialogue*, ed. Stephen Kresge and Leif Wenar (Chicago, 1994). Hayek's last book, *The Fatal Conceit: The Errors of Socialism* includes his speculation on cultural evolution and the survival of the most adaptively fit traditions. It was published in 1989 as volume one of *The Collected Works of F.A. Hayek*, now being published in English by the University of Chicago, with German and Japanese editions of the collected works also slated to appear.

For a useful overview of his economic thought, see the article on Hayek by Roger W. Garrison and Israel M. Kirzner in *The New Palgrave: A Dictionary of Economics*, four volumes (New York, 1987). The best book-length study of Hayek's political thought is John Gray, *Hayek on Liberty*, second edition (Oxford, 1986); also valuable is Chadran Kukathas, *Hayek and Modern Liberalism* (Oxford, 1989). For an extended critique of the cogency of Hayek's conception of cultural evolution, see Ronald Kley, *Hayek's Social and Political Thought* (Oxford, 1994), which builds on the earlier works of Gray and Kukathas. Many of the most significant articles about Hayek's work, as well as reviews of his major books have been collected in *Friedrich A. Hayek: Critical Assessments*, ed. John Cunningham Wood and Ronald N. Woods, four volumes (London, 1991). For a knowledgeable critique from the left, see David Miller, "F.A. Hayek: Dogmatic Skeptic," *Dissent* (Summer 1994), pp. 346–53, who argues that Hayek's skepticism does not extend to the market. The journal *Critical Review* devoted a special issue (vol. 3, no. 2, Spring 1989) to reflections on and critiques of Hayek's work. On the Humean elements of Hayek's thought, see Donald W. Livingston, "Hayek as Humean," *Critical Review* (Spring 1991), pp. 159–78.

Edward C. Banfield

The Unheavenly City Revisited (Boston, 1974) supersedes the original *The Unheavenly City: The Nature and Future of Our Urban Crisis* (Boston, 1970); it in turn has been reprinted with a brief new preface by the author (Prospect Heights, IL, 1990). Among Banfield's other most significant works are *The Moral Basis of a Backward Society* (Glencoe, 1960, rev. ed. 1967), written together with Laura F. Banfield; and the collection *Here the People Rule: Selected Essays* (2nd edition, Washington, 1991), which includes the essay "Policy Science as Metaphysical Madness" (1980), Banfield's biting attack on hubris in the social sciences. On the reception of *The Unheavenly City* and Banfield's replies to his critics, see the articles listed in "Appendix B" of *The Unheavenly City Revisited*.

Arnold Gehlen

Gehlen's writings are currently being published in a critical edition of his collected works, *Arnold Gehlen Gesamtausgabe*, published by Vittorio Klostermann Verlag in Frankfurt am Main. Gehlen's most systematic works of social theory are *Der Mensch: Seine Natur und seine Stellung in der Welt* and *Urmensch und Spätkultur: Philosophische Ergebnisse und Aussagen*. *Der Mensch* was first published in 1940 and then substantially revised in editions published in 1944 and 1950; it is now available in a critical edition edited by Karl-Siegbert Rehberg as volume 3 of the *Arnold Gehlen Gesamtausgabe*. The book has been translated into English as *Man: His Nature and Place in the World* by Clare McMillan and Karl Pillemer (New York, 1988); though not an easy work to begin with, and rendered slightly more opaque in translation, it is still digestible once one adjusts to the author's terminology. Gehlen's second major work of social theory, *Urmensch und Spätkultur* was first published in 1956, and in a revised fourth edition in 1977. A volume of contemporary social and cultural analysis, *Die Seele im technischen Zeitalter: Sozialpsychologische Probleme in der industriellen Gesellschaft* (Reinbek, 1957) went through many editions in Gehlen's lifetime, and is available in English as *Man in the Age of Technology*, translated by Patricia Lipscomb (New York, 1980), with a foreword by Peter L. Berger. Also available in English is Gehlen's influential essay of cultural analysis, first published in German in 1961, "The Crystallization of Cultural Forms," translated by Clare A. McMillan in *Modern German Sociology*, ed. Volker Meja et al. (New York, 1987). Many of his Gehlen's most engaging and penetrating essays on political, sociological, and cultural topics are collected in a volume edited by Karl-Siegbert Rehberg, *Einblicke* (Frankfurt am Main, 1978), which comprises volume 7 of the *Arnold Gehlen Gesamtausgabe*.

A good short introduction to Gehlen's thought is Peter Berger and Hanfried Kellner, "Arnold Gehlen and the Theory of Institutions," *Social Research*, vol. 32 (1965), pp. 110–15. Gehlen's own description of his intellectual development can be found in "An Anthropological Model," *The Human Context*, vol. 1, no. 1 (1968). For evaluations of Gehlen's work, see the excellent volume edited by Helmut Klages and Helmut Quaritsch, *Zur geisteswissenschaftlichen Bedeutung Arnold Gehlens* (Berlin, 1994). The volume includes a bibliography of Gehlen's works and a fifty-page bibliography of secondary works on Gehlen, compiled by Karl-Siegbert Rehberg. For an informed discussion of Gehlen's relationship to National Socialism, see the introduction and notes by Rehberg to the edition of *Der Mensch* in the *Arnold Gehlen Gesamtausgabe*.

Philip Rieff

Rieff's three major books are *Freud: The Mind of the Moralist* (New York, 1959); third edition, with a new epilogue, "One Step Further" (Chicago, 1979); *The Triumph of the Therapeutic: Uses of Faith after Freud* (New York, 1966); second edition with a new preface (Chicago, 1987); *Fellow Teachers* (New York, 1973), second edition published as *Fellow Teachers/Of Culture and Its Second Death*, with a new preface, "A Pretext of Proof Texts" (Chicago, 1984). Many of Rieff's essays are collected in Rieff, *The Feeling Intellect: Selected Writings*, ed. and with an introduction by Jonathan B. Imber (Chicago, 1990); this volume also includes a complete bibliography of Rieff's works through 1990. In the 1990s Rieff was at work on a trilogy, to be entitled *Sacred Order/Social Order*, portions of which have been published in the form of articles. They take the form of commentary on contemporary cultural phenomena, and betray the stylistic influence of Nietzsche and James Joyce, making Rieff's work increasingly aphoristic and allusive.

The volume *Psychological Man*, edited by Robert Boyers (New York, 1975) includes essays by Rieff and about his work. On Rieff's intellectual trajectory from conservative cultural theorist to apologist of a nondenominational, monotheistic orthodoxy, see Jerry Z. Muller, "A Neglected Conservative Thinker," *Commentary* (Feb. 1991), an expanded version of which appears as "Philip Rieff," in David Murray, ed., *American Cultural Critics* (Exeter, 1995); and Kenneth S. Piver, "Philip Rieff: The Critic of Psychoanalysis as Cultural Theorist," in *Discovering the History of Psychiatry*, ed. Mark S. Micale and Roy Porter (New York, 1994).

INDEX

◆

Note: The term "institution" appears so frequently in the text that it is not indexed separately; for the same reason, only selected subtopics of the terms "conservative" and "conservatism" are listed. Material in the footnotes is indexed by the page number on which the note appears. In regard to authors of secondary works, only those whose work is discussed at some length in the footnotes or in the "Guide to Further Reading" are included in the index.

Gronlund, Laurence, 234
guilds, 70–72, 124
guilt, 418

Haakonssen, Knud, 429
Habermas, Jürgen, 391, 403, 439
habit, 2, 11, 18, 19, 28, 35, 42, 46–49,
53–54, 65, 67, 109, 124, 134, 155,
174, 288, 292–94, 303–4, 307–9, 311,
321, 408
Habsburg empire, 313, 315, 317–18
Hamann, Johann Georg, 417
Hamilton, Alexander, 147, 49
Harrington, Michael, 335, 340
Harrison, Frederic, 171, 180, 183
Hartz, Louis, 146, 428
Harvard Law School, 154
Hayek, Friedrich, 8, 11, 14, 231, 303,
313–34, 439–40, 422
Hearnshaw, F.J.C., 427
Hegel, G.W.F., 372, 403, 422
Heine, Heinrich, 176
hierarchy. See elites; inequality
Hilferding, Rudolph, 222
Hindenburg, Paul von, 265
Hirschman, Albert O., 16, 19, 427
historical consequentialism, 8, 60, 89,
110–12, 119, 143, 145
historical utilitarianism, 6–9, 18, 22, 24,
28, 32–65, 84, 89, 99, 101, 124, 132,
164, 205, 236, 238, 294, 317, 323,
420–24
historicism, 11–12, 26, 84, 424. See also
historical utilitarianism
Hitler, Adolf, 265–66, 285
Hobbes, Thomas, 137
Hofstadter, Richard, 429, 435
Hofstätter, Peter, 407
Holmes, Stephen, 437
honor, 72
Hooker, Richard, 46
human imperfection. See imperfection,
human
human nature, 57–58, 64, 100, 188, 194,
202, 277–83, 403–11, 418
Hulme, T. E., 249–60, 436
human rights. See natural rights
humanitarianism. See anti-humanitarianism
Hume, David, 9, 10, 12, 13, 14, 17, 19,
20, 24, 25, 32–63, 134, 140, 148, 164,
212, 231, 291, 293, 316, 319–20, 403,
429
Huntington, Samuel, 2–3, 427
Hyde Park riots, 169, 175–77, 183

ideology, 295, 298, 303, 305, 311
illegitimacy, 16, 70–73, 204, 350

imperfection, human, 10, 48, 57, 104,
127, 189, 199, 291, 295, 303, 337,
342, 411–12
individualism, 171, 236, 402
inequality, 18, 210, 40–41, 74, 94–98,
210–32, 235, 240–41, 337, 344, 392
inheritance, 90–92
intellectuals, 65–66, 72, 79–80, 82–83,
106–7, 361, 412, 414–15, 417
intelligence. See aptitude
"interdicts" (Rieff), 412, 419
intermediary institutions, 70
intermediary powers, 372
international relations, 19. See also war
irony, 65–67, 71, 170, 337
Islam, 196
Isocrates, 67

Jacksonianism, 152
Jefferson, Thomas, 147, 283
Jencks, Christopher, 344
Jesus, 235
Jews, 352, 385, 398
Johnson, Lyndon B., 335
Joyce, James, 361, 442
Judaism, 399
Jünger, Ernst, 270
justice, 35–45, 48–49, 59, 98, 156, 330.
See also "social justice"
Justine, 363

Kant, Immanuel, 31
Keats, John, 293
Kennedy, John F., 335
Keynes, John Maynard, 313
Kidd, Benjamin, 212
King, Martin Luther, 373
Kirk, Russell, 4, 429
Knight, Frank H., 342
Knights of Labor, 234
knowledge, technical vs. practical (Oake-
shott), 297–302
Kristol, Irving, 7, 27, 358–71, 374, 438

labor unions, 263
Labour Party (British), 210, 290–91
Lagarde, Paul de, 28
L'Histoire d'O, 365
"laissez-faire conservatism," 236
language, 318, 321–22
latent functions, 7, 15–17, 28, 71, 100,
105, 237, 285, 311, 317, 319, 324,
421
law, 137–40, 156, 161–63, 165, 188,
195, 189, 200, 203–6, 321. See also
Common Law; rule of law
law, rule of, 18, 152–66. See also justice

Jerry Z. Muller is Professor of History
at the Catholic University of America in
Washington, D.C.

(continued from front flap)

Edmund Burke, Justus Möser); The Critique of Revolution (Burke, Louis de Bonald, Joseph de Maistre, James Madison, Rufus Choate); Authority (Matthew Arnold, James Fitzjames Stephen); Inequality (W. H. Mallock, Joseph A. Schumpeter); The Critique of Good Intentions (William Graham Sumner); War (T. E. Hulme); Democracy (Carl Schmitt, Schumpeter); The Limits of Rationalism (Winston Churchill, Michael Oakeshott, Friedrich Hayek, Edward Banfield); The Critique of Social and Cultural Emancipation (Irving Kristol, Peter Berger and Richard John Neuhaus, Hermann Lübbe); and Between Social Science and Cultural Criticism (Arnold Gehlen, Philip Rieff). The book contains an afterword on recurrent tensions and dilemmas of conservative thought.

Jerry Z. Muller is Professor of History at the Catholic University of America in Washington, D.C. His previous books, *Adam Smith in His Time and Ours: Designing the Decent Society* and *The Other God That Failed: Hans Freyer and the Deradicalization of German Conservatism* are available from Princeton in paperback.